# organizational behavior

## key concepts, skills & best practices

**fourth edition**

# organizational behavior

## key concepts, skills & best practices

### Angelo Kinicki
### Robert Kreitner

*Both of*
*Arizona State University*

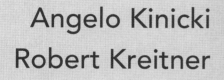

McGraw-Hill
Irwin

Boston    Burr Ridge, IL    Dubuque, IA    New York    San Francisco    St. Louis
Bangkok    Bogotá    Caracas    Kuala Lumpur    Lisbon    London    Madrid    Mexico City
Milan    Montreal    New Delhi    Santiago    Seoul    Singapore    Sydney    Taipei    Toronto

**McGraw-Hill**
**Irwin**

ORGANIZATIONAL BEHAVIOR: KEY CONCEPTS, SKILLS & BEST PRACTICES

This book is printed on acid-free paper.
Printed in China

3 4 5 6 7 8 9 0 CTP/CTP 0 9

ISBN 978-0-07-338141-1
MHID 0-07-338141-1

Vice president and editor-in-chief: *Brent Gordon*
Publisher: *Paul Ducham*
Executive editor: *John Weimeister*
Developmental editor: *Donielle Xu*
Editorial assistant: *Heather Darr*
Marketing manager: *Natalie Zook*
Marketing coordinator: *Michael Gedatus*
Project manager: *Dana M. Pauley*
Full service project manager: *Michelle Gardner, Pine Tree Composition, Inc.*
Senior manager, EDP: *Heather D. Burbridge*
Designer: *Matt Diamond*
Senior photo research coordinator: *Lori Kramer*
Photo researcher: *PoYee Oster*
Senior media project manager: *Susan Lombardi*
Typeface: *10.5/12 Times Roman*
Compositor: *Laserwords Private Limited*
Printer: *CTPS*

**Library of Congress Cataloging-in-Publication Data**
Kinicki, Angelo.
    Organizational behavior : key concepts, skills & best practices / Angelo Kinicki,
Robert Kreitner.—4th ed.
        p. cm.
    Includes index.
    ISBN-13: 978-0-07-338141-1 (alk. paper)
    ISBN-10: 0-07-338141-1 (alk. paper)
    1. Organizational behavior. I. Kreitner, Robert. II. Title.
HD58.7.K5265 2009
658.3—dc22                                        2008034246

www.mhhe.com

With respect and gratitude to John Weimeister, a supportive and talented editor who is now my friend.

———AK

With love to Margaret.

———BK

**Angelo Kinicki** is a professor, author, and consultant. He is a professor of management and is the recipient of the Weatherup/Overby Chair in Leadership. He also is a Dean's Council of 100 Distinguished Scholar at the W P Carey School of Business. He joined the faculty in 1982, the year he received his doctorate in business administration from Kent State University. His primary research interests include coping with job loss and organizational change, leadership,

have been translated into multiple languages.

Angelo is an award-winning researcher and teacher. He has received several awards, including a best research paper award from the Organizational Behavior (OB) division of the Academy of Management, the All Time Best Reviewer Award (1996–99) and the Excellent Reviewer Award (1997–98) from the *Academy of Management Journal,* and five teaching awards from Arizona State University

boards for the *Academy of Management Journal,* the *Journal of Management,* and the *Journal of Vocational Behavior.* Angelo has been an active member of the Academy of Management, including service as a representative at large for the Organizational Behavior division, member of the Best Paper Award committee for both the OB and Human Resources (HR) divisions, chair of the committee to select the best publication in the *Academy of Management Journal,* and program committee reviewer for the OB and HR divisions.

Angelo also is a busy international consultant and is a principal at Kinicki and Associates. Inc, a management consulting firm that works with top management teams to create organizational change aimed at increasing organizational effectiveness and profitability. He has worked with many Fortune 500 firms as well as numerous entrepreneurial organizations in diverse industries. His expertise includes facilitating strategic/operational planning sessions, diagnosing the causes of organizational and work-unit problems, conducting organizational culture interventions, implementing performance management systems, designing and implementing performance appraisal systems, developing and administering surveys to assess employee attitudes, and leading management/executive education programs. He developed a 360-degree leadership feedback instrument called the Performance Management Leadership Survey (PMLS) that is used by companies throughout the United States and Europe. The survey is used to assess an individual's

and multilevel issues associated with organizational culture, organizational climate, and organizational effectiveness. Angelo has published more than 80 articles in a variety of academic journals and is coauthor of seven textbooks (21 including revisions) that are used by hundreds of universities around the world. Several of his books

(Outstanding Teaching Award—MBA and Master's Program, John W Teets Outstanding Graduate Teacher Award, Outstanding Undergraduate Teaching Excellence Award, Outstanding Graduate Teaching Excellence Award, and Outstanding Executive Development Teaching Excellence Award). Angelo also has served on the editorial review

leadership style and to coach individuals interested in developing their leadership skills.

Angelo and his wife, Joyce, have enjoyed living in the beautiful Arizona desert for 25 years but are natives of Cleveland, Ohio. They enjoy traveling, golfing, hiking, and spending time in the White Mountains.

**Robert Kreitner, PhD,** is a professor emeritus of management at Arizona State University. Prior to joining ASU in 1975, Bob taught at Western Illinois University. He also has taught organizational behavior at Thunderbird. Bob is a popular speaker who has addressed a diverse array of audiences worldwide on management topics. He is a member of ASU's W P Carey School of Business Faculty Hall of Fame. Bob has authored articles for journals such as *Organizational Dynamics, Business Horizons,* and *Journal of Business Ethics.* He also is the coauthor (with Fred Luthans) of the award-winning book *Organizational Behavior Modification and Beyond: An Operant and Social Learning Approach,* and the author of *Management,* 11th edition, a best-selling introductory management text.

Among his consulting and executive development clients have been American Express, SABRE Computer Services, Honeywell, Motorola, Amdahl, the Hopi Indian Tribe, State Farm Insurance, Goodyear Aerospace, Doubletree Hotels, Bank One—Arizona, Nazarene School of Large Church Management, US Steel, Ford, Caterpillar, and Allied-Signal. In 1981–82 he served as chairman of the Academy of Management's Management Education and Development Division.

On the personal side, Bob was born in Buffalo, New York. After a four-year enlistment in the US Coast Guard, including service on the icebreaker *Eastwind* in Antarctica, Bob attended the University of Nebraska–Omaha on a football scholarship. Bob also holds an MBA from the University of Nebraska–Omaha and a PhD from the University of Nebraska–Lincoln. While working on his PhD in business at Nebraska, he spent six months teaching management courses for the University in Micronesia. In 1996, Bob taught two courses in Albania's first-ever MBA program (funded by the US Agency for International Development and administered by the University of Nebraska–Lincoln). He taught a summer leadership program in Switzerland from 1995 to 1998. Bob and his wife, Margaret, live in Phoenix and enjoy travel, hiking, woodcarving, and fishing.

# preface

In our many years of teaching organizational behavior and management to undergraduate and graduate students in various countries, we *never* had a student say, "I want a longer, more expensive textbook with more chapters." We got the message! Indeed, there is a desire for shorter and less expensive textbooks in today's fast-paced world where overload and tight budgets are a way of life. Within the field of organizational behavior, so-called "essentials" texts have attempted to satisfy this need. Too often, however, brevity has been achieved at the expense of up-to-date examples, artful layout, and learning enhancements. We believe "brief" does not have to mean outdated and boring.

## A New Standard

Kinicki and Kreitner's *Organizational Behavior: Key Concepts, Skills & Best Practices*, fourth edition, represents a new standard in OB essentials textbooks. The following guiding philosophy inspired our quest for this new standard: "Create a short, up-to-date, practical, user-friendly, interesting, and engaging introduction to the field of organizational behavior." Thus, in this book, you will find lean and efficient coverage of topics recommended by the accreditation organizations AACSB International and ACBSP conveyed with pedagogical features found in full-length OB textbooks. Among those pedagogical enhancements are current, real-life chapter-opening cases, a rich array of contemporary in-text examples, a strong skills emphasis including Skills & Best Practices boxes throughout the text, at least one interactive exercise integrated into each chapter, an appealing four-color presentation, interesting captioned photos, poignant cartoons, instructive chapter summaries, and chapter-closing Ethical Dilemma exercises.

## Efficient and Flexible Structure

The 16 chapters in this text (including the ethics module following Chapter 1) are readily adaptable to traditional 15-week semesters, 10-week terms, summer and inter-sessions, management development seminars, and distance learning programs via the Internet. Following up-front coverage of important topics—including ethics, international OB, and managing diversity—the topical flow of this text goes from micro (individuals) to macro (groups, teams, and organizations). Mixing and matching chapters (and topics within each chapter) in various combinations is not only possible but strongly encouraged to create optimum teaching/learning experiences.

## A Solid Base of Fresh and Relevant Source Material

Wise grocery shoppers gauge the freshness of essential purchases such as bread and milk by checking the sell by dates. So, too, OB textbooks need to be checked for freshness to ensure the reader's time is well spent on up-to-date and relevant theory, research, and practical examples. By our count, **you will find 414 and 329 chapter endnotes dated 2007 and 2008, respectively, indicating a thorough**

**updating of this new edition.** Additionally, 16 of the chapter-opening cases and 40 of the in-text Skills & Best Practices boxes are from timely 2007 and 2008 material.

# A Rich Array of OB Research Insights

To enhance the instructional value of our coverage of major topics, we systematically cite "hard" evidence from five different categories. Worthwhile evidence was obtained by drawing upon the following *priority* of research methodologies:

- *Meta-analyses.* A **meta-analysis** is a statistical pooling technique that permits behavioral scientists to draw general conclusions about certain variables from many different studies. It typically encompasses a vast number of subjects, often reaching the thousands. Meta-analyses are instructive because they focus on general patterns of research evidence, not fragmented bits and pieces or isolated studies.

- *Field studies.* In OB, a **field study** probes individual or group processes in an organizational setting. Because field studies involve real-life situations, their results often have immediate and practical relevance for managers.

- *Laboratory studies.* In a **laboratory study,** variables are manipulated and measured in contrived situations. College students are commonly used as subjects. The highly controlled nature of laboratory studies enhances research precision. But generalizing the results to organizational management requires caution.

- *Sample surveys.* In a **sample survey,** samples of people from specified populations respond to questionnaires. The researchers then draw conclusions about the relevant population. Generalizability of the results depends on the quality of the sampling and questioning techniques.

- *Case studies.* A **case study** is an in-depth analysis of a single individual, group, or organization. Because of their limited scope, case studies yield realistic but not very generalizable results.

**meta-analysis**

Pools the results of many studies through statistical procedures.

**field study**

Examination of variables in real-life settings.

**laboratory study**

Manipulation and measurement of variables in contrived situations.

**sample survey**

Questionnaire responses from a sample of people.

**case study**

In-depth study of a single person, group, or organization.

# Emphasis on Ethics in the Fourth Edition

We have continued (and updated) two features from the third edition—a comprehensive module on Ethics following Chapter 1 and an Ethical Dilemma exercise at the end of every chapter—to set a proper moral tone for managing people at work. The 16 Ethical Dilemma exercises raise contemporary ethical issues, ask tough questions, and have corresponding interpretations on our Web site at www.mhhe.com/kinickiob4e. An instructive Group Exercise, "Investigating the Difference in Moral Reasoning between Men and Women," follows the Ethics module. Ten of these dilemmas are new in this edition.

ethics learning module

## U.S. Lawmakers Believe that Yahoo Committed Ethical Breach in China

**How do you view Yahoo's actions? Explain. For an interpretation of this case and additional comments, visit our Online Learning Center at**

**www.mhhe.com/ kinickiob4e**

FOR DISCUSSION

The hearing by the House Foreign Affairs Committee on Yahoo's conduct in China was a rare public shaming of the Internet leader, whose actions led to the imprisonment of journalist Shi Tao.

Committee Chairman Tom Lantos (D-Burlingame) and other lawmakers pilloried Yang and Michael Callahan, Yahoo's executive vice president and general counsel, for providing Chinese officials with Shi's identity from his e-mail address in 2004, then misleading lawmakers last year [2006] about what it knew about the case.

"While technologically and financially you are giants, morally you are pygmies," Lantos said, scolding Yahoo executives. . . .

Yahoo, Google Inc., eBay Inc., and other major Web players have invested billions in China to capture a share of the country's exploding Internet population. But they have been largely overwhelmed by local competitors, such as Alibaba.com and Baidu.com, as well as by concessions they must make to local laws. Google, for example, has faced heavy criticism for proactively censoring Web search results to which it believes the government might object.

Yahoo provided Shi's name to Chinese authorities in 2004 after they demanded to

# ethical dilemma

## You Mean Cheating Is Wrong?

College students are disturbed by recent corporate scandals: Some 84% believe the U.S. is having a business crisis, and 77% think CEOs should be held personally responsible for it.

But when the same students are asked about their own ethics, it's another story. Some 59% admit cheating on a test (66% of men, 54% of women). And only 19% say they would report a classmate who cheated (23% of men, but 15% of women—even though recent whistle-blowers have been women).

The survey of 1,100 students on 27 U.S. campuses was conducted by Students in Free Enterprise (SIFE), a nonprofit that teams up with corporations to teach students ethical business practices. "There's a lack of understanding

### How Should We Interpret This Hypocritical Double Standard?

1. Don't worry, most students know the difference between school and real life. They'll do the right thing when it really counts. Explain your rationale.

2. Whether in the classroom or on the job, pressure for results is the problem. People tend to take shortcuts and bend the rules when they're pressured. Explain.

3. A cheater today is a cheater tomorrow. Explain.

4. College professors need to do a better job with ethics education. How?

## Assurance of Learning Ready

Assurance of learning is an important element of many accreditation standards. *Organizational Behavior: Key Concepts, Skills & Best Practices,* fourth edition is designed specifically to support your assurance of learning initiatives. We accomplish this goal by starting each chapter with a list of learning objectives. We then repeat these objectives in the text at the point they are being discussed. This enables students to focus their reading around the learning objectives. To complete the learning cycle, we then include end-of-chapter discussion questions and provide a summary of each learning objective. Every test bank question for *Organizational Behavior: Key Concepts, Skills & Best Practices,*

fourth edition is also linked to one of these objectives, in addition to level of difficulty, Bloom's Taxonomy level, and AACSB skill area. *EZ Test,* McGraw-Hill's easy-to-use test bank software, can search the test bank by these and other categories, providing an engine for targeted Assurance of Learning analysis and assessment.

## AACSB Statement

The McGraw-Hill Companies is a proud corporate member of AACSB International. Understanding the importance and value of AACSB accreditation, *Organizational Behavior: Key Concepts, Skills & Best Practices,* fourth edition has sought to recognize the curricula guidelines detailed in the AACSB standards for business accreditation by connecting selected questions in the test bank to

the general knowledge and skill guidelines found in the AACSB standards.

The statements contained in *Organizational Behavior: Key Concepts, Skills & Best Practices,* fourth edition are provided only as a guide for the users of this text. The AACSB leaves content coverage and assessment within the purview of individual schools, the mission of the school, and the faculty. While *Organizational Behavior: Key Concepts, Skills & Best Practices,* fourth edition and the teaching package make no claim of any specific AACSB qualification or evaluation, we have, within the test bank, labeled selected questions according to the six general knowledge and skills areas.

# Active Learning

## Engaging Pedagogy

We have a love and a passion for teaching organizational behavior in the classroom and via textbooks because it deals with the intriguing realities of working in modern organizations. Puzzling questions, insights, and surprises hide around every corner. Seeking useful insights about how and why people behave as they do in the workplace is a provocative, interesting, and oftentimes fun activity. After all, to know more about organizational behavior is to know more about both ourselves and life in general. We have designed this text to facilitate *active* learning by relying on the following learning enhancements:

### Chapter-Opening Cases—

For some real-world context, these brief cases use topics that are timely and relevant to actual life situations. The text's Web site also features interpretations for each case.

Apple's latest innovation is the MacBook Air.

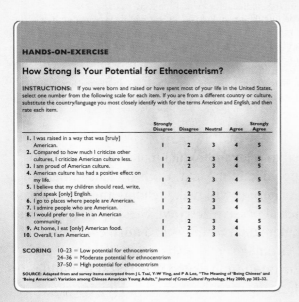

### Hands-On Exercises—

These 16 exercises are included to help readers personalize and expand upon key concepts as they are presented in the text. These exercises encourage active and thoughtful interaction rather than passive reading.

# Active Learning

## The Effective Manager's Skill Profile

1. *Clarifies goals and objectives* for everyone involved.

2. *Encourages participation*, upward communication, and suggestions.

3. *Plans and organizes* for an orderly work flow.

4. Has *technical and administrative expertise* to answer organization-related questions.

5. *Facilitates work* through team building, training, coaching, and support.

6. *Provides feedback* honestly and constructively.

7. *Keeps things moving* by relying on schedules, deadlines, and helpful reminders.

8. *Controls details* without being overbearing.

## Skills & Best Practices Boxes—

These additional readings and practical application items are designed to sharpen users' skills by either recommending how to apply a concept, theory, or model, or by giving an exemplary corporate application. Students will benefit from real-world experiences and direct skill-building opportunities.

**Test Your Knowledge**
Management's Historical Figures

standpoint of organizational behavior, the central feature of this definition is "working with and through others." In a recent survey, chief executive officers from more than three dozen countries said the challenge of greatest concern to them was "excellence in execution"—that is, getting their people to do a great job of carrying out their strategy.[12]

Managers play a constantly evolving role. Today's successful managers are no longer the I've-got-everything-under-control order givers of yesteryear. Rather, they need to creatively envision and actively sell bold new directions in an ethical and sensitive manner. Effective managers are team players empowered by the willing and active support of others who are driven by conflicting self-interests. Each of us has a

## A Dynamic Active Learning Feature for the Fourth Edition—

Sixty-eight Web-based readings and exercises keyed to relevant textual material with OLC (Online Learning Center) logos in the margin are included in the text. Both student-initiated and instructor-assigned access to these enrichment materials will make reading this book an active and robust learning process, rather than the usual passive activity. These Web resources fall into four categories: Test your Knowledge (supplemental readings and quizzes), Self-Assessment Exercises (for greater self-awareness), Group Exercises (for team building), and Manager's Hot Seat Video Applications (for realistic on-the-job experience and skill building). All this material can be easily accessed via the OLC at www.mhhe.com/kinickiob4e—just look for the *Group and Video Resource Manual* link.

# Active Learning

## Up-to-Date Real-World Examples—

Nothing brings material to life better than in-text examples featuring real companies, people, and situations. Hundreds of examples, including organizations such as Southwest Airlines, DaimlerChrysler, Seagate Technology, Baptist Health Care, US Marine Corp., Procter & Gamble, and General Electric, permeate the text.

## chapter summary

- *Identify at least four of Pfeffer's people-centered practices, and define the term* management. Pfeffer's seven people-centered practices are job security, careful hiring, power to the people, generous pay for performance, lots of training, less emphasis on status, and trust building. *Management* is the process of working with and through others to achieve organizational objectives in an efficient and ethical manner.

- *Contrast McGregor's Theory X and Theory Y assumptions about employees.* Theory X employees, according to traditional thinking, dislike work, require close supervision, and are primarily interested in security. According to the modern Theory Y view, employees are capable of self-direction, of seeking responsibility, and of being creative.

- *Explain the managerial significance of Deming's 85–15 rule, and identify the four principles of total quality management (TQM).* Deming claimed that about 85% of organizational failures are due to system breakdowns involving factors such as management, machinery, or work rules. He believed the workers themselves are responsible for failures only about 15% of the time. Consequently, Deming criticized the standard practice of blaming and punishing individuals for what are typically system failures beyond their immediate control. The four principles of TQM are (a) do it right the first time to eliminate costly rework; (b) listen to and learn from customers and employees; (c) make continuous improvement an everyday matter; and (d) build teamwork, trust, and mutual respect.

- *Contrast human and social capital, and identify five measurable outcomes when building human capital.* Human

capital involves *individual* characteristics and abilities; social capital involves *social* relationships. Human capital is the productive potential of an individual's knowledge and actions. Social capital is productive potential resulting from strong relationships, goodwill, trust, and cooperative effort. Five measurable outcomes of programs to build human capital are (a) leadership/managerial practices; (b) workforce optimization; (c) learning capacity; (d) knowledge accessibility; and (e) talent engagement.

- *Explain the impact of the positive psychology movement on the field of OB.* Reversing psychology's long-standing preoccupation with what is wrong with people, positive psychology instead focuses on identifying and building human strengths and potential. Accordingly, Luthans recommends positive organizational behavior (POB) and identifies its basic elements with the CHOSE model. This acronym stands for Confidence/self-efficacy, Hope, Optimism, Subjective well-being, and Emotional intelligence.

- *Define the term e-business, and explain at least three practical lessons about effective e-leadership in a virtual organization.* E-business involves using the Internet to more effectively and efficiently manage *every* aspect of a business. Today's employees are skilled in many aspects of digital communication: e-mail, blogs, social networking sites, and sites where users provide and refine content, such as Wikipedia. In such an environment, where employees have more control over the information they can access and share, the manager's role is evolving into one of providing the means for collaboration.

## Chapter Summaries—

This section includes responses to the learning objectives in each chapter, making it a handy review tool for all users.

# Active Learning

## discussion questions

1. Based on reading this chapter, why is IBM (see the chapter-opening case) having success with its global operations?
2. How would you describe the prevailing culture in your country to a stranger from another land, in terms of the nine GLOBE project dimensions?
3. Why are people from high-context cultures such as China and Japan likely to be misunderstood by low-context Westerners?
4. How strong is your desire for a foreign assignment? Why? If it is strong, where would you like to work? Why? How prepared are you for a foreign assignment? What do you need to do to be better prepared?
5. What is your personal experience with culture shock? Which of the OB trouble spots in Figure 3–2 do you believe is the greatest threat to expatriate employee success? Explain.

### Discussion Questions—
Focused and challenging, these questions help facilitate classroom discussion or review material.

### Ethical Dilemmas—
These 16 exercises raise contemporary ethical issues, ask tough questions, and have corresponding interpretations on the Online Learning Center at www.mhhe.com/kinickiob4e.

## ethical dilemma

### Should Countrywide Reimburse Angelo Mozilio for His Wife's Travel Expenses?[61]

The United States' largest mortgage lender, Countrywide Financial Corp., is under intense scrutiny from the U.S. government. Not only has the company lost billions of dollars in 2007 and part of 2008, but it is currently under investigation by the Securities and Exchange Commission for potential improper accounting and by the Federal Bureau of Investigation for possible securities fraud. Countrywide's actions and alleged problems are related to the mortgage crisis that occurred in 2007 and 2008.

The company's CEO, Angelo Mozilo, was paid roughly $250 million from 1998 through 2007 and received an additional $406 million from the sale of Countrywide stock. His actions were under scrutiny when he wrote an e-mail to the board asking them to reimburse him for taxes owed for his wife's use of the corporate jet. He threatened to resign and liquidate his 12 million shares if the board did not reimburse him. The sale of the stock would hurt the company's image in the marketplace.

**What would you have done if you were on the board of directors for Countrywide?**

1. Tell Mr. Mozilo that you will not reimburse him. His wife used the corporate jet, and the shareholders should not pay for this expense.
2. Reimburse him. Angelo co-founded the company and his wife should be able to use the jet when she wants.
3. Split the expense. This is a win-win solution.
4. Invent other options. Discuss.

For an interpretation of this situation, visit our Web site at **www.mhhe.com/kinickiob4e**

# Instructor supplements

*Organizational Behavior* 4e gives you all the support material you need for an enriched classroom experience.

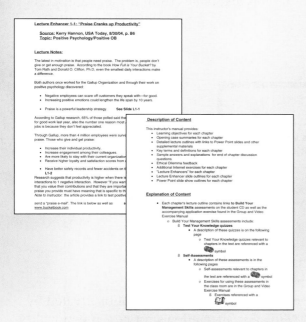

## Instructor's Resource Guide

The Instructor's Manual is a creative guide to understanding organizational behavior. It combines traditional elements of instructor's manuals with newer features such as teaching tips throughout the lecture outline, additional discussion ideas for the chapter opening cases, note pages for the PPT slides, a matrix from the Group & Video Resource Manual on how to incorporate Test Your Knowledge features, Self-Assessment Exercises, Group Exercises, and Manager Hot Seat Video Applications, answers to Discussion Questions and End of Chapter material, and much more. Each element will assist the instructor and students in maximizing the ideas, issues, concepts, and important organizational behavior approaches included in each chapter. We'd like to thank Mindy West of Arizona State University for helping us update our Instructor's Guide.

## Computerized Test Bank

We've aligned our Test Bank with new AACSB guidelines, tagging each question according to its knowledge and skills areas. Categories include Global, Ethics and Social Responsibility, Legal and other External Environment, Communication, Diversity, Group Dynamics, Individual Dynamics, Production, and IT. Previous designations aligning questions with Learning Objectives, boxes, and features still exist as well, with over 1,200 questions from which to choose. Our thanks to Eileen Hogan of Kutztown University for her help in developing our new Test Bank.

## Instructor's CD-ROM
ISBN: 0073364282

All of the above-mentioned materials, including Power-Point slides, can be located on the Instructor's CD-ROM. This CD-ROM allows professors to easily create their own custom presentation. They can pull from resources on the CD, like the Instructor's Manual, the Test Bank, and PowerPoint, or from their own files. Additional downloads of figures and tables from the text are available for use.

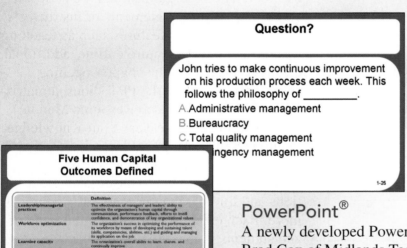

## PowerPoint®

A newly developed PowerPoint presentation created by Brad Cox of Midlands Tech allows for new functionality and variety in the classroom. With the inclusion of video usage suggestions and links to additional information, instructors have the availability to tailor their presentations to their class needs.

## Videos on DVD
ISBN: 0073337285

If you're looking for a way to bring real-life experience into the classroom, an all-new video collection delivered on DVD is available. Segments such as "Pike Place Fish Market," "Johnson & Johnson: Creating a Global Learning Organization," or "Wal-Mart's Public Image Campaign" demonstrate current OB topics, but also help students apply them to everyday organizations.

## The Manager's Hot Seat Videos Online
www.mhhe.com/MHS

In today's workplace, managers are confronted daily with issues like ethics, diversity, working in teams, and the virtual workplace. The manager's Hot Seat videos allow students to watch as 21 real managers apply their years of experience to confront these issues. Students assume the role of the manager as they watch the video and answer multiple-choice questions that pop up, forcing them to make decisions on the spot. They learn from the manager's mistakes and successes, and then write a report critiquing the manager's approach by defending their reasoning. Reports can be e-mailed or printed out for credit. These video segments are a powerful tool for your course that truly immerses your students in the learning experience. **The Manager's Hot Seat online is just an additional $10 when packaged with this text, and includes six new episodes with this edition.**

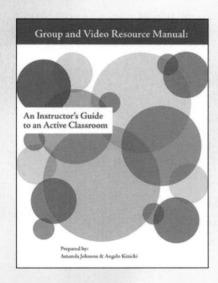

## Group and Video Resource Manual: An Instructor's Guide to an Active Classroom
in print ISBN: 9780073044347; MHID: 0073044342 or online at www.mhhe.com/mobmanual

Prepared by Amanda Johnson and Angelo Kinicki, this manual created for instructors contains everything needed to successfully integrate activities into the classroom. It includes a menu of items to use as teaching tools in class. All of our self-assessment exercises, Test Your Knowledge quizzes, group exercises, and Manager's Hot Seat exercises are located in this one manual along with teaching notes and PowerPoint slides to use in class. Group exercises include everything you would need to use the exercise in class—handouts, figures, and more.

This manual is organized into 25 topics including ethics, decision making, change, and leadership for easy inclusion in your lecture. A matrix is included at the front of the manual that references each resource by topic. Students access all of the exercises and self-assessments on their textbook's Web site. The Manager's Hot Seat exercises are located online at www.mhhe.com/MHS.

# Instructor supplements

## Online Learning Center
www.mhhe.com/kinickiob4e
More and more students are studying online. That's why we offer an Online Learning Center (OLC) that follows *Organizational Behavior* chapter by chapter. It doesn't require any building or maintenance on your part. It's ready to go the moment you and your students type in the URL.

As your students study, they can refer to the OLC Web site for such benefits as:

- Internet-based activities
- Self-grading quizzes
- Learning objectives
- Chapter summaries
- Additional video
- Narrated lectures

A secured Instructor Resource Center stores your essential course materials to save you prep time before class. The Instructor's Manual, PowerPoint, and sample syllabi are now just a couple of clicks away. You will also find useful packaging information and Video notes.

# Grateful Appreciation

Our sincere thanks and gratitude go to our editor, John Weimeister, and his first-rate team at McGraw-Hill/Irwin who encouraged and facilitated our pursuit of "something better." Key contributors include Donielle Xu, Developmental Editor; Natalie Zook, Marketing Manager; and Dana Pauley, Project Manager. We would also like to thank Mindy West of Arizona State University for her work on the Instructor's Guide, Eileen Hogan of Kutztown University for her help revising and updating the Test Bank, and Brad Cox of Midlands Tech for developing the PowerPoint presentation slides.

We'd also like to thank Karen Hill and her colleagues at Elm Street Publishing for their invaluable contributions toward completing this revision.

A special thank you also goes out to those colleagues who gave their comments and suggestions over the years to help us create all four editions. They are:

**Abe Bakhsheshy**
*University of Utah*

**Jodi Barnes-Nelson**
*NC State–Raleigh*

**Joy Benson**
*University of Illinois–Springfield*

**Linda Boozer**
*Suny AG & Tech College–Morrisville*

**Emilio Bruna**
*University of Texas at El Paso*

**Mark Butler**
*San Diego State University*

**Holly Buttner**
*University of North Carolina–Greensboro*

**John Byrne**
*St. Ambrose University*

**Diane Caggiano**
*Fitchburg State College*

**Dave Carmichel**
*Oklahoma City University*

**Xiao-Ping Chen**
*University of Washington*

**Jack Chirch**
*Hampton University*

**Bongsoon Cho**
*SUNY–Buffalo*

**Savannah Clay**
*Central Piedmont Community College*

**Ray Coye**
*DePaul University*

**Denise Daniels**
*Seattle Pacific University*

**W. Gibb Dyer, Jr.**
*Brigham Young University*

**Mark Fichman**
*Carnegie Mellon University*

**David A. Foote**
*Middle Tennessee State University*

**Lucy Ford**
*Rutgers University*

**Thomas Gainey**
*State University of West Georgia*

**Jacqueline Gilbert**
*Middle Tennessee State University*

**Leonard Glick**
*Northeastern University*

**Debi Griggs**
*Bellevue Community College*

**Barbara Hassell**
*IUPUI–Indianapolis*

**Hoyt Hayes**
*Columbia College–Columbia*

**Kim Hester**
*Arkansas State University*

**Chad Higgins**
*University of Washington*

**Kristine Hoover**
*Bowling Green State University*

**David Jalajas**
*Long Island University*

**Andrew Johnson**
*Bellevue Community College*

**Raymond Jones**
*University of Pittsburgh*

**Dong Jung**
*San Diego State University*

**Jordan Kaplan**
*Long Island University*

**John Keeling**
*Old Dominion University*

**Claire Killian**
*University of Wisconsin–River Falls*

**Bobbie Knoblauch**
*Witchita State University*

**Frances Kubicek**
*Kalamazoo Valley Community College*

**Gerald Levy**
*Franklin Career Institute*

**Karen Markel**
*Oakland University*

**Tom McDermott**
*Pittsburgh Technical Institute*

**Edward Miles**
*Georgia State University*

**Linda Morable**
*Richland College*

**Jay Nathan**
*St. John's University*

**Regina Oneil**
*Suffolk University*

**Joseph Petrick**
*Wright State University*

**Dave Phillips**
*Purdue University–Westville*

**Amy Randel**
*Wake Forest University*

**Clint Relyea**
*Arkansas State University*

**Patricia Rice**
*Finger Lakes Community College*

**Janet Romaine**
*St. Anselm College*

**Paula Silva**
*University of New Mexico*

**Randi Sims**
*Nova University*

**Peggy Takahashi**
*University of San Francisco*

**Jennie Carter Thomas**
*Belmont University*

**Tyra Townsend**
*University of Pittsburgh*

**Brian Usilaner**
*University of Maryland–University College*

**Matthew Valle**
*Elon University*

**Andrew Ward**
*Emory University*

**John Washbush**
*University of Wisconsin*

**John Watt**
*University of Central Arkansas*

**Ken Weidner**
*St. Josephs University*

**Scott Williams**
*Wright State University*

**Lynn Wilson**
*Saint Leo University*

Finally, we would like to thank our wives, Joyce and Margaret. Their love, support, and managerial experience are instrumental to *everything* we do. They lift our tired spirits when needed and encourage and coach us at every turn.

This project has been a fun challenge from start to finish. Not only did we enjoy reading and learning more about the latest developments within the field of organizational behavior, but completion of this edition has deepened our twenty-seven-year friendship. We hope you enjoy this textbook. Best wishes for success and happiness!

**Angelo & Bob**

# brief contents

# contents

# Part Two
# Managing Individuals   83

Part Three
Managing Social Processes and Making Decisions    221

## Part Four
## Managing Organizational Processes 295

# part One

# Managing People in a Global Economy

# Needed: People-Centered Managers and Workplaces

## LEARNING OBJECTIVES

**After reading the material in this chapter, you should be able to:**

1. Identify at least four of Pfeffer's people-centered practices, and define the term *management*.

2. Contrast McGregor's Theory X and Theory Y assumptions about employees.

3. Explain the managerial significance of Deming's 85–15 rule, and identify the four principles of total quality management (TQM).

4. Contrast human and social capital, and identify five measurable outcomes when building human capital.

5. Explain the impact of the positive psychology movement on the field of organizational behavior (OB).

6. Define the term *e-business*, and explain at least three practical lessons about effective e-leadership in a virtual organization.

Striving to be the best of the big four accounting firms, and an employer of choice, is challenging, but KPMG LLP U.S. knows where it's headed. The firm's strategy-driven approach integrates technical skills, such as auditing, tax, and advisory methodology, with executive education, including leadership development and global business ethics. With 23,000 employees to educate across the firm's audit, tax, advisory, and client support functions, KPMG uses everything from traditional classroom sessions to immersive virtual technology to get its message across.

"Our business model is all about building knowledge, and being able to bring that knowledge to the marketplace," says Jack Taylor, executive vice chair, operations, and regional chief operating officer, Americas. "Everything we have is based on starting with that core philosophy, and building a learning and development program that is the best of the big four."

Achieving that success led KPMG to change its approach to learning. Technical skills—such as understanding and applying standards and regulations, producing the necessary documentation, and understanding the proper protocol to follow with clients—are still crucial. But alongside that functional knowledge, the firm is emphasizing the executive know-how that will get up-and-comers through their first difficult conversation with clients, or provide them with a moral compass when faced with ethical conflicts. "We're beginning to build a huge cultural component to our training program, including business ethics, diversity, and inclusion training," says Taylor.

This emerging cultural education hinges on business ethics and an understanding of what it means to work in a global and diverse environment. "We're committed to giving each of our people, over a five-year period, some type of global immersion," he explains. . . .

**KPMG headquarters in Frankfurt, Germany.**

As important as it is to the success of KPMG that its young new hires acquire career-building skills that go beyond technical knowledge, teaching them how to interact effectively in the workforce also is helpful to the firm's recruitment and retention strategy. New hires are drawn to the firm, and enticed to stay, at least partly for the career development that will be provided to them. "Our whole employment proposition is built on being a great place to build a career," says Bruce Pfau, vice chair, human resources. "Not just a great place to work, but to gain the professional skills and development they will need to be a success here or elsewhere." The idea, he elaborates, is to provide employees with "successively marketable skills." . . .

Hand in hand with a need for leaders who know how to communicate KPMG's values to lower-level staff is a wide-ranging view of leadership in which there are not a few leaders, but many to spread the message. "Because we're a professional services firm," says Rodstein, "we define 'leadership' slightly differently. Everybody touches a client in some way or another. So, we really need 23,000 leaders. They all need client skills, business acumen, technical skills, and the ability to manage teams of people." Along with those hands-on skills, the firm, Rodstein points out, wants all employees to have self-awareness of their own values. "They're in tough situations much of the time," she says, "and we want them to have that inner balance that makes them mature in the face of difficult conversations and a changing regulatory environment."[1]

**HOW IMPORTANT ARE PEOPLE?** The chapter-opening case highlights that KPMG is betting its future success on the quality and job satisfaction of its people. The same is true of Southwest Airlines. As noted by Gary Kelly, the former accountant who is CEO of Southwest Airlines, "'My top priority is, as it always has been at Southwest, our people,' Kelly says. 'If our employees love working at Southwest Airlines, everything else will fall into place."[2] Considering that Kelly has more than 34,000 fellow employees at Southwest Airlines, he certainly has a full plate.[3]

A longer research-based answer comes from Stanford's Jeffrey Pfeffer: "There is a substantial and rapidly expanding body of evidence, some of it quite methodologically sophisticated, that speaks to the strong connection between how firms manage their people and the economic results achieved."[4] His review of research from the United States and Germany showed *people-centered practices* strongly associated with higher profits and lower employee turnover. Seven people-centered practices in successful companies are:

learning objective 1

Identify at least four of Pfeffer's people-centered practices, and define the term *management.*

1. Job security (to eliminate fear of layoffs).
2. Careful hiring (emphasizing a good fit with the company culture).
3. Power to the people (via decentralization and self-managed teams).
4. Generous pay for performance.
5. Lots of training.
6. Less emphasis on status (to build a "we" feeling).
7. Trust building (through the sharing of critical information).[5]

For example, research shows that sharing information about the work group's and company's performance is associated with better financial performance, and a focus on teamwork, including training for team participation, is associated with quality improvements.[6] Importantly, the seven factors are a *package* deal, meaning they need to be installed in a coordinated and systematic manner—not in bits and pieces.

Sadly, too many managers act counter to their declarations that people are their most important asset. Pfeffer blames a number of modern management trends and practices. For example, undue emphasis on short-term profit precludes long-term efforts to nurture human resources. Also, excessive layoffs, when managers view people as a cost rather than an asset, erode trust, commitment, and loyalty.[7] In a recent survey of workers in 18 countries, just over one out of five said they are engaged in their work—willing to do extra to contribute to their company's success. The remaining employees, explaining their lack of engagement, most often blamed it on the doubt that their company's senior management was "sincerely interested in their well-being."[8]

To us, this lack of engagement among workers represents a tragic loss, both to society and to the global economy. We all need to accept the challenge to do better.[9] *Fortune* magazine's annual list of "The 100 Best Companies to Work For" shows what is being done at progressive organizations that put people first. For example, JM Family Enterprises, a Toyota distributor in Florida, offers employees generous perks such as on-site child care and fitness centers. When the company's founder recently died, his stock went into a trust to keep those benefits funded.[10] Importantly, as documented in a recent study, companies making *Fortune*'s "100 Best" list tend to outperform the competition.[11]

**Test Your Knowledge**

Levels of Strategy

The mission of this book is to help increase the number of people-centered managers and organizations around the world. Our jumping-off point is the 4-P model of strategic results in Figure 1–1. The 4-P model emphasizes the larger strategic context for managing people. Of course, other factors such as planning, technology, and finances also require good management. Further, the 4-P model stresses the importance of day-to-day *continuous improvement* in all aspects of organizational endeavor to cope with more demanding customers and stiffer competition.

In this chapter, we discuss the manager's job, define and examine organizational behavior and its evolution, and explore new directions.

# Managers Get Results with and through Others

For better or for worse, managers touch our lives in many ways. Schools, hospitals, government agencies, and large and small businesses all require systematic management. Formally defined, **management** is the process of working with and through others to achieve organizational objectives in an efficient and ethical manner. From the

**management**

Process of working with and through others to achieve organizational objectives efficiently and ethically.

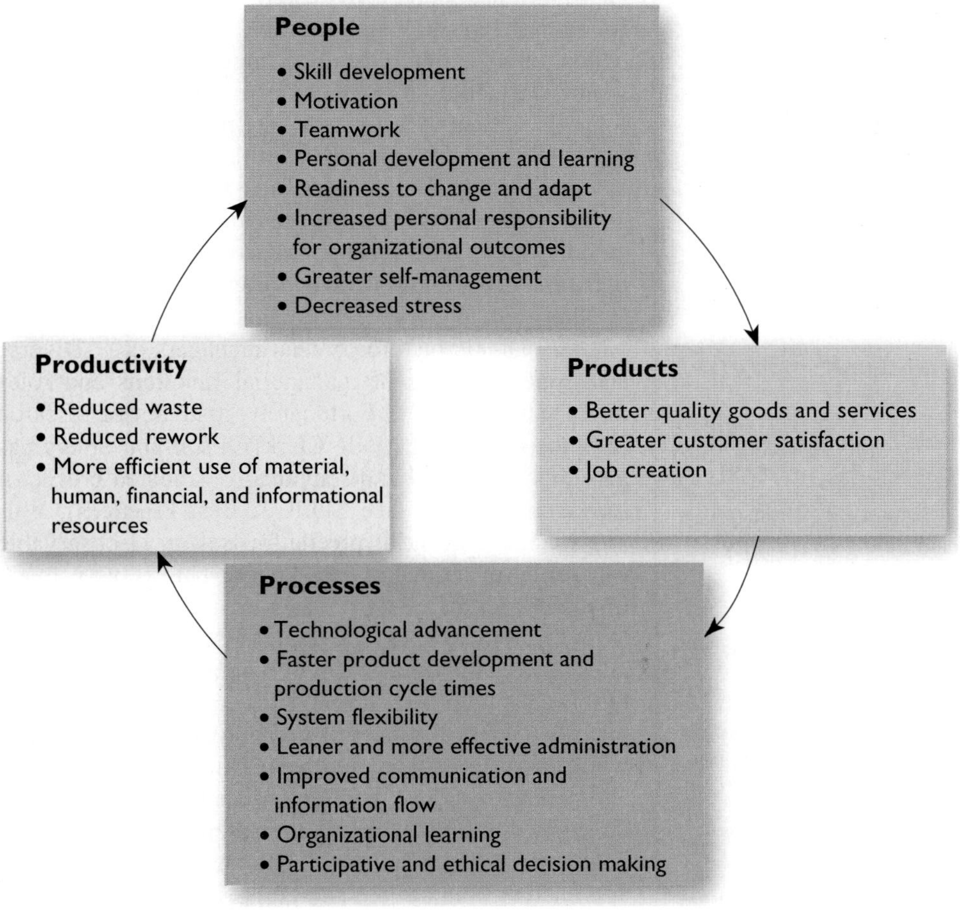

**FIGURE 1–1**
Strategic Results: The 4-P Cycle of Continuous Improvement

**People**
- Skill development
- Motivation
- Teamwork
- Personal development and learning
- Readiness to change and adapt
- Increased personal responsibility for organizational outcomes
- Greater self-management
- Decreased stress

**Productivity**
- Reduced waste
- Reduced rework
- More efficient use of material, human, financial, and informational resources

**Products**
- Better quality goods and services
- Greater customer satisfaction
- Job creation

**Processes**
- Technological advancement
- Faster product development and production cycle times
- System flexibility
- Leaner and more effective administration
- Improved communication and information flow
- Organizational learning
- Participative and ethical decision making

standpoint of organizational behavior, the central feature of this definition is "working with and through others." In a recent survey, chief executive officers from more than three dozen countries said the challenge of greatest concern to them was "excellence in execution"—that is, getting their people to do a great job of carrying out their strategy.[12]

Managers play a constantly evolving role. Today's successful managers are no longer the I've-got-everything-under-control order givers of yesteryear. Rather, they need to creatively envision and actively sell bold new directions in an ethical and sensitive manner. Effective managers are team players empowered by the willing and active support of others who are driven by conflicting self-interests. Each of us has a huge stake in how well managers carry out their evolving role. Henry Mintzberg, a respected management scholar, observed: "No job is more vital to our society than that of the manager. It is the manager who determines whether our social institutions serve us well or whether they squander our talents and resources."[13]

Extending our managerial thrust, let us take a closer look at the skills managers need to perform and the future direction of management.

**Test Your Knowledge**
Management's Historical Figures

## A Skills Profile for Managers

Observational studies by Mintzberg and others have found the typical manager's day to be a fragmented collection of brief episodes.[14] Interruptions are commonplace, while large blocks of time for planning and reflective thinking are not. In one particular study, four top-level managers spent 63% of their time on activities lasting less than nine minutes each. Only 5% of the managers' time was devoted to activities lasting more than an hour.[15] But what specific skills do effective managers perform during their hectic and fragmented workdays?

Many attempts have been made over the years to paint a realistic picture of what managers do.[16] Diverse and confusing lists of managerial functions and roles have been suggested. Fortunately, a stream of research over the past 25 years by Clark Wilson and others has given us a practical and statistically validated profile of managerial *skills*[17] (see Skills & Best Practices). Wilson's managerial skills profile focuses on 11 observable categories of managerial behavior. This is very much in tune with today's emphasis on managerial competency.[18] Wilson's unique skills-assessment technique goes beyond the usual self-report approach with its natural bias. In addition to surveying a given manager about his or her 11 skills, the Wilson approach also asks those who report directly to the manager to answer questions about their boss's skills. According to Wilson and his colleagues, the result is an assessment of skill *mastery*, not simply skill awareness.[19] The logic behind Wilson's approach is both simple and compelling. Who better to

**SKILLS & BEST PRACTICES**

### The Effective Manager's Skill Profile

1. *Clarifies goals and objectives* for everyone involved.

2. *Encourages participation,* upward communication, and suggestions.

3. *Plans and organizes* for an orderly work flow.

4. Has *technical and administrative expertise* to answer organization-related questions.

5. *Facilitates work* through team building, training, coaching, and support.

6. *Provides feedback* honestly and constructively.

7. *Keeps things moving* by relying on schedules, deadlines, and helpful reminders.

8. *Controls details* without being overbearing.

9. Applies reasonable *pressure for goal accomplishment.*

10. *Empowers and delegates* key duties to others while maintaining goal clarity and commitment.

11. *Recognizes good performance* with rewards and positive reinforcement.

SOURCE: Adapted from material in F Shipper, "A Study of the Psychometric Properties of the Managerial Skill Scales of the Survey of Management Practices," *Educational and Psychological Measurement,* June 1995, pp 468–79; and C L Wilson, *How and Why Effective Managers Balance Their Skills: Technical, Teambuilding, Drive* (Columbia, Maryland: Rockatech Multimedia Publishing, 2003).

assess a manager's skills than the people who experience those behaviors on a day-to-day basis—those who report directly to the manager?

The Wilson managerial skills research yields three useful lessons:

1. Dealing effectively with people is what management is all about. The 11 skills constitute a goal creation/commitment/feedback/reward/ accomplishment cycle with human interaction at every turn.
2. Managers with high skills mastery tend to have better subunit performance and employee morale than managers with low skills mastery.[20]
3. *Effective* female and male managers *do not* have significantly different skill profiles,[21] contrary to claims in the popular business press in recent years.[22]

# 21st-Century Managers

Today's workplace is indeed undergoing immense and permanent changes.[23] Organizations have been "reengineered" for greater speed, efficiency, and flexibility.[24] Teams are pushing aside the individual as the primary building block of organizations.[25] Command-and-control management is giving way to participative management and empowerment.[26] Ego-centered leaders are being replaced by customer-centered leaders. Employees increasingly are being viewed as internal customers. All this creates a mandate for a new kind of manager in the 21st century.[27] Table 1–1 contrasts the characteristics of past and future managers. As the balance of this book will demonstrate, the managerial shift in Table 1–1 is not just a good idea, it is an absolute necessity in the new workplace.

**Evolution of the 21st-Century Manager    TABLE 1–1**

|  | Past Managers | Future Managers |
|---|---|---|
| **Primary role** | Order giver, privileged elite, manipulator, controller | Facilitator, team member, teacher, advocate, sponsor, coach, partner |
| **Learning and knowledge** | Periodic learning, narrow specialist | Continuous life-long learning, generalist with multiple specialties |
| **Compensation criteria** | Time, effort, rank | Skills, results |
| **Cultural orientation** | Monocultural, monolingual | Multicultural, multilingual |
| **Primary source of influence** | Formal authority | Knowledge (technical and interpersonal) |
| **View of people** | Potential problem | Primary resource |
| **Primary communication Pattern** | Vertical | Multidirectional |
| **Decision-making style** | Limited input for individual decisions | Broad-based input for joint decisions |
| **Ethical considerations** | Afterthought | Forethought |
| **Nature of interpersonal relationships** | Competitive (win–lose) | Cooperative (win–win) |
| **Handling of power and key information** | Hoard and restrict access | Share and broaden access |
| **Approach to change** | Resist | Facilitate |

# The Field of Organizational Behavior: Past and Present

**organizational behavior (OB)**

Interdisciplinary field dedicated to better understanding and managing people at work.

**Organizational behavior,** commonly referred to as OB, is an interdisciplinary field dedicated to better understanding and managing people at work. By definition, organizational behavior is both research and application oriented. Three basic levels of analysis in OB are individual, group, and organizational. OB draws upon a diverse array of disciplines, including psychology, management, sociology, organization theory, social psychology, statistics, anthropology, general systems theory, economics, information technology, political science, vocational counseling, human stress management, psychometrics, ergonomics, decision theory, and ethics. This rich heritage has spawned many competing perspectives and theories about human work behavior. In fact, one researcher identified 73 established OB theories.[28]

Organizational behavior is an academic designation. With the exception of teaching/research positions, OB is not an everyday job category such as accounting, marketing, or finance. Students of OB typically do not get jobs in organizational behavior, per se. This reality in no way demeans OB or lessens its importance in effective organizational management. OB is a *horizontal* discipline that cuts across virtually every job category, business function, and professional specialty. Anyone who plans to make a living in a large or small, public or private, organization needs to study organizational behavior. Both managers and nonmanagers alike need a solid grounding in OB.

A historical perspective of the study of people at work helps in studying organizational behavior. According to a management history expert, this is important because

> Historical perspective is the study of a subject in light of its earliest phases and subsequent evolution. Historical perspective differs from history in that the object of historical perspective is to sharpen one's vision of the present, not the past.[29]

In other words, we can better understand where the field of OB is today and where it appears to be headed by appreciating where it has been. Let us examine three significant landmarks in the evolution of understanding and managing people:

1. The human relations movement.
2. The total quality management movement.
3. The contingency approach to management.

## The Human Relations Movement

A unique combination of factors during the 1930s fostered the human relations movement. First, following legalization of union–management collective bargaining in the United States in 1935, management began looking for new ways of handling employees. Second, behavioral scientists conducting on-the-job research started calling for more attention to the "human" factor. Managers who had lost the battle to keep unions out of their factories heeded the call for better human relations and improved working conditions. One such study, conducted at Western Electric's Chicago-area Hawthorne plant, was a prime stimulus for the human relations movement. Ironically, many of the Hawthorne findings have turned out to be more myth than fact.

**The Hawthorne Legacy**    Interviews conducted decades later with three subjects of the Hawthorne studies and reanalysis of the original data with modern statistical techniques do not support initial conclusions about the positive effect of supportive supervision. Specifically, money, fear of unemployment during the Great Depression, managerial discipline, and high-quality raw materials—not supportive supervision—turned out to be responsible for high output in the relay assembly test room experiments.[30] Nonetheless, the human relations movement gathered momentum through the 1950s, as academics and managers alike made stirring claims about the powerful effect that individual needs, supportive supervision, and group dynamics apparently had on job performance.

### The Writings of Mayo and Follett

Essential to the human relations movement were the writings of Elton Mayo and Mary Parker Follett. Australian-born Mayo, who headed the Harvard researchers at Hawthorne, advised managers to attend to employees' emotional needs in his 1933 classic, *The Human Problems of an Industrial Civilization.* Follett was a true pioneer, not only as a female management consultant in the male-dominated industrial world of the 1920s, but also as a writer who saw employees as complex bundles of attitudes, beliefs, and needs. Mary Parker Follett was way ahead of her time in telling managers to motivate job performance instead of merely demanding it, a "pull" rather than "push" strategy. She also built a logical bridge between political democracy and a cooperative spirit in the workplace.[31]

These relay assembly test room employees in the classic Hawthorne Western Electric studies turned in record performance. Why? No one knows for certain, and debate continues to this day. Supportive supervision was long believed to be the key factor. Whatever the reason, Hawthorne gave the budding human relations movement needed research credibility.

### McGregor's Theory Y

In 1960, Douglas McGregor wrote a book entitled *The Human Side of Enterprise,* which has become an important philosophical base for the modern view of people at work.[32] Drawing upon his experience as a management consultant, McGregor formulated two sharply contrasting sets of assumptions about human nature (see Table 1–2). His Theory X assumptions were pessimistic and negative and, according to McGregor's interpretation, typical of how managers traditionally perceived employees. To help managers break with this negative tradition, McGregor formulated his **Theory Y,** a modern and positive set of assumptions about people. McGregor believed managers could accomplish more through others by viewing them as self-energized, committed, responsible, and creative beings.

A survey of 10,227 employees from many industries across the United States challenges managers to do a better job of acting on McGregor's Theory Y assumptions. From the employees' perspective, Theory X management practices are the major barrier to productivity improvement and employee well-being. The researcher concluded:

> The most noteworthy finding from our survey is that an overwhelming number of American workers—some 97%—desire work conditions known to facilitate high productivity. Workers uniformly reported— regardless of the type of organization, age, gender, pay schedule, or level in the organizational hierarchy—that they needed and wanted in their own workplaces the conditions for collaboration, commitment, and creativity research has demonstrated as necessary for both productivity and health. Just as noteworthy, however, is the finding that the actual conditions of work supplied by management are those conditions that research has identified as *competence suppressors*—procedures, policies, and practices that prevent or punish expressions of competence and most characterize unproductive organizations.[33]

**Theory Y**

McGregor's modern and positive assumptions about employees being responsible and creative.

learning objective 2

Contrast McGregor's Theory X and Theory Y assumptions about employees.

**TABLE 1–2**    McGregor's Theory X and Theory Y

| Outdated (Theory X) Assumptions about People at Work | Modern (Theory Y) Assumptions about People at Work |
|---|---|
| 1. Most people dislike work; they avoid it when they can. | 1. Work is a natural activity, like play or rest. |
| 2. Most people must be coerced and threatened with punishment before they will work. People require close direction when they are working. | 2. People are capable of self-direction and self-control if they are committed to objectives. |
| 3. Most people actually prefer to be directed. They tend to avoid responsibility and exhibit little ambition. They are interested only in security. | 3. People generally become committed to organizational objectives if they are rewarded for doing so. |
| | 4. The typical employee can learn to accept and seek responsibility. |
| | 5. The typical member of the general population has imagination, ingenuity, and creativity. |

SOURCE: Adapted from D McGregor, *The Human Side of Enterprise* (New York: McGraw-Hill, 1960), Ch 4.

**New Assumptions about Human Nature**    Unfortunately, unsophisticated behavioral research methods caused the human relationists to embrace some naive and misleading conclusions. For example, human relationists believed in the axiom, "A satisfied employee is a hardworking employee." Subsequent research, as discussed later in this book, shows the satisfaction–performance linkage to be more complex than originally thought.

Despite its shortcomings, the human relations movement opened the door to more progressive thinking about human nature. Rather than continuing to view employees as passive economic beings, managers began to see them as active social beings and took steps to create more humane work environments.[34]

# The Total Quality Management Movement

In 1980, NBC aired a television documentary titled *If Japan Can . . . Why Can't We?* It was a wake-up call for North American companies to dramatically improve product quality or continue losing market share to Japanese electronics and automobile companies. A full-fledged movement ensued during the 1980s and 1990s. Much was written, said, and done about improving the quality of both goods and services.[35] Thanks to the concept of *total quality management (TQM),* the quality of much of what we buy today is significantly better than in the past. The underlying principles of TQM are more important than ever given the growth of both e-business on the Internet and the overall service economy. For example, when Ideal Supply Company consolidates and delivers orders for Vermont Teddy Bear Company, it has to get each gift to the right customer at the right time. But the logistics company has to do more: Especially for highly perishable shipments of flowers, Vermont Teddy Bear also wants its people to be able to look at up-to-the-minute data on upcoming orders so that the company can operate more efficiently. It wants zero defects in its information from Ideal, not just in the actual deliveries.[36]

**Group Exercise**

Exploring Total Quality Management

Managers know that customers expect top-quality goods, services, and information, and that places quality among managers' top concerns. In a recent survey of chief financial officers, meeting customer demands placed second only to finding skilled staff as the biggest challenge facing the executives' company.[37] TQM principles have profound practical implications for managing people today.[38]

> **total quality management (TQM)**
>
> An organizational culture dedicated to training, continuous improvement, and customer satisfaction.

**What Is TQM?** Experts on the subject offered this definition of **total quality management:**

> TQM means that the organization's culture is defined by and supports the constant attainment of customer satisfaction through an integrated system of tools, techniques, and training. This involves the continuous improvement of organizational processes, resulting in high-quality products and services.[39]

Quality consultant Richard J Schonberger sums up TQM as "continuous, customer-centered, employee-driven improvement."[40] TQM is necessarily employee driven because product/service quality cannot be continuously improved without the active learning and participation of *every* employee. Thus, in successful quality improvement programs, TQM principles are embedded in the organization's culture, and hiring is very selective (see Skills & Best Practices).

**The Deming Legacy** TQM is firmly established today thanks in large part to the pioneering work of W Edwards Deming.[41] Ironically, the mathematician credited with Japan's post–World War II quality revolution rarely talked in terms of quality. He instead preferred to discuss "good management" during the hard-hitting seminars he delivered right up until his death at age 93 in 1993.[42] Although Deming's passion was the statistical measurement and reduction of variations in industrial processes, he had much to say about how employees should be treated. Regarding the human side of quality improvement, Deming called for the following:

- Formal training in statistical process control techniques and teamwork.
- Helpful leadership, rather than order giving and punishment.
- Elimination of fear so employees will feel free to ask questions.
- Emphasis on continuous process improvements rather than on numerical quotas.
- Teamwork.
- Elimination of barriers to good workmanship.[43]

One of Deming's most enduring lessons for managers is his 85–15 rule.[44] Specifically, when things go wrong, there is roughly an 85% chance the *system* (including

## Hiring Decisions Deliver Quality at Four Seasons

Guests are willing to spend thousands of dollars for a night at a Four Seasons hotel because service there is extraordinary. Employees are attentive to each guest, looking for opportunities to be helpful with every detail.

That level of service requires an intense commitment to the company's goals by all employees, year after year. Four Seasons doesn't assume that just anyone will have that commitment. The company's hiring process focuses on finding people whose attitude is positive and helpful, who value treating others as they would like to be treated. Rather than simply screening résumés for experience, human resource personnel bring in candidates for interviews. Founder and chief executive Isadore Sharp explains, "We look for people who say, 'I'd be proud to be a doorman.'" To recognize such employees, Four Seasons has at least four people, including the general manager, interview each candidate.

Of course, having the best employees also requires benefits that make the company attractive. Besides paying its employees near-top earnings for the industry, the company offers retirement benefits and gives everyone access to a comfortable employee cafeteria in the hotel. Best of all, any employee with six months of experience can stay three nights at any Four Seasons hotel or resort each year at no charge. As employees' experience increases, so does the number of free nights. That's a luxurious way to learn firsthand the meaning of first-class service.

**SOURCE: Based on Jeffrey M O'Brien, "A Perfect Season,"** *Fortune,* **February 1, 2008, http://money.cnn.com.**

> **learning objective 3**
>
> Explain the managerial significance of Deming's 85–15 rule, and identify the four principles of total quality management (TQM).

management, machinery, and rules) is at fault. Only about 15% of the time is the individual employee at fault. Unfortunately, as Deming observed, the typical manager spends most of his or her time wrongly blaming and punishing individuals for system failures. Statistical analysis is required to uncover system failures.

**Principles of TQM**     Despite variations in the language and scope of TQM programs, it is possible to identify four common TQM principles:

1. Do it right the first time to eliminate costly rework.
2. Listen to and learn from customers and employees.
3. Make continuous improvement an everyday matter.
4. Build teamwork, trust, and mutual respect.[45]

Deming's influence is clearly evident in this list. Once again, as with the human relations movement, we see people as the key factor in organizational success. Daimler drives that point home for high-end customers who plunk down $190,000 for a new Mercedes-Benz CL65 AMG:

> Every CL65 sold this year will ease onto its owner's cobbled drive boasting an aluminum V-12 bi-turbo engine, signed on its carbon-fiber face by the exacting craftsman who assembled it by hand.[46]

For both producers and consumers of high-quality goods and services, quality is indeed a matter of *personal* importance.

In summary, TQM advocates have made a valuable contribution to the field of OB by providing a *practical* context for managing people. When people are managed according to TQM principles, everyone is more likely to get the employment opportunities and high-quality goods and services they demand. As you will see many times in later chapters, this book is anchored to Deming's philosophy and TQM principles.

# The Contingency Approach to Management

Scholars have wrestled for many years with the problem of how best to apply the diverse and growing collection of management tools and techniques. Their answer is the contingency approach. The **contingency approach** calls for using management concepts and techniques in a situationally appropriate manner, instead of trying to rely on "one best way."

**contingency approach**

Using management tools and techniques in a situationally appropriate manner; avoiding the one-best-way mentality.

**Manager's Hot Seat Application**

Project Management: Steering the Committee

The contingency approach encourages managers to view organizational behavior within a situational context. According to this modern perspective, evolving situations, not hard-and-fast rules, determine when and where various management techniques are appropriate. Harvard's Clayton Christensen put it this way: "Many of the widely accepted principles of good management are only situationally appropriate."[47] For example, as will be discussed in Chapter 14, contingency researchers have determined that there is no single best style of leadership. Organizational behavior specialists embrace the contingency approach because it helps them realistically interrelate individuals, groups, and organizations. Moreover, the contingency approach sends a clear message to managers in today's global economy: Carefully read the situation and then apply lessons learned from published research studies,[48] observing role models, self-study and training, and personal experience in situationally appropriate ways.

# New Directions in OB

The field of OB is a dynamic work in progress—not static and in final form. As such, OB is being redirected and reshaped by various forces both inside and outside the discipline, including new concepts, models, and technology. In this section, we explore three general new directions for OB: human and social capital, *positive* organizational behavior, and impacts of the Internet revolution.

## The Age of Human and Social Capital

Management is a lot like juggling. Everything is constantly in motion, with several things up in the air at any given time. Strategically speaking, managers juggle human, financial, material, informational, and technological resources. Each is vital to success in its own way. But jugglers remind us that some objects are rubber and some are glass. Dropped rubber objects bounce; dropped glass objects break. As more and more managers have come to realize, we cannot afford to drop the people factor (referred to in Figure 1–2 as human and social capital).

**FIGURE 1–2**
The Strategic Importance and Dimensions of Human and Social Capital

Strategic assumption: People, individually and collectively, are the key to organizational success

**Individual human capital**
- Intelligence/abilities/knowledge
- Visions/dreams/aspirations
- Technical and social skills
- Confidence/self-esteem
- Initiative/entrepreneurship
- Adaptability/flexibility
- Readiness to learn
- Creativity
- Enthusiasm
- Motivation/commitment
- Persistence
- Ethical standards/courage
- Honesty
- Emotional maturity

**Organizational learning**
(Shared knowledge)

**Social capital**
- Shared visions/goals
- Shared values
- Trust
- Mutual respect/goodwill
- Friendship/support groups
- Mentoring/positive role modeling
- Participation/empowerment
- Connections/sources
- Networks/affiliations
- Cooperation/collaboration
- Teamwork
- Camaraderie
- Assertive (rather than aggressive) communication
- Functional (rather than dysfunctional) conflict
- Win–win negotiations
- Philanthropy/volunteering

## What Is Human Capital? (Hint: Think BIG)

A team of human resource management authors recently offered this perspective:

> We're living in a time when a new economic paradigm—characterized by speed, innovation, short cycle times, quality, and customer satisfaction—is highlighting the importance of intangible assets, such as brand recognition, knowledge, innovation, and particularly human capital.[49]

**human capital**

The productive potential of one's knowledge and actions.

**Human capital** is the productive potential of an individual's knowledge and actions.[50] *Potential* is the operative word in this intentionally broad definition. When you are hungry, money in your pocket is good because it has the potential to buy a meal. Likewise, a present or future employee with the right combination of knowledge, skills, and motivation to excel represents human capital with the potential to give the organization a competitive advantage. For that reason, today's executives are very concerned about recruiting and retaining talented people, developing employees' skills, getting them fully engaged, and preparing for the day when valuable people retire or leave for another employer.[51] At DuPont, for example, Ellen Kullman is executive vice president of two divisions that together are responsible for generating 70% of the company's pretax income. That makes her valuable, of course, but Kullman is quick to credit her employees for their contributions. Much of her time is devoted to developing employees and assigning them to the projects to which they can contribute most effectively.[52]

Within the context of individual organizations, researchers have identified and defined five important human capital *outcomes* (see Table 1–3). These definitions are a necessary first step toward eventually measuring an organization's attempts to build its human capital.[53] Measurement, of course, is the key to accountability.

## What Is Social Capital?

Our focus now shifts from the individual to social units (e.g., friends, family, company, group or club, nation). Think *relationships*.

## TABLE 1–3 | Five Human Capital Outcomes Defined

| | Definition |
|---|---|
| **Leadership/managerial practices** | The effectiveness of managers' and leaders' ability to optimize the organization's human capital through communication, performance feedback, efforts to instill confidence, and demonstration of key organizational values |
| **Workforce optimization** | The organization's success in optimizing the performance of its workforce by means of developing and sustaining talent (skills, competencies, abilities, etc.) and guiding and managing its application on the job |
| **Learning capacity** | The organization's overall ability to learn, change, and continually improve |
| **Knowledge accessibility** | The extent of the organization's "collaborativeness" and its current efforts and ability to share knowledge and ideas across the organization |
| **Talent engagement** | The organization's ability to retain, engage, and optimize the value of its talent |

SOURCE: L Bassi and D McMurrer, "Developing Measurement Systems for Managing in the Knowledge Era," *Organizational Dynamics*, no. 2, 2005, Table 2, p 190.

**Social capital** is productive potential resulting from strong relationships, goodwill, trust, and cooperative effort.[54] Again, the word *potential* is key. According to experts on the subject: "It's true: the social capital that used to be a given in organizations is now rare and endangered. But the social capital we can build will allow us to capitalize on the volatile, virtual possibilities of today's business environment"[55] (see Skills & Best Practices). Relationships do matter. One general survey revealed that 77% of the women and 63% of the men rated "Good relationship with boss" extremely important. Other factors—including good equipment, resources, easy commute, and flexible hours—received lower ratings.[56]

> **social capital**
>
> **The productive potential of strong, trusting, and cooperative relationships.**

**Test Your Knowledge**

Training Methods

### How to Build Human and Social Capital

Making the leap from concept to practice within this broad domain appears to be a daunting task. But we have a handy shortcut to jump-start your imagination. *Fortune* magazine, as mentioned earlier, publishes its annual list of "The 100 Best Companies to Work For" every January. Reading the brief side comments about the 100 selected companies is time well spent because they are both interesting and inspiring (as well as being a great resource for job hunters). These model companies are good at building human and/or social capital. Another area to watch is the *social entrepreneurship* movement that challenges students and businesspeople to create businesses with a dual bottom line. Social entrepreneurs apply business methods, business capital, and businesspeople to solve social problems such as extreme poverty and environmental degradation. Examples are as varied as German-based Hasso Plattner Ventures Africa, which targets investment dollars to African business ventures, Indian Ratan Tata's idea for an inexpensive automobile,

Target has been recognized for its financial performance and strength. It has been honored as one of America's most admired companies, one of the best companies for both working mothers and Latinos, one of the best corporate citizens, and a leader in its commitment to the education and training of its people. To what extent do you think its positive work environment affects its financial success?

---

**SKILLS & BEST PRACTICES**

## Social Capital a Must in Development Projects

In Indonesia, the Kecamatan Development Program has helped more than 34,000 villages address poverty through projects such as repairing schools and building water supply systems. Although money comes from the United States through the World Bank, all the decisions about what to do with the money are made democratically in each village. Before projects receive funding, various groups in the village must be able to demonstrate that they are able to cooperate. In other words, while the World Bank provides financial capital, the projects also require social capital.

In fact, some researchers have found evidence that social capital is an important ingredient in development projects. For instance, political scientist Anirudh Krishna measured the social capital of villages in India. Krishna found that villagers where social capital was high used their resources more efficiently by cooperating instead of competing. He also found that aid organizations could not build social capital themselves. That's why the structure of the Kecamatan Development Program is so important; it gives the people of the local communities an incentive to build relationships themselves.

**SOURCE:** Based on S Vedantam, "One Thing We Can't Build Alone in Iraq," *Washington Post,* October 29, 2007, www.washingtonpost.com; World Bank, "Indonesia Kecamatan Development Program," Projects and Programs, accessed February 22, 2008; and World Bank, "Kecamatan Development Project in Indonesia," *PovertyNet,* July 25, 2003, http://poverty2.forumone.com.

and the Clinton Foundation's projects to make solutions to HIV/AIDS more practical in less-developed nations.[57] This promising initiative meshes nicely with the areas of corporate social responsibility and business ethics.

Meanwhile, relative to the field of OB, many of the ideas discussed in this book relate directly or indirectly to building human and social capital (e.g., managing diversity, self-efficacy, self-management, emotional intelligence, goal setting, positive reinforcement, group problem solving, group development, building trust, teamwork, managing conflict, communicating, empowerment, leadership, and organizational learning).

# The Emerging Area of Positive Organizational Behavior (POB)

OB draws heavily on the field of psychology. So major shifts and trends in psychology eventually ripple through to OB. One such shift being felt in OB is the positive psychology movement. This exciting new direction promises to broaden the scope and practical relevance of OB.

Employees at Google are a well-fed bunch. The company even has a rule—workers can never be more than 100 feet away from food. Elaborate free snack stations and restaurants are scattered throughout the company where this Google chef is making sushi for an employee. How does this environment contribute to the improvement of employees' positive attributes and capabilities?

## The Positive Psychology Movement

Something curious happened to the field of psychology during the last half of the 20th century. It took a distinctly negative turn. Theory and research became preoccupied with mental and behavioral pathologies; in other words, what was *wrong* with people! Following the traditional medical model, most researchers and practicing psychologists devoted their attention to diagnosing what was wrong with people and trying to make them better. At the turn of the 21st century, bits and pieces of an alternative perspective advocated by pioneering psychologists such as Abraham Maslow and Carl Rogers were pulled together under the label of positive psychology. This approach recommended focusing on human strengths and potential as a way to possibly *prevent* mental and behavioral problems and improve the general quality of life. A pair of positive psychologists described their new multilevel approach as follows:

> The field of positive psychology at the subjective level is about valued subjective experiences: well-being, contentment, and satisfaction (in the past); hope and optimism (for the future); and flow and happiness (in the present). At the individual level, it is about positive individual traits: the capacity for love and vocation, courage, interpersonal skill, aesthetic sensibility, perseverance, forgiveness, originality, future mindedness, spirituality, high talent, and wisdom. At the group level, it is about the civic virtues and the institutions that move individuals toward better citizenship: responsibility, nurturance, altruism, civility, moderation, tolerance, and work ethic.[58]

This is an extremely broad agenda for understanding and improving the human condition. However, we foresee a productive marriage between the concepts of human and social capital and the positive psychology movement, as it evolves into POB.[59]

## Positive Organizational Behavior: Definition and Key Dimensions

University of Nebraska OB scholar Fred Luthans defines **positive organizational behavior (POB)** as "the study and application of positively oriented human resource strengths and psychological capacities that can be measured, developed, and effectively managed for performance improvement in today's workplace."[60] His emphasis on study and measurement (meaning a coherent body of theory and research evidence) clearly sets POB apart from the quick-and-easy self-improvement books commonly found on best-seller lists. Also, POB focuses positive psychology more narrowly on the workplace.[61]

> **positive organizational behavior (POB)**
>
> The study and improvement of employees' positive attributes and capabilities.

Luthans created the CHOSE acronym to identify five key dimensions of POB (see Table 1–4). Recent research shows that POB is positively associated with employee engagement, organizational commitment, job satisfaction, performance, and customer satisfaction.[62] Progressive managers already know the value of a positive workplace atmosphere, as evidenced by the following situations: At Plante & Moran, the 1,356-employee accounting firm in Southfield, Michigan, the "goal is a 'jerk-free' workforce . . . , where the staff is encouraged to live by the Golden Rule and abide by the credo 'Speak up! If it's not right, we'll change it.'"[63] And at Sunnyvale, California–based Network Appliance, employees rate their top managers as "easy to approach." For example, when some employees asked for health benefits to be extended to cover the treatment of autism in family members, the data-storage company responded by adding that benefit.[64]

> **learning objective 6**
>
> Define the term *e-business*, and explain at least three practical lessons about effective e-leadership in a virtual organization.

# The Internet and E-Business Revolution

Experts on the subject draw an important distinction between *e-commerce* (buying and selling goods and services over the Internet) and **e-business,** using the Internet to facilitate *every* aspect of running a business.[65] Today's companies are using the Internet to share information among employees and with suppliers and customers. Employees can

> **E-business**
>
> Running the *entire* business via the Internet.

**Luthans' CHOSE Model of Key POB Dimensions (with cross-references to related topics in this textbook)**   **TABLE 1–4**

> **Confidence/self-efficacy:** One's belief (confidence) in being able to successfully execute a specific task in a given context. (See Chapter 5.)
>
> **Hope:** One who sets goals, figures out how to achieve them (identify pathways) and is self-motivated to accomplish them, that is, willpower and "waypower." (See Chapters 5 and 7.)
>
> **Optimism:** Positive outcome expectancy and/or a positive causal attribution, but is still emotional and linked with happiness, perseverance, and success. (See Chapters 4, 5, 7, and 16.)
>
> **Subjective well-being:** Beyond happiness emotion, how people cognitively process and evaluate their lives, the satisfaction with their lives. (See Chapters 4, 5, and 6.)
>
> **Emotional intelligence:** Capacity for recognizing and managing one's own and others' emotions—self-awareness, self-motivation, being empathetic, and having social skills. (See Chapters 5, 9, 11, 12, 13, and 14.)

SOURCE: From *The Academy of Management Executive: The Thinking Manager's Source* by F Luthans. Copyright © 2002 by Academy of Management. Reproduced with permission of Academy of Management via Copyright Clearance Center.

© 2002 Ted Goff

"So what's the problem with morale now?"

Copyright © 2002 Ted Goff. Reprinted with permission.

## Web 2.0 Requires Management 2.0

As more and more individuals went online, they began exerting control over the information they send and receive: writing blogs, building relationships on social networking sites, and contributing to user-created projects like Wikipedia. This active involvement, relying heavily on user-created content, has come to be called *Web 2.0.* And now employees are expecting to share information just as freely at work.

As a result, predicts Gary Hamel in *The Future of Management,* "Management 2.0 is going to look a lot like Web 2.0." He means managers of the future won't control the flow of information; instead, they will be expected to provide the means for employees to collaborate and share information with each other to achieve common goals. Ideally, this collaboration will bring the best ideas to the surface.

Dale Dauten, founder of the Innovators' Lab, was impressed with Hamel's idea and decided to try it with clients. He suggested that managers choose an issue and start a company blog about that topic. Anyone in the company would be able to contribute their thoughts and react to each other's contributions.

So far, Dauten says, no one has taken him up on the idea. But perhaps by the time you read this story, this type of collaboration will be the norm. The Internet moves that fast.

**SOURCE: Based on Dale Dauten, "Managers of Future Will Shake Things Up," *The Arizona Republic,* December 3, 2007, p. B7.**

collaborate online, whether developing new products, creating marketing plans, or resolving billing problems. They can demonstrate ideas and products or carry on conversation in virtual communities, such as Second Life, where they may be meeting with people from anywhere in the world.[66] The Internet also lets even tiny businesses link to powerful software for accounting, inventory, and other information-based systems. That means you don't have to be an industry giant to stay competitive in the Internet Age.

One development with important implications for managers is the ability to link to the Internet with small, portable devices, including cell phones, personal digital assistants (PDAs, such as the BlackBerry), and laptop computers. As discussed in Chapter 12, these devices free many workers to do their job anywhere they can log on—at a client's work site, at home, or in the neighborhood coffee shop.[67] Today's managers have to be able to select workers who have the self-discipline to work off-site, as well as to measure performance when they cannot directly observe their workers much of the time. On the flip side, employees and their managers are concerned that linking to the office everywhere means they cannot or will not ever disconnect. Managers have to be sure their people don't succumb to stress and exhaustion from being constantly tethered to their job.

E-business has significant implications for OB because it eventually will seep into every corner of life both on and off the job. Thanks to the Internet, we are able to make quicker and better decisions because of speedy access to vital information (see Skills & Best Practices). The Internet also allows us to seemingly defy the laws of physics by being in more than one place at a time. For example, consider the futuristic situation at Hackensack University Medical Center in New Jersey:

> Doctors can tap an interval Web site to examine X-rays from a PC anywhere. Patients can use 37-inch plasma TVs in their rooms to surf the Net for information about their medical conditions. There's even a life-size robot, Mr Rounder, that doctors can control from their laptops at home. They direct the digital doc, complete with white lab coat and stethoscope, into hospital rooms and use two-way video to discuss patients' conditions.[68]

In short, organizational life will never be the same because of e-mail, e-learning, e-management, e-leadership, virtual teams, and virtual organizations.[69] You will learn more about virtual teams and virtual organizations in later chapters.

# key terms

# chapter summary

- *Identify at least four of Pfeffer's people-centered practices, and define the term* management. Pfeffer's seven people-centered practices are job security, careful hiring, power to the people, generous pay for performance, lots of training, less emphasis on status, and trust building. *Management* is the process of working with and through others to achieve organizational objectives in an efficient and ethical manner.

- *Contrast McGregor's Theory X and Theory Y assumptions about employees.* Theory X employees, according to traditional thinking, dislike work, require close supervision, and are primarily interested in security. According to the modern Theory Y view, employees are capable of self-direction, of seeking responsibility, and of being creative.

- *Explain the managerial significance of Deming's 85–15 rule, and identify the four principles of total quality management (TQM).* Deming claimed that about 85% of organizational failures are due to system breakdowns involving factors such as management, machinery, or work rules. He believed the workers themselves are responsible for failures only about 15% of the time. Consequently, Deming criticized the standard practice of blaming and punishing individuals for what are typically *system* failures beyond their immediate control. The four principles of TQM are (a) do it right the first time to eliminate costly rework; (b) listen to and learn from customers and employees; (c) make continuous improvement an everyday matter; and (d) build teamwork, trust, and mutual respect.

- *Contrast human and social capital, and identify five measurable outcomes when building human capital.* Human capital involves *individual* characteristics and abilities; social capital involves *social* relationships. Human capital is the productive potential of an individual's knowledge and actions. Social capital is productive potential resulting from strong relationships, goodwill, trust, and cooperative effort. Five measurable outcomes of programs to build human capital are (a) leadership/managerial practices; (b) workforce optimization; (c) learning capacity; (d) knowledge accessibility; and (e) talent engagement.

- *Explain the impact of the positive psychology movement on the field of OB.* Reversing psychology's long-standing preoccupation with what is wrong with people, positive psychology instead focuses on identifying and building human strengths and potential. Accordingly, Luthans recommends positive organizational behavior (POB) and identifies its basic elements with the CHOSE model. This acronym stands for Confidence/self-efficacy, Hope, Optimism, Subjective well-being, and Emotional intelligence.

- *Define the term* e-business, *and explain at least three practical lessons about effective e-leadership in a virtual organization.* E-business involves using the Internet to more effectively and efficiently manage *every* aspect of a business. Today's employees are skilled in many aspects of digital communication: e-mail, blogs, social networking sites, and sites where users provide and refine content, such as Wikipedia. In such an environment, where employees have more control over the information they can access and share, the manager's role is evolving into one of providing the means for collaboration.

# discussion questions

1. Which of Pfeffer's seven people-centered practices are evident in the chapter-opening case? Explain.
2. In your opinion, what are the three or four most important strategic results in Figure 1–1? Why?
3. What is your personal experience with Theory X and Theory Y managers (see Table 1–2)? Which did you prefer? Why?
4. What are you doing to build human and social capital?
5. As the field of positive organizational behavior (POB) evolves, what potential impacts on the practice of management do you foresee?

# ethical dilemma

## You Mean Cheating Is Wrong?

College students are disturbed by recent corporate scandals: Some 84% believe the U.S. is having a business crisis, and 77% think CEOs should be held personally responsible for it.

But when the same students are asked about their own ethics, it's another story. Some 59% admit cheating on a test (66% of men, 54% of women). And only 19% say they would report a classmate who cheated (23% of men, but 15% of women—even though recent whistle-blowers have been women).

The survey of 1,100 students on 27 U.S. campuses was conducted by Students in Free Enterprise (SIFE), a non-profit that teams up with corporations to teach students ethical business practices. "There's a lack of understanding about ethics and how ethics are applied in real life," says Alvin Rohrs, SIFE'S CEO. "We have to get young people to stop and think about ethics and the decisions they're making." Otherwise, today's students may be tomorrow's criminals.[70] Unfortunately, a recent survey of 726 U.S. teens suggests that ethics may be a bigger problem than expected. Thirty-eight percent of the sample indicated that it is necessary to lie, cheat, plagiarize, or behave violently in order to succeed.[71]

### How Should We Interpret This Hypocritical Double Standard?

1. Don't worry, most students know the difference between school and real life. They'll do the right thing when it really counts. Explain your rationale.

2. Whether in the classroom or on the job, pressure for results is the problem. People tend to take shortcuts and bend the rules when they're pressured. Explain.

3. A cheater today is a cheater tomorrow. Explain.

4. College professors need to do a better job with ethics education. How?

5. Both students and managers need to be held personally accountable for their unethical behavior. How?

6. Invent other interpretations or options. Discuss.

For an interpretation of this situation, visit our Web site, **www.mhhe.com/kinickiob4e.**

If you're looking for additional study materials, be sure to check out the Online Learning Center at

**www.mhhe.com/kinickiob4e**

for more information and interactivities that correspond to this chapter.

# U.S. Lawmakers Believe that Yahoo Committed Ethical Breach in China

**FOR DISCUSSION**

How do you view Yahoo's actions? Explain. For an interpretation of this case and additional comments, visit our Online Learning Center at

www.mhhe.com/ kinickiob4e

The hearing by the House Foreign Affairs Committee on Yahoo's conduct in China was a rare public shaming of the Internet leader, whose actions led to the imprisonment of journalist Shi Tao.

Committee Chairman Tom Lantos (D-Burlingame) and other lawmakers pilloried Yang and Michael Callahan, Yahoo's executive vice president and general counsel, for providing Chinese officials with Shi's identity from his e-mail address in 2004, then misleading lawmakers last year [2006] about what it knew about the case.

"While technologically and financially you are giants, morally you are pygmies," Lantos said, scolding Yahoo executives. . . .

Yahoo, Google Inc., eBay Inc., and other major Web players have invested billions in China to capture a share of the country's exploding Internet population. But they have been largely overwhelmed by local competitors, such as Alibaba.com and Baidu.com, as well as by concessions they must make to local laws. Google, for example, has faced heavy criticism for proactively censoring Web search results to which it believes the government might object.

Yahoo provided Shi's name to Chinese authorities in 2004 after they demanded to know the owner of a Yahoo e-mail address from which a government memo had been forwarded to an international human rights group. The memo had forbidden new coverage of the anniversary of the Tiananmen Square massacre. After Yahoo disclosed his identity, Shi was sentenced to 10 years for divulging what China had deemed a state secret.

Yang and Callahan defended Yahoo during the hearing, arguing that the company was doing its best to compete in China's notoriously difficult business environment. They noted that Yahoo must respond to lawful requests by authorities for information about Internet users—just as they must when served with subpoenas in the United States.[1]

Balancing conflicting demands of governments, customers, shareholders, and others is difficult under any circumstances. It is especially delicate when operations extend to parts of the world where the standards for business behavior are different. To operate in China, Yahoo had to decide whether to comply with all of the Chinese government's requirements, even if they conflicted with moral standards generally applied to U.S. people and companies. One can argue both sides of this issue. The problem when discussing ethics is that there is no universal standard of ethical behavior.[2]

# The Ethics Challenge

Here are six reasons to be concerned about business ethics:

- Bernard Ebbers, former CEO of WorldCom, serving a 25-year prison sentence for fraud and conspiracy.

- Jeffrey Skilling, former CEO of Enron, serving a 24-year prison sentence for securities fraud and insider trading.

- John Rigas, former CEO of Aldelphia Communications, serving a 15-year prison sentence for conspiracy and bank fraud.

- Sanjay Kumar, former CEO of Computer Associates, serving a 12-year prison sentence for securities fraud and obstruction of justice.

- Dennis Kozlowski, former CEO of Tyco, serving an 8-year prison sentence for grand larceny and falsifying business records.

- Andrew Fastow, former chief financial officer of Enron, serving a 6-year prison sentence for wire fraud.[3]

Thanks to the highly publicized criminal acts of these and other executives, corporate officers in the United States are now subject to high accountability standards and harsh penalties under the Sarbanes-Oxley Act of 2002.[4] The general public and elected officials (who have their own criminal hall of shame) have called for greater attention to ethical conduct. The challenge is immense because unethical behavior is pervasive.

A nationwide survey of 581 human resource professionals revealed that 62% of the respondents occasionally observed unethical behavior at their companies.[5] Unethical behavior occurs from the bottom to the top of organizations. For example, a survey of 3,000 medical doctors revealed that 45% had not reported impaired or incompetent colleagues when they observed a serious medical mistake.[6] Job applicants, for their part, also have ethical lapses. An analysis of 2.6 million background checks by ADP Screening and Selection Services, revealed that "44% of applicants lied about their work histories, 41% lied about their education, and 23% falsified credentials or licenses."[7]

Experts estimated that U.S. companies lose about $600 billion a year from unethical and criminal behavior.[8] Studies in the United States and the United Kingdom further demonstrated that corporate commitment to ethics can be profitable. Evidence suggested that profitability is enhanced by a reputation for honesty and corporate citizenship.[9] Ethics can also impact the quality of people who apply to work in an organization. A recent online survey of 1,020 individuals indicated that 83% rated a company's record of business ethics as "very important" when deciding to accept a job offer. Only 2% rated it as "unimportant."[10]

Clearly, *everyone* needs to join in the effort to stem this tide of unethical conduct. There are a variety of individual and organizational factors that contribute to unethical behavior. OB is an excellent vantage point for better understanding and improving workplace ethics. If OB can provide insights about managing human work behavior, then it can teach us something about avoiding *misbehavior*.

**Ethics** involves the study of moral issues and choices. It is concerned with right versus wrong, good versus bad, and the many shades of gray in supposedly black-and-white issues. Moral implications spring from virtually every decision, both on and off the job. Managers are challenged to have more imagination and the courage to do the right thing to make the world a better place.

**Ethics**
**Study of moral issues and choices.**

To enhance our understanding of ethics within an OB context, we will discuss (1) a global model of corporate social responsibility, (2) a model of individual ethical behavior, (3) general moral principles for managers, and (4) how to improve an organization's ethical climate.

# A Global Model of Corporate Social Responsibility and Ethics

**corporate social responsibility**
Corporations are expected to go above and beyond following the law and making a profit.

**Corporate social responsibility** (CSR) is defined as "the notion that corporations have an obligation to constituent groups in society other than stockholders and beyond that prescribed by law or union contract."[11] CSR challenges businesses to go above and beyond just making a profit to serve the interests and needs of "stakeholders," including past and present employees, customers, suppliers, and countries and communities where facilities are located. Accordingly, some use the term *corporate citizenship*.[12] A good deal of controversy surrounds the drive for greater CSR because classical economic theory says businesses are responsible for producing goods and services to make profits, not solving the world's social, political, and environmental ills. What is your opinion?

University of Georgia business ethics scholar Archie B Carroll views CSR in broad terms. So broad, in fact, that he recently offered a model of CSR/business ethics with the global economy and multinational corporations in mind (see Figure A–1). This

**FIGURE A–1** Carroll's Global Corporate Social Responsibility Pyramid

Be a good global corporate citizen — Philanthropic Responsibility — Do what is *desired* by global stakeholders

Be ethical — Ethical Responsibility — Do what is *expected* by global stakeholders

Obey the law — Legal Responsibility — Do what is *required* by global stakeholder

Be profitable — Economic Responsibility — Do what is *required* by global capitalism

SOURCE: Academy of Management Executive: The Thinking Manager's Source by A B CARROLL. Copyright © 2004 by Academy of Management (NY). Reproduced with permission of Academy of Management (NY) in the format Textbook via Copyright Clearance Center.

model is very timely because it effectively triangulates three major trends: (1) economic globalization, (2) expanding CSR expectations, and (3) the call for improved business ethics. Carroll's global CSR pyramid, from the bottom up, advises organizations in the global economy to:

- *Make a profit* consistent with expectations for international businesses.
- *Obey the law* of host countries as well as international law.
- *Be ethical in its practices,* taking host-country and global standards into consideration.
- *Be a good corporate citizen,* especially as defined by the host country's expectations.[13]

In keeping with the pyramid idea, Carroll emphasizes that each level needs to be solid if the structure is to stand. A pick-and-choose approach to CSR is inappropriate. The top level of the pyramid, according to Carroll, reflects "global society's expectations that business will engage in social activities that are not mandated by law nor generally expected of business in an ethical sense."[14]

# A Model of Individual Ethical Behavior

Ethical and unethical conduct is the product of a complex combination of influences (see Figure A–2). At the center of the model in Figure A–2 is the individual decision maker. He or she has a unique combination of personality characteristics, values, and moral principles, leaning toward or away from ethical behavior. For example, people who think of themselves as being moral individuals tend to take stronger ethical stands.[15] Personal experience with being rewarded or reinforced for certain behaviors and punished for others also shapes the individual's tendency to act ethically or unethically. Finally, gender may play an important role in explaining ethical behavior.

## A Model of Ethical Behavior in the Workplace    FIGURE A–2

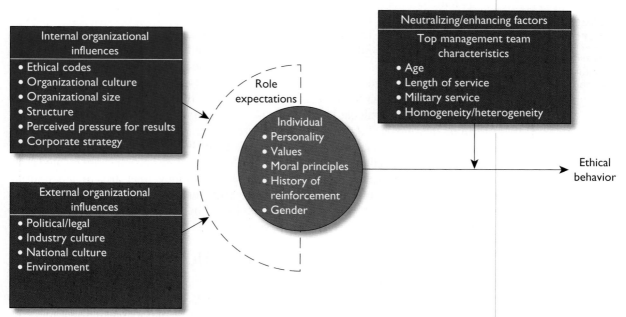

SOURCE: Based in part on A J Daboub, A M A Rasheed, R L Priem, and D A Gray, "Top Management Team Characteristics and Corporate Illegal Activity," *Academy of Management Review,* January 1995, pp 138–70.

**David Radler, former Chicago Sun-Times publisher, was convicted in a multimillion dollar fraud case in 2007. What accounts for such massive wrongdoing? Do actions like Radler's encourage poor ethical choices by others?**

**Self-Assessment Exercise**

Assessing Your Ethical Decision Making Skills

A traditional belief is that women and men have different moral orientations.[16] But a meta-analysis of 113 studies found that women were not more compassionate and caring (a *care* perspective) and less interested in rights and rules (a *justice* perspective) than men.[17] Importantly, this clarifies but does not rule out gender differences in moral reasoning.

Next, Figure A–2 illustrates two major sources of influence on one's role expectations. People assume many roles in life, including those of employee or manager. One's expectations for how those roles should be executed are shaped by a combination of internal and external organizational factors. Let us now examine how various internal and external organizational influences impact ethical behavior and how these effects are neutralized or enhanced by characteristics possessed by an organization's top management team.

## Internal Organizational Influences

Figure A–2 shows six key internal organizational influences on ethical behavior.[18] Corporate ethical codes of conduct and organizational culture, discussed in Chapter 2, clearly contribute to reducing the frequency of unethical behavior. But as ethics coach Karla Robertson says, "Ethics must be lived, not just talked about."[19] In other words, the organization's leaders must model ethical behavior, and they must ensure that the organization's people are aware that ethical choices are made—and valued. During meetings and informal conversations, leaders should talk about situations in which they or others have weighed the ethical implications of decisions related to hiring, sales, financing, and other areas of business. In contrast, if the organization protects an employee who misbehaves but is a top seller, that behavior signals that the company really doesn't value ethical standards as much as its code of conduct might say.

A number of studies have uncovered a positive relationship between organizational size and unethical behavior: Unethical behavior is more frequent in large organizations. Interestingly, research also reveals that managers are more likely to behave unethically in decentralized organizations. Unethical behavior is suspected to occur in this context because lower-level managers want to "look good" for the corporate office. In support of this conclusion, many studies have found a tendency among middle-and lower-level managers to act unethically in the face of perceived pressure for results. This tendency is particularly pronounced when individuals are rewarded for accomplishing their goals.[20] By fostering a pressure-cooker atmosphere for results, managers can unwittingly set the stage for unethical shortcuts by employees who seek to please and be loyal to the company. Unfortunately, the seeds of this problem are planted early in life. In a recent survey of 787 teenagers, 44% said they "feel they're under strong pressure to succeed in school, no matter the cost," and 81% of those pressured teens expect at least as much pressure in the workplace.[21] In the same survey, 69% of the students admitted to lying during the past year.

## External Organizational Influences

Figure A–2 identifies four key external influences on role expectations and ethical behavior. The political/legal system clearly impacts ethical behavior. As previously mentioned, the U.S. political/legal system is demanding and increasingly monitoring corporate ethical behavior. The official tolerance of corruption varies from country to country. Also, the prevailing norms of conduct in some countries promote unethical conduct. Globe-trotting businesspeople need to prepare accordingly.

Moreover, Figure A–2 shows that national culture affects ethical behavior (national cultures are discussed in Chapter 3). This conclusion was supported in a multination study (including the United States, Great Britain, France, Germany, Spain, Switzerland, India, China, and Australia) of management ethics. Managers from each country were asked to judge the ethicality of the 12 behaviors listed in the Hands-On Exercise on page 28. Results revealed significant differences across the 10 nations.[22] That is, managers did not agree about the ethicality of the 12 behaviors. What is your attitude toward these behaviors? (You can find out by completing the Hands-On Exercise.) Finally, the external environment influences ethical behavior. For example, unethical behavior is more likely to occur in environments that are characterized by less generosity and when industry profitability is declining.

CEO Paulette Cole wants to make ethical behavior part of the corporate strategy of ABC Carpet and Home, a trendy Manhattan department store with nearly $80 million in sales. Jewelry made by Ugandan women with AIDS and other products whose proceeds go to foster schools in Central America are being sold there as Cole begins a new business plan. "Knowing that your investment in a product actually has a positive effect on somebody's life makes the design in your hands more important," she says. "My goal is for the store to be 100 percent responsible design."

# Neutralizing/Enhancing Factors

In their search for understanding the causes of ethical behavior, OB researchers uncovered several factors that may weaken or strengthen the relationship between the internal and external influencers shown in Figure A–2 and ethical behavior. These factors all revolve around characteristics possessed by an organization's top management team (TMT): A TMT consists of the CEO and his or her direct reports.[23] The relationship between ethical influencers and ethical behavior is weaker with increasing average age and increasing tenure among the TMT. This result suggests that an older and more experienced group of leaders is less likely to allow unethical behavior to occur. Further, the ethical influencers are less likely to lead to unethical behavior as the number of TMT members with military experience increases and when the TMT possesses heterogenous characteristics (e.g., diverse in terms of gender, age, race, religion, etc.).

This conclusion has two important implications. First, it appears that prior military experience favorably influences the ethical behavior of executives. While OB researchers are uncertain about the cause of this relationship, it may be due to the military's practice of indoctrinating recruits to endorse the values of duty, discipline, and honor. Regardless of the cause, military experience within a TMT is positively related to ethical behavior. Organizations thus should consider the merits of including military experience as one of their selection criteria when hiring or promoting managers. Second, organizations are encouraged to increase the diversity of their TMT if they want to reduce the chances of unethical decision making. Chapter 4 thoroughly discusses how employee diversity can increase creativity, innovation, group problem solving, and productivity.

# HANDS-ON-EXERCISE

## How Ethical Are These Behaviors?

**INSTRUCTIONS** Evaluate the extent to which you believe the following behaviors are ethical. Circle your responses on the rating scales provided. Compute your average score and compare it to the norms.

| | Very Unethical | Unethical | Neither Ethical nor Unethical | Ethical | Very Ethical |
|---|---|---|---|---|---|
| Accepting gifts/favors in exchange for preferential treatment | 1 | 2 | 3 | 4 | 5 |
| Giving gifts/favors in exchange for preferential treatment | 1 | 2 | 3 | 4 | 5 |
| Divulging confidential information | 1 | 2 | 3 | 4 | 5 |
| Calling in sick to take a day off | 1 | 2 | 3 | 4 | 5 |
| Using the organization's materials and supplies for personal use | 1 | 2 | 3 | 4 | 5 |
| Doing personal business on work time | 1 | 2 | 3 | 4 | 5 |
| Taking extra personal time (breaks, etc.) | 1 | 2 | 3 | 4 | 5 |
| Using organizational services for personal use | 1 | 2 | 3 | 4 | 5 |
| Passing blame for errors to an innocent co-worker | 1 | 2 | 3 | 4 | 5 |
| Claiming credit for someone else's work | 1 | 2 | 3 | 4 | 5 |
| Not reporting others' violations of organizational policies | 1 | 2 | 3 | 4 | 5 |
| Concealing one's errors | 1 | 2 | 3 | 4 | 5 |
| Average score = _____ | | | | | |

Norms (average scores by country)

United States = 1.49

Great Britain = 1.70

Australia = 1.44

France = 1.66

China = 1.46

Average of all 10 countries = 1.67

**SOURCE:** The survey behaviors were taken from T Jackson, "Cultural Values and Management Ethics: A 10-Nation Study," *Human Relations,* October 2001, pp 1287–88.

Although China is the largest contributor to counterfeit business around the world, officials like these in Zhejiang Province have been increasing their efforts to confiscate fake products. These officials found 460,000 fake Sony batteries and 30,000 fake Sony earphones. Would you buy a designer knockoff if the price was right?

# A Decision Tree for Ethical Decisions

Ethical acts ultimately involve individual or group decisions. It thus is important to consider the issue of ethical decision making. Harvard Business School professor Constance Bagley suggests that decision trees can help managers to make more ethical decisions.[24] A **decision tree** is a graphical representation of the process underlying decisions and it shows the resulting consequences of making various choices. Decision trees are used as an aid in decision making.

**decision tree**

Graphical representation of the process underlying decision making.

Ethical decision making frequently involves trade-offs, and a decision tree helps managers to navigate through them. The decision tree shown in Figure A–3 can be applied to any type of decision or action that an individual manager or corporation is contemplating. Looking at the tree, the first question to ask is whether or not the proposed action is legal. If the action is illegal, do not do it. If the action is legal, then consider the impact of the action on shareholder value. A decision maximizes shareholder value when it results in a more favorable financial position (e.g., increased profits) for an organization. Whether or not an action maximizes shareholder value, the decision tree shows that managers still need to consider the ethical implications of the decision or action. For example, if an action maximizes shareholder value, the next question to consider is whether or not the action is ethical. The answer to this question is based on considering the positive effect of the action on an organization's other key constituents (i.e., customers, employees, the community, the environment, and suppliers) against the benefit to the shareholders. According to the decision tree framework, managers should make the decision to engage in an action if the benefits to the shareholders exceed the benefits to the other key constituents. Managers should not engage in the action if the other key constituents benefit more from the action than shareholders.

Figure A–3 illustrates that managers use a slightly different perspective when their initial conclusion is that an action does not maximize shareholder value. In this case, the question becomes "Would it be ethical not to take action?" This question necessitates that a manager consider the *harm or cost* of an action to shareholders against the *costs or benefits* to other key constituents. If the costs to shareholders from a managerial decision exceed the costs or benefits to other constituents, the manager or company should not engage in the action. Conversely, the manager or company

**Test Your Knowledge**

Ethics

**FIGURE A–3**
An Ethical
Decision Tree

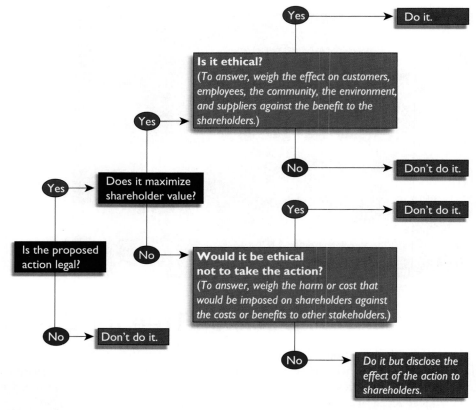

SOURCE: Reprinted by permission of *Harvard Business Review*. From Constance E. Bagley, "The Ethical Leader's Decision Tree," *Harvard Business Review*, February 2003, p 19. Copyright © 2003 by Harvard Business School Publishing Corporation; all rights reserved.

**Group Exercise**

Applying the Ethical Decision-Making Tree

should take action when the perceived costs or benefits to the other constituents are greater than the costs to shareholders. Let us apply this decision tree to the example of whether or not a company should decrease its contributions to retiree health-care benefits while simultaneously raising retirees' contributions. IBM, for example, made the decision to follow this practice.[25]

Is it legal for a company to decrease its contribution to retiree health-care benefits while simultaneously raising retirees' contributions? The answer is yes. Does an organization maximize shareholder value by decreasing its retiree health-care expenses? Again, the answer is yes. We now have to consider the overall benefits to shareholders against the overall benefits to other key constituents. The answer to this question is more complex than it appears and is contingent on an organization's corporate values. Consider the following two examples. In company one, the organization is losing money and needs cash in order to invest in new product development. Management believes that new products will fuel the company's economic growth and ultimate survival. This company's statement of corporate values also reveals that the organization values profits and shareholder return more than employee loyalty. In this case, the company should make the decision to increase retirees' health-care contributions. Company two, in contrast, is profitable and has been experiencing increased market share with its products. This company's statement of corporate values also indicates that employees are the most important constituent it has, even more than shareholders. Southwest Airlines is a good example of a company with these corporate values. In this case, the company should not make the decision to decrease its contribution to retirees' benefits.

It is important to keep in mind that the decision tree cannot provide a quick formula that managers and organizations can use to assess every ethical question. It does, however, provide a framework for considering the trade-offs between managerial and corporate actions and managerial and corporate ethics. Try using this decision tree the next time you are faced with an ethical question or problem.

**Manager's Hot Seat Application**

Ethics: Let's Make a Fourth Quarter Deal

# General Moral Principles

Management consultant and writer Kent Hodgson has helpfully taken managers a step closer to ethical decisions by identifying seven general moral principles (see Table A–1). Hodgson calls them "the magnificent seven" to emphasize their timeless and worldwide relevance. Importantly, according to Hodgson, there are no absolute ethical answers for decision makers. The goal

**TABLE A–1**

### The Magnificent Seven: General Moral Principles for Managers

1. *Dignity of human life: The lives of people are to be respected.* Human beings, by the fact of their existence, have value and dignity. We may not act in ways that directly intend to harm or kill an innocent person. Human beings have a right to live; we have an obligation to respect that right to life. Human life is to be preserved and treated as sacred.

2. *Autonomy: All persons are intrinsically valuable and have the right to self-determination.* We should act in ways that demonstrate each person's worth, dignity, and right to free choice. We have a right to act in ways that assert our own worth and legitimate needs. We should not use others as mere "things" or only as means to an end. Each person has an equal right to basic human liberty, compatible with a similar liberty for others.

3. *Honesty: The truth should be told to those who have a right to know it.* Honesty is also known as integrity, truth telling, and honor. One should speak and act so as to reflect the reality of the situation. Speaking and acting should mirror the way things really are. There are times when others have the right to hear the truth from us; there are times when they do not.

4. *Loyalty: Promises, contracts, and commitments should be honored.* Loyalty includes fidelity, promise keeping, keeping the public trust, good citizenship, excellence in quality of work, reliability, commitment, and honoring just laws, rules, and policies.

5. *Fairness: People should be treated justly.* One has the right to be treated fairly, impartially, and equitably. One has the obligation to treat others fairly and justly. All have the right to the necessities of life—especially those in deep need and the helpless. Justice includes equal, impartial, unbiased treatment. Fairness tolerates diversity and accepts differences in people and their ideas.

6. *Humaneness:* There are two parts: (1) *Our actions ought to accomplish good,* and (2) *we should avoid doing evil.* We should do good to others and to ourselves. We should have concern for the well-being of others; usually, we show this concern in the form of compassion, giving, kindness, serving, and caring.

7. *The common good: Actions should accomplish the "greatest good for the greatest number" of people.* One should act and speak in ways that benefit the welfare of the largest number of people, while trying to protect the rights of individuals.

SOURCE: From *A Rock and a Hard Place: How to Make Ethical Business Decisions When the Choices Are Tough,* by Kent Hodgson, 1992, American Management Association. Reprinted with permission of the author.

for managers should be to rely on moral principles so their decisions are *principled, appropriate,* and *defensible.*[26]

Business writer Suzy Welch recalls many people who have applied these principles at work.[27] For instance, a bank employee was troubled by a manager who repeatedly strengthened his own position in the organization by holding back people in his group. When the manager expected this employee to support this behavior, she decided she could not live up to her own principles while working for him, and she left to start her own business. In another situation, a manager asked an administrative assistant to prepare the paperwork for several people who were to be terminated a week later. The assistant was troubled about giving employees only one week's notice, but before acting, she sought more information. From a staffer in the human resource department, the assistant learned that the employees had in fact opted to accept a generous early retirement package. In this case, getting that information assured the assistant that following the manager's directions was in fact defensible and appropriate.

# How to Improve the Organization's Ethical Climate

A team of management researchers recommended the following actions for improving on-the-job ethics:[28]

**Sandra Williams, Director of Ethics & Compliance at American Electric Power (AEP) takes an optimistic and proactive approach to ethics and compliance. Her high profile position within the company helps to make ethics conduct a priority issue.**

- *Behave ethically yourself.* Managers are potent role models whose habits and actual behavior send clear signals about the importance of ethical conduct. Ethical behavior is a top-to-bottom proposition.

- *Screen potential employees.* Surprisingly, employers are generally lax when it comes to checking references, credentials, transcripts, and other information on applicant résumés. More diligent action in this area can screen out those given to fraud and misrepresentation. Integrity testing is fairly valid but is no panacea.[29]

- *Develop a meaningful code of ethics.* Codes of ethics can have a positive impact if they satisfy these four criteria:

    1. They are distributed to every employee.
    2. They are firmly supported by top management.
    3. They refer to *specific* practices and ethical dilemmas likely to be encountered by target employees (e.g., salespersons paying kickbacks, purchasing agents receiving payoffs, laboratory scientists doctoring data, or accountants "cooking the books").
    4. They are evenly enforced with rewards for compliance and strict penalties for noncompliance.

- *Provide ethics training.* Employees can be trained to identify and deal with ethical issues during orientation and through seminar, video, and Internet training sessions.[30]

- *Reinforce ethical behavior.* Behavior that is reinforced tends to be repeated, whereas behavior that is not reinforced tends to disappear. Ethical conduct too often is punished or ignored while unethical behavior is rewarded.

- *Create positions, units, and other structural mechanisms to deal with ethics.* Ethics needs to be an everyday affair, not a one-time announcement of a new ethical code that gets filed away and forgotten. A growing number of large companies in the United States have chief ethics officers who report directly to the CEO, thus making ethical conduct and accountability priority issues.

- *Create a climate in which whistle-blowing becomes unnecessary.* **Whistle-blowing** occurs when an employee reports a perceived unethical and/or illegal activity to a third party such as government agencies, news media, or public-interest groups. Enron's Sherron Watkins was a highly publicized whistle-blower.[31] Organizations can reduce the need for whistle-blowing by encouraging free and open expression of dissenting viewpoints and giving employees a voice through fair grievance procedures and/or anonymous ethics hot lines.

> **Whistle-blowing**
> Reporting unethical/illegal acts to outside third parties.

## A Personal Call to Action

In the final analysis, ethics comes down to individual motivation. Organizational climate, role models, structure, and rewards all can point employees in the right direction. But individuals must *want* to do the right thing. Bill George, the respected former CEO of Medtronic, the maker of life-saving devices such as heart pacemakers, gave us this call to action: "Each of us needs to determine . . . where our ethical boundaries are and, if asked to violate (them), refuse. . . . If this means refusing a direct order, we must be prepared to resign."[32] Rising to this challenge requires strong personal *values* and the *courage* to adhere to them during adversity.[33]

# chapter two

# Organizational Culture, Socialization, and Mentoring

**LEARNING OBJECTIVES**

**After reading the material in this chapter, you should be able to:**

1. Discuss the layers and functions of organizational culture.

2. Describe the general types of organizational culture and their associated characteristics.

3. Summarize the process by which organizations change their cultures.

4. Describe the three phases in Feldman's model of organizational socialization.

5. Discuss the various tactics used to socialize employees.

6. Explain the four types of developmental networks derived from a developmental network model of mentoring.

**The mass market is supposed to be dead,** but you would never know it from Apple. In February the iTunes Store became the second-largest music retailer in the U.S., right behind Wal-Mart. The iPod is to music players what Kleenex is to tissue or Xerox is to copiers. Almost everything Apple makes transcends gender, geography, age, and race. An Apple Store is a demographic melting pot, with computer games for kids and a Genius Bar for their parents and so much cool stuff to touch that it's a magnet for teens and twentysomethings.

Apple scoffs at the notion of a target market. It doesn't even conduct focus groups. "You can't ask people what they want if it's around the next corner," says Steve Jobs, Apple's CEO and cofounder. At Apple, new-product development starts in the gut and gets hatched in rolling conversations that go something like this: What do we hate? (Our cellphones.) What do we have the technology to make? (A cellphone with a Mac inside.) What would we like to own? (You guessed it, an iPhone.) "One of the keys to Apple is that we build products that really turn us on," says Jobs.

With that simple formula, Apple not only has upstaged the likes of Microsoft but has set the gold standard for corporate America with an entirely new business model: creating a brand, morphing it, and reincarnating it to thrive in a disruptive age. Now, just seven years after it unveiled the first iPod, *fully half of Apple's revenues come from music and iPods.* Interest in the iPod and iPhone has rubbed off on the Mac, whose sales growth outpaces the industry's. Apple has demonstrated how to create real, breathtaking growth by dreaming up products so new and ingenious that they have upended one industry after another: consumer electronics, the record industry, the movie industry, video and music production.

In the process the company that ranks as the new No. 1 among America's Most Admired Companies has become a roaring financial success. In the five years ended last September, sales tripled to

$24 billion and profits surged to $3.5 billion, up from $42 million. While Apple's stock is slumping along with the market, tumbling 40% this year on worries about less-than-stratospheric sales growth, it doesn't usually stay down for long. Apple ranks No. 1 among *Fortune* 500 companies for total return to shareholders over both the past five years (94%) and the past ten (51%).

The decade coincides exactly with the return of Jobs as Apple's maestro, bringing his particular mix of genius and obsession, as well as a tendency to play by his own rules. His utter dedication to discovery and excellence has created a culture that has made Apple a symbol of innovation. You won't find that word on a placard or a piece of propaganda at One Infinite Loop, Apple's headquarters in Cupertino, Calif. There innovation is a way of life. But it isn't like creating

**Apple's latest innovation is the MacBook Air.**

new variations on Crest toothpaste. At Apple, every endeavor is a moon shot. Sometimes the company misses, but the successes are huge. Apple's goal for iPhone sales this year is ten million units, up from 3.7 million during its six months on sale in 2007.

Apple requires a special kind of workforce. The place is divided by product but also by function along what COO Tim Cook calls "very faint lines." Collaboration is key. So is a degree of perfectionism. Apple hires people who are never satisfied. A designer has to be a borderline fanatic to care about the curve of a screw on the underside of a MacBook Air or the apparent weightlessness of the tiny door that hides its

connectors. You don't get a foot in the door here unless your eyes light up when you talk about your Mac. (Head designer Jonathan Ive referred to a new MacBook Air as "this guy" as he pointed out features in a recent interview.) The place is loaded with engineers, but it's not just the skills that are important, it's the ability to emote. ("Emotive" is a big word here.) The passion is what provides the push to overcome design and engineering obstacles, to bring projects in on time—and a peer pressure so great it sometimes causes a team to eject a weak link or revolt against an underperforming boss. "Apple," says Cook, "is not for the faint of heart."

Here there is no such thing as hedging your bets. "One traditional management philosophy that's taught in many business schools is diversification. Well, that's not us," says Cook. "We are the anti–business school." Apple's philosophy goes like this: Too many companies spread themselves thin, making a profusion of products to defuse risk, so they get mired in the mediocre. Apple's approach is to put every resource it has behind just a few products and make them exceedingly well. Apple is brutal about culling past hits: The company dropped its most popular iPod, the Mini, on the day it introduced the Nano (a better product, higher margins—why dilute your resources?).[1]

**How would you describe the organizational culture at Apple? Explain. For an interpretation of this case and additional comments, visit our Online Learning Center at**

**www.mhhe.com/ kinickiob4e**

FOR DISCUSSION

**THE OPENING CASE HIGHLIGHTS** the role of organizational culture in contributing to organizational effectiveness. Apple's culture, which highly values innovation, collaboration, and passion, significantly contributes to the organization's success. The case also highlights that an organization's culture is strongly influenced by the values and attitudes of top management, particularly the CEO.

This chapter will help you better understand how managers can use organizational culture as a competitive advantage. After defining and discussing the context of organizational culture, we examine (1) the dynamics of organizational culture, (2) the organization socialization process, and (3) the embedding of organizational culture through mentoring.

# Organizational Culture: Definition and Context

**Organizational culture** is "the set of shared, taken-for-granted implicit assumptions that a group holds and that determines how it perceives, thinks about, and reacts to its various environments."[2] This definition highlights three important characteristics of organizational culture. First, organizational culture is passed on to new employees through the process of socialization, a topic discussed later in this chapter. Second, organizational culture influences our behavior at work. Finally, organizational culture operates at different levels.

**organizational culture**

**Shared values and beliefs that underlie a company's identity.**

Figure 2–1 provides a conceptual framework for reviewing the widespread impact organizational culture has on organizational behavior.[3] It also shows the linkage between this chapter—culture, socialization, and mentoring—and other key topics in this book. Figure 2–1 reveals organizational culture is shaped by four key components: the founders' values, the industry and business environment, the national

**FIGURE 2–1** A Conceptual Framework for Understanding Organizational Culture

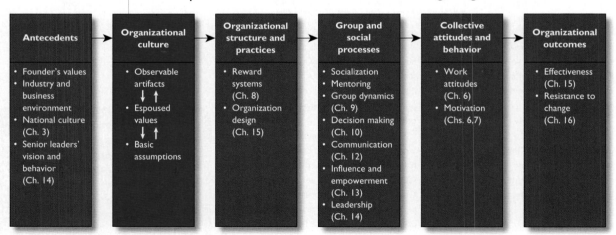

SOURCE: Adapted in part from C Ostroff, A Kinicki, and M Tamkins, "Organizational Culture and Climate," in *Handbook of Psychology,* Vol 12, eds W C Burman, D R Iigen, and R J Klimoski (New York: Wiley and Sons, 2003), pp 565–93.

culture, and the senior leaders' vision and behavior. In turn, organizational culture influences the type of organizational structure adopted by a company and a host of practices, policies, and procedures implemented in pursuit of organizational goals. These organizational characteristics then affect a variety of group and social processes. This sequence ultimately affects employees' attitudes and behavior and a variety of organizational outcomes. All told, Figure 2–1 reveals that organizational culture is a contextual variable influencing individual, group, and organizational behavior.

# Dynamics of Organizational Culture

learning objective 1

Discuss the layers and functions of organizational culture.

To provide a better understanding of how organizational culture is formed and used by employees, this section begins by discussing the layers of organizational culture. It then reviews the four functions of organizational culture, types of organizational culture, outcomes associated with organizational culture, and how cultures are embedded within organizations.

## Layers of Organizational Culture

Figure 2–1 shows the three fundamental layers of organizational culture. Each level varies in terms of outward visibility and resistance to change, and each level influences another level.[4]

**Observable Artifacts**    At the more visible level, culture represents observable artifacts. Artifacts consist of the physical manifestation of an organization's culture. Organizational examples include acronyms, manner of dress, awards, myths and stories told about the organization, published lists of values, observable rituals and ceremonies, special parking spaces, decorations, and so on. For example, the Ritz-Carlton hotel uses storytelling to reinforce a culture that is focused on exceeding customers' expectations. The company shares "wow stories" at meetings each week that relay guests' tales of staff members going above and beyond the call of duty. Each "wow" winner, such as a laundry attendant who dove into a dumpster to retrieve one young guest's stuffed gingerbread man, gets $100.[5] This level also includes visible behaviors exhibited by people and groups. Artifacts are easier to change than the less visible aspects of organizational culture.

**Espoused Values**    Values possess five key components. "**Values** (1) are concepts or beliefs, (2) pertain to desirable end-states or behaviors, (3) transcend situations, (4) guide selection or evaluation of behavior and events, and (5) are ordered by relative importance."[6] It is important to distinguish between values that are espoused versus those that are enacted.

**Espoused values** represent the explicitly stated values and norms that are preferred by an organization. They are generally established by the founder of a new or small company and by the top management team in a larger organization. Consider, for example, the espoused values of Williams-Sonoma, Inc. (see Skills & Best Practices on page 38). At a growing number of companies, one of the espoused values is *sustainability,* which

**values**

Enduring belief in a mode of conduct or end-state.

**espoused values**

The stated values and norms that are preferred by an organization.

# Williams-Sonoma's Espoused Values Focus on Employees, Customers, Shareholders, Ethical Behavior, and the Environment

**People First** We believe the potential of our company has no limit and is driven by our associates and their imagination. We are committed to an environment that attracts, motivates and recognizes high performance.

**Customers** We are here to please our customers—without them nothing else matters.

**Quality** We must take pride in everything we do. From our people, to our products and in our relationships with business partners and our community, quality is our signature.

**Shareholders** We must provide a superior return to our shareholders. It's everyone's job.

**Ethical Sourcing** Williams-Sonoma, Inc., and all of its brands are committed to maintaining the highest level of integrity and honesty throughout all aspects of our business, and strive to ensure that our business associates, including agents, vendors and suppliers, share our commitment to socially responsible employment conditions.

**Environmental Paper Procurement Policy** Williams-Sonoma, Inc., is committed to environmental stewardship, and more specifically, to sound paper procurement practices that ensure the sustainability of forests and other natural resources.

**Recycling** The launch of Williams-Sonoma, Inc.'s, *Recycle 100* brings our companywide *Greening Our Home* initiative to our customers' homes. 50% of American households recycle their paper products. Our customers recycle 60%, but, in sharing their environmental concern, we're making 100% recycling the goal for this innovative new program.

**SOURCE: Excerpted from "Corporate Values," www.williams-sonomainc.com/car/car_val.cfm, accessed February 26, 2008.**

involves meeting "humanity's needs without harming future generations." Ways of achieving sustainability include using renewable resources and avoiding waste and pollution. A recent article in *BusinessWeek* identified 24 companies committed to sustainability; they include Toyota, Nokia, Hewlett-Packard, and Sony.[7]

Because espoused values constitute aspirations that are explicitly communicated to employees, managers hope that espoused values will directly influence employee behavior. Unfortunately, aspirations do not automatically produce the desired behaviors because people do not always "walk the talk."

**Enacted values,** on the other hand, represent the values and norms that actually are exhibited or converted into employee behavior. They represent the values that employees ascribe to an organization based on their observations of what occurs on a daily basis.

The enacted values may differ from the values an organization espouses. For example, under Charles Prince, Citibank espoused the value of "One Citi," a "universal" bank where employees would make available a wide variety of financial services to its customers. That culture required a spirit of collaboration among employees brought together by a series of mergers. But in fact, many of the employees were unhappy to be part of Citigroup and placed more value on the culture of the company Citigroup had acquired. For instance, several years after Citigroup acquired Salomon Brothers, some of its bond traders were still answering the phone "Salomon." Such values enacted within the bond-trading group directly conflicted with Citigroup's espoused value of unity.[8]

It is important for managers to reduce gaps between espoused and enacted values because they can significantly influence employee attitudes and organizational performance. When Control Data Corporation (now Ceridian) introduced total quality management (TQM), its managers saw a potential conflict between espoused and enacted values. If embracing TQM led employees to focus only on avoiding variances from processes or product specifications, the enacted value of avoiding defects could conflict with Control Data's espoused value of innovation. So Control Data rolled out its TQM program with a "guiding principle" that reinforced innovation *and* quality:

Control Data wants each employee to believe two things:

What I think and do matters to Control Data's success. Always think and act on the statement "There's gotta be a better way!"[9]

**enacted values**

The values and norms that are exhibited by employees.

Managers can use a "cultural fit assessment" survey to determine the match between espoused and enacted values. Results can then be used to improve the work environment and to align the organization's espoused and enacted values.[10]

## Basic Assumptions

Basic underlying assumptions are unobservable and represent the core of organizational culture. They constitute organizational values that have become so taken for granted over time that they become assumptions that guide organizational behavior. They thus are highly resistant to change. When basic assumptions are widely held among employees, people will find behavior based on an inconsistent value inconceivable. Google, for example, is noted for its innovative culture. Employees at Google would be shocked to see management act in ways that did not value creativity and innovation.[11]

An observable artifact of the culture at the offices of Bloomberg, the financial news and information company in New York, is the office itself, a glass-walled structure that has been compared to a beehive cut open. There are no private offices and no cubicles in a space intended to express the company's energy and sense of style. And, says CEO Lex Fenwick, a big benefit is the information the view from his office affords him. "I know quicker than any piece of damn software when we have a problem," he says. "I can see it right in front of me when it happens. . . . What does it allow me to do? Get on someone to fix it in seconds. The communication this setup affords is staggering."

# Four Functions of Organizational Culture

As illustrated in Figure 2–2, an organization's culture fulfills four functions.[12] To help bring these four functions to life, let us consider how each of them has taken shape at Southwest Airlines.[13] Southwest is a particularly instructive example because it has grown to become the fourth-largest U.S. airline since its inception in 1971 and has achieved 33 consecutive years of profitability. *Fortune* ranked Southwest in the top five of the Best Companies to Work For in America from 1997–2000; Southwest has chosen not to participate in this ranking process since 2000. Southwest also was ranked as the twelfth most admired company in the United States by *Fortune* in 2008, partly due to its strong and distinctive culture.

**FIGURE 2–2**
Four
Functions of
Organizational
Culture

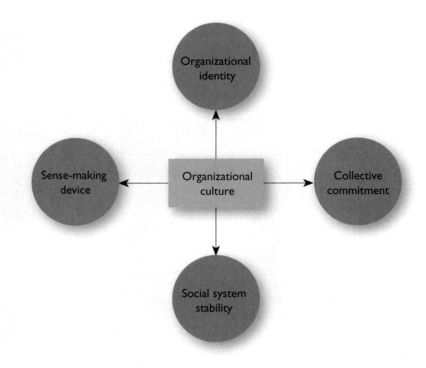

SOURCE: Adapted from discussion in L Smircich, "Concepts of Culture and Organizational Analysis," *Administrative Science Quarterly,* September 1983, pp 339–58. Reprinted with permission.

1. *Give members an organizational identity.* Southwest Airlines is known as a fun place to work that values employee satisfaction and customer loyalty over corporate profits. Herb Kelleher, executive chairman, commented on this issue.

   > Who comes first? The employees, customers, or shareholders? That's never been an issue to me. The employees come first. If they're happy, satisfied, dedicated, and energetic, they'll take real good care of the customers. When the customers are happy, they come back. And that makes the shareholders happy.[14]

   The company also has a catastrophe fund based on voluntary contributions for distribution to employees who are experiencing serious personal difficulties. Southwest's people-focused identity is reinforced by the fact that it is an employer of choice. For example, Southwest received 329,200 résumés and hired 4,200 new employees in 2007. The company also was noted as an employer of choice among college students by *Fortune.*

2. *Facilitate collective commitment.* The mission of Southwest Airlines "is dedication to the highest quality of Customer Service delivered with a sense of warmth, friendliness, individual pride, and Company Spirit."[15] Southwest's more than 34,000 employees are committed to this mission. According to the Department of Transportation's Air Travel Consumer Report, Southwest has had the fewest complaints per customer since 1987.

3. *Promote social system stability.* Social system stability reflects the extent to which the work environment is perceived as positive and reinforcing, and the extent to which conflict and change are effectively managed. Southwest is noted for its philosophy of having fun, having parties, and celebrating. For example, each city in which the firm operates is given a budget for parties. Southwest also uses a variety of performance-based awards and service awards to reinforce employees. The company's positive and enriching environment is supported by the lowest turnover rates in the airline industry and the employment of 1,165 married couples.

4. *Shape behavior by helping members make sense of their surroundings.* This function of culture helps employees understand why the organization does what it does and how it intends to accomplish its long-term goals. Keeping in mind that Southwest's leadership originally viewed ground transportation as their main competitor in 1971, employees come to understand why the airline's primary vision is to be the best primarily short-haul, low-fare, high-frequency, point-to-point carrier in the United States. Employees understand they must achieve exceptional performance, such as turning a plane in 20 minutes, because they must keep costs down in order to compete against Greyhound and the use of automobiles. In turn, the company reinforces the importance of outstanding customer service and high performance expectations by using performance-based awards and profit sharing. Employees own at least 8% of the company stock.

Fun and celebrating are the norm at Southwest Airlines. Colleen Barrett, President of Southwest Airlines (standing on right side) takes great pride in fostering a positive work environment. Would you like to work at Southwest?

# Types of Organizational Culture

Organizational behavior researchers have proposed three different frameworks to capture the various types of organizational culture: the Organizational Culture Inventory, the Competing Values Framework, and the Organizational Culture Profile. This section discusses the Competing Values Framework because it is the most widely used approach for classifying organizational culture. It also was named as one of the 40 most important frameworks in the study of organizations and has been shown to be a valid approach for classifying organizational culture.[16]

The **competing values framework** (CVF) provides a practical way for managers to understand, measure, and change organizational culture. It was originally developed by a team of researchers who were trying to classify different ways to assess organizational effectiveness. This research showed that measures of organizational effectiveness vary along two fundamental dimensions or axes. One axis pertains to whether an organization focuses its attention and efforts on internal dynamics and employees or outward toward its external environment and its customers and shareholders. The second is concerned with an organization's preference for flexibility and

learning objective 2

Describe the general types of organizational culture and their associated characteristics.

**competing values framework**

**A framework for categorizing organizational culture.**

discretion or control and stability. Combining these two axes creates four types of organizational culture that are based on different core values and different sets of criteria for assessing organizational effectiveness. The CVF is shown in Figure 2–3.[17]

Figure 2–3 shows the strategic thrust associated with each cultural type along with the means used to accomplish this thrust and the resulting ends or goals pursued by each cultural type. Before beginning our exploration of the CVF, it is important to note that organizations can possess characteristics associated with each culture type. That said, however, organizations tend to have one type of culture that is more dominant than the others. Let us begin our discussion of culture types by starting in the upper-left-hand quadrant of the CVF.

**clan culture**

**A culture that has an internal focus and values flexibility rather than stability and control.**

**Clan Culture**    A **clan culture** has an internal focus and values flexibility rather than stability and control. It resembles a family-type organization in which effectiveness is achieved by encouraging collaboration between employees. This type of culture is very "employee-focused" and strives to instill cohesion through consensus and job satisfaction and commitment through employee involvement. Clan organizations devote considerable resources to hiring and developing their employees, and they view customers as partners.

A company with a strong clan culture is Badger Mining Corporation. The company may be small, but its benefits package is generous, including employer contributions to a 401(k) retirement savings plan, full premiums paid for health insurance, and a wellness package with health coaching. Schedules are flexible, and employees are encouraged to contribute ideas to Badger's safety training program. Employees also were

## FIGURE 2–3  |  Competing Values Framework

**Flexibility and discretion**

|  | **Clan** | **Adhocracy** |  |
|---|---|---|---|
| | **Thrust:** Collaborate | **Thrust:** Create | |
| | **Means:** Cohesion, participation, communication, empowerment | **Means:** Adaptability, creativity, agility | |
| **Internal focus and integration** | **Ends:** Morale, people development, commitment | **Ends:** Innovation, Growth, cutting-edge output | **External focus and differentiation** |
| | **Hierarchy** | **Market** | |
| | **Thrust:** Control | **Thrust:** Compete | |
| | **Means:** Capable processes, consistency, process control, measurement | **Means:** Customer focus, productivity, enhancing competitiveness | |
| | **Ends:** Efficiency, timeliness, smooth functioning | **Ends:** Market share, profitability, goal achievement | |

**Stability and control**

SOURCE: Adapted from K S Cameron, R E Quinn, J Degraff, and A V Thakor, *Competing Values Leadership* (Northampton, MA: Edward Elgar, 2006), p 32.

involved in planning a major expansion of one of the company's mining facilities. The facility's vice president for operations, Dan Valiquette, noted that this collaborative approach achieved "the support of the whole company" for the changes. Badger's president, Timothy J Wuest, says this type of teamwork is the basis for the company's success. And benefits specialist Barbara Swanson says the focus on employees is obvious even to a newcomer. When she applied to work for Badger, Swanson says, "I immediately felt that this was a place that cared about who they wanted to hire."[18]

### Adhocracy Culture

An **adhocracy culture** has an external focus and values flexibility. As demonstrated in the chapter-opening case on Apple, this type of culture fosters the creation of innovative products and services by being adaptable, creative, and fast to respond to changes in the marketplace. Adhocracy cultures do not rely on the type of centralized power and authority relationships that are part of market and hierarchical cultures. They also encourage employees to take risks, think outside the box, and experiment with new ways of getting things done. This type of culture is well suited for start-up companies, those in industries undergoing constant change, and those in mature industries that are in need of innovation to enhance growth. Consider how Jeff Immelt, CEO of General Electric, is trying to instill characteristics of an adhocracy in order to fuel revenue growth.

> The company, which is well-known for sharing best practices across its many units, has recently begun formally discussing failures, too. Last September the company set up a two-hour conference call for managers of eight "imagination breakthroughs" that didn't live up to expectations and were being shelved, or "retired," in GE's parlance. ("Imagination breakthrough"—Ibs—are new businesses or products that have potential sales of $100 million within three to five years.)
>
> Such discussions can be nerve-racking, especially in companies where failure has traditionally been met with tough consequences. . . . "I had some offline conversations with some of the IB leaders reassuring them that this was not a call where they were going to get their pink slips," says Patia McGrath, a GE marketing director who helped put together the call. "The notion of taking big swings, and that it's O.K. to miss the swing, is something that's quite new with Jeff."[19]

W L Gore and Intel are two other companies that possess cultural characteristics consistent with an Adhocracy.

### Market Culture

A **market culture** has a strong external focus and values stability and control. Organizations with this culture are driven by competition and a strong desire to deliver results and accomplish goals. Because this type of culture is focused on the external environment,

---

**adhocracy culture**

A culture that has an external focus and values flexibility.

---

**SKILLS & BEST PRACTICES**

## The Mayo Clinic's Market Culture

The mission statement of the prestigious Mayo Clinic is "The best interest of the patient is the only interest to be considered." Evidence of the value placed on the patient's interest appears in artifacts such as mottos displayed in high-traffic areas of the facilities. The institution refers to its physicians as "consultants," emphasizing their role in supporting and conferring with patients. Pay practices also reinforce the value: physicians earn a salary so they can focus completely on patients' needs, rather than considering how decisions might affect the amount they can bill for services.

People at the Mayo Clinic recount stories about how staff members go beyond the usual job requirements to attend to patients. In one remarkable case, a woman whose daughter was to be married became critically ill. When the doctors learned how anxious the bride was to have her mother be able to attend the wedding, they notified the critical-care manager. While the doctors controlled the mother's illness, staff members went to work setting up the hospital atrium for a wedding, complete with flowers, balloons, and confetti. The mother was wheeled to the atrium, where the hospital chaplain performed the wedding ceremony.

**SOURCE: C Jarnagin and J W Slocum Jr., "Creating Corporate Cultures through Mythopoetic Leadership," *Organizational Dynamics*, vol. 36, no. 3, 2007, pp 288–302.**

---

**market culture**

A culture that has a strong external focus and values stability and control.

customers and profits take precedence over employee development and satisfaction. (For an example, see Skills & Best Practices about Mayo Clinic.) The major goal of managers is to drive toward productivity, profits, and customer satisfaction. Employees are expected to react fast, work hard, and deliver quality work on time. Organizations with this culture tend to reward people who deliver results. Byung Mo Ahn, president of Kia Motors, is a good example of a leader who desires to promote a market culture. He fired two senior executives from Kia Motors America in February 2008 because they were not meeting their expected sales goals. Employees from North America note that Mr. Ahn has created a very aggressive and competitive work environment. Some describe the environment as militaristic. Intel is another example of a company with a market culture. The company eliminated more than 10,000 jobs between 2006 and 2007 in a restructure to reduce costs and improve efficiency and profitability.[20]

**hierarchy culture**

A culture that has an internal focus and values stability and control over flexibility.

**Hierarchy Culture**    Control is the driving force within a hierarchical culture. The **hierarchy culture** has an internal focus, which produces a more formalized and structured work environment, and values stability and control over flexibility. This orientation leads to the development of reliable internal processes, extensive measurement, and the implementation of a variety of control mechanisms. For example, companies with a hierarchical culture are more likely to use the type of total quality management (TQM) programs discussed in Chapter 1. Effectiveness in a company with this type of culture is likely to be assessed with measures of efficiency, timeliness, and reliability of producing and delivering products and services. Exelon, the No. 1 U.S. nuclear power generator, and Dell are good examples of companies with hierarchical cultures. Both companies focus on efficiency and cost-cutting in order to compete.[21]

**Cultural Types Represent Competing Values**    It is important to note that certain cultural types reflect opposing core values. These contradicting cultures are found along the two diagonals in Figure 2–3. For example, the Clan culture—upper-left quadrant—is represented by values that emphasize an internal focus and flexibility, whereas the market culture—bottom-right quadrant—has an external focus and concern for stability and control. You can see the same conflict between an adhocracy culture that values flexibility and an external focus and a hierarchical culture that endorses stability and control along with an internal focus. Why are these contradictions important?

They are important because an organization's success may depend on its ability to possess core values that are associated with competing cultural types. While this is difficult to pull off, it can be done. Consider Nortel Networks, for example. The company is trying to encourage innovation at the same time it is trying to implement Six Sigma quality processes. The Ritz-Carlton, a high-end luxury hotel, has similarly found a way to overcome competing values associated with clan and market cultures. The company spends 10% of its payroll on employee training and empowers its employees to determine the best way to provide customer service. At the same time, the company is fiercely focused on providing world-class customer service.[22]

# Outcomes Associated with Organizational Culture

Both managers and academic researchers believe that organizational culture can be a driver of employee attitudes and organizational effectiveness and performance. To test this possibility, various measures of organizational culture have been correlated with a variety of individual and organizational outcomes. So what have we learned?

First, several studies demonstrated that organizational culture was significantly correlated with employee behavior and attitudes. For example, a clan culture was positively associated with employees' job satisfaction, organizational commitment, intentions to stay at the company, and the quality of communication received from one's supervisor. Employees in clan cultures also reported having more positive relationships with their managers than employees working in organizations with an external focus, such as those with adhocracy or market cultures. Employees working in organizations with hierarchical or market-based cultures also reported lower job satisfaction and organizational commitment, and greater intentions to quit their jobs.[23] These results suggest that employees prefer to work in organizations that value flexibility over stability and control and those that are more concerned with satisfying employees' needs than customer or shareholder desires.

Second, results from several studies revealed that the congruence between an individual's values and the organization's values was significantly associated with organizational commitment, job satisfaction, intention to quit, performance, and turnover.[24]

**Farcus** by David Waisglass / Gordon Coulthart

© 1994 Farcus Cartoons    WAISGLASS/COULTHART

www.farcus.com

**"I don't think this change in corporate culture is gonna pay-off."**

Third, there is not a clear pattern of relationships between organizational culture and outcomes such as service quality, customer satisfaction, and an organization's financial performance. For example, organizations with a market culture have been shown to exhibit both higher and lower levels of financial performance.[25] While the aforementioned conclusion is supported by data obtained from employees' assessments of organizational culture, it must be tempered by results from two recent studies. A study of 200 companies in more than 40 industries showed that an organization's financial performance was significantly related to customer satisfaction.[26] These results imply that it is important for organizations to have an external focus on its customers if they want to make money. In contrast, a recent meta-analysis of 92 studies revealed that a firm's financial performance was positively associated with the extent to which it employed high performance work practices. High performance work practices reflect an internal cultural orientation and include such things as incentive compensation, employee involvement, employee training, and the use of flexible work schedules.[27] All told, these results suggest that it is important for managers to effectively accommodate the potential conflict between cultures that have both an internal and external focus.

This conclusion is consistent with findings from a study of 207 companies in 22 industries over an 11-year period. Results demonstrated that an organization's financial performance was higher among companies that had adaptive or flexible cultures.[28] Stated differently, successful companies modified their cultures over time so that they were appropriate or consistent with the market or business situation at hand. We encourage managers to evaluate the extent to which their organization's culture is aligned with its business or strategic context and to respond accordingly.

Finally, studies of mergers indicated that they frequently failed due to incompatible cultures. Due to the increasing number of corporate mergers around the world, and the conclusion that 7 out of 10 mergers and acquisitions failed to meet their financial promise, managers within merged companies would be well advised to consider the role of organizational culture in creating a new organization.[29]

In summary, research underscores the significance of organizational culture. It also reinforces the need to learn more about the process of cultivating and changing an organization's culture. An organization's culture is not determined by fate. It is formed and shaped by the combination and integration of everyone who works in the organization. A change-resistant culture, for instance, can undermine the effectiveness of any type of organizational change. Although it is not an easy task to change an organization's culture, the next section provides a preliminary overview of how this might be done.

## The Process of Culture Change

**3**  learning objective

Summarize the process by which organizations change their cultures.

An organization's culture can be changed. The process essentially begins with targeting one of the three layers of organizational culture—observable artifacts, espoused values, and basic assumptions—for change. Ultimately, culture change involves changing people's minds and their behavior.[30] Edgar Schein, an OB scholar, notes that changing organizational culture involves a teaching process. That is, organizational members teach each other about the organization's preferred values, beliefs, expectations, and behaviors. This is accomplished by using one or more of the following mechanisms:[31]

1. *Formal statements of organizational philosophy, mission, vision, values, and materials used for recruiting, selection, and socialization.* Sam Walton, the founder of Wal-Mart, established three basic beliefs or values that represent the core of the organization's culture. They are (1) respect for the individual, (2) service to our customer, and (3) striving for excellence. Further, Nucor Corp. attempts to emphasize the value it places on its people by including every employee's name on the cover of the annual report. This practice also

Training programs help preserve and embed the culture in an organization. Infosys Technologies, the rapidly growing software firm headquartered in Bangalore, India, hires about 40 new employees every day and trains them by the thousands at one of the world's largest corporate training centers, in Mysore. Here chairman and founder Narayana Murthy welcomes "freshers" via video.

reinforces the family-type culture the company wants to encourage.[32] Would you be attracted to work there?

2. *The design of physical space, work environments, and buildings.* Intel originally had all its staff work in uniform cubicles, consistent with the value it places on equality. (Top managers don't have reserved parking spaces either.) However, the cubicle arrangement conflicted with another Intel value—innovation—so the company is experimenting with open seating arrangements combined with small conference rooms. Not only are open-seating arrangements thought to encourage collaboration, they can reduce noise because employees can see when their activities are annoying to other workers. Intel hopes that this environment will better support creative thinking.[33]

3. *Slogans, language, acronyms, and sayings.* For example, Robert Mittelstaedt, Dean of the W P Carey School of Business at Arizona State University, promotes his vision of having one of the best business schools in the world through the slogan "Top-of-mind business school." Employees are encouraged to engage in activities that promote the quality and reputation of the school's academic programs.

4. *Deliberate role modeling, training programs, teaching, and coaching by managers and supervisors.* Triage Consulting Group, a health care financial consulting firm in California, places a high value on superior performance and achieving measurable goals. New employees are immediately prepared with a four-day orientation in Triage's culture and methods, followed by 15 training modules scheduled in six-week intervals. After less than a year, the best performers are ready to begin managing their own project, thereby furthering their career development. Performance evaluations take place four times a year, reinforcing the drive for results.[34]

5. *Explicit rewards, status symbols (e.g., titles), and promotion criteria.* At Triage Consulting Group, employees at the same level of their career earn the same pay, but employees are eligible for merit bonuses, reinforcing the culture of achievement. The merit bonuses are partly based on coworkers' votes for who contributed most to the company's success, and the employees who received the most votes are recognized each year at the company's "State of Triage" meeting.[35]

6. *Stories, legends, and myths about key people and events.* Time is a highly valued resource at the Associates, a financial services firm. To reinforce the importance of not wasting time, many stories circulate about senior managers missing planes or being locked out of meetings because they were late.[36] The Skills & Best Practices contains recommendations for how managers can find stories with impact.

## SKILLS & BEST PRACTICES

### Developing Stories That Have Impact

Managers can develop and tell motivating stories by noticing relevant actions and tying them to values. They need to observe day-to-day activities, watching for successful individuals, risk takers, informal leaders, organizational heroes, and people who go beyond the call of duty, live the organization's values, and help others succeed. Other stories may come from listening carefully to satisfied customers and suppliers. Managers can ask what happened that made them happy.

When telling the story, the manager needs to point out how it reflects the company's mission and values. Who were the heroes? Who benefited from what the heroes did? What does the story say about what kind of organization the company is? What does the story say about what is expected of employees?

The strongest stories have emotional content. Telling stories that move the listener is easier when the storyteller personally believes in the values being taught.

SOURCES: Based on B Kaufman, "Stories That Sell, Stories That Tell," *Journal of Business Strategy*, March/April 2003, pp 11–15; and C Jarnagin and J W Slocum Jr., "Creating Corporate Cultures through Mythopoetic Leadership," *Organizational Dynamics* 36(3) (2007), pp. 288–302.

7. *The organizational activities, processes, or outcomes that leaders pay attention to, measure, and control.* When Ron Sargent took over as chief executive of Staples, he wanted to increase the focus on customer service. He started by investigating what values the office supply retailer's employees already held, and they told him they cared about helping others. Sargent used that value as the basis for developing their skill in serving customers. Staples began teaching employees more about the products they sell and now offers bonuses for team performance. Sargent also pays frequent visits to stores so he can talk directly to employees about what customers like and dislike.[37]

8. *Leader reactions to critical incidents and organizational crises.*[38]

9. *The workflow and organizational structure.* Hierarchical structures are more likely to embed an orientation toward control and authority than a flatter organization. One way that Staples enables its employees to focus on the company's commitment to customer service is by giving employees wide latitude in decision making.[39]

10. *Organizational systems and procedures.* Companies are increasingly using electronic networks to enhance collaboration among employees in order to achieve innovation, quality, and efficiency. For example, Serena Software Inc., a California-based company with 800 employees located in 29 offices across 14 countries, encouraged its employees to sign up for Facebook for free, and to use the network as a vehicle for getting to know each other. In contrast to using a public site for networking, Dow Chemical launched its own internal social network in order to create relationships between current, past, and temporary employees.[40]

11. *Organizational goals and the associated criteria used for recruitment, selection, development, promotion, layoffs, and retirement of people.* PepsiCo reinforces a high-performance culture by setting challenging goals.

# The Organizational Socialization Process

**Organizational socialization** is defined as "the process by which a person learns the values, norms, and required behaviors which permit him to participate as a member of the organization."[41] As previously discussed, organizational socialization is a key mechanism used by organizations to embed their organizational cultures. In short, organizational socialization turns outsiders into fully functioning insiders by promoting and reinforcing the organization's core values and beliefs. This section introduces a three-phase model of organizational socialization and examines the practical application of socialization research.

**organizational socialization**

Process by which employees learn an organization's values, norms, and required behaviors.

**4** learning objective

Describe the three phases in Feldman's model of organizational socialization.

## A Three-Phase Model of Organizational Socialization

One's first year in a complex organization can be confusing. There is a constant swirl of new faces, strange jargon, conflicting expectations, and apparently unrelated events. Some organizations treat new members in a rather haphazard, sink-or-swim manner. More typically, though, the socialization process is characterized by a sequence of identifiable steps.

## A Model of Organizational Socialization | **FIGURE 2–4**

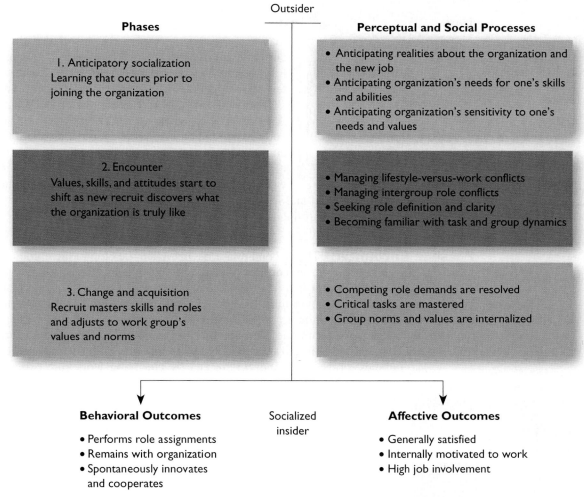

Outsider

**Phases**

I. Anticipatory socialization
Learning that occurs prior to joining the organization

2. Encounter
Values, skills, and attitudes start to shift as new recruit discovers what the organization is truly like

3. Change and acquisition
Recruit masters skills and roles and adjusts to work group's values and norms

**Perceptual and Social Processes**

- Anticipating realities about the organization and the new job
- Anticipating organization's needs for one's skills and abilities
- Anticipating organization's sensitivity to one's needs and values

- Managing lifestyle-versus-work conflicts
- Managing intergroup role conflicts
- Seeking role definition and clarity
- Becoming familiar with task and group dynamics

- Competing role demands are resolved
- Critical tasks are mastered
- Group norms and values are internalized

**Behavioral Outcomes**

- Performs role assignments
- Remains with organization
- Spontaneously innovates and cooperates

Socialized insider

**Affective Outcomes**

- Generally satisfied
- Internally motivated to work
- High job involvement

SOURCE: Adapted from material in D C Feldman, "The Multiple Socialization of Organization Members," *Academy of Management Review*, April 1981, pp 309–18.

Organizational behavior researcher Daniel Feldman has proposed a three-phase model of organizational socialization that promotes deeper understanding of this important process. As illustrated in Figure 2–4, the three phases are (1) anticipatory socialization, (2) encounter, and (3) change and acquisition. Each phase has its associated perceptual and social processes. Feldman's model also specifies behavioral and affective outcomes that can be used to judge how well an individual has been socialized. The entire three-phase sequence may take from a few weeks to a year to complete, depending on individual differences and the complexity of the situation.

**Phase 1: Anticipatory Socialization**   **Anticipatory socialization** occurs before an individual actually joins an organization. It is represented by the information people have learned about different careers, occupations, professions, and organizations. For example, anticipatory

**anticipatory socialization**

**Occurs before an individual joins an organization, and involves the information people learn about different careers, occupations, professions, and organizations.**

Boot camp, which is part of the encounter phase, is used by the military to quickly and firmly instill values endorsed by the military.

socialization partially explains the different perceptions you might have about working for the U.S. government versus a high-technology company like Intel or Microsoft. Anticipatory socialization information comes from many sources. An organization's current employees are a powerful source of anticipatory socialization. Consider the case of Sedona Center, which includes Amara Creekside Resort, two shopping plazas, and three restaurants in Sedona, Arizona. The organization's 200 employees apparently like to tell others in the labor market about the company's employee-focused organizational culture. In turn, job openings are filled with employees who better "fit" within Sedona Center's culture and ultimately are more satisfied and less likely to quit. The company's turnover rate—13% to 18%—is less than half the national average for this industry.[42]

**Phase 2: Encounter**    This second phase begins when the employment contract has been signed. During the **encounter phase** employees come to learn what the organization is really like. It is a time for reconciling unmet expectations and making sense of a new work environment. Many companies use a combination of orientation and training programs to socialize employees during the encounter phase. Onboarding is one such technique. **Onboarding** programs help employees to integrate, assimilate, and transition to new jobs by making them familiar with corporate policies, procedures, and culture and by clarifying work role expectations and responsibilities.[43] The Chubb Group of insurance companies has a service-oriented culture to meet the expectations of its clients, who are paying for extensive coverage and expect to be treated as the valuable clients they are. To prepare its new claims center employees to succeed in this culture, Chubb gives them 30 days of training in the company's products and procedures, followed by 30 days in which trainees practice what they have learned by applying it to a variety of claims. During the six months that follow, each of the new employees is assigned to a mentor, who helps the employee understand Chubb's customers and how to be attentive to them.[44]

> **encounter phase**
>
> Employees learn what the organization is really like and reconcile unmet expectations.

> **onboarding**
>
> Programs aimed at helping employees integrate, assimilate, and transition to new jobs.

> **change and acquisition**
>
> Requires employees to master tasks and roles and to adjust to work group values and norms.

**Phase 3: Change and Acquisition**    The **change and acquisition** phase requires employees to master important tasks and roles and to adjust to their work group's values and norms. To achieve that adjustment, employees should be clear about their roles, feel confident they can do what is expected of them, and have the acceptance of their coworkers.[45] Additionally, organizations such as Schlumberger, a large multinational oil company, use incentives and social gatherings to reinforce the new behaviors expected of employees.

The company is gradually changing its old Soviet culture of blame. Luc Ollivier, a 50-year-old Frenchman, was installed as the boss of regional operations Siberian Geophysical. He's trying to reward performance and, more critical, systematically eliminate mistakes rather than simply punish the people who make them. Ollivier says the company's veteran drillers have immense experience, "but they don't like to teach the young people." So he is working to forge better ties through daylong get-togethers that conclude with a beer bash. Ollivier says the pace of work is up by more than 30% in the past two years, and Siberian Geophysical's drilling revenues reached about $250 million last year [2007], about double their level in 2006.[46]

Table 2–1 presents a list of socialization processes or tactics used by organizations to help employees through this adjustment process. Returning to Table 2–1, can you identify the socialization tactics used by Schlumberger?

Socialization Tactics | **TABLE 2–1**

learning objective **5**

Discuss the various tactics used to social-ize employees.

| Tactic | Description |
|---|---|
| Collective vs. individual | Collective socialization consists of grouping new-comers and exposing them to a common set of experiences rather than treating each newcomer individually and exposing him or her to more or less unique experiences. |
| Formal vs. informal | Formal socialization is the practice of segregating a newcomer from regular organization members during a defined socialization period versus not clearly distinguishing a newcomer from more experienced members. Army recruits must attend boot camp before they are allowed to work along-side established soldiers. |
| Sequential vs. random | Sequential socialization refers to a fixed progres-sion of steps that culminate in the new role, com-pared to an ambiguous or dynamic progression. The socialization of doctors involves a lock-step sequence from medical school, to internship, to residency before they are allowed to practice on their own. |
| Fixed vs. variable | Fixed socialization provides a timetable for the assumption of the role, whereas a variable process does not. American university students typically spend one year apiece as freshmen, sophomores, juniors, and seniors. |
| Serial vs. disjunctive | A serial process is one in which the newcomer is socialized by an experienced member, whereas a disjunctive process does not use a role model. |
| Investiture vs. divestiture | Investiture refers to the affirmation of a newcom-er's incoming global and specific role identities and attributes. Divestiture is the denial and stripping away of the newcomer's existing sense of self and the reconstruction of self in the organization's image. During police training, cadets are required to wear uniforms and maintain an immaculate appearance, they are addressed as "officer," and told they are no longer ordinary citizens but are representatives of the police force. |

SOURCE: Descriptions were taken from B E Ashforth, *Role Transitions in Organizational Life: An Identity-Based Perspective* (Mahwah, NJ: Lawrence Erlbaum Associates, 2001), pp 149–83.

# Have You Been Adequately Socialized?

**INSTRUCTIONS:** Complete the following survey items by considering either your current job or one you held in the past. If you have never worked, identify a friend who is working and ask that individual to complete the questionnaire for his or her organization. Read each item and circle your response by using the rating scale shown below. Compute your total score by adding up your responses and compare it to the scoring norms.

| | Strongly Disagree | Disagree | Neutral | Agree | Strongly Agree |
|---|---|---|---|---|---|
| 1. I have been through a set of training experiences that are specifically designed to give newcomers a thorough knowledge of job-related skills. | 1 | 2 | 3 | 4 | 5 |
| 2. This organization puts all newcomers through the same set of learning experiences. | 1 | 2 | 3 | 4 | 5 |
| 3. I did not perform any of my normal job responsibilities until I was thoroughly familiar with departmental procedures and work methods. | 1 | 2 | 3 | 4 | 5 |
| 4. There is a clear pattern in the way one role leads to another, or one job assignment leads to another, in this organization. | 1 | 2 | 3 | 4 | 5 |
| 5. I can predict my future career path in this organization by observing other people's experiences. | 1 | 2 | 3 | 4 | 5 |
| 6. Almost all of my colleagues have been supportive of me personally. | 1 | 2 | 3 | 4 | 5 |
| 7. My colleagues have gone out of their way to help me adjust to this organization. | 1 | 2 | 3 | 4 | 5 |
| 8. I received much guidance from experienced organizational members as to how I should perform my job. | 1 | 2 | 3 | 4 | 5 |
| Total Score | _____ | _____ | _____ | _____ | _____ |

## SCORING NORMS

8–18 = Low socialization     19–29 = Moderate socialization     30–40 = High socialization

**SOURCE:** Adapted from survey items excerpted from D Cable and C Parsons, "Socialization Tactics and Person-Organization Fit," *Personnel Psychology*, Spring 2001, pp 1–23.

# Practical Application of Socialization Research

Past research suggests four practical guidelines for managing organizational socialization.

1. Managers should avoid a haphazard, sink-or-swim approach to organizational socialization because formalized socialization tactics positively affect new hires. Formalized orientation programs are more effective.[47]

2. Managers play a key role during the encounter phase. Studies of newly hired accountants demonstrated that the frequency and type of information obtained during their first six months of employment significantly affected their job performance, their role clarity, and the extent to which they were socially integrated.[48] Managers need to help new hires integrate within the organizational culture. Consider the approach used by John Chambers, CEO of Cisco Systems. "He meets with groups of new hires to welcome them soon after they start, and at monthly breakfast meetings workers are encouraged to ask him tough questions.[49]

   Take a moment now to complete the Hands-On Exercise on page 52. It measures the extent to which you have been socialized into your current work organization. Have you been adequately socialized? If not, you may need to find a mentor. Mentoring is discussed in the next section.

3. The organization can benefit by training new employees to use proactive socialization behaviors. A study of 154 entry-level professionals showed that effectively using proactive socialization behaviors influenced the newcomers' general anxiety and stress during the first month of employment and their motivation and anxiety six months later.[50]

4. Managers should pay attention to the socialization of diverse employees. Research demonstrated that diverse employees, particularly those with disabilities, experienced different socialization activities than other newcomers. In turn, these different experiences affected their long-term success and job satisfaction.[51]

# Embedding Organizational Culture through Mentoring

The modern word *mentor* derives from Mentor, the name of a wise and trusted counselor in Greek mythology. Terms typically used in connection with mentoring are *teacher, coach, sponsor,* and *peer.* **Mentoring** is defined as the process of forming and maintaining intensive and lasting developmental relationships between a variety of developers (i.e., people who provide career and psychosocial support) and a junior person (the protégé, if male; or protégée, if female).[52] Mentoring can serve to embed an organization's culture when developers and the protégé/protégée work in the same organization for two reasons. First,

**mentoring**

Process of forming and maintaining developmental relationships between a mentor and a junior person.

mentoring contributes to creating a sense of oneness by promoting the acceptance of the organization's core values throughout the organization. Second, the socialization aspect of mentoring also promotes a sense of membership.

Not only is mentoring important as a tactic for embedding organizational culture, but research suggests it can significantly influence the protégé/protégée's future career. For example, mentored employees performed better on the job and experienced more rapid career advancement than nonmentored employees. Mentored employees also reported higher job and career satisfaction and working on more challenging job assignments.[53] With this information in mind, this section focuses on how people can use mentoring to their advantage. We discuss the functions of mentoring, the developmental networks underlying mentoring, and the personal and organizational implications of mentoring.

**Test Your Knowledge**

Mentoring

## Functions of Mentoring

Kathy Kram, a Boston University researcher, conducted in-depth interviews with both members of 18 pairs of senior and junior managers. As a by-product of this study, Kram identified two general functions—career and psychosocial—of the mentoring process. Five *career functions* that enhanced career development were sponsorship, exposure-and-visibility, coaching, protection, and challenging assignments. Four *psychosocial functions* were role modeling, acceptance-and-confirmation, counseling, and friendship. The psychosocial functions clarified the participants' identities and enhanced their feelings of competence.[54]

**6 learning objective**

Explain the four types of developmental networks derived from a developmental network model of mentoring.

## Developmental Networks Underlying Mentoring

Historically, it was thought that mentoring was primarily provided by one person who was called a mentor. Today, however, the changing nature of technology, organizational structures, and marketplace dynamics requires that people seek career information and support from many sources. Mentoring is currently viewed as a process in which protégés and protégées seek developmental guidance from a network of people, who are referred to as developers. McKinsey & Company tells its associates, "Build your own McKinsey." This slogan means the consulting firm expects its people to identify partners, colleagues, and subordinates who have related goals and interests so that they can help one another develop their expertise. Each McKinsey associate is thus responsible for his or her own career development—and for mentoring others.[55] As McKinsey's approach recognizes, the diversity and strength of a person's network of relationships is instrumental in obtaining the type of career assistance needed to manage his or her career. Figure 2–5 presents a developmental network typology based on integrating the diversity and strength of developmental relationships.[56]

**diversity of developmental relationships**

The variety of people in a network used for developmental assistance.

The **diversity of developmental relationships** reflects the variety of people within the network an individual uses for developmental assistance. There are two subcomponents associated with network diversity: (1) the number of different people the person is networked with and (2) the various social systems from which the networked relationships stem (e.g., employer, school, family, community, professional associations, and religious affiliations). As shown in Figure 2–5, developmental relationship diversity ranges from low (few people or social systems) to high (multiple people or social systems). **Developmental relationship strength** reflects the quality of relationships among an individual and those involved in his or her developmental network. For example, strong ties are reflective of relationships based on frequent interactions, reciprocity, and positive affect. Weak ties, in contrast, are based more on superficial relationships. Together, the diversity and strength of developmental relationships results in four types of developmental networks (see Figure 2–5): receptive, traditional, entrepreneurial, and opportunistic.

> **developmental relationship strength**
> The quality of relationships among people in a network.

A *receptive* developmental network is composed of a few weak ties from one social system such as an employer or a professional association. The single oval around D1 and D2 in Figure 2–5 is indicative of two developers who come from one social system. In contrast, a *traditional* network contains a few strong ties between an employee and developers that all come from one social system. An *entrepreneurial* network, which is the strongest type of developmental network, is made up of strong ties among several developers (D1–D4) who come from four different social systems. Finally, an *opportunistic* network is associated with having weak ties with multiple developers from different social systems.

## Developmental Networks Associated with Mentoring    FIGURE 2–5

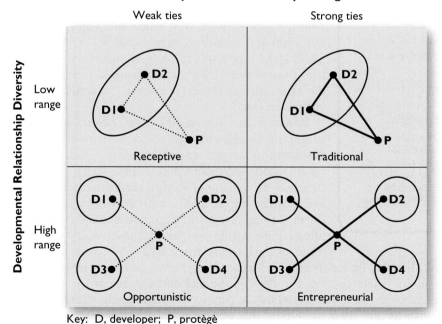

Key: D, developer; P, protègè

## Building an Effective Mentoring Network

1. *Invest in your relationships.* Devote the time and energy necessary to develop trust and respect in your mentors. Get to know each mentor's personality and background before plunging into specific problems.

2. *Engage in 360-degree networking.* Share information and maintain good relationships with people above, below, and at your level of the organization's hierarchy.

3. *Plan your network.* Assess what competencies you need to build, identify mentors who can help with those competencies, and change mentors as your competencies develop.

4. *Develop diverse connections.* Be open to informal and formal relationships.

5. *Agree on the process.* At the first meeting, the mentor and protégé/protégée should agree how often they will meet and how they will communicate outside the scheduled meetings.

6. *Be ready to move on.* The average mentoring relationship lasts five years. When a relationship is no longer beneficial, the parties should end it and free their time for more productive relationships.

SOURCES: Based on S C de Janasz, S E Sullivan, and V Whiting, "Mentor Networks and Career Success: Lessons for Turbulent Times," *Academy of Management Executive,* November 2003, pp 78–91; and N Anand and J Conger, "Capabilities of the Consummate Networker," *Organizational Dynamics,* 2007, pp 13–27.

# Personal and Organizational Implications

There are three key personal implications to consider. First, job and career satisfaction are likely to be influenced by the consistency between an individual's career goals and the type of developmental network at his or her disposal. For example, people with an entrepreneurial developmental network are more likely to experience change in their careers and to benefit from personal learning than people with receptive, traditional, and opportunistic networks. If this sounds attractive to you, you should try to increase the diversity and strength of your developmental relationships. In contrast, lower levels of job satisfaction are expected when employees have receptive developmental networks and they desire to experience career advancement in multiple organizations. Receptive developmental networks, however, can be satisfying to someone who does not desire to be promoted up the career ladder. Second, a developer's willingness to provide career and psychosocial assistance is a function of the protégé/protégée's ability, potential, and the quality of the interpersonal relationship.[57] This implies that you must take ownership for enhancing your skills, abilities, and developmental networks if you desire to experience career advancement throughout your life (see Skills & Best Practices). Third, put effort into finding a mentor. A recent study of 4,559 leaders and 944 human resource professionals from 42 countries showed that 91% of those who used a mentor found the experience moderately or greatly beneficial to their career success.[58]

Research also supports the organizational benefits of mentoring. In addition to the obvious benefit of employee development, mentoring enhances the effectiveness of organizational communication. Specifically, mentoring increases the amount of vertical communication both up and down an organization, and it provides a mechanism for modifying or reinforcing organizational culture. An effective mentoring program can also reduce employee turnover and increase productivity. A star associate at the law firm of Milbank, Tweed, Hadley & McCloy was restless and ready to leave when a practice group leader happened to offer praise and encouragement for a job well done. The associate felt so reinforced by the partner's interest that he decided to stay with the firm after all.[59] Benefits such as this are leading more and more companies to set up formal mentoring programs. A recent survey found that 6 out of 10 companies already have programs for coaching or mentoring, and of the remaining companies, 8 out of 10 are planning such a program.[60]

# key terms

# chapter summary

- *Discuss the layers and functions of organizational culture.* The three layers of organizational culture are observable artifacts, espoused values, and basic underlying assumptions. Each layer varies in terms of outward visibility and resistance to change. Four functions of organizational culture are organizational identity, collective commitment, social system stability, and sense-making device.

- *Discuss the general types of organizational culture and their associated characteristics.* According to the competing values framework, defining culture along two axes (internal or external focus and preference for stability or flexibility) defines four types of organizational cultures. A clan culture has an internal focus and values flexibility; it achieves effectiveness through employee involvement. An adhocracy culture has an external focus and values flexibility; it emphasizes innovation and fast responses to change. A market culture has a strong external focus and values stability and control; such organizations are driven by competition and emphasize customer satisfaction. A hierarchy culture has an internal focus and values stability and control; it emphasizes formal, structured work to meet high standards.

- *Summarize the process by which organizations change their cultures.* The process essentially begins with targeting one of the three layers of organizational culture—observable artifacts, espoused values, and basic assumptions—for change. This is accomplished by using one or more of the following 11 mechanisms: (a) formal statements of organizational philosophy, mission, vision, values, and materials used for recruiting, selection, and socialization; (b) the design of physical space, work environments, and buildings; (c) slogans, language, acronyms, and sayings; (d) deliberate role modeling, training programs, teaching, and coaching by managers and supervisors; (e) explicit rewards, status symbols, and promotion criteria; (f) stories, legends, and myths about key people and events; (g) the organizational activities, processes, or outcomes that leaders pay attention to, measure, and control; (h) leader reactions to critical incidents and organizational crises; (i) the workflow and organizational structure; (j) organizational systems and procedures; and (k) organizational goals and associated criteria used for recruitment, selection, development, promotion, layoffs, and retirement of people.

- *Describe the three phases in Feldman's model of organizational socialization.* The three phases of Feldman's model are anticipatory socialization, encounter, and change and acquisition. Anticipatory socialization begins before an individual actually joins the organization. The encounter phase begins when the employment contract has been signed. Phase 3 involves the period in which employees master important tasks and resolve any role conflicts.

- *Discuss the various socialization tactics used to socialize employees.* There are six key socialization tactics. They are collective versus individual, formal versus informal, sequential versus random, fixed versus variable, serial versus disjunctive, and investiture versus divestiture (see Table 2–1). Each tactic provides organizations with two opposing options for socializing employees.

- *Explain the four types of development networks derived from a developmental network model of mentoring.* The four development networks are receptive, traditional, entrepreneurial, and opportunistic. A receptive network is composed of a few weak ties from one social system. A traditional network contains a few strong ties between an employee and developers that all come from one social system. An entrepreneurial network is made up of strong ties among developers from several social systems, and an opportunistic network is associated with having weak ties with multiple developers from different social systems.

# discussion questions

1. Using the competing values framework, how would you describe the type of organizational culture that exists at Apple?
2. How would you respond to someone who made the following statement? "Organizational cultures are not important as far as managers are concerned."
3. Can you think of any organizational heroes who have influenced your work behavior? Describe them, and explain how they affected your behavior.
4. Why is socialization essential to organizational success?
5. Have you ever had a mentor? Explain how things turned out.

# ethical dilemma

## Should Countrywide Reimburse Angelo Mozilo for His Wife's Travel Expenses?[61]

The United States' largest mortgage lender, Countrywide Financial Corp., is under intense scrutiny from the U.S. government. Not only has the company lost billions of dollars in 2007 and part of 2008, but it is currently under investigation by the Securities and Exchange Commission for potential improper accounting and by the Federal Bureau of Investigation for possible securities fraud. Countrywide's actions and alleged problems are related to the mortgage crisis that occurred in 2007 and 2008.

The company's CEO, Angelo Mozilo, was paid roughly $250 million from 1998 through 2007 and received an additional $406 million from the sale of Countrywide stock. His actions were under scrutiny when he wrote an e-mail to the board asking them to reimburse him for taxes owed for his wife's use of the corporate jet. He threatened to resign and liquidate his 12 million shares if the board did not reimburse him. The sale of the stock would hurt the company's image in the marketplace.

### What would you have done if you were on the board of directors for Countrywide?

1. Tell Mr. Mozilo that you will not reimburse him. His wife used the corporate jet, and the shareholders should not pay for this expense.
2. Reimburse him. Angelo co-founded the company and his wife should be able to use the jet when she wants.
3. Split the expense. This is a win-win solution.
4. Invent other options. Discuss.

For an interpretation of this situation, visit our Web site at **www.mhhe.com/kinickiob4e**

If you're looking for additional study materials, be sure to check out the Online Learning Center at

**www.mhhe.com/kinickiob4e**

for more information and interactivities that correspond to this chapter.

# chapter Three

# Developing Global Managers

**After reading the material in this chapter, you should be able to:**

1. Define *ethnocentrism,* and explain what Hofstede concluded about applying American management theories in other countries.

2. Identify and describe the nine cultural dimensions from the GLOBE project.

3. Draw a distinction between individualistic cultures and collectivist cultures.

4. Demonstrate your knowledge of these two distinctions: high-context versus low-context cultures and monochronic versus polychronic cultures.

5. Explain what the GLOBE project has taught us about leadership.

6. Identify an OB trouble spot for each stage of the foreign assignment cycle.

This is not the IBM of the 20th century, when Big Blue defined what it meant to be a multinational. Back then, its subsidiaries in 160 countries behaved like mini-IBMs—essentially, standalone operations serving their local customers. But replicating itself became too costly for IBM. So now the company is reorganizing around the principle that it will perform work for customers where the jobs can best be done—tapping the right talent at the right price.

That philosophy has produced a monumental shift in how IBM operates. In the past three years, the company has hired some 90,000 people in low-cost countries including Brazil, China, and India. These people, working in so-called global service delivery centers, provide a wide array of services for clients. The work goes beyond software programming to include data center operations, help-desk call centers, financial accounting, and benefits management. Initially, cheap labor was the big attraction of this move, with pay in India 70% to 80% lower than in the U.S. But these days, tapping the abundant talent pools—and new ideas—in emerging markets such as India and China is important as well.

Many of those global service employees report both to local supervisors and to managers thousands of miles away . . . .

But there's still plenty of work to be done before IBM, with 375,000 people on six continents, is a smooth-running global machine. Says Chief Executive Samuel J. Palmisano: "The big issues for us are: Where do you put them? How do you retain them? How do you develop them? How do you move work to them or them to work?"

Cost-cutting alone wouldn't do the job: Palmisano had to transform how

service work was done. He assigned Robert W. Moffat Jr., 51, a longtime IBMer, to the task. Moffat had already wrung $5 billion of annual costs out of IBM's manufacturing supply chain . . . .

Moffat figured that the same approach could be taken with services. His team surveyed countries for costs, available talent, educational pipelines, languages spoken, proximity to markets, and political stability. They used this information to choose locations where IBM would serve clients anywhere around the world. Moffat set up finance and administration back-office centers, for example, in Bangalore, Buenos Aires, Krakow, Shanghai, and Tulsa . . . .

Moffat and his colleagues also have used their manufacturing experience to

**Actress Shabana Azmi addresses IBM women employees at Winspiration 2008, and IBM India leadership conference in Bangalore India. IBM's global presence is developing managers around the world.**

keep track of IBM's far-flung employees. Just as every component used in an IBM computer is described in detail on inventory and planning documents, new databases contain profiles of employees that list their capabilities and their up-to-the-minute availability. Yet while a computer part doesn't change over time, people do. So the databases can be continuously updated by employees and their managers as employees gain skills and experience.

Before, project managers assembled teams largely made up of people they had worked with. But as IBM expanded

around the globe, managers found it harder to pull teams together. Now project managers post detailed requests in one of the databases called Professional Marketplace that lists more than 170,000 employees along with their skills, pay rate, and availability. Other managers monitor the database and serve as matchmakers between jobs and people. The databases have shaved 20% from the average time it takes to assemble a team and have saved IBM $500 million overall . . . .

IBM Brazil is a true microcosm of the enterprise. In five years the workforce has grown from 4,000 to 13,000 people, many of them based in Hortolandia, Brazil's Silicon Valley, about a 90-minute drive from São Paulo. Employees fly the national flags of their clients on their cubicles. Walk down the aisles and you'll hear English, French, Portuguese, and Spanish spoken. Salaries are about half of what IBM pays in the U.S. for similar work.

While most of the management team in Brazil is local, IBM mixes in people from other countries to hasten the global integration process. One such "assignee" is American Robert Payne, a 22-year IBM executive who runs part of the tech services organization in Brazil. Payne, 48, immerses himself in the cultures of the countries where he's assigned. He learned Japanese for his Tokyo gig. When he arrived in Brazil three years ago, he promised to conduct all of his meetings in Portuguese within nine months. And he did.[1]

**FOR DISCUSSION**

How is IBM using technology to manage its global operations? For an interpretation of this case and additional comments, visit our Online Learning Center at

www.mhhe.com/ kinickiob4e

**THE CHAPTER-OPENING CASE ILLUSTRATES** the complexity of trying to manage an international business. One only has to read the paper or watch the nightly news to hear something about the global economy. Signs and symptoms of economic globalization making headlines in recent years have been the controversial North American Free Trade Agreement, riots at World Trade Organization meetings, complaints about the offshoring of jobs, trade imbalances, foreign sweatshops, immigration restrictions, and intellectual property abuses.[2] No less than a global economic earthquake is underway:

> For more than half a century, Americans could take for granted that the world economy would orbit around them. No longer . . . .
>
> Assuming continued economic growth in the developing world, the ranks of the global middle class are expected to triple by 2030 to 1.2 billion, according to the World Bank. Today, a bit more than half of that free-spending group resides in developing countries. By 2030, almost all of it, 92%, will call the developing world home.
>
> For multinational corporations, that means paying ever more attention to what's happening outside the United States and especially in Asia, Latin America, parts of the Middle East and Africa.[3]

Courtesy of Vahan Shirvanian.

Not only does rising demand mean companies have to pay attention to global markets, but managers also have to lead employees in various parts of the world. KLA-Tencor makes equipment and systems for semiconductor (computer chip) manufacturers. As the manufacturers have set up operations in China, Singapore, and India, so does KLA-Tencor. In each of those locations, KLA-Tencor has to plan ways to train local employees in how to operate its machines productively and then teach chip manufacturers' employees what they have learned.[4] This requires a combination of cross-cultural communication, teaching, problem-solving, technical, and leadership skills.

Global managers such as Coke's Muhtar Kent, who can move comfortably from one culture to another while conducting business, have an advantage in the new global economy.[5] Indeed, according to one study, U.S. multinational companies headed by CEOs with international assignments on their résumés tended to outperform the competition.[6] Even managers and employees who stay in their native country will find it hard to escape today's global economy. Many will be thrust into international relationships by working for foreign-owned companies or by dealing with foreign suppliers, customers, and coworkers.

Competition for both businesses and those seeking good-paying jobs in the global economy promises to be very tough. The purpose of this chapter is to help you move toward meeting the challenge. To do that, the chapter draws on cultural anthropology to explore the impact of culture in today's increasingly globalized organizations. We begin by discussing how to develop a global mind-set. Next, we examine key dimensions of societal culture with the goal of enhancing cross-cultural awareness. Then we review practical lessons from research into cross-cultural management. The chapter concludes by exploring the challenges of foreign assignments and ways organizations can prepare their people to meet those challenges.

# Developing a Global Mind-Set

Managing in a global economy is as much about patterns of thinking and behavior as it is about trade agreements, goods and services, and currency exchange rates. Extended periods in a single dominant culture ingrain assumptions about how things are and should be. Today's managers, whether they work at home for a foreign-owned company or actually work in a foreign country, need to develop a global mind-set (involving open-mindedness, adaptability, and a strong desire to learn).[7]

This section encourages a global mind-set by defining societal culture and contrasting it with organizational culture, discussing ethnocentrism, exploring ways to become a global manager, and examining the applicability of American management theories in other cultures.

## A Model of Societal and Organizational Cultures

**Societal culture** involves "beliefs and values about what is desirable and undesirable in a community of people, and a set of formal or informal practices to support the values."[8] Elements of culture therefore may be prescriptive (what people should do) and descriptive (what they actually do). Culture is passed from one generation to the next by family, friends, teachers, and relevant others. Most cultural lessons are learned by observing and imitating role models as they go about their daily affairs or as observed in the media.

> **societal culture**
>
> **Socially derived, taken-for-granted assumptions about how to think and act.**

**Peeling the Cultural Onion**   Culture is difficult to grasp because it is multi-layered. International management experts Fons Trompenaars (from the Netherlands) and Charles Hampden-Turner (from Britain) offer this instructive analogy in their landmark book, *Riding the Waves of Culture:*

> Culture comes in layers, like an onion. To understand it you have to unpeel it layer by layer.
>
> On the outer layer are the products of culture, like the soaring skyscrapers of Manhattan, pillars of private power, with congested public streets between them. These are expressions of deeper values and norms in a society that are not directly visible (values such as upward mobility, "the more-the-better," status, material success). The layers of values and norms are deeper within the "onion," and are more difficult to identify.[9]

Thus, the September 11, 2001, destruction of the New York World Trade Center towers by terrorists was as much an attack on American cultural values as it was on lives and property. That deepened the hurt and made the anger more profound for Americans and their friends around the world. In both life and business, culture is a serious matter.

**Merging Societal and Organizational Cultures**    As illustrated in Figure 3–1, culture influences organizational behavior in two ways. Employees bring their societal culture to work with them in the form of customs and language. Organizational culture, a by-product of societal culture, in turn affects the individual's values, ethics, attitudes, assumptions, and expectations.[10] The term *societal culture* is used here instead of national culture because the boundaries of many modern nation-states were not drawn along cultural lines. The former Soviet Union, for example, included 15 republics and more than 100 ethnic nationalities, many with their own distinct language.[11] Meanwhile, English-speaking Canadians in Vancouver are culturally closer to Americans in Seattle than to their French-speaking compatriots in Quebec. Societal culture is shaped by the various environmental factors listed in the left-hand side of Figure 3–1.

Once inside the organization's sphere of influence, the individual is further affected by the *organization's* culture, which was discussed in Chapter 2. Mixing of societal and organizational cultures can produce interesting dynamics in multinational companies. For example, several years ago, when BOSS International expanded operations to India, the software company's chief executive, Chris Maeder, a Wisconsin native, found cultural differences with his 65 Indian employees. They all spoke English, but the cultures didn't interpret words the same way. If Maeder asked a question, he merely wanted information, but the Indian employees thought he was making a less-than-polite request for action. When he established project schedules, he would find out later that jobs weren't getting done. Often, the problem was that a goal was impossible but no one wanted to say so. In Indian culture, as in much of the East and Middle East, a direct no is considered impolite. Rather than refusing to do something, Indian employees might simply remain silent, in order not to disappoint their boss. One way Maeder has coped is by hiring an Indian manager to help him interpret Indian culture.[12]

At work, managers need to consider individual employees' societal culture, the organizational culture, and any interaction between the two. For example, as Japanese

## FIGURE 3–1    Cultural Influences on Organizational Behavior

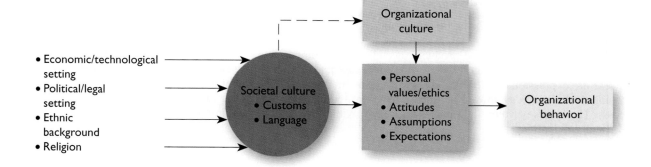

firms have had to address the problems of economic slowdown at home and stiffer competition from abroad, they have had to reevaluate their management practices. In so doing, they are likely to adapt Western-style emphasis on rewarding performance without abandoning such traditional values as "respect and care for people [notably employees], the consideration of their interest and needs, and a long-term commitment in these relationships."[13]

## Ethnocentrism: Removing a Cultural Roadblock in the Global Economy

**Ethnocentrism,** the belief that one's native country, culture, language, and modes of behavior are superior to all others, has its roots in the dawn of civilization. First identified as a behavioral science concept in 1906, involving the tendency of groups to reject outsiders,[14] the term *ethnocentrism* generally has a more encompassing (national or societal) meaning today. Worldwide evidence of ethnocentrism is plentiful. Militant ethnocentrism led to deadly "ethnic cleansing" in Bosnia, Kosovo, and Kenya and genocide in Rwanda, Burundi, and Sudan.

Less dramatic, but still troublesome, is ethnocentrism within managerial and organizational contexts. Experts on the subject framed the problem this way:

> [Ethnocentric managers have] a preference for putting home-country people in key positions everywhere in the world and rewarding them more handsomely for work, along with a tendency to feel that this group is more intelligent, more capable, or more reliable. . . . Ethnocentrism is often not attributable to prejudice as much as to inexperience or lack of knowledge about foreign persons and situations. This is not too surprising, since most executives know far more about employees in their home environments. As one executive put it, "At least I understand why our own managers make mistakes. With our foreigners, I never know. The foreign managers may be better. But if I can't trust a person, should I hire him or her just to prove we're multinational?"[15]

**Research Insight** Research suggests ethnocentrism is bad for business. A survey of 918 companies with home offices in the United States (272 companies), Japan (309), and Europe (337) found ethnocentric staffing and human resource policies to be associated with increased personnel problems. Those problems included recruiting difficulties, high turnover rates, and lawsuits over personnel policies. Among the three regional samples, Japanese companies had the most ethnocentric human resource practices and the most international human resource problems.[16]

**Dealing with Ethnocentrism in Ourselves and Others** Current and future managers can effectively deal with ethnocentrism through education, greater cross-cultural awareness, international experience, and a conscious effort to value cultural diversity.[17] (Take a moment to complete the Hands-On Exercise on page 66.) Results of the Hands-On Exercise need to be interpreted cautiously because this version has not been scientifically validated; thus, it is for instructional and discussion purposes only.

**learning objective** 1

Define *ethnocentrism,* and explain what Hofstede concluded about applying American management theories in other countries.

**ethnocentrism**

Belief that one's native country, culture, language, and behavior are superior.

**Manager's Hot Seat Application**

Cultural Differences: Let's Break a Deal

Prominent Americans such as George Clooney (left) and Chris Rock have spoken publicly to draw the world's attention to the devastating genocide in Darfur. Non-Arab Muslims in the war-torn African nation are in rebellion against the mostly Arab central government and its militia. By 2006, as many as 180,000 had died and about 2 million were homeless.

## How Strong Is Your Potential for Ethnocentrism?

**INSTRUCTIONS:** If you were born and raised or have spent most of your life in the United States, select one number from the following scale for each item. If you are from a different country or culture, substitute the country/language you most closely identify with for the terms *American* and *English,* and then rate each item.

| | Strongly Disagree | Disagree | Neutral | Agree | Strongly Agree |
|---|---|---|---|---|---|
| 1. I was raised in a way that was [truly] American. | 1 | 2 | 3 | 4 | 5 |
| 2. Compared to how much I criticize other cultures, I criticize American culture less. | 1 | 2 | 3 | 4 | 5 |
| 3. I am proud of American culture. | 1 | 2 | 3 | 4 | 5 |
| 4. American culture has had a positive effect on my life. | 1 | 2 | 3 | 4 | 5 |
| 5. I believe that my children should read, write, and speak [only] English. | 1 | 2 | 3 | 4 | 5 |
| 6. I go to places where people are American. | 1 | 2 | 3 | 4 | 5 |
| 7. I admire people who are American. | 1 | 2 | 3 | 4 | 5 |
| 8. I would prefer to live in an American community. | 1 | 2 | 3 | 4 | 5 |
| 9. At home, I eat [only] American food. | 1 | 2 | 3 | 4 | 5 |
| 10. Overall, I am American. | 1 | 2 | 3 | 4 | 5 |

**SCORING**  10–23 = Low potential for ethnocentrism
24–36 = Moderate potential for ethnocentrism
37–50 = High potential for ethnocentrism

**SOURCE:** Adapted from and survey items excerpted from J L Tsai, Y-W Ying, and P A Lee, "The Meaning of 'Being Chinese' and 'Being American': Variation among Chinese American Young Adults," *Journal of Cross-Cultural Psychology,* May 2000, pp 302–32.

# Becoming a Global Manager

On any given day in today's global economy, a manager can interact with colleagues from several different countries or cultures. For instance, at PolyGram, the British music company, the top 33 managers are from 15 different countries.[18] If they are to be effective, present and future managers in such multicultural situations need to develop a global mind-set and cross-cultural skills (see Skills & Best Practices). Developing skilled managers who move comfortably from culture to culture takes time. Consider, for example, this comment by the head of Gillette, who wants twice as many global managers on the payroll. "We could try to hire the best and the brightest, but it's the experience with Gillette that we need. About half of our [expatriates] are now on their fourth country—that kind of experience. It takes 10 years to make the kind of Gillette manager I'm talking about."[19]

Importantly, these global skills will help managers in culturally diverse countries such as the United States and Canada do a more effective job on a day-to-day basis.

# The Hofstede Study: How Well Do U.S. Management Theories Apply in Other Countries?

The short answer to this important question: *not very well.* This answer derives from a landmark study conducted nearly 30 years ago by Dutch researcher Geert Hofstede. His unique cross-cultural comparison of 116,000 IBM employees from 53 countries worldwide focused on four cultural dimensions:

- *Power distance.* How much inequality does someone expect in social situations?[20]
- *Individualism-collectivism.* How loosely or closely is the person socially bonded?
- *Masculinity-femininity.* Does the person embrace stereotypically competitive, performance-oriented masculine traits or nurturing, relationship-oriented feminine traits?
- *Uncertainty avoidance.* How strongly does the person desire highly structured situations?

The U.S. sample ranked relatively low on power distance, very high on individualism, moderately high on masculinity, and low on uncertainty avoidance.[21]

The high degree of variation among cultures led Hofstede to two major conclusions: (1) Management theories and practices need to be adapted to local cultures. This is particularly true for made-in-America management theories (e.g., Maslow's need hierarchy) and Japanese team management practices. *There is no one best way to manage across cultures.*[22] (2) Cultural arrogance is a luxury individuals, companies, and nations can no longer afford in a global economy.

## Two Global Managers

One manager who has developed skills to succeed in the global economy is Lin Chase. Accenture put Chase in charge of its research and development operations in Bangalore, India. At her new job, Chase quickly discovered that common values in U.S. business culture are not always the same in India. She would make plans during meetings and then assume everyone was devoted to meeting the plan's requirements. But when no progress occurred, Chase realized she would have to follow up actively and frequently. She eventually came to see this effort as part of maintaining strong business relationships. Chase has learned to adjust her leadership style to the work style of her employees.

Another successful global manager is Vicki Ho, who works for General Electric. Born in Taiwan, raised in the United States, and armed with a business degree from the University of Chicago, Ho actively sought an overseas position. GE sent her to China to head up the company's equipment leasing there. Ho believes her family's ethnic background gave her an edge in adapting to Chinese culture while the networking skills she learned in America help her maintain relationships with colleagues at GE's headquarters. Her track record supports that view. When GE closed the Chinese equipment-leasing unit, it put her in charge of a division selling security equipment in China, and revenues under Ho quintupled.

**SOURCE: Based on L T Cullen, "The New Expatriates,"** *Time,* **October 22, 2007, Global Business pp 1–2, 4.**

**Test Your Knowledge**
Hofstede's Model of National Culture

# Becoming Cross-Culturally Competent

Cultural anthropologists believe interesting and valuable lessons can be learned by comparing one culture with another. Many dimensions have been suggested over the years to help contrast and compare the world's rich variety of cultures. Five cultural perspectives, especially relevant to present and aspiring global managers, discussed in this section are basic cultural dimensions, individualism versus collectivism, high-context and low-context cultures, monochronic and polychronic time orientation, and cross-cultural leadership. Separately or together these cultural distinctions can become huge stumbling blocks

Jackie Fouse is CFO of Alcon, one of the world's biggest producers of eye-care products. Before taking the number 2 job at the $4.4 billion global manufacturer, she had spent nine years working abroad, adding subtle skills like cultural sensitivity to her management expertise. Of her global experience at Nestlé and Swissair, Fouse, who is fluent in French and German, says, "Everything else being equal—educational background, years of experience—that was the thing more than any other that set me apart from other people."

when doing business across cultures. But first we need to think about cultural stereotyping and the need for *cultural intelligence.*

## Cultural Paradoxes Require Cultural Intelligence

An important qualification needs to be offered at this juncture. All of the cultural differences in this chapter and elsewhere need to be viewed as *tendencies* and *patterns* rather than as absolutes.[23] As soon as one falls into the trap of assuming *all* Italians are this, and *all* Koreans will do that, and so on, potentially instructive generalizations become mindless stereotypes. A pair of professors with extensive foreign work experience advises, "As teachers, researchers, and managers in cross-cultural contexts, we need to recognize that our original characterizations of other cultures are best guesses that we need to modify as we gain more experience."[24] Consequently, they contend, we will be better prepared to deal with inevitable *cultural paradoxes.* By paradox, they mean there are always exceptions to the rule: individuals who do not fit the expected cultural pattern. A good example is the head of Canon. "By Japanese CEO standards, Canon, Inc.'s Fujio Mitarai is something of an anomaly. For starters, he's fast and decisive—a far cry from the consensus builders who typically run Japan, Inc."[25] One also encounters lots of cultural paradoxes in large and culturally diverse nations such as the United States and Brazil. This is where the need for cultural intelligence arises.

**Cultural intelligence,** the ability to accurately interpret ambiguous cross-cultural situations, is an important skill in today's diverse workplaces. Two OB scholars explain:

> A person with high cultural intelligence can somehow tease out of a person's or group's behavior those features that would be true of all people and all groups, those peculiar to this person or this group, and those that are neither universal nor idiosyncratic. The vast realm that lies between those poles is culture.[26]

**cultural intelligence**

The ability to interpret ambiguous cross-cultural situations accurately.

Those interested in developing their cultural intelligence need to first develop their *emotional intelligence,* discussed in detail in Chapter 5, and then practice in ambiguous cross-cultural situations. Of course, as in all human interaction, there is no adequate substitute for really getting to know, listen to, and care about others.

## Nine Basic Cultural Dimensions from the GLOBE Project

2  learning objective

Identify and describe the nine cultural dimensions from the GLOBE project.

Project GLOBE (Global Leadership and Organizational Behavior Effectiveness) is the brainchild of University of Pennsylvania professor Robert J House.[27] It is a massive and ongoing attempt to "develop an empirically based theory to describe, understand, and predict the impact of specific cultural variables on leadership and organizational processes and the effectiveness of these processes."[28] GLOBE has evolved into a network of more than 160 scholars from 62 societies since the project was launched in Calgary, Canada, in 1994. Most of the researchers are native to the particular cultures they study, thus greatly enhancing the credibility of the project. During the first two phases of the GLOBE project, a list of nine basic cultural dimensions was developed and statistically validated. Translated questionnaires based on the nine dimensions were administered to thousands of managers in the banking, food, and telecommunications industries around the world to build a database. Results are being published on a regular basis.[29] Much work and many years are needed if the project's goal, as stated above, is to be achieved. In the meantime, we have been given a comprehensive, valid, and up-to-date tool for better understanding cross-cultural similarities and differences.

**Anthropologists employed by large companies have been researching how people use technology in Asia and the Pacific to learn more about values and habits in emerging markets. A result of this research is the phone shown here. Targeted toward Muslim consumers, it has features such as the automatic listing and announcement of prayer times anywhere in the world, a compass showing the direction of prayer toward Mecca, and a complete transcription of the Koran in Arabic with accompanying English translation.**

The nine cultural dimensions from the GLOBE project are:

- *Power distance:* How much unequal distribution of power should there be in organizations and society?
- *Uncertainty avoidance:* How much should people rely on social norms and rules to avoid uncertainty and limit unpredictability?
- *Institutional collectivism:* How much should leaders encourage and reward loyalty to the social unit, as opposed to the pursuit of individual goals?
- *In-group collectivism:* How much pride and loyalty should individuals have for their family or organization?
- *Gender egalitarianism:* How much effort should be put into minimizing gender discrimination and role inequalities?
- *Assertiveness:* How confrontational and dominant should individuals be in social relationships?
- *Future orientation:* How much should people delay gratification by planning and saving for the future?
- *Performance orientation:* How much should individuals be rewarded for improvement and excellence?
- *Humane orientation:* How much should society encourage and reward people for being kind, fair, friendly, and generous?[30]

Notice how the two forms of collectivism, along with the dimensions of power distance and uncertainty avoidance, correspond to the similarly labeled variables in Hofstede's classic study, discussed earlier.

### Bringing the GLOBE Cultural Dimensions to Life

A fun and worthwhile exercise is to reflect on your own cultural roots, family traditions, and belief system and develop a personal cultural profile, using as many of the GLOBE dimensions as possible. As a case in point, which of the GLOBE cultural dimensions relates to the following biographical sketch?

> Christopher Jones, 24, [is] a UCLA grad who's a musician, playing with his rock band at clubs in Los Angeles.
>
> Like many his age, he has no money for rainy-day savings, let alone the long term. "At this point, my attitude of life is 'carpe diem.' If I have some money, take a trip, something like that," Jones said.

"I understand that being a young person and saving money is the right thing to do. But finding happiness is more important to me than having a little money down the line."[31]

If you said "future orientation," you're right! Indeed, like too many Americans (of all ages), Christopher Jones scores low on future orientation and thus has inadequate savings for the future.

**Country Profiles and Practical Implications**   How do different countries score on the GLOBE cultural dimensions? Data from 18,000 managers yielded the profiles in Table 3–1. A quick overview shows a great deal of cultural diversity around the world. But thanks to the nine GLOBE dimensions, we have more precise understanding of *how* cultures vary. Closer study reveals telling cultural patterns, or cultural fingerprints for nations. The U.S. managerial sample, for instance, scored high on assertiveness and performance orientation. Accordingly, Americans are widely perceived as pushy and hardworking. Switzerland's high scores on uncertainty avoidance and future orientation help explain its centuries of political neutrality and world-renowned banking industry. Singapore is known as a great place to do business because it is clean and safe and its people are well educated and hardworking. This is no surprise, considering Singapore's high scores on institutional collectivism, future orientation, and performance orientation. In contrast, Russia's low scores on future

**TABLE 3–1**   Countries Ranking Highest and Lowest on the GLOBE Cultural Dimensions

| Dimension | Highest | Lowest |
|---|---|---|
| Power distance | Morocco, Argentina, Thailand, Spain, Russia | Denmark, Netherlands, South Africa—black sample, Israel, Costa Rica |
| Uncertainty avoidance | Switzerland, Sweden, Germany—former West, Denmark, Austria | Russia, Hungary, Bolivia, Greece, Venezuela |
| Institutional collectivism | Sweden, South Korea, Japan, Singapore, Denmark | Greece, Hungary, Germany—former East, Argentina, Italy |
| In-group collectivism | Iran, India, Morocco, China, Egypt | Denmark, Sweden, New Zealand, Netherlands, Finland |
| Gender egalitarianism | Hungary, Poland, Slovenia, Denmark, Sweden | South Korea, Egypt, Morocco, India, China |
| Assertiveness | Germany—former East, Austria, Greece, US, Spain | Sweden, New Zealand, Switzerland, Japan, Kuwait |
| Future orientation | Singapore, Switzerland, Netherlands, Canada—English speaking, Denmark | Russia, Argentina, Poland, Italy, Kuwait |
| Performance orientation | Singapore, Hong Kong, New Zealand, Taiwan, US | Russia, Argentina, Greece, Venezuela, Italy |
| Humane orientation | Philippines, Ireland, Malaysia, Egypt, Indonesia | Germany—former West, Spain, France, Singapore, Brazil |

SOURCE: Adapted from M Javidan and R J House, "Cultural Acumen for the Global Manager: Lessons from Project GLOBE," *Organizational Dynamics,* Spring 2001, pp 289–305.

orientation and performance orientation could foreshadow a slower than hoped for transition from a centrally planned economy to free enterprise capitalism.

These illustrations bring us to an important practical lesson: *Knowing the cultural tendencies of foreign business partners and competitors can give you a strategic competitive advantage.* For example, when managers need to discipline employees for shortcomings, they should keep in mind that employees in a collectivist culture are likely to feel they have let down their group. And in cultures with high power distance, employees are most likely to accept discipline when delivered by someone who is clearly of higher status—or to ignore it if the person does not obviously rank higher.[32]

# Individualism versus Collectivism: A Closer Look

Have you ever been torn between what you personally wanted and what the group, organization, or society expected of you? If so, you have firsthand experience with a fundamental and important cultural distinction in both the Hofstede and GLOBE studies: individualism versus collectivism. Awareness of this distinction, as we will soon see, can spell the difference between success and failure in cross-cultural business dealings.

**Individualistic cultures,** characterized as "I" and "me" cultures, give priority to individual freedom and choice. Senior citizens in individualistic U.S. culture are more likely to see themselves as responsible for their own well-being, in contrast to Europeans, who more often expect help at this stage of their lives.[33] **Collectivist cultures,** oppositely called "we" and "us" cultures, rank shared goals higher than individual desires and goals. People in collectivist cultures are expected to subordinate their own wishes and goals to those of the relevant social unit. A worldwide survey of 30,000 managers by Trompenaars and Hampden-Turner, who prefer the term *communitarianism* to collectivism, found the highest degree of individualism in Israel, Romania, Nigeria, Canada, and the United States. Countries ranking lowest in individualism—thus qualifying as collectivist cultures—were Egypt, Nepal, Mexico, India, and Japan. Brazil, China, and France also ended up toward the collectivist end of the scale.[34]

learning objective 3

Draw a distinction between individualistic cultures and collectivist cultures.

**individualistic culture**

Primary emphasis on personal freedom and choice.

**collectivist culture**

Personal goals less important than community goals and interests.

**A Business Success Factor**    Of course, one can expect to encounter both individualists and collectivists in culturally diverse countries such as the United States.[35] For example, imagine the frustration of Dave Murphy, a Boston-based mutual fund salesperson, when he recently tried to get Navajo Indians in Arizona interested in saving money for their retirement. After several fruitless meetings with groups of Navajo employees, he was given this cultural insight by a local official: "If you come to this environment, you have to understand that money is different. It's there to be spent. If you have some, you help your family."[36] To traditional Navajos, enculturated as collectivists, saving money is an unworthy act of selfishness. Subsequently, the sales pitch was tailored to emphasize the *family* benefits of individual retirement savings plans.

**Allegiance to Whom?**    The Navajo example brings up an important point about collectivist cultures. Specifically, which unit of society predominates? For the Navajos, family is the key reference group. But, as Trompenaars and Hampden-Turner observe, important differences exist among collectivist (or communitarian) cultures:

> For each single society, it is necessary to determine the group with which individuals have the closest identification. They could be keen to identify with their trade union,

their family, their corporation, their religion, their profession, their nation, or the state apparatus. The French tend to identify with *la France, la famille, le cadre;* the Japanese with the corporation; the former eastern bloc with the Communist Party; and Ireland with the Roman Catholic Church. Communitarian goals may be good or bad for industry depending on the community concerned, its attitude and relevance to business development.[37]

**4** learning objective

Demonstrate your knowledge of these two distinctions: high-context versus low-context cultures and monochronic versus polychronic cultures.

# High-Context and Low-Context Cultures

People from **high-context cultures**—including China, Korea, Japan, Vietnam, Mexico, and Arab cultures—rely heavily on situational cues for meaning when perceiving and communicating with others.[38] Nonverbal cues such as one's official position, status, or family connections convey messages more powerfully than do spoken words (see Skills & Best Practices). Thus, we come to better understand the ritual of exchanging *and reading* business cards in Japan. Japanese culture is relatively high context. One's business card, listing employer and official position, conveys vital silent messages about one's status to members of Japan's homogeneous society. Also, people from high-context cultures who are not especially talkative during a first encounter with a stranger are not necessarily being unfriendly; they are simply taking time to collect "contextual" information.

**high-context cultures**

**Primary meaning derived from nonverbal situational cues.**

**Reading the Fine Print in Low-Context Cultures**    In **low-context cultures,** written and spoken words carry the burden of shared meanings. Low-context cultures include those found in Germany, Switzerland, Scandinavia, North America, and Great Britain. True to form, Germany has precise written rules for even the smallest details of daily life. In *high*-context cultures, agreements tend to be made on the basis of someone's word or a handshake, after a rather prolonged get-acquainted and trust-building period. Low-context Americans and Canadians, who have cultural roots in Northern Europe, see the handshake as a signal to get a signature on a detailed, lawyer-approved, iron-clad contract.

**low-context cultures**

**Primary meaning derived from written and spoken words.**

**Avoiding Cultural Collisions**    Misunderstanding and miscommunication often are problems in international business dealings when the parties are from high- versus low-context cultures. A Mexican business professor made this instructive observation:

> Over the years, I have noticed that across cultures there are different opinions on what is expected from a business report. U.S. managers, for instance, take a pragmatic, get-to-the-point approach, and expect reports to be concise and action-oriented. They don't have time to read long explanations: "Just the facts, ma'am."
>
> Latin American managers will usually provide long explanations that go beyond the simple facts . . . .
>
> I have a friend who is the Latin America representative for a United States firm and has been asked by his boss to provide regular reports on sales activities. His reports are long, including detailed explanations on the context in which the events he is reporting on occur and the possible interpretations that they might have. His boss regularly answers these reports with very brief messages, telling him to "cut the crap and get to the point!"[39]

Awkward situations such as this can be avoided when those on both sides of the context divide make good-faith attempts to understand and accommodate their counterparts. For instance, people from low-context cultures should make the effort to provide information about the history and personalities involved in a situation, and people from high-context cultures should ask questions when they aren't given information that will help them.[40]

# Cultural Perceptions of Time

In North American and Northern European cultures, time seems to be a simple matter. It is linear, relentlessly marching forward, never backward, in standardized chunks. To the American who received a watch for his or her third birthday, time is like money. It is spent, saved, or wasted.[41] Americans are taught to show up 10 minutes early for appointments. When working across cultures, however, time becomes a very complex matter. For example, consider that it took years for Kanawha Scales & Systems to complete its first deal to sell its coal-loading machines in China:

> [CEO Jim] Bradbury, 61, made his first trip to China in 1986, spending a month in Beijing in a fruitless quest for an order. Six years later, the company finally landed its first deal, a $3 million contract to install coal load-out systems at a Chinese coal mine.[42]

After Bradbury took the time to establish business relationships, however, his Poca, West Virginia, company began bringing in sales of more than $10 million a year from China.

The need for patience in this cross-cultural business deal can be explained in part by the distinction between **monochronic time** and **polychronic time**:

> The former is revealed in the ordered, precise, schedule-driven use of public time that typifies and even caricatures efficient Northern Europeans and North Americans. The latter is seen in the multiple and cyclical activities and concurrent involvement with different people in Mediterranean, Latin American, and especially Arab cultures.[43]

**A Matter of Degree**   Monochronic and polychronic are relative rather than absolute concepts. Generally, the more things a person tends to do at once, the more polychronic that person is.[44] Thanks to computers and advanced telecommunications systems, highly polychronic managers can engage in "multitasking."[45] For instance, it is possible to talk on the telephone, read and respond to e-mail messages, print a report, check an instant phone message, *and* eat a stale sandwich all at the same time. Unfortunately, this extreme polychronic behavior too often is not as efficient as hoped and can be very stressful.[46] Monochronic people prefer to do one thing at a time. What is your attitude toward time?

## Learning to Navigate a High-Context Culture

For managers from a low-context culture such as the United States, doing business in a high-context culture requires the ability to learn how their behavior—not just their words—will be interpreted.

When C Roe Goddard was part of a group looking for a Chinese drug manufacturer to participate in a joint venture, he tried to follow Chinese business customs by winding up his trip to China with a fancy luncheon and gifts to his Chinese colleagues. He purchased beautiful leather-bound travel clocks for each colleague. But to the recipients, a gift is not simply a gift; even the name of the gift carries a meaning. In Chinese, the word for *giving* is *song,* and the word for *clock* is *zhong,* which sounds similar to the word meaning the end of life. Putting all those meanings together, a gift of a clock signals a death wish—hardly Goddard's intended message.

Fortunately for Goddard, his colleagues preserved the relationship by educating him. After the banquet, one of the Chinese businessmen sent Goddard a note explaining the problem and enclosing a penny from each recipient, turning the gift into a symbolic purchase. The Chinese colleagues' willingness to share information about their culture, coupled with Goddard's humility and willingness to learn, saved a deal that was important to both parties. And now Goddard knows that in China, a visitor should stick to "safe" gifts such as pens, stationery, or books about his or her own part of the world.

**SOURCE: Based on E Flitter, "How Not to Give Partners a 'Death Wish' in China," *The Wall Street Journal,* October 10, 2007, http://online.wsj.com.**

**monochronic time**

Preference for doing one thing at a time because time is limited, precisely segmented, and schedule driven.

**polychronic time**

Preference for doing more than one thing at a time because time is flexible and multidimensional.

**Practical Implications**    Low-context cultures, such as that of the United States, tend to run on monochronic time while high-context cultures, such as that of Mexico, tend to run on polychronic time. People in polychronic cultures view time as flexible, fluid, and multidimensional. The Germans and Swiss have made an exact science of monochronic time. In fact, a radio-controlled watch made by a German company, Junghans, is "guaranteed to lose no more than one second in 1 million years."[47] Many a visitor has been a minute late for a Swiss train, only to see its taillights leaving the station. Time is more elastic in polychronic cultures. During the Islamic holy month of Ramadan in Middle Eastern nations, for example, the faithful fast during daylight hours, and the general pace of things markedly slows. Managers need to reset their mental clocks when doing business across cultures.

## Leadership Lessons from the GLOBE Project

**5** learning objective

Explain what the GLOBE project has taught us about leadership.

In phase 2, the GLOBE researchers set out to discover which, if any, attributes of leadership were universally liked or disliked. They surveyed 17,000 middle managers working for 951 organizations across 62 countries. Their results, summarized in Table 3–2, have important implications for trainers and present and future global managers. Visionary and inspirational *charismatic leaders* who are good team builders generally do the best. On the other hand, *self-centered leaders* seen as loners or face-savers generally receive a poor reception worldwide. (See Chapter 14 for a comprehensive treatment of leadership.) Local and foreign managers who heed these results are still advised to use a contingency approach to leadership after using their cultural intelligence to read the local people and culture.[48] David Whitwam, the longtime CEO of appliance maker Whirlpool, recently framed the challenge this way:

**Test Your Knowledge**

International Cultural Diversity

> Leading a company today is different from the 1980s and '90s, especially in a global company. It requires a new set of competencies. Bureaucratic structures don't work anymore. You have to take the command-and-control types out of the system. You need to allow and encourage broad-based involvement in the company. Especially in consumer kinds of companies, we need a diverse workforce with diverse leadership. You need strong regional leadership that lives in the culture. We have a North American running the North American business, and a Latin American running the Latin American business.[49]

# Preparing for a Foreign Assignment

As the reach of global companies continues to grow, many opportunities for living and working in foreign countries will arise. Not only do employers want to develop employees with global-business capabilities, but in some locations, the demand for local talent with necessary skills continues to outstrip the supply. In China, for example, fast-growing businesses are hard-pressed to find enough managers with leadership and teamwork skills. Companies therefore need talented people who are willing to work in China and help to develop the leaders of the future.[50] Global players need a vibrant and growing cadre of employees who are willing and able to do business across cultures. Thus, the purpose of this final section is to help you prepare yourself and others to work successfully in foreign countries. In fact, when *Fortune* recently listed "Five Ways to Ignite Your Career," the number one suggestion was this: "Go global. International operations aren't a backwater—they're a way to prove you get it."[51]

Leadership Attributes Universally Liked and Disliked across 62 Nations | **TABLE 3–2**

| Universally Positive Leader Attributes | Universally Negative Leader Attributes |
|---|---|
| Trustworthy | Loner |
| Just | Asocial |
| Honest | Noncooperative |
| Foresight | Irritable |
| Plans ahead | Nonexplicit |
| Encouraging | Egocentric |
| Positive | Ruthless |
| Dynamic | Dictatorial |
| Motive arouser | |
| Confidence builder | |
| Motivational | |
| Dependable | |
| Intelligent | |
| Decisive | |
| Effective bargainer | |
| Win–win problem solver | |
| Administrative skilled | |
| Communicative | |
| Informed | |
| Coordinator | |
| Team builder | |
| Excellence oriented | |

SOURCE: Excerpted and adapted from P W Dorfman, P J Hanges, and F C Brodbeck, "Leadership and Cultural Variation: The Identification of Culturally Endorsed Leadership Profiles," in *Culture, Leadership, and Organizations: The GLOBE Study of 62 Societies,* eds R J House, P J Hanges, M Javidan, P W Dorfman, and V Gupta (Thousand Oaks, CA: Sage, 2004), Tables 21.2 and 21.3, pp 677–78.

# A Poor Track Record for American Expatriates

As we use the term here, **expatriate** refers to anyone living and/or working outside their home country. Hence, they are said to be *expatriated* when transferred to another country and *repatriated* when transferred back home. U.S. expatriate managers usually are characterized as culturally inept and prone to failure on international assignments. Sadly, research supports this view.

**expatriate**

**Anyone living or working in a foreign country.**

Studies showed that expatriates tended to leave their assignments early due to job dissatisfaction and problems adjusting to the culture of the host country.[52] Further, a recent study by Pricewaterhouse Coopers revealed that over 25 percent of repatriated employees quit their jobs within one year of returning from an international assignment.[53] These results suggest that U.S. multinationals clearly need to do a better job of preparing employees and their families for foreign assignments. This section presents suggested ways to accomplish this goal.

## Some Good News: North American Women on Foreign Assignments

Historically, a woman from the United States or Canada on a foreign assignment was a rarity. Things are changing, albeit slowly. A review of research evidence and anecdotal accounts uncovered these insights:

- The proportion of corporate women from North America on foreign assignments grew from about 3% in the early 1980s to between 11% and 15% in the late 1990s.
- Self-disqualification and management's assumption that women would not be welcome in foreign cultures—not foreign prejudice, itself—are the primary barriers for potential female expatriates.
- Expatriate North American women are viewed first and foremost by their hosts as being foreigners, and only secondarily as being female.
- North American women have a very high success rate on foreign assignments.[54]

Considering the rapidly growing demand for global managers, self-disqualification and management's prejudicial policies are counterproductive. Our advice to women who have their heart set on a foreign assignment: "Go for it!"

## Avoiding OB Trouble Spots in the Foreign Assignment Cycle

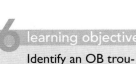

**6 learning objective**

Identify an OB trouble spot for each stage of the foreign assignment cycle.

Finding the right person (often along with a supportive and adventurous family) for a foreign position is a complex, time-consuming, and costly process.[55] For our purposes, it is sufficient to narrow the focus to common OB trouble spots in the foreign assignment cycle. As illustrated in Figure 3–2, the first and last stages of the cycle occur at

**FIGURE 3–2**

The Foreign Assignment Cycle (with OB Trouble Spots)

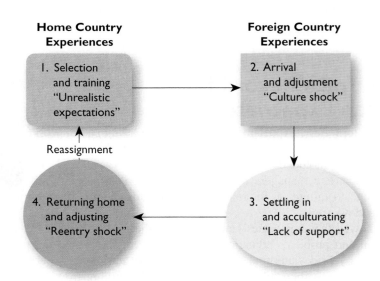

home. The middle two stages occur in the foreign or host country. Each stage hides an OB-related trouble spot that needs to be anticipated and neutralized. Otherwise, the bill for another failed foreign assignment will grow.

**Avoiding Unrealistic Expectations with Cross-Cultural Training** Realistic job previews (RJPs) have proven effective at bringing people's unrealistic expectations about a pending job assignment down to earth by providing a realistic balance of good and bad news. People with realistic expectations tend to quit less often and be more satisfied than those with unrealistic expectations. RJPs are a must for future expatriates. In addition, cross-cultural training is required.

   **Cross-cultural training** is any type of structured experience designed to help departing employees adjust to a foreign culture. The trend is toward more of this type of training. Although costly, companies believe cross-cultural training is less expensive than failed foreign assignments. Programs vary widely in type and also in rigor. Of course, the greater the difficulty, the greater the time and expense:

**SKILLS & BEST PRACTICES**

## Key Cross-Cultural Competencies

| Cross-Cultural Competency Cluster | Knowledge or Skill Required |
|---|---|
| Building relationships | Ability to gain access to and maintain relationships with members of host culture |
| Valuing people of different cultures | Empathy for difference; sensitivity to diversity |
| Listening and observation | Knows cultural history and reasons for certain cultural actions and customs |
| Coping with ambiguity | Recognizes and interprets implicit behavior, especially nonverbal cues |
| Translating complex information | Knowledge of local language, symbols or other forms of verbal language, and written language |
| Taking action and initiative | Understands intended and potentially unintended consequences of actions |
| Managing others | Ability to manage details of a job including maintaining cohesion in a group |
| Adaptability and flexibility | Views change from multiple perspectives |
| Managing stress | Understands own and other's mood, emotions, and personality |

SOURCE: Excerpted from Y Yamazaki and D C Kayes, "An Experiential Approach to Cross-Cultural Learning: A Review and Integration of Competencies for Successful Expatriate Adaptation," *Academy of Management Learning and Education*, December 2004, Table 2, p 372.

- *Easiest.* Predeparture training is limited to informational materials, including books, lectures, films, videos, and Internet searches.

- *Moderately difficult.* Experiential training is conducted through case studies, role playing, assimilators (simulated intercultural incidents), and introductory language instruction.

**cross-cultural training**

Structured experiences to help people adjust to a new culture/country.

- *Most difficult.* Departing employees are given some combination of the preceding methods plus comprehensive language instruction and field experience in the target culture.

   Which approach is the best? Research to date does not offer a final answer. One study involving U.S. employees in South Korea led the researcher to recommend a *combination* of informational and experiential predeparture training.[56] As a general rule of thumb, the more rigorous the cross-cultural training, the better. The nine competencies

**Group Exercise**

Applying Hofstede's Cultural Values

detailed in Skills & Best Practices on page 77 should be the core of any comprehensive cross-cultural training program. Fluor Corporation prepares employees for overseas assignments by using a diversity-training tool that identifies specific cultural areas where an individual requires development before beginning an assignment in a particular country or region.[57]

Our personal experience with teaching OB to foreign students both in the United States and abroad reminds us that there really is no substitute for an intimate knowledge of the local culture, language, customs, and etiquette. Bill Roedy, President of MTV Networks International, used this advice to land an important deal in Saudi Arabia.

> His job requires getting often risqué programming into as many countries as he can without offending local sensibilities. . . . Roedy was in town to persuade the mayor of Mecca to give his blessing to MTV Arabia, the network's biggest global launch, which had the potential to reach 2,000 million Arabs across the region. "Presidents and sheiks don't normally watch MTV, so we have to help them overcome stereotypical views they have," says Roedy. "Nobody was more important than the mayor of Mecca, the religious center of Islam. We had to get it right."
>
> While there he attended recording sessions with the Arab rappers Jeddah Legends, where he learned that their lyrics tended to be about family and religion—themes that he would draw on during his meeting with the mayor of Mecca.[58]

**Avoiding Culture Shock**   Have you ever been in a totally unfamiliar situation and felt disoriented and perhaps a bit frightened? If so, you already know something about culture shock. According to anthropologists, **culture shock** involves anxiety and doubt caused by an overload of unfamiliar expectations and social cues. For Chinese people who come to the United States to work, one of the challenges they face is that their U.S. colleagues generally are far less interested in socializing and disclosing their personal lives. *Wall Street Journal* columnist Li Yuan, a Chinese native, explains, "In China, the office is both a work space and a social space . . . . It's quite common for co-workers to go out for dinner, karaoke and team sports after work a couple of times a week, and those who rarely participate in group activities are considered arrogant or lacking in social graces." Coworkers are eager to learn about one another's marital status, salary, housing costs, love life, and so on. To people coming from this culture, American workers seem cold and detached, and life in America seems lonely. For her part, Yuan has come to see Americans' reluctance to talk about certain subjects as a way to maintain harmony in a diverse culture. She has grown accustomed to the difference—but when she gets a raise, she shares the news with her friends in China.[59]

College freshmen often experience a variation of culture shock. An expatriate manager, or family member, may be thrown off balance by an avalanche of strange sights, sounds, and behaviors. Among them may be unreadable road signs, strange-tasting food, inability to use your left hand for social activities (in Islamic countries, the left hand is the toilet hand), or failure to get a laugh with your sure-fire joke. For the expatriate manager trying to concentrate on the fine details of a business negotiation, culture shock is more than an embarrassing inconvenience. It is a disaster! Like the confused college freshman who quits and goes home, culture-shocked employees often panic and go home early.

The best defense against culture shock is comprehensive cross-cultural training, including intensive language study. Once again, the only way to pick up subtle—yet

**culture shock**

Anxiety and doubt caused by an overload of new expectations and cues.

Despite classes like Christine Wang's, in which first-graders in Maryland learn basic Chinese, managers in the United States are likely to lag behind those in China in their ability to understand and appreciate someone else's language and culture. Many experts worry that lack of foreign language skills goes hand-in-hand with a general lack of global awareness in the United States.

important—social cues is via the local language. And as today's businesspeople are discovering, learning a language is a lot more than translating words from one language to another. At Computer Sciences Corporation, which has offices in 49 countries, a French employee was offended by a British colleague's dry humor. At Reuters Group, American programmers thought they were giving directions by saying when they would "like" work to be done, while their Thai colleagues saw the statement more literally as a description of their preferences. Responding to miscommunications such as these, language-training programs are beginning to broaden their curriculum to include strategies for avoiding cross-cultural misunderstandings.[60]

**Support During the Foreign Assignment** Especially during the first six months, when everything is so new to the expatriate, a support system needs to be in place. *Host-country sponsors,* assigned to individual managers or families, are recommended because they serve as "cultural seeing-eye dogs." In a foreign country, where even the smallest errand can turn into an utterly exhausting production, sponsors can get things done quickly because they know the cultural and geographical territory. Honda's Ohio employees, for example, enjoyed the help of family sponsors when training in Japan:

> Honda smoothed the way with Japanese wives who once lived in the U.S. They handled emergencies such as when Diana Jett's daughter Ashley needed stitches in her chin. When Task Force Senior Manager Kim Smalley's daughter, desperate to fit in at elementary school, had to have a precisely shaped bag for her harmonica, a Japanese volunteer stayed up late to make it.[61]

Another way to support expatriates during the transition phase of a new foreign assignment is to maintain an active dialog with established *mentors* from back home. Technology such as e-mail and teleconferencing is efficient and practical but not a substitute for spending time with mentors or colleagues. AchieveGlobal operates in 44 countries, helping clients manage multinational teams. Whether working with clients or strengthening its own teamwork, the company insists that team members gather for several face-to-face meetings each year, because this level of communication is essential for mutual understanding and problem solving.[62]

**Avoiding Reentry Shock**    Strange as it may seem, many otherwise successful expatriate managers encounter their first major difficulty only after their foreign assignment is over. Why? Returning to one's native culture is taken for granted because it seems so routine and ordinary. But having adjusted to another country's way of doing things for an extended period of time can put one's own culture and surroundings in a strange new light. Three areas for potential reentry shock are work, social activities, and general environment (e.g., politics, climate, transportation, food). Ira Caplan's return to New York City exemplifies reentry shock:

> During the past 12 years, living mostly in Japan, he and his wife had spent their vacations cruising the Nile or trekking in Nepal. They hadn't seen much of the U.S. They are getting an eyeful now . . . .
>
> Prices astonish him. The obsession with crime unnerves him. What unsettles Mr Caplan more, though, is how much of himself he has left behind.
>
> In a syndrome of return no less stressful than that of departure, he feels displaced, disregarded, and diminished . . . .
>
> In an Italian restaurant, crowded at lunchtime, the waiter sets a bowl of linguine in front of him. Mr Caplan stares at it. "In Asia, we have smaller portions and smaller people," he says.
>
> Asia is on his mind. He has spent years cultivating an expertise in a region of huge importance. So what? This is New York.[63]

*Work-related* adjustments were found to be a major problem for samples of repatriated Finnish, Japanese, and American employees.[64] Upon being repatriated, a 12-year veteran of one U.S. company said: "Our organizational culture was turned upside down. We now have a different strategic focus, different 'tools' to get the job done, and different buzzwords to make it happen. I had to learn a whole new corporate 'language'."[65] Reentry shock can be reduced through employee career counseling and home-country mentors and sponsors. Simply being forewarned about the problem of reentry shock is a big step toward effectively dealing with it.

Overall, the key to a successful foreign assignment is making it a well-integrated link in a career chain rather than treating it as an isolated adventure.

# key terms

| | | |
|---|---|---|
| collectivist culture   71 | ethnocentrism   65 | low-context cultures   72 |
| cross-cultural training   77 | expatriate   75 | monochronic time   73 |
| cultural intelligence   68 | high-context cultures   72 | polychronic time   73 |
| culture shock   78 | individualistic culture   71 | societal culture   63 |

# chapter summary

- *Define* ethnocentrism, *and explain what Hofstede concluded about applying American management theories in other countries.* Ethnocentrism is a prejudicial belief that one's native country, culture, language, behavior, and traditions are better than all others. Due to the wide variations in key dimensions Hofstede found among cultures, he warned against directly applying American-made management theories to other cultures without adapting them first. He said there is no one best way to manage across cultures.

- *Identify and describe the nine cultural dimensions from the GLOBE project.* (1) *Power distance*—How equally should power be distributed? (2) *Uncertainty avoidance*—How much should social norms and rules reduce uncertainty and unpredictability? (3) *Institutional collectivism*—How much should loyalty to the social unit override individual interests? (4) *In-group collectivism*—How strong should one's loyalty be to family or organization? (5) *Gender egalitarianism*—How much should gender discrimination and role inequalities be minimized? (6) *Assertiveness*—How confrontational and dominant should one be in social relationships? (7) *Future orientation*—How much should one delay gratification by planning and saving for the future? (8) *Performance orientation*—How much should individuals be rewarded for improvement and excellence? (9) *Humane orientation*—How much should individuals be rewarded for being kind, fair, friendly, and generous?

- *Draw a distinction between individualistic cultures and collectivist cultures.* People in individualistic cultures think primarily in terms of "I" and "me" and place a high value on freedom and personal choice. Collectivist cultures teach people to be "we" and "us" oriented and to subordinate personal wishes and goals to the interests of the relevant social unit (such as family, group, organization, or society).

- *Demonstrate your knowledge of these two distinctions: high-context versus low-context cultures and monochronic versus polychronic cultures.* People in high-context cultures (such as China, Japan, and Mexico) derive great meaning from situational cues, above and beyond written and spoken words. Low-context cultures (including Germany, the United States, and Canada) derive key information from precise and brief written and spoken messages. In monochronic cultures (e.g., the United States), time is precise and rigidly measured. Polychronic cultures, such as those found in Latin America and the Middle East, view time as multidimensional, fluid, and flexible. Monochronic people prefer to do one thing at a time, while polychronic people like to tackle multiple tasks at the same time.

- *Explain what the GLOBE project has taught us about leadership.* Across 62 cultures, they identified leader attributes that are universally liked and universally disliked. The universally liked leader attributes—including trustworthy, dynamic, motive arouser, decisive, and intelligent—are associated with the charismatic/transformational leadership style that is widely applicable. Universally disliked leader attributes—such as noncooperative, irritable, egocentric, and dictatorial—should be avoided in all cultures.

- *Identify an OB trouble spot for each stage of the foreign assignment cycle.* The four stages of the foreign assignment cycle (and OB trouble spots) are (a) selection and training (unrealistic expectations), (b) arrival and adjustment (culture shock), (c) settling in and acculturating (lack of support), and (d) returning home and adjusting (reentry shock).

# discussion questions

1. Based on reading this chapter, why is IBM (see the chapter-opening case) having success with its global operations?
2. How would you describe the prevailing culture in your country to a stranger from another land, in terms of the nine GLOBE project dimensions?
3. Why are people from high-context cultures such as China and Japan likely to be misunderstood by low-context Westerners?
4. How strong is your desire for a foreign assignment? Why? If it is strong, where would you like to work? Why? How prepared are you for a foreign assignment? What do you need to do to be better prepared?
5. What is your personal experience with culture shock? Which of the OB trouble spots in Figure 3–2 do you believe is the greatest threat to expatriate employee success? Explain.

# ethical dilemma

## Chiquita Brands International Discloses Payments to Columbian Terrorists

Assume that you are on a grand jury in the United States and you are debating whether or not to file charges against Roderick Hills, former head of Chiquita Brands International, Inc.'s audit committee and former chairman of the Securities and Exchange Commission.

The case involves payments that the company made to a violent Colombian group that has been determined to be a terrorist group by the U.S. government. Mr Mills was in charge of the company's audit committee during the time of the payments. The facts of the case indicate that "a paramilitary organization had threatened to kidnap or kill employees on the banana farms of Chiquita's Columbian subsidiary, Banadex, and Chiquita was concerned that its employees could be harmed if it cut the payments immediately." Mr Hill and other executives viewed the expense payments as "security payments" that were saving employees' lives. "Lawyers familiar with the case say Mr Hills and Mr Olson [former general counsel] believe senior Justice Department officials understood this and were deferring any demand to stop the payments to the

United Self-Defense Forces, known by its Spanish abbreviation AUC. Chiquita ultimately paid $1.7 million over seven years." Chiquita never hid the payments from its accountants or Ernst & Young, its auditor.[66]

### What Would You Do?

1. Charge Mr Mills. He knew that it was against U.S. policy to have dealings with terrorist organizations.

2. The company should have folded its operations in Colombia rather than make payments to a terrorist organization. You should fine the company $25 million.

3. Don't charge Mr Mills. He was trying to protect his employees' lives and he fully disclosed the company's actions to U.S. authorities.

4. Invent other options.

For an interpretation of this situation, visit our Web site, **www.mhhe.com/kinickiob4e**.

---

If you're looking for additional study materials, be sure to check out the Online Learning Center at

**www.mhhe.com/kinickiob4e**

for more information and interactivities that correspond to this chapter.

# part two

# Managing Individuals

# chapter Four

# Understanding Social Perception and Managing Diversity

**LEARNING OBJECTIVES**

**After reading the material in this chapter, you should be able to:**

1. Describe *perception* in terms of the social information processing model.

2. Identify and briefly explain six managerial implications of social perception.

3. Explain, according to Kelley's model, how external and internal causal attributions are formulated.

4. Demonstrate your familiarity with the demographic trends that are creating an increasingly diverse workforce.

5. Identify the barriers and challenges to managing diversity.

6. Discuss organizational practices used to manage diversity.

In a recent class at Abraham Clark High School in Roselle, NJ, business teacher Barbara Govahn distributed glossy classroom materials that invited students to think about what they want to be when they grow up. Eighteen career paths were profiled, including a writer, a magician, a town mayor—and five employees from accounting giant Deloitte LLP.

"Consider a career you may never have imagined," the book suggests. "Working as a professional auditor."

The curriculum, provided free to the public school by a nonprofit arm of Deloitte, aims to persuade students to join the company's ranks. One 18-year-old senior in Ms Govahn's class, Hipolito Rivera, says the company-sponsored lesson drove home how professionals in all fields need accountants. "They make it sound pretty good," he says.

Deloitte and other corporations are reaching out to classrooms—drafting curricula while also conveying the benefits of working for the sponsor companies. Hoping to create a pipeline of workers far into the future, these corporations furnish free lesson plans and may also underwrite classroom materials, computers or training seminars for teachers.

The programs represent a new dimension of the business world's influence in public schools. Companies such as McDonald's Corp and Yum Brands Inc's Pizza Hut have long attempted to use school promotions to turn students into customers. The latest initiatives would turn them into employees.

Companies that employ engineers, fearful of a coming labor shortage, are at the movement's forefront. Lockheed Martin Corp began funding engineering courses two years ago at schools near its aircraft testing and development site in Palmdale, Calif, saying it hopes to replenish its local workforce. Starting in 2004, British engine-maker Rolls-Royce PLC has helped fund high-school courses in topics such as engine propulsion. Intel Corp supports curricula in school districts where engineering concepts are taught as early as the elementary level.

Schools, for their part, have embraced corporate support as state education funding has remained flat for a decade and declining housing values now threaten to eat into property-tax revenues. Teachers, meanwhile, often welcome the lesson plans, classroom equipment and the corporate-sponsored professional development sessions. . . .

Lockheed is bracing for a worker shortage. The company estimates that about half of its science- and engineering-based workforce will

be retiring in the next decade or so. Meanwhile, interest in engineering as a career is declining among US students. In a 2007 survey of more than 270,000 college freshmen conducted by the Higher Education Research Institute at UCLA, 7.5% said they intended to major in engineering—the lowest level since the 1970s. National-security restrictions preclude the Bethesda, Md, company and other major defense contractors from outsourcing many jobs overseas.

"We're already within the window of criticality to get tomorrow's engineers in the classroom today," says Jim Knotts, director of corporate citizenship for Lockheed. "We want to address a national need to develop the next generation of engineers—but with some affinity toward Lockheed Martin."

Lockheed is particularly eager to refresh the engineer pool at its giant facility in Palmdale, Calif. Here, at the southern edge of the Mojave desert, the company works alongside aerospace giants Boeing Co and Northrop Grumman Corp, designing aircraft and testing them near an Air Force facility known as Plant 42. Luring workers to this flat, parched area is a challenge, Lockheed and local officials concede. So the company, working with local schools, is hoping to grow its own talent.[1]

This Lockheed Martin engineer speaks to a high school classroom about a career in engineering. Interest in engineering as a career is declining among US students, and this effort to send engineers into classrooms may reverse that trend.

**FOR DISCUSSION**

Are school systems compromising their academic freedom or integrity by involving corporations in curriculum development? Explain. For an interpretation of this case and additional comments, vist our Online Learning Center at

www.mhhe.com/kinickiob4e.

**THE CHAPTER-OPENING CASE HIGHLIGHTS** the broad implications of perceptions and managing diversity. Some people perceive that organizations are going too far in trying to influence curriculum development, while others see this as a proactive strategy. What is your perception of this growing trend?

Our perceptions and feelings are influenced by information we receive from newspapers, magazines, television, radio, family, and friends. You see, we all use information stored in our memories to interpret the world around us, and our interpretations, in turn, influence how we respond and interact with others. As human beings, we constantly strive to make sense of our surroundings. The resulting knowledge influences our behavior and helps us navigate our way through life. Think of the perceptual process that occurs when meeting someone for the first time. Your attention is drawn to the individual's physical appearance, mannerisms, actions, and reactions to what you say and do. You ultimately arrive at conclusions based on your perceptions of this social interaction. The brown-haired, green-eyed individual turns out to be friendly and fond of outdoor activities. You further conclude that you like this person and then ask him or her to go to a concert, calling the person by the name you stored in memory.

The reciprocal process of perception, interpretation, and behavioral response also applies at work. Ruth Simmons, who grew up in rural East Texas, absorbed from her hardworking mother's example the idea that a woman's role is second to a man's and that she should not "pretend to be smart." However, she excelled in college, and in her junior year at Wellesley College, she was impressed by President Margaret Clapp, who broadened her ideas of what a woman can do. Mentored by professors, Simmons began to see herself as an achiever, earning a PhD, landing faculty jobs, and eventually becoming the first black president of a Seven Sisters school and later the first female president of Brown University. There, she is widely respected and serves as a mentor to others. Personally recruiting students to Brown, says Simmons, is "probably the most important thing I can do on a national basis."[2]

Managing diversity is a sensitive, potentially volatile, and sometimes uncomfortable issue. Yet managers are required to deal with it in the name of organizational survival. Accordingly, the purpose of this chapter is to enhance your understanding of the perceptual process and how it influences the manner in which managers manage diversity. We begin by focusing on a social information processing model of perception and then discuss the perceptual outcome of causal attributions. Next, we define diversity and describe the organizational practices used to effectively manage diversity.

# A Social Information Processing Model of Perception

**perception**

**Process of interpreting one's environment.**

**Perception** is a cognitive process that enables us to interpret and understand our surroundings. Recognition of objects is one of this process's major functions.[3] For example, both people and animals recognize familiar objects in their environments. You would recognize a picture of your best friend; dogs and cats can recognize their food dishes or a favorite toy. Reading involves recognition of visual patterns representing letters in the alphabet. People must recognize objects to meaningfully interact with their environment. But since OB's principal focus is on people, the following discussion emphasizes *social* perception rather than object perception.

## Social Perception: A Social Information Processing Model | FIGURE 4–1

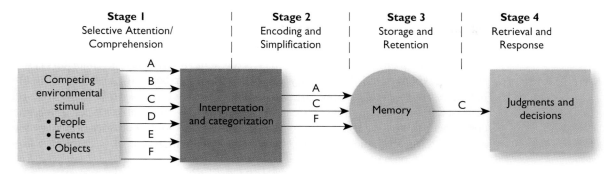

SOURCE: R Kreitner and A Kinicki, *Organizational Behavior,* 7th ed (Burr Ridge, IL: McGraw-Hill), p 207.

Social perception involves a four-stage information processing sequence (hence, the label "social information processing"). Figure 4–1 illustrates a basic social information processing model. Three of the stages in this model—selective attention/comprehension, encoding and simplification, and storage and retention—describe how specific social information is observed and stored in memory. The fourth and final stage, retrieval and response, involves turning mental representations into real-world judgments and decisions.

Keep the following everyday example in mind as we look at the four stages of social perception. Suppose you were thinking of taking a course in, say, personal finance. Three professors teach the same course, using different types of instruction and testing procedures. Through personal experience, you have come to prefer good professors who rely on the case method of instruction and essay tests. According to social perception theory, you would likely arrive at a decision regarding which professor to take following the steps outlined in the following sections.

learning objective 1
Describe *perception* in terms of the social information processing model.

# Stage 1: Selective Attention/Comprehension

People are constantly bombarded by physical and social stimuli in the environment. Because they do not have the mental capacity to fully comprehend all this information, they selectively perceive subsets of environmental stimuli. This is where attention plays a role. **Attention** is the process of becoming consciously aware of something or someone. Attention can be focused on information either from the environment or from memory. Regarding the latter situation, if you sometimes find yourself thinking about totally unrelated events or people while reading a textbook, your memory is the focus of your attention. Research has shown that people tend to pay attention to salient stimuli.

**attention**

**Being consciously aware of something or someone.**

**Salient Stimuli** Something is *salient* when it stands out from its context. For example, a 250-pound man would certainly be salient in a women's aerobics class but not at a meeting of the National Football League Players' Association. One's needs and goals often dictate which stimuli are salient. For a driver whose gas gauge is on empty, an Exxon or Shell sign is more salient than a McDonald's or Burger King sign. The Centers for Medicare and Medicaid Services made the prevention of bedsores more salient at hospitals by announcing that it will stop reimbursing hospitals for treatment of bedsores and other conditions that can be prevented with proper care.

The prospect of bearing the full cost of treatment has spurred some hospitals to draw nurses' attention to the need to reposition frail patients every two hours. To make that task more salient to the nursing staff, hospitals are using pagers and timed musical alerts played over their PA systems.[4]

Moreover, research shows that people have a tendency to pay more attention to negative than positive information. This leads to a negativity bias.[5] Perhaps this is why surveys regularly find that employees undervalue their benefits packages, including health insurance and paid time off. Given that benefits play a key role in boosting job satisfaction and that employees are more prone to focus on negatives, such as a higher copayment in next year's health insurance, managers should consider drawing more attention to the good news about employee benefits, which typically represent $4 out of every $10 spent on payroll.[6]

**Back to Our Example**    You begin your search for the "right" personal finance professor by asking friends who have taken classes from the three professors. You also may interview the various professors who teach the class to gather still more relevant information. Returning to Figure 4–1, all the information you obtain represents competing environmental stimuli labeled A through F. Because you are concerned about the method of instruction (e.g., line A in Figure 4–1), testing procedures (e.g., line C), and past grade distributions (e.g., line F), information in those areas is particularly salient to you. Figure 4–1 shows that these three salient pieces of information thus are perceived, and you then progress to the second stage of information processing. Meanwhile, competing stimuli represented by lines B, D, and E in Figure 4–1 fail to get your attention and are discarded from further consideration.

# Stage 2: Encoding and Simplification

Observed information is not stored in memory in its original form. Encoding is required; raw information is interpreted or translated into mental representations. To accomplish this, perceivers assign pieces of information to **cognitive categories.** "By *category* we mean a number of objects that are considered equivalent. Categories are generally designated by names, e.g., *dog, animal.*"[7] People, events, and objects are interpreted and evaluated by comparing their characteristics with information contained in schemata (or schema in singular form).

**cognitive categories**

Mental depositories for storing information.

**Schema**    According to social information processing theory, a **schema** represents a person's mental picture or summary of a particular event or type of stimulus. For example, picture your image of a sports car. Does it contain a smaller vehicle with two doors? Is it red? If you answered yes, you would tend to classify all small, two-door, fire-engine-red vehicles as sports cars because this type of car possesses characteristics that are consistent with your "sports car schema."[8]

**schema**

Mental picture of an event or object.

**Group Exercise**

Win, Lose or Schema

**Stereotypes Are Used During Encoding**    People use stereotypes during encoding in order to organize and simplify social information. "A **stereotype** is an individual's set of beliefs about the characteristics or attributes of a group."[9] Stereotypes are not always negative. For example, the belief that engineers are good at math is certainly part of a stereotype. Stereotypes may or may not be accurate. Engineers may in fact be better at math than the general population. Especially given that stereotypes are not accurate for every individual,

**stereotype**

Beliefs about the characteristics of a group.

the evidence is mixed on whether individuals are helped or hurt by positive stereotypes about them.[10] In general, stereotypic characteristics are used to differentiate a particular group of people from other groups.

Unfortunately, stereotypes can lead to poor decisions; can create barriers for women, older individuals, people of color, and people with disabilities; and can undermine loyalty and job satisfaction. For example, a study of 427 members of the National Association of Black Accountants revealed that 59% believed that they received biased performance evaluations because of their race, and 63% felt no obligation to remain with their current employer.[11] It thus is not surprising that the turnover rate for African and Hispanic Americans is significantly greater than white Americans.[12] Another example is the widely shared stereotype that women talk more than men, a stereotype that might discourage women from speaking up when they have ideas. Perhaps you have heard the untested assertion that women typically speak 20,000 words per day, versus only 7,000 words for men. In fact, until recently, no technology could accurately record the amount of words a person uses in an entire day. In a study conducted over the past few years, however, electronically activated digital recorders carried by university students in the United States and Mexico showed that the men and women each used on average about 16,000 words a day.[13]

Stereotyping is a four-step process. It begins by categorizing people into groups according to various criteria, such as gender, age, race, and occupation. Next, we infer that all people within a particular category possess the same traits or characteristics (e.g., all women are nurturing, older people have more job-related accidents, all African-Americans are good athletes, all professors are absentminded). Then, we form expectations of others and interpret their behavior according to our stereotypes. Finally, stereotypes are maintained by (1) overestimating the frequency of stereotypic behaviors exhibited by others, (2) incorrectly explaining expected and unexpected behaviors, and (3) differentiating minority individuals from oneself. Although these steps are self-reinforcing, there are ways to break the chain of stereotyping.

Research shows that the use of stereotypes is influenced by the amount and type of information available to an individual and his or her motivation to accurately process information.[14] People are less apt to use stereotypes to judge others when they encounter salient information that is highly inconsistent with a stereotype. For instance, you are unlikely to assign stereotypic "professor" traits to a new professor you have this semester if he or she rides a Harley-Davidson, wears leather pants to class, and has a pierced nose. People also are less likely to rely on stereotypes when they are motivated to avoid using them. That is, accurate information processing requires mental effort. Stereotyping is generally viewed as a less effortful strategy of information processing.

### Encoding Outcomes

We use the encoding process to interpret and evaluate our environment. Interestingly, this process can result in differing interpretations and evaluations of the same person or event. Table 4–1 describes five common perceptual errors that influence our judgments about others. Because these perceptual errors often distort the evaluation of job applicants and of employee performance, managers need to guard against them.

Denis Hennequin, a Parisian and president of McDonald's operations in Europe, discovered the power of stereotypes when his family in France learned he would be working for the American fast-food chain, a job that entails overseeing more than 6,000 restaurants in 41 countries. "My grandmother thought I was selling French fries on the Boulevard Saint-Michel," he said.

**TABLE 4–1**    Commonly Found Perceptual Errors

| Perceptual Error | Description | Example | Recommended Solution |
|---|---|---|---|
| Halo | A rater forms an overall impression about an object and then uses that impression to bias ratings about the object. | Rating a professor high on the teaching dimensions of ability to motivate students, knowledge, and communication because we like him or her. | Remember that an employee's behavior tends to vary across different dimensions of performance. Keep a file or diary to record examples of positive and negative employee performance throughout the year. |
| Leniency | A personal characteristic that leads an individual to consistently evaluate other people or objects in an extremely positive fashion. | Rating a professor high on all dimensions of performance regardless of his or her actual performance. The rater who hates to say negative things about others. | It does not help employees when they are given positive feedback that is inaccurate. Try to be fair and realistic when evaluating others. |
| Central tendency | The tendency to avoid all extreme judgments and rate people and objects as average or neutral. | Rating a professor average on all dimensions of performance regardless of his or her actual performance. | It is normal to provide feedback that contains both positive and negative information. The use of a performance diary can help to remember examples of employee performance. |
| Recency effects | The tendency to remember recent information. If the recent information is negative, the person or object is evaluated negatively. | Although a professor has given good lectures for 12 to 15 weeks, he or she is evaluated negatively because lectures over the last 3 weeks were done poorly. | It is critical to accumulate examples of performance that span the entire rating period. Keep a file or diary to record examples of performance throughout the year. |
| Contrast effects | The tendency to evaluate people or objects by comparing them with characteristics of recently observed people or objects. | Rating a good professor as average because you compared his or her performance with three of the best professors you have ever had in college. You are currently taking courses from the three excellent professors. | It is important to evaluate employees against a standard rather than your memory of the best or worst person in a particular job. |

**Back to Our Example**    Having collected relevant information about the three personal finance professors and their approaches, you compare this information with other details contained in schemata. This leads you to form an impression and evaluation of what it would be like to take a course from each professor. In turn, the relevant information contained on paths A, C, and F in Figure 4–1 are passed along to the third stage of information processing.

# Stage 3: Storage and Retention

This phase involves storage of information in long-term memory. Long-term memory is like an apartment complex consisting of separate units connected to one another. Although different people live in each apartment, they sometimes interact. In addition, large apartment complexes have different wings (such as A, B, and C). Long-term memory similarly consists of separate but related categories. Like the individual apartments inhabited by unique residents, the connected categories contain different types of information. Information also passes among these categories. Finally, long-term memory is made up of three compartments (or wings) containing categories of information about events, semantic materials, and people.[15]

**Event Memory**   This compartment is composed of categories containing information about both specific and general events. These memories describe appropriate sequences of events in well-known situations, such as going to a restaurant, going on a job interview, going to a food store, or going to a movie.

**Semantic Memory**   Semantic memory refers to general knowledge about the world. In so doing, it functions as a mental dictionary of concepts. Each concept contains a definition (e.g., a good leader) and associated traits (outgoing), emotional states (happy), physical characteristics (tall), and behaviors (works hard). Just as there are schemata for general events, concepts in semantic memory are stored as schemata. Given our previous discussion of international OB in Chapter 3, it should come as no surprise that there are cultural differences in the type of information stored in semantic memory.

**Person Memory**   Categories within this compartment contain information about a single individual (your supervisor) or groups of people (managers).

**Back to Our Example**   As the time draws near for you to decide which personal finance professor to take, your schemata of them are stored in the three categories of long-term memory. These schemata are available for immediate comparison and/or retrieval.

# Stage 4: Retrieval and Response

People retrieve information from memory when they make judgments and decisions. Our ultimate judgments and decisions are either based on the process of drawing on, interpreting, and integrating categorical information stored in long-term memory or on retrieving a summary judgment that was already made.

Concluding our example, it is registration day and you have to choose which professor to take for personal finance. After retrieving from memory your schemata-based impressions of the three professors, you select a good one who uses the case method and gives essay tests (line C in Figure 4–1). In contrast, you may choose your preferred professor by simply recalling the decision you made two weeks ago.

# Managerial Implications

Social cognition is the window through which we all observe, interpret, and prepare our responses to people and events. A wide variety of managerial activities, organizational processes, and quality-of-life issues are thus affected by perception. Consider, for example, the following implications.

learning objective 2

Identify and briefly explain six managerial implications of social perception.

**Hiring**   Interviewers make hiring decisions based on their impression of how an applicant fits the perceived requirements of a job. Inaccurate impressions in either direction produce poor hiring decisions. Moreover, interviewers with racist or sexist schemata

© 2002 Ted Goff

**"Let me guess.
You're a salesperson, right?"**

Copyright © Ted Goff. Reprinted with permission

can undermine the accuracy and legality of hiring decisions. Those invalid schemata need to be confronted and
improved through coaching and training.[16] Failure to do
so can lead to poor hiring decisions. For example, a study
of 46 male and 66 female financial institution managers
revealed that their hiring decisions were biased by the
physical attractiveness of applicants. More attractive men
and women were hired over less attractive applicants with
equal qualifications.[17] On the positive side, however, a
study demonstrated that interviewer training can reduce
the use of invalid schema. Training improved interviewers' ability to obtain high-quality, job-related information
and to stay focused on the interview task. Trained interviewers provided more balanced judgments about applicants than did nontrained interviewers.[18]

**Performance Appraisal**    Faulty schemata about
what constitutes good versus poor performance can lead
to inaccurate performance appraisals, which erode work
motivation, commitment, and loyalty. For example, a
study of 166 production employees indicated that they
had greater trust in management when they perceived that the performance appraisal
process provided accurate evaluations of their performance.[19] Therefore, it is important for managers to accurately identify the behavioral characteristics and results

Perception colors
our interpretation of
management behaviors.
An employee whose
manager multitasks
while talking to her is
likely to believe that
their conversation—and
therefore the employee's
work and even the
employee herself—are
not very important. Have
you ever been treated
this way?

indicative of good performance at the beginning of a
performance review cycle. These characteristics then
can serve as the benchmarks for evaluating employee
performance. The importance of using objective rather
than subjective measures of employee performance
was highlighted in a meta-analysis involving 50 studies and 8,341 individuals. Results revealed that objective and subjective measures of employee performance
were only moderately related. The researchers concluded that objective and subjective measures of performance are not interchangeable.[20] Managers are thus
advised to use more objectively based measures of
performance as much as possible because subjective
indicators are prone to bias and inaccuracy. In those
cases where the job does not possess objective measures of performance, however, managers should still
use subjective evaluations. Furthermore, because memory for specific instances of
employee performance deteriorates over time, managers need a mechanism for accurately recalling employee behavior. Research reveals that individuals can be trained to
be more accurate raters of performance.[21]

**Leadership**    Research demonstrates that employees' evaluations of leader effectiveness are influenced strongly by their schemata of good and poor leaders. A leader
will have a difficult time influencing employees when he or she exhibits behaviors
contained in employees' schemata of poor leaders. A team of researchers investigated
the behaviors contained in our schemata of good and poor leaders. Good leaders were
perceived as exhibiting the following behaviors: (1) assigning specific tasks to group

members, (2) telling others that they had done well, (3) setting specific goals for the group, (4) letting other group members make decisions, (5) trying to get the group to work as a team, and (6) maintaining definite standards of performance. In contrast, poor leaders were perceived to exhibit these behaviors: (1) telling others that they had performed poorly, (2) insisting on having their own way, (3) doing things without explaining themselves, (4) expressing worry over the group members' suggestions, (5) frequently changing plans, and (6) letting the details of the task become overwhelming.[22]

### Communication and Interpersonal Influence

Managers must remember that social perception is a screening process that can distort communication, both coming and going. Because people interpret oral and written communications by using schemata developed through past experiences, your ability to influence others is affected by information contained in others' schemata regarding age, gender, ethnicity, appearance, speech, mannerisms, personality, and other personal characteristics. It is important to keep this in mind when trying to influence others or when trying to sell your ideas. The Skills & Best Practices box describes ways that young employees can effectively manage the impressions that others form of them in the workplace.

### Physical and Psychological Well-Being

The negativity bias can lead to both physical and psychological problems. Specifically, research shows that perceptions of fear, harm, and anxiety are associated with the onset of illnesses such as asthma and depression.[23] We should all attempt to avoid the tendency of giving negative thoughts too much attention. Try to let negative thoughts roll off yourself just like water off a duck.

### Designing Web Pages

Researchers have recently begun to explore what catches viewers' attention on Web pages by using sophisticated eye-tracking equipment. This research can help organizations to spend their money wisely when designing Web pages. Kara Pernice Coyne, director of a research project studying Web page design, praised the Web pages of JetBlue Airways and Sears while noting problems with the one used by Agree Systems.[24] One expert provided the following recommendation for designing an effective Web page:

- Individuals read Web pages in an "F" pattern. They're more inclined to read longer sentences at the top of a page and less and less as they scroll down. That makes the first two words of a sentence very important. . . .

## Demonstrating That You're Ready to Do Business

All too often, a young employee's coworkers don't take him or her seriously. Sometimes young workers unconsciously reinforce negative stereotypes that people may have of their generation. Here are some ways to contribute to coworkers' perceptions that you mean business:

- *Convey a positive attitude.* When situations get stressful, focus on problem solving, and hang on to your sense of humor.

- *Dress professionally.* Coworkers draw negative conclusions about the professionalism of employees who wear wrinkled shirts or expose their cleavage, navel, or underwear.

- *When interacting with others, don't check your cell phone or listen to your music.* What might seem to be multitasking to some younger employees is often perceived as a failure to pay careful attention to others.

- *Take sexual harassment seriously.* Don't flirt at work, and if someone makes you uncomfortable, speak up.

- *Ask for feedback.* Don't wait for criticism (or praise) at your annual performance review. Even if criticism makes you uncomfortable, listen, and then show you listened by trying to apply what you learned.

SOURCES: Based on M E Slayter, "What Young Women at Work Should Know," *Arizona Republic*, June 3, 2007, p EC1; P Bathurst, "Success: Share, Play Nice," *Arizona Republic*, December 23, 2007, p EC1; C Binkley, "Want to Be CEO? You Have to Dress the Part," *The Wall Street Journal*, January 10, 2008, pp D1–D2; and K Tyler, "Generation Gaps," *HR Magazine*, January 2008, pp 69–72.

- Surfers connect well with images of people looking directly at them. It helps if the person in the photo is attractive, but not too good looking. . . .
- Images in the middle of a page can present an obstacle course.
- People respond to pictures that provide useful information, not just decoration.[25]

# Causal Attributions

Attribution theory is based on the premise that people attempt to infer causes for observed behavior. Rightly or wrongly, we constantly formulate cause-and-effect explanations for our own and others' behavior. Attributional statements such as the following are common: "Joe drinks too much because he has no willpower; but I need a couple of drinks after work because I'm under a lot of pressure." Formally defined, **causal attributions** are suspected or inferred causes of behavior. Even though our causal attributions tend to be self-serving and are often invalid, it is important to understand how people formulate attributions because they profoundly affect organizational behavior. For example, a supervisor who attributes an employee's poor performance to a lack of effort might reprimand that individual. However, training might be deemed necessary if the supervisor attributes the poor performance to a lack of ability.

**causal attributions**

Suspected or inferred causes of behavior.

Generally speaking, people formulate causal attributions by considering the events preceding an observed behavior. This section introduces Harold Kelley's model of attribution and two important attributional tendencies.

## Kelley's Model of Attribution

Current models of attribution, such as Kelley's, are based on the pioneering work of the late Fritz Heider. Heider, the founder of attribution theory, proposed that behavior can be attributed either to **internal factors** within a person (such as ability) or to **external factors** within the environment (such as a difficult task). Building on Heider's work, Kelley attempted to pinpoint major antecedents of internal and external attributions. Kelley hypothesized that people make causal attributions after gathering information about three dimensions of behavior: consensus, distinctiveness, and consistency.[26] These dimensions vary independently, thus forming various combinations and leading to differing attributions.

**internal factors**

Personal characteristics that cause behavior.

**external factors**

Environmental characteristics that cause behavior.

Figure 4–2 presents performance charts showing low versus high consensus, distinctiveness, and consistency. These charts are now used to help develop a working knowledge of all three dimensions in Kelley's model.

3 learning objective

Explain, according to Kelley's model, how external and internal causal attributions are formulated.

- *Consensus* involves a comparison of an individual's behavior with that of his or her peers. There is high consensus when one acts like the rest of the group and low consensus when one acts differently. As shown in Figure 4–2, high consensus is indicated when persons A, B, C, D, and E obtain similar levels of individual performance. In contrast, person C's performance is low in consensus because it significantly varies from the performance of persons A, B, D, and E.
- *Distinctiveness* is determined by comparing a person's behavior on one task with his or her behavior on other tasks. High distinctiveness means the individual has performed the task in question in a significantly different manner than he or she has performed other tasks. Low distinctiveness means stable performance

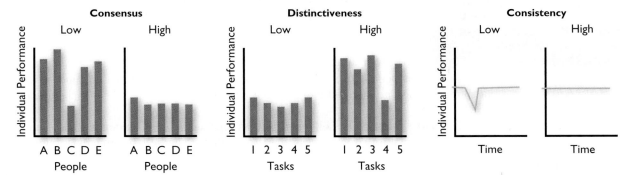

**FIGURE 4-2**

**Performance Charts Showing Low and High Consensus, Distinctiveness, and Consistency Information**

SOURCE: K A Brown, "Explaining Group Poor Performance: An Attributional Analysis," *Academy of Management Review*, January 1984, p 56. Copyright © 2001 by Academy of Management. Reproduced with permission of Academy of Management via Copyright Clearance Center.

or quality from one task to another. Figure 4-2 reveals that the employee's performance on task 4 is highly distinctive because it significantly varies from his or her performance on tasks 1, 2, 3, and 5.

- *Consistency* is determined by judging if the individual's performance on a given task is consistent over time. High consistency implies that a person performs a certain task the same, time after time. Unstable performance of a given task over time would mean low consistency. The downward spike in performance depicted in the consistency graph of Figure 4-2 represents low consistency. In this case, the employee's performance on a given task varied over time.

It is important to remember that consensus relates to other *people,* distinctiveness relates to other *tasks,* and consistency relates to *time.* The question now is: How does information about these three dimensions of behavior lead to internal or external attributions?

Kelley hypothesized that people attribute behavior to *external* causes (environmental factors) when they perceive high consensus, high distinctiveness, and low consistency. *Internal* attributions (personal factors) tend to be made when observed behavior is characterized by low consensus, low distinctiveness, and high consistency. So, for example, when all employees are performing poorly (high consensus), when the poor performance occurs on only one of several tasks (high distinctiveness), and the poor performance occurs during only one time period (low consistency), a supervisor will probably attribute an employee's poor performance to an external source such as peer pressure or an overly difficult task. In contrast, performance will be attributed to an employee's personal characteristics (an internal attribution) when only the individual in question is performing poorly (low consensus), when the inferior performance is found across several tasks (low distinctiveness), and when the low performance has persisted over time (high consistency). Many studies supported this predicted pattern of attributions.[27]

# Attributional Tendencies

Researchers have uncovered two attributional tendencies that distort one's interpretation of observed behavior—*fundamental attribution bias* and *self-serving bias.*

### Fundamental Attribution Bias

The **fundamental attribution bias** reflects one's tendency to attribute another person's behavior to his or her personal character-

istics, as opposed to situational factors. This bias causes perceivers to ignore important environmental forces that often significantly affect behavior. For example, a study of 1,420 employees of a large utility company demonstrated that supervisors tended to make more internal attributions about worker accidents than did the workers. Interestingly, research also shows that people from Westernized cultures tend to exhibit the fundamental attribution bias more than individuals from East Asia.[28]

### Self-Serving Bias

The **self-serving bias** represents one's tendency to take more personal responsibility for success than for failure. The self-serving bias suggests

employees will attribute their success to internal factors (high ability or hard work) and their failures to uncontrollable external factors (tough job, bad luck, unproductive coworkers, or an unsympathetic boss). This tendency seems to have been in play at companies where employees filed high-profile discrimination lawsuits.[29] In one case, an employee of a major accounting firm was, as the court judge wrote, "generally viewed as

a highly competent project leader who worked long hours, pushed vigorously to meet deadlines, and demanded much from the multidisciplinary staffs." She was denied a partnership. The employee blamed the firm for discriminating against her because she was a woman; the firm blamed her for being "sometimes overly aggressive, unduly harsh, difficult to work with, and impatient with staff." And in another case, a woman who was not promoted to dean blamed the university for discriminating against her, while the university, like the accounting firm, said this employee was hard to get along with. In both cases, the courts could not take either point of view for granted but had to look for objective performance measures and evidence of how the organization treated its male employees.

### Managerial Application and Implications

Attribution models can be used to explain how managers handle poorly performing employees. One study revealed that managers gave employees more immediate, frequent, and negative feedback when they attributed their performance to low effort. This reaction was even more pronounced when the manager's success was dependent on an employee's performance. A second study indicated that managers tended to transfer employees whose poor performance was attributed to a lack of ability. These same managers also decided to take no immediate action when poor performance was attributed to external factors beyond an individual's control.[30]

The preceding situations have several important implications for managers. First, managers tend to disproportionately attribute behavior to *internal* causes.[31] This can result in inaccurate evaluations of performance, leading to reduced employee motivation. No one likes to be blamed because of factors they perceive to be beyond their control. Further, because managers' responses to employee performance vary according to their attributions, attributional biases may lead to inappropriate managerial actions, including promotions, transfers, layoffs, and so forth. This can dampen motivation and performance. Attributional training sessions for managers are in order. Basic attributional processes can be explained, and managers can be taught to detect and avoid attributional biases. Finally, an employee's attributions for his or her own performance have dramatic effects on subsequent motivation, performance, and personal attitudes such as self-esteem. For instance, people tend to give up, develop lower expectations for future success, and experience decreased self-esteem when they attribute failure to a lack of ability. In contrast, employees are more likely to display high performance and job satisfaction when they attribute success to internal factors such as ability and effort.[32] Fortunately, attributional realignment can improve both motivation and performance. The goal of attributional realignment is to shift failure attributions away from ability and towards attributions of low effort or some other external cause (e.g., lack of resources).

# Defining and Managing Diversity

**Diversity** represents the multitude of individual differences and similarities that exist among people. This definition underscores a key issue about managing diversity. There are many different dimensions or components of diversity. This implies that diversity pertains to everybody. It is not an issue of age, race, or gender. It is not an issue of being heterosexual, gay, or lesbian or of being Catholic, Jewish, Protestant, or Muslim. Diversity also does not pit white males against all other groups of people. Diversity pertains to the host of individual differences that make all of us unique and different from others.

> **diversity**
>
> The host of individual differences that make people different from and similar to each other.

This section begins our journey into managing diversity by first reviewing the key dimensions of diversity. Because many people associate diversity with affirmative action, we then compare affirmative action with managing diversity. Next, we review the demographic trends that are creating an increasingly diverse workforce. This section concludes by describing the organizational practices used to effectively manage diversity.

**Self-Assessment Exercise**

Appreciating and Valuing Diversity

## Layers of Diversity

Like seashells on a beach, people come in a variety of shapes, sizes, and colors. This variety represents the essence of diversity. Lee Gardenswartz and Anita Rowe, a team of diversity experts, identified four layers of diversity to help distinguish the important ways in which people differ (see Figure 4–3). Taken together, these layers define your personal identity and influence how each of us sees the world.[33]

Figure 4–3 shows that personality is at the center of the diversity wheel. Personality is at the center because it represents a stable set of characteristics that is responsible for a person's identity: The dimensions of personality are discussed later in Chapter 5. The next layer of diversity consists of a set of internal dimensions that are referred to as the primary dimensions of diversity. These dimensions, for the most part, are not within our control, but strongly influence our attitudes and expectations and assumptions about others, which, in turn, influence our behavior. Take the encounter experienced by an African-American woman in middle management while vacationing at a resort:

> While she was sitting by the pool, "a large 50-ish white male approached me and demanded that I get him extra towels. I said, 'Excuse me?' He then said, 'Oh, you don't work here,' with no shred of embarrassment or apology in his voice."[34]

Stereotypes regarding one or more of the primary dimensions of diversity most likely influenced this man's behavior toward the woman.

# FIGURE 4–3 | The Four Layers of Diversity

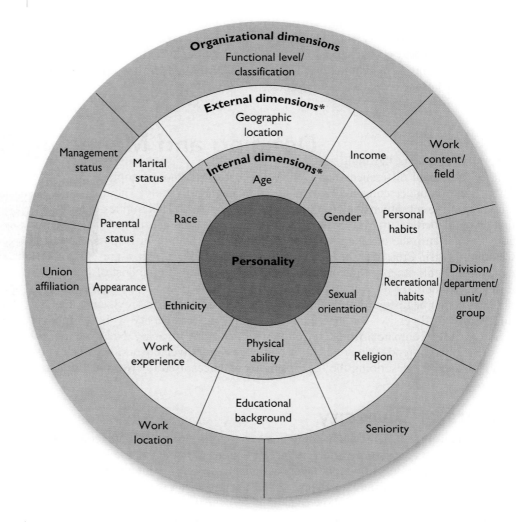

*Internal Dimensions and External Dimensions are adapted from Loden and Rosener, *Workforce America!* (Homewood, IL: Business One Irwin, 1991).

SOURCE: From L Gardenswartz and A Rowe, *Diverse Teams at Work: Capitalizing on the Power of Diversity*, 1994, 2003, p 33. Published by the Society for Human Resource Management. Reprinted with permission.

Figure 4–3 reveals that the next layer of diversity is composed of external influences, which are referred to as secondary dimensions of diversity. They represent individual differences that we have a greater ability to influence or control. Examples include where you grew up and live today, your religious affiliation, whether you are married and have children, and your work experiences. These dimensions also exert a significant influence on our perceptions, behavior, and attitudes. The final layer of diversity includes organizational dimensions such as seniority, job title and function, and work location.

# Affirmative Action and Managing Diversity

Effectively managing diversity requires organizations to adopt a new way of thinking about differences among people. Rather than pitting one group against another, managing diversity entails recognition of the unique contribution every employee can make.[35] For example, Aetna Inc, EMC Corporation, IBM, PepsiCo, and Nordstrom focus on hiring and promoting diverse employees as part of a strategy to create and market products appealing to a broader and more diverse customer base.[36] This section highlights the differences between affirmative action and managing diversity.

**Affirmative Action**    Affirmative action is an outgrowth of equal employment opportunity (EEO) legislation. The goal of this legislation is to outlaw discrimination and to encourage organizations to proactively prevent discrimination. **Discrimination** occurs when employment decisions about an individual are due to reasons not associated with performance or are not related to the job. Table 4–2 provides a review of major federal laws pertaining to equal employment opportunity. As you can see from this table, many forms of discrimination are outlawed. For example, organizations cannot discriminate on the basis of race, color, religion, national origin, sex, age, physical and mental disabilities, and pregnancy. Many of these federal laws are enforced by the Equal Employment Opportunity Commission (EEOC), and individuals may sue for back pay and punitive damages when they feel that they have been discriminated against.[37]

In contrast to the proactive perspective of EEO legislation, **affirmative action** is an artificial intervention aimed at giving management a chance to correct an imbalance, an injustice, a mistake, or outright discrimination that occurred in the past.

Affirmative action does not legitimize quotas. Quotas are illegal. They can only be imposed by judges who conclude that a company has engaged in discriminatory practices. It also is important to note that under no circumstances does affirmative action require companies to hire unqualified people.

Although affirmative action created tremendous opportunities for women and minorities, it does not foster the type of thinking that is needed to effectively manage diversity. For example, a recent meta-analysis summarizing 35 years of research involving 29,000 people uncovered the following results: (1) affirmative action plans are perceived more negatively by white males than women and minorities because it is perceived to work against their own self-interests; (2) affirmative action plans are viewed more positively by people who are liberals and Democrats than conservatives and Republicans; and (3) affirmative action plans are not supported by people who possess racist or sexist attitudes.[38]

Affirmative action programs also were found to negatively affect the women and minorities expected to benefit from them. Research demonstrated that women and minorities, supposedly hired on the basis of affirmative action, felt negatively stigmatized as unqualified or incompetent. They also experienced lower job satisfaction and more stress than

Achieving diversity remains a challenge for many organizations, including the New York City Fire Department, which despite efforts to recruit more blacks, Hispanics, Asian-Americans, and women, remains predominantly white and male. Fewer women and minorities apply than white men, and fewer still complete the five steps needed to reach the final hiring pool. One Brooklyn councilwoman applauded the department's diversity recruiting efforts but noted that "women have not necessarily been embraced once they've gotten on the force, notwithstanding their own intestinal fortitude."

**discrimination**

Occurs when employment decisions are based on factors that are not job related.

**affirmative action**

Focuses on achieving equality of opportunity in an organization.

**TABLE 4.2** Some Important U.S. Federal Laws and Regulations Protecting Employees

| Year | Law or Regulation | Provisions |
|---|---|---|
| **Labor relations** | | |
| 1974 | Privacy Act | Gives employees legal right to examine letters of reference concerning them |
| 1986 | Immigration Reform & Control Act | Requires employers to verify the eligibility for employment of all their new hires (including U.S. citizens) |
| 1988 | Polygraph Protection Act | Limits employer's ability to use lie detectors |
| 1988 | Worker Adjustment & Retraining Notification Act | Requires organizations with 100 or more employees to give 60 days' notice for mass layoffs or plant closings |
| 2003 | Sarbanes-Oxley Act | Prohibits employers from demoting or firing employees who raise accusations of fraud to a federal agency |
| **Compensation and Benefits** | | |
| 1974 | Employee Retirement Income Security Act (ERISA) | Sets rules for managing pension plans; provides federal insurance to cover bankrupt plans |
| 1993 | Family & Medical Leave Act | Requires employers to provide 12 weeks of unpaid leave for medical and family reasons, including for childbirth, adoption, or family emergency |
| 1996 | Health Insurance Portability & Accountability Act (HIPPA) | Allows employees to switch health insurance plans when changing jobs and receive new coverage regardless of preexisting health conditions; prohibits group plans from dropping ill employees |
| **Health and Safety** | | |
| 1970 | Occupational Safety & Health Act (OSHA) | Establishes minimum health and safety standards in organizations |
| 1985 | Consolidated Omnibus Budget Reconciliation Act (COBRA) | Requires an extension of health insurance benefits after termination |
| **Equal Employment Opportunity** | | |
| 1963 | Equal Pay Act | Requires men and women be paid equally for performing equal work |
| 1964, amended 1972 | Civil Rights Act, Title VII | Prohibits discrimination on basis of race, color, religion, national origin, or sex |
| 1967, amended 1978 and 1986 | Age Discrimination in Employment Act (ADEA) | Prohibits discrimination in employees over 40 years old; restricts mandatory retirement |
| 1978 | Pregnancy Discrimination Act | Broadens discrimination to cover pregnancy, childbirth, and related medical conditions; protects job security during maternity leave |
| 1990 | Americans with Disabilities Act (ADA) | Prohibits discrimination against essentially qualified employees with physical or mental disabilities or chronic illness; requires "reasonable accommodation" be provided so they can perform duties |
| 1991 | Civil Rights Act | Amends and clarifies Title VII, ADA, and other laws; permits suits against employers for punitive damages in cases of intentional discrimination |

SOURCE: A Kinicki and B Williams, *Management: A Practical Introduction,* 3rd ed, (New York: McGraw-Hill, 2008), p 293. Reprinted by permission of McGraw-Hill Companies, Inc.

employees supposedly selected on the basis of merit.[39] Another study, however, showed that these negative consequences were reduced for women when a merit criterion was included in hiring decisions. In other words, women hired under affirmative action programs felt better about themselves and exhibited higher performance when they believed they were hired because of their competence rather than their gender.[40]

**Managing Diversity**    **Managing diversity** enables people to perform up to their maximum potential. It focuses on changing an organization's culture and infrastructure such that people provide the highest productivity possible. For example, few would doubt that female employees would be most satisfied and productive in an environment free of sexual harassment. But in addition, a recent study of about 1,700 university employees found that when employees of *either* sex observed hostility toward women and perceived the organization was lax in punishing such behavior, they felt uncomfortable and burned out, were less satisfied with their jobs, and were less committed to their work.[41]

Ann Morrison, a diversity expert, conducted a study of 16 organizations that successfully managed diversity. Her results uncovered three key strategies for success: education, enforcement, and exposure. She describes them as follows:

> The education component of the strategy has two thrusts: one is to prepare nontraditional managers for increasingly responsible posts, and the other is to help traditional managers overcome their prejudice in thinking about and interacting with people who are of a different sex or ethnicity. The second component of the strategy, enforcement, puts teeth in diversity goals and encourages behavior change. The third component, exposure to people with different backgrounds and characteristics, adds a more personal approach to diversity by helping managers get to know and respect others who are different.[42]

In summary, both consultants and academics believe that organizations should strive to manage diversity rather than only valuing it or simply using affirmative action.

# Increasing Diversity in the Workforce

This section explores four demographic trends that are creating an increasingly diverse workforce: (1) women are encountering a glass ceiling, (2) racial groups are encountering a glass ceiling and perceived discrimination, (3) there is a mismatch between workers' educational attainment and occupational requirements, and (4) the workforce is aging.

**Women Are Encountering a Glass Ceiling**    In spite of the fact that women constitute slightly more than 46% of the labor force,[43] they continue to encounter the glass ceiling. The **glass ceiling** represents an invisible barrier that separates women and minorities from advancing into top management positions. Women, therefore, find themselves stuck in lower level jobs, ones that do not have profit-and-loss responsibility, and those with less visibility and influence. In general, these positions result in a lack of power because the job holder does not have control over others, resources, or technology. The end result is that women face legitimate power deficits while trying to climb the corporate ladder.[44]

There are a variety of statistics that support the existence of a glass ceiling. As of 2006, women were still underpaid relative to men: women who worked full time were

**Test Your Knowledge**

Comparing Affirmative Action, Valuing Diversity, and Managing Diversity

**managing diversity**

Creating organizational changes that enable all people to perform up to their maximum potential.

learning objective **4**

Demonstrate your familiarity with the demographic trends that are creating an increasingly diverse workforce.

**glass ceiling**

Invisible barrier blocking women and minorities from top management positions.

Andrea Jung (at left),
Chairman and CEO
of Avon Products,
actress and Avon Global
Ambassador Resse
Witherspoon (second
from left), UNIFEM
Executive Director,
Joanne Sandler and
television personality
Suze Orman (far right)
pose at the UNIFEM and
AVON press conference
announcing partnership
to end violence against
women and advance
women's empowerment
at the second annual
Global Summit for a
Better Tomorrow. As a
result of the partnership,
Avon is committing
$1 million to the UN
Trust Fund to End
Violence against Women.
How does this work
contribute to helping
break the glass ceiling for
women in the future?

paid 81% of men's median earnings.[45] Even when women are paid the same as men, they may suffer in other areas of job opportunities. For example, a study of 69 male and female executives from a large multinational financial services corporation revealed no differences in base salary or bonus. However, the women in this sample received fewer stock options than the male executives, even after controlling for level of education, performance, and job function, and reported less satisfaction with future career opportunities.[46] A follow-up study of 13,503 female managers and 17,493 male managers from the same organization demonstrated that women at higher levels in the managerial hierarchy received fewer promotions than males at comparable positions.[47] Would you be motivated if you were a woman working in this organization?

Women still have not broken into the highest echelon of corporate America to a significant extent. For example, in 2007, only one woman—Angela Braly of WellPoint—was chief executive officer of a Fortune 50 company. Out of the larger Fortune 500, just 2.4% of CEOs are women, and that was a record (at 12). In addition, only 14.8% of board directors were women.[48] Further, the majority of women in top jobs have traditionally worked in staff rather than line positions. In general, roles associated with line jobs contain more power and influence than staff positions.

How can women overcome the glass ceiling? A team of researchers attempted to answer this question by surveying 461 executive women who held titles of vice president or higher in Fortune 1000 companies. Respondents were asked to evaluate the extent to which they used 13 different career strategies to break through the glass ceiling. The 13 strategies are shown in the Hands-On Exercise on page 103. Before discussing the results from this study, we would like you to complete the Hands-On Exercise.

Findings indicated that the top nine strategies were central to the advancement of these female executives. Within this set, however, four strategies were identified as critical toward breaking the glass ceiling: consistently exceeding performance expectations, developing a style with which male managers are comfortable, seeking out difficult or challenging assignments, and having influential mentors.[50] Of these, the second strategy can be especially tricky for women, because the kinds of behavior that are in the typical schema of a leader (for example, assertiveness and commitment to results) tend to be associated in women with a personality that is not as likable.[51]

**Racial Groups Are Encountering a Glass Ceiling and Perceived Discrimination**    Historically, the United States has been a black-and-white country. Today, however, one in three U.S. residents is a member of a minority group, and Hispanics are the largest and fastest-growing of those groups. With the black and non-Hispanic white populations growing more slowly than those of Hispanics and Asian-Americans, the cultural makeup of the United States will become increasingly diverse. The Census Bureau projects that in 2015, the U.S. population will be 17% Hispanic, 13% black, and 5% Asian. Several states—Hawaii, New Mexico, California, and Texas—and the District of Columbia have populations that are "majority minority."[52]

Unfortunately, three additional trends suggest that current-day minority groups are experiencing their own glass ceiling. First, minorities are advancing even less in the

# What Are the Strategies for Breaking the Glass Ceiling?

**INSTRUCTIONS:** Read the 13 career strategies shown below that may be used to break the glass ceiling. Next, rank order each strategy in terms of its importance for contributing to the advancement of a woman to a senior management position. Rank the strategies from 1 (most important) to 13 (least important). Once this is completed, compute the gap between your rankings and those provided by the women executives who participated in this research. Their rankings are presented in Endnote[49] at the back of the book. In computing the gaps, use the absolute value of the gap. (Absolute values are always positive, so just ignore the sign of your gap.) Finally, compute your total gap score. The larger the gap, the greater the difference in opinion between you and the women executives. What does your total gap score indicate about your recommended strategies?

| Strategy | My Rating | Survey Rating | Gap \|Your Rating _ Survey Rating\| |
|---|---|---|---|
| 1. Develop leadership outside office | _____ | _____ | _____ |
| 2. Gain line management experience | _____ | _____ | _____ |
| 3. Network with influential colleagues | _____ | _____ | _____ |
| 4. Change companies | _____ | _____ | _____ |
| 5. Be able to relocate | _____ | _____ | _____ |
| 6. Seek difficult or high-visibility assignments | _____ | _____ | _____ |
| 7. Upgrade educational credentials | _____ | _____ | _____ |
| 8. Consistently exceed performance expectations | _____ | _____ | _____ |
| 9. Move from one functional area to another | _____ | _____ | _____ |
| 10. Initiate discussion regarding career aspirations | _____ | _____ | _____ |
| 11. Have an influential mentor | _____ | _____ | _____ |
| 12. Develop style that men are comfortable with | _____ | _____ | _____ |
| 13. Gain international experience | _____ | _____ | _____ |

**SOURCE:** Strategies and data were taken from B R Ragins, B Townsend, and M Mattis, "Gender Gap in the Executive Suite: CEOs and Female Executives Report on Breaking the Glass Ceiling," *The Academy of Management Executive*, February 1998, pp 28–42.

managerial and professional ranks than women. For example, blacks and Hispanics held 8.4% and 7.0%, respectively, of all managerial and professional jobs in 2007; women held 50.5% of these positions.[53] Second, the number of race-based charges of discrimination that were deemed to show reasonable cause by the US Equal Employment Opportunity Commission increased from 918 in 1997 to 2,397 in 2001; they have since fallen to 998 in 2007. Companies paid a total of $67.7 million to resolve these claims outside of litigation in 2007.[54] Third, minorities also tend to earn less than whites. Median weekly earnings in 2007 were $569, $503, and $716 for African-Americans, Hispanics, and whites, respectively. Interestingly, Asians had the highest median income—$830 per week.[55] Finally, a number of studies showed that minorities experience more perceived discrimination than whites.[56]

**Mismatch between Educational Attainment and Occupational Requirements**    Approximately 28% of the labor force has a college degree, and college graduates typically earn substantially more than workers with less education.[57] At the same time, however, three trends suggest a mismatch between educational attainment and the knowledge and skills needed by employers. First, recent studies show that college graduates, while technically and functionally competent, are lacking in terms of teamwork skills, critical thinking, and analytic reasoning. Second, there is a shortage of college graduates in technical fields related to science, math, and engineering. Third, organizations are finding that high school graduates working in entry-level positions do not possess the basic skills needed to perform effectively.[58] This latter trend is partly due to a national high-school dropout rate estimated at over 9% and the existence of about 30 million adults in the United States who lack basic skills in reading prose. Even more lack basic skills in number-related tasks such as balancing a checkbook.[59] These statistics underscore the issue of employees' literacy. Literacy is defined as "an individual's ability to read, write, and speak English, compute and solve problems at levels of proficiency necessary to function on the job and in society, to achieve one's goals, and develop one's knowledge and potential."[60] Illiteracy costs corporate America around $60 billion a year in lost productivity.[61] These statistics are worrisome to both government officials and business leaders.

The key issue confronting organizations in the United States, and any country that wants to compete in a global economy, is whether or not the population has the skills and abilities needed to drive economic growth. Unfortunately, results from a study commissioned by the National Center on Education and the Economy suggest that the United States is losing ground on this issue. Findings were summarized in a book titled *Tough Choice or Tough Times: The Report of the New Commission on the Skills of the American Workforce.* The authors arrived at the following conclusions based on their analysis.

> Whereas for most of the 20th century the United States could take pride in having the best-educated workforce in the world, that is no longer true. Over the past 30 years, one country after another has surpassed us in the proportion of their entering workforce with the equivalent of a high school diploma, and many more are on the verge of doing so. Thirty years ago, the United States could lay claim to having 30 percent of the world's population of college students. Today that proportion has fallen to 14 percent and is continuing to fall.
>
> While our international counterparts are increasingly getting more education, their young people are getting a better education as well. American students and young adults place anywhere from the middle to the bottom of the back in all three continuing comparative studies of achievement in mathematics, science, and general literacy in the advanced industrial nations.
>
> While our relative position in the world's education league tables has continued its long slow decline, the structure of the global economy has continued to evolve. Every day, more and more of the work that people do ends up in a digitized form. From X-rays used for medical diagnostic purposes, to songs, movies, architectural drawings, technical papers, and novels, that work is saved on a hard disk and transmitted instantly over the Internet to someone near or far who makes use of it in an endless variety of ways. Because this is so, employers everywhere have access to a worldwide workforce composed of people who do not have to move to participate in work teams that are truly global. Because this is so, a swiftly rising number of American workers at every skill level are in direct competition with workers in every corner of the globe.[62]

These conclusions underscore the fact that the mismatch between educational attainment and occupational requirements have both short- and long-term implications for

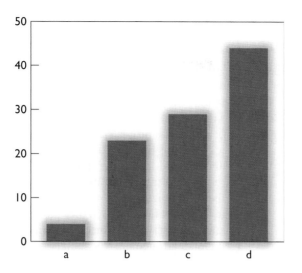

a. Formal process of transferring knowledge from retiring boomers to other employees.
b. Informal process of transferring knowledge from retiring boomers to other employees.
c. No knowledge transfer process but plans to implement one.
d. No knowledge transfer process and no plans for one.

**Percent of organizations that report taking the specified steps**

Source: "What Is the Baby Boomers' Workforce Impact?" *HR Magazine*, January 2008, p 24.

organizations and countries alike. American companies are more likely to outsource technical work to countries like India and China, to hire more immigrants to fill entry-level positions, and to spend more money on employee training.[63]

**The Aging Workforce**   America's population and workforce are getting older. Between 2010 and 2050, the population aged 65 and over is expected to more than double while the population aged 18 to 24 increases by 21%. By 2025, the share of the workforce that is under 25 will have fallen a percentage point to 8.9%.[64] So far, however, as shown in Figure 4–4, U.S. employers have only begun to take steps to ensure that their retiring employees are sharing their knowledge with the organization.

Life expectancy is increasing as well. The number of people living into their 80s is increasing rapidly, and this group disproportionately suffers from chronic illness. The United States is not the only country with an aging population. Japan, Eastern Europe, and former Soviet republics, for example, are expected to encounter significant economic and political problems due to an aging population.

**Managerial Implications of Demographic Diversity**   Regardless of gender, race, or age, all organizations need employees who possess the skills and abilities needed to successfully complete their jobs. Hiring, retaining, and developing a diverse workforce not only gives an organization access to a deeper pool of talent, it also may introduce perspectives that help the organization identify and meet the needs of a diverse customer base.[65] To attract the best workers, companies need to

**Manager's Hot Seat Applications**

Office Romance: Groping for Answers

Diversity: Mediating Morality

Personal Disclosure: Confession Coincidence

Diversity in Hiring: Candidate Conundrum

## Retaining Older Workers

Here are some ways that companies are recruiting and retaining older workers and benefiting from their knowledge:

- Home Depot has a recruiting slogan "Passion Never Retires," and its Web site features pictures of older workers. The screening process for job applicants is set up to give equal opportunity to workers of all ages.

- At ACUITY, a Wisconsin insurance company, employees with long service are asked to participate in strategic planning.

- CXtec, an information technology company in New York, keeps long-term employees interested by cross-training them to learn jobs in new areas so they can step in when other employees are away. As employees begin thinking about retirement and what they want to do beyond work, CXtec lets its top performers fashion more flexible schedules so that it won't lose them.

- Kahler Slater, an architecture firm, assigns experienced employees to projects with new employees so that the older workers can serve as mentors. The firm also gives its experienced employees increasingly complex projects to keep them learning and engaged.

SOURCES: Based on D Cadrain, "Employers Prepare to Keep, Not Lose, Baby Boomers," *2008 HR Trendbook*, pp 23–24; and K Tyler, "Leveraging Long Tenure," *HR Magazine*, May 2007, pp 55–60.

adopt policies and procedures that meet the needs of all employees. Programs such as day care, elder care, flexible work schedules, and benefits such as paternal leaves, less rigid relocation policies, concierge services, and mentoring programs are likely to become more popular.[66] Pfizer, for example, offers on-site child care at four locations and elder care.[67]

Given the projected increase in the number of Hispanics entering the workforce over the next 20 years, managers should consider progressive methods to recruit, retain, and integrate this segment of the population into their organizations. Maricopa Medical Center, located in central Phoenix, Arizona has had to recruit actively and aggressively to meet the need for translators who understand medical vocabulary as well as a second language. The supervisor of the hospital's interpreters and translators is Martha Martinez, who started more than 15 years ago as a housekeeper. Other employees often asked Martinez to help them communicate with Spanish-speaking patients and their families, so Martinez built on this opportunity by completing English as a Second Language classes and training in medical terminology. The medical center offered her a position as translator, and Martinez worked her way up to the supervisor's job. Even with this success story, Maricopa Medical Center is still struggling to fill its fast-growing need for interpreters. On some shifts, says the department's manager, Luis Gendreau, only one Spanish speaker is available to serve the whole hospital.[68]

Mismatches between the amount of education needed to perform current jobs and the amount of education possessed by members of the workforce are growing. This trend creates two potential problems for organizations. First, there will be a shortage of qualified people in technical fields. To combat this issue, both Lockheed Martin and Agilent Technologies offer some type of paid apprenticeship or internship to attract high-school students interested in the sciences.[69] Second, underemployment among college graduates threatens to erode job satisfaction and work motivation. As well-educated workers begin to look for jobs commensurate with their qualifications and expectations, absenteeism and turnover likely will increase. This problem underscores the need for job redesign (see the discussion in Chapter 6). In addition, organizations will need to consider interventions, such as realistic job previews and positive reinforcement programs, to reduce absenteeism and turnover. On-the-job remedial skills and literacy training will be necessary to help the growing number of dropouts and illiterates cope with job demands.

There are two general recommendations for helping organizations effectively adapt to an aging workforce. The first involves the need to help employees deal with personal issues associated with elder care. Elder care is a critical issue for employees who have aging parents, and failing to deal with it can drive up an employer's costs. For example, MetLife estimates that a lack of elder care costs organizations billions of dollars a year in lost productivity and increased absenteeism, workday interruptions, and turnover. Second, employers need to make a concerted effort to keep older workers engaged and committed and their skills current (see Skills & Best Practices on page 106). The following seven initiatives can help accomplish this objective.[70]

1. Provide challenging work assignments that make a difference to the firm.
2. Give the employee considerable autonomy and latitude in completing a task.
3. Provide equal access to training and learning opportunities when it comes to new technology.
4. Provide frequent recognition for skills, experience, and wisdom gained over the years.
5. Provide mentoring opportunities whereby older workers can pass on accumulated knowledge to younger employees.
6. Ensure that older workers receive sensitive, high-quality supervision.
7. Design a work environment that is both stimulating and fun.

Of course, many of these practices can make the workplace more appealing to younger workers as well. Many organizations, in valuing diversity, look for management practices and policies that are suited to each generation of workers.[71]

# Organizational Practices Used to Effectively Manage Diversity

Many organizations throughout the United States are unsure of what it takes to effectively manage diversity. In addition, the sensitive and potentially volatile nature of managing diversity has led to significant barriers when trying to move forward with diversity initiatives. This section reviews the barriers to managing diversity and discusses a framework for categorizing organizational diversity initiatives.

## Barriers and Challenges to Managing Diversity

Organizations encounter a variety of barriers when attempting to implement diversity initiatives. It thus is important for present and future managers to consider these barriers before rolling out a diversity program. The following is a list of the most common barriers to implementing successful diversity programs.[72]

learning objective 5
Identify the barriers and challenges to managing diversity.

1. *Inaccurate stereotypes and prejudice.* This barrier manifests itself in the belief that differences are viewed as weaknesses. In turn, this promotes the view that diversity hiring will mean sacrificing competence and quality.
2. *Ethnocentrism.* The ethnocentrism barrier represents the feeling that one's cultural rules and norms are superior or more appropriate than the rules and norms of another culture.
3. *Poor career planning.* This barrier is associated with the lack of opportunities for diverse employees to get the type of work assignments that qualify them for senior management positions.

4. *An unsupportive and hostile working environment for diverse employees.* Diverse employees are frequently excluded from social events and the friendly camaraderie that takes place in most offices.

5. *Lack of political savvy on the part of diverse employees.* Diverse employees may not get promoted because they do not know how to "play the game" of getting along and getting ahead in an organization. Research reveals that women and people of color are excluded from organizational networks.[73]

6. *Difficulty in balancing career and family issues.* Women still assume the majority of the responsibilities associated with raising children. This makes it harder for women to work evenings and weekends or to frequently travel once they have children. Even without children in the picture, household chores take more of a woman's time than a man's time.

7. *Fears of reverse discrimination.* Some employees believe that managing diversity is a smoke screen for reverse discrimination. This belief leads to very strong resistance because people feel that one person's gain is another's loss.

8. *Diversity is not seen as an organizational priority.* This leads to subtle resistance that shows up in the form of complaints and negative attitudes. Employees may complain about the time, energy, and resources devoted to diversity that could have been spent doing "real work."

9. *The need to revamp the organization's performance appraisal and reward system.* Performance appraisals and reward systems must reinforce the need to effectively manage diversity. This means that success will be based on a new set of criteria. Employees are likely to resist changes that adversely affect their promotions and financial rewards.

10. *Resistance to change.* Effectively managing diversity entails significant organizational and personal change. As discussed in Chapter 16, people resist change for many different reasons.

Recent research suggests that an important first step in overcoming these obstacles is for leaders to convey to their employees why the organization values diversity. In a study of 184 college students, groups of students performed better if they had first received information supporting the value of diversity for group performance.[74]

# R Roosevelt Thomas Jr's Generic Action Options

**6** learning objective

Discuss organizational practices used to manage diversity.

So what are organizations doing to effectively manage diversity? Answering this question requires that we provide a framework for categorizing organizational initiatives. Researchers and practitioners have developed relevant frameworks. One was developed by R Roosevelt Thomas Jr, a diversity expert. He identified eight generic action options that can be used to address any type of diversity issue. After describing each action option, we discuss relationships among them.[75]

**Option I: Include/Exclude**     This choice is an outgrowth of affirmative action programs. Its primary goal is to either increase or decrease the number of diverse people at all levels of the organization. Shoney's restaurant represents a good example of a company that attempted to include diverse employees after settling a discrimination lawsuit. The company subsequently hired African-Americans into positions of dining-room supervisors and vice presidents, added more franchises owned by African-Americans, and purchased more goods and services from minority-owned companies.[76]

**Option 2: Deny**    People using this option deny that differences exist. Denial may manifest itself in proclamations that all decisions are color, gender, and age blind and that success is solely determined by merit and performance. Consider State Farm Insurance, for example. "Although it was traditional for male agents and their regional managers to hire male relatives, State Farm Insurance avoided change and denied any alleged effects in a nine-year gender-bias suit that the company lost."[77]

**Option 3: Assimilate**    The basic premise behind this alternative is that all diverse people will learn to fit in or become like the dominant group. It only takes time and reinforcement for people to see the light. Organizations initially assimilate employees through their recruitment practices and the use of company orientation programs. New hires generally are put through orientation programs that aim to provide employees with the organization's preferred values and a set of standard operating procedures. Employees then are encouraged to refer to the policies and procedures manual when they are confused about what to do in a specific situation. These practices create homogeneity among employees.

**Option 4: Suppress**    Differences are squelched or discouraged when using this approach. This can be done by telling or reinforcing others to quit whining and complaining about issues. The old "you've got to pay your dues" line is another frequently used way to promote the status quo.

**Option 5: Isolate**    This option maintains the current way of doing things by setting the diverse person off to the side. In this way the individual is unable to influence organizational change. Managers can isolate people by putting them on special projects. Entire work groups or departments are isolated by creating functionally independent entities, frequently referred to as "silos." Shoney Inc's employees commented to a *Wall Street Journal* reporter about isolation practices formerly used by the company:

> White managers told of how Mr Danner [previous chairman of the company] told them to fire blacks if they became too numerous in restaurants in white neighborhoods; if they refused, they would lose their jobs, too. Some also said that when Mr Danner was expected to visit their restaurant, they scheduled black employees off that day or, in one case, hid them in the bathroom. Others said blacks' applications were coded and discarded.[78]

**Option 6: Tolerate**    Toleration entails acknowledging differences but not valuing or accepting them. It represents a live-and-let-live approach that superficially allows organizations to give lip service to the issue of managing diversity. Toleration is different from isolation in that it allows for the inclusion of diverse people. However, differences are not really valued or accepted when an organization uses this option.

**Option 7: Build Relationships**    This approach is based on the premise that good relationships can overcome differences. It addresses diversity by fostering quality relationships—characterized by acceptance and understanding—among diverse groups. Rockwell Collins, Inc, a producer of aviation electronics in Cedar Rapids,

## Mutual Adaptation Draws Women to Principal Financial

The CEO of Principal Financial Group, Barry Griswell, says his childhood experiences helped to shape his commitment to equal opportunity: "My mother was a single parent who raised my brother and me and worked two jobs. It's been important to me to know that women have equal pay, equal access—all the things that men have." In fact, his company has gone beyond that level of fairness to create a culture in which female and male employees feel valued.

In the 1970s, many companies still saw flexible scheduling as a costly concession, but Principal was already offering flexibility as a way to retain talent. The effort was validated years later, when an HR consultant determined that employees who stayed three years were likely to become the company's most committed employees. Griswell concluded that if the company could help women arrange flexible schedules through such short-term challenges as returning to work after the birth of a child, that flexibility would pay off in terms of an experienced and loyal workforce.

Key executives at Principal have actually been offered their promotions while working part time or on maternity leave. They have come to expect being evaluated based on their talent rather than on their schedules. And the company has hardly suffered; it has enjoyed greater productivity, sales, and profits.

**SOURCE: Based on J Hempel, "In the Land of Women," *Fortune*, January 22, 2008, http://money.cnn.com.**

Iowa, is a good example of a company attempting to use this diversity option. Rockwell is motivated to purse this option because it needs to hire around 7,000 employees between 2005 and 2010 in order to meet its revenue goals. The problem in recruiting is that the state is about 6% nonwhite. To attract minority candidates the company "is building closer relationships with schools that have strong engineering programs as well as sizable minority populations. It also is working more closely with minority-focused professional societies."[79] The city of Cedar Rapids is also getting involved in the effort by trying to offer more cultural activities and ethnic-food stores that cater to a more diverse population base.

**Option 8: Foster Mutual Adaptation**    In this option, people are willing to adapt or change their views for the sake of creating positive relationships with others. This implies that employees and management alike must be willing to accept differences, and most important, agree that everyone and everything is open for change. Companies can foster mutual adaptation through their recruitment and retention strategies as well as their benefit packages (see Skills & Best Practices). Consider the amount of mutual adaptation that has occurred with respect to the issue of sexual preferences. In 1990, for example, Cracker Barrel fired 11 gay employees because it did not want to employ people whose "sexual preferences fail to demonstrate normal heterosexual values."[80] As an aside, it is important to note that it is legal to fire employees simply for being gay in 34 states. In contrast, 263 firms in the Fortune 500 provided domestic partner benefits in 2006 whereas only 28 did in 1996. Hayward Bell, Chief Diversity Officer at Raytheon, offers keen insight about why organizations should consider fostering mutual adaptation. "Over the next ten years we're going to need anywhere from 30,000 to 40,000 new employees" and "we can't afford to turn our backs on anyone in the talent pool."[81]

**Conclusions about Action Options**    Although the action options can be used alone or in combination, some are clearly better than others. Exclusion, denial, assimilation, suppression, isolation, and toleration are among the least preferred options. Inclusion, building relationships, and mutual adaptation are the preferred strategies.[82] That said, Thomas reminds us that mutual adaptation is the only approach that unquestionably endorses the philosophy behind managing diversity. In closing this discussion, it is important to note that choosing how to best manage diversity is a dynamic process that is determined by the context at hand. For instance, some organizations are not ready for mutual adaptation. The best one might hope for in this case is the inclusion of diverse people.

# key terms

affirmative action   99

attention   87

causal attributions   94

cognitive categories   88

discrimination   99

diversity   97

external factors   94

fundamental attribution bias   96

glass ceiling   101

internal factors   94

managing diversity   101

perception   86

schema   88

self-serving bias   96

stereotype   88

# chapter summary

- *Describe perception in terms of the social information processing model.* Perception is a mental and cognitive process that enables us to interpret and understand our surroundings. Social perception, also known as social cognition and social information processing, is a four-stage process. The four stages are selective attention/comprehension, encoding and simplification, storage and retention, and retrieval and response. During social cognition, salient stimuli are matched with schemata, assigned to cognitive categories, and stored in long-term memory for events, semantic materials, or people.

- *Identify and briefly explain six managerial implications of social perception.* Social perception affects hiring decisions, performance appraisals, leadership perceptions, communication, and interpersonal influence, physical and psychological well-being, and the design of Web pages. Inaccurate schemata or racist and sexist schemata may be used to evaluate job applicants. Similarly, faulty schemata about what constitutes good versus poor performance can lead to inaccurate performance appraisals. Invalid schemata need to be identified and replaced with appropriate schemata through coaching and training. Further, managers are advised to use objective rather than subjective measures of performance. With respect to leadership, a leader will have a difficult time influencing employees when he or she exhibits behaviors contained in employees' schemata of poor leaders. Because people interpret oral and written communications by using schemata developed through experiences, an individual's ability to influence others is affected by information contained in others' schemata regarding age, gender, ethnicity, appearance, speech, mannerisms, personality, and other personal characteristics.

  Research also shows a connection between negative thinking and one's physical and psychological health. We should all attempt to avoid the tendency of giving negative thoughts too much attention. Finally, the extent to which a Web page garners interests and generates sales is partly a function of perceptual processes. Organizations are encouraged to consider the characteristics of effective Web page design.

- *Explain, according to Kelley's model, how external and internal causal attributions are formulated.* Attribution theory attempts to describe how people infer causes for observed behavior. According to Kelley's model of causal attribution, external attributions tend to be made when consensus and distinctiveness are high and consistency is low. Internal (personal responsibility) attributions tend to be made when consensus and distinctiveness are low and consistency is high.

- *Demonstrate your familiarity with the demographic trends that are creating an increasingly diverse workforce.* There are four key demographic trends: (a) women are encountering a glass ceiling, (b) racial groups are encountering a glass ceiling and perceived discrimination, (c) a mismatch exists between workers' educational attainment and occupational requirements, and (d) the workforce is aging.

- *Identify the barriers and challenges to managing diversity.* There are 10 barriers to successfully implementing diversity initiatives: (a) inaccurate stereotypes and prejudice, (b) ethnocentrism, (c) poor career planning, (d) an unsupportive and hostile working environment for diverse employees, (e) lack of political savvy on the part of diverse employees, (f) difficulty in balancing career and family issues, (g) fears of reverse discrimination, (h) diversity is not seen as an organizational priority, (i) the need to revamp the organization's performance appraisal and reward system, and (j) resistance to change.

• *Discuss organizational practices used to manage diversity.* Organizations have eight options that they can use to address diversity issues: (a) include/exclude the number of diverse people at all levels of the organization, (b) deny that differences exist, (c) assimilate diverse people into the dominant group, (d) suppress differences, (e) isolate diverse members from the larger group, (f) tolerate differences among employees, (g) build relationships among diverse employees, and (h) foster mutual adaptation to create positive relationships.

# discussion questions

1. Referring back to the chapter-opening case, to what extent are Deloitte and Lockheed Martin effectively managing diversity? Explain.
2. Why is it important for managers to have a working knowledge of perception and attribution?
3. How would you formulate an attribution, according to Kelley's model, for the behavior of a classmate who starts arguing in class with your professor?
4. Does diversity suggest that managers should follow the rule, "Do unto others as you would have them do unto you"?
5. How can diversity initiatives be helpful in overcoming the barriers and challenges to managing diversity?

# ethical dilemma

## Should Brain Scans Be Used to Craft Advertising?[83]

### BusinessWeek

It might soon be time to redefine MRI machines as "market research imaging" devices. At Harvard's McLean Hospital not long ago, six male whiskey drinkers, ages 25 to 34, lined up to have their brains scanned for Arnold Worldwide. The Boston-based ad shop was using functional magnetic resonance imaging (fMRI) to gauge the emotional power of various images, including college kids drinking cocktails on spring break, twentysomethings with flasks around a campfire, and older guys at a swanky bar. The scans "help give us empirical evidence of the emotion of decision making," says Baysie Wightman, head of Arnold's new, science-focused Human Nature Dept. The results will help shape the 2007 ad campaign for client Brown-Forman, which owns Jack Daniels.

The idea of peeking into the brain for consumer insights isn't new. More than a dozen universities have been using fMRI to study how people respond to products (prompting Ralph Nader's Commercial Alert group to assert that "it's wrong to use a medical technology for marketing, not healing"). But now a few agencies like Arnold—whose clients also include McDonald's and Fidelity—and Digitas, another Boston-based shop, are offering fMRI research "Neuromarketing" consultants, like Los Angeles-based FKF Applied Research, are springing up, too, to link companies with hospitals seeking to lease time on their pricey MRI machines.

### Should we allow companies to use brain scans to test advertising campaigns?

1. Absolutely not! Ralph Nader is right; it's wrong to use medical equipment for marketing.
2. Why not? People participate voluntarily in these studies and they get paid for the experience.
3. Ad campaigns are expensive, and it is good business sense to test their effectiveness with brain scans.

**4.** Using medical equipment in this way is a good way to share the costs of an expensive MRI. In the end, reducing the costs of medical equipment is good for society at large.

**5.** Invent other options.

For an interpretation of this situation, visit our Web site at **www.mhhe.com/kinickiob4e.**

If you're looking for additional study materials, be sure to check out the Online Learning Center at

**www.mhhe.com/kinickiob4e**

for more information and interactivities that correspond to this chapter.

# chapter

## five

# Appreciating Individual Differences: Self-Concept, Personality, Attitudes, and Emotions

**LEARNING OBJECTIVES**

**After reading the material in this chapter, you should be able to:**

1. Distinguish between self-esteem and self-efficacy.

2. Contrast high and low self-monitoring individuals, and describe resulting problems each may have.

3. Identify and describe the Big Five personality dimensions, specify which one is correlated most strongly with job performance, and describe the proactive personality.

4. Explain the difference between an internal and external locus of control.

5. Identify the three components of attitudes and discuss cognitive dissonance.

6. Identify at least five of Gardner's eight multiple intelligences, and explain "practical intelligence."

7. Explain the concepts of emotional intelligence, emotional contagion, and emotional labor.

Reneé Trubiano and Kelly Roy are talented women who used self-knowledge about their personalities to advance their careers.

**Reneé Trubiano, 31, Marketing Manager. Maracay Homes, Scottsdale.**

Trubiano, who joined Maracay about two years ago, describes herself as bubbly and outgoing. "I've always wanted to try it all, experience things firsthand, know more about people and places," she says. That pushes her ahead in the workplace. "I want to find out what I can do to better the company and bring it to the next level."

Trubiano describes herself as creative, a critical strength in her job, whether leading employees in a holiday project to raise money for charity or establishing an employee-recognition program.

Not surprisingly, Trubiano is outwardly passionate about her job and the company. She believes that's an important motivating trait.

"I love what I do. I think that's a big key when you do have a staff . . . That shows through to everyone else you work with," she says.

One thing Trubiano has changed about herself at work is her inclination to work at warp speed. "I've had to sit back and say, 'I need to slow down, so other people in the office don't think I'm too busy for them,' " she says.

In doing that, she says, another one of her traits comes through: an "openness" to other people's ideas, creativity and energy.

Roy joined Infusion two years ago to oversee customer experience from end to end.

She has taken personality tests in different jobs, and the latest one pegs her as an extrovert, a description that fits her well. That trait, and what she calls her natural ability to think creatively, are key for her job.

She's also a self-described "rescuer," which is a great match with her work overseeing operations. Roy says that trait also makes her empathize with customers and truly care about how the company designs its processes around them.

When Roy needs to fill a position on her team, she looks at the skills required, who might be successful and personality traits the team is missing. That way, the team challenges and develops each member.

Roy has made a few notable changes to her work style. She's a multitasker and finds that trait clashes with her male peers, who tend to do things in serial order. So instead of just popping into a colleague's office, she now makes a list of things she needs to discuss and schedules time to do it.

Roy also wears her passion on her sleeve, not a bad thing unless the person she's dealing with doesn't. In those cases, she reels in the passion.

Being self-aware isn't easy. Roy relies on mentors to help her step back and look at herself. She's also a believer in taking personality tests every few years. Her advice about the results: "Don't obsess about them, but take things away from them."[1]

**What personal characteristics and traits have helped Reneé Trubiano and Kelly Roy succeed in the business world? Explain. For an interpretation of this case and additional comments, visit our Online Learning Center at**

**www.mhhe.com/ kinickiob4e.**

**FOR DISCUSSION**

**THE CHAPTER-OPENING CASE ILLUSTRATES** the differences in personalities between two successful women. This comparison reinforces the notion that there is not one type of person that is universally successful. Thanks to a vast array of individual differences, modern organizations have a rich and interesting human texture. However, these individual differences make the manager's job endlessly challenging. According to research, "variability among workers is substantial at all levels but increases dramatically with job complexity. In life insurance sales, for example, variability in performance is around six times as great as in routine clerical jobs."[2]

Growing workforce diversity, detailed in Chapter 4, compels managers to view individual differences in a fresh new way. Rather than limiting diversity, as in the past, today's managers need to better understand and accommodate employee diversity and individual differences.

This chapter explores the following important dimensions of individual differences: (1) self-concept, (2) personality traits, (3) attitudes, (4) mental abilities, and (5) emotions. Figure 5–1 is a conceptual model showing the relationship between self-concept (how you view yourself), personality (how you appear to others), and key forms of self-expression. Considered as an integrated package, these factors provide a foundation for better understanding yourself and others as unique and special individuals.

# Focusing on the "Self"

**self-concept**

Person's self-perception as a physical, social, spiritual being.

**cognitions**

A person's knowledge, opinions, or beliefs.

*Self* is the core of one's conscious existence. Awareness of self is referred to as one's self-concept. Individualistic North American cultures have been called self-centered. Not surprisingly, when people ages 16 to 70 were asked in a recent survey what they would do differently if they could live life over again, 48% chose the response category "Get in touch with self."[3] To know more about self-concept is to understand more about life in general.[4] Sociologist Viktor Gecas defines **self-concept** as "the concept the individual has of himself as a physical, social, and spiritual or moral being."[5] In other words, because you have a self-concept, you recognize yourself as a distinct human being. A self-concept would be impossible without the capacity to think. This brings us to the role of cognitions. **Cognitions** represent "any knowledge, opinion, or belief about the environment, about

**FIGURE 5–1**
An OB Model for Studying Individual Differences

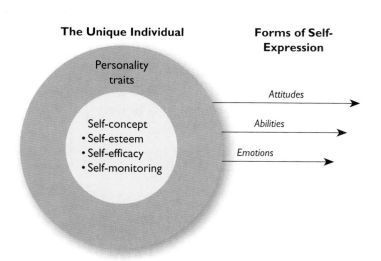

oneself, or about one's behavior."[6] Among many different types of cognitions, those involving anticipation, planning, goal setting, evaluating, and setting personal standards are particularly relevant to OB. Cognitively based topics covered in this book include social perception, modern motivation theories, decision-making styles, and change management.

Importantly, ideas of self and self-concept vary from one historical era to another, from one socio-economic group to another, and from culture to culture.[7] How well one detects and adjusts to different cultural notions of self can spell the difference between success and failure in international dealings. For example, Japanese–U.S. communication and understanding often are hindered by significantly different degrees of self-disclosure. With a comparatively large public self, Americans pride themselves in being open, honest, candid, and to the point. Meanwhile, Japanese, who culturally discourage self-disclosure, typically view Americans as blunt, prying, and insensitive to formalities. For their part, Americans tend to see Japanese as distant, cold, and evasive.[8] One culture is not right and the other wrong. They are just different, and a key difference involves culturally rooted conceptions of self and self-disclosure.

Keeping this cultural qualification in mind, let us explore three topics invariably mentioned when behavioral scientists discuss self-concept. They are self-esteem, self-efficacy, and self-monitoring. Each of these areas deserves a closer look by those who want to better understand and effectively manage people at work. Terri Kelly, CEO of W L Gore & Associates, the maker of Gore-Tex fabrics popular among outdoor enthusiasts, recently told *Fast Company* magazine, "Leaders have to be very self-aware. They have to understand their flaws, their own behavior, and the impact they have on others."[9]

**Terri Kelly, CEO of W L Gore & Associates,** understands the importance of self-awareness in managers. In fact, in a company famous for its lack of hierarchy, Kelly has an acute perception about her own role. "The idea of me as CEO managing the company is a misperception," she says. "My goal is to provide the overall direction. I spend a lot of time making sure we have the right people in the right roles."

# Self-Esteem

**Self-esteem** is a belief about one's own self-worth based on an overall self-evaluation.[10] Self-esteem is measured by having survey respondents indicate their agreement or disagreement with both positive and negative statements. A positive statement on one general self-esteem survey is: "I feel I am a person of worth, the equal of other people."[11] Among the negative items is: "I feel I do not have much to be proud of."[12] Those who agree with the positive statements and disagree with the negative statements have high self-esteem. They see themselves as worthwhile, capable, and acceptable. People with low self-esteem view themselves in negative terms. They do not feel good about themselves and are hampered by self-doubts.[13]

> **self-esteem**
> One's overall self-evaluation.

**A Cross-Cultural Perspective**    What are the cross-cultural implications for self-esteem, a concept that has been called uniquely Western? In a survey of 13,118 students from 31 countries worldwide, a moderate positive correlation was found between self-esteem and life satisfaction. But the relationship was stronger in individualistic cultures (e.g., United States, Canada, New Zealand, Netherlands) than in collectivist cultures (e.g., Korea, Kenya, Japan). The researchers concluded that individualistic cultures socialize people to focus more on themselves, while people in collectivist cultures "are socialized to fit into the community and to do their duty. Thus, how a collectivist feels about him- or herself is less relevant to . . . life satisfaction."[14] Global managers need to remember to deemphasize self-esteem when doing business in collectivist ("we") cultures, as opposed to emphasizing it in individualistic ("me") cultures.[15]

**Can General Self-Esteem Be Improved?** The short answer is *yes*. More detailed answers come from research. In one study, youth-league baseball coaches who were trained in supportive teaching techniques had a positive effect on the self-esteem of young boys. A control group of untrained coaches had no such positive effect.[16] Another study led to this conclusion: "Low self-esteem can be raised more by having the person think of *desirable* characteristics *possessed* rather than of undesirable characteristics from which he or she is free."[17]

Yet another comprehensive study threw cold water on the popular view that high self-esteem is the key to better performance. The conclusion:

> . . . self-esteem and school or job performance are correlated. But long overdue scientific scrutiny points out the foolishness of supposing that people's opinion of themselves can be the *cause* of achievement. Rather, high-esteem is the *result* of good performance.[18]

This is where self-efficacy comes to the forefront.

# Self-Efficacy ("I can do that.")

Have you noticed how those who are confident about their ability tend to succeed, while those who are preoccupied with failing tend to fail? Perhaps that explains the comparative golfing performance of your authors! One consistently stays in the fairways and hits the greens. The other spends the day thrashing through the underbrush, wading in water hazards, and blasting out of sand traps. At the heart of this performance mismatch is a specific dimension of self-esteem called self-efficacy.

**self-efficacy**

Belief in one's ability to do a task.

**Self-efficacy** is a person's belief about his or her chances of successfully accomplishing a specific task. According to one OB writer, "Self-efficacy arises from the gradual acquisition of complex cognitive, social, linguistic, and/or physical skills through experience."[19]

Helpful nudges in the right direction from parents, role models, and mentors are central to the development of high self-efficacy. Consider, for example, how former U.S. Army Green Beret Earl Woods used his tough-love style to build his son Tiger's self-efficacy on the golf links:

> Long after Tiger Woods is finished playing golf, people will study Earl Woods. They will want to hear the stories of exactly how he raised this generation's most popular athlete. . . .
> "I tried to break him down mentally, tried to intimidate him verbally, by saying. 'Water on the right, OB [out of bounds] on the left,' just before his downswing," Earl Woods once told the Associated Press. "He would look at me with the most evil look, but he wasn't permitted to say anything. . . . One day I did all my tricks, and he looked at me and smiled. At the end of the round, I told him, 'Tiger, you've completed the training.' And I made him a promise. 'You'll never run into another person as mentally tough as you.' He hasn't. And he won't."[20]

The relationship between self-efficacy and performance is a cyclical one. Efficacy → performance cycles can spiral upward toward success or downward toward failure.[21] Researchers have documented a strong linkage between high self-efficacy expectations and success in widely varied physical and mental tasks, anxiety reduction, addiction control, pain tolerance, and illness recovery.[22] Oppositely, those with low self-efficacy expectations tend to have low success rates. Chronically low self-efficacy is associated with a condition called **learned helplessness,** the severely debilitating belief that one has no control over one's environment.[23] Although self-efficacy sounds like some sort of mental magic, it operates in a very straightforward manner, as the model discussed below will show.

Golfer Tiger Woods unveils a bronze statue bearing the likeness of himself with his late father Earl Woods, at the Tiger Woods Learning Center, while also announcing the launch of a nationwide youth program called the "Fist Pump Challenge." Do you think that Earl Woods influenced Tiger's self-efficacy? How?

**Mechanisms of Self-Efficacy**  A basic model of self-efficacy is displayed in Figure 5–2. It draws upon the work of Stanford psychologist Albert Bandura.[24] Let us explore this model with a simple illustrative task. Imagine you have been told to prepare and deliver a 10-minute talk to an OB class of 50 students on the workings of the self-efficacy model in Figure 5–2. Your self-efficacy calculation would involve cognitive appraisal of the interaction between your perceived capability and situational opportunities and obstacles.

As you begin to prepare for your presentation, the four sources of self-efficacy beliefs would come into play. Because prior experience is the most potent source, according to Bandura, it is listed first and connected to self-efficacy beliefs with a solid line.[25] Past success in public speaking would boost your self-efficacy. But bad experiences with delivering speeches would foster low self-efficacy. Regarding behavior models as a source of self-efficacy beliefs, you would be influenced by the success or failure of your classmates in delivering similar talks. Their successes would tend to bolster you (or perhaps their failure would if you were very competitive and had high self-esteem). Likewise, any supportive persuasion from your classmates that you

**learned helplessness**

Debilitating lack of faith in one's ability to control the situation.

will do a good job would enhance your self-efficacy. Physical and emotional factors also might affect your self-confidence. A sudden case of laryngitis or a bout of stage fright could cause your self-efficacy expectations to plunge. Your cognitive evaluation of the situation then would yield a self-efficacy belief—ranging from high to low expectations for success. Importantly, self-efficacy beliefs are not merely boastful statements based on bravado; they are deep convictions supported by experience.

Moving to the *behavioral patterns* portion of Figure 5–2, we see how self-efficacy beliefs are acted out. In short, if you have high self-efficacy about giving your 10-minute speech you will work harder, more creatively, and longer when preparing for your talk than will your low-self-efficacy classmates. The results would then take shape accordingly. People program themselves for success or failure by enacting their self-efficacy expectations. Positive or negative results subsequently become feedback for one's base of personal experience. Bob Schmonsees, a software entrepreneur, is an inspiring example of the success pathway through Figure 5–2:

A contender in mixed-doubles tennis and a former football star, Mr Schmonsees was standing near a ski lift when an out-of-control skier rammed him. His legs were paralyzed. He would spend the rest of his life in a wheelchair.

## FIGURE 5–2 │ Self-Efficacy Beliefs Pave the Way for Success or Failure

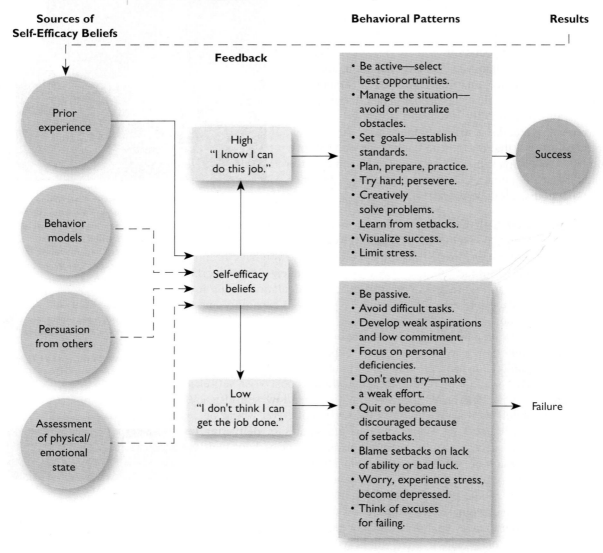

**Sources of Self-Efficacy Beliefs**

**Behavioral Patterns**

**Results**

Feedback

Prior experience

Behavior models

Persuasion from others

Assessment of physical/ emotional state

Self-efficacy beliefs

High "I know I can do this job."

Low "I don't think I can get the job done."

- Be active—select best opportunities.
- Manage the situation— avoid or neutralize obstacles.
- Set goals—establish standards.
- Plan, prepare, practice.
- Try hard; persevere.
- Creatively solve problems.
- Learn from setbacks.
- Visualize success.
- Limit stress.

- Be passive.
- Avoid difficult tasks.
- Develop weak aspirations and low commitment.
- Focus on personal deficiencies.
- Don't even try—make a weak effort.
- Quit or become discouraged because of setbacks.
- Blame setbacks on lack of ability or bad luck.
- Worry, experience stress, become depressed.
- Think of excuses for failing.

Success

Failure

SOURCES: Adapted from discussion in A Bandura, "Regulation of Cognitive Processes through Perceived Self-Efficacy," *Developmental Psychology,* September 1989, pp 729–35; and R Wood and A Bandura, "Social Cognitive Theory of Organizational Management," *Academy of Management Review,* July 1989, pp 361–84.

Fortunately, he discovered a formula for his different world: Figure out the new rules for any activity, then take as many small steps as necessary to master those rules. After learning the physics of a tennis swing on wheels and the geometry of playing a second bounce (standard rules), he became the world's top wheelchair player over age 40.[26]

**Managerial Implications**    On-the-job research evidence encourages managers to nurture self-efficacy, both in themselves and in others. In fact, a meta-analysis encompassing 21,616 subjects found a significant positive correlation between self-efficacy and job performance.[27] Self-efficacy requires constructive action in each of the following managerial areas:

1. *Recruiting/selection/job assignments.* Interview questions can be designed to probe job applicants' general self-efficacy as a basis for determining orientation and training needs. Pencil-and-paper tests for self-efficacy are not in an advanced stage of development and validation. Care needs to be taken not to hire solely on the basis of self-efficacy because studies have detected below-average self-esteem and self-efficacy among women and protected minorities.[28]

2. *Job design.* Complex, challenging, and autonomous jobs tend to enhance perceived self-efficacy.[29] Boring, tedious jobs generally do the opposite.

3. *Training and development.* Employees' self-efficacy expectations for key tasks can be improved through guided experiences, mentoring, and role modeling.[30]

4. *Self-management.* Systematic self-management training involves enhancement of self-efficacy expectations.[31]

5. *Goal setting and quality improvement.* Goal difficulty needs to match the individual's perceived self-efficacy.[32] As self-efficacy and performance improve, goals and quality standards can be made more challenging.

6. *Creativity.* Supportive managerial actions can enhance the strong linkage between self-efficacy beliefs and workplace creativity.[33]

7. *Coaching.* Those with low self-efficacy and employees victimized by learned helplessness need lots of constructive pointers and positive feedback.[34]

8. *Leadership.* Needed leadership talent surfaces when top management gives high self-efficacy managers a chance to prove themselves under pressure.

9. *Rewards.* Small successes need to be rewarded as stepping-stones to a stronger self-image and greater achievements.

# Self-Monitoring

Consider these contrasting scenarios:

learning objective 2

Contrast high and low self-monitoring individuals, and describe resulting problems each may have.

1. You are rushing to an important meeting when a coworker pulls you aside and starts to discuss a personal problem. You want to break off the conversation, so you glance at your watch. He keeps talking. You say, "I'm late for a big meeting." He continues. You turn and start to walk away. The person keeps talking as if he never received any of your verbal and nonverbal signals that the conversation was over.

2. Same situation. Only this time, when you glance at your watch, the person immediately says, "I know, you've got to go. Sorry. We'll talk later."

In the first all-too-familiar scenario, you are talking to a "low self-monitor." The second scenario involves a "high self-monitor." But more is involved here than an irritating situation. A significant and measurable individual difference in self-expression behavior, called self-monitoring, is highlighted. **Self-monitoring** is the extent to which a person observes his or her own self-expressive behavior and adapts it to the demands of the situation.[35] Experts on the subject offer this explanation:

**self-monitoring**

**Observing one's own behavior and adapting it to the situation.**

> Individuals high in self-monitoring are thought to regulate their expressive self-presentation for the sake of desired public appearances, and thus be highly

responsive to social and interpersonal cues of situationally appropriate performances. Individuals low in self-monitoring are thought to lack either the ability or the motivation to so regulate their expressive self-presentations. Their expressive behaviors, instead, are thought to functionally reflect their own enduring and momentary inner states, including their attitudes, traits, and feelings.[36]

In organizational life, both high and low self-monitors are subject to criticism. High self-monitors are sometimes called *chameleons,* who readily adapt their self-presentation to their surroundings. Low self-monitors, on the other hand, often are criticized for being on their own planet and insensitive to others. Importantly, within an OB context, self-monitoring is like any other individual difference—not a matter of right or wrong or good versus bad, but rather a source of diversity that needs to be adequately understood by present and future managers.

**A Matter of Degree**    Self-monitoring is not an either-or proposition. It is a matter of degree; a matter of being relatively high or low in terms of related patterns of self-expression. The Hands-On Exercise on page 123 is a self-assessment of your self-monitoring tendencies. It can help you better understand your*self.* Take a short break from your reading to complete the 10-item survey. Does your score surprise you in any way? Are you unhappy with the way you present yourself to others? What are the ethical implications of your score (particularly with regard to items 9 and 10)?

**Research Insights and Practical Recommendations**    According to field research, there is a positive relationship between high self-monitoring and career success. Among 139 MBA graduates who were tracked for five years, high self-monitors enjoyed more internal and external promotions than did their low self-monitoring classmates.[37] Another study of 147 managers and professionals found that high self-monitors had a better record of acquiring a mentor (someone to act as a personal career coach and professional sponsor).[38] These results mesh well with an earlier study that found managerial success (in terms of speed of promotions) tied to political savvy (knowing how to socialize, network, and engage in organizational politics).[39] High self-monitors also may contribute to the group's well-being. A study of employees in a recruiting agency found that when managers were high self-monitors, they were more likely to provide emotional help to employees struggling with anxiety, stress, or other emotion-related problems.[40]

The foregoing evidence and practical experience lead us to make these practical recommendations:

*For high, moderate, and low self-monitors:* Become more consciously aware of your self-image and how it affects others (the Hands-On Exercise is a good start).

*For high self-monitors:* Don't overdo it by turning from a successful chameleon into someone who is widely perceived as insincere, dishonest, phoney, and untrustworthy. You cannot be everything to everyone.

*For low self-monitors:* You can bend without breaking, so try to be a bit more accommodating while being true to your basic beliefs. Don't wear out your welcome when communicating. Practice reading and adjusting to nonverbal cues in various public situations. More is said about this in Chapter 12. If your conversation partner is bored or distracted, stop—because he or she is not really listening.

# Personality Dynamics

Individuals have their own way of thinking and acting, their own unique style or *personality*. **Personality** is defined as the combination of stable physical and mental characteristics that give the individual his or her identity. These characteristics or traits—including how one looks, thinks, acts, and feels—are the product of interacting genetic and environmental influences.[41] In this section, we introduce the Big Five personality dimensions and discuss key personality dynamics including locus of control, attitudes, intelligence, and mental abilities.

**personality**

Stable physical and mental characteristics responsible for a person's identity.

## The Big Five Personality Dimensions

Long and confusing lists of personality dimensions have been distilled in recent years to the Big Five.[42] They are extraversion, agreeableness, conscientiousness, emotional stability, and openness to experience (see Table 5–1 for descriptions). Standardized personality tests determine how positively or negatively a person scores on each of the Big Five. For example, someone scoring negatively on extraversion would

**Self-Assessment Exercise**

Assessing How Personality Type Impacts Your Goal Setting Skills

## TABLE 5–1    The Big Five Personality Dimensions

| Personality Dimension | Characteristics of a Person Scoring Positively on the Dimension |
|---|---|
| 1. Extraversion | Outgoing, talkative, sociable, assertive |
| 2. Agreeableness | Trusting, good-natured, cooperative, softhearted |
| 3. Conscientiousness | Dependable, responsible, achievement oriented, persistent |
| 4. Emotional stability | Relaxed, secure, unworried |
| 5. Openness to experience | Intellectual, imaginative, curious, broad-minded |

SOURCE: Adapted from M R Barrick and M K Mount, "Autonomy as a Moderator of the Relationships between the Big Five Personality Dimensions and Job Performance," *Journal of Applied Psychology,* February 1993, pp 111–18.

be an introverted person prone to shy and withdrawn behavior.[43] Someone scoring negatively on emotional stability would be nervous, tense, angry, and worried. A person's scores on the Big Five reveal a personality profile as unique as his or her fingerprints.

But one important question lingers: Are personality models ethnocentric and unique to the culture in which they were developed? At least as far as the Big Five model goes, cross-cultural research evidence points in the direction of "no." Specifically, the Big Five personality structure held up very well in a study of women and men from Russia, Canada, Hong Kong, Poland, Germany, and Finland.[44] A recent comprehensive analysis of Big Five studies led the researchers to this conclusion: "To date, there is no compelling evidence that culture affects personality structure."[45]

**Personality and Job Performance**    Those interested in OB want to know the connection between the Big Five and job performance. Ideally, Big Five personality dimensions that correlate positively and strongly with job performance would be helpful in the selection, training, and appraisal of employees. A meta-analysis of 117 studies involving 23,994 subjects from many professions offers guidance.[46] Among the Big Five, *conscientiousness* had the strongest positive correlation with job performance and training performance. According to the researchers, "those individuals who exhibit traits associated with a strong sense of purpose, obligation, and persistence generally perform better than those who do not."[47] Conscientiousness or a sixth personality measure, honesty-humility, also has been associated with high scores on integrity tests and less counterproductive behavior.[48] So it comes as no surprise that British researchers recently found that people scoring *low* on conscientiousness tended to have significantly more accidents both on and off the job.[49] Likewise, a meta-analysis found that people low in conscientiousness are more likely to procrastinate (see Skills & Best Practices on page 125).

Another expected finding: Extraversion (an outgoing personality) was associated with success for managers and salespeople. Also, extraversion was a stronger predictor of job performance than agreeableness, across all professions. The researchers concluded, "It appears that being courteous, trusting, straightforward, and softhearted has a smaller impact on job performance than being talkative, active, and assertive."[50] Not surprisingly, another study found a strong linkage between conscientiousness and performance among those with polished social skills.[51] As an added bonus for extraverts, a recent positive psychology study led to this conclusion: "All you have to do is act extraverted and you can get a happiness boost."[52] So the next time you are on the job, go initiate a conversation with someone and be more productive *and* happier!

Despite these findings, a panel of psychologists reviewing the history of personality testing concluded that the typical personality test, which asks individuals to rate themselves, is not a valid predictor of job performance.[53] One reason might be that many test-takers don't describe themselves accurately but instead try to guess what answers the employer is looking for. In that case, personality actually may be related to performance, but managers need a better way to measure personality than the current tests if they want to select employees based on personality traits.

**The Proactive Personality**   As suggested by the above discussion, someone who scores high on the Big Five dimension of conscientiousness is probably a *better* and *safer* worker. Thomas Bateman and J Michael Crant took this important linkage an additional step by formulating the concept of the proactive personality. They define and characterize the **proactive personality** in these terms: "someone who is relatively unconstrained by situational forces and who effects environmental change. Proactive people identify opportunities and act on them, show initiative, take action, and persevere until meaningful change occurs."[54] In short, people with proactive personalities are "hardwired" to change the status quo. In a review of relevant studies, Crant found the proactive personality to be positively associated with individual, team, and organizational success.[55]

Successful entrepreneurs exemplify the proactive personality. Consider Joaquin Galan, founder of Galypso International, an export company with $13 million in revenues. Following the death of his father when Galan was just 15, he worked hard to help support his family, took a sales job with a company that would help pay for classes toward a master's degree in business administration, and launched a furniture business that failed and left him with tremendous debt. Undaunted, Galan started Galypso with his last $1,000 and a small line of credit. With similar resilience, Rachel Coleman founded Two Little Hands Productions, which produces DVDs that teach American Sign Language to children, after discovering that her baby daughter was severely hearing impaired. When Coleman learned of her daughter's disability, she abandoned her career as singer/songwriter, taught herself to sign, and began teaching children at local preschools. She and her sister made their first video just to teach others, but when the *Today Show* inquired, Coleman saw an opportunity and started building a business.[56]

## Why We Procrastinate— and How to Get Busy

A meta-analysis by Piers Steel at the University of Calgary found several qualities associated with procrastination. One of those is the personality trait of conscientiousness; people who score lower on conscientiousness tend to procrastinate. Changing that personality trait might not be possible, but Steel identifies ways to minimize the consequences of the other factors:

- *Low self-efficacy:* If you worry that you can't complete a big project, identify small steps you feel confident about. Get started on the small steps. Learn the skills you need; get a tutor, coach, or mentor.

- *Task aversiveness:* If the job is boring, connect it to something fun—say, putting together a work or study group with people you like, adding an interesting dimension to the task (build a computer model to go with the report), or planning a reward. If your energy level is low, see the Skills & Best Practices box about stamina (p. 127).

- *Impulsiveness and lack of control:* These personality traits are difficult to influence directly, but you can cope by removing temptations, surrounding yourself with reminders, and getting into work-related habits, such as set hours for certain tasks.

- *Task delay:* The further away your deadline, the easier it is to procrastinate. Create a schedule with interim goals.

SOURCE: Based on P Steel, "The Nature of Procrastination: A Meta-Analytic and Theoretical Review of Quintessential Self-Regulatory Failure," *Psychological Bulletin,* January 2007, pp 65–94.

**proactive personality**

Action-oriented person who shows initiative and perseveres to change things.

After starting and managing a number of billion-dollar firms, some of which he has sold, Robert Louis Johnson is opening a bank. The Urban Trust Bank will offer mortgages, investment opportunities, and student loans mainly to African-Americans and other minorities. Johnson is a prime example of a proactive personality, having let few things stand in the way of becoming the first African-American billionaire, the owner of the first black-owned business to go public on the New York Stock Exchange, and the first African-American to be the sole owner of a professional sports team.

People with proactive personalities truly are valuable *human capital,* as defined in Chapter 1. Those wanting to get ahead would do well to cultivate the initiative, drive, and perseverance of someone with a proactive personality.

**There Is No "Ideal Employee" Personality**   A word of caution is in order here. The Big Five personality dimensions of conscientiousness and extraversion and the proactive personality are generally desirable in the workplace, but they are not panaceas. Given the complexity of today's work environments, the diversity of today's workforce, and recent research evidence,[57] the quest for an ideal employee personality profile is sheer folly. Just as one shoe does not fit all people, one personality profile does not fit all job situations. Good management involves taking the time to get to know *each* employee's *unique combination* of personality traits, abilities, and potential and then creating a productive and satisfying person-job fit.

# Locus of Control: Self or Environment?

Individuals vary in terms of how much personal responsibility they take for their behavior and its consequences. Julian Rotter, a personality researcher, identified a dimension of personality he labeled *locus of control* to explain these differences. He proposed that people tend to attribute the causes of their behavior primarily to either themselves or environmental factors.[58] This personality trait produces distinctly different behavior patterns.

People who believe they control the events and consequences that affect their lives are said to possess an **internal locus of control.** For example, such a person tends to attribute positive outcomes, such as getting a passing grade on an exam, to her or his own abilities. Similarly, an "internal" tends to blame negative events, such as failing an exam, on personal shortcomings—not studying hard enough, perhaps. Many entrepreneurs eventually succeed because their *internal* locus of control helps them overcome setbacks and disappointments. They see themselves as masters of their own fate and not as simply lucky. Likewise, when people with an internal locus of control must shoulder a heavy workload, they look for solutions, such as the advice in Skills & Best Practices on page 127.

On the other side of this personality dimension are those who believe their performance is the product of circumstances beyond their immediate control. These individuals are said to possess an **external locus of control** and tend to attribute outcomes to environmental causes, such as luck or fate. Unlike someone with an internal locus of control, an "external" would attribute a passing grade on an exam to something external (an easy test or a good day) and attribute a failing grade to an unfair test or problems at home.

**Research Lessons**   Researchers have found important behavioral differences between internals and externals:

- Internals display greater work motivation.
- Internals have stronger expectations that effort leads to performance.

**4**  learning objective

Explain the difference between an internal and external locus of control.

**internal locus of control**

Attributing outcomes to one's own actions.

- Internals exhibit higher performance on tasks involving learning or problem solving, when performance leads to valued rewards.

- There is a stronger relationship between job satisfaction and performance for internals than for externals.

- Internals obtain higher salaries and greater salary increases than externals.

- Externals tend to be more anxious than internals.[59]

**external locus of control**

Attributing outcomes to circumstances beyond one's control.

### Tempering an Internal Locus of Control with Humility

Do you have an internal locus of control? Odds are high that you do, judging from the "typical" OB student we have worked with over the years. Good thing, because it should pay off in the workplace with opportunities, raises, and promotions. But before you declare yourself Grade A executive material, here is one more thing to toss into your tool kit: a touch of humility. **Humility** is "a realistic assessment of one's own contribution and the recognition of the contribution of others, along with luck and good fortune that made one's own success possible."[60] Humility has been called the silent virtue. How many truly humble people brag about being humble? Two OB experts recently offered this instructive perspective:

> Humble individuals have a down-to-earth perspective of themselves and of the events and relationships in their lives. Humility involves a capability to evaluate success, failure, work, and life without exaggeration. Furthermore, humility enables leaders to distinguish the delicate line between such characteristics as healthy self-confidence, self-esteem, and self-assessment, and those of over-confidence, narcissism, and stubbornness. Humility is the mid-point between the two negative extremes of arrogance and lack of self-esteem. This depiction allows one to see that a person can be humble and competitive or humble and ambitious at the same time, which contradicts common—but mistaken—views about humility.[61]

Cuban-born Carlos Gutierrez, U.S. secretary of commerce and former CEO of Kellogg Company, learned about humility from his father:

> He taught me that you have to keep your perspective and have a sense of humility. As he used to say, "Tell me what you brag about, and I'll tell you what you lack."[62]

---

**SKILLS & BEST PRACTICES**

## Build Your Stamina and Get More Done

In today's workplace, you'll see exhausted and frustrated workers say, "There aren't enough hours in the day" to get their work done. But some people focus less on the clock, which they cannot control, and more on their energy level, which they can. Here are some stamina-boosting ideas from the Energy Project, a New York City research group:

- **Take care of your body.** You already know you should eat nutritious meals, exercise, and get to bed at a regular bedtime. Not only do those practices keep you in good health, they also give you a consistent energy supply.

- **Take breaks.** When you start yawning and can't concentrate, walk around for a few minutes. Clear your mind by listening to music, and get your blood pumping by walking up and down the stairs a few times.

- **Notice what brings on negative emotions.** When that happens, defuse stress with deep breathing.

- **Cultivate positive feelings** by expressing appreciation to others. Be positive about negative events by looking at the big picture: what the other person's viewpoint is, whether the situation will still be important a year from now, and what you can learn from it.

- **When you can, do one thing at a time.** Wait until a meeting ends to check phone messages. Read e-mail at set times, rather than as each message arrives.

- **Set priorities** to do the things that really matter to you and express your values.

**SOURCE:** Based on T Schwartz, "Manage Your Energy, Not Your Time," *Harvard Business Review,* October 2007, pp 63–73.

**humility**

Considering the contributions of others and good fortune when gauging one's success.

**5** learning objective

Identify the three components of attitudes and discuss cognitive dissonance.

**attitude**

Learned predisposition toward a given object.

**affective component**

The feelings or emotions one has about an object or situation.

**cognitive component**

The beliefs or ideas one has about an object or situation.

# Attitudes

Hardly a day goes by without the popular media reporting the results of another attitude survey. The idea is to take the pulse of public opinion. What do we think about candidate X, the war on drugs, gun control, or abortion? In the workplace, meanwhile, managers conduct attitude surveys to monitor such things as job and pay satisfaction. All this attention to attitudes is based on the assumption that attitudes somehow influence our behavior. For example, research demonstrated that seniors with a positive attitude about aging had better memory, better hearing, and lived longer than those with negative attitudes.[63] In a work setting, a recent meta-analysis involving more than 50,000 people revealed that overall job attitudes were positively related to performance and negatively associated with indicators of withdrawal—lateness, absenteeism, and turnover.[64] In this section, we discuss the components of attitudes and examine the connection between attitudes and behavior.

**The Nature of Attitudes**   An **attitude** is defined as "a learned predisposition to respond in a consistently favorable or unfavorable manner with respect to a given object."[65] Consider your attitude toward chocolate ice cream. You are more likely to purchase a chocolate ice cream cone if you have a positive attitude toward chocolate ice cream. In contrast, you are more likely to purchase some other flavor, say vanilla caramel swirl, if you have a positive attitude toward vanilla and a neutral or negative attitude toward chocolate ice cream.

As in this example, attitudes propel us to act in a specific way in a specific context. That is, attitudes affect behavior at a different level than do values. While values represent global beliefs that influence behavior across *all* situations, attitudes relate only to behavior directed toward *specific* objects, persons, or situations. Values and attitudes generally, but not always, are in harmony. A manager who strongly values helpful behavior may have a negative attitude toward helping an unethical coworker.

The difference between attitudes and values is clarified by considering the three components of attitudes:[66]

- *Affective component.* The **affective component** of an attitude contains the feelings or emotions one has about a given object or situation. For example, how do you *feel* about people who talk on cell phones in restaurants? If you feel annoyed or angry with such people you are expressing negative affect or feelings toward people who talk on cell phones in restaurants. In contrast, the affective component of your attitude is neutral if you are indifferent about people talking on cell phones in restaurants.

- *Cognitive component.* What do you *think* about people who talk on cell phones in restaurants? Do you believe this behavior is inconsiderate, productive, completely acceptable, or rude? Your answer represents the cognitive component of your attitude toward people talking on cell phones in restaurants. The **cognitive component** of an attitude reflects the beliefs or ideas one has about an object or situation.

- *Behavioral component.* The **behavioral component** refers to how one intends or expects to act toward someone or something. For example, how would you intend to respond to someone talking on a cell phone during dinner at a restaurant if this individual were sitting in close proximity to you and your guest? Attitude theory suggests that your ultimate behavior in this situation is a function of all three attitudinal components. You are unlikely to say anything to someone using a cell phone in a restaurant if you are not irritated by this behavior (affective), if you believe cell phone use helps people to manage their lives (cognitive), and you have no intention of confronting this individual (behavioral).

> **behavioral component**
>
> **How one intends to act or behave toward someone or something.**

Your overall attitude toward someone or something is a function of the combined influence of all three components. For example, consulting firm Towers Perrin measures an attitude called "employee engagement," which describes people's attitude toward contributing fully at work, in terms of all three components: feeling emotionally connected to their job and company (affective), knowing what they should do at work (cognitive), and actually going above and beyond job requirements (behavioral). Towers Perrin has found that only one out of five employees are fully engaged. Most are lacking the emotional component, which managers can supply by offering opportunities for career development and communicating a vision in which the things that employees do make a real difference.[67]

**When Attitudes and Reality Collide: Cognitive Dissonance** What happens when a strongly held attitude is contradicted by reality? One widely held belief is that meetings are a waste of time. People routinely grumble about how much they could get done if they weren't "tied up" in meetings. But recent research has suggested that a majority of people actually enjoy meetings and would make them part of an ideal workday.[68] According to social psychologist Leon Festinger, this situation, in which negative beliefs about meetings are inconsistent with people's choice to schedule them, would create cognitive dissonance.

**Cognitive dissonance** represents the psychological discomfort a person experiences when his or her attitudes or beliefs are incompatible with his or her behavior.[69] Festinger proposed that people are motivated to maintain consistency between their attitudes and beliefs and their behavior. He therefore theorized that people will seek to reduce the "dissonance" or psychological tension through one of three main methods.

> **cognitive dissonance**
>
> **Psychological discomfort experienced when attitudes and behavior are inconsistent.**

1. *Change your attitude or behavior, or both.* This is the simplest solution when confronted with cognitive dissonance. For mechanical engineer John McKay, a behavior change led to an attitude change about meetings. He left a company where meetings took up most of his time and joined a company where meetings are rare. He discovered that he misses the "human contact" and now admits that he actually looks forward to meetings.

2. *Belittle the importance of the inconsistent behavior.* This happens all the time. In the case of meetings, insurance agent Joe Adams quips, "I learned long ago that I am not going to meet myself to greatness." Although meetings seem unimportant to Adams, he attends them and uses the time to make lists of things to do later.

3. *Find consonant elements that outweigh the dissonant ones.* This approach entails rationalizing away the dissonance. Tom Landis, president of a restaurant company, finds a logical explanation for the apparently illogical choice to hold meetings: "While people detest [meetings], they hate actually working more."

**How Stable Are Attitudes?** In one landmark study, researchers found the *job* attitudes of 5,000 middle-aged male employees to be very stable over a five-year period.

Positive job attitudes remained positive; negative ones remained negative. Even those who changed jobs or occupations tended to maintain their prior job attitudes.[70] More recent research suggests the foregoing study may have overstated the stability of attitudes because it was restricted to a middle-aged sample. This time, researchers asked: What happens to attitudes over the entire span of adulthood? *General* attitudes were found to be more susceptible to change during early and late adulthood than during middle adulthood. Three factors accounted for middle-age attitude stability: (1) greater personal certainty, (2) perceived abundance of knowledge, and (3) a need for strong attitudes. Thus, the conventional notion that general attitudes become less likely to change as the person ages was rejected. Elderly people, along with young adults, can and do change their general attitudes because they are more open and less self-assured.[71]

Some evidence suggests that attitudes toward work can vary between generations. Many people at or nearing retirement age, like Kathy Swartout, shown here with her husband, Mark, and their dog, are discovering that they crave the intangible benefits of working, such as the chance to learn new things, socialize with others, and feel appreciated. Swartout spent eight months sailing, gardening, and practicing yoga after retirement. Then she returned to a full-time job that she plans to cut back soon to three days a week. "Working part time balances financial security with family and all the other fun things I want to do," she says.

Because our cultural backgrounds and experiences vary, our attitudes and behavior vary. Attitudes are translated into behavior via behavioral intentions. Let us examine an established model of this important process.

**Attitudes Affect Behavior via Intentions** Building on Leon Festinger's work on cognitive dissonance, Icek Ajzen and Martin Fishbein further delved into understanding the reason for discrepancies between individuals' attitudes and behavior. Ajzen ultimately developed and refined a model focusing on intentions as the key link between attitudes and planned behavior. His theory of planned behavior in Figure 5–3 shows three separate but interacting determinants of one's intention (a person's readiness to perform a given behavior) to exhibit a specific behavior.

Importantly, this model only predicts behavior under an individual's control, not behavior due to circumstances beyond one's control. For example, this model can predict the likelihood of someone skipping work if the person says his intention is to stay in bed tomorrow morning. But it would be a poor model for predicting getting to work on time, because uncontrolled circumstances such as traffic delays or an accident could intervene.

*Determinants of Intention* Ajzen has explained the nature and roles of the three determinants of intention as follows:

> The first is the *attitude toward the behavior* and refers to the degree to which a person has a favorable or unfavorable evaluation or appraisal of the behavior in question. The second predictor is a social factor termed *subjective norm;* it refers to the perceived social pressure to perform or not to perform the behavior. The third antecedent of intention is the degree of *perceived behavior control,* which . . . refers to the perceived ease or difficulty of performing the behavior and it is assumed to reflect past experience as well as anticipated impediments and obstacles.[72]

To bring these three determinants of intention to life, let us return to our lazy soul who chose to stay in bed rather than go to work. He feels overworked and underpaid and thus has a favorable attitude about skipping work occasionally. His perceived

**FIGURE 5–3**
Ajzen's Theory
of Planned
Behavior

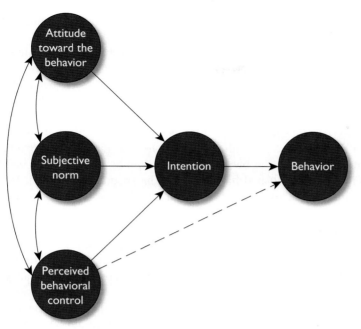

SOURCE: Reprinted from I Ajzen, "The Theory of Planned Behavior," *Organizational Behavior and Human Decision Processes*, Figure I, p 182. Copyright 1991, with permission from Elsevier Science.

subjective norm is favorable because he sees his coworkers skipping work with no ill effects (in fact, they collect sick pay). Regarding perceived behavior control, he is completely in charge of acting on his intention to skip work today. So he turns off the alarm clock and pulls the covers over his head. Sweet dreams!

***Intentions and Behavior Research Lessons and Implications***    According to the model of planned behavior, someone's intention to engage in a given behavior is a strong predictor of that behavior. For example, the quickest and possibly most accurate way of determining whether an individual will quit his or her job is to have an objective third party ask if he or she intends to quit. A meta-analysis of 34 studies of employee turnover involving more than 83,000 employees validated this direct approach. The researchers found stated behavioral intentions to be a better predictor of employee turnover than job satisfaction, satisfaction with the work itself, or organizational commitment.[73] A recent study took these findings one step further by considering whether or not job applicants' intention to quit a job before they were hired would predict voluntary turnover six months after being hired. Results demonstrated that intentions to quit significantly predicted turnover.[74]

Research has demonstrated that Ajzen's model accurately predicted a host of intentions and behaviors including intentions to buy products online, donate blood, pirate digital materials, adhere to a physical training program, vote for specific political candidates, lose weight, and be

*Today someone called me pompous, overpaid, and out of touch.
I think it's beginning to happen for me."*

HARVARD BUSINESS REVIEW

Copyright © Leo Collum 2006.

absent from work.[75] The theory of planned behavior also was found to explain the behavior of people from Turkey and the Netherlands.[76]

From a practical standpoint, the theory of planned behavior has important managerial implications. Managers are encouraged to use prescriptions derived from the model to implement interventions aimed at changing employees' behavior. According to this model, changing behavior starts with the recognition that behavior is modified through intentions, which in turn are influenced by three different determinants (see Figure 5–3). Managers can thus influence behavioral change by doing or saying things that affect the three determinants of employees' intentions to exhibit a specific behavior: attitude toward the behavior, subjective norms, and perceived behavioral control.[77] This is accomplished by modifying the specific beliefs that foster each of these determinants. For example, behavioral beliefs, normative beliefs, and control beliefs directly affect attitude toward the behavior, subjective norms, and perceived behavioral control, respectively. As a case in point, a study showed that employees had lower perceptions of job security and more negative attitudes toward temporary workers when they had the behavioral belief that temporaries posed a threat to their jobs.[78] Ultimately, managers change both attitudes and behavior by changing employees' beliefs.

Employee beliefs can be influenced through the information management provides on a day-by-day basis, organizational cultural values, role models, and rewards that are targeted to reinforce certain beliefs. For instance, management can foster the belief that teamwork is valued by setting and rewarding team-based goals instead of individual goals. Beliefs can also be modified through education and training.

## Intelligence and Cognitive Abilities

**intelligence**

Capacity for constructive thinking, reasoning, problem solving.

Although experts do not agree on a specific definition, **intelligence** represents an individual's capacity for constructive thinking, reasoning, and problem solving.[79] Historically, intelligence was believed to be an innate capacity, passed genetically from one generation to the next. Research since has shown, however, that intelligence (like personality) also is a function of environmental influences.[80] Organic factors have more recently been added to the formula as a result of mounting evidence of the connection between alcohol and drug abuse by pregnant women and intellectual development problems in their children.[81]

Researchers have produced some interesting findings about abilities and intelligence in recent years. A unique five-year study documented the tendency of people to "gravitate into jobs commensurate with their abilities."[82] This prompts the vision of the labor market acting as a giant sorting or sifting machine, with employees tumbling into various ability bins. Meanwhile, a steady and significant rise in average intelligence among those in developed countries has been observed over the last 70 years. Why? Experts at an American Psychological Association conference concluded, "Some combination of better schooling, improved socioeconomic status, healthier nutrition, and a more technologically complex society might account for the gains in IQ scores."[83] So if you think you're smarter than your parents and your teachers, you're probably right! Also, recent research has demonstrated that you can maintain your cognitive abilities as you grow older (see Skills & Best Practices on page 133).

**Two Types of Abilities**   Human intelligence has been studied predominantly through the empirical approach. By examining the relationships between measures of mental abilities and behavior, researchers have statistically isolated major components of intelligence. Using this empirical procedure, pioneering psychologist Charles Spearman proposed in 1927 that all cognitive performance is determined by two types of abilities. The first can be characterized as a general mental ability needed for *all* cognitive tasks. The second is unique to the task at hand. For example, an individual's ability to complete crossword puzzles is a function of his or her broad mental abilities as well as the specific ability to perceive patterns in partially completed words.

**Seven Major Mental Abilities** Through the years, much research has been devoted to developing and expanding Spearman's ideas on the relationship between cognitive abilities and intelligence.[84] One research psychologist listed 120 distinct mental abilities. Table 5–2 on page 134 contains definitions of the seven most frequently cited mental abilities. Of the seven abilities, personnel selection researchers have found verbal ability, numerical ability, spatial ability, and inductive reasoning to be valid predictors of job performance for both minority and majority applicants. Also, according to a recent comprehensive research review, standard intelligence (IQ) tests do a good job of predicting both academic achievement and job performance.[85] This contradicts the popular notion that different cognitive abilities are needed for school and work. Plainly stated: "smarts" are "smarts."

**Do We Have Multiple Intelligences?** Howard Gardner, a professor at Harvard's Graduate School of Education, offered a new paradigm for human intelligence in his 1983 book *Frames of Mind: The Theory of Multiple Intelligences.*[86] He has subsequently identified eight different intelligences that vastly broaden the long-standing concept of intelligence. Gardner's concept of multiple intelligences (MI) includes not only cognitive abilities but social and physical abilities and skills as well:

- *Linguistic intelligence:* potential to learn and use spoken and written languages.
- *Logical-mathematical intelligence:* potential for deductive reasoning, problem analysis, and mathematical calculation.
- *Musical intelligence:* potential to appreciate, compose, and perform music.
- *Bodily-kinesthetic intelligence:* potential to use mind and body to coordinate physical movement.
- *Spatial intelligence:* potential to recognize and use patterns.

## Fitness Isn't Just about Your Body Anymore

Until the past decade, people used to assume that the brain's function necessarily deteriorates with age. However, brain research has since shown that how we use our brain affects how well it functions. That means there are things we can do to help how well we think:

- *Expose yourself to important experiences.* Observe experts in action. Visit the employees you manage or the customers you serve, and listen to their opinions.

- *Take time to play.* Games, sports, and imagination engage and develop parts of the brain that are important for solving complex problems. Even the joy associated with playing is important for cognitive development.

- *Study and analyze.* The brain's ability to scan the environment and see patterns is a powerful information-processing ability. To develop this capacity, challenge your thinking by seeking out different viewpoints in what you read, listen to, and view. Make a point of seeking out people with different perspectives.

- *Try something new.* It's never too late to learn, and the very process of learning exercises your brain. Talk to people about what you're learning.

- *Exercise.* The biochemical changes from exercising literally flow to your brain as well as to the rest of your body.

**SOURCES:** Based on R Gilkey and C Kilts, "Cognitive Fitness," *Harvard Business Review,* November 2007, pp 53–66; and B Azar, "The Expert's Advantage," *Monitor on Psychology,* September 2007, pp 26–27.

learning objective **6**

Identify at least five of Gardner's eight multiple intelligences, and explain "practical intelligence."

**TABLE 5–2** | Mental Abilities

| Ability | Description |
|---------|-------------|
| 1. Verbal comprehension | The ability to understand what words mean and to readily comprehend what is read. |
| 2. Word fluency | The ability to produce isolated words that fulfill specific symbolic or structural requirements (such as all words that begin with the letter b and have two vowels). |
| 3. Numerical | The ability to make quick and accurate arithmetic computations such as adding and subtracting. |
| 4. Spatial | Being able to perceive spatial patterns and to visualize how geometric shapes would look if transformed in shape or position. |
| 5. Memory | Having good rote memory for paired words, symbols, lists of numbers, or other associated items. |
| 6. Perceptual speed | The ability to perceive figures, identify similarities and differences, and carry out tasks involving visual perception. |
| 7. Inductive reasoning | The ability to reason from specifics to general conclusions. |

SOURCE: Adapted from M D Dunnette, "Aptitudes, Abilities, and Skills," in *Handbook of Industrial and Organizational Psychology,* ed M D Dunnette (Skokie, IL: Rand McNally, 1976), pp 478–83.

- *Interpersonal intelligence:* potential to understand, connect with, and effectively work with others.
- *Intrapersonal intelligence:* potential to understand and regulate oneself.
- *Naturalist intelligence:* potential to live in harmony with one's environment.[87]

Many educators and parents have embraced MI because it helps explain how a child could score poorly on a standard IQ test yet be obviously gifted in one or more ways (e.g., music, sports, relationship building). Moreover, they believe the concept of MI underscores the need to help each child develop in his or her own unique way and at his or her own pace. They say standard IQ tests deal only with the first two intelligences on Gardner's list. Meanwhile, most academic psychologists and intelligence specialists continue to criticize Gardner's model as too subjective and poorly integrated. They prefer the traditional model of intelligence as a unified variable measured by a single test.

While the academic debate continues, we can draw some practical benefits from Gardner's notion of MI. In the final section of this chapter, you will encounter the concept of *emotional intelligence.* Yale's Robert J Sternberg recently applied Gardner's "naturalist intelligence" to the domain of leadership under the heading *practical intelligence.* He explains,

Practical intelligence is the ability to solve everyday problems by utilizing knowledge gained from experience in order to purposefully adapt to, shape, and select environments. It thus involves changing oneself to suit the environment (adaptation), changing the environment to suit oneself (shaping), or finding a new environment within which to work (selection). One uses these skills to (a) manage oneself, (b) manage others, and (c) manage tasks.[88]

Others believe MI has important implications for employee selection and training.[89] One-size-fits-all training programs fall short when MI diversity is taken into consideration. We look forward to breakthroughs in this area as MI attracts OB researchers and practicing managers.

# OB Gets Emotional

In the ideal world of management theory, employees pursue organizational goals in a logical and rational manner. Emotional behavior seldom is factored into the equation. Yet day-to-day organizational life shows us how prevalent and powerful emotions can be. Anger and jealousy, both potent emotions, often push aside logic and rationality in the workplace. Managers use fear and other emotions to both motivate and intimidate. For example, Eliot Spitzer, former governor of New York who resigned after a sex scandal in 2008, was known for his emotional outbursts. Here is what the former CEO of General Electric Jack Welch told a reporter from *Fortune* about an interaction he had with Spitzer about Ken Lagone. Lagone was a former director at both GE and the New York Stock Exchange.

> "We were having an amiable chat," Welch recalled. "Then—boom—he flipped his lid. He snapped. He started sticking his finger in my chest and said, 'You can tell your friend Lagone that I'm gonna put a stake through his heart!'"[90]

A combination of curiosity and fear is said to drive Barry Diller, one of the media world's legendary dealmakers. Says Diller, "I and my friends succeeded because we were scared to death of failing."[91] These admired corporate leaders would not have achieved what they have without the ability to be logical and rational decision makers *and* be emotionally charged. Too much emotion, however, could have spelled career and organizational disaster for either one of them. In contrast, Patricia Russo, CEO of Alcatel-Lucent, addresses business challenges with emotional stability. Her recent response to criticism over the telecom company's turnaround plans: "Pressure comes with the job. Someone else could come in here and have a different view of what to do, but I think this is the path we should be on. Now it is our job to execute."[92]

In this final section, our examination of individual differences turns to defining emotions, reviewing a typology of 10 positive and negative emotions, and discussing the topics of emotional contagion, emotional labor, and emotional intelligence.

**learning objective 7**

Explain the concepts of emotional intelligence, emotional contagion, and emotional labor.

## Positive and Negative Emotions

Richard S Lazarus, a leading authority on the subject, defines **emotions** as "complex, patterned, organismic reactions to how we think we are doing in our lifelong efforts to survive and flourish and to achieve what we wish for ourselves."[93] The word *organismic* is appropriate because emotions involve the *whole* person—biological, psychological, and social.

**emotions**

**Complex human reactions to personal achievements and setbacks that may be felt and displayed.**

Importantly, psychologists draw a distinction between *felt* and *displayed* emotions.[94] For example, when a boss makes repeated demands that sound impossible, you might feel angry or frightened (felt emotion); you might keep your feelings to yourself or begin to cry (either response is the displayed emotion). The boss might feel alarmed by your tears (felt emotion) but could react constructively (displayed emotion) by asking if you'd like to talk about the situation when you feel calmer.[95] Emotions play roles in both causing and adapting to stress and its associated biological and psychological problems.[96] The destructive effect of emotional behavior on social relationships is all too obvious in daily life.

Lazarus's definition of emotions centers on a person's goals. Accordingly, his distinction between positive and negative emotions is goal oriented. Some emotions are triggered by frustration and failure when pursuing one's goals. Lazarus calls these *negative* emotions. They are said to be goal incongruent. For example, which of the six negative emotions in Figure 5–4 are you likely to experience if you fail the final exam in a required course? Failing the exam would be incongruent with your goal of graduating on time. On the other hand, which of the four *positive* emotions in Figure 5–4 would you probably experience if you graduated on time and with honors? The emotions you would experience in this situation are positive because they are congruent (or consistent) with an important lifetime goal. The individual's goals, it is important to note, may or may not be socially acceptable. Thus, a positive emotion, such as love/affection, may be undesirable if associated with sexual harassment. Oppositely, slight pangs of guilt, anxiety, and envy can motivate extra effort. On balance, the constructive or destructive nature of a particular emotion must be judged in terms of both its intensity and the person's relevant goal.

**FIGURE 5–4**
Positive and Negative Emotions

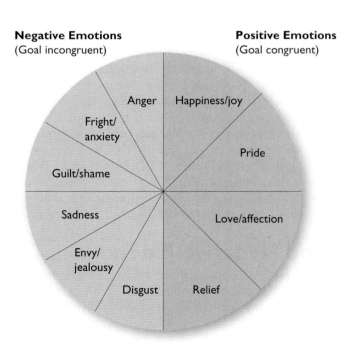

**Negative Emotions**
(Goal incongruent)

**Positive Emotions**
(Goal congruent)

Anger
Fright/anxiety
Guilt/shame
Sadness
Envy/jealousy
Disgust

Happiness/joy
Pride
Love/affection
Relief

SOURCE: Adapted from discussion in R S Lazarus, *Emotion and Adaptation* (New York: Oxford University Press, 1991), Chs 6, 7.

# Developing Emotional Intelligence

People cope with powerful emotions in lots of different ways. Take Taryn Rose, for example. She followed in her physician father's footsteps by attending medical school. However, near the end of her residency, she was bitten by the entrepreneurial bug and set her sights on developing and selling stylish shoes that would not ruin women's feet. But she did not want to disappoint her family. "I feared regret more than I feared failure,"[97] she recalled for *Fast Company* magazine, so she followed her dream. Now that she is the CEO of her own $20-million-a-year company, her family understands. For Taryn Rose, it took a good idea and determination to conquer her fears. Another way to deal effectively with fear and other emotions is to become more emotionally mature by developing emotional intelligence.

In 1995, Daniel Goleman, a psychologist turned journalist, created a stir in education and management circles with the publication of his book *Emotional Intelligence.* Hence, an obscure topic among positive psychologists became mainstream. According to Goleman, traditional models of intelligence (IQ) are too narrow, failing to consider interpersonal competence. Goleman's broader agenda includes "abilities such as being able to motivate oneself and persist in the face of frustrations; to control impulse and delay gratification; to regulate one's moods and keep distress from swamping the ability to think; to empathize and to hope."[98] Thus, **emotional intelligence** is the ability to manage oneself and one's relationships in mature and constructive ways. Referred to by some as EI and others as EQ, emotional intelligence is said to have four key components: self-awareness, self-management, social awareness, and relationship management.[99] The first two constitute *personal competence;* the second two feed into *social competence* (see Skills & Best Practices).

As an integrated package, the proactive personality discussed earlier and the components of emotional intelligence constitute a challenging self-development agenda for each of us. Indeed, Goleman and his followers believe greater emotional intelligence can boost individual, team, and organizational effectiveness.[100]

---

## Developing Emotional Intelligence

**Personal Competence:** These capabilities determine how we manage ourselves.

**Self-Awareness**
- *Emotional self-awareness:* Reading one's own emotions and recognizing their impact; using "gut sense" to guide decisions.
- *Accurate self-assessment:* Knowing one's strengths and limits.
- *Self-confidence:* A sound sense of one's self-worth and capabilities.

**Self-Management**
- *Emotional self-control:* Keeping disruptive emotions and impulses under control.
- *Transparency:* Displaying honesty and integrity; trustworthiness.
- *Adaptability:* Flexibility in adapting to changing situations or overcoming obstacles.
- *Achievement:* The drive to improve performance to meet inner standards of excellence.
- *Initiative:* Readiness to act and seize opportunities.
- *Optimism:* Seeing the upside in events.

**Social Competence:** These capabilities determine how we manage relationships.

**Social Awareness**
- *Empathy:* Sensing others' emotions, understanding their perspective, and taking active interest in their concerns.
- *Organizational awareness:* Reading the currents, decision networks, and politics at the organizational level.
- *Service:* Recognizing and meeting follower, client, or customer needs.

**Relationship Management**
- *Inspirational leadership:* Guiding and motivating with a compelling vision.
- *Influence:* Wielding a range of tactics for persuasion.
- *Developing others:* Bolstering others' abilities through feedback and guidance.
- *Change catalyst:* Initiating, managing, and leading in a new direction.
- *Conflict management:* Resolving disagreements.
- *Building bonds:* Cultivating and maintaining a web of relationships.
- *Teamwork and collaboration:* Cooperation and team building.

**SOURCE: Reprinted by permission of Harvard Business School Press. D Goleman, R Boyatzis, and A McKee, *Primal Leadership: Realizing the Power of Emotional Intelligence* (Boston: Harvard Business School Press, 2002), p 39. Copyright © 2002 by the Harvard Business School Publishing Corporation; all rights reserved.**

# Practical Research Insights about Emotional Contagion and Emotional Labor

Two streams of OB research on emotions are beginning to yield interesting and instructive insights:

**emotional intelligence**

Ability to manage oneself and interact with others in mature and constructive ways.

Self-Assessment Exercise

Assessing Your Emotional Intelligence

- *Emotional contagion.* Have you ever had someone's bad mood sour your mood? That person could have been a parent, supervisor, coworker, friend, or someone serving you in a store or restaurant. Appropriately, researchers call this *emotional contagion.* We, quite literally, can catch another person's bad mood or displayed negative emotions. This effect was documented in a recent study of 131 bank tellers (92% female) and 220 exit interviews with their customers. Tellers who expressed positive emotions tended to have more satisfied customers.[101] Two field studies with nurses and accountants as subjects found a strong linkage between the work group's collective mood and the individual's mood.[102] Both foul moods and good moods turned out to be contagious. Management professor Sigal Barsade says you cannot necessarily change your coworkers' bad moods but you can inoculate yourself against them. For example, you can decide ahead of time not to let a negative person bother you or take up your attention. One manager started each day by passing the desk of an employee who was grumpy in the morning. The manager simply found a different route through the office and thus avoided this negative start to the day.[103]

- *Emotional labor.* Although they did not have the benefit of a catchy label or a body of sophisticated research, generations of managers have known about the power of emotional contagion in the marketplace. "Smile, look happy for the customers," employees are told over and over. But what if the employee is having a rotten day? What if they have to mask their true feelings and emotions? What if they have to fake it? Researchers have begun studying the dynamics of what they call *emotional labor.* A pair of authors, one from Australia, the other from the United States, recently summarized the research lessons to date:

  Emotional labor can be particularly detrimental to the employee performing the labor and can take its toll both psychologically and physically. Employees . . . may bottle up feelings of frustration, resentment, and anger, which are not appropriate to express. These feelings result, in part, from the constant requirement to monitor one's negative emotions and express positive ones. If not given a healthy expressive outlet, this emotional repression can lead to a syndrome of emotional exhaustion and burnout.[104]

A recent review of the literature finds that emotional labor may cause less stress and burnout if the employees work on actually feeling the emotions they express—for example, by trying to empathize with why a difficult customer may be acting that way and then expressing sympathy with the customer's plight.[105] Interestingly, a pair of laboratory studies with U.S. college students as subjects found no gender difference in *felt* emotions. But the women were more emotionally *expressive* than the men.[106] This stream of research on emotional labor has major practical implications for productivity and job satisfaction, as well as for workplace anger, aggression, and violence. Clearly, managers need to be attuned to (and responsive to) the emotional states and needs of their people. This requires emotional intelligence.

# key terms

affective component   128
attitude   128
behavioral component   129
cognitions   116
cognitive component   128
cognitive dissonance   129
emotional intelligence   138

emotions   135
external locus of control   127
humility   128
intelligence   132
internal locus of control   126
learned helplessness   119
personality   123

proactive personality   125
self-concept   116
self-efficacy   118
self-esteem   117
self-monitoring   121

# chapter summary

- *Distinguish between self-esteem and self-efficacy.* Self-esteem is an overall evaluation of oneself, one's perceived self-worth. Self-efficacy is the belief in one's ability to successfully perform a task.

- *Contrast high and low self-monitoring individuals, and describe resulting problems each may have.* A high self-monitor strives to make a good public impression by closely monitoring his or her behavior and adapting it to the situation. Very high self-monitoring can create a "chameleon" who is seen as insincere and dishonest. Low self-monitors do the opposite by acting out their momentary feelings, regardless of their surroundings. Very low self-monitoring can lead to a one-way communicator who seems to ignore verbal and nonverbal cues from others.

- *Identify and describe the Big Five personality dimensions, specify which one is correlated most strongly with job performance, and describe the proactive personality.* The Big Five personality dimensions are extraversion (social and talkative), agreeableness (trusting and cooperative), conscientiousness (responsible and persistent), emotional stability (relaxed and unworried), and openness to experience (intellectual and curious). Conscientiousness is the best predictor of job performance. A person with a proactive personality shows initiative, takes action, and perseveres until a desired change occurs.

- *Explain the difference between an internal and external locus of control.* People with an *internal* locus of control, such as entrepreneurs, believe they are masters of their own fate. Those with an *external* locus of control attribute their behavior and its results to situational forces.

- *Identify the three components of attitudes and discuss cognitive dissonance.* The three components of attitudes are affective, cognitive, and behavioral. The affective component

represents the feelings or emotions one has about a given object or situation. The cognitive component reflects the beliefs or ideas one has about an object or situation. The behavioral component refers to how one intends or expects to act toward someone or something. Cognitive dissonance represents the psychological discomfort an individual experiences when his or her attitudes or beliefs are incompatible with his or her behavior. There are three main methods for reducing cognitive dissonance: change an attitude or behavior, belittle the importance of the inconsistent behavior, and find consonant elements that outweigh dissonant ones.

- *Identify at least five of Gardner's eight multiple intelligences, and explain "practical intelligence."* Harvard's Howard Gardner broadens the traditional cognitive abilities model of intelligence to include social and physical abilities. His eight multiple intelligences include: linguistic, logical-mathematical, musical, bodily-kinesthetic, spatial, interpersonal, intrapersonal, and naturalist. Someone with practical intelligence, according to Sternberg, is good at solving everyday problems and learning from experience by adapting to the environment, reshaping their environment, and selecting new environments in which to work.

- *Explain the concepts of emotional intelligence, emotional contagion, and emotional labor.* Four key components of emotional intelligence are self-awareness and self-management (for personal competence) and social awareness and relationship management (for social competence). Emotions are indeed contagious, with good and bad moods "infecting" others. Emotional labor occurs when people need to repress their emotional reactions when serving others. Resentment, frustration, and even anger can result when "putting on a happy face" for customers and others.

# discussion questions

1. In the context of the *chapter-opening vignette,* do you have what it takes to become a high-level executive? Explain.
2. How is someone you know with low self-efficacy, relative to a specified task, "programming themselves for failure"? What could be done to help that individual develop high self-efficacy?
3. On scales of low = 1 to high = 10, how would you rate yourself on the Big Five personality dimensions? Is your personality profile suitable for your present (or chosen) line of work? Explain.
4. Based on the three components underlying attitudes, what is your attitude toward the president of the United States?
5. Which of the four key components of emotional intelligence is (or are) your strong suit? Which is (or are) your weakest? What are the everyday implications of your EI profile?

# ethical dilemma

## Can We Talk about Your Body Art?

As tattoos and piercings gain popularity with a younger generation of employees, interviewers and supervisors are developing new dress code criteria.

While there are industries and companies that are tolerant of body art, it is still more common for businesses to hold a hard line, especially in jobs that require frequent customer interaction.

For example, at the Fairmont Scottsdale Princess in Scottsdale [Arizona], recruitment specialist Melisa Leserance said the company has definitive guidelines about on-the-job appearances and applicants are told during the interview process what is acceptable. . . .

Leserance recalled one employee who had a tattoo across his wrist. "He wore a jacket, but you could still see it. And as long as he worked here, he wore a bandage over the tattoo."

"If the company has a written or stated dress code," . . . [says an employment attorney], then "the company gets to determine what constitutes a professional image or appearance."[107]

### How should employers deal with self-expression through body art?

1. Many businesses have carefully cultivated images to protect, so they have a moral responsibility to their shareholders to monitor their employees' appearance. Explain.

2. Companies may have the legal right to force people to look a certain way, but they don't have the moral right to stifle self-expression in arbitrary ways. Explain.

3. The style of a new generation calls for new employment policies. Where should lines be drawn about employees' personal appearance?

4. The business case for diversity declares that an organization's employees should look like its customer base. If a growing number of customers have body art, why can't employees? Should this vary by industry or type of business? Explain.

5. Today's discrimination against those with body art is equivalent to now-illegal racial and gender discrimination years ago. Do you agree or disagree? Explain.

6. Invent other options. Discuss.

If you're looking for additional study materials, be sure to check out the Online Learning Center at

**www.mhhe.com/kinickiob4e**

for more information and interactivities that correspond to this chapter.

# chapter six

# Motivation I: Needs, Job Design, Intrinsic Motivation, and Satisfaction

# what is your dream job?

Asked what job they would take if they could have any, people unleash their imaginations and dream of exotic places, powerful positions or work that involves alcohol and a paycheck at the same time.

Or so you'd think.

None of that appeals to Lori Miller who, as a lead word processor has to do things that don't seem so dreamy, including proofreading, spell checking and formatting. But she loves it.

"I like and respect nearly all my coworkers, and most of them feel the same way about me," she says. "Just a few things would make it a little better," she says, including a

ask for much. One could attribute it to lack of imagination, setting the bar low or "anchoring," the term referring to the place people start and never move far from. One could chalk it up to rationalizing your plight.

But maybe people simply like what they do and aren't, as some management would have you believe, asking for too much—just the elimination of a small but disproportionately powerful amount of office inanity.

That may be one reason why two-thirds of Americans would take the same job again "without hesitation" and why 90% of Americans are

never completed, with the title of "Contractor of the Year."

Thus: "My dream job would be one free of politics," she says. "All advancement would be based on merit. The people who really did the work would be the ones who received the credit."

Frank Gastner has a similar ideal: "VP in charge of destroying inane policies." Over the years; he's had to hassle with the simplest of design flaws that would cost virtually nothing to fix were it not for the bureaucracies that entrenched them. So, the retired manufacturer's representative says he would address product and process problems with the attitude, "It's not right; let's fix it now without a committee meeting."

Monique Huston actually has her dream job—and many tell her it's theirs, too. She's general manager of a pub in Omaha, the Dundee Dell, which boasts 650 single-malt scotches on its menu. She visits bars, country clubs, people's homes and Scotland for whiskey tastings. "I stumbled on my passion in life," she says.

Still, some nights she doesn't feel like drinking—or smiling. "Your face hurts," she complains. And when you have your dream job you wonder what in the world you'll do next.[1]

One person's idea of a dream job is as simple as a place where coworkers would put their dishes in the dishwasher. What is your idea of a dream job?

shorter commute and the return of some great people who used to work there. And one more thing: She'd appreciate if everyone would put their dishes in the dishwasher.

*It's not a lot to ask for* and, it turns out a surprising number of people dreaming up their dream job don't

at least somewhat satisfied with their jobs, according to a Gallup Poll. . . .

So, money doesn't interest Elizabeth Gray as much as a level playing field. "I like what I do," says the city project manager who once witnessed former colleagues award a contractor, paid for work he

**What is your dream job? For an interpretation of this case and additional comments, visit our Online Learning Center at**

**www.mhhe.com/kinickiob4e**

FOR DISCUSSION

# The Fundamentals of Employee Motivation

**motivation**

**Psychological processes that arouse and direct goal-directed behavior.**

The term *motivation* derives from the Latin word *movere,* meaning "to move." In the present context, **motivation** represents "those psychological processes that cause the arousal, direction, and persistence of voluntary actions that are goal directed."[2] Managers need to understand these psychological processes if they are to successfully guide employees toward accomplishing organizational objectives. This section thus provides a conceptual framework for understanding motivation and examines need theories of motivation.

## A Job Performance Model of Motivation

1 learning objective

Discuss the job performance model of motivation.

**Group Exercise**

What Motivates You?

Terence Mitchell, a well-known OB researcher, proposed a broad conceptual model that explains how motivation influences job behaviors and performance. This model, which is shown in Figure 6–1, integrates elements from several of the theories we discuss in this book. It identifies the causes and consequences of motivation.[3]

Figure 6–1 shows that individual inputs and job context are the two key categories of factors that influence motivation. As discussed in Chapter 5, employees bring ability, job knowledge, dispositions and traits, emotions, moods, beliefs, and values to the work setting. The job context includes the physical environment, the tasks one completes, the organization's approach to recognition and rewards, the adequacy of supervisory support and coaching, and the organization's culture (recall our discussion in Chapter 2). These two categories of factors influence each other as well as the motivational processes of arousal, direction, and persistence. Consider how Heinfeld, Meech & Company manages the interplay between individual inputs and job context. Heinfeld, Meech & Company, an accounting firm in Arizona, selects employees who have "a positive attitude, a strong interest in the job and the energy to do it well."[4] The goal is to have happy employees, because—in the words of Gary Heinfeld, cofounder of the firm—"Happy employees equal happy clients." Job context factors that reinforce employees' positive attitudes include an emphasis on friendliness and teamwork, opportunities for professional growth and development,

A Job Performance Model of Motivation | **FIGURE 6–1**

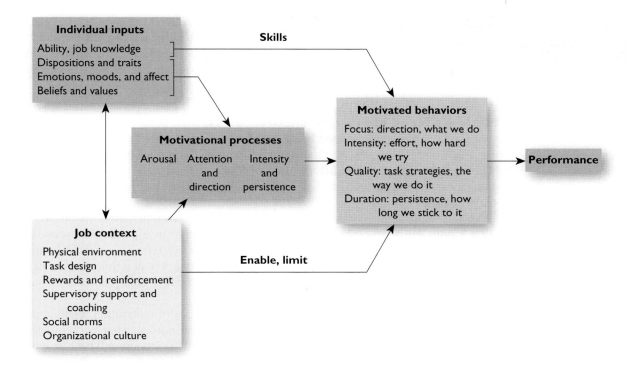

SOURCE: Adapted from T R Mitchell and D Daniels, "Motivation," in *Handbook of Psychology* (Vol 12), eds W C Borman, D R Ilgen, and R J Klimoski (Hoboken, NJ: John Wiley & Sons, Inc., 2003), p 226.

and scheduling flexibility. Employees conclude that the firm cares about them, and they respond by giving their best work.

In support of the idea that job context influences employee motivation and performance, economics professors Sandra Black and Lisa Lynch estimated that 89% of the growth in multifactor productivity in the 1990s (i.e., the growth in productivity that goes beyond investments in new technology) was due to innovative workplace practices.[5] Examples include job rotation, which is discussed later in this chapter, tying compensation to performance (see Chapters 7 and 8), and employee empowerment (see Chapter 13).

Figure 6–1 further reveals that *motivated behaviors* are directly affected by an individual's ability and job knowledge (skills), motivation, and a combination of enabling and limiting job context factors. For instance, it would be difficult to persist on a project if you were working with defective raw materials or broken equipment. In contrast, motivated behaviors are likely to be enhanced when managers supply employees with adequate resources to get the job done and provide effective coaching. This coaching might entail furnishing employees with successful role models, showing employees how to complete complex tasks, and helping them maintain high self-efficacy and self-esteem (recall the discussion in Chapter 5). Likewise, researchers found that workers tackling a complex task did better when they were experts, but novices outperformed experts on a simpler task, perhaps because they were less bored and more focused on important aspects of the job.[6] Performance is, in turn, influenced by motivated behavior.

# Need Theories of Motivation

**needs**

**Physiological or psychological deficiencies that arouse behavior.**

Need theories attempt to pinpoint internal factors that energize behavior. **Needs** are physiological or psychological deficiencies that arouse behavior. They can be strong or weak and are influenced by environmental factors. Human needs thus vary over time and place. Two popular need theories are discussed in this section: Maslow's need hierarchy theory and McClelland's need theory.

**2 learning objective**

Contrast Maslow's and McClelland's need theories.

**Maslow's Need Hierarchy Theory**    In 1943, psychologist Abraham Maslow published his now-famous need hierarchy theory of motivation. Although the theory was based on his clinical observation of a few neurotic individuals, it has subsequently been used to explain the entire spectrum of human behavior. Maslow proposed that motivation is a function of five basic needs—physiological, safety, love, esteem, and self-actualization.

Maslow said these five need categories are arranged in a prepotent hierarchy. In other words, he believed human needs generally emerge in a predictable stair-step fashion. Accordingly, when one's physiological needs are relatively satisfied, one's safety needs emerge, and so on up the need hierarchy, one step at a time. Once a need is satisfied it activates the next higher need in the hierarchy. This process continues until the need for self-actualization is activated.[7]

Although research does not clearly support this theory of motivation, there is one key managerial implication of Maslow's theory worth noting. That is, a satisfied need may lose its motivational potential. Therefore, managers are advised to motivate employees by devising programs or practices aimed at satisfying emerging or unmet needs. Many companies have responded to this recommendation by offering employees targeted benefits that meet their specific needs. Consider Joie de Vivre, a hotel chain in California's Bay Area. Management uses Maslow's principles to verify that the company is building employee satisfaction and loyalty in a variety of ways. For example, Joie de Vivre managers provide recognition with formal processes to identify and comment on occasions when employees have provided exceptional service. They try to help housekeepers derive meaning from their jobs by bringing them together to talk about what the guests' experience would be like if the housekeepers weren't making their stay more comfortable.[8] Managers also can use customized surveys in order to assess the specific needs of their employees.[9] In conclusion, managers are more likely to fuel employee motivation by offering benefits and rewards that meet individual needs.

**McClelland's Need Theory**    David McClelland, a well-known psychologist, has been studying the relationship between needs and behavior since the late 1940s. Although he is most recognized for his research on the need for achievement, he also investigated the needs for affiliation and power. Let us consider each of these needs:

- The **need for achievement** is defined by the following desires:

**need for achievement**

**Desire to accomplish something difficult.**

To accomplish something difficult. To master, manipulate, or organize physical objects, human beings, or ideas. To do this as rapidly and as independently as possible. To overcome obstacles and attain a high standard. To excel one's self. To rival and surpass others. To increase self-regard by the successful exercise of talent.[10]

Achievement-motivated people share three common characteristics: (1) a preference for working on tasks of moderate difficulty; (2) a preference for situations in which performance is due to their efforts rather than other factors, such as luck; and (3) they desire more feedback on their successes and failures than do low achievers. A review of research on the "entrepreneurial" personality showed that entrepreneurs were found to have a higher need for achievement than nonentrepreneurs.[11]

Elon Musk, one of the founders of Paypal, was named Inc. Magazine's 2007 Entrepreneur of the Year. Entrepreneurs have been found to have a higher need for achievement. Do you agree?

- People with a high **need for affiliation** prefer to spend more time maintaining social relationships, joining groups, and wanting to be loved. Individuals high in this need are not the most effective managers or leaders because they have a hard time making difficult decisions without worrying about being disliked.

- The **need for power** reflects an individual's desire to influence, coach, teach, or encourage others to achieve. People with a high need for power like to work and are concerned with discipline and self-respect. There is a positive and negative side to this need. The negative face of power is characterized by an "if I win, you lose" mentality. In contrast, people with a positive orientation to power focus on accomplishing group goals and helping employees obtain the feeling of competence. More is said about the two faces of power in Chapter 13. Because effective managers must positively influence others, McClelland proposes that top managers should have a high need for power coupled with a low need for affiliation. He also believes that individuals with high achievement motivation are *not* best suited for top management positions. Several studies support these propositions.[12]

**need for affiliation**

Desire to spend time in social relationships and activities.

**need for power**

Desire to influence, coach, teach, or encourage others to achieve.

There are three managerial implications associated with McClelland's need theory. First, given that adults can be trained to increase their achievement motivation, and achievement motivation is correlated with performance, organizations should consider the benefits of providing achievement training for employees.[13] Second, achievement, affiliation, and power needs can be considered during the selection process, for better placement. For example, a study revealed that people with a high need for achievement were more attracted to companies that had a pay-for-performance environment than were those with a low achievement motivation.[14] Finally, managers should create challenging task assignments or goals because the need for achievement is positively correlated with goal commitment, which, in turn, influences performance.[15]

# Motivating Employees through Job Design

**Job design,** also referred to as job redesign, "refers to any set of activities that involve the alteration of specific jobs or interdependent systems of jobs with the intent of improving the quality of employee job experience and their on-the-job productivity."[16] A team of researchers examined the various methods for conducting job design and integrated them into an interdisciplinary framework that contains four major

**job design**

Changing the content and/or process of a specific job to increase job satisfaction and performance.

approaches: mechanistic, motivational, biological, and perceptual-motor.[17] As you will learn, each approach to job design emphasizes different outcomes. This section discusses these four approaches to job design and focuses most heavily on the motivational methods.

# The Mechanistic Approach

The mechanistic approach draws from research in industrial engineering and scientific management and is most heavily influenced by the work of Frederick Taylor. Taylor, a mechanical engineer, developed the principles of scientific management based on research and experimentation to determine the most efficient way to perform jobs. Because jobs are highly specialized and standardized when they are designed according to the principles of scientific management, this approach to job design targets efficiency, flexibility, and employee productivity.

Designing jobs according to the principles of scientific management has both positive and negative consequences. Positively, employee efficiency and productivity are increased. On the other hand, research reveals that simplified, repetitive jobs also lead to job dissatisfaction, poor mental health, higher levels of stress, and low sense of accomplishment and personal growth.[18] These negative consequences paved the way for several motivational approaches to job design.

"You seem to be bored and listless. How about a little 300 volt electric shock to perk you up?"

*Copyright © Ted Goff. Reprinted with permission.*

# Motivational Approaches

The motivational approaches to job design attempt to improve employees' affective and attitudinal reactions such as job satisfaction and intrinsic motivation as well as a host of behavioral outcomes such as absenteeism, turnover, and performance. We discuss three key motivational techniques: job enlargement, job enrichment, and a contingency approach called the job characteristics model.

**Job Enlargement** This technique was first used in the late 1940s in response to complaints about tedious and overspecialized jobs. **Job enlargement** involves putting more variety into a worker's job by combining specialized tasks of comparable difficulty. Some call this *horizontally loading* the job. Researchers recommend using job enlargement as part of a broader approach that uses multiple motivational methods because it does not have a significant and lasting positive effect on job performance by itself.[19]

**job enlargement**

Putting more variety into a job.

**job rotation**

Moving employees from one specialized job to another.

**Job Rotation** As with job enlargement, job rotation's purpose is to give employees greater variety in their work. **Job rotation** calls for moving employees from one specialized job to another. Rather than performing only one job, workers are trained and given the opportunity to perform two or more separate jobs on a rotating basis. By rotating employees from job to job, managers believe they can stimulate interest and motivation while providing employees with a broader perspective of the organization. Other proposed advantages of job rotation include increased worker flexibility and easier scheduling because employees are cross-trained to perform different jobs. General Electric, for example, experienced many of these benefits from its rotation program for human resource (HR) entry-level employees.

> The goal of the program is to hire talented people who can become senior HR leaders in the company. . . . The program offers tremendous opportunities to participants, says Peters [Susan Peters is vice president for executive development]. "The big attraction is the variety they get in the first few years," she says. "They see different businesses and different functions. You might start in labor relations, and then go to compensation, then to staffing, then benefits."
>
> About a decade ago, GE added a cross-functional rotation to the mix, and it has become a key component of the program's success. "You have to go on the audit staff or become a marketing person for one rotation," Peters says. "We've learned that the HR function has to have good connectivity with the business operations and it improves the credibility of the individual later on."[20]

Despite positive experiences from companies like GE, it is not possible to draw firm conclusions about the value of job rotation programs because they have not been adequately researched.

**Job Enrichment** Job enrichment is the practical application of Frederick Herzberg's motivator–hygiene theory of job satisfaction. Herzberg's theory is based on a landmark study in which he interviewed 203 accountants and engineers.[21] These interviews sought to determine the factors responsible for job satisfaction and dissatisfaction. Herzberg found separate and distinct clusters of factors associated with job satisfaction and dissatisfaction. Job satisfaction was more frequently associated with achievement, recognition, characteristics of the work, responsibility, and advancement.

> **motivators**
>
> **Job characteristics associated with job satisfaction.**

These factors were all related to outcomes associated with the *content* of the task being performed. Herzberg labeled these factors **motivators** because each was associated with strong effort and good performance. He hypothesized that motivators cause a person to move from a state of no satisfaction to satisfaction (see Figure 6–2). Therefore, Herzberg's theory predicts managers can motivate individuals by incorporating "motivators" into an individual's job.

Jesse Kiefer, a gumologist, is a good example of someone who is energized by the motivators contained in his job. Here is what he said to a reporter from *Fortune* about his job.

> Some days I don't blow any bubbles. Other days I have to blow a lot. It depends on what stage we are in the project. A piece of gum weighs just one to seven grams, but it's packed with a lot of different technology. It has to deliver a burst of flavor, a lot of sweetness, and a lot of tartness if it's a fruit gum. Our team figures out how to combine all those. For example, Trident Splash Strawberry with Lime—it's not easy to pick lime and strawberry flavors that complement each other. . . . When we work on the gum in its raw form, sometimes we use a hatchet to chop it up.

Jesse Kiefer (right) finds many rewards in his job as gumologist for Cadbury Schweppes, maker of Trident gum. Would you like to be a gumologist?

**FIGURE 6–2**
Herzberg's
Motivator–
Hygiene Model

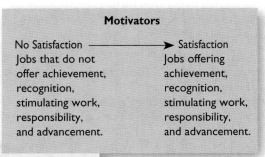

SOURCE: Adapted in part from D A Whitsett and E K Winslow, "An Analysis of Studies Critical of the Motivator–Hygiene Theory," *Personnel Psychology,* Winter 1967, pp 391–415.

> I did my graduate work as a chemical engineer, and I started out working on detergent and soaps. But with gum there's just so many flavors! I find the job very stimulating.[22]

Herzberg found job *dissatisfaction* to be associated primarily with factors in the work *context* or environment. Specifically, company policy and administration, technical supervision, salary, interpersonal relations with one's supervisor, and working conditions were most frequently mentioned by employees expressing job dissatisfaction.

**hygiene factors**

**Job characteristics associated with job dissatisfaction.**

Herzberg labeled this second cluster of factors **hygiene factors.** He further proposed that they were not motivational. At best, according to Herzberg's interpretation, an individual will experience no job dissatisfaction when he or she has no grievances about hygiene factors (refer to Figure 6–2).

The key to adequately understanding Herzberg's motivator–hygiene theory is recognizing that he believes that satisfaction is not the opposite of dissatisfaction. Herzberg concludes that "the opposite of job satisfaction is not job dissatisfaction, but rather no job satisfaction; and similarly, the opposite of job dissatisfaction is not job satisfaction, but no dissatisfaction."[23] Herzberg thus asserts that the dissatisfaction–satisfaction continuum contains a zero midpoint at which dissatisfaction and satisfaction are absent. Conceivably, an organization member who has good supervision, pay, and working conditions but a tedious and unchallenging task with little chance of advancement would be at the zero midpoint. That person would have no dissatisfaction (because of good hygiene factors) and no satisfaction (because of a lack of motivators).

Herzberg's theory generated a great deal of research and controversy. Although research does not support the two-factor aspect of his theory, it does support many of the theory's implications for job design.[24] Job enrichment is based on the application of Herzberg's ideas. Specifically, **job enrichment** entails modifying a job such that an employee has the opportunity to experience achievement, recognition, stimulating work, responsibility, and advancement. These characteristics are incorporated into a job through vertical loading. Rather than giving employees additional tasks of similar difficulty (horizontal loading), *vertical loading* consists of giving workers more responsibility. In other words, employees take on chores normally performed by their supervisors.

> **job enrichment**
> Building achievement, recognition, stimulating work, responsibility, and advancement into a job.

**The Job Characteristics Model**   Two OB researchers, J Richard Hackman and Greg Oldham, played a central role in developing the job characteristics approach. These researchers tried to determine how work can be structured so that employees are internally or intrinsically motivated. **Intrinsic motivation** occurs when an individual is "turned on to one's work because of the positive internal feelings that are generated by doing well, rather than being dependent on external factors (such as incentive pay or compliments from the boss) for the motivation to work effectively."[25] These positive feelings power a self-perpetuating cycle of motivation. As shown in Figure 6–3, internal work motivation is determined by three psychological states. In turn, these psychological states are fostered by the presence of five core job characteristics. As you can see in Figure 6–3, the object of this approach is to promote high intrinsic motivation by designing jobs that possess the five core job characteristics shown in Figure 6–3. Let us examine the core job characteristics.

> **intrinsic motivation**
> Motivation caused by positive internal feelings.

The Job Characteristics Model   **FIGURE 6–3**

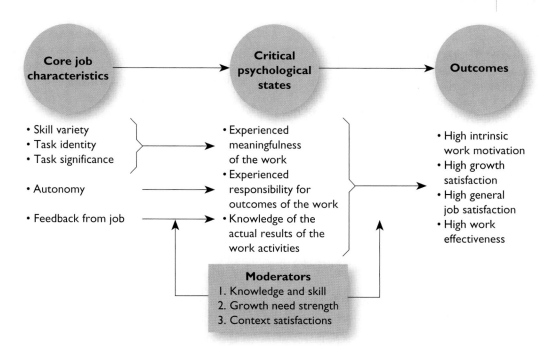

**core job characteristics**

Job characteristics found to various degrees in all jobs.

In general terms, **core job characteristics** are common characteristics found to a varying degree in all jobs. Three of the job characteristics shown in Figure 6–3 combine to determine experienced meaningfulness of work:

- *Skill variety.* The extent to which the job requires an individual to perform a variety of tasks that require him or her to use different skills and abilities.
- *Task identity.* The extent to which the job requires an individual to perform a whole or completely identifiable piece of work. In other words, task identity is high when a person works on a product or project from beginning to end and sees a tangible result.
- *Task significance.* The extent to which the job affects the lives of other people within or outside the organization.

Experienced responsibility is elicited by the job characteristic of autonomy, defined as follows:

- *Autonomy.* The extent to which the job enables an individual to experience freedom, independence, and discretion in both scheduling and determining the procedures used in completing the job.

Finally, knowledge of results is fostered by the job characteristic of feedback, defined as follows:

- *Feedback.* The extent to which an individual receives direct and clear information about how effectively he or she is performing the job.[26]

Hackman and Oldham recognized that not everyone wants a job containing high amounts of the five core job characteristics. They incorporated this conclusion into their model by identifying three attributes that affect how individuals respond to job enrichment. These attributes are concerned with the individual's knowledge and skill, growth need strength (representing the desire to grow and develop as an individual), and context satisfactions (see the box labeled Moderators in Figure 6–3). Context satisfactions represent the extent to which employees are satisfied with various aspects of their job, such as satisfaction with pay, coworkers, and supervision.

There are several practical implications associated with using the job characteristics model to enhance intrinsic motivation: Steps for applying this model are shown in Skills & Best Practices. Managers may want to use this model to increase employee job satisfaction. Research overwhelmingly demonstrates a moderately strong relationship between job characteristics and satisfaction.[27] Consistent with this finding, researchers investigating the consequences of telecommuting found that it increased workers' autonomy, and their sense of greater autonomy contributed to higher levels of job satisfaction and performance.[28]

Moreover, research suggests that managers can enhance employees' intrinsic motivation, initiative, creativity,

## SKILLS & BEST PRACTICES

## Steps for Applying the Job Characteristics Model

1. Diagnose the work environment to determine the level of employee motivation and job satisfaction. Job design should be used when employee motivation ranges from low to moderately high. The diagnosis can be made using employee surveys.

2. Determine whether job redesign is appropriate for a given group of employees. Job redesign is most likely to work in a participative environment in which employees have the necessary knowledge and skills to perform the enriched tasks and their job satisfaction is average to high.

3. Determine how to best redesign the job. The focus of this effort is to increase those core job characteristics that are low. Employee input is essential during this step to determine the details of a redesign initiative.

innovation, and commitment to their performance goals by increasing the core job characteristics.[29] Two separate meta-analyses also support the practice of using the job characteristics model to help managers reduce absenteeism and turnover.[30] On the negative side, however, job redesign appears to reduce the quantity of output just as often as it has a positive effect. Caution and situational appropriateness are advised. For example, one study demonstrated that job redesign works better in less complex organizations (small plants or companies).[31] Nonetheless, managers are likely to find noticeable increases in the quality of performance after a job redesign program. Results from 21 experimental studies revealed that job redesign resulted in a median increase of 28% in the quality of performance.[32]

Job characteristics research also underscores an additional implication for companies undergoing reengineering. Reengineering potentially leads to negative work outcomes because it increases job characteristics beyond reasonable levels. This occurs for two reasons: (1) reengineering requires employees to use a wider variety of skills to perform their jobs, and (2) reengineering typically results in downsizing and short-term periods of understaffing.[33] The unfortunate catch is that understaffing was found to produce lower levels of group performance, and jobs with either overly low or high levels of job characteristics were associated with higher stress.[34] Managers are advised to carefully consider the level of perceived job characteristics when implementing reengineering initiatives.

# Biological and Perceptual-Motor Approaches

The biological approach to job design is based on research from biomechanics, work physiology, and ergonomics and focuses on designing the work environment to reduce employees' physical strain, fatigue, and health complaints. An attempt is made to redesign jobs so that they eliminate or reduce the amount of repetitive motions from a worker's job. Ford Motor Company uses virtual reality in its biological approach to job design. In a Dearborn, Michigan, laboratory, technicians wearing sensors and virtual-reality goggles go through the motions required to assemble newly designed vehicles. Cameras and motion-capture software collect data from the sensors and create animated images of the assembly jobs. Then ergonomics specialists

Ford Motor Co. ergonomics specialist places virtual reality goggles on an employee. How does this approach lower costs and boost quality of their vehicles and their jobs?

analyze each job, looking for potentially painful, difficult, or repetitive movements that could cause discomfort and injuries. Jobs—or the vehicles themselves—are redesigned to prevent these problems before the vehicle assembly even begins. Besides making assembly line jobs less painful, the approach has lowered costs and boosted quality.[35]

The perceptual-motor approach is derived from research that examines human factors engineering, perceptual and cognitive skills, and information processing. This approach to job design emphasizes the reliability of work outcomes by examining error rates, accidents, and workers' feedback about facilities and equipment.[36]

Toyota Motor Company applies such principles in developing standard procedures and training for its manufacturing plants around the world. To prepare workers in China, the company taught 3,000 detailed assembly line tasks by displaying videos above workstations simulating factory setups. The videos teach workers how to perform tasks as basic as holding a screw or air gun in the way that is most efficient, delivers consistent quality, and is least tiring. As the company simplifies jobs for inexperienced workers in places like China, it discovers solutions that can apply anywhere in the world. For example, instead of asking workers to go to bins to choose parts, Toyota started delivering all the needed parts to workers inside containers placed in the otherwise empty car bodies. The process is so efficient that Toyota is starting to use it in its Mississippi factory.[37]

The frequency of using both the biological and perceptual-motor approaches to job redesign is increasing in light of the number of workers who experience injuries related to overexertion or repetitive motion. **Repetitive motion disorders (RMDs)** are "a family of muscular conditions that result from repeated motions performed in the course of normal work or daily activities. RMDs include carpal tunnel syndrome, bursitis, tendonitis, epicondyliltis, ganglion cyst, tenosynovitis, and trigger finger. RMDs are caused by too many uninterrupted repetitions of an activity or motion, unnatural or awkward motions such as twisting the arm or wrist, overexertion, incorrect posture, or muscle fatigue."[38] According to data from the Bureau of Labor Statistics, the incidence of some types of RMDs—in particular, carpal tunnel syndrome—has declined, but among the types of events that led to injury, repetitive motion resulted in the longest absences from work (a median of 19 days).[39] Injuries caused by repetitive motion are by far most likely in production jobs, especially among meat cutters, plumbers, and welders. To combat this problem, the Occupational Safety and Health Administration (OSHA) implemented guidelines regarding ergonomic standards in the workplace.

**repetitive motion disorders (RMDs)**

Muscular disorder caused by repeated motions.

Recent research suggests that the biological approach should be combined with other job design considerations, because physical ailments are not always completely caused by physical strain. In this study, researchers in the United Kingdom studied more than 900 call center workers and found that they were more likely to experience upper-body and lower-back disorders if they experienced psychological strain in the form of anxiety and depression. Heavy workloads also contributed to the physical symptoms, but adding psychological strain made the disorders worse.[40]

# Cultivating Intrinsic Motivation

The Gallup Organization has been studying employee engagement around the world for many years. It completed a study of employee engagement in the United States and 10 other countries. Sadly, results reveal that 31%, 52%, and 17% of the U.S. workforce is actively engaged at work (i.e., loyal, productive, and satisfied), not engaged (i.e., not psychologically committed to their work role), and actively disengaged (i.e., disenchanted with their workplace) at work, respectively. Gallup estimates that the behavior and lower productivity of actively disengaged workers cost the U.S. economy about $370 billion a year.[41] Results further reveal that the pattern of employee engagement is lower among the other 10 countries. These countries include Canada, Germany, Japan, Great Britain, Chile, France, Israel, Australia, New Zealand, and Singapore. Singapore, for instance, ranks among the lowest in the world in employee engagement, costing about $6 billion annually in lost productivity.[42]

Managers play a major role in the extent to which employees are engaged at work. Quite simply, employees tend to engage at work when they are intrinsically motivated. It thus is important to have an understanding of how managers can influence employees' intrinsic motivation.

We begin our exploration of intrinsic motivation by discussing the difference between intrinsic and extrinsic motivation and then presenting a model of intrinsic motivation. We conclude by reviewing the research and managerial implications pertaining to the model of intrinsic motivation.

## The Foundation of Intrinsic Motivation

*Intrinsic motivation* was defined earlier as being driven by positive feelings associated with doing well on a task or job. Intrinsically motivated people are driven to act for the fun or challenge associated with a task rather than because of external rewards, pressures, or requests. Motivation comes from the psychological rewards associated with doing well on a task that one enjoys (see Skills & Best Practices). It is important to note that individual differences exist when it comes to intrinsic motivation. People are intrinsically motivated for some activities and not others, and everyone is not intrinsically motivated by the same tasks.[43] For example, while the authors of this book are intrinsically motivated to write, we do not jump for joy when asked to proofread hundreds of pages. In contrast, someone else may hate to write but love the task of finding typos in a document.

In contrast to completing tasks for the joy of doing them, **extrinsic motivation** drives people's behavior when they do things in order to attain a specific outcome. In other words, extrinsic motivation is fueled by a person's desire to avoid or achieve some type of consequence for his or her behavior.[44] For example, a student who completes homework because he or she wants to avoid the embarrassment of being called on in class without knowing the answer is extrinsically motivated because he or she is doing it to avoid the negative outcome of being embarrassed. Similarly, a student who does homework because he or she believes it will help him or her obtain a job also is extrinsically motivated because he or she is studying for its instrumental value rather than because of pure interest. As you can see, extrinsic motivation is related to the receipt of extrinsic rewards. *Extrinsic rewards* do not come from the work itself; they are given by others (e.g., teachers, managers, parents, friends, or customers). At work, they include things like salaries, bonuses, promotions, benefits, awards, and titles.

**Group Exercise**

What Rewards Motivate Student Achievement?

**extrinsic motivation**

Motivation caused by the desire to attain specific outcomes.

## SKILLS & BEST PRACTICES

### Motivation at Massachusetts Medical Society

The Massachusetts Medical Society is an association of physicians whose mission and goals include advancing medical knowledge and ensuring a high quality of health care. The group's day-to-day activities, including publication of the *New England Journal of Medicine,* are carried about by more than 400 staff members.

Overall, these employees cite a high level of satisfaction with their work. Why? You might start with benefits like on-site exercise facilities and backup day care for workers' children. Or you might look at compensation that is fair, if not up to the level of high-tech companies in the surrounding Boston area.

But what employees most often mention are intrinsic benefits of meaningful, quality-driven work. They talk about the organization's "sense of mission" and its "culture of excellence." Newsletter editor Catherine Ryan says the organization's people and their work are both respected. And employees appreciate that they are helping to improve a profession on which—for better or worse—most of us depend. Theresa Sciarappa, the society's vice president for human resources, says a former president once told employees, "At some point in your life, you or someone you love will be sick, and you'll realize the value of what you do."

**SOURCES: Based on L Rubis, "Compassion, Commitment Fuel Society on a Mission," *HR Magazine,* July 2007, p 57; and Massachusetts Medical Society, "About: Mission & Goals," May 22, 2007, www .massmed.org.**

There has been an extensive amount of research on the topic of intrinsic motivation. The majority of this research relied on students performing tasks in laboratory experiments to determine whether or not the use of extrinsic rewards dampened their intrinsic motivation. Unfortunately, the overall pattern of results has created controversy and debate among researchers. Nonetheless, this conclusion does not detract from the value of focusing on the positive application of intrinsic motivation at work.

# A Model of Intrinsic Motivation

Kenneth Thomas proposed the most recent model of intrinsic motivation. He developed his model by integrating research on empowerment, which is discussed in Chapter 13, with two previous models of intrinsic motivation.[45] Thomas specifically linked components of the job characteristics model of job design discussed in the last section with Edward Deci and Richard Ryan's cognitive evaluation theory. Deci and Ryan proposed people must satisfy their needs for autonomy and competence when completing a task for it to be intrinsically motivating.[46] Thomas's model is shown in Figure 6–4.

Figure 6–4 illustrates the four key intrinsic rewards underlying an individual's level of intrinsic motivation. Looking across the rows, rewards of meaningfulness and progress are derived from the purpose for completing various tasks, while the sense of choice and sense of competence come from the specific tasks one completes. Looking down the columns, the sense of choice and meaningfulness are related to the opportunity to use one's own judgment and to pursue a worthwhile purpose. In contrast, accomplishment rewards—a sense of competence and progress—are derived from the extent to which individuals feel competent in completing tasks and successful in attaining their original task purpose, respectively. Thomas believes intrinsic motivation is a direct result of the extent to which an individual experiences these four intrinsic rewards while working. Let us examine these intrinsic rewards in more detail.

**Sense of Meaningfulness**  "A **sense of meaningfulness** is the opportunity you feel to pursue a worthy task purpose. The feeling of meaningfulness is the feeling that you are on a path that is worth your time and energy—that you are on a valuable mission, that your purpose

**sense of meaningfulness**

The task purpose is important and meaningful.

**FIGURE 6–4**
A Model
of Intrinsic
Motivation

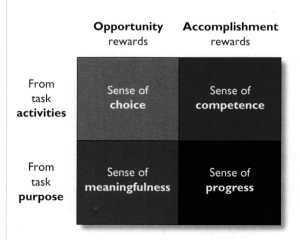

| | Opportunity rewards | Accomplishment rewards |
|---|---|---|
| From task **activities** | Sense of **choice** | Sense of **competence** |
| From task **purpose** | Sense of **meaningfulness** | Sense of **progress** |

matters in the larger scheme of things."[47] This description reveals that it is not the task itself that drives intrinsic motivation, but rather the overall purpose for completing tasks. People have a desire to do meaningful work, work that makes a difference. That desire is especially challenging to meet in today's information economy, where many workers have intangible goals and products, and the impact on lives may be difficult to see.[48] David Fahl used to work for an energy reseller, a company that buys energy from generating companies and sells it to energy users. He felt little satisfaction from a task that seemed to create nothing: "Not even the marketing people could come up with a plausible explanation for why the company existed." Jon Williams recalls that when he worked in the auto claims department of an insurance company, management measured his accomplishments in terms of the number of calls he fielded each day, but he gained more satisfaction from calming a frustrated customer, an accomplishment he found more meaningful.

**Sense of Choice**    "A **sense of choice** is the opportunity you feel to select task activities that make sense to you and to perform them in ways that seem appropriate. The feeling of choice is the feeling of being free to choose—of being able to use your own judgment and act out of your own understanding of the task."[49] Nordstrom's, for example, grants employees much latitude in determining how best to provide customer service. The company tells employees to use good judgment and to treat their job as if they were running their own business.[50]

> **sense of choice**
>
> The ability to use judgment and freedom when completing tasks.

**Sense of Competence**    "A **sense of competence** is the accomplishment you feel in skillfully performing task activities you have chosen. The feeling of competence involves the sense that you are doing good, high-quality work on a task."[51] A sense of competence also is related to the level of challenge associated with completing tasks. In general, people feel a greater sense of competence by completing challenging tasks.

> **sense of competence**
>
> Feelings of accomplishment associated with doing high-quality work.

**Sense of Progress**    "A **sense of progress** is the accomplishment you feel in achieving the task purpose. The feeling of progress involves the sense that the task is moving forward, that your activities are really accomplishing something."[52] A sense of progress promotes intrinsic motivation because it reinforces the feeling that one is wisely spending his or her time. A low sense of progress leads to discouragement. Over time, a low sense of progress can lower enthusiasm and lead to feelings of being stuck or helpless. Here again, progress is often harder to see in information industry jobs, which have intangible results. Management consultant Jane Vawter has taught herself to seek satisfaction from the quality of her presentations, rather than from clients' response to them. She also seeks a sense of accomplishment outside work by completing needlepoint projects, which provide defined starting and ending points.[53]

> **sense of progress**
>
> Feeling that one is accomplishing something important.

# Research and Managerial Implications

Before discussing research and managerial implications, we would like you to complete the Hands-On Exercise entitled "Are You Intrinsically Motivated at Work?" It assesses the level of intrinsic motivation in your current or past job. How did you stack up? Does your job need a dose of intrinsic rewards? If it does, the following discussion outlines how you or your manager might attempt to increase your intrinsic motivation.

# Are You Intrinsically Motivated at Work?

**INSTRUCTIONS:** The following survey was designed to assess the extent to which you are deriving intrinsic rewards from your current job: If you are not working, use a past job or your role as a student to complete the survey. There are no right or wrong answers to the statements. Circle your answer by using the rating scale provided. After evaluating each of the survey statements, complete the scoring guide.

| | Strongly Disagree | Disagree | Neither Agree or Disagree | Agree | Strongly Agree |
|---|---|---|---|---|---|
| **1.** I am passionate about my work. | 1 | 2 | 3 | 4 | 5 |
| **2.** I can see how my work tasks contribute to my organization's corporate vision. | 1 | 2 | 3 | 4 | 5 |
| **3.** I have significant autonomy in determining how I do my job. | 1 | 2 | 3 | 4 | 5 |
| **4.** My supervisor/manager delegates important projects/tasks to me that significantly impact my department's overall success. | 1 | 2 | 3 | 4 | 5 |
| **5.** I have mastered the skills necessary for my job. | 1 | 2 | 3 | 4 | 5 |
| **6.** My supervisor/manager recognizes when I competently perform my job. | 1 | 2 | 3 | 4 | 5 |
| **7.** Throughout the year, my department celebrates its progress toward achieving its goals. | 1 | 2 | 3 | 4 | 5 |
| **8.** I regularly receive evidence/information about my progress toward achieving my overall performance goals. | 1 | 2 | 3 | 4 | 5 |

## SCORING KEY

Sense of meaningfulness (add items 1–2) _____

Sense of choice (add items 3–4) _____

Sense of competence (add items 5–6) _____

Sense of progress (add items 7–8) _____

Overall score (add all items) _____

## ARBITRARY NORMS

For each intrinsic reward, a score of 2–4 indicates low intrinsic motivation, 5–7 represents moderate intrinsic motivation, and 8–10 indicates high intrinsic motivation. For the overall score, 8–19 is low, 20–30 is moderate, and 31–40 is high.

Thomas's model of intrinsic motivation has not been subjected to much research at this point in time. This is partly due to its newness in the field of organizational behavior and the fact that the model is based on integrating theories—the job characteristics model and cognitive evaluation theory—that have been supported by past research. This leads us to conclude that the basic formulation of the model appears to be on solid ground, and future research is needed to study the specific recommendations for leading others toward intrinsic motivation.[54] In the meantime, managers are encouraged to use a different set of managerial behaviors to increase each of the four intrinsic rewards. Let us consider these managerial behaviors.

Managers can foster a sense of *meaningfulness* by inspiring their employees and modeling desired behaviors. This can be done by helping employees to identify their passions at work and creating an exciting organizational vision that employees are motivated to pursue. As Starbucks recently sought to rekindle excitement for its brand, it brought employees together to retrain and recommit them to "the soul of the past." They watched a videotape of the company's founder say, "This is about the love and compassion and commitment that we all need to have for the customer."[55] Managers can lead for *choice* by empowering employees and delegating meaningful assignments and tasks. Managers can enhance a sense of *competence* by supporting and coaching their employees. At its employee retraining sessions, Starbucks strengthened choice and competence by emphasizing the barista's role in crafting drinks by, for example, pouring espresso into shot glasses to examine its color, rather than relying on automation to get the product just right. Employees practiced their technique and discussed ways to improve the quality of their drinks.[56] Finally, managers can increase employees' sense of *progress* by monitoring and rewarding them. On-the-spot incentives are a useful way to reward a broader-based group of employees. "If an employee's performance has been exceptional—such as filling in for a sick colleague, perhaps, or working nights or weekends or cutting costs for the company—the employer may reward the worker with a one-time bonus of $50, $100, or $500 shortly after the noteworthy actions."[57]

# Job Satisfaction

An individual's work motivation is related to his or her job satisfaction, which in turn is associated with employee performance and ultimately customer satisfaction.[58]

**Job satisfaction** is an affective or emotional response toward various facets of one's job. This definition means job satisfaction is not a unitary concept. Rather, a person can be relatively satisfied with one aspect of his or her job and dissatisfied with one or more other aspects. The Hands-On Exercise on page 160, for instance, assesses your satisfaction with recognition, compensation, and supervision. Please take a moment now to determine how satisfied you are with three aspects of your present or most recent job, and then use the norms to compare your score.[59] How do you feel about your job?

> **job satisfaction**
> **An affective or emotional response to one's job.**

> learning objective **5**
> Discuss the causes and consequences of job satisfaction.

Research revealed that job satisfaction varied across countries. A study of 9,300 adults in 39 countries identified the percentage of workers who said they were "very satisfied with their jobs." The top five countries were Denmark (61%), India (urban middle and upper class only; 55%), Norway (54%), United States (50%), and Ireland (49%). Experts suggest that job satisfaction is highest in Denmark because labor and management have a great working relationship. The bottom five countries were Estonia (11%), China (11%), Czech Republic (10%), Ukraine (10%), and Hungary

# How Satisfied Are You with Your Present Job?

| | Very<br>Dissatisfied | | | | Very<br>Satisfied |
|---|---|---|---|---|---|
| 1. The way I am noticed when I do a good job | 1 | 2 | 3 | 4 | 5 |
| 2. The recognition I get for the work I do | 1 | 2 | 3 | 4 | 5 |
| 3. The praise I get for doing a good job | 1 | 2 | 3 | 4 | 5 |
| 4. How my pay compares with that for similar jobs in other companies | 1 | 2 | 3 | 4 | 5 |
| 5. My pay and the amount of work I do | 1 | 2 | 3 | 4 | 5 |
| 6. How my pay compares with that of other workers | 1 | 2 | 3 | 4 | 5 |
| 7. The way my boss handles employees | 1 | 2 | 3 | 4 | 5 |
| 8. The way my boss takes care of complaints brought to him/her by employees | 1 | 2 | 3 | 4 | 5 |
| 9. The personal relationship between my boss and his/her employees | 1 | 2 | 3 | 4 | 5 |

Total score for satisfaction with recognition (add questions 1–3), compensation (add questions 4–6), and supervision (add questions 7–9).

Comparative norms for each dimension of job satisfaction are: Total score of 3–6 = Low job satisfaction; 7–11 = Moderate satisfaction; 12 and above = High satisfaction.

SOURCE: Adapted from D J Weiss, R V Dawis, G W England, and L H Lofquist, Manual for the *Minnesota Satisfaction Questionnaire* (Minneapolis: Industrial Relations Center, University of Minnesota, 1967). Used with permission of Vocational Psychology Research, University of Minnesota.

(9%). Why do Hungarian employees indicate the lowest job satisfaction? An average monthly salary of $302 and poor labor management relations are two possible causes.[60] OB researchers have identified other causes of job satisfaction and dissatisfaction.

# The Causes of Job Satisfaction

Five predominant models of job satisfaction specify its causes. They are need fulfillment, discrepancy, value attainment, equity, and dispositional/genetic components. A brief review of these models will provide insight into the complexity of this seemingly simple concept.[61]

**Need Fulfillment** These models propose that satisfaction is determined by the extent to which the characteristics of a job allow an individual to fulfill his or her needs. For example, a recent survey by the Society for Human Resource Management asked employees to choose the aspects of their job that were very important to their job satisfaction. Their top four choices were compensation, benefits, job security, and work/life balance—all directly related to employees' ability to meet a variety of basic needs.[62] Although these models generated a great degree of controversy, it is generally accepted that need fulfillment is correlated with job satisfaction.[63]

**Discrepancies**   These models propose that satisfaction is a result of met expectations. **Met expectations** represent the difference between what an individual expects to receive from a job, such as good pay and promotional opportunities, and what he or she actually receives. When expectations are greater than what is received, a person will be dissatisfied. In contrast, this model predicts the individual will be satisfied when he or she attains outcomes above and beyond expectations. A meta-analysis of 31 studies that included 17,241 people demonstrated that met expectations were significantly related to job satisfaction.[64] Many companies use employee attitude or opinion surveys to assess employees' expectations and concerns. Joanne G Sujansky, founder of KEYGroup, which provides speakers on leadership topics, says it's also important to give prospective employees honest information about the type of organization for which they will be working. Sujansky advises, "If your culture isn't quite where you'd like it to be, tell your new hires about the type of company you are striving to become. Tell them how you are going to get there, and how they can help you get there."[65]

> **met expectations**
>
> The extent to which one receives what he or she expects from a job.

Methodist Hospital System instituted a program for employees to volunteer their time to spend with terminal patients. How would this program help to achieve a sense of value attainment within the hospital?

**Value Attainment**   The idea underlying **value attainment** is that satisfaction results from the perception that a job allows for fulfillment of an individual's important work values.[66] In general, research consistently supports the prediction that value fulfillment is positively related to job satisfaction.[67] Managers can thus enhance employee satisfaction by structuring the work environment and its associated rewards and recognition to reinforce employees' values.

**Equity**   In this model, satisfaction is a function of how "fairly" an individual is treated at work. Satisfaction results from one's perception that work outcomes, relative to inputs, compare favorably with a significant other's outcomes/inputs. A meta-analysis involving 190 studies and 64,757 people supported this model. Employees' perceptions of being treated fairly at work were highly related to overall job satisfaction.[68] Managers thus are encouraged to monitor employees' fairness perceptions and to interact with employees in such a way that they feel equitably treated. Chapter 7 explores this promising model in more detail.

> **value attainment**
>
> The extent to which a job allows fulfillment of one's work values.

**Dispositional/Genetic Components**   Have you ever noticed that some of your coworkers or friends appear to be satisfied across a variety of job circumstances, whereas others always seem dissatisfied? This model of satisfaction attempts to explain this pattern.[69] Specifically, the dispositional/genetic model is based on the belief that job satisfaction is partly a function of both personal traits and genetic factors. As such, this model implies that stable individual differences are just as important in explaining job satisfaction as are characteristics of the work environment. Although only a few studies have tested these propositions, results support a positive, significant relationship between personal traits and job satisfaction over time periods ranging from 2 to 50 years.[70] Genetic factors also were found to significantly predict life satisfaction, well-being, and general job satisfaction.[71] Overall, researchers estimate that 30% of an individual's job satisfaction is associated with dispositional and genetic components.[72]

# Major Correlates and Consequences of Job Satisfaction

This area has significant managerial implications because thousands of studies have examined the relationship between job satisfaction and other organizational variables. Because it is impossible to examine them all, we will consider a subset of the more important variables from the standpoint of managerial relevance.

Table 6–1 summarizes the pattern of results. The relationship between job satisfaction and these other variables is either positive or negative. The strength of the relationship ranges from weak (very little relationship) to strong. Strong relationships imply that managers can significantly influence the variable of interest by increasing job satisfaction. Let us now consider several of the key correlates of job satisfaction.

**Motivation**    A recent meta-analysis of nine studies and 1,739 workers revealed a significant positive relationship between motivation and job satisfaction. Because satisfaction with supervision also was significantly correlated with motivation, managers are advised to consider how their behavior affects employee satisfaction.[73] Managers can potentially enhance employees' motivation through various attempts to increase job satisfaction.

**Job Involvement**    Job involvement represents the extent to which an individual is personally involved with his or her work role. A meta-analysis involving 27,925 individuals from 87 different studies demonstrated that job involvement was moderately related with job satisfaction.[74] Managers are thus encouraged to foster satisfying work environments in order to fuel employees' job involvement.

**TABLE 6–1**    Correlates of Job Satisfaction

| Variables Related with Satisfaction | Direction of Relationship | Strength of Relationship |
| --- | --- | --- |
| Motivation | Positive | Moderate |
| Job involvement | Positive | Moderate |
| Organizational commitment | Positive | Moderate |
| Organizational citizenship behavior | Positive | Moderate |
| Absenteeism | Negative | Weak |
| Tardiness | Negative | Weak |
| Withdrawal cognitions | Negative | Strong |
| Turnover | Negative | Moderate |
| Heart disease | Negative | Moderate |
| Perceived stress | Negative | Strong |
| Pro-union voting | Negative | Moderate |
| Job performance | Positive | Moderate |
| Life satisfaction | Positive | Moderate |
| Mental health | Positive | Moderate |

**Organizational Commitment**    Organizational commitment reflects the extent to which an individual identifies with an organization and is committed to its goals. A meta-analysis of 879 studies and 490,624 individuals uncovered a significant and moderate relationship between organizational commitment and satisfaction.[75] Managers are advised to increase job satisfaction in order to elicit higher levels of commitment. In turn, higher commitment can facilitate higher productivity.

**Organizational Citizenship Behavior**    Organizational citizenship behaviors (OCBs) consist of employee behaviors that are beyond the call of duty. Examples include "such gestures as constructive statements about the department, expression of personal interest in the work of others, suggestions for improvement, training new people, respect for the spirit as well as the letter of housekeeping rules, care for organizational property, and punctuality and attendance well beyond standard or enforceable levels."[76] Managers certainly would like employees to exhibit these behaviors. A meta-analysis covering 7,031 people and 21 separate studies revealed a significant and moderately positive correlation between organizational citizenship behaviors and job satisfaction.[77] Moreover, additional research demonstrated that employees' citizenship behaviors were determined more by leadership and characteristics of the work environment than by an employee's personality.[78] It thus appears that managerial behavior significantly influences an employee's willingness to exhibit citizenship behaviors.

> **organizational citizenship behaviors (OCBs)**
>
> Employee behaviors that exceed work-role requirements.

This relationship is important to recognize because employees' OCBs were positively correlated with customer satisfaction, organizational commitment, and performance ratings.[79] Another recent study demonstrated a broader impact of OCBs on organizational effectiveness. Results revealed that the amount of OCBs exhibited by employees working in 28 regional restaurants was significantly associated with each restaurant's corporate profits one year later.[80] Because employees' perceptions of being treated fairly at work are related to their willingness to engage in OCBs, managers are encouraged to make and implement employee-related decisions in an equitable fashion. More is said about equity in Chapter 7. Managers also should be sure they are rewarding OCBs. For example, time spent helping others learn or making suggestions for improvement is time not available for job-specific duties. If the organization only rewards successful performance of job-specific duties, it is in effect discouraging people from engaging in OCBs.[81]

**Absenteeism**    Absenteeism is not always what it appears to be, and it can be costly. For example, a 2004 study of 305 human resource executives throughout the U.S. revealed that 35% of all absences are due to illness. The remaining 65% result from family issues (21%), personal needs (18%), entitlement mentality (14%), and stress (12%). While it is difficult to provide a precise estimate of the cost of absenteeism, findings from this study project it to be $660 per employee.[82] This would suggest that absenteeism costs $198,000 for a company with 300 employees. Imagine the costs for a company with 100,000 employees! Because of these costs, managers are constantly on the lookout for ways to reduce it. One recommendation has been to increase job satisfaction. If this is a valid recommendation, there should be a strong negative relationship (or negative correlation) between satisfaction and absenteeism. In other words, as satisfaction increases, absenteeism should decrease. A researcher tracked this prediction by synthesizing three separate meta-analyses containing a total of 74 studies. Results revealed a weak negative relationship between satisfaction and absenteeism.[83] It is unlikely, therefore, that managers will realize any significant decrease in absenteeism by increasing job satisfaction.

**Withdrawal Cognitions**    Although some people quit their jobs impulsively or in a fit of anger, most go through a process of thinking about whether or not they should quit. **Withdrawal cognitions** encapsulate this thought process by representing an individual's overall thoughts and feelings about quitting. What causes an individual to think about quitting his or her job? Job satisfaction is believed to be one of the most significant contributors. For example, a study of managers, salespersons, and auto mechanics from a national automotive retail store chain demonstrated that job dissatisfaction caused employees to begin the process of thinking about quitting. In turn, withdrawal cognitions had a greater impact on employee turnover than job satisfaction in this sample.[84] Results from this study imply that managers can indirectly help to reduce employee turnover by enhancing employee job satisfaction.

**withdrawal cognitions**

**Overall thoughts and feelings about quitting a job**

**Turnover**    Recent statistics show that turnover is on the rise for managers, salespeople, manufacturing workers, and chief financial officers.[85] This is a problem because turnover disrupts organizational continuity and is very costly. Costs of turnover fall into two categories: separation costs and replacement costs.

> Separation costs may include severance pay, costs associated with an exit interview, out-placement fees, and possible litigation costs, particularly for involuntary separation. Replacement costs are the well-known costs of a hire, including sourcing expenses, HR processing costs for screening and assessing candidates, the time spent by hiring managers interviewing candidates, travel and relocation expenses, signing bonuses, if applicable, and orientation and training costs.[86]

Experts estimate that the cost of turnover for an hourly employee is roughly 30% of annual salary, whereas the cost can range up to 150% of yearly salary for professional employees.[87]

Although there are various things a manager can do to reduce employee turnover, many of them revolve around attempts to improve employees' job satisfaction. This trend is supported by results from a meta-analysis of 67 studies covering 24,556 people. Job satisfaction obtained a moderate negative relationship with employee turnover.[88] Given the strength of this relationship, managers are advised to try to reduce employee turnover by increasing employee job satisfaction.

**Perceived Stress**    Stress can have very negative effects on organizational behavior and an individual's health. Stress is positively related to absenteeism, turnover, coronary heart disease, and viral infections. Based on a meta-analysis of seven studies covering 2,659 individuals, Table 6–1 reveals that perceived stress has a strong, negative relationship with job satisfaction.[89] It is hoped that managers would attempt to reduce the negative effects of stress by improving job satisfaction.

**Job Performance**    One of the biggest controversies within OB research centers on the relationship between job satisfaction and job performance. Although researchers have identified seven different ways in which these variables are related, the dominant beliefs are either that satisfaction causes performance or performance causes satisfaction.[90] A team of researchers recently attempted to resolve this controversy through a meta-analysis of data from 312 samples involving 54,417 individuals.[91]

There were two key findings from this study. First, job satisfaction and performance are moderately related. This is an important finding because it supports the belief that employee job satisfaction is a key work attitude managers should consider when attempting to increase employees' job performance. Second, the relationship between job satisfaction and performance is much more complex than originally thought. It is not as simple as satisfaction causing performance or performance causing satisfaction. Rather, researchers now believe both variables indirectly influence each other through a host of individual differences and work-environment characteristics.[92] There is one additional consideration to keep in mind regarding the relationship between job satisfaction and job performance.

Researchers believe the relationship between satisfaction and performance is understated due to incomplete measures of individual-level performance. For example, if performance ratings used in past research did not reflect the actual interactions and interdependencies at work, inaccurate measures of performance served to lower the reported correlations between satisfaction and performance. Examining the relationship between *aggregate* measures of job satisfaction and organizational performance is one solution to correct this problem.[93] In support of these ideas, a team of researchers conducted a recent meta-analysis of 7,939 business units in 36 companies. Results uncovered significant positive relationships between business-unit-level employee satisfaction and business-unit outcomes of customer satisfaction, productivity, profit, employee turnover, and accidents.[94] It thus appears managers can positively affect a variety of important organizational outcomes, including performance, by increasing employee job satisfaction.

# Motivational Challenges

As organizations seek to foster job satisfaction and motivate employees to contribute to goals, they often run into two motivation-related challenges: counterproductive work behavior and conflicts between work and family life.

# Counterproductive Work Behavior

**learning objective** 6

Identify the causes of counterproductive work behavior and measures to prevent it.

In our discussion of job satisfaction, we noted that an absence of satisfaction may be associated with some types of undesirable behavior, such as absenteeism and employee turnover. These costly behaviors, along with some that are even more disturbing, are part of a category of behavior known as **counterproductive work behaviors (CWBs),** types of behavior that harm employees and the organization as a whole. CWBs "include but are not limited to theft, white collar crime, absenteeism, tardiness, drug and alcohol abuse, disciplinary problems, accidents, sabotage, sexual harassment, and violence."[95] A well-publicized example involves an executive secretary at the Coca-Cola Company who approached PepsiCo executives with an offer of trade secrets in exchange for cash. PepsiCo reported the secretary to Coca-Cola and government officials, she was fired, and eventually a federal judge sentenced her to eight years in prison.[96]

> **counterproductive work behaviors (CWBs)**
>
> Types of behavior that harm employees and the organization as a whole.

**Mistreatment of Others**  Some forms of CWBs involve mistreatment of coworkers, subordinates, or even customers. For example, employees engage in harassment, bullying, or blatant unfairness. Unfortunately, in a recent survey of U.S. employees, 45% said they have had a boss who was abusive.[97] Abuse by supervisors is especially toxic because employees report that when they feel they have been intimidated, humiliated, or undermined by an abusive supervisor, they are more likely to retaliate with counterproductive behavior aimed at the supervisor or their coworkers.[98] This type of response is especially likely when the organization does not provide channels through which employees can complain and find a resolution to the problem of mistreatment.[99]

**Violence at Work** Terrifying images of the shootings at Virginia Tech and Northern Illinois University have brought home the urgency of protecting people in organizations from sudden acts of violence committed by insiders or outsiders. Often, coworkers are first to notice that an employee explodes in anger or seems depressed or troubled. Psychiatrist and consultant Roger Brunswick says, "Violence rarely begins with someone walking in and shooting others. Violence usually builds slowly and starts with bullying, intimidation and threats."[100] A first line of defense should be for the organization to set up and publicize how employees can report troubling behavior to their supervisor or human resource department. Pitney Bowes set up a hotline that employees can call anonymously to report any concerns, and it has trained managers in identifying signs that something is wrong with an employee.[101]

**Causes and Prevention of CWBs** Employers obviously want to prevent CWBs, so they need to know the causes of such behavior. A study that followed the work behaviors of more than 900 young adults for 23 years found that a diagnosis of conduct disorder in adolescence was associated with CWBs, but criminal convictions before entering the workforce were not associated with CWBs.[102] Personality traits and job conditions also could make CWBs more likely. For example, young adults who scored higher on compulsion to adhere to norms, control their impulses, and avoid hostility tended not to use CWBs. They also were less likely to engage in CWBs if they had satisfying jobs that offered autonomy—and more likely to engage in CWBs if they had more resource power (such as more people to supervise). Intelligence may play a role, too. A study of applicants for law enforcement jobs found that higher scores for cognitive ability were associated with fewer reports of CWBs such as violence and destruction of property after candidates were hired.[103]

These findings suggest the following implications for management:

- Organizations can limit CWBs by hiring individuals who are less prone to engage in this type of behavior. Cognitive ability is associated with many measures of success, so it is a logical quality to screen for in hiring decisions. Personality tests also may be relevant.

- Organizations should ensure they are motivating desired behaviors and not CWBs, for example, by designing jobs that promote satisfaction and by preventing abusive supervision. A study of 265 restaurants found that CWBs were greater in restaurants where employees reported abuse by supervisors and where managers had more employees to supervise.[104] CWBs in these restaurants were associated with lower profits and lower levels of customer satisfaction, so adequate staffing and management development could not only make employees' lives more pleasant but also improve the bottom line.

- If an employee does engage in CWBs, the organization should respond quickly and appropriately, defining the specific behaviors that are unacceptable and the requirements for acceptable behavior.[105] Chapter 8 describes guidelines for effective feedback.

# Work versus Family Life Conflict

**learning objective** **7**
Describe the values model of work–family conflict.

Motivation is not independent of an employee's work environment or personal life. For example, your desire to study for your next OB test is jointly affected by how much you like the course and the state of your health at the time you are studying. It is very hard to study when you have a bad cold or the flu. Because of the dynamic relationships between motivation and work–family relationships, understanding ways to manage work–family relationships will increase your understanding about how to motivate others as well as yourself.

A complex web of demographic and economic factors makes the balancing act between job and life very challenging for most of us. Demographically, there are more women in the workforce, more dual-income families, more single working parents, and an aging population that gives mid-career employees child care or elder care responsibilities, or both. On the economic front, years of downsizing and corporate cost-cutting have given employees heavier workloads. Meanwhile, an important trend was recently documented in a unique 25-year study of values in the United States: "employees have become less convinced that work should be an important part of one's life or that working hard makes one a better person."[106] Something has to give in this collision of trends. More men and women are asking that some of the concessions come from work, for example, less travel and more family time.[107] Eric Sonntag left his job as a management circulation director altogether for what he thought would be a year and a half; after a difficult job hunt, he found another job at 20% less pay and says the decision "set my career back half a decade." Psychologist Eileen Kennedy-Moore chose to forgo a fast-paced academic career in favor of writing books and running a small clinical practice so that she would have more time for her four children. Although her career path is less prestigious than it might have been, it has provided its own measure of success in terms of published books, speaking engagements, and clients for her practice.

In this section, we try to better understand work versus family life conflict by introducing a values-based model and discussing organizational responses to work–family issues.

**A Values-Based Model of Work–Family Conflict**    Pamela L Perrewé and Wayne A Hochwarter constructed the model in Figure 6–5 (see page 169). On the left, we see one's general life values feeding into one's family-related values and work-related values. Family values involve enduring beliefs about the importance of family and who should play key family roles (e.g., child rearing, housekeeping, and income earning). Work values center on the relative importance of work and career goals in one's life. *Value similarity* relates to the degree of consensus among family members about family values. When a housewife launches a business venture despite her husband's desire to be the sole breadwinner, lack of family value similarity causes work–family conflict. *Value congruence,* on the other hand, involves the amount of value agreement between employee and employer. If, for example, refusing to go on a business trip to stay home for a child's birthday is viewed as disloyalty to the company, lack of value congruence can trigger work–family conflict.

In turn, "work–family conflict can take two distinct forms: work interference with family and family interference with work."[108] For example, suppose two managers in the same department have daughters playing on the same soccer team. One manager misses the big soccer game to attend a last-minute department meeting; the other manager skips the meeting to attend the game. Both may experience work–family conflict, but for different reasons.

## Helping Employees Live by Their Values

Today, as workers address the challenges of careers, relationships with family and friends, and various personal interests, many are choosing to have a "kaleidoscope" career that is dynamic—changing along with their abilities and needs. As they do so, they look for work that is authentic (consistent with their values and abilities), allows balance among conflicting demands, and provides a stimulating level of challenge. Companies can support these desires—and retain these workers—with work–life programs aimed at authenticity, balance, and challenge.

Ways to support authenticity include paid sabbaticals so that employees can pursue personal goals, wellness programs, career coaching, opportunities to participate in socially responsible activities, and training in life skills such as negotiating.

Ways to support balance include flexible work hours, phased retirement, child care benefits, leave for parenting and other family needs, and job reentry programs for employees who took time away from work.

Ways to support challenge include employee empowerment, mentoring programs, career development, training in technology applications, and rewards based on accomplishments rather than face time.

SOURCE: Based on S E Sullivan and L A Mainiero, "Benchmarking Ideas for Fostering Family-Friendly Workplaces," *Organizational Dynamics*, 2007, pp 45–62.

The last two boxes in the model—value attainment and job and life satisfaction—are a package deal. Satisfaction tends to be higher for those who live according to their values and lower for those who do not. For some ideas on how organizations can enable employees to get to this happy situation, see Skills & Best Practices. Overall, this model reflects much common sense. How does *your* life track through the model? Sadly, it is a painful trip for many these days.

**Organizational Response to Work–Family Issues** A study that investigated the experiences of telephone call center representatives found that, as expected, they were less satisfied with their work–life balance if they worked longer hours. However, they were more satisfied with balancing the two when they had some control over their work hours and when their jobs were more complex.[109] These relationships follow from the values-based model, as well as the impact of autonomy on satisfaction. Similarly, a group of top female executives discussed how using technology to stay in touch at all hours of the day or night can be either an aid to flexibility or a source of added work–life conflict, depending on whether employees feel free to send and reply to messages at the times that are most convenient for them.[110] So far, most organizations have addressed work–life issues mainly by offering scheduling flexibility and by making it easier to stay at work, thanks to programs such as child-care services, dry-cleaning services, concierge services, ATM at work, and stress reduction programs.[111] In addition, companies help with work–life balance when they offer paid time off for maternity leave, illness, or to care for a sick relative (such paid leave is required by law in most countries and voluntary in the United States).[112]

Although these programs are positively received by employees, experts now believe that such efforts are partially misguided because they focus on balancing work–family issues rather than integrating them. Balance is needed for opposites, and work and family are not opposites. Rather, our work and personal lives should be a well-integrated whole.[113]

What does integration look like in practice? Melanie Healey, group president of Procter & Gamble's Global Feminine and Health Care division, exemplifies one possible answer. Born in Rio de Janeiro, Brazil, Healey has had a career with international responsibility in her native country as well as in Mexico, Venezuela, and the United States. This challenging work not only enabled her to achieve goals for herself but also helped her realize her dream of allowing her children to experience various cultures.[114]

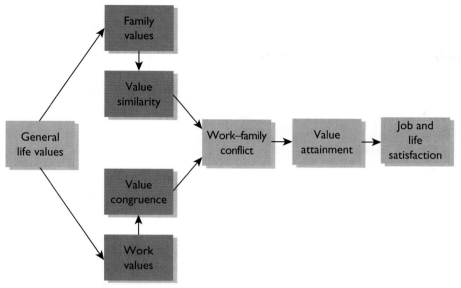

FIGURE 6–5
A Values
Model of
Work–Family
Conflict

SOURCE: From Pamela L Perrewé and Wayne A Hochwarter, "Can We Really Have It All? The Attainment of Work and Family Values," *Current Directions in Psychological Science*, February 2001 Copyright © Association for Psychological Science. Reprinted with permission of Blackwell Publishing. © American Psychological Society.

# key terms

core job characteristics   152
counterproductive work behaviors
  (CWBs)   165
extrinsic motivation   155
hygiene factors   150
intrinsic motivation   151
job design   147
job enlargement   148
job enrichment   151
job rotation   148

job satisfaction   159
met expectations   161
motivation   144
motivators   149
need for achievement   146
need for affiliation   147
need for power   147
needs   146
organizational citizenship behaviors
  (OCBs)   163

repetitive motion disorders
  (RMDs)   154
sense of choice   157
sense of competence   157
sense of meaningfulness   156
sense of progress   157
value attainment   161
withdrawal cognitions   164

# chapter summary

- *Discuss the job performance model of motivation.* Individual inputs and job context variables are the two key categories of factors that influence motivation. In turn, motivation leads to motivated behaviors, which then affect performance.

- *Contrast Maslow's and McClelland's need theories.* Two well-known need theories of motivation are Maslow's need hierarchy and McClelland's need theory. Maslow's notion of a prepotent or stair-step hierarchy of five levels of needs has not stood up well under research. McClelland believes that motivation and performance vary according to the strength of an individual's need for achievement. High achievers prefer moderate risks and situations where they can control their own destiny. Top managers should have a high need for power coupled with a low need for affiliation.

- *Describe the mechanistic, motivational, biological, and perceptual-motor approaches to job design.* The mechanistic approach is based on industrial engineering and scientific management and focuses on increasing efficiency, flexibility, and employee productivity. Motivational approaches aim to improve employees' affective and attitudinal reactions and behavioral outcomes. Job enlargement, job enrichment, and a contingency approach called the job characteristics model are motivational approaches to job design. The biological approach focuses on designing the work environment to reduce employees' physical strain, effort, fatigue, and health complaints. The perceptual-motor approach emphasizes the reliability of work outcomes.

- *Review the four intrinsic rewards underlying intrinsic motivation, and discuss how managers can cultivate intrinsic motivation in others.* Intrinsic motivation is driven by the opportunity rewards of a sense of meaningfulness and a sense of choice, and the accomplishment rewards of a sense of competence and a sense of progress. Senses of meaningfulness and progress are driven by the purpose underlying task completion, whereas senses of choice and competence revolve around the tasks one performs at work. Managers specifically lead for meaningfulness, choice, competence, and progress by inspiring and modeling, empowering and delegating, supporting and coaching, and monitoring and rewarding, respectively.

- *Discuss the causes and consequences of job satisfaction.* Job satisfaction is an affective or emotional response toward various facets of one's job. Five models of job satisfaction specify its causes. They are need fulfillment, discrepancy, value attainment, equity, and trait/genetic components. Job satisfaction has been correlated with hundreds of consequences. Table 6–1 summarizes the pattern of results found for a subset of the more important variables.

- *Identify the causes of counterproductive work behavior and measures to prevent it.* Counterproductive work behaviors (CWBs) may result from personal characteristics coupled with a lack of autonomy and job satisfaction. CWBs are more likely in situations where supervisors are abusive and responsible for many employees. Organizations can limit CWBs by hiring individuals with appropriate cognitive skills and personality traits. They can design jobs to promote satisfaction. They can develop managers to supervise effectively without abuse and should deliver immediate feedback and discipline if anyone engages in CWBs.

- *Describe the values model of work–family conflict.* General life values determine one's values about family and work. Work–family conflict can occur when there is a lack of value similarity with family members. Likewise, work–family conflict can occur when one's own work values are not congruent with the company's values. When someone does not attain his or her values because of work–family conflicts, job or life satisfaction, or both, can suffer.

# discussion questions

1. Returning to the chapter opening case, what are causes of Lori Miller, Frank Gastner, and Monique Huston's motivation? Explain.

2. Which of the four types of job design is most likely to be used in the future? Explain your rationale.

3. To what extent is your behavior and performance as a student a function of intrinsic and extrinsic motivation? Explain.

4. Have you ever observed someone exhibiting counterproductive work behavior? What was the cause and consequence of this behavior?

5. What are the three most valuable lessons about employee motivation that you have learned from this chapter?

# ethical dilemma

## How Would You Handle a Confrontation between an Employee and a Customer?

Mala Amarsingh, a JetBlue Airways Corp attendant, was standing in the Las Vegas airport in June, waiting to hitch a ride to New York to start her shift. An intoxicated female passenger approached her, started cursing, threatened to beat her up, and then spit in her face. The flight attendant says she lost her cool, cursed back at the passenger, and later was terminated by the airline for "inappropriate behavior." JetBlue won't comment about personnel matters but says "Customers traveling today are more frustrated by delays and perceived service lapses."

Ms Amarsingh thinks "uniformed flight attendants are walking targets for passenger frustrations," which "absolutely" have gotten worse in her more than six years in the job.[115]

**Assume that you are a vice president of JetBlue and that you just became aware of the situation involving Ms Amarsingh. What would you do?**

**1.** Nothing. Ms Amarsingh's behavior violated corporate policy about the treatment of customers, so she deserved to be fired. Changing the decision would set a bad precedent for other employees.

**2.** Acknowledge that the employee's behavior violates corporate policy but hire her back given the extenuating circumstances. Provide Ms Amarsingh with back pay for any lost time.

**3.** Hire the employee back and use company resources to sue the customer. The customer committed assault and battery by purposely spitting in Ms Amarsingh's face. Rehiring Ms Amarsingh would send a clear message that you care about your employees and that JetBlue managers will not allow their employees to be assaulted.

**4.** Invent other options.

---

If you're looking for additional study materials, be sure to check out the Online Learning Center at

### www.mhhe.com/kinickiob4e

for more information and interactivities that correspond to this chapter.

# Motivation II: Equity, Expectancy, and Goal Setting

## LEARNING OBJECTIVES

**After reading the material in this chapter, you should be able to:**

1. Discuss the role of perceived inequity in employee motivation.

2. Describe the practical lessons derived from equity theory.

3. Explain Vroom's expectancy theory.

4. Describe the practical implications of expectancy theory.

5. Identify five practical lessons to be learned from goal-setting research.

6. Specify issues that should be addressed before implementing a motivational program.

# many CEOs are not paid according to the principles of expectancy theory

You might suppose that the stars are in near-perfect alignment for major reform of CEO pay. The mammoth pay and disastrous performance of Countrywide Financial's Angelo Mozilo, Citigroup's Chuck Prince, and Merrill Lynch's Stan O'Neal should be enough to make the public furious. Each CEO departed with $100-million-plus compensation after misadventures with subprime mortgages. Now add the economic slowdown to the mix; ordinary Americans are worried about making ends meet while failed pooh-bahs rake it in. Then throw in one more element—a presidential election. Put it all together, and how could change *not* be imminent?

The answer is that whatever remedies reformers enact, corporate boards can always find a way to pay the boss whatever they like. Over the past 25 years CEO pay has risen regardless of the economic or political climate. It rises faster than corporate profits, economic growth, or average workforce compensation. A recent study by the compensation consulting firm DolmatConnell & Partners found that CEO pay in the companies of the Dow Jones industrials increased at a blowout 15.1% annual rate over the past decade.

A more sensible alternative to the current compensation system would require CEOs to own a lot of company stock. If the stock is given to the boss, his salary and bonus should be docked to reflect its value. As for bonuses, they should be based on improving a company's cash earnings relative to its cost of capital, not to more easily manipulated measures like earnings per share. They should not be capped, but they should be banked—unavailable to the CEO for some period of years—to prevent short-term gaming.

To see why that is unlikely to happen, check out this spring's crop of corporate proxy statements, which are still being filed. You'll note that this year many companies are reporting the specific performance targets on which CEO pay is based—saying not just that pay is based partly on free cash flow, for example, but reporting the amount that must be achieved. Companies are doing that because the SEC is making them. But by wangling pay formulas in a dozen ways, they can still pay CEOs as crazily as they like. Look, for example, at one of America's legendary pay abusers, Occidental Petroleum. Its latest proxy is full of impressive-looking targets and formulas, but the bottom line is that the company has consistently paid CEO Ray Irani huge sums ($110 million for 2007) during his 17 years at the top, regardless of performance, which has mostly been terrible.[1]

**CEO Ray Irani of Occidental Petroleum has been paid millions of dollars despite consistently poor performance. This practice is inconsistent with the principles of Expectancy Theory.**

**FOR DISCUSSION**

**Do you think that CEOs' pay should be tied to corporate performance? Explain. For an interpretation of this case and additional comments, visit our Online Learning Center at**

**www.mhhe.com/kinickiob4e**

# Adams's Equity Theory of Motivation

Defined generally, **equity theory** is a model of motivation that explains how people strive for *fairness* and *justice* in social exchanges or give-and-take relationships. Equity theory is based on cognitive dissonance theory, developed by social psychologist Leon Festinger in the 1950s.[2]

**equity theory**

Holds that motivation is a function of fairness in social exchanges.

According to Festinger's theory, people are motivated to maintain consistency between their cognitive beliefs and their behavior. Perceived inconsistencies create cognitive dissonance (or psychological discomfort), which, in turn, motivates corrective action. For example, a cigarette smoker who sees a heavy-smoking relative die of lung cancer probably would be motivated to quit smoking if he or she attributes the death to smoking. Accordingly, when victimized by unfair social exchanges, our resulting cognitive dissonance prompts us to correct the situation. Corrective action may range from a slight change in attitude or behavior to stealing to the extreme case of trying to harm someone. For example, researchers have demonstrated that people attempt to "get even" for perceived injustices by using either direct (e.g., theft, sabotage, violence, or absenteeism) or indirect (e.g., intentionally working slowly, lower motivation, being less cooperative, or displaying less organizational citizenship behavior) examples of counter productive work behaviors (CWB), which were discussed in the previous chapter.[3]

Psychologist J Stacy Adams pioneered application of the equity principle to the workplace. Central to understanding Adams's equity theory of motivation is an awareness of key components of the individual–organization exchange relationship. This relationship is pivotal in the formation of employees' perceptions of equity and inequity.

## The Individual–Organization Exchange Relationship

Adams points out that two primary components are involved in the employee–employer exchange, *inputs* and *outcomes*. An employee's inputs, for which he or she expects a just return, include education/training, skills, creativity, seniority, age, personality traits, effort expended, and personal appearance. On the outcome side of the exchange, the organization provides such things as pay/bonuses, fringe benefits, challenging assignments, job security, promotions, status symbols, recognition, and participation in important decisions.[4] These outcomes vary widely, depending on one's organization and rank.

# Negative and Positive Inequity

On the job, feelings of inequity revolve around a person's evaluation of whether he or she receives adequate rewards to compensate for his or her contributive inputs. People perform these evaluations by comparing the perceived fairness of their employment exchange to that of relevant others. This comparative process, which is based on an equity norm, was found to generalize across countries.[5] People tend to compare themselves to other individuals with whom they have close interpersonal ties—such as friends—and/or to similar others—such as people performing the same job or individuals of the same gender or educational level—rather than dissimilar others. Consider, for example, the situation faced by two Houston firefighters, Alison Stein and Michelle McLeod. A few years ago, they got the highest scores on the exam to become arson investigators and were promoted to that job, becoming the Houston Fire Department's top-ranked female employees. But when they later applied for promotions to district chief, the rules had changed to place less emphasis on test scores and more on seniority. Stein and McLeod complained that the change was unfair to females in the department, which had not been hiring women two decades ago.[6] Do you agree with their qualifications emphasizing achievements or with the union's position that years of service should define the proper criteria?

Three different equity relationships are illustrated in Figure 7–1: equity, negative inequity, and positive inequity. Assume the two people in each of the equity relationships in Figure 7–1 have equivalent backgrounds (equal education, seniority, and so forth) and perform identical tasks. Only their hourly pay rates differ. Equity exists for an individual when his or her ratio of perceived outcomes to inputs is equal to the ratio of outcomes to inputs for a relevant coworker (see part A in Figure 7–1). Because equity is based on comparing *ratios* of outcomes to inputs, inequity will not necessarily be perceived just because someone else receives greater rewards. If the other person's additional outcomes are due to his or her greater inputs, a sense of equity may still exist. However, if the comparison person enjoys greater outcomes for similar inputs, **negative inequity** will be perceived (see part B in Figure 7–1). On the other hand, a person will experience **positive inequity** when his or her outcome to input ratio is greater than that of a relevant coworker (see part C in Figure 7–1).

## Dynamics of Perceived Inequity

Managers can derive practical benefits from Adams's equity theory by recognizing that (1) people have varying sensitivities to perceived equity and inequity and (2) inequity can be reduced in a variety of ways.

**Thresholds of Equity and Inequity**   Have you ever noticed that some people become very upset over the slightest inequity whereas others are not bothered at all? Research has shown that people respond differently to the same level of inequity due to an individual difference called equity sensitivity. **Equity sensitivity** reflects an individual's "different preferences for, tolerances for, and reactions to the level of equity associated with any given situation."[7] Equity sensitivity spans a continuum ranging from benevolents to sensitives to entitled.

*Benevolents* are people who have a higher tolerance for negative inequity. They are altruistic in the sense that they prefer their outcome/input ratio to be lower than ratios

**learning objective 1**

Discuss the role of perceived inequity in employee motivation.

**negative inequity**

Comparison in which another person receives greater outcomes for similar inputs.

**positive inequity**

Comparison in which another person receives lesser outcomes for similar inputs.

**equity sensitivity**

An individual's tolerance for negative and positive equity.

## FIGURE 7–1 │ Negative and Positive Inequity

**A. An Equitable Situation**                                    **B. Negative Inequity**

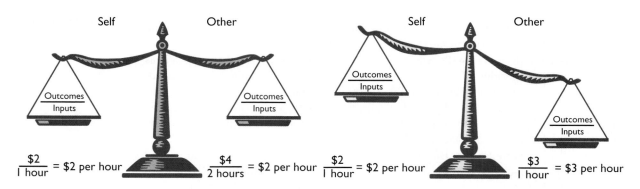

**C. Positive Inequity**

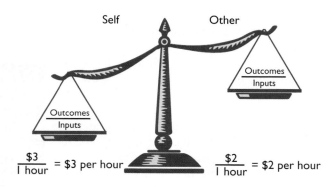

from comparison others. In contrast, equity *sensitives* are described as individuals who adhere to a strict norm of reciprocity and are quickly motivated to resolve both negative and positive inequity. Finally, *entitleds* have no tolerance for negative inequity. They actually expect to obtain greater output/input ratios than comparison others and become upset when this is not the case.[8]

**Reducing Inequity**   Equity ratios can be changed by attempting to alter one's outcomes or adjusting one's inputs. For example, negative inequity might be resolved by asking for a raise or a promotion (i.e., raising outputs) or by reducing inputs (i.e., working fewer hours or exerting less effort).[9] It also is important to note that equity can be restored by altering one's equity ratios behaviorally and/or cognitively. A cognitive strategy entails psychologically distorting perceptions of one's own or one's comparison person's outcomes and inputs (e.g., conclude that comparison other has more experience or works harder).

For example, consider how Peter Brockman adjusted his thinking and then his behavior when he perceived inequity while working for a high-tech company:

He witnessed a peer get a promotion to a job Mr. Brockman thought was well over [the peer's] head. Holy cow, he thought to himself, how did that happen?

At first it was a blow to his confidence, he says. "But then it helps it. I was emboldened." His colleague's success prompted him to start discussions with his boss that led to a promotion, 30% raise and options just three months later.[10]

First Brockman saw only the perceived inequity, but he restored equity by seeing that promotions were more readily available at his company than he had expected.

## Expanding the Concept of Equity: Organizational Justice

Beginning in the later 1970s, researchers began to expand the role of equity theory in explaining employee attitudes and behavior. This led to a domain of research called *organizational justice*. Organizational justice reflects the extent to which people perceive that they are treated fairly at work. This, in turn, led to the identification of three different components of organizational justice: distributive, procedural, and interactional.[11] **Distributive justice** reflects the perceived fairness of how resources and rewards are distributed or allocated. During the recent economic slowdown, some chief executives have turned down bonuses offered by their board of directors, but several have generated more goodwill and motivation by asking instead that their bonuses be distributed among employees. For example, after First American Corporation suffered a loss in a recent year, CEO Parker S Kennedy asked that his salary be cut and that his bonus of about $800,000 be added to employees' bonus pool.[12] This request showed not only a concern for whether Kennedy's own pay was fair compensation for his work but also concern for how the company's rewards are distributed among its employees.

**distributive justice**

The perceived fairness of how resources and rewards are distributed.

**Procedural justice** is defined as the perceived fairness of the process and procedures used to make allocation decisions. Research shows that positive perceptions of distributive and procedural justice are enhanced by giving employees a "voice" in decisions that affect them. Voice represents the extent to which employees who are affected by a decision can

**procedural justice**

The perceived fairness of the process and procedures used to make allocation decisions.

Whole Foods Market has over 270 stores in North America and the United Kingdom. The company's CEO, John Mackey (fourth from the left), has implemented a pay program that encourages equity among employees. He implemented a salary cap that limits the pay of top executives to 19 times the average full-time employee, and even reduced his own salary to $1. How do you think his decisions to cut his pay and cap executive salaries affect employee motivation?"

present relevant information about the decision to others. Voice is analogous to asking employees for their input into the decision-making process.

The last justice component, **interactional justice,** relates to the "quality of the interpersonal treatment people receive when procedures are implemented."[13]

**interactional justice**

**Extent to which people feel fairly treated when procedures are implemented.**

This form of justice does not pertain to the outcomes or procedures associated with decision making, but rather it focuses on whether or not people believe they are treated fairly when decisions are implemented. Fair interpersonal treatment necessitates that managers communicate truthfully and treat people with courtesy and respect. Consider the role of interactional justice in how a manager of information-management systems responded to being laid off by a New Jersey chemical company. The man gained access to the company's computer systems from home by using another executive's password and deleted critical inventory and personnel files. The sabotage ultimately caused $20 million in damage and postponed a public stock offering that had been in the works. Why would a former employee do something like this?

> An anonymous note that he wrote to the company president sheds light on his motive. "I have been loyal to the company in good and bad times for over 30 years," he wrote. "I was expecting a member of top management to come down from his ivory tower to face us with the layoff announcement, rather than sending the kitchen supervisor with guards to escort us off the premises like criminals. You will pay for your senseless behavior."[14]

This employee's direct retaliation against the company was caused by the insensitive manner—interactional justice—in which employees were notified about the layoffs.

## Practical Lessons from Equity Theory

**2** learning objective

Describe the practical lessons derived from equity theory.

Equity theory has at least nine important practical implications. First, equity theory provides managers with yet another explanation of how beliefs and attitudes affect job performance. According to this line of thinking, the best way to manage job behavior is to adequately understand underlying cognitive processes. Indeed, we are motivated powerfully to correct a situation when our ideas of fairness and justice are offended.

Second, research on equity theory emphasizes the need for managers to pay attention to employees' perceptions of what is fair and equitable. No matter how fair management thinks the organization's policies, procedures, and reward system are, each employee's *perception* of the equity of those factors is what counts. People respond positively when they perceive organizational and interpersonal justice and negatively when they do not. For example, employees were more likely to complete organizationally sponsored surveys when they felt a sense of procedural justice, and employees also reported greater insomnia when they experienced poor interactional justice.[15] Moreover, research demonstrates that employees' perceptions of distributive, procedural, and interactional justice are positively associated with job performance, job satisfaction, organizational commitment, and organizational citizenship behavior and negatively with intentions to quit.[16] Managers thus are encouraged to make hiring and promotion decisions on merit-based, job-related information. Moreover, because justice perceptions are influenced by the extent to which managers explain their decisions, managers are encouraged to explain the rationale behind their decisions. For some further practical advice, see Skills & Best Practices on page 179.

Third, managers benefit by allowing employees to participate in making decisions about important work outcomes. In general, employees' perceptions of procedural justice are enhanced when they have a voice in the decision-making process.[17] For example, employees were more satisfied with their performance appraisals and resultant outcomes when they had a "voice" during the appraisal review.[18] Fourth, employees should be given the opportunity to appeal decisions that affect their welfare. Being able to appeal a decision promotes the belief that management treats employees fairly.

Fifth, employees are more likely to accept and support organizational change when they believe it is implemented fairly and when it produces equitable outcomes.[19]

Sixth, managers can promote cooperation and teamwork among group members by treating them equitably. Research reveals that people are just as concerned with fairness in group settings as they are with their own personal interests.[20] Seventh, treating employees inequitably can lead to litigation and costly court settlements. Employees denied justice at work are more likely to file employee grievances, to seek arbitration, and to ultimately seek relief from the courts.[21] Even when discipline is necessary, managers can minimize this risk of retaliation by demonstrating the justice of their actions. A series of experiments with undergraduate students found that when outcomes were negative (as in the case of low pay and layoffs), the students were more likely to blame the outcome on the organizational authority if they believed procedural fairness was lacking.[22] In a work context, if managers cannot demonstrate that negative actions are done fairly, employees may be more likely to blame the organization—and thus to retaliate.

Eighth, employees' perceptions of justice are strongly influenced by the leadership behavior exhibited by their managers (leadership is discussed in Chapter 14).[23] It thus is important for managers to consider the justice-related implications of their decisions, actions, and public communications. This requirement is particularly important—and challenging—in light of a recent study in which employees were more likely to perceive interpersonal justice if their supervisor had positive feelings toward them.[24] Supervisors must therefore put extra effort toward justice if they find some employees more appealing than others.

Finally, managers should pay attention to the organization's climate for justice. For example, an organization's climate for justice was found to significantly influence employees' organizational citizenship behavior.[25] Researchers also believe that a

## Fair Pay

Retired General Electric CEO Jack Welch and business journalist Suzy Welch acknowledge that although most employers set out to pay their people fairly, employees often see their pay in a different light. Employees who think they contributed a lot but were rewarded just a little end up feeling not motivated but "confused, frustrated, even cynical." The Welches offer some ideas for improving employees' perception of fairness when it comes to pay:

- *Don't be a "skinflint."* If the organization isn't measuring up to industry norms for pay, employees will know it, and creativity and productivity will suffer. If times are really bad, you'll have to say so, but don't use that argument all the time.

- *Distinguish between fairness and equal treatment.* If some people work hard and produce a lot while others are coasting, it's not fair to give everyone the same reward—or to spread the pain of cutbacks equally in bad times.

- *Speak the truth.* Give employees accurate feedback about their performance so they know whether they deserve a big raise or bonus.

- *Link rewards to performance.* If one employee is a star performer, that employee should get a noticeably bigger reward. Not only is that policy likely to be perceived as fair, but it is also likely to get employees' attention and help the company hang on to people with star potential.

**SOURCE: Based on J Welch and S Welch, "Give Till It Doesn't Hurt,"** *BusinessWeek,* **January 31, 2008, www .businessweek.com.**

## Measuring Perceived Fair Interpersonal Treatment

**INSTRUCTIONS:** The following survey was designed to assess the extent to which you are treated fairly at your current job: If you are not working, use a past job or your role as a student to complete the survey. There is no right or wrong answer to the statements. Circle your answers by using the rating scale provided. After evaluating each of the survey statements, complete a total score and compare your total to the arbitrary norms.

| | Strongly Disagree | Disagree | Neither | Agree | Strongly Agree |
|---|---|---|---|---|---|
| 1. Employees are praised for good work. | 1 | 2 | 3 | 4 | 5 |
| 2. Supervisors do not yell at employees. | 1 | 2 | 3 | 4 | 5 |
| 3. Employees are trusted. | 1 | 2 | 3 | 4 | 5 |
| 4. Employees' complaints are dealt with effectively. | 1 | 2 | 3 | 4 | 5 |
| 5. Employees are treated with respect. | 1 | 2 | 3 | 4 | 5 |
| 6. Employees' questions and problems are responded to quickly. | 1 | 2 | 3 | 4 | 5 |
| 7. Employees are treated fairly. | 1 | 2 | 3 | 4 | 5 |
| 8. Employees' hard work is appreciated. | 1 | 2 | 3 | 4 | 5 |
| 9. Employees' suggestions are used. | 1 | 2 | 3 | 4 | 5 |
| 10. Employees are told the truth. | 1 | 2 | 3 | 4 | 5 |

Total score = _____

**ARBITRARY NORMS**

Very fair organization = 38–50
Moderately fair organization = 24–37
Unfair organization = 10–23

SOURCE: Adapted in part from M A Donovan, F Drasgow, and L J Munson, "The Perceptions of Fair Interpersonal Treatment Scale Development and Validation of a Measure of Interpersonal Treatment in the Workplace," *Journal of Applied Psychology*, October 1998, pp 683–92.

climate of justice can significantly influence the type of customer service provided by employees. In turn, this level of service is likely to influence customers' perceptions of "fair service" and their subsequent loyalty and satisfaction.

Managers can attempt to follow these practical implications by monitoring equity and justice perceptions through informal conversations, interviews, or attitude surveys. For example, researchers have developed and validated a host of surveys that can be used for this purpose. Please take a moment now to complete the Hands-On Exercise shown above. It contains part of a survey that was developed to measure employees' perceptions of fair interpersonal treatment. If you perceive your work organization as interpersonally unfair, you are probably dissatisfied and have contemplated quitting. In contrast, your organizational loyalty and attachment are likely greater if you believe you are treated fairly at work.

# Expectancy Theory of Motivation

**Expectancy theory** holds that people are motivated to behave in ways that produce desired combinations of expected outcomes. Perception plays a central role in expectancy theory because it emphasizes cognitive ability to anticipate likely consequences of behavior. Embedded in expectancy theory is the principle of hedonism. Hedonistic people strive to maximize their pleasure and minimize their pain. Generally, expectancy theory can be used to predict behavior in any situation in which a choice between two or more alternatives must be made. For instance, it can be used to predict whether to quit or stay at a job; whether to exert substantial or minimal effort at a task; and whether to major in management, computer science, accounting, marketing, psychology, or communication.

> **expectancy theory**
>
> Holds that people are motivated to behave in ways that produce valued outcomes.

This section explores Victor Vroom's version of expectancy theory. Understanding the cognitive processes underlying this theory can help managers develop organizational policies and practices that enhance employee motivation.

## Vroom's Expectancy Theory

Victor Vroom formulated a mathematical model of expectancy theory in his 1964 book *Work and Motivation*. Vroom's theory has been summarized as follows:

learning objective 3

Explain Vroom's expectancy theory.

> The strength of a tendency to act in a certain way depends on the strength of an expectancy that the act will be followed by a given consequence (or outcome) and on the value or attractiveness of that consequence (or outcome) to the actor.[26]

Motivation, according to Vroom, boils down to the decision of how much effort to exert in a specific task situation. This choice is based on a two-stage sequence of expectations (effort → performance and performance → outcome). First, motivation is affected by an individual's expectation that a certain level of effort will produce the intended performance goal. For example, if you do not believe increasing the amount of time you spend studying will significantly raise your grade on an exam, you probably will not study any harder than usual. Motivation also is influenced by the employee's perceived chances of getting various outcomes as a result of accomplishing his or her performance goal. Finally, individuals are motivated to the extent that they value the outcomes received.

Vroom used a mathematical equation to integrate these concepts into a predictive model of motivational force or strength. For our purposes, however, it is sufficient to define and explain the three key concepts within Vroom's model—*expectancy, instrumentality,* and *valence.*

**Expectancy** An **expectancy,** according to Vroom's terminology, represents an individual's belief that a particular degree of effort will be followed by a particular level of performance. In other words, it is an effort → performance expectation. Expectancies take the form of subjective probabilities. As you may recall from a course in statistics, probabilities range from zero to one. An expectancy of zero indicates effort has no anticipated impact on performance.

> **expectancy**
>
> Belief that effort leads to a specific level of performance.

For example, suppose you do not know how to type on a keyboard. No matter how much effort you exert, your perceived probability of typing 30 error-free words per minute likely would be zero. An expectancy of one suggests that performance is totally dependent on effort. If you decided to take a typing course as well as practice a couple of hours a day for a few weeks (high effort), you should be able to type 30 words per minute without any errors. In contrast, if you do not take a typing course and only practice an hour or two per week (low effort), there is a very low probability (say, a 20% chance) of being able to type 30 words per minute without any errors.

The following factors influence an employee's expectancy perceptions:

- Self-esteem.
- Self-efficacy.
- Previous success at the task.
- Help received from others.
- Information necessary to complete the task.
- Good materials and equipment to work with.[27]

**instrumentality**

**A performance → outcome perception.**

**Instrumentality**  An **instrumentality** is a performance → outcome perception. It represents a person's belief that a particular outcome is contingent on accomplishing a specific level of performance. Performance is instrumental when it leads to something else. For example, passing exams is instrumental to graduating from college.

Instrumentalities range from −1.0 to 1.0. An instrumentality of 1.0 indicates attainment of a particular outcome is totally dependent on task performance. An instrumentality of zero indicates there is no relationship between performance and receiving an outcome. For example, most companies link the number of vacation days to seniority, not job performance. Finally, an instrumentality of −1.0 reveals that high performance reduces the chance of obtaining an outcome while low performance increases the chance. For example, the more time you spend studying to get an A on an exam (high performance), the less time you will have for enjoying leisure activities. Similarly, as you lower the amount of time spent studying (low performance), you increase the amount of time that may be devoted to leisure activities.

The concept of instrumentality may help to explain why some employees are more willing than others to make suggestions for improvement. In general, if employees speak up to say there is a better way to get something done, some managers will be open-minded, while others typically ignore suggestions. When managers make a habit of trying out valid ideas, their behavior creates a positive instrumentality. A study of restaurant employees found that employees do indeed offer more suggestions when they have this type of leader.[28]

**valence**

**The value of a reward or outcome.**

**Valence**  As Vroom used the term, **valence** refers to the positive or negative value people place on outcomes. Valence mirrors our personal preferences. For example, most employees have a positive valence for receiving additional money or recognition. In contrast, being laid off or being ridiculed for making a suggestion would likely be negatively valent for most individuals. In Vroom's expectancy model, *outcomes* refer to different consequences that are contingent on performance, such as pay, promotions, or recognition. An outcome's valence depends on an individual's needs and can be measured for research purposes with scales ranging from a negative value to a positive value. For example, an individual's valence toward more recognition can be assessed on a scale ranging from −2 (very undesirable) to 0 (neutral) to +2 (very desirable).

## Vroom's Expectancy Theory in Action

Vroom's expectancy model of motivation can be used to analyze a real-life motivation program. Consider the following performance problem described by Frederick W Smith, founder and chief executive officer of Federal Express Corporation:

> . . . we were having a helluva problem keeping things running on time. The airplanes would come in, and everything would get backed up. We tried every kind of control mechanism that you could think of, and none of them worked. Finally, it became obvious that the underlying problem was that it was in the interest of the employees at the cargo terminal—they were college kids, mostly—to run late, because it meant that they made more money. So what we did was give them all a minimum guarantee and say, "Look, if you get through before a certain time, just go home, and you will have beat the system." Well, it was unbelievable. I mean, in the space of about 45 days, the place was way ahead of schedule. And I don't even think it was a conscious thing on their part.[29]

"My computer has the strangest virus. It bombards me with messages that say how wonderful you are and that you deserve a promotion."

Copyright © Ted Goff. Reprinted with permission.

How did Federal Express get its college-age cargo handlers to switch from low effort to high effort? According to Vroom's model, the student workers originally exerted low effort because they were paid on the basis of time, not output. It was in their best interest to work slowly and accumulate as many hours as possible. By offering to let the student workers *go home early if and when they completed their assigned duties,* Federal Express prompted high effort. This new arrangement created two positively valued outcomes: guaranteed pay plus the opportunity to leave early. The motivation to exert high effort became greater than the motivation to exert low effort.

# Research on Expectancy Theory and Managerial Implications

Many researchers have tested expectancy theory. In support of the theory, a meta-analysis of 77 studies indicated that expectancy theory significantly predicted performance, effort, intentions, preferences, and choice.[30] Another summary of 16 studies revealed that expectancy theory correctly predicted occupational or organizational choice 63.4% of the time; this was significantly better than chance predictions.[31]

**learning objective 4**

Describe the practical implications of expectancy theory.

Nonetheless, expectancy theory has been criticized for a variety of reasons. For example, the theory is difficult to test, and the measures used to assess expectancy, instrumentality, and valence have questionable validity.[32] In the final analysis, however, expectancy theory has important practical implications for individual managers and organizations as a whole (see Table 7–1).

Managers are advised to enhance effort → performance expectancies by helping employees accomplish their performance goals. Managers can do this by providing support and coaching and by increasing employees' self-efficacy. To read about how a real estate development company applies these principles to motivate its workforce, see Skills & Best Practices on page 185.

**TABLE 7–1**    Managerial and Organizational Implications of Expectancy Theory

| Implications for Managers | Implications for Organizations |
|---|---|
| Determine the outcomes employees value. | Reward people for desired performance, and do not keep pay decisions secret. |
| Identify good performance so appropriate behaviors can be rewarded. | Design challenging jobs. |
| Make sure employees can achieve targeted performance levels. | Tie some rewards to group accomplishments to build teamwork and encourage cooperation. |
| Link desired outcomes to targeted levels of performance. | Reward managers for creating, monitoring, and maintaining expectancies, instrumentalities, and outcomes that lead to high effort and goal attainment. |
| Make sure changes in outcomes are large enough to motivate high effort. | Monitor employee motivation through interviews or anonymous questionnaires. |
| Monitor the reward system for inequities. | Accommodate individual differences by building flexibility into the motivation program. |

**One way to link rewards to performance is to pay employees on the selling floor commissions on the products they sell. Sears has expanded its policy so that employees earn commissions in all departments of the store, not just in specialized areas like appliances or tools.**

It also is important for managers to influence employees' instrumentalities and to monitor valences for various rewards. This raises the issue of whether organizations should use monetary rewards as the primary method to reinforce performance. Although money is certainly a positively valent reward for most people, there are three issues to consider when deciding on the relative balance between monetary and nonmonetary rewards.

First, research shows that some workers value interesting work and recognition more than money.[33] Second, extrinsic rewards can lose their motivating properties over time and may undermine intrinsic motivation.[34] This conclusion, however, must be balanced by the fact that performance is related to the receipt of financial incentives. A recent meta-analysis of 39 studies involving 2,773 people showed that financial incentives were positively related to performance quantity but not to performance quality.[35] Third, monetary rewards must be large enough to generate motivation. For example, Robert Heneman, professor of management at Ohio State University, estimates that monetary awards must be at least 7% above employees' base pay to truly motivate people.[36] Although this percentage is well above the typical salary increase received by most employees, some organizations have designed their incentive systems with this recommendation in mind. The law firm of Arnold & Porter pays its staffers profit sharing equal to 7.5% of their salary, and American Express recently announced that if the company meets stiff performance requirements, its chief executive, Kenneth Chenault, will receive a generous compensation package including stock options that could be worth hundreds of millions of dollars.[37]

In summary, there is no one best type of reward. Individual differences and need theories tell us that people are motivated by different rewards. Managers should therefore focus on linking employee performance to valued rewards regardless of the type of reward used to enhance motivation. There are four prerequisites to effectively linking performance and rewards:

1. Managers need to develop and communicate performance standards to employees. Baptist Health Care is well known for its challenging and specific standards of performance, "developed so that every employee would know exactly what behaviors are acceptable."[38] For example, all employees are required to "acknowledge a customer's presence immediately. Smile and introduce yourself at once." Everyone is responsible for answering patient call lights, which are to be acknowledged within three minutes. Even elevator etiquette is covered with standards such as "Hold the door open for others" and "When transporting patients in wheelchairs, always face them toward the door." Because Baptist Health Care sets and communicates these high standards, the organization is known for exceptional patient satisfaction.

2. Managers need valid and accurate performance ratings with which to compare employees. Inaccurate ratings create perceptions of inequity and thereby erode motivation.

3. Managers need to determine the relative mix of individual versus team contribution to performance and then reward accordingly. For example, pharmaceutical giant Pharmacia designed its reward system around its belief in creating an organizational culture that reinforced collaboration, customer focus, and speed. "The company's reward system reinforced this collaborative model by explicitly linking compensation to the actions of the group. Every member's compensation would be based on the time to bring the drug to market, the time for the drug to reach peak profitable share, and total sales. The system gave group members a strong incentive to talk openly with one another and to share information freely."[39]

4. Managers should use the performance ratings to differentially allocate rewards among employees. That is, it is critical that managers allocate significantly different amounts of rewards for various levels of performance.

---

**SKILLS & BEST PRACTICES**

## The Right People in the Right Place at McWhinney

McWhinney Real Estate Services is a fast-growing real estate development company located north of Denver in Loveland, Colorado. Asked to explain how the company managed to run smoothly as it grew, the founders—brothers Chad and Troy McWhinney—gave much of the credit to Johnna Bavoso, who left her consulting practice to become the company's vice president of people services.

Under Bavoso, McWhinney focuses on helping employees discover what they care about and are good at, then puts them in positions where they can grow into the new role they have defined. Chad McWhinney describes the practice as "getting the right people on the right seats on the bus." One person who moved to a new "seat" is a former maintenance technician who realized that if he had a job in the design phase of the company's projects, he could "prevent some of the problems he has to fix later." So the company created a position where he could do just that. Bavoso also brought in two employees with stellar "character and competence" and began coaching them to help them find the position where they can best contribute to McWhinney's future successes.

Coaching employees as they look for a "seat on the bus" is an unusual strategy, but it works because it helps people find goals they care about and then prepares them to achieve those goals. In a positive environment focused on problem solving, McWhinney employees believe they can achieve—and they do.

**SOURCE: Based on A Fox, "Open, Honest Communication Sustains McWhinney,"** *HR Magazine,* **July 2007, p 46.**

# Motivation through Goal Setting

Regardless of the nature of their specific achievements, successful people tend to have one thing in common. Their lives are goal oriented. This is as true for politicians seeking votes as it is for world-class athletes. Within the context of employee motivation, this section explores the theory, research, and practice of goal setting.

## Goals: Definition and Background

**goal**

**What an individual is trying to accomplish.**

Edwin Locke, a leading authority on goal setting, and his colleagues define a **goal** as "what an individual is trying to accomplish; it is the object or aim of an action."[40] The motivational effect of performance goals and goal-based reward plans has been recognized for a long time. At the turn of the century, Frederick Taylor attempted to scientifically establish how much work of a specified quality an individual should be assigned each day. He proposed that bonuses be based on accomplishing those output standards. More recently, goal setting has been promoted through a widely used management technique called management by objectives (MBO).

**management by objectives (MBO)**

**Management system incorporating participation in decision making, goal setting, and feedback.**

**Management by objectives** is a management system that incorporates participation in decision making, goal setting, and objective feedback. A meta-analysis of MBO programs showed productivity gains in 68 of 70 different organizations. Specifically, results uncovered an average gain in productivity of 56% when top management commitment was high. The average gain was only 6% when commitment was low. A second meta-analysis of 18 studies further demonstrated that employees' job satisfaction was significantly related to top management's commitment to an MBO implementation.[41] These impressive results highlight the positive benefits of implementing MBO and setting goals. To further understand how MBO programs can increase both productivity and satisfaction, let us examine the process by which goal setting works.

## How Does Goal Setting Work?

Despite abundant goal-setting research and practice, goal-setting theories are surprisingly scarce. An instructive model was formulated by Locke and his associates. According to Locke's model, goal setting has four motivational mechanisms.[42]

**Goals Direct Attention**    Goals direct one's attention and effort toward goal-relevant activities and away from goal-irrelevant activities. If, for example, you have a term project due in a few days, your thoughts and actions tend to revolve around completing that project. The power of goals directs the attention of employees at Wyeth Pharmaceuticals. CEO Robert Ruffolo shook up the ranks of its research and development staff by setting a goal for how many drug compounds each scientist must produce per year. Following establishment of that goal, the number of drug compounds produced in a year tripled with no increase in resources. For the firm's sales representatives, a key goal is to be "the best in the business," measured in terms of specific scores for customer satisfaction. The company provided sales reps with training in the behaviors associated with customer satisfaction, and in just over a year, their scores had jumped 20%.[43]

**Goals Regulate Effort**  Not only do goals make us selectively perceptive, they also motivate us to act. The instructor's deadline for turning in your term project would prompt you to complete it, as opposed to going out with friends, watching television, or studying for another course. Generally, the level of effort expended is proportionate to the difficulty of the goal.

**Goals Increase Persistence**  Within the context of goal setting, persistence represents the effort expended on a task over an extended period of time: It takes effort to run 100 meters; it takes persistence to run a 26-mile marathon. Persistent people tend to see obstacles as challenges to be overcome rather than as reasons to fail. A difficult goal that is important to an individual is a constant reminder to keep exerting effort in the appropriate direction. This is a fundamental reason why investors are keenly interested in the goals executives must meet in order to earn incentives such as stock grants and bonuses. In today's highly competitive marketplace, companies are linking a growing share of executives' pay to profits and share price. Executives know that investors are watching to see whether they meet the targets and won't hesitate to push for their ouster if they fail to deliver. Therefore, says Ira Kay, a director of the consulting firm Watson Wyatt, "Setting sufficiently challenging performance goals and appropriate corporate performance metrics is an extremely important part of the executive pay process."[44] Similarly, in the world of sports, after Irish golfer Padraig Harrington won the British Open, he announced that his goal was to win more major titles, saying, "You have to have goals to keep you moving forward. If your goal is to win one major, then that would be it. I am definitely focused on winning more than one."[45]

Padraig Harrington, Irish golfer and winner of 19 tournaments worldwide, including the 2007 British Open sets his goals high. He has earned over $12 million since turning pro in 1995. His current goal is to win more major championships and to increase the contributions to his charitable foundation. What type of goals might a golfer of Padraig's caliber set at the start of every year?

**Goals Foster the Development and Application of Task Strategies and Action Plans**  If you are here and your goal is out there somewhere, you face the problem of getting from here to there. For example, think about the challenge of starting a business. Do you want to earn profits, grow larger, or make the world a better place? To get there, you have to make a tremendous number of decisions and complete a myriad of tasks. Goals can help because they encourage people to develop strategies and action plans that enable them to achieve their goals. A series of studies conducted in South Africa, Zimbabwe, and Namibia found that small businesses were more likely to grow and succeed if their owners engaged in "elaborate and proactive planning."[46]

# Insights from Goal-Setting Research

Research consistently has supported goal setting as a motivational technique. Setting performance goals increases individual, group, and organizational performance. Further, the positive effects of goal setting were found in six other countries or regions: Australia, Canada, the Caribbean, England, West Germany, and Japan. Goal setting works in different cultures. Reviews of the many goal-setting studies conducted over the past few decades have given managers five practical insights:

**learning objective 5**

Identify five practical lessons to be learned from goal-setting research.

1. *Difficult goals lead to higher performance.* **Goal difficulty** reflects the amount of effort required to meet a goal. It is more difficult to sell nine cars a month than it is to sell three cars a month.

> **goal difficulty**
> **The amount of effort required to meet a goal.**

A meta-analysis spanning 4,000 people and 65 separate studies revealed that goal difficulty was positively related to performance.[47] As illustrated in Figure 7–2, however, the positive relationship between goal difficulty and performance breaks down when goals are perceived to be impossible. Figure 7–2 reveals that performance goes up when employees are given hard goals as opposed to easy or moderate goals (section A). Performance then plateaus (section B) and drops (section C) as the difficulty of a goal goes from challenging to impossible.

2. *Specific, difficult goals lead to higher performance for simple rather than complex tasks.* **Goal specificity** pertains to the quantifiability of a goal. For example, a goal of selling nine cars a month is more specific than telling a salesperson to do his or her best. In an early review of goal-setting research, 99 of 110 studies (90%) found that specific, hard goals led to better performance than did easy, medium, do-your-best, or no goals. This result was confirmed in a meta-analysis of 70 studies conducted between 1966 and 1984, involving 7,407 people.[48]

In contrast to these positive effects, several recent studies demonstrated that setting specific, difficult goals leads to poorer performance under certain circumstances. For example, a meta-analysis of 125 studies indicated that goal-setting effects were strongest for easy tasks and weakest for complex tasks.[49] There are two explanations for this finding. First, employees are not likely to put forth increased effort to achieve complex goals unless they "buy-in" or support them. Thus, it is important for managers to obtain employee buy-in to the goal-setting process. Second, novel and complex tasks can make employees anxious about succeeding, which in turn causes them to develop strategies in an unsystematic way and to fail to learn what strategies or actions are effective. This can further create pressure and performance anxiety. According to Locke and his colleagues, the antidote is to set specific challenging learning goals aimed at identifying the best way to accomplish the task or goal.[50]

**goal specificity**

Quantifiability of a goal.

**FIGURE 7–2**
Relationship between Goal Difficulty and Performance

A   Performance of committed individuals with adequate ability
B   Performance of committed individuals who are working at capacity
C   Performance of individuals who lack commitment to high goals

SOURCE: From *A Theory of Goal Setting and Task Performance,* by Locke/Latham. Copyright © 1990 Pearson Education. Reprinted by permission of Pearson Education, Inc., Upper Saddle River, NJ.

Specific, difficult goals thus impair performance on novel, complex tasks when employees do not have clear strategies for solving these types of problems. On a positive note, however, a study demonstrated that goal setting led to gradual improvements in performance on complex tasks when people were encouraged to explicitly solve the problem at hand.[51]

3. *Feedback enhances the effect of specific, difficult goals.* Feedback plays a key role in all of our lives. For example, consider the role of feedback in bowling. Imagine going to the bowling lanes only to find that someone had hung a sheet from the ceiling to the floor in front of the pins. How likely is it that you would reach your goal score or typical bowling average? Not likely, given your inability to see the pins. Regardless of your goal, you would have to guess where to throw your second ball if you did not get a strike on your first shot. The same principles apply at work.

   Feedback lets people know if they are headed toward their goals or if they are off course and need to redirect their efforts. Goals plus feedback is the recommended approach.[52] Goals inform people about performance standards and expectations so that they can channel their energies accordingly. In turn, feedback provides the information needed to adjust direction, effort, and strategies for goal accomplishment.

4. *Participative goals, assigned goals, and self-set goals are equally effective.* Both managers and researchers are interested in identifying the best way to set goals. Should goals be participatively set, assigned, or set by the employee him- or herself? A summary of goal-setting research indicated that no single approach was consistently more effective than others in increasing performance.[53]

   Managers are advised to use a contingency approach by picking a method that seems best suited for the individual and situation at hand. For example, employees' preferences for participation should be considered. Some employees desire to participate in the process of setting goals, whereas others do not. Employees are also more likely to respond positively to the opportunity to participate in goal setting when they have greater task information, higher levels of experience and training, and greater levels of task involvement. Finally, a participative approach stimulates information exchange, which in turn results in the development of more effective task strategies and higher self-efficacy.[54]

5. *Goal commitment and monetary incentives affect goal-setting outcomes.* **Goal commitment** is the extent to which an individual is personally committed to achieving a goal. In general, an individual is expected to persist in attempts to accomplish a goal when he or she is committed to it. Researchers believe that goal commitment moderates the relationship between the difficulty of a goal and performance. That is, difficult goals lead to higher performance only when employees are committed to their goals. Conversely, difficult goals are hypothesized to lead to lower performance when people are not committed to their goals. A meta-analysis of 21 studies based on 2,360 people supported these predictions.[55] It also is important to note that people are more likely to commit to difficult goals when they have high self-efficacy about successfully accomplishing their goals. Managers thus are encouraged to consider employees' self-efficacy when setting goals.

   **goal commitment**

   **Amount of commitment to achieving a goal.**

   Like goal setting, the use of monetary incentives to motivate employees is seldom questioned. Unfortunately, research uncovered some negative consequences when goal achievement is linked to individual incentives. Case studies, for example, reveal that pay should not be linked to goal achievement unless (a) performance goals are under the employees' control; (b) goals are quantitative and measurable; and (c) frequent, relatively large payments are made for performance achievement.[56] Goal-based incentive systems are more likely to produce undesirable effects if these three conditions are not satisfied.

Moreover, empirical studies demonstrated that goal-based bonus incentives produced higher commitment to easy goals and lower commitment to difficult goals. People were reluctant to commit to difficult goals that were tied to monetary incentives. People with high goal commitment also offered less help to their coworkers when they received goal-based bonus incentives to accomplish difficult individual goals. Individuals also neglected aspects of the job that were not covered in the performance goals.[57]

These findings underscore some of the dangers of using goal-based incentives, particularly for employees in complex, interdependent jobs requiring cooperation. Managers need to consider the advantages, disadvantages, and dilemmas of goal-based incentives prior to implementation.

**Self-Assessment Exercise**

Assessing How Personality Impacts Your Goal-Setting Skills

## Practical Application of Goal Setting

There are three general steps to follow when implementing a goal-setting program. Serious deficiencies in one step cannot make up for strength in the other two. The three steps need to be implemented in a systematic fashion.

**Guitar Center is one of the fastest-growing retailers in the United States. At its 165 stores, service as a core value translates into a specific goal—salespeople are expected to answer the phone before the fourth ring. Company executives place calls periodically to make sure the goal is being met. Do you like this approach to monitoring employee performance?**

**Step I: Set Goals** Amazingly, this commonsense first step is not always followed. A recent survey of 1,900 managers revealed that nearly 46% of their project teams are not given specific, attainable goals. It thus should not be surprising to learn that only 33% of these managers indicated that their project teams complete their work on time and within budget.[58] Let us consider how managers can set goals with their employees or project teams.

A number of sources can be used as input during this goal-setting stage. Time and motion studies are one source. Goals also may be based on the average past performance of job holders. Third, the employee and his or her manager may set the goal participatively, through give-and-take negotiation. Fourth, goals can be set by conducting external or internal benchmarking. Benchmarking is used when an organization wants to compare its performance or internal work processes to those of other organizations (external benchmarking) or to other internal units, branches, departments, or divisions within the organization (internal benchmarking). For example, a company might set a goal to surpass the customer service levels or profit of a benchmarked competitor. Finally, the overall strategy of a company (e.g., become the lowest-cost producer) may affect the goals set by employees at various levels in the organization.

In accordance with available research evidence, goals should be "SMART." SMART is an acronym that stands for specific, measurable, attainable, results oriented, and time bound. Table 7–2 contains a set of guidelines for writing SMART goals. There are two additional recommendations to consider when setting goals. First, for complex

Guidelines for Writing SMART Goals   **TABLE 7–2**

| Specific | Goals should be stated in precise rather than vague terms. For example, a goal that provides for 20 hours of technical training for each employee is more specific than stating that a manager should send as many people as possible to training classes. Goals should be quantified when possible. |
|---|---|
| Measurable | A measurement device is needed to assess the extent to which a goal is accomplished. Goals thus need to be measurable. It also is critical to consider the quality aspect of the goal when establishing measurement criteria. For example, if the goal is to complete a managerial study of methods to increase productivity, one must consider how to measure the quality of this effort. Goals should not be set without considering the interplay between quantity and quality of output. |
| Attainable | Goals should be realistic, challenging, and attainable. Impossible goals reduce motivation because people do not like to fail. Remember, people have different levels of ability and skill. |
| Results oriented | Corporate goals should focus on desired end-results that support the organization's vision. In turn, an individual's goals should directly support the accomplishment of corporate goals. Activities support the achievement of goals and are outlined in action plans. To focus goals on desired end-results, goals should start with the word "to," followed by verbs such as complete, acquire, produce, increase, and decrease. Verbs such as develop, conduct, implement, or monitor imply activities and should not be used in a goal statement. |
| Time bound | Goals specify target dates for completion. |

SOURCE: A J Kinicki, *Performance Management Systems* (Superstition Mt., AZ: Kinicki and Associates, Inc., 1992), pp 2–9. Reprinted with permission; all rights reserved.

tasks, managers should train employees in problem-solving techniques and encourage them to develop a performance action plan. Action plans specify the strategies or tactics to be used in order to accomplish a goal.

Second, because of individual differences (recall our discussion in Chapter 5), it may be necessary to establish different goals for employees performing the same job. For example, a study of 103 undergraduate business students revealed that individuals high in conscientiousness had higher motivation, had greater goal commitment, and obtained higher grades than students low in conscientiousness.[59] An individual's goal orientation is another important individual difference to consider when setting goals. Three types of goal orientations are a learning goal orientation, a performance-prove goal orientation, and a performance-avoid goal orientation. A team of researchers described the differences and implications for goal setting in the following way:

People with a high learning goal orientation view skills as malleable. They make efforts not only to achieve current tasks but also to develop the ability to accomplish future tasks. People with a high performance-prove goal orientation tend to focus on performance and try to demonstrate their ability by looking better than others.

SKILLS & BEST PRACTICES

## Managerial Actions for Enhancing Goal Commitment

1. Provide valued outcomes for goal accomplishment.

2. Raise employees' self-efficacy about meeting goals by (a) providing adequate training, (b) role modeling desired behaviors and actions, and (c) persuasively communicating confidence in the employees' ability to attain the goal.

3. Have employees make a public commitment to the goal.

4. Communicate an inspiring vision and explain how individual goals relate to accomplishing the vision.

5. Allow employees to participate in setting the goals.

6. Behave supportively rather than punitively.

7. Break a long-term goal (i.e., a yearly goal) into short-term subgoals.

8. Ensure that employees have the resources required to accomplish the goal.

SOURCE: These recommendations were derived from E A Locke and G P Latham, "Building a Practically Useful Theory of Goal Setting and Task Motivation," *American Psychologist*, September 2002, pp 705–17. Copyright © 2002 by the American Psychological Association. Adapted with permission.

People with a high performance-avoid goal orientation also focus on performance, but this focus is grounded in trying to avoid negative outcomes.[60]

Although some studies showed that people set higher goals, exerted more effort, had higher self-efficacy, and achieved higher performance when they possessed a learning goal orientation as opposed to either a performance-prove or performance-avoid goal orientation, other research demonstrated a more complex series of relationships.[61] The best we can conclude is that an individual's goal orientation influences the actions that he or she takes in the pursuit of accomplishing goals in specific situations.[62] In conclusion, managers are encouraged to consider individual differences when setting goals.

**Step 2: Promote Goal Commitment**  Obtaining goal commitment is important because employees are more motivated to pursue goals they view as reasonable, obtainable, and fair. Goal commitment may be increased through a variety of methods. The Skills & Best Practices, for example, presents eight managerial actions that can be used to increase employees' goal commitment.

**Step 3: Provide Support and Feedback**  Step 3 calls for providing employees with the necessary support elements or resources to get the job done. This includes ensuring that each employee has the necessary abilities, training, and information needed to achieve his or her goals. At Verizon Wireless, for example, all training must be explicitly linked to business goals. Not only does this focus ensure that training equips employees to meet goals, but it also provides a basis for measuring whether the training itself is meeting objectives.[63] Moreover, managers should pay attention to employees' perceptions of effort → performance expectancies, self-efficacy, and valence of rewards. Finally, as we discuss in detail in Chapter 8, employees should be provided with timely, specific feedback (knowledge of results) on how they are doing.

# Putting Motivational Theories to Work

6  learning objective

Specify issues that should be addressed before implementing a motivational program.

Successfully designing and implementing motivational programs is not easy. Managers cannot simply take one of the theories discussed in this book and apply it word for word. Dynamics within organizations interfere with applying motivation theories in "pure" form. According to management scholar Terence Mitchell,

> There are situations and settings that make it exceptionally difficult for a motivational system to work. These circumstances may involve the kinds of jobs or people

present, the technology, the presence of a union, and so on. The factors that hinder the application of motivational theory have not been articulated either frequently or systematically.[64]

With Mitchell's cautionary statement in mind, this section uses Figure 6–1 (see page 145 in Chapter 6) to raise issues that need to be addressed before implementing a motivational program. Our intent is not to discuss all relevant considerations but rather to highlight a few important ones.

Assuming a motivational program is being considered to improve productivity, quality, or customer satisfaction, the first issue revolves around the difference between motivation and performance. As shown in Figure 6–1, motivation and performance are not one and the same. Motivation is only one of several factors that influence performance. For example, poor performance may be more a function of outdated or inefficient materials and machinery, not having goals to direct one's attention, a monotonous job, feelings of inequity, a negative work environment characterized by political behavior and conflict, poor supervisory support and coaching, or poor work flow. Motivation cannot make up for a deficient job context (see Figure 6–1). Managers, therefore, need to carefully consider the causes of poor performance and employee misbehavior. Employee surveys can be used to help determine the contextual causes of low motivation.

Importantly, managers should not ignore the individual inputs identified in Figure 6–1. As discussed in this chapter as well as Chapters 5 and 6, individual differences are an important input that influence motivation and motivated behavior. Managers are advised to develop employees so that they have the ability and job knowledge to effectively perform their jobs. In addition, attempts should be made to nurture positive employee characteristics, such as self-esteem, self-efficacy, positive emotions, a learning goal orientation, and need for achievement.

Because motivation is goal directed, the process of developing and setting goals should be consistent with our previous discussion. Moreover, the method used to evaluate performance also needs to be considered. Without a valid performance appraisal system, it is difficult, if not impossible, to accurately distinguish good and poor performers. Managers need to keep in mind that both equity and expectancy theory suggest that employee motivation is squelched by inaccurate performance ratings. Consider the approach that General Electric takes in terms of developing and evaluating its employees.

> The company takes a lot of heat for getting rid of the bottom 10% of its employees every year, but that's only the end point of a process of constant appraisal. The fired ones are not surprised when the ax comes down. . . . Dan Mudd is the president and CEO of Fannie Mae; as president and CEO of GE Capital Japan from 1999 to mid-2005, he saw this dynamic from the inside. "GE, like anywhere else, has a little bit of politics, a little bit of personal stuff and all that," he says, "but compared with all the other organizations I know, it's minimized. It's upfront. You know what you have to do to succeed." Most companies, frankly, don't have the stomach to give frequent, rigorous evaluations—and to fire those who need to be fired.[65]

Finally, it is important for organizations to train their managers to properly assess people. Consistent with expectancy theory, managers should make extrinsic rewards contingent on performance. In doing so, however, it is important to consider three

**Group Exercise**
What Motivates You?

issues. First, managers need to ensure that performance goals are directed to achieve the "right" end-results. For example, health insurers and medical groups wrestle over the relative focus on cost savings versus patient satisfaction. Consider the case of Oakland-based Kaiser Permanente:

> Telephone clerks at California's largest HMO received bonuses for keeping calls with patients brief and limiting the number of doctor visits they set up. . . . The California Nurses Association, the union representing Kaiser's registered nurses, derided the program as deceitful and harmful to patients with serious medical problems.
>
> "Patients don't understand they're talking to a high school graduate with no nursing background," [Jim] Anderson said.
>
> The clerks, who generally have little to no medical training, answer phone calls from customers wanting to set up doctor appointments or asking simple medical questions.
>
> Cash bonuses were paid to those who made appointments for fewer than 35% of callers and spent less than an average of three minutes, 45 seconds on the phone with each patient. Clerks were also encouraged to transfer fewer than 50% of the calls to registered nurses for further evaluation.[66]

How do you feel about Kaiser Permanente's plan? How might it be changed to more effectively motivate employees to provide higher quality care?

Second, the promise of increased rewards will not prompt higher effort and good performance unless those rewards are clearly tied to performance and they are large enough to gain employees' interest or attention.[67] Third, rewards may shift how employees allocate their effort among various goals. An experiment with 252 college students found that if they were given two goals but received an incentive for achieving just one of those goals, they directed more of their effort toward the goal that would be rewarded.[68] In a business setting, most employees are expected to achieve more than one goal; if the organization rewards only some kinds of achievement, employees may direct their attention away from activities that are important but are not specifically rewarded.

Moreover, equity theory tells us that motivation is influenced by employee perceptions about the fairness of reward allocations. Motivation is decreased when employees believe rewards are inequitably allocated. Rewards also need to be integrated appropriately into the appraisal system. If performance is measured at the individual level, individual achievements need to be rewarded. On the other hand, when performance is the result of group effort, rewards should be allocated to the group.

Feedback also should be linked with performance. Feedback provides the information and direction needed to keep employees focused on relevant tasks, activities, and goals. Managers should strive to provide specific, timely, and accurate feedback to employees.

Finally, we end this chapter by noting that an organization's culture significantly influences employee motivation and behavior. A positive self-enhancing culture is more likely to engender higher motivation and commitment than a culture dominated by suspicion, fault finding, and blame.

# key terms

# chapter summary

- *Discuss the role of perceived inequity in employee motivation.* Equity theory is a model of motivation that explains how people strive for fairness and justice in social exchanges. On the job, feelings of inequity revolve around a person's evaluation of whether he or she receives adequate rewards to compensate for his or her contributive inputs. People perform these evaluations by comparing the perceived fairness of their employment exchange with that of relevant others. Perceived inequity creates motivation to restore equity.

- *Describe the practical lessons derived from equity theory.* Equity theory has at least nine practical implications. First, because people are motivated to resolve perceptions of inequity, managers should not discount employees' feelings and perceptions when trying to motivate workers. Second, managers should pay attention to employees' *perceptions* of what is fair and equitable. It is the employee's view of reality that counts when trying to motivate someone, according to equity theory. Third, employees should be given a voice in decisions that affect them. Fourth, employees should be given the opportunity to appeal decisions that affect their welfare. Fifth, employees are more likely to accept and support organizational change when they believe it is implemented fairly and when it produces equitable outcomes. Sixth, managers can promote cooperation and teamwork among group members by treating them equitably. Seventh,

treating employees inequitably can lead to litigation and costly court settlements. Eighth, managers need to pay attention to the organization's climate for justice because it influences employee attitudes and behavior. Finally, employees' perceptions of justice are strongly influenced by the leadership behavior exhibited by their managers.

- *Explain Vroom's expectancy theory.* Expectancy theory assumes motivation is determined by one's perceived chances of achieving valued outcomes. Vroom's expectancy model of motivation reveals how effort → performance expectancies and performance → outcome instrumentalities influence the degree of effort expended to achieve desired (positively valent) outcomes.

- *Describe the practical implications of expectancy theory.* Managers are advised to enhance effort → performance expectancies by helping employees accomplish their performance goals. With respect to instrumentalities and valences, managers should attempt to link employee performance and valued rewards. There are four prerequisites to linking performance and rewards: (a) Managers need to develop and communicate performance standards to employees, (b) managers need valid and accurate performance ratings, (c) managers need to determine the relative mix of individual versus team contribution to performance and then reward accordingly, and (d) managers should use performance ratings to differentially allocate rewards among employees.

- *Identify five practical lessons to be learned from goal-setting research.* Difficult goals lead to higher performance than easy or moderate goals: goals should not be impossible to achieve. Specific, difficult goals lead to higher performance for simple rather than complex tasks. Third, feedback enhances the effect of specific, difficult goals. Fourth, participative goals, assigned goals, and self-set goals are equally effective. Fifth, goal commitment and monetary incentives affect goal-setting outcomes.

- *Specify issues that should be addressed before implementing a motivational program.* Managers need to consider the variety of causes of poor performance and employee

misbehavior. Undesirable employee performance and behavior may be due to a host of deficient individual inputs (e.g., ability, dispositions, emotions, and beliefs) or job context factors (e.g., materials and machinery, job characteristics, reward systems, supervisory support and coaching, and social norms). The method used to evaluate performance as well as the link between performance and rewards must be examined. Performance must be accurately evaluated and rewards should be equitably distributed. Managers should also recognize that employee motivation and behavior are influenced by organizational culture.

# discussion questions

1. Explain why the CEO pay practices described in the chapter-opening case violate expectancy theory.
2. Could a manager's attempt to treat his or her employees equally lead to perceptions of inequity? Explain.
3. If someone who reported to you at work had a low expectancy for successful performance, what could you do to increase this person's expectancy?
4. Goal-setting research suggests that people should be given difficult goals. How does this prescription mesh with expectancy theory? Explain.
5. How could a professor use equity, expectancy, and goal-setting theory to motivate students?

# ethical dilemma

## A High School Teacher Must Deal with Plagiarizing Students[69]

High school teacher Christine Pelton wasted no time after discovering that nearly a fifth of her biology students had plagiarized their semester projects from the Internet.

She had received her rural Kansas district's backing before when she accused students of cheating, and she expected it again this time after failing the 28 sophomores.

Her principal and superintendent agreed: It was plagiarism, and the students should get a zero for the assignment.

But after parents complained, the Piper School Board ordered her to go easier on the guilty. . . . The board ordered her to give the students partial credit and to decrease the project's value from 50% of the final course grade to 30%.

One of the complaining parents, Theresa Woolley, told the *Kansas City Star* that her daughter did not plagiarize but was not sure how much she needed to rewrite research material.

But Pelton said the course syllabus, which she required students to sign, warned of the consequences of cheating and plagiarism. . . .

What is worse, McCabe said [Donald McCabe is a professor of management at Rutgers University], is that tolerance of dishonesty disheartens other students, who have to compete with the cheaters to get into college.

"If they see teachers looking the other way, students feel compelled to participate even though it makes them uncomfortable," McCabe said.

# What Would You Do If You Were Christine Pelton?

1. Resign your position in protest over the school board's lack of support. Explain your rationale.

2. Do what the school board ordered. Discuss the impact of this choice on the students who plagiarized and those who did not.

3. Ignore the school board's order and give the failing grades. Explain your rationale.

4. Invent other options. Discuss.

For an interpretation of this situation, visit our Web site, **www.mhhe.com/kinickiob4e.**

If you're looking for additional study materials, be sure to check out the Online Learning Center at

**www.mhhe.com/kinickiob4e**

for more information and interactivities that correspond to this chapter.

# Improving Performance with Feedback, Rewards, and Positive Reinforcement

**After reading the material in this chapter, you should be able to:**

1. Specify the two basic functions of feedback and three sources of feedback.

2. Define upward feedback and 360-degree feedback, and summarize the general tips for giving good feedback.

3. Distinguish between extrinsic and intrinsic rewards, and give a job-related example of each.

4. Summarize the research lessons about pay for performance, and explain why rewards often fail to motivate employees.

5. State Thorndike's "law of effect" and explain Skinner's distinction between respondent and operant behavior.

6. Demonstrate your knowledge of positive reinforcement, negative reinforcement, punishment, and extinction, and explain behavior shaping.

Pictured is Sue Nokes of T-Mobile. Given the case you read about her on these pages, how would you like to work for her?

But this isn't just any suit; It's Sue Nokes. She's the flashy, feisty spark plug of a woman who runs sales and customer service at T-Mobile USA, the fast-growing $17 billion subsidiary of Deutsche Telekom. In that capacity she's in charge of more than 15,000 employees around the U.S. . . .

Though T-Mobile is ranked fourth, with 11% of the U.S. market, behind Verizon, AT&T, and Sprint Nextel, since the end of 2002 it has gained more than five share points, according to Mark Cardwell of Sanford C. Bernstein. Even more impressive, within two years of Nokes's arrival in 2002, the company catapulted to the top of J.D. Power's rankings of customer care in the wireless industry. It has now won the biannual title six times in a row. . . .

That's a huge turnaround from 2002, when T-Mobile ranked dead last according to internal surveys. (J.D. Power started its national wireless surveys in 2003.) Dotson, who had just been named CEO, reached out to Nokes, then at Wal-Mart.com, telling her that the company's customer organization needed a complete overhaul. Before committing to the job, Nokes visited a few call centers and was horrified by what she saw. Absenteeism averaged 12% daily; turnover was a staggering 100%-plus annually. The company used "neighborhood seating," a common technique at call centers in which employees don't have desks but instead drag their stuff from cubicle to cubicle. "I asked [managers], 'Are

you losing any good people?' They said, 'Yeah,'" Nokes says. "I said, 'Anybody feeling bad about that?'" . . .

Although Nokes loves to talk, she actually spends much of her day listening. In a focus group in the Menaul center, dressed in a natty black jacket with white trim, tons of gold jewelry, and funky black-and-white-checked glasses to match, Nokes, 52, says what she says at virtually every such meeting (after, that is, making a bunch of wisecracks about her weight, age, and declining mental functions). "I have two questions: What's going well, and what's broken?"

One rep suggests a feature that lets customers turn off incoming text messages so that they don't have to be charged; another, Sergio Juardo, wonders why T-Mobile.com has no web page in Spanish. Nokes listens carefully, seemingly unfazed by the fact that Juardo's cheek is painted with the words I HEART SUE NOKES. In the focus groups and in the larger town hall meetings, Nokes is brutally honest, telling the group, for instance, that the company erred by not adding enough service reps to support T-Mobile's new pay-as-you-go service. Responding to a complaint that it's too time-consuming to log in to the system, she tells employees that a quick fix is impossible given the company's other technological priorities. "It's important that we build an environment where you can tell me my baby is ugly," Nokes says, her hard A's revealing her Midwestern roots. "And when you ask what's wrong, you'd better fix some stuff." . . .

Connecting to everyday workers was particularly important when Nokes landed at Wal-Mart.com, working for then-CEO Jeanne Jackson to build a customer-service organization nearly from scratch. "Sue, to me, is the world's perfect executive," says Jackson, now with MSP Capital. "You don't have to go to sleep at night worrying about her decisions. And on the other hand she makes you feel like a brilliant boss—not by sucking up but by giving you honest feedback." Jackson recalls Nokes "reading me the riot act" one day. "I was spending most of my time with the engineering staff, and

she said [I needed to] get out there and show my face to call-center employees. She was absolutely right."

Nokes quickly gave workers their own seats and asked for $17 million to bring salaries up to the 50th percentile. She also overhauled the training process (reps now go through 132 hours of training and team meetings each year) and began hiring based more on attitude than experience. She also created a standard set of metrics to measure reps on, tracking call quality, attendance, and schedule reliability along with the speed of the call resolution. "I will never hold you accountable for things that don't matter to your customer or to fellow employees," Nokes tells her Albuquerque acolytes before explaining—in her own inimitable way—what she's looking for. Absenteeism ("pimping your peers," she calls it) is bad. Solving problems in one phone call (one-call resolution, or OCR), she says, is critical. "We have frigged up [our customers'] day," she says. "They need to go to the john and do other things."

To motivate employees in what has long been considered a dead-end job, Nokes promised when she joined that 80% of promotions would eventually go to existing employees. By August 2007 that number had hit 82%. Her team also created a new "rewards and recognition system" in which high performers—using the new metrics—were rewarded with trips to Las Vegas or Hawaii and prizes. Today absenteeism is at 3% annually and attrition is at 42%. Employee satisfaction—at 80%—is the highest it's ever been.[1]

> **How would you like to work for Sue Nokes? Explain. For an interpretation of this case and additional comments, visit our Online Learning Center at**
>
> **www.mhhe.com/ kinickiob4e**

FOR DISCUSSION

**THIS FINAL CHAPTER OF PART TWO SERVES** as a practical capstone for what we have learned so far in Parts One and Two. Our focus here is on improving individual job performance. We need to put to work what we have learned about cultural and individual differences, perception, and motivation. Some organizations apply these principles effectively, as Sue Nokes has done at T-Mobile USA. Unfortunately, a longitudinal study of more than 500 managers found that hardly any of them provided their employees with daily information about performance requirements, measurable goals, feedback on their work performance, and rewards for achievement.[2]

The popular term these days for doing things the right way is performance management. **Performance management** is an organizationwide system whereby managers integrate the activities of goal setting, monitoring and evaluating, providing feedback and coaching, and rewarding employees on a continuous basis.[3] This contrasts with the haphazard tradition of annual performance appraisals,[4] a largely unsatisfying experience for everyone involved.[5] OB can shed valuable light on key aspects of performance management: goal setting (discussed in Chapter 7), feedback and coaching, and rewards and positive reinforcement.

As indicated in Figure 8–1, job performance needs a life-support system. Like an astronaut drifting in space without the protection and support of a space suit, job performance will not thrive without a support system. First, people with the requisite abilities, skills, and job knowledge need to be hired. Next training is required to correct any job knowledge shortfalls. The organization's culture, job design, and supervisory practices also can facilitate or hinder job performance. At the heart of the model in Figure 8–1 are the key aspects of the performance improvement cycle. First, as we saw in Chapter 7, effective goals show employees where to direct their efforts. Next, as we will discuss in this chapter, feedback shows employees when they are succeeding and where they need to improve, while rewards and positive reinforcement give them reasons to continue their efforts.

**performance management**

Continuous cycle of improving job performance with goal setting, feedback and coaching, and rewards and positive reinforcement.

**FIGURE 8–1** Improving Individual Job Performance: A Continuous Process

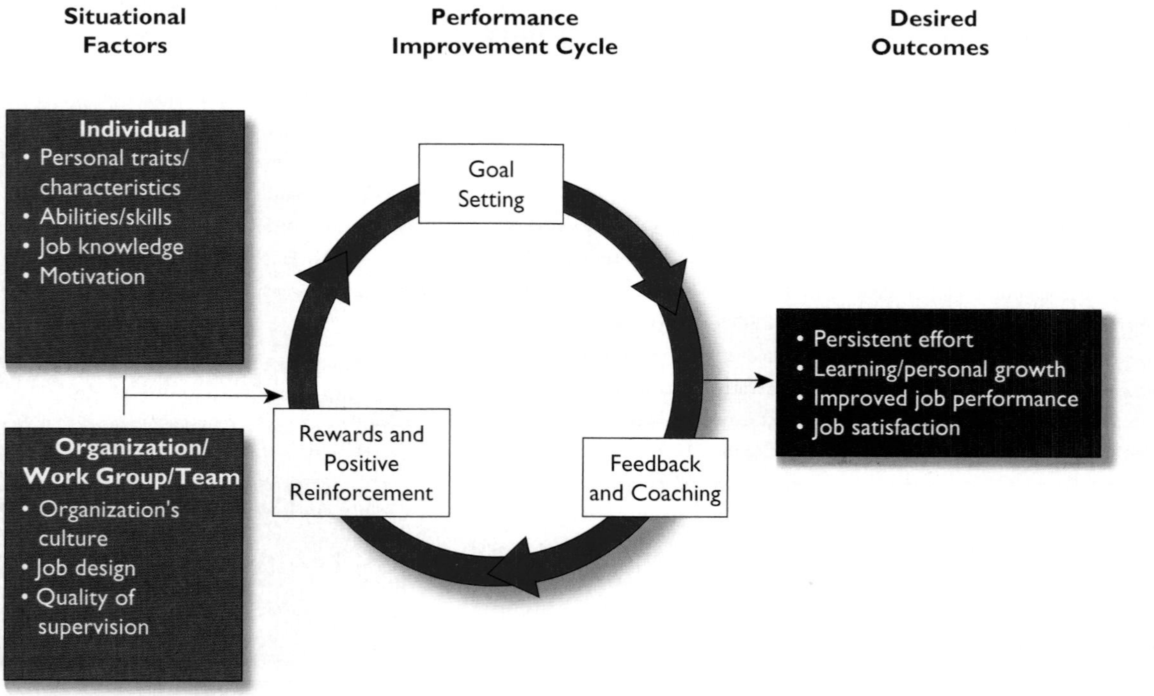

Situational Factors

Performance Improvement Cycle

Desired Outcomes

**Individual**
- Personal traits/characteristics
- Abilities/skills
- Job knowledge
- Motivation

Goal Setting

Rewards and Positive Reinforcement

Feedback and Coaching

**Organization/Work Group/Team**
- Organization's culture
- Job design
- Quality of supervision

- Persistent effort
- Learning/personal growth
- Improved job performance
- Job satisfaction

# Providing Effective Feedback

Numerous surveys tell us employees have a hearty appetite for feedback.[6] So also do achievement-oriented students. Following a difficult exam, for instance, students want to know two things: how they did and how their peers did. By letting students know how their work measures up to grading and competitive standards, an instructor's feedback permits the students to adjust their study habits so they can reach their goals. Likewise, managers in well-run organizations follow up goal setting with a feedback program to provide a rational basis for adjustment and improvement. For example, notice the importance Fred Smith, the founder and head of Federal Express, places on feedback when outlining his philosophy of leadership:

> When people walk in the door, they want to know: What do you expect out of me? What's in this deal for me? What do I have to do to get ahead? Where do I go in this organization to get justice if I'm not treated appropriately? They want to know how they're doing. They want some feedback. And they want to know that what they are doing is important.
>
> If you take the basic principles of leadership and answer those questions over and over again, you can be successful dealing with people.[7]

Feedback too often gets shortchanged. In a survey by Watson Wyatt Worldwide, 43% of employees said they "feel they don't get enough guidance to improve their performance."[8]

As the term is used here, **feedback** is objective information about individual or collective performance shared with those in a position to improve the situation. Subjective assessments such as, "You're lazy" do not qualify as *objective* feedback. But hard data such as units sold, days absent, dollars saved, projects completed, customers satisfied, and quality rejects are all candidates for objective feedback programs. Christopher D Lee, author of *Performance Conversations: An Alternative to Appraisals,* clarifies the concept of feedback by contrasting it with performance appraisals:

> Feedback is the exchange of information about the status and quality of work products. It provides a road map to success. It is used to motivate, support, direct, correct and regulate work efforts and outcomes. Feedback ensures that the manager and employees are in sync and agree on the standards and expectations of the work to be performed.
>
> Traditional appraisals, on the other hand, discourage two-way communication and treat employee involvement as a bad thing. Employees are discouraged from participating in a performance review, and when they do, their responses are often considered "rebuttals."[9]

**"I work best when someone is looking over my shoulder and telling me that I'm a screw-up."**

SOURCE: *Harvard Business Review,* December 2005, p 97. Copyright © 2005 Bob Vejtko. Reprinted with permission.

**feedback**
Objective information about performance.

**learning objective**

Specify the two basic functions of feedback and three sources of feedback.

# Two Functions of Feedback

Experts say feedback serves two functions for those who receive it; one is *instructional* and the other *motivational*. Feedback instructs when it clarifies roles or teaches new behavior. For example, an assistant accountant might be advised to handle a certain entry as a capital item rather than as an expense item. Feedback motivates when it serves as a reward or promises a reward.[10] Hearing the boss say, "Take the rest of the day off," is a pleasant reward for hard work, but many employees also appreciate the attention and interest expressed by the very act of providing feedback, whatever its content (see Skills & Best Practices).

As documented in one study, the motivational function of feedback can be significantly enhanced by pairing *specific,* challenging goals with *specific* feedback about results.[11] A recent laboratory study with college students divided into superior-subordinate pairs demonstrated not only the positive impact of helpful feedback on performance, but a dampening effect on perceived organizational politics as well.[12] As discussed in Chapter 13, organizational politics is often dysfunctional.

# Three Sources of Feedback: Others, Task, and Self

It almost goes without saying that employees receive objective feedback from *others* such as peers, supervisors, lower-level employees, and outsiders. Perhaps less obvious is the fact that the *task* itself is a ready source of objective feedback.[13] Anyone who has spent hours on a "quick" Google search can appreciate the power of task-provided feedback. Similarly, skilled tasks such as computer programming or landing a jet airplane provide a steady stream of feedback about how well or poorly one is doing. A third source of feedback is *oneself,* but self-serving bias and other perceptual problems can contaminate this source. Those high in self-confidence tend to rely on personal feedback more than those with low self-confidence. Although circumstances vary, an employee can be bombarded by feedback from all three sources simultaneously. This is where the gatekeeping functions of perception and cognitive evaluation are needed to help sort things out.

**Self-Assessment Exercise**

Assessing Your Empathy Skills

# The Recipient's Perception of Feedback

The need for feedback is variable, across both individuals and situations[14] (see Hands-On Exercise). Feedback can be positive or negative. Generally, people tend to perceive and recall positive feedback more accurately than they do negative feedback.[15] But negative feedback (e.g., being told your performance is below average) can have a *positive* motivational effect. In fact, in one study, those who were told they were below average on a creativity test subsequently outperformed those who were led to believe their results were above average. The subjects apparently took the negative feedback as a challenge and set and pursued higher goals. Those receiving positive feedback apparently were less motivated to do better.[16] Nonetheless, feedback with a negative message or threatening content needs to be administered carefully to avoid creating insecurity and defensiveness.[17] Self-efficacy also can be damaged by negative feedback, as discovered in a pair of experiments with business students. The researchers concluded, "To facilitate the development of strong efficacy beliefs, managers should be careful about the provision of negative feedback. Destructive criticism by managers which attributes the cause of poor performance to internal factors reduces both the beliefs of self-efficacy and the self-set goals of recipients."[18]

## Correcting the Workplace "Jerk"

Unfortunately, the same employees who make coworkers miserable because they ignore rules, intimidate and harass others, and express a negative attitude are prone to retaliate when confronted about their behavior. This problem is especially sensitive when the difficult employee might be able to claim that the employer's complaints were really an expression of discrimination or violated a union contract. Still, if organizations are afraid to act, the damage to morale and productivity can be devastating. Here are some guidelines for giving feedback to an employee who is being a jerk at work:

- Act when the problem starts; don't try to tolerate counterproductive work behavior. Waiting will only make you look inconsistent and arbitrary later on.

- Use direct and specific words. Identify attitudes and behaviors that must change, and define what attitudes and behaviors will be acceptable in the future.

- Evaluate responses to make sure they are consistent with company policy and with the treatment of other employees.

- Document every step of this feedback process, including what was said.

- Verify that the employee understands, and give him or her time to correct the problem.

**SOURCE:** Based on J Janove, "Jerks at Work," *HR Magazine,* May 2007, pp 111–17.

Upon receiving feedback, people cognitively evaluate factors such as its accuracy, the credibility of the source, the fairness of the system (e.g., performance appraisal system), their performance-reward expectancies, and the reasonableness of the standards. Any feedback that fails to clear one or more of these cognitive hurdles will be rejected or downplayed. Personal experience largely dictates how these factors are weighed. For example, a review of research on disciplinary practices found that people have different perceptions of a disciplinary act based on the sex of the person delivering the discipline, the cultural characteristics of the people involved, and the supervisor's use of apologies and explanations.[19] Given these differences in perception, the writers recommend that the supervisor follow up with the employee to make sure the discipline was understood, use apologies or empathy to lessen the employee's anger, and focus on an objective of helping the employee in the long run. Two-way communication in the delivery of feedback is especially important for female supervisors, as a way to address expectations that they will lead in a more nurturing manner.

## Behavioral Outcomes of Feedback

In Chapter 7, we discussed how goal setting gives behavior direction, increases expended effort, and fosters persistence. Because feedback is intimately related to the goal-setting process, it involves the same behavioral outcomes: direction, effort, and persistence. However, while the fourth outcome of goal setting involves formulating goal-attainment strategies, the fourth possible outcome of feedback is *resistance.* Feedback schemes that smack of manipulation or fail one or more of the perceptual and cognitive evaluation tests mentioned previously breed resistance.[20] For ideas on how to deliver negative feedback in a way that avoids resistance and other counterproductive work behaviors, see Skills & Best Practices. Also, desirable work outcomes are more likely when feedback is part of a comprehensive *mentoring* or *coaching* process.[21]

## Nontraditional Upward Feedback and 360-Degree Feedback

Traditional top-down feedback programs have given way to some interesting variations in recent years. Two newer approaches, discussed in this section, are upward feedback and 360-degree feedback. Aside from breaking away from a strict superior-to-subordinate feedback loop, these newer approaches are different because they typically involve *multiple sources* of feedback.[22] Instead of getting feedback from one boss, often during an annual performance appraisal, more and more managers are getting structured feedback from superiors, lower-level employees, peers, and even outsiders such as customers. Nontraditional feedback is growing in popularity for at least six reasons:

1. Traditional performance appraisal systems have created widespread dissatisfaction. This was clearly evident in a survey of 96 human resource managers:

   > Sixty-one percent said managers have not been trained on how to properly assess people; 40 percent say the competencies managers are using to assess their employees do not accurately reflect the job and 28 percent report that managers play favorites.[23]

2. Team-based organization structures are replacing traditional hierarchies. This trend requires managers to have good interpersonal skills that are best evaluated by team members.

3. Multiple-rater systems are said to make feedback more valid than single-source feedback.[24]

4. Advanced computer network technology (the Internet and company intranets) greatly facilitates multiple-rater systems.[25]

5. Bottom-up feedback meshes nicely with the trend toward participative management and employee empowerment.

6. Coworkers and lower-level employees are said to know more about a manager's strengths and limitations than the boss.[26]

Together, these factors make a compelling case for looking at better ways to give and receive performance feedback.

**Upward Feedback** Upward feedback stands the traditional approach on its head by having lower-level employees provide feedback on a manager's style and performance. This type of feedback is generally anonymous. Most students are familiar with upward feedback programs from years of filling out anonymous teacher evaluation surveys. At MATRIX Resources, an Atlanta professional services firm, the CEO solicits feedback at quarterly meetings with groups of employees. This process fits well with the company's culture of employee involvement; employees also participate in setting corporate goals.[27]

> **upward feedback**
>
> **Employees evaluate their boss.**

Managers often resist upward feedback programs because they believe it erodes their authority. Other critics say anonymous upward feedback can become little more than a personality contest or, worse, be manipulated by managers who make promises or threats. What does the research literature tell us about upward feedback? Studies with diverse samples have given us these useful insights:

- The question of whether upward feedback should be *anonymous* was addressed by a study at a large U.S. insurance company. All told, 183 employees rated the skills and effectiveness of 38 managers. Managers who received anonymous upward feedback received *lower* ratings and liked the process *less* than did those receiving feedback from identifiable employees. This finding confirmed the criticism that employees will tend to go easier on their boss when not protected by confidentiality.[28]

- A large-scale study at the U.S. Naval Academy, where student leaders and followers live together day and night, discovered a positive impact of upward feedback on leader behavior.[29]

- In a field study of 238 corporate managers, upward feedback had a positive impact on the performance of low-to-moderate performers.[30]

**360-degree feedback**

Comparison of anonymous feedback from one's superior, subordinates, and peers with self-perceptions.

**360-Degree Feedback** Letting individuals compare their own perceived performance with behaviorally specific (and usually anonymous) performance information from their manager, subordinates, and peers is known as **360-degree feedback.** Even outsiders may be involved in what is sometimes called full-circle feedback. The idea is to let individuals know how their behavior affects others, with the goal of motivating change. For example, at both Scientific Atlanta, a Cisco Company, and Hanover Healthcare Plus, employees receive 360-degree feedback regarding a host of managerial and interpersonal skills and then review results with an external coach who helps employees to create a development plan.[31]

A G Lafley, CEO of Procter & Gamble, has the courage to handle 360-degree feedback and the common sense to make changes.

A recent meta-analysis of 24 studies of 360-degree feedback in which the recipients were rated two or more times prompted this helpful conclusion about when improvement is most likely to follow:

> [W]hen feedback indicates that change is necessary, recipients have a positive feedback orientation, perceive a need to change their behavior, react positively to the feedback, believe change is feasible, set appropriate goals to regulate their behavior, and take actions that lead to skill and performance improvement.[32]

Top-management support and an organizational climate of openness can help 360-degree feedback programs succeed. Procter & Gamble offers a good example:

> CEO A G Lafley finds out what his employees really think about him when he receives the results of his 360-degree feedback evaluation.
>
> The human resources tool that assesses strengths and weaknesses can be brutally honest because it lets a circle of people from executives on down give him anonymous performance reviews. The results show that others at P&G think Lafley is impatient. Lafley must also test the patience of others, because he is excoriated for being chronically late to meetings.[33]

**Practical Recommendations** Research evidence on upward and 360-degree feedback leads us to *favor* anonymity and *discourage* use for pay and promotion decisions. Otherwise, managerial resistance and self-serving manipulation would prevail.[34] We enthusiastically endorse the use of upward and/or 360-degree feedback for management development and training purposes.

## Why Feedback Often Fails

According to Annie Stevens and Greg Gostanian, managing partners at ClearRock, an outplacement and executive coaching firm, "Giving feedback to employees—and receiving feedback yourself—is one of the most misunderstood and poorly executed human resource processes."[35] Experts on the subject cite the following six common trouble signs for organizational feedback systems:

1.  Feedback is used to punish, embarrass, or put down employees.
2.  Those receiving the feedback see it as irrelevant to their work.
3.  Feedback information is provided too late to do any good.
4.  People receiving feedback believe it relates to matters beyond their control.
5.  Employees complain about wasting too much time collecting and recording feedback data.
6.  Feedback recipients complain about feedback being too complex or difficult to understand.[36]

Managers can provide effective feedback by consciously avoiding these pitfalls and by following some commonsense guidelines. Keep feedback relevant by relating it to existing goals and key result areas and by delivering it as soon as possible. Help employees understand the feedback by being specific and identifying observable behaviors or measurable results. Focus feedback on things employees can control: improvement, not just results, and performance rather than personality. Cultivate a fair and constructive climate by including positive feedback, giving one or two examples instead of "dumping" on employees, and taking time to listen to employees' reactions.

# Organizational Reward Systems

Rewards are an ever-present and always controversial feature of organizational life.[37] Some employees see their job as the source of a paycheck and little else. Others derive great pleasure from their job and association with co-workers. Even volunteers who donate their time to charitable organizations, such as the Red Cross, walk away with rewards in the form of social recognition and pride of having given unselfishly of their time. Hence, the subject of organizational rewards includes, but goes far beyond, monetary compensation.[38] This section examines key components of organizational reward systems.

Despite the fact that reward systems vary widely, it is possible to identify and interrelate some common components. The model in Figure 8–2 focuses on three important components: (1) types of rewards, (2) distribution criteria, and (3) desired outcomes. Let us examine these components and then discuss pay for performance.

**learning objective 3**

Distinguish between extrinsic and intrinsic rewards, and give a job-related example of each.

## Types of Rewards

Including the usual paycheck, the variety and magnitude of organizational rewards boggles the mind—from subsidized day care to college tuition reimbursement to stock

**FIGURE 8–2**
Key Factors in
Organizational
Reward
Systems

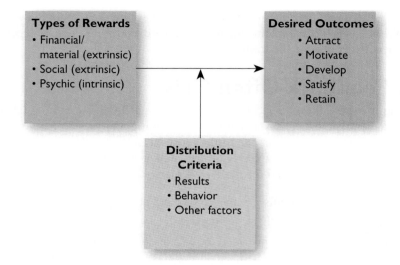

Types of Rewards
- Financial/
  material (extrinsic)
- Social (extrinsic)
- Psychic (intrinsic)

Desired Outcomes
- Attract
- Motivate
- Develop
- Satisfy
- Retain

Distribution
Criteria
- Results
- Behavior
- Other factors

grants and options.[39] A U.S. Bureau of Labor Statistics economist offered the following historical perspective of employee compensation:

> One of the more striking developments . . . over the past 75 years has been the growing complexity of employee compensation. Limited at the outbreak of World War I largely to straight-time pay for hours worked, compensation now includes a variety of employer-financed benefits, such as health and life insurance, retirement income, and paid time off. Although the details of each vary widely, these benefits are today standard components of the compensation package, and workers generally have come to expect them.[40]

Today, it is common for nonwage benefits to be 50% or more of total compensation.

In addition to the obvious pay and benefits, there are less obvious social and psychic rewards. Social rewards include praise and recognition from others both inside and outside the organization. Psychic rewards come from personal feelings of self-esteem, self-satisfaction, and accomplishment.

An alternative typology for organizational rewards is the distinction between extrinsic and intrinsic rewards. Financial, material, and social rewards qualify as **extrinsic rewards** because they come from the environment. Psychic rewards, however, are **intrinsic rewards** because they are self-granted. An employee who works to obtain extrinsic rewards, such as money or praise, is said to be extrinsically motivated. As we discussed in Chapter 6, one who derives pleasure from the task itself or experiences a sense of competence, pride, or self-determination is said to be intrinsically motivated.[41] The relative importance of extrinsic and intrinsic rewards is a matter of culture, personal tastes, and pressing circumstances. For example, employees of Digital Federal Credit Union in Massachusetts get extrinsic benefits like health insurance and a company match to their retirement savings. In addition, the company helps employees see how their work matters to others; in stories posted on the company's intranet, customers tell how employees have helped them. For many employees, this knowledge would be a source of intrinsic benefits.[42] And although it

**extrinsic rewards**

Financial, material, or social rewards from the environment.

**intrinsic rewards**

Self-granted, psychic rewards.

**Group Exercise**

What Rewards Motivate Student Achievement?

might seem hard to find intrinsic benefits in running a retailer during an economic slowdown, Carol Tomé, chief financial officer of The Home Depot, told a reporter that she has gained satisfaction from working to turn around that company because she is "passionate about finding out what we can be best at."[43]

**Test Your Knowledge**

Appraisal Methods

## Distribution Criteria

According to one expert on organizational reward systems, three general criteria for the distribution of rewards are as follows:

- *Performance: results.* Tangible outcomes such as individual, group, or organization performance; quantity and quality of performance.
- *Performance: actions and behaviors.* Such as teamwork, cooperation, risk taking, creativity.
- *Nonperformance considerations.* Customary or contractual, where the type of job, nature of the work, equity, tenure, level in hierarchy, etc., are rewarded.[44]

As illustrated in the following example, the trend today is toward *performance* criteria and away from nonperformance criteria:

> Del Wallick wears his pride under his sleeve. A handshake reveals his prized wristwatch, given to mark his 25th anniversary with Timken Co. "I only take it off to shower and sleep," he says.
>
> The hallways of Mr. Wallick's home in Canton, Ohio, are filled with an array of certificates marking the milestones in his 31-year career as a Timken steel-mill worker. Down in his rec room, a mantel clock that he and his wife picked out from a Timken gift catalog rests atop the family television.
>
> But these days, once-paternal companies like Timken are trying to move away from rewarding employees for long service. Many are reducing service-award programs—and a few are eliminating them entirely. Besides wanting to save money, these companies hope to tilt recognition more toward performance and away from years of loyal service.[45]

We turn our attention to pay for performance after rounding out the reward system model in Figure 8–2.

**For Urban Outfitters, the trendy clothing chain, everyone is expected to help with trend spotting, and they're well rewarded. Employees from managers to interns who bring back news of hot trends and styles to the buyers and design teams receive free concert tickets and evenings out, courtesy of the company. The chain won't give away exactly who it's spying on.**

## Desired Outcomes

As listed in Figure 8–2, a good reward system should attract talented people and motivate and satisfy them once they have joined the organization.[46] Further, a good reward system should foster personal growth and development and keep talented people from leaving.

## Pay for Performance

**Pay for performance** is the popular term for monetary incentives linking at least some portion of the paycheck directly to results or accomplishments. Many refer to it

learning objective **4**

Summarize the research lessons about pay for performance, and explain why rewards often fail to motivate employees.

**pay for performance**

Monetary incentives tied to one's results or accomplishments.

simply as *incentive pay,* while others call it *variable pay.*[47] The general idea behind pay-for-performance schemes—including but not limited to merit pay, bonuses, and profit sharing—is to give employees an incentive for working harder or smarter. Pay for performance is something extra, compensation above and beyond basic wages and salaries. Proponents of incentive compensation say something extra is needed because hourly wages and fixed salaries do little more than motivate people to show up at work and put in the required hours.[48] The most basic form of pay for performance is the traditional piece-rate plan, whereby the employee is paid a specified amount of money for each unit of work. For example, 2,500 artisans at Longaberger's, in Frazeyburg, Ohio, are paid a fixed amount for each handcrafted wooden basket they weave. Together, they produce 40,000 of the prized maple baskets daily.[49] Sales commissions, whereby a salesperson receives a specified amount of money for each unit sold, are another long-standing example of pay for performance. Today's service economy is forcing management to creatively adapt and go beyond piece rate and sales commission plans to accommodate greater emphasis on product and service quality, interdependence, and teamwork.[50]

Research results show mixed outcomes from pay for performance. In a recent experiment with college students, paying for performance resulted in greater productivity than paying a fixed amount for completing the task.[51] Not only did the subjects put forth more effort under the pay-for-performance scheme, but higher-performing individuals also tended to opt for performance-based pay. These results suggest that companies can improve productivity by offering pay for performance, which should help them attract workers with the best skills. However, in another study, incentive pay had a *negative* effect on the performance of 150,000 managers from 500 financially distressed companies.[52] A meta-analysis of 39 studies found only a modest positive correlation between financial incentives and performance *quantity* and no impact on performance *quality.*[53] Other researchers have found only a weak statistical link between large executive bonuses paid out in good years and subsequent improvement in corporate profitability.[54] Linking teachers' merit pay to student performance, an exciting school reform idea, turned out to be a big disappointment: "The bottom line is that despite high hopes, none of the 13 districts studied was able to use teacher pay incentives to achieve significant, lasting gains in student performance."[55] Clearly, the pay-for-performance area is still very much up in the air.

## Why Rewards Often Fail to Motivate

Despite huge investments of time and money for organizational reward systems, the desired motivational effect often is not achieved. A management consultant/writer recently offered these eight reasons:

1. Too much emphasis on monetary rewards.
2. Rewards lack an "appreciation effect."
3. Extensive benefits become entitlements.
4. Counterproductive behavior is rewarded. For example:

   In one case, city officials in Albuquerque, N.M., decided to pay trash truck crews for eight hours of work, no matter how long it actually took them to finish their routes. They wanted this move to encourage workers to finish the job quickly and thus lower the city's overtime expenses.

Instead, the crews began to cut corners. They missed pickups, resulting in numerous complaints from customers. Some drove too fast and caused accidents. Others incurred fines for driving to the dump with overloaded trucks.[56]

5. Too long a delay between performance and rewards.

6. Too many one-size-fits-all rewards.

7. Use of one-shot rewards with a short-lived motivational impact.

8. Continued use of demotivating practices such as layoffs, across-the-board raises and cuts, and excessive executive compensation.[57]

These stubborn problems have fostered a growing interest in more effective reward and compensation practices (see Skills & Best Practices).[58] For example, companies are going to greater lengths to communicate with employees about the value of their total rewards, including salary, benefits, and incentive pay. Boeing employees can go online to look up their pay and benefits profile, which shows salary, bonuses, and the value of medical and retirement benefits, as well as services such as wellness programs and child care referral services. "We have all sorts of great programs that [employees] might not have been aware of," says Tom Acker, the program manager for this information tool, but online access to the information makes it easy for them to learn—and to appreciate their rewards.[59] Other organizations are addressing the problem of one-size-fits-all rewards by offering flexible benefits packages. Harrisburg University of Science and Technology gives each employee a set value to allocate among a variety of benefits, such as retirement and insurance plans. The flexibility makes Harrisburg an attractive employer for a diverse group of talented employees.[60]

# Positive Reinforcement

Feedback and reward programs all too often are ineffective because they are administered in haphazard ways.[61] For example, consider these scenarios:

- A young programmer stops e-mailing creative suggestions to his boss because she never responds.

- The office politician gets a great promotion while her more skilled coworkers scratch their heads and gossip about the injustice.

**5** learning objective

State Thorndike's "law of effect" and explain Skinner's distinction between respondent and operant behavior.

In the first instance, a productive behavior faded away for lack of encouragement. In the second situation, unproductive behavior was unwittingly rewarded. Feedback and rewards need to be handled more precisely. Fortunately, the field of behavioral psychology can help. Thanks to the pioneering work of Edward L Thorndike, B F Skinner, and many others, a behavior modification technique called *positive reinforcement* helps managers achieve needed discipline and desired effect when providing feedback and granting rewards.[62]

## Thorndike's Law of Effect

**law of effect**

**Behavior with favorable consequences is repeated; behavior with unfavorable consequences disappears.**

During the early 1900s, Edward L Thorndike observed in his psychology laboratory that a cat would behave randomly and wildly when placed in a small box with a secret trip lever that opened a door. However, once the cat accidentally tripped the lever and escaped, the animal would go straight to the lever when placed back in the box. Hence, Thorndike formulated his famous **law of effect,** which says *behavior with favorable consequences tends to be repeated, while behavior with unfavorable consequences tends to disappear.*[63] This was a dramatic departure from the prevailing notion a century ago that behavior was the product of inborn instincts.

## Skinner's Operant Conditioning Model

Skinner refined Thorndike's conclusion that behavior is controlled by its consequences. Skinner's work became known as *behaviorism* because he dealt strictly with observable behavior.[64] As a behaviorist, Skinner believed it was pointless to explain behavior in terms of unobservable inner states such as needs, drives, attitudes, or thought processes.[65] He similarly put little stock in the idea of self-determination.

In his 1938 classic, *The Behavior of Organisms,* Skinner drew an important distinction between two types of behavior: respondent and operant behavior.[66] He labeled unlearned reflexes or stimulus–response (S–R) connections **respondent behavior.** This category of behavior was said to describe a very small proportion of adult human behavior. Examples of respondent behavior would include shedding tears while peeling onions and reflexively withdrawing one's hand from a hot stove.[67] Skinner attached the label **operant behavior** to behavior that is learned when one "operates on" the environment to produce desired consequences. Some call this the response–stimulus (R–S) model. Years of controlled experiments with pigeons in "Skinner boxes" helped Skinner develop a sophisticated technology of behavior control, or operant conditioning. For example, he taught pigeons how to pace figure eights and how to bowl by reinforcing the underweight (and thus hungry) birds with

Renowned behavioral psychologist **B F Skinner** and your coauthor **Bob Kreitner** met and posed for a snapshot at an Academy of Management meeting in Boston. As a behaviorist, Skinner preferred to deal with observable behavior and its antecedents and consequences in the environment rather than with inner states such as attitudes and cognitive processes. Professor Skinner was a fascinating man who left a permanent mark on modern psychology.

**respondent behavior**

**Skinner's term for unlearned stimulus–response reflexes.**

**operant behavior**

**Skinner's term for learned, consequence-shaped behavior.**

food whenever they more closely approximated target behaviors. Skinner's work has significant implications for OB because the vast majority of organizational behavior falls into the operant category.[68]

## Contingent Consequences

**learning objective 6**

Demonstrate your knowledge of positive reinforcement, negative reinforcement, punishment, and extinction, and explain behavior shaping.

Contingent consequences, according to Skinner's operant theory, control behavior in four ways: positive reinforcement, negative reinforcement, punishment, and extinction.[69] The term *contingent* means there is a systematic if-then linkage between the target behavior and the consequence. Remember Mom (and Pink Floyd) saying something to this effect: "If you don't finish your dinner, you don't get dessert" (see Figure 8–3)? To avoid the all-too-common mislabeling of these consequences, let us review some formal definitions.

**Test Your Knowledge**

Reinforcement Theory

**Positive Reinforcement Strengthens Behavior** **Positive reinforcement** is the process of strengthening a behavior by contingently presenting something pleasing. (Importantly, a behavior is strengthened when it increases in frequency and weakened when it decreases in frequency.) The watchwords for using positive reinforcement are "catch them doing something *right*!"[70] The "something right" that managers of Target want to see includes new product ideas that are attractive, appealing, and affordable. The retailer delivers positive reinforcement for innovation by setting up Big Idea contests where employees are invited to present new ideas on a particular topic, such as "the product in your pantry [that] frustrates you the most" or ideas for reducing energy consumption. Winners get recognition and a cash prize.[71]

**positive reinforcement**

**Making behavior occur more often by contingently presenting something positive.**

**Negative Reinforcement Also Strengthens Behavior** **Negative reinforcement** is the process of strengthening a behavior by contingently withdrawing something displeasing. For example, an army sergeant who stops yelling when a recruit jumps out of bed has negatively reinforced that particular behavior. Similarly, the behavior

**negative reinforcement**

**Making behavior occur more often by contingently withdrawing something negative.**

**FIGURE 8–3** Contingent Consequences in Operant Conditioning

**Nature of Consequence**

| Behavior–Consequence Relationship | Positive or Pleasing | Negative or Displeasing |
|---|---|---|
| Contingent Presentation | Positive Reinforcement<br>*Behavioral outcome:*<br>Target behavior occurs *more* often. | Punishment<br>*Behavioral outcome:*<br>Target behavior occurs *less* often. |
| Contingent Withdrawal | Punishment (Response Cost)<br>*Behavioral outcome:*<br>Target behavior occurs *less* often. | Negative Reinforcement<br>*Behavioral outcome:*<br>Target behavior occurs *more* often. |

**(no contingent consequence)**
Extinction
*Behavioral outcome:*
Target behavior occurs *less* often.

of clamping our hands over our ears when watching a jumbo jet take off is negatively reinforced by relief from the noise. Negative reinforcement is often confused with punishment. But the two strategies have opposite effects on behavior. Negative reinforcement, as the word *reinforcement* indicates, strengthens a behavior because it provides relief from an unpleasant situation.

**Punishment Weakens Behavior**  **Punishment** is the process of weakening behavior through either the contingent presentation of something displeasing or the contingent withdrawal of something positive. A manager assigning a tardy employee to a dirty job exemplifies the first type of punishment. At Target, missing out on a bonus because your new idea didn't have the expected market appeal would be an example of the second kind of punishment. Because Target doesn't want to weaken innovative behavior, it recognizes that trying new ideas involves risk, and in the words of Target president Gregg Steinhafel, "We don't penalize the teams that have made these calculated risks."[72] Other examples of withdrawing something positive include docking a tardy employee's pay or levying a fine for violating a law. Salespeople who must make up any cash register shortages out of their own pockets are being managed through response cost punishment. Ethical questions can and should be raised about this type of on-the-job punishment.[73]

> **punishment**
>
> **Making behavior occur less often by contingently presenting something negative or withdrawing something positive.**

> **extinction**
>
> **Making behavior occur less often by ignoring or not reinforcing it.**

At Granite Construction in Watsonville, California, 20% of every manager's bonus depends on the person's "people skills." For most of its 80 years, a call from the boss's office meant bad news. "Employees were only contacted when something went wrong," says division manager Bruce McGowan, a 20-year veteran who oversees a staff of 700. Now the emphasis is on positive reinforcement.

**Extinction Also Weakens Behavior**  **Extinction** is the weakening of a behavior by ignoring it or making sure it is not reinforced. Getting rid of a former boyfriend or girlfriend by refusing to return their phone calls is an extinction strategy. A good analogy for extinction is to imagine what would happen to your houseplants if you stopped watering them. Like a plant without water, a behavior without occasional reinforcement eventually dies. Although very different processes, both punishment and extinction have the same weakening effect on behavior.

# Schedules of Reinforcement

As just discussed, contingent consequences are an important determinant of future behavior. The *timing* of behavioral consequences can be even more important. Based on years of tedious laboratory experiments with pigeons in highly controlled environments, Skinner and his colleagues discovered distinct patterns of responding for various schedules of reinforcement.[74] Although some of their conclusions can be generalized to negative reinforcement, punishment, and extinction, it is best to think only of positive reinforcement when discussing schedules.

**Continuous Reinforcement**  As indicated in Table 8–1, every instance of a target behavior is reinforced when a **continuous reinforcement** (CRF) schedule is in effect. For instance, when your television set is operating properly, you are reinforced with a picture every time you turn it on (a CRF schedule). But, as with any CRF

## Schedules of Reinforcement | TABLE 8–1

| Schedule | Description | Probable Effects on Responding |
|---|---|---|
| **Continuous (CRF)** | Reinforcer follows every response. | Steady high rate of performance as long as reinforcement continues to follow every response. |
| | | High frequency of reinforcement may lead to early satiation. |
| | | Behavior weakens rapidly (undergoes extinction) when reinforcers are withheld. |
| | | Appropriate for newly emitted, unstable, or low-frequency responses. |
| **Intermittent** | Reinforcer does not follow every response. | Capable of producing high frequencies of responding. |
| | | Low frequency of reinforcement precludes early satiation. |
| | | Appropriate for stable or high-frequency responses. |
| Fixed ratio (FR) | A fixed number of responses must be emitted before reinforcement occurs. | A fixed ratio of 1:1 (reinforcement occurs after every response) is the same as a continuous schedule. |
| | | Tends to produce a high rate of response, which is vigorous and steady. |
| Variable ratio (VR) | A varying or random number of responses must be emitted before reinforcement occurs. | Capable of producing a high rate of response, which is vigorous, steady, and resistant to extinction. |
| Fixed interval (FI) | The first response after a specific period of time has elapsed is reinforced. | Produces an uneven response pattern varying from a very slow, unenergetic response immediately following reinforcement to a very fast, vigorous response immediately preceding reinforcement. |
| Variable interval (VI) | The first response after varying or random periods of time have elapsed is reinforced. | Tends to produce a high rate of response, which is vigorous, steady, and resistant to extinction. |

SOURCE: F Luthans and R Kreitner, *Organizational Behavior Modification and Beyond: An Operant and Social Learning Approach* (Glenview, IL: Scott, Foresman, 1985), p 58. Used with permission of the authors.

schedule of reinforcement, the behavior of turning on the television will undergo rapid extinction if the set breaks.

**Intermittent Reinforcement**   Unlike CRF schedules, **intermittent reinforcement** involves reinforcement of some but not all instances of a target behavior. Four subcategories of intermittent schedules, described in Table 8–1, are fixed and variable ratio schedules and fixed and variable interval schedules. Reinforcement in *ratio* schedules is

**continuous reinforcement**

Reinforcing every instance of a behavior.

**intermittent reinforcement**

Reinforcing some but not all instances of behavior.

contingent on the number of responses emitted. *Interval* reinforcement is tied to the passage of time. Some common examples of the four types of intermittent reinforcement are as follows:

- *Fixed ratio*—piece-rate pay; bonuses tied to the sale of a fixed number of units.
- *Variable ratio*—slot machines that pay off after a variable number of lever pulls; lotteries that pay off after the purchase of a variable number of tickets.
- *Fixed interval*—hourly pay; annual salary paid on a regular basis.
- *Variable interval*—random supervisory praise and pats on the back for employees who have been doing a good job.

**Proper Scheduling Is Important**    The schedule of reinforcement can more powerfully influence behavior than the magnitude of reinforcement. Although this proposition grew out of experiments with pigeons, subsequent on-the-job research confirmed it. Consider, for example, a field study of 12 unionized beaver trappers employed by a lumber company to keep the large rodents from eating newly planted tree seedlings.[75]

The beaver trappers were randomly divided into two groups that alternated weekly between two different bonus plans. Under the first schedule, each trapper earned his regular $7 per hour wage plus $1 for each beaver caught. Technically, this bonus was paid on a CRF schedule. The second bonus plan involved the regular $7 per hour wage plus a one-in-four chance (as determined by rolling the dice) of receiving $4 for each beaver trapped. This second bonus plan qualified as a variable ratio (VR-4) schedule. In the long run, both incentive schemes averaged out to a $1-per-beaver bonus. Surprisingly, however, when the trappers were under the VR-4 schedule, they were 58% more productive than under the CRF schedule, despite the fact that the net amount of pay averaged out the same for the two groups during the 12-week trapping season.

**Work Organizations Typically Rely on the Weakest Schedule**    Generally, variable ratio and variable interval schedules of reinforcement produce the strongest behavior that is most resistant to extinction. As gamblers will attest, variable schedules hold the promise of reinforcement after the next target response. For example, the following drama at a Laughlin, Nevada, gambling casino is one more illustration of the potency of variable ratio reinforcement:

> An elderly woman with a walker had lost her grip on the slot [machine] handle and had collapsed on the floor.
> "Help," she cried weakly.
> The woman at the machine next to her interrupted her play for a few seconds to try to help her to her feet, but all around her the army of slot players continued feeding coins to the machines.
> A security man arrived to soothe the woman and take her away.
> "Thank you," she told him appreciatively.
> "But don't forget my winnings."[76]

Organizations without at least some variable reinforcement are less likely to prompt this type of dedication to task. Consider the mix of reinforcement schedules at Kimley Horn & Associates, a Cary, North Carolina, engineering firm. Employees work

**Test Your Knowledge**

Reinforcing Performance

nine-hour days so that they can go home before noon every Friday (fixed interval), and employees are authorized to award any coworker a "$50 on-the-spot bonus" (variable ratio).[77] Despite the trend toward pay-for-performance, time-based pay schemes such as hourly wages and yearly salaries that rely on the weakest schedule of reinforcement (fixed interval) are still the rule in today's workplaces.

# Shaping Behavior with Positive Reinforcement

Have you ever wondered how trainers at aquarium parks manage to get bottle-nosed dolphins to do flips, killer whales to carry people on their backs, and seals to juggle balls? The results are seemingly magical. Actually, a mundane learning process called shaping is responsible for the animals' antics.

Two-ton killer whales, for example, have a big appetite, and they find buckets of fish very reinforcing. So if the trainer wants to ride a killer whale, he or she reinforces very basic behaviors that will eventually lead to the whale being ridden. The killer whale is contingently reinforced with a few fish for coming near the trainer, then for being touched, then for putting its nose in a harness, then for being straddled, and eventually for swimming with the trainer on its back. In effect, the trainer systematically raises the behavioral requirement for reinforcement. Thus, **shaping** is defined as the process of reinforcing closer and closer approximations to a target behavior.

Shaping works very well with people, too, especially in training and quality programs involving continuous improvement. Praise, recognition, and instructive and credible feedback cost managers little more than moments of their time.[78] Yet, when used in conjunction with a behavior-shaping program, these consequences can efficiently foster significant improvements in job performance.[79] The key to successful behavior shaping lies in reducing a complex target behavior to easily learned steps and then faithfully (and patiently) reinforcing any improvement. For example, Continental Airlines used a cash bonus program to improve its on-time arrival record from one of the worst in the industry to one of the best. Employees originally were promised a $65 bonus each month Continental earned a top-five ranking. Now it takes a second- or third-place ranking to earn the $65 bonus and a $100 bonus awaits employees when they achieve a No. 1 ranking.[80] The airline handed out a total of $33 million in on-time bonuses in 2007.[81] (Skills & Best Practices lists practical tips on shaping.)

## How to Effectively Shape Job Behavior

1. *Accommodate the process of behavioral change.* Behaviors change in gradual stages, not in broad, sweeping motions.

2. *Define new behavior patterns specifically.* State what you wish to accomplish in explicit terms and in small amounts that can be easily grasped.

3. *Give individuals feedback on their performance.* A once-a-year performance appraisal is not sufficient.

4. *Reinforce behavior as quickly as possible.*

5. *Use powerful reinforcement.* To be effective, rewards must be important to the employee—not to the manager.

6. *Use a continuous reinforcement schedule.* New behaviors should be reinforced every time they occur. This reinforcement should continue until these behaviors become habitual.

7. *Use a variable reinforcement schedule for maintenance.* Even after behavior has become habitual, it still needs to be rewarded, though not necessarily every time it occurs.

8. *Reward teamwork—not competition.* Group goals and group rewards are one way to encourage cooperation in situations in which jobs and performance are interdependent.

9. *Make all rewards contingent on performance.*

10. *Never take good performance for granted.* Even superior performance, if left unrewarded, will eventually deteriorate.

**SOURCE:** Adapted from A T Hollingsworth and D Tanquay Hoyer, "How Supervisors Can Shape Behavior," *Personnel Journal,* May 1985, pp 86, 88.

**shaping**

**Reinforcing closer and closer approximations to a target behavior.**

# key terms

# chapter summary

- *Specify the two basic functions of feedback and three sources of feedback.* Feedback, in the form of objective information about performance, both instructs and motivates. Individuals receive feedback from others, the task, and from themselves.

- *Define upward feedback and 360-degree feedback, and summarize the general tips for giving good feedback.* Lower-level employees provide upward feedback (usually anonymous) to their managers. A focal person receives 360-degree feedback from subordinates, the manager, peers, and selected others such as customers or suppliers. Good feedback is tied to performance *goals* and clear *expectations,* linked with *specific* behavior and/or results, reserved for *key result* areas, given as soon as possible, provided for *improvement* as well as for final results, focused on *performance* rather than on personalities, and based on *accurate* and *credible* information.

- *Distinguish between extrinsic and intrinsic rewards, and give a job-related example of each.* Extrinsic rewards, which are granted by others, include pay and benefits, recognition and praise, and favorable assignments and schedules. Intrinsic rewards are experienced internally or, in a sense, self-granted. Common intrinsic rewards include feelings of satisfaction, pride, and a sense of accomplishment.

- *Summarize the research lessons about pay for performance, and explain why rewards often fail to motivate employees.* Research on pay for performance has yielded mixed results, with no clear pattern of effectiveness. Reward systems can fail to motivate employees for these reasons:

overemphasis on money, no appreciation effect, benefits become entitlements, wrong behavior is rewarded, rewards are delayed too long, use of one-size-fits-all rewards, one-shot rewards with temporary effect, and demotivating practices such as layoffs.

- *State Thorndike's "law of effect," and explain Skinner's distinction between respondent and operant behavior.* According to Edward L Thorndike's law of effect, behavior with favorable consequences tends to be repeated, while behavior with unfavorable consequences tends to disappear. B F Skinner called unlearned stimulus–response reflexes *respondent behavior.* He applied the term *operant behavior* to all behavior learned through experience with environmental consequences.

- *Demonstrate your knowledge of positive reinforcement, negative reinforcement, punishment, and extinction, and explain behavior shaping.* Positive and negative reinforcement are consequence management strategies that strengthen behavior, whereas punishment and extinction weaken behavior. These strategies need to be defined objectively in terms of their actual impact on behavior frequency, not subjectively on the basis of intended impact. Behavior shaping occurs when closer and closer approximations of a target behavior are reinforced. In effect, the standard for reinforcement is made more difficult as the individual learns. The process begins with continuous reinforcement, which gives way to intermittent reinforcement when the target behavior becomes strong and habitual.

# discussion questions

1. Returning to the chapter-opening case, what recommendations or principles discussed in this chapter are being used by Sue Nokes?
2. How has feedback instructed or motivated you lately?
3. How would you summarize the practical benefits and drawbacks of 360-degree feedback?
4. How would you respond to a manager who said, "Employees cannot be motivated with money"?
5. What real-life examples of positive reinforcement, negative reinforcement, both forms of punishment, and extinction can you draw from your recent experience? Were these strategies appropriately or inappropriately used?

# ethical dilemma

## You Have 20 Minutes to Surf the Web. Go.

It's getting harder than ever to wheedle a raise out of the boss. So maybe at this year's annual review you should ask for more Web browsing time instead. Several employers are turning to a software program from Websense in San Diego that puts workers on the clock for their personal Net use. Kozy Shack Enterprises, a Hicksville (N.Y.) maker of ready-to-eat pudding, uses the "quota time" feature in Websense Enterprise to give employees one hour each day to shop, chat, and otherwise browse.

Info-tech managers can choose what sites are available during that time and adjust access depending on job titles. "We have sales people who travel extensively, so we give them much more access to travel sites," says Kozy's IT director, Richard Lehan. At Bates County Memorial Hospital in Butler, Mo., staff get 20 minutes a day for personal Internet use; department managers get 40.

For some companies, that's just too Big Brother-esque. Employees at London-based high-end retailer Harvey Nichols sign an honor code stating that personal Web use will be limited to their lunch break or after hours. The chain uses Websense to block gambling, pornography, and other inappropriate sites, but it doesn't limit time. "We have quite a bit of trust in people in the company," says Lee Smith, technology business systems manager. And most tech outfits figure they can't be Web innovators while restricting its use. Says Microsoft spokesman Lou Gellos: "We expect all employees to exercise common sense and good judgment and shop on MSN shopping—and I say that kind of tongue in cheek."[81]

## What Is Your Ethical Interpretation of This Situation?

1. There are no real ethical problems here because what an employee does on the company's time with the company's equipment is the company's business. Explain your ethical reasoning.

2. Employers either trust their employees or they don't. Any sort of monitoring of their Internet use says the employer doesn't trust them. Playing Big Brother only serves to erode loyalty and motivation. Explain the implications for hiring, along with your ethical reasoning.

3. Having employees sign an honor code about not abusing their Internet privileges is okay, but putting them on an electronic meter is going too far. Explain your ethical reasoning, and explore the practical implications.

**4.** Employers have a moral obligation to protect their employees from pornography, gambling, and other inappropriate Web sites with Internet blocks and filters. Explain.

**5.** Invent other options. Discuss.

For an interpretation of this situation, visit our Web site, **www.mhhe.com/kinickiob4e.**

If you're looking for additional study materials, be sure to check out the Online Learning Center at

**www.mhhe.com/kinickiob4e**

for more information and interactivities that correspond to this chapter.

# part Three

# Managing Social Processes and Making Decisions

# chapter
## Nine

# Effective Groups and Teamwork

**LEARNING OBJECTIVES**

**After reading the material in this chapter, you should be able to:**

1. Describe the five stages of Tuckman's theory of group development.

2. Contrast roles and norms, and specify four reasons why norms are enforced in organizations.

3. Explain how a work group becomes a team, and identify five teamwork competencies.

4. List at least four things managers can do to build trust.

5. Describe self-managed teams and virtual teams.

6. Describe groupthink, and identify at least four of its symptoms.

American corporations love teamwork. But few companies are as smitten as *ICU Medical Inc.*

At the San Clemente, Calif., maker of medical devices, any worker can form a team to tackle any project. Team members set meetings, assign tasks and create deadlines themselves. Chief Executive George Lopez says he's never vetoed a team decision, even when he disagreed with it. These teams have altered production processes and set up a 401(k) plan, among other changes. . . .

**Managers like George Lopez play an important role in creating an environment that supports teamwork.**

Most big companies assign teams for projects. ICU, which has around 1,480 employees, is unusual in that it allows workers to initiate the teams. . . .

Dr. Lopez, an internist, founded ICU in 1984. By the early 1990s, the company had about $10 million in annual revenue and was preparing for a public offering. Demand for the company's Clave product, used in connecting a patient's IV systems, was skyrocketing; Dr. Lopez needed to figure out how to ramp up production.

ICU had fewer than 100 employees but was expanding rapidly. Handling the booming growth and demand "was an overwhelming task for one entrepreneur CEO," says Dr. Lopez, 59 years old. He was still making most decisions himself, often sleeping at the office.

Then, he had an epiphany watching his son play hockey. The opposing team had a star, but his son's team ganged up on him and won. "The team was better than one player," says Dr. Lopez. He decided to delegate power by letting employees form teams hoping it would help him spread out the decisionmaking and encourage input from people closest to the problems.

Some executives hated the idea; his chief financial officer quit. Putting the new system in place, Dr. Lopez told employees to form teams to come up with ways to boost production. It didn't work. With no leaders, and no rules, "nothing was getting done, except people were spending a lot of time talking," he says.

After about a year and a half, he decided teams should elect leaders, which brought a vast improvement. In 1995 he hired Jim Reitz now the human-resources director, who helped him create a structure with a minimum of bureaucracy. They developed core values—"take risks"—and so-called rules of engagement—"challenge the issue, not the person." At the same time, ICU started paying teams rewards based on a percentage of the cumulative salaries of their members.

It worked. Employees embraced teams. Today 12 to 15 teams finish projects each quarter, often meeting once a week or so. The typical team has five to seven members, and the company allots $75,000 quarterly to reward those that succeed.

Teams have propelled changes over the objections of top executives. Dr. Lopez, worried about the cost, didn't want to institute a 401(k) plan, but acquiesced after a team recommended one. He now concedes the plan has helped in retaining employees.

Dr. Lopez can veto team decisions but says he hasn't yet. For teams to work, employees need to feel they have authority, he says. A veto would really have to be worth it, Dr. Lopez says. The team would have to be putting the company "on a pathway to destruction."

So far, that hasn't happened. ICU's revenue grew 28% last year to $201.6 million though the company projects that revenue will decline this year. Its stock has climbed more than sixfold in the past decade. . . .

At ICU, team members don't get a break from their regular jobs. Serving on teams is technically voluntary but some employees with special expertise are "requested" to join. "It's above and beyond your job," says business-applications manager Colleen Wilder, who has served on many teams in the 10 years at ICU, "You still have to get your job done."

The rewards can create tension. Ms. Wilder once balked at sharing a reward with coworkers she thought had joined a team solely for the money. She proposed dividing the money based on what tasks team members performed. "I said, 'You did nothing, and I propose you get nothing,' " she says. The team agreed.

The payment system has been changed to peg the size of the reward to the importance of the project. "People started thinking, 'We created a whole new product for the company and these guys painted the lunch room, and they're getting the same amount of money that we are?' " Mr. Reitz says. He encourages employees to question whether teams really met their goals, or whether a project is significant enough to merit high reward levels.

Over the years, ICU has instituted more rules to help teams function smoothly. A group of employees created a 25-page handbook that concretely spells out team operations—for instance, listing eight items for "What should we do at the first meeting?"—and addresses frequently asked questions. Teams must post notes of each meeting to the company intranet, where any employee can offer feedback.[1]

**How are teams helping ICU Medical to grow its business? For an interpretation of this case and additional comments, visit our Online Learning Center at**

**www.mhhe.com/ kinickiob4e.**

**FOR DISCUSSION**

BOTH DAILY EXPERIENCE and research reveal the importance of social skills for individual and organizational success. An ongoing study by the Center for Creative Leadership (involving diverse samplings from Belgium, France, Germany, Italy, Spain, the United Kingdom, and the United States), for example, found four stumbling blocks that tend to derail executives' careers. According to the researchers, "A derailed executive is one who, having reached the general manager level, finds that there is little chance of future advancement due to a misfit between job requirements and personal skills."[2] The four stumbling blocks, consistent across the cultures studied, are as follows:

1. Problems with interpersonal relationships.
2. Failure to meet business objectives.
3. Failure to build and lead a team.
4. Inability to change or adapt during a transition.[3]

Notice how both the first and third career stumbling blocks involve interpersonal skills—the ability to get along and work effectively with others. Managers with interpersonal problems typically were described as manipulative and insensitive. Interestingly, two-thirds of the derailed European managers studied had problems with interpersonal relationships. That same problem reportedly plagued one-third of the derailed US executives. Management, as defined in Chapter 1, involves getting things done with and through others. The job is simply too big to do it alone.

The purpose of this chapter is to shift the focus from individual behavior to collective behavior. As illustrated in the chapter-opening case, the collective ideas and effort put forth by teams can significantly contribute to organizational success. It thus is important to understand the dynamics of teamwork and the role that managers like George Lopez play in creating an environment that supports teamwork. This chapter will help you to understand these issues. We explore groups and teams, key features of modern life, and discuss how to make them effective while avoiding common pitfalls. Among the interesting variety of topics in this chapter are group development, trust, self-managed teams, virtual teams, and groupthink.

# Fundamentals of Group Behavior

**group**

Two or more freely interacting people with shared norms and goals and a common identity.

Drawing from the field of sociology,[4] we define a **group** as two or more freely interacting individuals who share collective norms and goals and have a common identity.[5] Organizational psychologist Edgar Schein shed additional light on this concept by drawing instructive distinctions between a group, a crowd, and an organization:

> The size of a group is thus limited by the possibilities of mutual interaction and mutual awareness. Mere aggregates of people do not fit this definition because they do not interact and do not perceive themselves to be a group even if they are aware of each other as, for instance, a crowd on a street corner watching some event. A total department, a union, or a whole organization would not be a group in spite of thinking of themselves as "we," because they generally do not all interact and are not all aware of each other. However, work teams, committees, subparts of departments, cliques, and various other informal associations among organizational members would fit this definition of a group.[6]

Take a moment now to think of various groups of which you are a member. Does each of your "groups" satisfy the four criteria in our definition?

# Formal and Informal Groups

Individuals join groups, or are assigned to groups, to accomplish various purposes. If the group is formed by a manager to help the organization accomplish its goals, then it qualifies as a **formal group.** Formal groups typically wear such labels as work group, team, committee, or task force. An **informal group** exists when the members' overriding purpose of getting together is friendship.[7] Formal and informal groups often overlap, such as when a team of corporate auditors heads for the tennis courts after work. A recent survey of 1,385 office workers in the US found 71% had attended important events with coworkers, such as weddings and funerals.[8] Indeed, friendships forged on the job can be so strong as to outlive the job itself in an era of job hopping, reorganizations, and mass layoffs:

> **formal group**
> Formed by the organization.
>
> **informal group**
> Formed by friends.

> Many employees are finding that leaving their employer doesn't always mean saying goodbye: Membership in organized corporate "alumni" groups is increasingly in vogue.
>
> There are now alumni groups for hundreds of companies, including Hewlett-Packard, Ernst & Young and Texas Instruments. Yahoo alone lists more than 500 such ex-employee groups.
>
> Some groups are started by former employees, while others are formally sanctioned by employers as a way to stay in touch, creating a potential pool of boomerang workers that employers can draw from when hiring picks up.[9]

The desirability of overlapping formal and informal groups is problematic.[10] Some managers firmly believe personal friendship fosters productive teamwork on the job while others view workplace "bull sessions" as a serious threat to productivity. Both situations are common, and it is the manager's job to strike a workable balance, based on the maturity and goals of the people involved.

# Functions of Formal Groups

Researchers point out that formal groups fulfill two basic functions: *organizational* and *individual*.[11] The various functions are listed in Table 9–1. Complex combinations of these functions can be found in formal groups at any given time.

Consider, for example, the Love Team at InsureMe, a 70-person company that provides online referrals to people shopping for insurance. The team operates within a culture based on four values: love, integrity, leadership, and innovation.[12] The Love Team is an expression of the first value, and its duties include organizing support for employees who are undergoing difficulties and coordinating regular volunteer activities for employees to serve their community. This team's functions support InsureMe's organizational goals of maintaining a caring organizational culture and increasing employee satisfaction. At the same time, employees who serve on the team most likely would be fulfilling individual functions such as building strong work relationships and living according to their values.

Teams serve many purposes at Whole Foods Market, where all employees belong to teams. Team members share equally in any savings they achieve for the company and vote on whether newcomers will be permanently hired. Would you like to work in this environment? Why?

**TABLE 9–1**    Formal Groups Fulfill Organizational and Individual Functions

| Organizational Functions | Individual Functions |
|---|---|
| 1. Accomplish complex, interdependent tasks that are beyond the capabilities of individuals. | 1. Satisfy the individual's need for affiliation. |
| 2. Generate new or creative ideas and solutions. | 2. Develop, enhance, and confirm the individual's self-esteem and sense of identity. |
| 3. Coordinate interdepartmental efforts. | 3. Give individuals an opportunity to test and share their perceptions of social reality. |
| 4. Provide a problem-solving mechanism for complex problems requiring varied information and assessments. | 4. Reduce the individual's anxieties and feelings of insecurity and powerlessness. |
| 5. Implement complex decisions. | 5. Provide a problem-solving mechanism for personal and interpersonal problems. |
| 6. Socialize and train newcomers. | |

SOURCE: Adapted from E H Schein, *Organizational Psychology*, 3rd ed (Englewood Cliffs. NJ: Prentice-Hall, 1980), pp. 149–51.

# The Group Development Process

**1 learning objective**

Describe the five stages of Tuckman's theory of group development.

Groups and teams in the workplace go through a maturation process, such as one would find in any life-cycle situation (e.g., humans, organizations, products). While there is general agreement among theorists that the group development process occurs in identifiable stages, they disagree about the exact number, sequence, length, and nature of those stages.[13] One oft-cited model is the one proposed in 1965 by educational psychologist Bruce W Tuckman. His original model involved only four stages (forming, storming, norming, and performing). The five-stage model in Figure 9–1 evolved when Tuckman and a doctoral student added "adjourning" in 1977.[14] A word of caution is in order. Somewhat akin to Maslow's need hierarchy theory, Tuckman's theory has been repeated and taught so often and for so long that many have come to view it as documented fact, not merely a theory. Even today, it is good to remember Tuckman's own caution that his group development model was derived more from group therapy sessions than from natural-life groups. Still, many in the OB field like Tuckman's five-stage model of group development because of its easy-to-remember labels and commonsense appeal.

Let us briefly examine each of the five stages in Tuckman's model. Notice in Figure 9–1 how individuals give up a measure of their independence when they join and participate in a group.[15] Also, the various stages are not necessarily of the same duration or intensity. For instance, the storming stage may be practically nonexistent or painfully long, depending on the goal clarity and the commitment and maturity of the members. You can make this process come to life by relating the various stages to your own experiences with work groups, committees, athletic teams, social or religious groups, or class project teams. Some group happenings that surprised you when they occurred may now make sense or strike you as inevitable when seen as part of a natural development process.

**Stage 1: Forming**    During this "ice-breaking" stage, group members tend to be uncertain and anxious about such things as their roles, the people in charge, and the group's goals. Mutual trust is low, and there is a good deal of holding back to see who takes charge and how. In life-and-death situations, which are sometimes faced by

**FIGURE 9–1**
Tuckman's
Five-Stage
Theory
of Group
Development

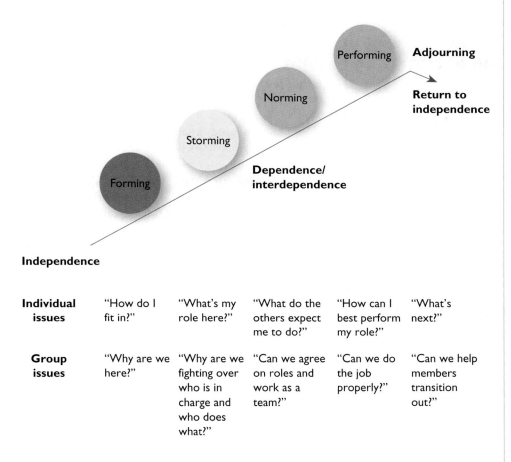

| | | | | | |
|---|---|---|---|---|---|
| **Individual issues** | "How do I fit in?" | "What's my role here?" | "What do the others expect me to do?" | "How can I best perform my role?" | "What's next?" |
| **Group issues** | "Why are we here?" | "Why are we fighting over who is in charge and who does what?" | "Can we agree on roles and work as a team?" | "Can we do the job properly?" | "Can we help members transition out?" |

surgical teams and airline cockpit crews, the period of uncertainty can be dangerous. According to the National Transportation Safety Board, "73% of commercial airline pilots' serious mistakes happen on crews' first day together."[16] If the formal leader (e.g., a supervisor) does not assert his or her authority, an emergent leader will eventually step in to fulfill the group's need for leadership and direction. Leaders typically mistake this honeymoon period as a mandate for permanent control. But later problems may force a leadership change.

**Stage 2: Storming**    This is a time of testing. Individuals test the leader's policies and assumptions as they try to determine how they fit into the power structure.[17] Subgroups take shape, and subtle forms of rebellion, such as procrastination, occur. Many groups stall in stage 2 because power politics erupts into open rebellion. For an example of a small company that successfully navigated the storming phase, see Skills & Best Practices on page 228.

**Stage 3: Norming**    Groups that make it through stage 2 generally do so because a respected member, other than the leader, challenges the group to resolve its power struggles so something can be accomplished. Questions about authority and power are resolved through unemotional, matter-of-fact group discussion. A feeling of team spirit is experienced because members believe they have found their proper roles. **Group cohesiveness,** defined as the "we feeling" that binds members of a group together, is the principal by-product of stage 3.[18]

**group cohesiveness**

**A "we feeling" binding group members together.**

## Big Foote Music Weathers the Storm

In the 1990s, brothers Ray and Sherman Foote founded Big Foote Music, bringing together a small group of composers, musicians, and producers to develop music for commercials and movie trailers. As more and more clients signed on with the New York company, work became more stressful, and the brothers began to argue.

At this point, the group might have splintered. But the brothers got help from Lou Cox, a clinical psychologist who specializes in communication. During four long sessions, Cox taught the Foote brothers to work together more effectively. Ray Foote recalls, "The most powerful piece of it was separating the emotional stuff from the task."

Impressed with how much better their own communication became, the Foote brothers had Cox teach the whole company how to communicate openly. Instead of letting negative feelings fester, the staff members now speak constructively about whatever is bothering them. Cox taught them names for problem behaviors, such as the "merry-go-round," a situation in which complaints go round and round the workplace. When employees identify a destructive behavior, everyone understands and can focus on a solution. That helps them realize the founders' goal of meeting clients' needs through the power of collaboration—group harmony in service of catchy music.

**SOURCES: Based on S Garmhausen, "Music Maker Finds Inner Harmony,"** *Crain's New York Business,* **February 18, 2008, downloaded from General Reference Center Gold, http://find.galegroup.com; and C Bunish, "A Big Foote in the Big Apple,"** *Post,* **May 1, 2002, downloaded from FindArticles, http://findarticles.com.**

**roles**

Expected behaviors for a given position.

**task roles**

Task-oriented group behavior.

**maintenance roles**

Relationship-building group behavior.

**Stage 4: Performing** Activity during this vital stage is focused on solving task problems. As members of a mature group, contributors get their work done without hampering others. There is a climate of open communication, strong cooperation, and lots of helping behavior. Conflicts and job boundary disputes are handled constructively and efficiently.[19] Cohesiveness and personal commitment to group goals help the group achieve more than could any one individual acting alone.

**Stage 5: Adjourning** The work is done; it is time to move on to other things. Having worked so hard to get along and get something done, many members feel a compelling sense of loss. The return to independence can be eased by rituals celebrating "the end" and "new beginnings." Parties, award ceremonies, graduations, or mock funerals can provide the needed punctuation at the end of a significant group project. Leaders need to emphasize valuable lessons learned in group dynamics to prepare everyone for future group and team efforts.

## Group Member Roles

Four centuries have passed since William Shakespeare had his character Jaques speak the following memorable lines in Act II of *As You Like It:* "All the world's a stage, And all the men and women merely players; They have their exits and their entrances; And one man in his time plays many parts. . . ." This intriguing notion of all people as actors in a universal play was not lost on 20th-century sociologists who developed a complex theory of human interaction based on roles. According to an OB scholar, **roles** are sets of behaviors that persons expect of occupants of a position."[20] For employees, roles can go beyond duties in a job description to include, for example, helping coworkers and suggesting improvements.[21] As described in Table 9–2, both task and maintenance roles need to be performed if a work group is to accomplish anything.[22]

**Task versus Maintenance Roles** **Task roles** enable the work group to define, clarify, and pursue a common purpose. Meanwhile, **maintenance roles** foster supportive and constructive interpersonal relationships. In short, task roles keep the group *on track* while maintenance roles keep the group *together.* A project team member is performing a task function when he or she says at an update meeting, "What is the real issue here? We don't seem to be getting anywhere." Another individual who says, "Let's hear from those who oppose this plan," is performing a maintenance function. Importantly, each of the various task and maintenance roles may be played in varying combinations and sequences by either the group's leader or any of its members.

**Checklist for Managers** The task and maintenance roles listed in Table 9–2 on page 230 can serve as a handy checklist for managers and group leaders who wish to ensure proper group development. Roles that are not always performed when needed, such as those of coordinator, evaluator, and gatekeeper, can be performed in a timely manner by the formal leader or assigned to other members. Leaders can further ensure that roles are fulfilled by clarifying specifically what is expected of employees in the group. A study of more than 20,000 US workers found that they were most likely to agree on their roles when job requirements were defined in terms of specific tasks. They had less agreement about their role as defined in terms of general responsibilities and least consensus for requirements defined by the traits the employee should possess.[23]

Danica Patrick, one of the only female racecar drivers, and all other professional racecar drivers rely on there teams to develop strategies to win races. How do the stages of team development apply to racecar teams?

The task roles of initiator, orienter, and energizer are especially important because they are *goal-directed* roles. Research studies on group goal setting confirm the motivational power of challenging goals. As with individual goal setting (in Chapter 7), difficult but achievable goals are associated with better group results.[24] Also in line with individual goal-setting theory and research, group goals are more effective if group members clearly understand them and are both individually and collectively committed to achieving them. Initiators, orienters, and energizers can be very helpful in this regard.

International managers need to be sensitive to cultural differences regarding the relative importance of task and maintenance roles. In Japan, for example, cultural tradition calls for more emphasis on maintenance roles, especially the roles of harmonizer and compromiser:

> Courtesy requires that members not be conspicuous or disputatious in a meeting or classroom. If two or more members discover that their views differ—a fact that is tactfully taken to be unfortunate—they adjourn to find more information and to work toward a stance that all can accept. They do not press their personal opinions through strong arguments, neat logic, or rewards and threats. And they do not hesitate to shift their beliefs if doing so will preserve smooth interpersonal relations. (To lose is to win.)[25]

**learning objective** 2
Contrast roles and norms, and specify four reasons why norms are enforced in organizations.

**Group Exercise**
Identifying Task and Maintenance Roles Within Groups

# Norms

Norms are more encompassing than roles. While roles involve behavioral expectations for specific positions, norms help organizational members determine right from wrong and good from bad. According to one respected team of management consultants: "A **norm** is an attitude, opinion, feeling, or action—shared by two or more people—that guides their behavior."[26] Although norms are typically unwritten and seldom discussed openly, they have a powerful influence on group and organizational behavior.[27] One of Google's norms, for instance, is that employees should be innovative and constantly looking for new products and better ways of working. That norm is seen in the company's requirement that employees devote part of their time to projects they come up

**norm**
Shared attitudes, opinions, feelings, or actions that guide social behavior.

## TABLE 9–2 | Task and Maintenance Roles

| Task Roles | Description |
|---|---|
| Initiator | Suggests new goals or ideas. |
| Information seeker/giver | Clarifies key issues. |
| Opinion seeker/giver | Clarifies pertinent values. |
| Elaborator | Promotes greater understanding through examples or exploration of implications. |
| Coordinator | Pulls together ideas and suggestions. |
| Orienter | Keeps group headed toward its stated goal(s). |
| Evaluator | Tests group's accomplishments with various criteria such as logic and practicality. |
| Energizer | Prods group to move along or to accomplish more. |
| Procedural technician | Performs routine duties (e.g., handing out materials or rearranging seats). |
| Recorder | Performs a "group memory" function by documenting discussion and outcomes. |

| Maintenance Roles | Description |
|---|---|
| Encourager | Fosters group solidarity by accepting and praising various points of view. |
| Harmonizer | Mediates conflict through reconciliation or humor. |
| Compromiser | Helps resolve conflict by meeting others "half way." |
| Gatekeeper | Encourages all group members to participate. |
| Standard setter | Evaluates the quality of group processes. |
| Commentator | Records and comments on group processes/dynamics. |
| Follower | Serves as a passive audience. |

SOURCE: Adapted from discussion in K D Benne and P Sheats, "Functional Roles of Group Members," *Journal of Social Issues,* Spring 1948, pp. 41–49.

with, the wide latitude granted to groups that want to take initiative, and the company's focus on hiring people who, in the words of founder Sergey Brin, "love to work here, . . . love to create things, and they're not here primarily for the money."[28]

At Google and elsewhere, group members positively reinforce those who adhere to current norms with friendship and acceptance. On the other hand, nonconformists experience criticism and even **ostracism,** or rejection by group members. Anyone who has experienced the "silent treatment" from a group of friends knows what a potent social weapon ostracism can be.[29] Norms can be put into proper perspective by understanding how they develop and why they are enforced.

**ostracism**

Rejection by other group members.

**How Norms Are Developed**    Experts say norms evolve in an informal manner as the group or organization determines what it takes to be effective. Generally speaking, norms develop in various combinations of the following four ways:

1. *Explicit statements by supervisors or coworkers.* For instance, a group leader might explicitly set norms about not drinking alcohol at lunch.

2. *Critical events in the group's history.* At times there is a critical event in the group's history that establishes an important precedent. For example, commercial jet manufacturer Airbus, a consortium formed among France, Germany,

Great Britain, and Spain, had a norm that employee groups drawn from one nation worked independently from groups located elsewhere. However, that approach recently caused so much inefficiency and poor communication that it threatened the company's ability to launch its innovative superjumbo A380 aircraft. As delivery dates were pushed further and further into the future, management in desperation required German engineers to travel to France, where their French colleagues would help them use newer, more efficient design software than they had in Germany. Eventually, successes began to reinforce the new norm of information sharing.[30]

3. *Primacy.* The first behavior pattern that emerges in a group often sets group expectations. For example, when Commonwealth Health Insurance Connector, a group of 10 representatives from business, labor, and consumer groups, began to sort out how Massachusetts might implement universal health coverage, the differences among group members led to fierce arguments. But on the first tough decision, which involved whether to charge low-income citizens a premium for participating, Celia Wcislo, an organizer with the Service Employees International Union, decided that although she had argued forcefully, she would compromise for the sake of unity and a chance to move forward. Ultimately, according to an analysis of the group's work, Wcislo's cooperative behavior established a norm that other group members followed on other issues.[31]

4. *Carryover behaviors from past situations.* Such carryover of individual behaviors from past situations can increase the predictability of group members' behaviors in new settings and facilitate task accomplishment. For instance, students and professors carry fairly constant sets of expectations from class to class.[32]

We would like you to take a few moments and think about the norms that are currently in effect in your classroom. List the norms on a sheet of paper. Do these norms help or hinder your ability to learn? Norms can affect performance either positively or negatively.

**Why Norms Are Enforced**  Norms tend to be enforced by group members when they

- Help the group or organization survive.
- Clarify or simplify behavioral expectations.
- Help individuals avoid embarrassing situations.
- Clarify the group's or organization's central values and/or unique identity.[33]

# Teams, Trust, and Teamwork

The team approach to managing organizations is having diverse and substantial impacts on organizations and individuals. Teams promise to be a cornerstone of progressive management for the foreseeable future. General Electric's CEO, Jeffrey Immelt, offers this blunt overview: "You lead today by building teams and placing others first. It's not about you."[34] This means virtually all employees will need to polish their team skills. Fortunately, the trend toward teams has a receptive audience today. Both women and younger employees, according to research, thrive in team-oriented organizations.[35]

In this team-focused environment, organizations need leaders who are adept at teamwork themselves and can cultivate the level of trust necessary to foster constructive teamwork. In a recent survey by consulting firm Development Dimensions International, the top three traits of a boss admired by employees were trust in employees, honesty/authenticity, and great team-building skills.[36] In this section, we define the term *team,* look at teamwork competencies and team building, discuss trust as a key to real teamwork, and explore two evolving forms of teamwork—self-managed teams and virtual teams.

## A Team Is More Than Just a Group

**team**

**Small group with complementary skills who hold themselves mutually accountable for common purpose, goals, and approach.**

Jon R Katzenbach and Douglas K Smith, management consultants at McKinsey & Company, say it is a mistake to use the terms *group* and *team* interchangeably. After studying many different kinds of teams—from athletic to corporate to military—they concluded that successful teams tend to take on a life of their own. Katzenbach and Smith define a **team** as "a small number of people with complementary skills who are committed to a common purpose, performance goals, and approach for which they hold themselves mutually accountable."[37]

Thus, a group becomes a team when the following criteria are met:

1. *Leadership* becomes a shared activity.
2. *Accountability* shifts from strictly individual to both individual and collective.
3. The group develops its own *purpose* or mission.
4. *Problem solving* becomes a way of life, not a part-time activity.
5. *Effectiveness* is measured by the group's collective outcomes and products.[38]

Bob Lane, CEO of Deere & Company, emphasizes the purpose and effectiveness of teams when he talks about his company being a team, not a family. A reporter summarized his words this way: "While family members who don't pull their weight may not be welcome at the Thanksgiving dinner table, they remain members of the family. But if you're not pulling your weight here, I'm sorry, you're not part of the team."[39]

Relative to Tuckman's theory of group development covered earlier—forming, storming, norming, performing, and adjourning—teams are task groups that have matured to the *performing* stage. Because of conflicts over power and authority and unstable interpersonal relations, many work groups never qualify as a real team.[40] Katzenbach and Smith clarified the distinction this way: "The essence of a team is common commitment. Without it, groups perform as individuals; with it, they become a powerful unit of collective performance."[41]

When Katzenbach and Smith refer to "a small number of people" in their definition, they mean between 2 and 25 team members. They found effective teams to typically have fewer than 10 members. This conclusion was echoed in a survey of 400 workplace team members in the United States and Canada: "The average North American team consists of 10 members. Eight is the most common size."[42]

## Developing Teamwork Competencies

Forming workplace teams and urging employees to be good team players are good starting points on the road to effective teams. But they are not enough today. Teamwork skills and competencies need to be role modeled and taught. These include group problem solving, mentoring, conflict management skills, and emotional intelligence. Research has found that teams collaborate most effectively when companies develop and encourage teamwork skills through the factors listed in Skills & Best Practices. Teamwork competencies should be rewarded, too. For example, consider what has taken place at Internet equipment maker Cisco Systems:

> [CEO John] Chambers took . . . steps to rein in Cisco's Wild West culture during 2002. Most pointedly, he made teamwork a critical part of top execs' bonus plans. He told them 30% of their bonuses for the 2003 fiscal year would depend on how well they collaborated with others. "It tends to formalize the discussion around how can I help you and how can you help me," says Sue Bostrom, head of Cisco's Internet consulting group.[43]

# Team Building

**Team building** is a catch-all term for a host of techniques aimed at improving the internal functioning of work groups. Whether conducted by company trainers or hired consultants (and done on-site or off-site), team-building workshops strive for greater cooperation, better communication, and less dysfunctional conflict. Rote memorization and lectures or discussions are discouraged by team builders who prefer *active* versus passive learning. Greater emphasis is placed on *how* work groups get the job done than on the task itself. Experiential learning techniques such as interpersonal trust exercises, conflict role-play sessions, and competitive games are common.[44] Some prefer off-site gatherings to get participants away from their work and out of their comfort zones. An exotic (and expensive) case in point is Seagate Technology:

> Plenty of companies try to motivate the troops, but few go as far as Seagate Technology. In February [2006] the $9.8 billion maker of computer storage hardware flew 200 staffers to New Zealand for its sixth annual Eco Seagate—an intense week of team-building topped off by an all-day race in which Seagaters had to kayak, hike, bike, swim, and rappel down a cliff. The tab? $9,000 per person. . . .
>
> This event, or social experiment, is [CEO Bill] Watkins' pet project. He dreamed up Eco Seagate as a way to break down barriers, boost confidence, and, yes, make staffers better team players. "Some of you will learn about teamwork because you have a great team," he . . . [said during his opening pep talk]. "Some of you will learn because your team is a disaster."[45]

Seagate's chief financial officer, Charles Pope, originally a nonparticipant who doubted the program's worth, has since joined in and now sees Eco Seagate as an investment, not a vacation.

## SKILLS & BEST PRACTICES

# Eight Factors That Lead to Successful Team Collaboration

In companies that used the following practices, teams collaborated more effectively.

1. *Investing in signature relationship practices.* Executives can encourage collaborative behavior by making highly visible investments—in facilities with open floor plans to foster communication, for example—that demonstrate their commitment to collaboration.

2. *Modeling collaborative behavior.* At companies where the senior executives demonstrate highly collaborative behavior themselves, teams collaborate well.

3. *Creating a "gift culture."* Mentoring and coaching—especially on an informal basis—help people build the networks they need to work across corporate boundaries.

4. *Ensuring the requisite skills.* Human resource departments that teach employees how to build relationships, communicate well, and resolve conflicts creatively can have a major impact on team collaboration.

5. *Supporting a strong sense of community.* When people feel a sense of community, they are more comfortable reaching out to others and more likely to share knowledge.

6. *Assigning team leaders that are both task- and relationship-oriented.* The debate has traditionally focused on whether a task or a relationship orientation creates better leadership, but in fact both are key to successfully leading a team. Typically, leaning more heavily on a task orientation at the outset of a project and shifting toward a relationship orientation once the work is in full swing works best.

7. *Building on heritage relationships.* When too many team members are strangers, people may be reluctant to share knowledge. The best practice is to put at least a few people who know one another on the team.

8. *Understanding role clarity and task ambiguity.* Cooperation increases when the roles of individual team members are sharply defined yet the team is given latitude on how to achieve the task.

**SOURCE:** List reprinted from L Gratton and T J Erickson, "Eight Ways to Build Collaborative Teams," *Harvard Business Review*, November 2007, p 104.

**team building**

**Experiential learning aimed at better internal functioning of groups.**

Seagate's CEO Bill Watkins is an enthusiastic participant in the sometimes bizarre rituals managers experience during the company's annual week of team-building exercises. "You're going to think some of this is pretty dumb," he tells attendees. "Just get involved. Don't be too cool to participate." What do you think of this sort of "extreme" team building?

But does team building work? Often, these exercises build good feelings about the team but don't translate that success into meeting business goals such as greater productivity or strong sales of new products. According to Deborah Ancona, a professor at MIT's Sloan School of Management, the problem is that most team-building efforts focus only on the internal dynamics of a team—how team members work with each other. Ancona says, "Research and the actual experience of many managers demonstrate that a team can function very well internally and still not deliver desired results."[46] She and her colleague Henrik Bresman explain that teams need strong internal dynamics but also need to "augment their internal focus with an external approach that enables them to innovate and align with leadership up and down the organizational hierarchy."[47] In practice, this external focus includes scouting for new ideas, gaining support and insights from management, and obtaining cooperation and ideas from other groups inside and outside the organization. Teams also need to shift their focus over time from exploring externally, to exploiting what they have learned, to exporting their ideas and excitement to the organization and its customers.

# Trust: A Key Ingredient of Teamwork

These have not been good times for trust in the corporate world. Years of mergers, layoffs, bloated executive bonuses, and corporate criminal proceedings have left many of us justly cynical about trusting management. For example, consider these recent news clippings:

- Merck recently agreed to pay more than $650 million "to settle charges that it routinely overbilled the government for its most popular medicines," following a complaint by a whistleblower, Dean Steinke. Steinke "said he was prompted to go to authorities after his direct supervisor told him: 'I don't care how you do it, but get the damn business,' when he questioned the sales practices."[48]
- American Airlines grounded hundreds of flights for maintenance, stranding passengers without warning, after "the Federal Aviation Administration began a series of compliance audits and found that bundles of wires stored in the [MD-80] jets' wheel wells had not been secured according to a September 2006 agency directive."[49] The cancellations angered passengers, many of whom blamed the company for not doing adequate maintenance, while pilots criticized the FAA for acting out of political, rather than safety, concerns. The public was left wondering whom to trust.

Public opinion polls show the resulting damage: In a recent survey by Harris Interactive, almost seven out of ten respondents said the reputation of "corporate America" is either "not good" or "terrible."[50]

While challenging readers of *Harvard Business Review* to do a better job of investing in social capital, experts offered this constructive advice:

No one can manufacture trust or mandate it into existence. When someone says, "You can trust me," we usually don't, and rightly so. But leaders can make deliberate investments in trust. They can give people reasons to trust one another instead of reasons to watch their backs. They can refuse to reward successes that are built on untrusting behavior. And they can display trust and trustworthiness in their own actions, both personally and on behalf of the company.[51]

These efforts are important for creating an ethical climate. And on a practical note, recent research found that people are more likely to be cooperative in situations where they believe the person in authority is trustworthy.[52]

**Three Dimensions of Trust**   Trust is defined as reciprocal faith in others' intentions and behavior.[53] Experts on the subject explain the reciprocal (give-and-take) aspect of trust as follows:

> When we see others acting in ways that imply that they trust us, we become more disposed to reciprocate by trusting in them more. Conversely, we come to distrust those whose actions appear to violate our trust or to distrust us.[54]

In short, we tend to give what we get: Trust begets trust; distrust begets distrust.

Trust is expressed in different ways. Three dimensions of trust are *overall trust* (expecting fair play, the truth, and empathy), *emotional trust* (having faith that someone will not misrepresent you to others or betray a confidence), and *reliableness* (believing that promises and appointments will be kept and commitments met).[55] These different dimensions contribute to a wide and complex range of trust, from very low to very high.

**How to Build Trust**   Management professor/consultant Fernando Bartolomé offers the following six guidelines for building and maintaining trust:

1. *Communication.* Keep team members and employees informed by explaining policies and decisions and providing accurate feedback. Be candid about one's own problems and limitations. Tell the truth.[56]

2. *Support.* Be available and approachable. Provide help, advice, coaching, and support for team members' ideas.

3. *Respect.* Delegation, in the form of real decision-making authority, is the most important expression of managerial respect. Actively listening to the ideas of others is a close second. That kind of respect builds trust for teamwork at Duoline Technologies, where a group composed of "employees from each business department created [safety] standards and 'non-negotiable safety criteria' based on the assumption that each worker knows his or her job better than anyone else."[57] Employees continue to suggest improvements to the company's safety team, and one of the initiatives has included training a team of 16 workers in skills such as first aid so they can serve as safety response specialists.

4. *Fairness.* Be quick to give credit and recognition to those who deserve it. Make sure all performance appraisals and evaluations are objective and impartial.

**trust**

**Reciprocal faith in others' intentions and behavior.**

*"Day 24: Haven't gained their trust. Still can't get past secretary."*

Copyright Scott Arthur Mesear. Reprinted with permission.

**5.** *Predictability.* Be consistent and predictable in your daily affairs. Keep both expressed and implied promises.

**6.** *Competence.* Enhance your credibility by demonstrating good business sense, technical ability, and professionalism.[58]

Trust needs to be earned; it cannot be demanded.

# Self-Managed Teams

**5** learning objective

Describe self-managed teams and virtual teams.

Have you ever thought you could do a better job than your boss? Well, if the trend toward self-managed work teams continues to grow as predicted, you just may get your chance. Entrepreneurs and artisans often boast of not having a supervisor. The same generally cannot be said for employees working in offices and factories. But things are changing. In fact, an estimated half of the employees at Fortune 500 companies are working on teams.[59] A growing share of those teams are self-managing. For example, teams at Google have wide latitude to evaluate and launch projects. One team, whose business responsibility is encouraging programmers outside the company to develop more open-source software, decided to do this by recruiting students. Without the need to go through an extensive process to get management approval, they launched the program, quickly expanding it "from 400 paid interns to 900 in 90 countries."[60] Typically, self-managed teams schedule work and assign duties, with managers present to serve as trainers and facilitators. However, self-managed teams come in every conceivable format today, some more autonomous than others (see Hands-On Exercise).

**self-managed teams**

**Groups of employees granted administrative oversight for their work.**

**Self-managed teams** are defined as groups of workers who are given administrative oversight for their task domains. Administrative oversight involves delegated activities such as planning, scheduling, monitoring, and staffing. These are chores normally performed by managers. In short, employees in these unique work groups act as their own supervisor. Accountability is maintained *indirectly* by outside managers and leaders. According to a recent study of a company with 300 self-managed teams, 66 "team advisors" relied on these four indirect influence tactics:

- *Relating* (understanding the organization's power structure, building trust, showing concern for individual team members).

- *Scouting* (seeking outside information, diagnosing teamwork problems, facilitating group problem solving).

- *Persuading* (gathering outside support and resources, influencing team to be more effective and pursue organizational goals).

- *Empowering* (delegating decision-making authority, facilitating team decision-making process, coaching).[61]

Self-managed teams are variously referred to as semiautonomous work groups, autonomous work groups, and superteams.

**Managerial Resistance**    Something much more complex is involved than this apparently simple label suggests. The term *self-managed* does not mean simply turning workers loose to do their own thing. Indeed, an organization embracing self-managed teams should be prepared to undergo revolutionary changes in management philosophy, structure, staffing and training practices, and reward systems. Moreover, the traditional notions of managerial authority and control are turned on their heads.

Not surprisingly, many managers strongly resist giving up the reins of power to people they view as subordinates. They see self-managed teams as a threat to their job security.

**Cross-Functionalism**   A common feature of self-managed teams, particularly among those above the shop-floor or clerical level, is **cross-functionalism.**[62] In other words, specialists from different areas are put on the same team. Mark Stefik, a manager at the world-renowned Palo Alto Research Center in California, explains the wisdom of cross-functionalism:

**cross-functionalism**

**Team made up of technical specialists from different areas.**

> Something magical happens when you bring together a group of people from different disciplines with a common purpose. It's a middle zone, the breakthrough zone. The idea is to start a team on a problem—a hard problem, to keep people motivated. When there's an obstacle, instead of dodging it, bring in another point of view: an electrical engineer, a user interface expert, a sociologist, whatever spin on the market is needed. Give people new eyeglasses to cross-pollinate ideas.[63]

The current drive for more efficient research and development (R&D) and better and faster innovation leans heavily on cross-functional teams. To develop the Nike Plus iPod kit—a sensor that is embedded in a Nike Plus running shoe and a receiver that attaches to an iPod Nano to measure and display the runner's speed, distance, and

**Manager's Hot Seat Application**

Working in Teams: Cross-Functional Dysfunction

calories burned—Nike assembled a cross-functional team: "Marketing chief Trevor Edwards brought together managers from apparel, technology, research, footwear design and music, all working with Apple on the technology."[64] Later, as team members began to think runners might want to do more with the collected data than check it on their iPod, they brought in Stefan Olander, Nike's director of digital content, who helped the team expand the offerings to include nikeplus.com, a site where runners can post their achievements, share stories, and view related information.

**Are Self-Managed Teams Effective? The Research Evidence**    Among companies with self-managed teams, the most commonly delegated tasks are work scheduling and dealing directly with outside customers. The least common team chores are hiring and firing.[65] Most of today's self-managed teams remain bunched at the shop-floor level in factory settings. Experts predict growth of the practice in the managerial ranks and in service operations.[66]

Much of what we know about self-managed teams comes from testimonials and case studies. Fortunately, a body of higher quality field research is slowly developing. A review of three meta-analyses covering 70 individual studies concluded that self-managed teams had

- A positive effect on productivity.
- A positive effect on specific attitudes relating to self-management (e.g., responsibility and control).
- No significant effect on general attitudes (e.g., job satisfaction and organizational commitment).
- No significant effect on absenteeism or turnover.[67]

In a recent review of 28 studies, Dutch researchers found a positive relationship between self-managed teamwork and job satisfaction.[68] Although encouraging, these results do not qualify as a sweeping endorsement of self-managed teams. Nonetheless, experts say the trend toward self-managed work teams will continue upward in North America because of a strong cultural bias in favor of direct participation. Managers need to be prepared for the resulting shift in organizational administration.

Managers also need information about the circumstances under which self-managed teams are most likely to realize their potential. Teams are *not* all created equal. For example, in a study of teams of customer service technicians in Canada, team performance was better when teams were interdependent and worked in a climate of openness.[69] A study of graduate students who participated in teams over a four-month period found that when conflict arose, trust tended to decline.[70] These teams reacted by restructuring their work so that individual team members had less autonomy and divided up tasks so they were less interdependent. These changes made the teams less effective, suggesting that managers can help improve the outcomes of self-managed teams by heading off conflict and setting limits on the ways teams can restructure their work. Selection decisions also can make a difference in teams' effectiveness. For example, a meta-analysis of 89 studies found that team performance was better when team members scored high in cognitive ability and emotional intelligence; possessed the personality traits of agreeableness, conscientiousness, and openness to experience; and valued collectivism and teamwork.[71] Finally, attention to emotional states is important because the overall mood of the team can influence the mood of each team member.[72]

# Virtual Teams

Virtual teams are a product of modern times. They take their name from *virtual reality* computer simulations, where "it's almost like the real thing." Thanks to evolving information technologies discussed in Chapter 12 such as the Internet, e-mail, videoconferencing, groupware, and fax machines, you can be a member of a work team without really being there. Traditional team meetings are location specific. Team members are either physically present or absent. Virtual teams, in contrast, convene electronically with members reporting in from different locations, different organizations, and even different time zones. *BusinessWeek* recently offered this broad perspective:

Trevor Edwards, Nike's marketing chief, leads cross company, multispecialty teams to develop and brainstorm new product ideas including the Nike Plus iPod kit. What would be different in the process if the teams didn't include members from different companies or specialties?

> More and more, the creative class is becoming post-geographic. Location-independent. Office-agnostic. Demographers and futurists call this trend the rise of "the distributed workforce." Distributed workers are those who have no permanent office at their companies, preferring to work in home offices, cafes, airport lounges, high school stadium bleachers, client conference rooms, or some combination of what [author Richard] Florida calls the "no-collar workplace." They are people who do team projects over the Web and report to bosses who may be thousands of miles away. Currently, about 12% of the U.S. workforce qualifies as distributed, estimates . . . [one expert] who predicts that 40% of the workforce will be distributed by 2012. "We're at a tipping point."[73]

Because virtual teams are so new, there is no consensual definition. Our working definition of a **virtual team** is a physically dispersed task group that conducts its business through modern information technology.[74] Advocates say virtual teams are very flexible and efficient because they are driven by information and skills, not by time and location.[75] People with needed information and/or skills can be team members, regardless of where or when they actually do their work. For example, Volvo's new station wagon grew out of a global collaboration among designers in Sweden, Spain, and the United States:

**virtual team**

**Group members in different locations who conduct business using information technology.**

> Using software called Alias, designers in Sweden and Detroit can change the curve of a fender or the shape of a headlight in real time. And if they want the big picture, they don 3-D goggles in special theaters that can project a full-size image of the car in two places at once. When Volvo's European designers put down their laser pens for the day, their counterparts in Irvine, Calif., pick up their pens and keep going. "We have almost 24-hour design," says [chief designer Peter] Horbury.[76]

On the negative side, lack of face-to-face interaction can weaken trust, communication, and accountability.

**Research Insights**    As one might expect with a new and ill-defined area, research evidence to date is a bit spotty. Here is what we have learned so far from recent studies of computer-mediated groups:

- Virtual groups formed over the Internet follow a group development process similar to that for face-to-face groups.[77]
- Internet chat rooms create more work and yield poorer decisions than face-to-face meetings and telephone conferences.[78]

SKILLS & BEST PRACTICES

## Overcoming Barriers to Knowledge Sharing in Virtual Teams

When teams are dispersed, they need effective systems to enhance their communication and share information. Here are some tips to help overcome barriers.

- *Leaders shape a psychologically safe team culture.* Hold face-to-face meetings at least monthly to develop trust and clear up misunderstandings. Team leaders point out good work and ensure that everyone has a chance to weigh in on an issue.

- *Overcome time constraints and deadline pressures.* Schedule regular conference calls to ensure sharing of information. Set clear objectives. When people have ideas about meeting objectives, team leader encourages sharing the idea with the full team.

- *Adapt technology to team's needs.* Create a Web site for posting and retrieving information. Provide training on new technologies. Monitor e-mail discussions and suggest conference calls or meetings when issues become complex.

- *Leaders serve as role models.* Agree on rules for team participation, including information sharing. Leaders share information and request frequent updates. Leaders encourage conversation about ideas that are shared.

- *Build a "transactive memory system."* Create a document itemizing each team member's areas of expertise. Look for answers and knowledge from team members before going outside the team.

- *Overcome cultural barriers to knowledge sharing.* Educate team members about potential cultural differences in communication and conflict styles. Avoid using jargon. Talk privately with group members who may need help understanding issues.

SOURCE: Adapted from Table 2 in B Rosen, S Furst, and R Blackburn, "Overcoming Barriers to Knowledge Sharing in Virtual Teams," *Organizational Dynamics,* 2007, pp 259–73.

- Successful use of groupware (software that facilitates interaction among virtual group members) requires training and hands-on experience.[79]
- Inspirational leadership has a positive impact on creativity in electronic brainstorming groups.[80]

**Practical Considerations**   Virtual teams may be in fashion, but they are not a cure-all. In fact, they may be a giant step backward for those not well versed in modern information technology and group dynamics.[81] Managers who rely on virtual teams agree on one point: *Meaningful face-to-face contact, especially during early phases of the group development process, is absolutely essential.* Virtual group members need "faces" in their minds to go with names and electronic messages. Additionally, virtual teams cannot succeed without some old-fashioned factors such as top-management support, hands-on training, a clear mission and specific objectives, effective leadership, and schedules and deadlines (see Skills & Best Practices).[82]

# Threats to Group and Team Effectiveness

No matter how carefully managers staff and organize task groups and teams, group dynamics can still go haywire. Forehand knowledge of two major threats to group effectiveness—groupthink and social loafing—can help managers and team members alike take necessary preventive steps.

## Groupthink

Systematic analysis of the decision-making processes underlying the war in Vietnam and other US foreign policy fiascoes prompted Yale University's Irving Janis to coin the term *groupthink*.[83] Modern managers can all too easily become victims of groupthink, just like professional politicians, if they passively ignore the danger.

Janis defines **groupthink** as "a mode of thinking that people engage in when they are deeply involved in a cohesive in-group, when members' strivings for unanimity override their motivation to realistically appraise alternative courses of action."[84] He adds, "Groupthink refers to a deterioration of mental efficiency, reality testing, and moral judgment that results from in-group pressures."[85] Members of groups victimized by groupthink tend to be friendly and tightly knit.

According to Janis's model, there are eight classic symptoms of groupthink. The greater the number of symptoms, the higher the probability of groupthink:

learning objective **6**
Describe groupthink, and identify at least four of its symptoms.

1. *Invulnerability.* An illusion that breeds excessive optimism and risk taking.
2. *Inherent morality.* A belief that encourages the group to ignore ethical implications.
3. *Rationalization.* Protects pet assumptions.
4. *Stereotyped views of opposition.* Cause group to underestimate opponents.
5. *Self-censorship.* Stifles critical debate.
6. *Illusion of unanimity.* Silence interpreted to mean consent.
7. *Peer pressure.* Loyalty of dissenters is questioned.
8. *Mindguards.* Self-appointed protectors against adverse information.[86]

**groupthink**

**Janis's term for a cohesive in-group's unwillingness to realistically view alternatives.**

These conditions often create a climate of fear in participants, described by Fuqua School of Business professor Richard Larrick as, for example, "the fear that everyone else knows more, so I'll just go along . . . [and] the fear that the boss has already really decided, so why bother to stick my neck out?"[87]

Janis believes that prevention is better than cure when dealing with groupthink (see Skills & Best Practices for his preventive measures).[88] At pharmaceutical company Alkermes, chief financial officer Jim Frates applies these principles when groups assemble to make major decisions. He avoids revealing his own opinion, questions assumptions, and speaks in favor of ideas not getting much attention, to see if there is quiet support. For example, when Frates and others were interviewing candidates for a senior finance job, group members were eager to extend an offer to one individual. To proceed carefully and ensure that all views were being aired, Frates asked the group to state negatives as well as positives about the candidate they were rushing to hire. It quickly became clear that they had hoped for someone with more management experience, so the group backed away from its first choice and continued recruiting until they found the right person for this key job.[89]

## Social Loafing

Is group performance less than, equal to, or greater than the sum of its parts? Can three people, working together, for example, accomplish less than, the same as, or more than they would working separately? An interesting study conducted more than a half century ago by a French agricultural engineer named Ringelmann found the answer to be "less than."[90] In a rope-pulling exercise, Ringelmann reportedly found that three people pulling together could achieve only two

### How to Prevent Groupthink

1. Each member of the group should be assigned the role of critical evaluator. This role involves actively voicing objections and doubts.
2. Top-level executives should not use policy committees to rubber-stamp decisions that have already been made.
3. Different groups with different leaders should explore the same policy questions.
4. Subgroup debates and outside experts should be used to introduce fresh perspectives.
5. Someone should be given the role of devil's advocate when discussing major alternatives. This person tries to uncover every conceivable negative factor.
6. Once a consensus has been reached, everyone should be encouraged to rethink their position to check for flaws.

**SOURCE:** Adapted from discussion in I L Janis, *Groupthink,* 2nd ed. (Boston: Houghton Mifflin, 1982), ch 11.

**SKILLS & BEST PRACTICES**

**social loafing**

Decrease in individual effort as group size increases.

and a half times the average individual rate. Eight pullers achieved less than four times the individual rate. This tendency for individual effort to decline as group size increases has come to be called **social loafing.**[91] Let us briefly analyze this threat to group effectiveness and synergy with an eye toward avoiding it.

**Social Loafing Theory and Research**   Among the theoretical explanations for the social loafing effect are (1) equity of effort ("Everyone else is goofing off, so why shouldn't I?"), (2) loss of personal accountability ("I'm lost in the crowd, so who cares?"), (3) motivational loss due to the sharing of rewards ("Why should I work harder than the others when everyone gets the same reward?"), and (4) coordination loss as more people perform the task ("We're getting in each other's way.").

Laboratory studies refined these theories by identifying situational factors that moderated the social loafing effect. Social loafing occurred when

- The task was perceived to be unimportant, simple, or not interesting.[92]
- Group members thought their individual output was not identifiable.[93]
- Group members expected their coworkers to loaf.[94]

But social loafing did *not* occur when group members in two laboratory studies expected to be evaluated.[95] Also, research suggests that self-reliant "individualists" are more prone to social loafing than are group-oriented "collectivists." But individualists can be made more cooperative by keeping the group small and holding each member personally accountable for results.[96]

**Practical Implications**   These findings demonstrate that social loafing is not an inevitable part of group effort. Management can curb this threat to group effectiveness by making sure the task is challenging and perceived as important. Additionally, it is a good idea to hold group members personally accountable for identifiable portions of the group's task.[97] (Recall our discussion about the power of goal setting in Chapter 7.)

# key terms

# chapter summary

- *Describe the five stages of Tuckman's theory of group development.* The five stages in Tuckman's theory are *forming* (the group comes together), *storming* (members test the limits and each other), *norming* (questions about authority and power are resolved as the group becomes more cohesive), *performing* (effective communication and cooperation help the group get things done), and *adjourning* (group members go their own way).

- *Contrast roles and norms, and specify four reasons why norms are enforced in organizations.* While roles are specific to the person's position, norms are shared attitudes that differentiate appropriate from inappropriate behavior in a variety of situations. Norms evolve informally and are enforced because they help the group or organization survive, clarify behavioral expectations, help people avoid embarrassing situations, and clarify the group's or organization's central values.

- *Explain how a work group becomes a team, and identify five teamwork competencies.* A team is a mature group where leadership is shared, accountability is both individual and collective, the members have developed their own purpose, problem solving is a way of life, and effectiveness is measured by collective outcomes. Five teamwork competencies are (1) orients team to problem-solving situations; (2) organizes and manages team performance; (3) promotes a positive team environment; (4) facilitates and manages task conflict; and (5) appropriately promotes perspective.

- *List at least four things managers can do to build trust.* Six recommended ways to build trust are through communication, support, respect (especially delegation), fairness, predictability, and competence.

- *Describe self-managed teams and virtual teams.* Self-managed teams are groups of workers who are given administrative oversight for various chores normally performed by managers—such as planning, scheduling, monitoring, and staffing. They are typically cross-functional, meaning they are staffed with a mix of specialists from different areas. Self-managed teams vary widely in the autonomy or freedom they enjoy. A virtual team is a physically dispersed task group that conducts its business through modern information technology such as the Internet. Periodic and meaningful face-to-face contact seems to be crucial for virtual team members, especially during the early stages of group development.

- *Describe groupthink, and identify at least four of its symptoms.* Groupthink plagues cohesive in-groups that shortchange moral judgment while putting too much emphasis on unanimity. Symptoms of groupthink include invulnerability, inherent morality, rationalization, stereotyped views of opposition, self-censorship, illusion of unanimity, peer pressure, and mindguards. Critical evaluators, outside expertise, and devil's advocates are among the preventive measures recommended by Irving Janis, who coined the term *groupthink*.

# discussion questions

1. Relative to the chapter-opening case, how important is trust in the smooth functioning of teams. Explain.

2. What is your opinion about managers being friends with the people they supervise (in other words, overlapping formal and informal groups)?

3. In your personal relationships, how do you come to trust someone? How fragile is that trust? Explain.

4. Are virtual teams likely to be a passing fad? Why or why not?

5. Have you ever witnessed groupthink or social loafing first-hand? Explain the circumstances and how things played out.

# ethical dilemma

## Let's Have Our Business Meeting at a Strip Club

Nicolette Hart explains how she can make up to $2,500 a night with investment bankers and their clients in a Manhattan strip club's private rooms. . . . Hart, who once worked for a venture-capital firm, always asks what brought the men together. They often say they're having a meeting.

"I say, 'You're having a *business meeting* in a *strip club?*' " Hart says in an interview in the dressing room at Rick's Cabaret here.

It's not just strippers who have questions. Some women on Wall Street want to know how it can be fair—or legal—for their managers and male colleagues to exclude them when they fraternize at strip clubs, often with the women's clients. Strip club clientele is hardly limited to Wall Street. Adult entertainment is enjoyed by men—and women—in most every industry in the USA, and it's a tax-deductible business expense allowed by the IRS.[98]

### As a Top Executive, What Should Your Organization's Policy on This Practice Be?

1. Boys will be boys. Besides, there's nothing illegal about having business meetings in strip clubs. Take no action.

2. While the company doesn't officially support doing business in strip clubs, it can be an effective marketing tactic to loosen up clients, which the company should continue to ignore.

3. This is one good-old-boy tradition that should die because it demeans women in general and sends out the wrong signal for the company's fight against sexual harassment.

4. Having business meetings in strip clubs may be perfectly legal, but that doesn't make it right. The company should take an ethical stand by refusing to reimburse strip club business meeting expenses.

5. The company should be proactive by forbidding the practice and lobbying Congress to outlaw adult entertainment as a legitimate business expense.

6. Invent other interpretations or options. Discuss.

One study suggests that females entering male-dominated fields, such as law enforcement, face greater challenges than do males entering female-dominated fields, such as nursing.

For an interpretation of this situation, visit our Web site at **www.mhhe.com/kinickiob4e**.

---

If you're looking for additional study materials, be sure to check out the Online Learning Center at

**www.mhhe.com/kinickiob4e**

for more information and interactivities that correspond to this chapter.

# chapter
## Ten

# Making Decisions

**LEARNING OBJECTIVES**

**After reading the material in this chapter, you should be able to:**

1. Compare and contrast the rational model of decision making, Simon's normative model, and the garbage can model.

2. Identify common decision-making biases.

3. Discuss knowledge management and techniques used by companies to increase knowledge sharing.

4. Describe the model of decision-making styles, the role of intuition in decision making, and the stages of the creative process.

5. Summarize the pros and cons of involving groups in the decision-making process.

6. Contrast brainstorming, the nominal group technique, the Delphi technique, and computer-aided decision making.

McDonald's baristas were added to the employee positions in an effort to drive business. Are you surprised by the successes they've had in selling specialty coffee?

This fall, a McDonald's here added a position to its crew: barista.

McDonald's is setting out to poach Starbucks customers with the biggest addition to its menu in 30 years. Starting this year, the company's nearly 14,000 U.S. locations will install coffee bars with "baristas" serving cappuccinos, lattes, mochas and the Frappe, similar to Starbucks' ice-blended Frappuccino. . . .

The confrontation between Starbucks Corp. and McDonald's Corp once seemed improbable. Hailing from very different corners of the restaurant world, the two chains have gradually encroached on each other's turf. McDonald's upgraded its drip coffee and its interiors, while Starbucks added drive-through windows and hot breakfast sandwiches. . . .

The growing overlap between the chains shows how convenience has become the dominant force shaping the food-service industry. . . .

It also shows how the chains' efforts to adapt to a changing market have had drastically different results on their bottom lines. McDonald's is entering the sixth year of a successful turnaround,

while Starbucks has begun struggling after years of strong earnings and stock growth.

Still, the new coffee program is a risky bet for McDonald's. It could slow down operations and alienate customers who come to McDonald's for cheap, simple fare rather than theatrics. . . .

McDonald's executives watching the growth of Starbucks at the beginning of this decade realized that they were missing out on the fastest-growing parts of the beverage business. Data showed that soda sales had flattened while sales of specialty coffee and smoothies were growing at a double-digit rate outside McDonald's. Customers were buying food at McDonald's, then going to convenience stores to get bottled energy drinks, sports drinks and tea, as well as sodas by Coke competitors.

Early on, Starbucks didn't see the Golden Arches as a competitor "because McDonald's was selling hot, brown liquid masquerading as coffee," says John Moore, who spent almost a decade in Starbucks's marketing department before leaving in 2003. . . .

At McDonald's, the success of its upgraded drip coffee emboldened the chain. In 2005, it began testing drinks sold under the McCafe banner at a handful of franchises in Michigan. It sold lattes and cappuccinos from the front counter so it could pass them to the drive-through windows.

McDonald's researchers contacted customers of Starbucks and other coffee purveyors and conducted three-hour interviews where they videotaped the customers talking about their coffee-buying habits. The researchers got in the cars of the customers and drove with them to their favorite coffee place, then took them to McDonald's and had them try the espresso drinks.

"There was a surprise factor," says Patrick Roney, a director of U.S. consumer and business insights at McDonald's. "The people who were on the fence . . . there was an opportunity to get those."

Restaurants that tested the drinks began passing out complimentary small mochas and lattes. "A lot of our customers don't know what a latte is," says John DeVera, an Overland Park, Kan., franchisee who is testing the drinks.

Management advised restaurant operators to hire baristas who are "very friendly" and show a "willingness to learn about the competitor's product," according to a 2006 internal memo about how to start selling the drinks. "For example, a typical Starbucks customer would ask for a Grande Latte; our Baristas need to know that this is a medium size drink," the memo says.

Unlike at Starbucks, where baristas steam pitchers of milk then combine it with the espresso, McDonald's process is more automated. It uses a single machine to make all the components of each drink. . . .

Only about 800 of McDonald's U.S. restaurants have the specialty coffee drinks now, and some may not get the full beverage program until 2009. Executives and franchisees will not give specifics on how well the espresso drinks have sold in tests.

McDonald's has already made some headway in gaining coffee credibility. In February, the magazine Consumer Reports rated the chain's drip coffee as better-tasting than Starbucks. Starbucks responded that taste is subjective and its millions of customer visits per week demonstrated the popularity of its coffee.[1]

**Are you surprised by McDonald's success in selling specialty coffee? Explain. For an interpretation of this case and additional comments, visit our Online Learning Center at**

**www.mhhe.com/ kinickiob4e**

FOR DISCUSSION

**THOMAS STEWART,** the editor of *Harvard Business Review,* recently concluded that "decisions are the essence of management."[2] The quality of a manager's decisions is important for two principal reasons. First, the quality of a manager's decisions directly affects his or her career opportunities, rewards, and job satisfaction. The second reason is highlighted in the chapter-opening vignette. Managerial decisions contribute to the success or failure of an organization.

The chapter-opening vignette highlights how a successful company such as McDonald's uses analytics to make decisions. **Analytics** involve a conscientious and explicit process of making decisions on the basis of the best available evidence. This process includes targeted approaches at collecting relevant information and data, studying or analyzing the information and data, and then making decisions on the basis of results. A recent study of 450 executives across 35 countries and 19 industries demonstrated that high-performance companies were five times more likely than low-performing companies to use analytics.[3]

**Decision making** entails identifying and choosing alternative solutions that lead to a desired state of affairs. The process begins with a problem and ends when a solution has been chosen. To gain an understanding of how managers can make better decisions, this chapter focuses on (1) models of decision making, (2) decision-making biases, (3) the dynamics of decision making, and (4) group decision making.

> **analytics**
>
> A conscientious and explicit process of making decisions on the basis of the best available evidence.
>
> **decision making**
>
> Identifying and choosing solutions that lead to a desired end result.

# Models of Decision Making

**1** learning objective

Compare and contrast the rational model of decision making, Simon's normative model, and the garbage can model.

You can use two broad approaches to make decisions. You can follow a *rational model* or various *nonrational models.* Let us consider how each of these approaches works.

## The Rational Model

The **rational model** proposes that managers use a rational, four-step sequence when making decisions: (1) identifying the problem, (2) generating alternative solutions, (3) selecting a solution, and (4) implementing and evaluating the solution. According to this model, managers are completely objective and possess complete information to make a decision. Despite criticism for being unrealistic, the rational model is instructive because it analytically breaks down the decision-making process and serves as a conceptual anchor for newer models.[4] Let us now consider each of these four steps.

**Test Your Knowledge**

The Vroom/ Yetton/Jago Decision Model

**Identifying the Problem** A **problem** exists when an actual situation and a desired situation differ. For example, a problem exists when you have to pay rent at the end of the month and don't have enough money. Your problem is not that you have to pay rent. Your problem is obtaining the needed funds. Mattel's CEO, Bob Eckert, learned that his company had a problem when two of his top managers arrived in his office to tell him lead had been discovered in one of the company's toys.[5] Around the same time, newspapers were publishing reports that magnets were becoming dislodged from other Mattel toys: If a small child swallowed them, they could cause serious damage by attaching themselves together in the child's intestines. Eckert had to decide whether his company had a publicity problem, a design problem, or a production problem—and if it were a production problem, where that problem was occurring and why.

> **rational model**
>
> Logical four-step approach to decision making.
>
> **problem**
>
> Gap between an actual and desired situation.

In general, how do individuals or organizations know when a problem exists or will occur soon? Three methods are commonly used for identifying problems.

1. Using historical cues, assuming the recent past is the best predictor of the future. For example, comparing current sales with last year's sales for the same period may uncover signs of a problem.

2. Using projections or scenarios to estimate what will happen in the next year or later. The **scenario technique** is a speculative, conjectural forecast tool used to identify future states, given a certain set of environmental conditions. Decision makers can devise responses for each scenario.

> **scenario technique**
>
> **A speculative forecast tool for identifying future states, given a set of conditions.**

3. Relying on the perceptions of others. For instance, feedback from customers or employees may provide valuable evidence of a problem.

**Generating Solutions**    After identifying a problem, the next logical step is generating alternative solutions. For repetitive and routine decisions such as deciding when to send customers a bill, alternatives are readily available through decision rules. For example, a company might routinely bill customers three days after shipping a product. This is not the case for novel and unstructured decisions. Because there are no simple procedures for dealing with novel problems, managers must creatively generate alternative solutions. Managers can use a number of techniques to stimulate creativity.

**Selecting a Solution**    Optimally, decision makers want to choose the alternative with the greatest value. Decision theorists refer to this as maximizing the expected utility of an outcome. This is no easy task. First, assigning values to alternatives is complicated and prone to error. Not only are values subjective, but they also vary according to the preferences of the decision maker. Research demonstrates that people vary in their preferences for safety or risk when making decisions. For example, a meta-analysis summarizing 150 studies revealed that males displayed more risk taking than females.[6] Further, evaluating alternatives assumes they can be judged according to some standards or criteria. This further assumes that (1) valid criteria exist, (2) each alternative can be compared against these criteria, and (3) the decision maker actually uses the criteria. As you know from making your own key life decisions, people frequently violate these assumptions. Finally, the ethics of the solution should be considered. In the earlier example of Mattel's problems, CEO Eckert said, "How you achieve success is just as important as success itself."[7] He announced a recall of 18.2 million toys, the largest recall in Mattel's history. The company also announced that its magnet toys had been redesigned to make them safer and that it had investigated the Chinese contractor that had used the paint containing lead. Would you conclude that these options maximized utility for Mattel?

Managers at Mattel had some serious decisions to make when they learned that toys on store shelves were contaminated with lead paint and magnets that could come loose. Do you think they made the right decision to recall several million toys?

**Implementing and Evaluating the Solution**    Once a solution is chosen, it needs to be implemented. After a solution is implemented, the evaluation phase is used to assess its effectiveness. If the solution is effective, it should reduce the

SKILLS & BEST PRACTICES

## How Good Leaders Exercise Judgment

Leaders who demonstrate good judgment understand that judgment is a process that unfolds through phases and includes "redo loops," opportunities to try again if something isn't working. Here's what good leaders do during each phase:

*Preparation Phase*

1. *Sense and identify.* Pick up signals in the environment and feel energized about the future.

2. *Frame and name.* Find the essence of an issue, set clear limits, and provide a context and shared language for everyone to understand the issue.

3. *Mobilize and align.* Identify important stakeholders, engage and energize them, and tap the best ideas coming from any source. If the organization can't be mobilized, reconsider the context, the limits, and the way the goal has been defined to find new definitions people will accept.

*Call Phase*

4. *Call.* Make a clear decision and explain it thoroughly. If resistance arises, redo step 3.

*Execution Phase*

5. *Make it happen.* Stay involved during execution, support those who are involved, and set clear milestones for progress.

6. *Learn and adjust.* Ask for continuous feedback, listen to it, and make adjustments to the execution.

**SOURCE: Based on N M Tichy and W G Bennis, "Making Judgment Calls," *Harvard Business Review*, October 2007, pp 94–102, especially exhibit on p 97.**

**optimizing**

**Choosing the best possible solution.**

**nonrational models**

**Decision models that explain how decisions actually are made.**

difference between the actual and desired states that created the problem. If the gap is not closed, the implementation was not successful, and one of the following is true: Either the problem was incorrectly identified, or the solution was inappropriate. In the first case, the decision maker should return to the beginning of the process and redefine the problem. In the second case, the decision maker should try to generate more solutions and select a different solution to implement.

**Summarizing the Rational Model**   The rational model is based on the premise that managers optimize when they make decisions. **Optimizing** involves solving problems by producing the best possible solution. As noted by Herbert Simon, a decision theorist who in 1978 earned the Nobel Prize for his work on decision making, "The assumptions of perfect rationality are contrary to fact. It is not a question of approximation; they do not even remotely describe the processes that human beings use for making decisions in complex situations."[8]

That said, there are three benefits of trying to follow a rational process as much as realistically possible.

1. The quality of decisions may be enhanced, in the sense that they follow more logically from all available knowledge and expertise.

2. It makes the reasoning behind a decision transparent and available to scrutiny.

3. If made public, it discourages the decider from acting on suspect considerations (such as personal advancement or avoiding bureaucratic embarrassment).[9]

To learn how successful leaders use this process, see Skills & Best Practices.

# Nonrational Models of Decision Making

In contrast to the rational model's focus on how decisions should be made, **nonrational models** attempt to explain how decisions actually are made. They are based on the assumption that decision making is uncertain, that decision makers do not possess complete information, and that it is difficult for managers to make optimal decisions. Two nonrational models are Herbert Simon's *normative* model and the *garbage can model.*

**Simon's Normative Model**   Herbert Simon proposed this model to describe the process that managers actually use when making decisions. The process is guided by a decision maker's bounded rationality. **Bounded**

**rationality** represents the notion that decision makers are "bounded" or restricted by a variety of constraints when making decisions. These constraints include any personal or environmental characteristics that reduce rational decision making. Examples are the limited capacity of the human mind, problem complexity and uncertainty, amount and timeliness of information at hand, criticality of the decision, and time demands.[10]

**bounded rationality**

**Constraints that restrict rational decision making.**

Ultimately, these limitations result in the tendency to acquire manageable rather than optimal amounts of information. In turn, this practice makes it difficult for managers to identify all possible alternative solutions. In the long run, the constraints of bounded rationality cause decision makers to fail to evaluate all potential alternatives, thereby causing them to satisfice.

**Satisficing** consists of choosing a solution that meets some minimum qualifications, one that is "good enough." Satisficing resolves problems by producing solutions that are satisfactory, as opposed to optimal. Finding a radio station to listen to in your car is a good example of satisficing. You cannot optimize because it is impossible to listen to all stations at the same time. You thus stop searching for a station when you find one playing a song you like or do not mind hearing.

**satisficing**

**Choosing a solution that meets a minimum standard of acceptance.**

A recent national survey by the Business Performance Management Forum underscores the existence of satisficing: only 26% of respondents indicated that their companies had formal, well-understood decision-making processes. Respondents noted that the most frequent causes of poor decision making included:

- Poorly defined processes and practices.
- Unclear company vision, mission, and goals.
- Unwillingness of leaders to take responsibility.
- A lack of reliable, timely information.[11]

**The Garbage Can Model**  Another response to the rational model's inability to explain how decisions are actually made assumes that organizational decision making is a sloppy and haphazard process. According to the **garbage can model,** decisions result from a complex interaction between four independent streams of events: problems, solutions, participants, and choice opportunities.[12] The interaction of these events creates "a collection of choices looking for problems, issues and feelings looking for decision situations in which they might be aired, solutions looking for issues to which they might be the answer, and decision makers looking for work."[13] A similar type of process occurs in your kitchen garbage basket. We randomly discard our trash, and it gets mashed together based on chance interactions and timing. Just like the process of mixing garbage in a trash container, the garbage can model of decision making assumes that decision making does not follow an orderly series of steps. Rather, attractive solutions can get matched up with whatever handy problems exist at a given point in time, or people get assigned to projects because their work load is low at that moment. This model of decision making thus attempts to explain how problems, solutions, participants, and choice opportunities interact and lead to a decision.

**garbage can model**

**Holds that decision making is sloppy and haphazard.**

The garbage can model has four practical implications.[14] First, many decisions are made by oversight or by the presence of a salient opportunity. For example, the Campbell Soup Company needed to find a way to motivate supermarkets to give them more space on the shelves. They thus decided to create a new shelving system that automatically slides soup cans to the front when a shopper picks up a can. The decision was a success. Customers bought more soup, increasing the revenue for both Campbell and the supermarkets, and the supermarkets reduced their restocking costs.[15]

Second, political motives frequently guide the process by which participants make decisions. It thus is important for you to consider the political ramifications of your decisions. Organizational politics are discussed in Chapter 13.

Third, the decision-making process is sensitive to load. That is, as the number of problems increases, relative to the amount of time available to solve them, problems are less likely to be solved. Finally, important problems are more likely to be solved than unimportant ones because they are more salient to organizational participants.[16]

Applying the idea that decisions are shaped by characteristics of problems and decision makers, consultants David Snowden and Mary Boone have come up with their own approach that is not as haphazard as the garbage can model but acknowledges the challenges facing today's organizations. They identify four kinds of decision environments and an effective method of decision making for each.[17]

1. A *simple* context is stable, and clear cause-and-effect relationships can be discerned, so the best answer can be agreed on. This context calls for the rational model, where the decision maker gathers information, categorizes it, and responds in an established way.

2. In a *complicated* context, there is a clear relationship between cause and effect, but some people may not see it, and more than one solution may be effective. Here, too, the rational model applies, but it requires the investigation of options, along with analysis of them.

3. In a *complex* context, there is one right answer, but there are so many unknowns that decision makers don't understand cause-and-effect relationships. Decision makers therefore need to start out by experimenting, testing options, and probing to see what might happen as they look for a creative solution.

4. In a *chaotic* context, cause-and-effect relationships are changing so fast that no pattern emerges. In this context, decision makers have to act first to establish order and then find areas where it is possible to identify patterns so that aspects of the problem can be managed.

Some situations are in the even more troubling state of *disorder,* where those involved cannot even agree on the context. The solution then is to see aspects of the situation as a separate context and address them accordingly. For example, following the murder of seven people in a fast-food restaurant, Deputy Chief Walter Gasior had to

> take immediate action via the media to stem the tide of initial panic by keeping the community informed (chaotic); . . . help keep the department running routinely and according to established procedure (simple); . . . call in experts (complicated); and . . . continue to calm the community . . . (complex). That last situation proved the most challenging. . . . Gasior set up a forum for business owners, high school students, teachers, and parents to share concerns and hear the facts. . . . He allowed solutions to emerge from the community itself rather than trying to impose them.[18]

# Decision-Making Biases

People make a variety of systematic mistakes when making decisions. These mistakes are generally associated with a host of biases that occur when we use judgmental heuristics. **Judgmental heuristics** represent rules of thumb or shortcuts that people use to reduce information-processing demands.[19] We automatically use them without conscious awareness. The use of heuristics helps decision makers reduce the uncertainty inherent within the decision-making process. Because these shortcuts represent knowledge gained from experience, they can help decision makers evaluate current problems. But they also can lead to systematic errors that erode the quality of decisions. For example, a recent study found that investment decisions were influenced by subjects' overconfidence about their retirement situation, tendency to make uninformed choices, and practice of judging advisers based on how they were dressed.[20]

More specifically, eight biases may affect decision making:[21]

learning objective **2**

Identify common decision-making biases.

**judgmental heuristics**

**Rules of thumb or shortcuts that people use to reduce information-processing demands.**

1. **Availability heuristic.** The availability heuristic represents a decision maker's tendency to base decisions on information that is readily available in memory. Information is more accessible in memory when it involves an event that recently occurred, when it is salient (e.g., a plane crash), and when it evokes strong emotions (e.g., a college student shooting other students). This heuristic is likely to cause people to overestimate the occurrence of unlikely events such as a plane crash or a college shooting. This bias also is partially responsible for the recency effect discussed in Chapter 4. For example, a manager is more likely to give an employee a positive performance evaluation if the employee exhibited excellent performance over the last few months.

2. **Representativeness heuristic.** The representativeness heuristic is used when people estimate the probability of an event occurring. It reflects the tendency to assess the likelihood of an event occurring based on one's impressions about similar occurrences. A manager, for example, may hire a graduate from a particular university because the past three people hired from this university turned out to be good performers. In this case, the "school attended" criterion is used to facilitate complex information processing associated with employment interviews. Unfortunately, this shortcut can result in a biased decision. Similarly, an individual may believe that he or she can master a new software package in a short period of time because a different type of software was easy to learn. This estimate may or may not be accurate. For example, it may take the individual much longer to learn the new software because it involves learning a new programming language.

3. **Confirmation bias.** The confirmation bias has two components. The first is to subconsciously decide something before investigating why it is the right decision. This directly leads to the second component, which is to seek information that supports our point of view and to discount information that does not.

These stock traders make investment decisions in a pressure filled environment. What type of decision-making biases are likely to influence their decisions?

4. **Anchoring bias.** How would you answer the following two questions? Is the population of Iraq greater than 40 million? What's your best guess about the population of Iraq? Was your answer to the second question influenced by the number *40 million* suggested by the first question? If yes, you were affected by the anchoring bias. The anchoring bias occurs when decision makers are influenced by the first information received about a decision, even if it is irrelevant. This bias happens because initial information, impressions, data, feedback, or stereotypes anchor our subsequent judgments and decisions.

5. **Overconfidence bias.** The overconfidence bias relates to our tendency to be overconfident about estimates or forecasts. This bias is particularly strong when you are asked moderate to extremely difficult questions rather than easy ones. Research shows that overoptimism significantly influences entrepreneurs' decisions to start and sustain new ventures.[22] Imagine the challenges this bias might create for managers in difficult and dangerous situations. Recently, five U.S. Forest Service firefighters died while fighting a fire in the mountains east of Los Angeles because their command officers were overconfident about their ability to protect a vacation home. According to an investigation, the highly motivated firefighters tackled the hazardous situation, even though they lacked an adequate escape route.[23]

6. **Hindsight bias.** Imagine yourself in the following scenario: You are taking an OB course that meets Tuesday and Thursday, and your professor gives unannounced quizzes each week. It's the Monday before a class, and you are deciding whether to study for a potential quiz or to watch Monday night football. Two of your classmates have decided to watch the game rather than study because they don't think there will be a quiz the next day. The next morning you walk into class and the professor says, "Take out a sheet of paper for the quiz." You turn to your friends and say, "I knew we were going to have a quiz; why did I listen to you?" The hindsight bias occurs when knowledge of an outcome influences our belief about the probability that we could have predicted the outcome earlier. We are affected by this bias when we look back on a decision and try to reconstruct why we decided to do something.

7. **Framing bias.** This bias relates to the manner in which a question is posed. Consider the following scenario: Imagine that the United States is preparing for the outbreak of an unusual Asian disease that is expected to kill 600 people. Two alternative programs to combat the disease have been proposed. Assume that the exact scientific estimates of the consequences of the programs are as follows:

   *Program A:* If Program A is adopted, 200 people will be saved.

   *Program B:* If Program B is adopted, there is a one-third probability that 600 people will be saved and a two-thirds probability that no people will be saved. Which of the two programs would you recommend?[24]

Research shows that most people chose Program A even though the two programs produce the same results. This result is due to the framing bias. The framing bias is the tendency to consider risks about gains—saving lives—differently than risks pertaining to losses—losing lives. You are encouraged to frame decision questions in alternative ways in order to avoid this bias.

8. **Escalation of commitment bias.** The escalation of commitment bias refers to the tendency to stick to an ineffective course of action when it is unlikely that the bad situation can be reversed. Personal examples include investing more money into an old or broken car, waiting an extremely long time for a bus to take you somewhere when you could have walked just as easily, or trying to save a disruptive personal relationship that has already lasted 10 years. Case studies indicate that this bias is partially responsible for some of the worst financial losses experienced by organizations.[25] Researchers recommend the following actions to reduce the escalation of commitment:

- Set minimum targets for performance, and have decision makers compare their performance against these targets.
- Regularly rotate managers in key positions throughout a project.
- Encourage decision makers to become less ego-involved with a project.
- Make decision makers aware of the costs of persistence.[26]

A desire to avoid biases in decision making leads to the understandable conclusion that a rational and unemotional approach would generate the best decisions. In contrast, people experiencing strong emotions tend to make judgments consistent with their feelings (for example, adopting an overconfidence bias if they feel positive), and if those strong emotions are unpleasant, they look for decisions that will bring a quick change in their situation. But a recent study offered this surprise: when 101 stock investors participated in a simulation, those who experienced more intense feelings actually performed *better*. Further investigation found that investors who were insightful about their feelings were better at watching out for decision-making biases.[27] One logical implication is that, for making decisions, emotional intelligence, which was discussed in Chapter 5, is a valuable complement to rational thinking.

# Dynamics of Decision Making

Decision making is part science and part art. Accordingly, this section examines four dynamics of decision making—knowledge management, decision-making styles, intuition, and creativity—that affect the "science" component. An understanding of these dynamics can help managers make better decisions.

learning objective **3**

Discuss knowledge management and techniques used by companies to increase knowledge sharing.

## Improving Decision Making through Effective Knowledge Management

Have you ever had to make a decision without complete information? If you have, then you know the quality of a decision is only as good as the information used to make the decision. The same is true for managerial decision making. In this case, however, managers frequently need information or knowledge possessed by people working in other parts of the organization. This realization has spawned a growing interest in the concept of knowledge management. **Knowledge management (KM)** is "the development of tools, processes, systems, structures, and cultures explicitly to improve the creation, sharing, and use of knowledge critical for

**knowledge management (KM)**

Implementing systems and practices that increase the sharing of knowledge and information throughout an organization.

decision making."[28] The effective use of KM helps organizations improve the quality of their decision making and correspondingly reduce costs and increase efficiency.[29]

This section explores the fundamentals of KM so that you can use them to improve your decision making.

**Knowledge Comes in Different Forms**     There are two types of knowledge that impact the quality of decisions: tacit knowledge and explicit knowledge. **Tacit knowledge** "entails information that is difficult to express, formalize, or share. It . . . is unconsciously acquired from the experiences one has while immersed in an environment."[30] Many skills, for example, such as swinging a golf club or writing a speech, are difficult to describe in words because they involve tacit knowledge. Tacit knowledge is intuitive and is acquired by having considerable experience and expertise at some task or job. In contrast, **explicit knowledge** can easily be put into words and explained to others. This type of knowledge is shared verbally or in written documents or numerical reports. In summary, tacit knowledge represents private information that is difficult to share, whereas explicit knowledge is external or public and is more easily communicated. Although both types of knowledge affect decision making, experts suggest competitive advantages are created when tacit knowledge is shared among employees.[31] Let us now examine how companies foster this type of information sharing.

**tacit knowledge**

Information gained through experience that is difficult to express and formalize.

**explicit knowledge**

Information that can be easily put into words and shared with others.

**Knowledge Sharing**     Organizations increasingly rely on sophisticated KM software to share explicit knowledge. This software allows companies to amass large amounts of information that can be accessed quickly from around the world. These systems can also be used to obtain information and feedback from customers and other organizations. For example, sales representatives for ExactTarget used to bombard headquarters staff with details about the company's software products. Now they efficiently and effectively help each other at a secure Web site, where any sales rep can post a question, answer it, or search for answers to questions that have already been addressed. The headquarters staff has also posted links to frequently requested information.[32] This type of networking to share information is pervasive in successful organizations, where people realize that the Internet lets any individual tap into a node of "a living information ecosystem, whose central purpose is to promote learning and growth."[33]

Tacit knowledge is shared most directly by observing, participating, or working with experts or coaches. Mentoring, which was discussed in Chapter 2, is another method for spreading tacit knowledge. Finally, informal networking, periodic meetings, and the design of office space can be used to facilitate KM. Alcoa, for example, designed its headquarters with the aim of increasing information sharing among its executives:

> Alcoa, the world's leading producer of aluminum, wanted to improve access between its senior executives. When designing their new headquarters they focused on open offices, family-style kitchens in the center of each floor, and plenty of open spaces. Previously, top executives would only interact with a couple of people in the elevator and those they had scheduled meetings with. Now, executives bump into each other more often and are more accessible for serendipitous conversations. This change in space has increased general accessibility as well as narrowed the gap between top executives and employees.[34]

It is important to remember that the best-laid plans for increasing KM are unlikely to succeed without the proper organizational culture. Effective KM requires a knowledge-sharing culture that both encourages and reinforces the spread of tacit knowledge. IBM Global Services has taken this recommendation to heart:

> IBM Global Services has incorporated knowledge creation, sharing, and reuse measurements into performance metrics. Performance metrics and incentives, particularly at the executive rank, have driven collaborative behavior into the day-to-day work practices of executive networks. Further, knowledge sharing has been incorporated into personal business commitments, which are required for certification and affect promotion decisions. This encourages employees at all levels to be collaborative with and accessible to each other.[35]

# General Decision-Making Styles

learning objective 4

Describe the model of decision-making styles, the role of intuition in decision making, and the stages of the creative process.

This section focuses on how an individual's decision-making style affects his or her approach to decision making. A **decision-making style** reflects the combination of how an individual perceives and comprehends stimuli and the general manner in which he or she chooses to respond to such information.[36] A team of researchers developed a model of decision-making styles that is based on the idea that styles vary along two different dimensions: value orientation and tolerance for ambiguity.[37] *Value orientation* reflects the extent to which an individual focuses on either task and technical concerns or people and social concerns when making decisions. The second dimension pertains to a person's *tolerance for ambiguity.* This individual difference indicates the extent to which a person has a high need for structure or control in his or her life. When the dimensions of value orientation and tolerance for ambiguity are combined, they form four styles of decision making (see Figure 10–1): directive, analytical, conceptual, and behavioral.

**decision-making style**

**A combination of how individuals perceive and respond to information.**

**Self-Assessment Exercise**

Your Preferred Decision-Making Style

**Directive**    People with a directive style have a low tolerance for ambiguity and are oriented toward task and technical concerns when making decisions. They are efficient, logical, practical, and systematic in their approach to solving problems. People with this style are action oriented and decisive and like to focus on facts. In their pursuit of speed and results, however, these individuals tend to be autocratic, exercise power and control, and focus on the short run. Interestingly, a directive style seems

**FIGURE 10–1**
Decision-Making Styles

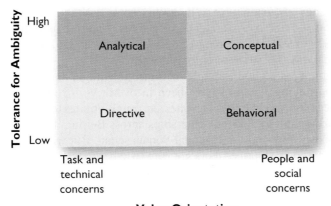

**Value Orientation**

SOURCE: Based on discussion contained in A J Rowe and R O Mason, *Managing with Style: A Guide to Understanding, Assessing, and Improving Decision Making* (San Francisco: Jossey-Bass, 1987), pp 1–17.

Air-traffic controller Paul Rinaldi uses a directive style to make quick decisions at Dulles International Airport. Would you like to work in this role?

well-suited for an air-traffic controller. Here is what Paul Rinaldi had to say about his decision-making style to a reporter from *Fortune*.

> It's not so much analytical as it is making a decision quickly and sticking with it. You have to do that knowing that some of the decisions you're going to make are going to be wrong, but you're going to make that decision be right. You can't back out. You've constantly got to be taking into account the speed of the airplane, its characteristics, the climb rate, and how fast it's going to react to your instructions. You're taking all that in and processing it in a split second, hoping that it'll all work together. If it doesn't, then you go to plan B. . . . The percentage of us that make it to retirement is not real high. It takes a toll on you. We can't make mistakes.[38]

**Analytical** This style has a much higher tolerance for ambiguity and is characterized by the tendency to overanalyze a situation. People with this style like to consider more information and alternatives than do directives. Analytic individuals are careful decision makers who take longer to make decisions but who also respond well to new or uncertain situations. They can often be autocratic.

Zhang Guangming is a good example of someone with an analytical style. "Zhang Guangming's car-buying synapses have been in overdrive for months. He has spent hours poring over Chinese car buff magazines, surfing Web sites to mine data on various models, and trekking out to a dozen dealerships across Beijing. Finally, Zhang settled on either a Volkswagen Bora or a Hyundai Sonata sedan. But with cutthroat competition forcing dealers to slash prices, he's not sure whether to buy now or wait."[39]

**Conceptual** People with a conceptual style have a high tolerance for ambiguity and tend to focus on the people or social aspects of a work situation. They take a broad perspective to problem solving and like to consider many options and future possibilities. Conceptual types adopt a long-term perspective and rely on intuition and discussions with others to acquire information. They also are willing to take risks and are good at finding creative solutions to problems. On the downside, however, a conceptual style can foster an idealistic and indecisive approach to decision making. Howard Stringer, Sony Corporation's first non-Japanese CEO, possesses characteristics of a conceptual style.

> Mr Stringer . . . says he recognizes the risk of falling behind amid breakneck changes in electronics. But he says there's an equal risk of moving too aggressively. "I don't want to change Sony's culture to the point where it's unrecognizable from the founder's vision," he says. . . . He tried gently persuading managers to cooperate with one another and urged them to think about developing products in a new way.[40]

**Behavioral**   People with a behavioral style work well with others and enjoy social interactions in which opinions are openly exchanged. Behavioral types are supportive, receptive to suggestions, show warmth, and prefer verbal to written information. Although they like to hold meetings, people with this style have a tendency to avoid conflict and to be too concerned about others. This can lead behavioral types to adopt a "wishy-washy" approach to decision making, to have a hard time saying no to others, and to have a hard time making difficult decisions.

**Research and Practical Implications**   Please take a moment now to complete the Hands-On Exercise on page 261. It assesses your decision-making style. How do your scores compare with the following norms: directive (75), analytical (90), conceptual (80), and behavioral (55)?[41] What do the differences between your scores and the survey norms suggest about your decision-making style?

Research shows that very few people have only one dominant decision-making style. Rather, most managers have characteristics that fall into two or three styles. Studies also show that decision-making styles vary across occupations, job level, and countries.[42] You can use knowledge of decision-making styles in three ways. First, knowledge of styles helps you to understand yourself. Awareness of your style assists you in identifying your strengths and weaknesses as a decision maker and facilitates the potential for self-improvement. Second, you can increase your ability to influence others by being aware of styles. For example, if you are dealing with an analytical person, you should provide as much information as possible to support your ideas. This same approach is more likely to frustrate a directive type. Finally, knowledge of styles gives you an awareness of how people can take the same information and yet arrive at different decisions by using a variety of decision-making strategies. It is important to conclude with the caveat that there is not a best decision-making style that applies in all situations. We should all strive to capitalize on the strengths of the various decision-making styles while trying to achieve a "state of clarity" when making decisions. According to a decision-making expert, "the clarity state is characterized by a balance of physical, mental and emotional systems. . . . it is actually a measurable physical and emotional state of being relaxed, positive and focused."[43]

**Self-Assessment Exercise**

Assessing Your Ethical Decision-Making Skills

# Intuition in Decision Making

If you have ever had a hunch or gut feeling about something, you have experienced the effects of intuition. **Intuition** "is a capacity for attaining direct knowledge or understanding without the apparent intrusion of rational thought or logical inference."[44] As a process, intuition is automatic and involuntary. In many decisions, it is as important as rational

**intuition**

**Capacity for attaining knowledge or understanding without rational thought or logic.**

analysis. Ray Kroc, for example, recalls that intuition drove his decision to buy the McDonald's brand: "I'm not a gambler, and I didn't have that kind of money, but my funny bone instinct kept urging me on."[45]

Unfortunately, the use of intuition does not always lead to blockbuster decisions such as Ray Kroc's. To enhance your understanding of intuition's role in decision making, this section presents a model of intuition and discusses the pros and cons of using intuition to make decisions.

**A Model of Intuition**    Figure 10–2 presents a model of intuition. Starting at the far right, the model shows there are two types of intuition:[46]

1. A *holistic hunch* represents a judgment that is based on a subconscious integration of information stored in memory. People using this form of intuition may not be able to explain why they want to make a certain decision, except that the choice "feels right."

2. *Automated experiences* represent a choice that is based on a familiar situation and a partially subconscious application of previously learned information related to that situation. For example, when you have years of experience driving a car, you react to a variety of situations without conscious analysis.

Returning to Figure 10–2, you can see that there are two sources of intuition: expertise and feelings. *Expertise* represents an individual's combined explicit and tacit knowledge regarding an object, person, situation, or decision opportunity. This source of intuition increases with age and experience. The *feelings* component reflects the automatic, underlying effect one experiences in response to an object, person, situation, or decision opportunity. An intuitive response is based on the interaction between one's expertise and feelings in a given situation.

**Pros and Cons of Using Intuition**    On the positive side, intuition can speed up the decision-making process.[47] Intuition thus can be valuable in our complex and ever-changing world. Intuition may be a practical approach when resources are limited and deadlines are tight. Intuition based on deep knowledge and active preparation informs quick and complicated decisions in an effective hospital emergency department. Recalling her work as director of an emergency department, Kathleen Gallo

**FIGURE 10–2**
A Model of
Intuition

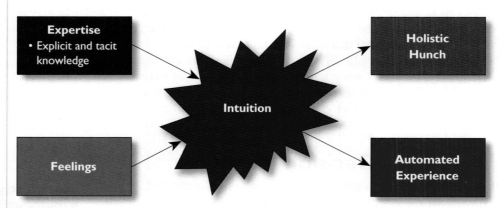

SOURCES: Based in part on E Sadler-Smith and E Shefy, "The Intuitive Executive: Understanding and Applying 'Gut Feel' in Decision-Making," *Academy of Management Executive*, November 2004, pp 76–91; and C C Miller and R D Ireland, "Intuition in Strategic Decision Making: Friend or Foe in the Fast-Paced 21st Century," *Academy of Management Executive*, February 2005, pp 19–30.

# What Is Your Decision-Making Style?

**INSTRUCTIONS:** This survey consists of 20 questions, each with four responses. You must consider each possible response for a question and then rank them according to how much you prefer each response. Because many of the questions are anchored to how individuals make decisions at work, you can feel free to use your student role as a frame of reference to answer the questions. For each question, use the space on the survey to rank the four responses with either a 1, 2, 4, or 8. Use the number 8 for the responses that are **most** like you, a 4 for those that are **moderately** like you, a 2 for those that are **slightly** like you, and a 1 for the responses that are **least** like you. For example, a question could be answered [8], [4], [2], [1]. Do not repeat any number when answering a question, and place the numbers in the boxes next to each of the answers. Once all of the responses for the 20 questions have been ranked, total the scores in each of the four columns. The total score for column one represents your directive style, column two your analytical style, column three your conceptual style, and column four your behavioral style.

| | | | |
|---|---|---|---|
| **1.** My prime objective in life is to: | have a position with status | be the best in whatever I do | be recognized for my work | feel secure in my job |
| **2.** I enjoy work that: | is clear and well defined | is varied and challenging | lets me act independently | involves people |
| **3.** I expect people to be: | productive | capable | committed | responsive |
| **4.** My work lets me: | get things done | find workable approaches | apply new ideas | be truly satisfied |
| **5.** I communicate best by: | talking with others | putting things in writing | being open with others | having a group meeting |
| **6.** My planning focuses on: | current problems | how best to meet goals | future opportunities | needs of people in the organization |
| **7.** I prefer to solve problems by: | applying rules | using careful analysis | being creative | relying on my feelings |
| **8.** I prefer information: | that is simple and direct | that is complete | that is broad and informative | that is easily understood |
| **9.** When I'm not sure what to do: | I rely on my intuition | I search for alternatives | I try to find a compromise | I avoid making a decision |
| **10.** Whenever possible, I avoid: | long debates | incomplete work | technical problems | conflict with others |
| **11.** I am really good at: | remembering details | finding answers | seeing many options | working with people |
| **12.** When time is important, I: | decide and act quickly | apply proven approaches | look for what will work | refuse to be pressured |
| **13.** In social settings, I: | speak with many people | observe what others are doing | contribute to the conversation | want to be part of the discussion |
| **14.** I always remember: | people's names | places I have been | people's faces | people's personalities |
| **15.** I prefer jobs where I: | receive high rewards | have challenging assignments | can reach my personal goals | am accepted by the group |
| **16.** I work best with people who: | are energetic and ambitious | are very competent | are open minded | are polite and understanding |
| **17.** When I am under stress, I: | speak quickly | try to concentrate on the problem | become frustrated | worry about what I should do |
| **18.** Others consider me: | aggressive | disciplined | imaginative | supportive |
| **19.** My decisions are generally: | realistic and direct | systematic and logical | broad and flexible | sensitive to the other's needs |
| **20.** I dislike: | losing control | boring work | following rules | being rejected |

Total score _____

**SOURCE:** © Dr. Alan J Rowe, Distinguished Emeritus Professor. Revised 12/18/98. Reprinted with permission.

says, "While the arrival of a helicopter with a whole family of car-wreck victims might look like a crisis and might be a crisis for the family, it is not a crisis for the staff . . . because they are prepared."[48]

On the downside, intuition is subject to the same types of biases associated with rational decision making. It is particularly susceptible to the availability and representativeness heuristics, as well as the overconfidence and hindsight biases.[49] In addition, the decision maker may have difficulty convincing others that the intuitive decision makes sense, so a good idea may be ignored.

Where does that leave us? We believe intuition and rationality are complementary, so managers should try to use both. For example, rational analysis can be used to verify or validate a hunch. We thus encourage managers to have the courage to use intuition.[50] Conversely, managers can use intuition to evaluate a rational choice by asking questions such as What does my experience suggest about this decision?

# Creativity

**creativity**

**Process of developing something new or unique.**

In light of today's need for fast-paced decisions, an organization's ability to stimulate the creativity and innovation of its employees is becoming increasingly important. Although many definitions have been proposed, **creativity** is defined here as the process of using intelligence, imagination, and skill to develop a new or novel product, object, process, or thought.[51] It can be as simple as locating a new place to hang your car keys or as complex as developing a pocket-size microcomputer. This definition highlights three broad types of creativity. One can create something new (creation), one can combine or synthesize things (synthesis), or one can improve or change things (modification).

Researchers are not absolutely certain how creativity takes place. Nonetheless, we do know that creativity involves "making remote associations" between unconnected events, ideas, information stored in memory (recall our discussion in Chapter 4), or physical objects. Consider how Dr William Foege, then working for the U.S. Centers for Disease Control and Prevention, led the effort to eradicate smallpox in Nigeria. Foege realized that his supply of vaccine was insufficient for the whole population. But he observed how people congregated to shop in markets, so he targeted his campaign to vaccinate the people in those crowded areas, even if they were merely visitors. In so doing, Foege (now a senior fellow with the Carter Center and the Bill and Melinda Gates Foundation) created a model for future vaccination campaigns that efficiently interrupt the paths by which a virus spreads.[52]

The idea of "remote associations" describes thinking such as Foege's connection of shopping behavior and a virus's spread. But it doesn't explain how Foege was able to make this creative link. Researchers, however, have identified five stages underlying the creative process: preparation, concentration, incubation, illumination, and verification. Let us consider these stages.

The *preparation* stage reflects the notion that creativity starts from a base of knowledge. Experts suggest that creativity involves a convergence between tacit or implied knowledge and explicit knowledge. Renowned

© 2005 Ted Goff

**"We need something to come after this part. Any ideas?"**

*COPYRIGHT © Ted Goff. Reprinted with permission.*

choreographer Twyla Tharp emphasizes the significance of preparation in the creative process: "I think everyone can be creative, but you have to prepare for it with routine."[53] Tharp's creativity-feeding habits include reading literature, keeping physically active (which stimulates the brain as well as the rest of the body), and choosing new projects that are very different from whatever she has just completed. Even an activity as simple as looking up a word in the dictionary offers an opportunity for preparation: Tharp looks at the word before and after, too, just to see if it gives her an idea.

During the *concentration* stage, an individual focuses on the problem at hand. Research shows that creative ideas at work are often triggered by work-related problems, incongruities, or failures. This was precisely the case for Jason Jiang, 35-year-old founder of Focus Media Holding.

> Focus was born of a simple observation. In 2002, Jiang was waiting for an elevator at a Shanghai shopping mall and found himself staring at a poster featuring sultry Taiwanese actress Shu Qi pushing Red Earth cosmetics. Jiang figured he'd make buckets of money by replacing such posters with video screens. His hunch was that people would be grateful for something to watch—yes, even ads—while they waited for the ride up to their office or apartment. (In China, it's not uncommon to wait several minutes for an elevator.)[54]

Jiang's creative idea was a hit. Focus's advertising sales surpassed $489 million in 2007 and the stock has increased sixfold since 2005. Interestingly, Japanese companies are noted for encouraging this stage as part of a quality improvement process more than American companies. For example, the average number of ideas per employee was 37.4 for Japanese workers versus 0.12 for U.S. workers.[55]

*Incubation* is done unconsciously. During this stage, people engage in daily activities while their minds simultaneously mull over information and make remote associations. These associations ultimately are generated in the *illumination* stage. Finally, *verification* entails going through the entire process to verify, modify, or try out the new idea.

Let us examine the stages of creativity to determine why Japanese organizations propose and implement more ideas than do American companies. To address this issue, a creativity expert visited and extensively interviewed employees from five major Japanese companies. He observed that Japanese firms have created a management infrastructure that encourages and reinforces creativity. People were taught to identify problems (discontents) on their first day of employment. In turn, discontents were referred to as "golden eggs" to reinforce the notion that it is good to identify problems.

These organizations also promoted the stages of incubation, illumination, and verification through teamwork and incentives. For example, some companies posted the golden eggs on large wall posters in the work area; employees were then encouraged to interact with each other to execute the final three stages of the creative process. Employees eventually received monetary awards for any suggestions that passed all five phases of this process.[56] This research underscores the conclusion that creativity can be enhanced by effectively managing the creativity process and by fostering a positive and supportive work environment.[57] Ways to create such an environment include leadership that values innovation, a focus on long-term goals as well as short-term results, and allocation of resources and rewards to innovative activities. To learn how companies sustain an innovation-friendly culture, see Skills & Best Practices on page 264.

## Crafting an Innovative Culture

An innovative organization has the following qualities:

- *Awareness.* The organization understands how existing tools and ideas can solve a problem. To go beyond having just one or two creative employees, the organization challenges all employees with problem-solving opportunities and treats problems as a chance to tap employees' creativity.

- *Intense motivation.* Employees receive extrinsic and intrinsic rewards for innovating. The company provides visible and sustained support for innovative projects, even if they suffer setbacks. If an innovation fails, the project may be discontinued, but its leader is not punished as "a failure."

- *Surfeit of skills and competence.* The organization hires talented people and encourages them to continue learning and developing their skills. Technical experts and leaders of sales and production teams are actively involved in recruiting employees.

- *Supportive infrastructure.* Goals for innovation are not limited to a research and development function, but apply to the entire organization. For example, measurement of success and related rewards might be tied to the percentage of revenues coming from new products or cost reductions resulting from new ideas to boost productivity.

SOURCE: Based on R M Price, "Infusing Innovation in Corporate Culture," *Organizational Dynamics,* 2007, pp 320–28.

5 learning objective

Summarize the pros and cons of involving groups in the decision-making process.

Managers need to balance these efforts against concern for efficiency. Developing new ideas can be risky and expensive but can generate big returns in the long run. Cutting costs by making processes more routine and efficient can boost profits in the short term but draw attention away from breakthrough innovations. For example, 3M has a reputation as an innovative company; until recently, at least one-third of its sales came from products released during the preceding few years. But when James McNerney came on board as CEO in 2000, he was able to dramatically improve the company's stock performance through wide-scale initiatives to improve efficiency, even in the research and development group. The pace of innovation fell during McNerney's four-and-a-half-year tenure, and now only one-fourth of the company's income results from new products. Under 3M's current CEO, George Buckley, 3M is again focusing on innovation in research and development by no longer pressuring its scientists to focus on efficient processes. The efficiency drive is concentrated on the manufacturing activities, where incremental improvements are more significant.[58]

# Group Decision Making

This section explores issues associated with group decision making. Specifically, we discuss (1) group involvement in decision making, (2) advantages and disadvantages of group-aided decision making, and (3) group problem-solving techniques.

## Group Involvement in Decision Making

Whether groups assemble in face-to-face meetings or rely on other technologically based methods to communicate, they can contribute to each stage of the decision-making process. In order to maximize the value of group-aided decision making, however, it is important to create an environment in which group members feel free to participate and express their opinions. A study sheds light on how managers can create such an environment.

A team of researchers conducted two studies to determine whether a group's innovativeness was related to *minority dissent,* defined as the extent to which group members feel comfortable disagreeing with other group members, and a group's level of participation in decision making. Results showed that the most innovative groups possessed high levels of both minority dissent and participation in decision making.[59]

# Assessing Participation in Group Decision Making

**INSTRUCTIONS:**  The following survey measures minority dissent, participation in group decision making, and satisfaction with a group. For each of the items, use the rating scale shown below to circle the answer that best represents your feelings based on a group project you were or currently are involved in. Next, use the scoring key to compute scores for the levels of minority dissent, participation in decision making, and satisfaction with the group.

1 = Strongly disagree

2 = Disagree

3 = Neither agree nor disagree

4 = Agree

5 = Strongly agree

| | | | | | |
|---|---|---|---|---|---|
| 1. Within my team, individuals disagree with one another. | 1 | 2 | 3 | 4 | 5 |
| 2. Within my team, individuals do not go along with majority opinion. | 1 | 2 | 3 | 4 | 5 |
| 3. Within my team, individuals voice their disagreement with the majority opinion. | 1 | 2 | 3 | 4 | 5 |
| 4. Within my team, I am comfortable voicing my disagreement of the majority opinion. | 1 | 2 | 3 | 4 | 5 |
| 5. Within my team, individuals do not immediately agree with one another. | 1 | 2 | 3 | 4 | 5 |
| 6. As a team member, I have a real say in how work is carried out. | 1 | 2 | 3 | 4 | 5 |
| 7. Within my team, most members have a chance to participate in decisions. | 1 | 2 | 3 | 4 | 5 |
| 8. My team is designed so that everyone has the opportunity to participate in decisions. | 1 | 2 | 3 | 4 | 5 |
| 9. I am satisfied with my group. | 1 | 2 | 3 | 4 | 5 |
| 10. I would like to work with this group on another project. | 1 | 2 | 3 | 4 | 5 |

## SCORING KEY

Minority dissent (add scores for items 1, 2, 3, 4, 5): _____

Participation in decision making (add scores for items 6, 7, 8): _____

Satisfaction (add scores for items 9, 10): _____

## ARBITRARY NORMS

Low minority dissent = 5–15

High minority dissent = 16–25

Low participation in decision making = 3–8

High participation in decision making = 9–15

Low satisfaction = 2–5

High satisfaction = 6–10

**SOURCE:** The items in the survey were developed from C K W De Dreu and M A West, "Minority Dissent and Team Innovation: The Importance of Participation in Decision Making," *Journal of Applied Psychology*, December 2001, pp 119–201.

Those findings are consistent with a recent study of research and development teams.[60] These teams generated the most innovative, significant, and useful ideas when the team was more diverse (in terms of educational background) and also had transformational leadership (a type of leadership, defined in Chapter 14, which inspires people to make changes). These findings encourage managers to seek divergent views from group members during decision making. They also support the practice of not seeking compliance from group members or punishing group members who disagree with a majority opinion. Take a moment now to complete the Hands-On Exercise on page 265. It assesses the amount of minority dissent and participation in group decision making for a group project you have completed or are currently working on in school or on the job. Is your satisfaction with the group related to minority dissent and participation in decision making? If not, what might explain this surprising result?

The previously discussed study about minority dissent reinforces the notion that the quality of group decision making varies across groups. This, in turn, raises the issue of how to best assess a group's decision-making effectiveness. Although experts do not agree on the one "best" criterion, there is agreement that groups need to work through various aspects of decision making in order to be effective. One expert proposed that decision-making effectiveness in a group is dependent on successfully accomplishing the following:[61]

1. Developing a clear understanding of the decision situation.
2. Developing a clear understanding of the requirements for an effective choice.
3. Thoroughly and accurately assessing the positive qualities of alternative solutions.
4. Thoroughly and accurately assessing the negative qualities of alternative solutions.

To increase the probability of groups making high-quality decisions, managers, team leaders, and individual group members are encouraged to focus on satisfying these four requirements.[62]

## Advantages and Disadvantages of Group-Aided Decision Making

Including groups in the decision-making process has both pros and cons (see Table 10–1). On the positive side, groups contain a greater pool of knowledge, provide more varied perspectives, create more comprehension of decisions, increase decision acceptance, and create a training ground for inexperienced employees. These advantages must be balanced, however, with the disadvantages listed in Table 10–1. In doing so, managers need to determine the extent to which the advantages and disadvantages apply to the decision situation. The following three guidelines may then be applied to help decide whether groups should be included in the decision-making process:

1. If additional information would increase the quality of the decision, managers should involve those people who can provide the needed information.
2. If acceptance is important, managers need to involve those individuals whose acceptance and commitment are important.
3. If people can be developed through their participation, managers may want to involve those whose development is most important.[63]

## Advantages and Disadvantages of Group-Aided Decision Making   TABLE 10–1

| Advantages | Disadvantages |
|---|---|
| 1. *Greater pool of knowledge.* A group can bring much more information and experience to bear on a decision or problem than can an individual acting alone. | 1. *Social pressure.* Unwillingness to "rock the boat" and pressure to conform may combine to stifle the creativity of individual contributors. |
| 2. *Different perspectives.* Individuals with varied experience and interests help the group see decision situations and problems from different angles. | 2. *Domination by a vocal few.* Sometimes the quality of group action is reduced when the group gives in to those who talk the loudest and longest. |
| 3. *Greater comprehension.* Those who personally experience the give-and-take of group discussion about alternative courses of action tend to understand the rationale behind the final decision. | 3. *Logrolling.* Political wheeling and dealing can displace sound thinking when an individual's pet project or vested interest is at stake. |
| 4. *Increased acceptance.* Those who play an active role in group decision making and problem solving tend to view the outcome as "ours" rather than "theirs." | 4. *Goal displacement.* Sometimes secondary considerations such as winning an argument, making a point, or getting back at a rival displace the primary task of making a sound decision or solving a problem. |
| 5. *Training ground.* Less experienced participants in group action learn how to cope with group dynamics by actually being involved. | 5. *"Groupthink."* Sometimes cohesive "in-groups" let the desire for unanimity override sound judgment when generating and evaluating alternative courses of action. (Groupthink is discussed in Chapter 9.) |

SOURCE: R Kreitner, *Management,* 10th ed (Boston: Houghton Mifflin, 2007), p 231. Used with permission.

**Group versus Individual Performance**   Before recommending that managers involve groups in decision making, it is important to examine whether groups perform better or worse than individuals. After reviewing 61 years of relevant research, a decision-making expert concluded that "Group performance was generally qualitatively and quantitatively superior to the performance of the average individual."[64] Although subsequent research of small-group decision making generally supported this conclusion, additional research suggests that managers should use a contingency approach when determining whether to include others in the decision-making process. Let us now consider these contingency recommendations.

**Practical Contingency Recommendations**   If the decision occurs frequently, such as deciding on promotions or who qualifies for a loan, use groups because they tend to produce more consistent decisions than do individuals. Given time constraints, let the most competent individual, rather than a group, make the decision. In the face of environmental threats such as time pressure and the potentially serious effects of a decision, groups use less information and fewer communication channels. This increases the probability of a bad decision.[65] This conclusion underscores a general recommendation that managers should keep in mind: Because the quality of communication strongly affects a group's productivity, on complex tasks it is essential to devise mechanisms to enhance communication effectiveness.

**Group Exercise**

Stranded in the Desert: An Exercise in Decision Making

# Group Problem-Solving Techniques

Using groups to make decisions generally requires that they reach a consensus. According to a decision-making expert, a **consensus** "is reached when all members can say they either agree with the decision or have had their 'day in court' and were unable to convince the others of their viewpoint. In the final analysis, everyone agrees to support the outcome."[66] This definition indicates that consensus does not require unanimous agreement because group members may still disagree with the final decision but are willing to work toward its success.

**consensus**

**Presenting opinions and gaining agreement to support a decision.**

Groups can experience roadblocks when trying to arrive at a consensus decision. For one, groups may not generate all relevant alternatives to a problem because an individual dominates or intimidates other group members. This is both overt and/or subtle. For instance, group members who possess power and authority, such as a CEO, can be intimidating, regardless of interpersonal style, simply by being present in the room. Moreover, shyness inhibits the generation of alternatives. Shy or socially anxious individuals may withhold their input for fear of embarrassment or lack of confidence. Satisficing is another hurdle to effective group decision making. As previously noted, groups satisfice due to limited time, information, or ability to handle large amounts of information.[67]

A management expert offered the following "do's" and "don'ts" for successfully achieving consensus: Groups should use active listening skills, involve as many members as possible, seek out the reasons behind arguments, and dig for the facts. At the same time, groups should not horse trade (I'll support you on this decision because you supported me on the last one), vote, or agree just to avoid "rocking the boat."[68] Voting works against consensus by splitting the group into winners and losers, but in some situations, speedy arrival at a decision is the greater priority (see Skills & Best Practices) on page 269.

Decision-making experts have developed three group problem-solving techniques—brainstorming, the nominal group technique, and the Delphi technique—to reduce the above roadblocks. Knowledge of these techniques can help current and future managers to more effectively use group-aided decision making. Further, the advent of computer-aided decision making enables managers to use these techniques to solve complex problems with large groups of people.

**Brainstorming** Brainstorming was developed by A F Osborn, an advertising executive, to increase creativity.[69] **Brainstorming** is used to help groups generate multiple ideas and alternatives for solving problems. This technique is effective because it helps reduce interference caused by critical and judgmental reactions to one's ideas from other group members.

**brainstorming**

**Process to generate a quantity of ideas.**

When brainstorming, a group is convened, and the problem at hand is reviewed. Individual members then are asked to silently generate ideas/alternatives for solving the problem. Silent idea generation is recommended over the practice of having group members randomly shout out their ideas because it leads to a greater number of unique ideas. Next, these ideas/alternatives are solicited and written on a board or flip chart. A recent study suggests that managers or team leaders may want to collect the brainstormed ideas anonymously. Results demonstrated that more controversial ideas and more nonredundant ideas were generated by anonymous than nonanonymous brainstorming groups.[70] Finally, a second session is used to critique and evaluate the alternatives. Managers are advised to follow the seven rules for brainstorming used by IDEO.[71]

1. *Defer judgment.* Don't criticize during the initial stage of idea generation. Phrases such as "we've never done it that way," "it won't work," "it's too expensive," and "our manager will never agree" should not be used.

2. *Build on the ideas of others.* Encourage participants to extend others' ideas by avoiding "buts" and using "ands."

3. *Encourage wild ideas.* Encourage out-of-the-box thinking. The wilder and more outrageous the ideas, the better.

4. *Go for quantity over quality.* Participants should try to generate and write down as many new ideas as possible. Focusing on quantity encourages people to think beyond their favorite ideas.

5. *Be visual.* Use different colored pens (e.g., red, purple, blue) to write on big sheets of flip chart paper, white boards, or poster board that are put on the wall.

6. *Stay focused on the topic.* A facilitator should be used to keep the discussion on target.

7. *One conversation at a time.* The ground rules are that no one interrupts another person, no dismissing of someone's ideas, no disrespect, and no rudeness.

Brainstorming is an effective technique for generating new ideas/alternatives. It is not appropriate for evaluating alternatives or selecting solutions.

**The Nominal Group Technique**　The **nominal group technique (NGT)** helps groups generate ideas and evaluate and select solutions. NGT is a structured group meeting that follows this format:[72] A group is convened to discuss a particular problem or issue. After the problem is understood, individuals silently generate ideas in writing. Each individual, in round-robin fashion, then offers one idea from his or her list. Ideas are recorded on a blackboard or flip chart; they are not discussed at this stage of the process. Once all ideas are elicited, the group discusses them. Anyone may criticize or defend any item. During this step, clarification is provided as well as general agreement or disagreement with the idea. The "30-second soap box" technique, which entails giving each participant a maximum of 30 seconds to argue for or against any of the ideas under consideration, can be used to facilitate this discussion. Finally, group members anonymously vote for their top choices with a weighted voting procedure (e.g., 1st choice = 3 points; 2nd choice = 2 points; 3rd choice = 1 point). Alternatively, group members can vote by placing colored dots next to their top choices. The group leader then adds the votes to determine the group's choice. Prior to making a final decision, the group may decide to discuss the top ranked items and conduct a second round of voting.

---

## Accelerating Decisions at Hewlett-Packard

Hewlett-Packard (HP) has recognized and addressed two big challenges to decision making: (1) in a complex environment, it is hard to move from analysis to action; and (2) when rapid change gives rise to uncertainty, decision makers are more comfortable with familiar practices than true innovation. HP helped its people tackle these challenges by establishing an internal consulting group known as Acceleration Services, charged with helping groups push decisions forward.

One component of Acceleration Services, the Decision-Accelerator, focused on the first challenge. When top executives launched initiatives but managers got stuck on how to carry them out, the Decision-Accelerator would bring them together in a bare room furnished only with rows of chairs and some tables. Decision-Accelerator staff kept everyone focused on defining goals and scheduling tasks, reminding participants to keep conversations on topic. Although these meetings aimed for consensus, differences of opinion were resolved with a simple vote, aimed at practical short-term results. The Decision-Accelerator helped implement HP's merger with Compaq. To decide how the joint company would combine processes such as human resource systems and e-mail, the group voted for either HP's system or Compaq's, with no side conversations about combining systems; this approach pushed managers to move quickly.

The second component of Acceleration Services, GarageWorks, addressed reluctance to innovate. Groups facing a situation that required creative thinking could assemble in the bright and inviting space devoted to GarageWorks, which encouraged playfulness with games, costumes, and books on diverse topics. Clocks were missing, and participants could choose music to play. Facilitators from GarageWorks helped the group agree on objectives and engage in team-building activities. As participants discussed the problem situation, they were encouraged to be open-minded about possibilities, generating ideas through brainstorming and the nominal group technique. Although GarageWorks didn't press for rapid action, it accelerated creative decisions by providing an environment for the creative process to move forward.

**SOURCE: Based on D M Zell, A M Glassman, and S A Duron, "Strategic Management in Turbulent Times: The Short and Glorious History of Accelerated Decision Making at Hewlett-Packard,"** *Organizational Dynamics,* **2007, pp 93–104.**

**nominal group technique (NGT)**

Process to generate ideas and evaluate solutions.

The nominal group technique reduces the roadblocks to group decision making by (1) separating brainstorming from evaluation, (2) promoting balanced participation among group members, and (3) incorporating mathematical voting techniques in order to reach consensus. NGT has been successfully used in many different decision-making situations, and has been found to generate more ideas than a standard brainstorming session.[73]

Brainstorming is a technique used to generate as many ideas as possible to solve a problem. You have probably engaged in brainstorming sessions for various class or work projects. Which of the seven rules for brainstorming do you think is most important?

**The Delphi Technique**    This problem-solving method was originally developed by the Rand Corporation for technological forecasting.[74] It now is used as a multipurpose planning tool. The **Delphi technique** is a group process that anonymously generates ideas or judgments from physically dispersed experts. Unlike the NGT, experts' ideas are obtained from questionnaires or via the Internet as opposed to face-to-face group discussions.

A manager begins the Delphi process by identifying the issue(s) he or she wants to investigate. For example, a manager might want to inquire about customer demand, customers' future preferences, or the effect of locating a plant in a certain region of the country. Next, participants are identified and a questionnaire is developed. The questionnaire is sent to participants and returned to the manager. In today's computer-networked environments, this often means that the questionnaires are e-mailed to participants. The manager then summarizes the responses and sends feedback to the participants. At this stage, participants are asked to (1) review the feedback, (2) prioritize the issues being considered, and (3) return the survey within a specified time period. This cycle repeats until the manager obtains the necessary information.

The Delphi technique is useful when face-to-face discussions are impractical, when disagreements and conflict are likely to impair communication, when certain individuals might severely dominate group discussion, and when groupthink is a probable outcome of the group process.

**Delphi technique**

Process to generate ideas from physically dispersed experts.

**Computer-Aided Decision Making**    The purpose of computer-aided decision making is to reduce consensus roadblocks while collecting more information in a shorter period of time. There are two types of computer-aided decision-making systems: chauffeur driven and group driven.[75] Chauffeur-driven systems ask participants to answer predetermined questions on electronic keypads or dials. Live television audiences on shows such as *Who Wants to Be a Millionaire* are frequently polled with this system. The computer system tabulates participants' responses in a matter of seconds.

Group-driven electronic meetings are conducted in one of two major ways. First, managers can use e-mail systems, which are discussed in Chapter 12, or the Internet to collect information or brainstorm about a decision that must be made. For example,

Miami Children's Hospital uses a combination of the Internet and a conferencing software technology to make decisions about the design of its training programs. Here is what Loubna Noureddin, director of staff and community education, had to say about the organization's computer-aided decision making:

> "What I truly like about it is my connection to other hospitals," Noureddin says. "I'm able to understand what other hospitals are doing about specific things. I put my question out, and people can respond, and I can answer back." She explains, for instance, that using the system, she and her colleagues have received guidance from other corporate educators, and even subject matter experts, on how to best train workers in such fields as critical care. "You get many other hospitals logging into the system, and telling us what they do," she says.[76]

Noureddin claims that the system has saved the company time and money.

The second method of computer-aided, group-driven meetings are conducted in special facilities equipped with individual workstations that are networked to each other. Instead of talking, participants type their input, ideas, comments, reactions, or evaluations on their keyboards. The input simultaneously appears on a large projector screen at the front of the room, thereby enabling all participants to see all input. This computer-driven process reduces consensus roadblocks because input is anonymous, everyone gets a chance to contribute, and no one can dominate the process. Research demonstrated that computer-aided decision making produced greater quality and quantity of ideas than either traditional brainstorming or the nominal group technique for both small and large groups of people.[77]

Interestingly, however, another recent study suggests caution when determining what forms of computer-aided decision making to use. This meta-analysis of 52 studies compared the effectiveness of face-to-face decision-making groups with "chat" groups. Results revealed that the use of chat groups led to decreased group effectiveness and member satisfaction and increased time to complete tasks compared to face-to-face groups.[78] These findings underscore the need to use a contingency approach for selecting the best method of computer-aided decision making in a given situation.

# key terms

# chapter summary

- *Compare and contrast the rational model of decision making, Simon's normative model, and the garbage can model.* The rational decision-making model consists of identifying the problem, generating alternative solutions, evaluating and selecting a solution, and implementing and evaluating the solution. Research indicates that decision makers do not follow the series of steps outlined in the rational model.

  Simon's normative model is guided by a decision maker's bounded rationality. Bounded rationality means that decision makers are bounded or restricted by a variety of constraints when making decisions. The normative model suggests that decision making is characterized by (a) limited information processing, (b) the use of judgmental heuristics, and (c) satisficing.

  The garbage can model holds that decision making in practice is sloppy and haphazard, resulting from a complex interaction of problems, solutions, participants, and choice opportunities. Thus, many decisions are the result of oversight or a salient opportunity, often guided by political motives. Specific problems are less likely to be solved as the total number of problems increases, and important problems are more likely to be solved than unimportant ones.

- *Identify common decision-making biases.* When people use judgmental heuristics, they tend to make systematic mistakes. The availability heuristic is a tendency to base decisions on information that is readily recalled. The representativeness heuristic is the tendency to assess an event's likelihood based on impressions about similar occurrences. Confirmation bias consists of (1) subconsciously deciding something before investigating the alternative's value and (2) seeking information that supports this preconceived opinion and discounting information that does not. The anchoring bias occurs when decision makers are influenced by the first information they receive about a decision, whether or not it is relevant. The overconfidence bias is a tendency to be overconfident about estimates or forecasts. The hindsight bias occurs when knowledge of an outcome causes the decision maker to overestimate the probability he or she could have predicted that outcome. Framing bias is the tendency to evaluate risks about gains differently from risks about losses. And escalation of commitment is the tendency to stick to an ineffective course of action on the (illogical) basis that an investment has already been made in that decision.

- *Discuss knowledge management and techniques used by companies to increase knowledge sharing.* Knowledge management involves the implementation of systems and practices that increase the sharing of knowledge and information throughout an organization. There are two types of knowledge that impact the quality of decisions: tacit knowledge and explicit knowledge. Organizations use computer systems to share explicit knowledge. Tacit knowledge is shared by observing, participating, or working with experts or coaches. Mentoring, informal networking, meetings, and design of office space also influence knowledge sharing.

- *Describe the model of decision-making styles, the role of intuition in decision making, and the stages of the creative process.* The model of decision-making styles is based on the idea that styles vary along two different dimensions: value orientation and tolerance for ambiguity. When these two dimensions are combined, they form four styles of decision making: directive, analytical, conceptual, and behavioral. People with a directive style have a low tolerance for ambiguity and are oriented toward task and technical concerns. Analytics have a higher tolerance for ambiguity and are characterized by a tendency to overanalyze a situation. People with a conceptual style have a high threshold for ambiguity and tend to focus on people or social aspects of a work situation. The behavioral style is the most people oriented of the four styles.

  Intuition is a capacity for getting direct knowledge or understanding without consciously applying logic or thought. It results from a combination of expertise and feelings and is expressed as a holistic hunch or automated experience. Intuition can speed up decision making but is subject to biases. It can be used as a complementary tool with rationality, where one is used as a check on the other.

  Creativity is defined as the process of using intelligence, imagination, and skill to develop a new or novel product, object, process, or thought. There are five stages of the creative process: preparation, concentration, incubation, illumination, and verification.

- *Summarize the pros and cons of involving groups in the decision-making process.* There are both pros and cons to involving groups in the decision-making process (see Table 10–1). Although research shows that groups typically outperform the average individual, managers need to use a contingency approach when determining whether to include others in the decision-making process.

- *Contrast brainstorming, the nominal group technique, the Delphi technique, and computer-aided decision making.* Group problem-solving techniques facilitate better decision making within groups. Brainstorming is used to help groups generate multiple ideas and alternatives for solving problems. The nominal group technique assists groups both to generate ideas and to evaluate and select solutions. The Delphi technique is a group process that anonymously generates ideas or judgments from physically dispersed experts. The purpose of computer-aided decision making is to reduce consensus roadblocks while collecting more information in a shorter period of time.

# discussion questions

1. Returning to the chapter-opening case, to what extent was McDonald's decision to pursue specialty coffee based on intuition? Explain.

2. Do you think knowledge management will become more important in the future? Explain your rationale.

3. Why would decision-making styles be a source of interpersonal conflict?

4. Describe a situation in which you exhibited escalation of commitment. Why did you escalate a losing situation?

5. Given the time it takes to get a group to reach consensus in decision making and the potential for conflict, are groups worth the effort?

# ethical dilemma

## Should the Principal of Westwood High Allow an Exception to the Graduation Dress Code?[79]

This dilemma involves a situation faced by Helen Riddle, the principal of Mesa, Arizona's, Westwood High. "Westwood High has 225 Native American students, including 112 from the Salt River Pima-Maricopa Indian Community, most of which lies within the boundaries of the Mesa Unified School District." Districtwide, there are 452 Native American high school students, 149 of whom are from the Salt River Reservation. Here is the situation.

Native American students asked the principal for permission to wear eagle feathers during their graduation ceremony. While this may seem like a reasonable request given these students' customs and traditions, Westwood High had a rule stating that "students were only allowed to wear a traditional cap and gown for graduation with no other adornments or clothing, including military uniforms. The rules were based on past practice and tradition at schools, not School Board policy."

Advocates for the Native American students argued that students should be allowed to wear the eagle feathers because they represent a significant achievement in the lives of those individuals. In contrast, one school board member opposed the exception to the rule because "it would open the door for other students wanting to display symbols of their own culture or background."

### What Would You Do If You Were the Principal of Westwood High?

1. Allow the Native American students to wear the eagle feathers now and in the future. This shows an appreciation for diversity.

2. Not allow the Native American students to wear the eagle feathers because it violates an existing rule. Allowing an exception opens the door for additional requests about changing the dress code. It would be difficult to defend one exception over another.

3. Allow the students to wear the eagle feathers only in this year's ceremony. Then form a committee to review the dress code requirements.

4. Invent other options. Discuss.

For an interpretation of this situation, visit our Web site, at
**www.mhhe.com/kinickiob4e**

If you're looking for additional study materials, be sure to check out the Online Learning Center at

## www.mhhe.com/kinickiob4e

for more information and interactivities that correspond to this chapter.

# Managing Conflict and Negotiating

**After reading the material in this chapter, you should be able to:**

1.  Define the term *conflict,* distinguish between functional and dysfunctional conflict, and identify three desired outcomes of conflict.

2.  Define *personality conflicts,* and explain how they should be managed.

3.  Discuss the role of in-group thinking in intergroup conflict, and explain what can be done to avoid cross-cultural conflict.

4.  Explain how managers can program functional conflict, and identify the five conflict-handling styles.

5.  Identify and describe at least four alternative dispute resolution (ADR) techniques.

6.  Draw a distinction between distributive and integrative negotiation, and explain the concept of added-value negotiation.

**Employees who spend much of their day on eBay or other online time-killers create tension for their colleagues. As a manager, how would you react if you witnessed an employee frequently cyberloafing?**

Lowrie Beacham didn't like confronting people or making decisions that favored one staffer over another, including the time two of his people were vying to be in charge of the new fitness center.

"Instead of having one bad day and getting over it, it went on for literally years," he recalls. "You just kick the can a little farther down the road—'Let's have a meeting on this next month'—anything you can try to keep from having that confrontation."

Anytime his employees bristled at his gentle criticisms, he'd change the subject: "You're getting to work on time; that's wonderful!" he'd say, "Never mind that your clients say you're difficult to work with."

What resulted was a dysfunctional department, he admits, "with no discipline, no confidence in where they stood, lots of scheming and kvetching, backstabbing." He gave up his management role. "I'm extremely happy not managing," he says.

The bad manager tends to conjure images of the blood-vessel-bursting screamer looking for a handle to fly off. But these types are increasingly rare. Far more common, and more insidious, are the managers who won't say a critical word to the staffers who need to hear it. In avoiding an unpleasant conversation,

they allow something worse to ferment in the delay. They achieve kindness in the short term but heartlessness in the long run, dooming the problem employee to nonimprovement. You can't fix what you can't say is broken. . . .

John Hardcastle, formerly in financial reporting, was one of the countless people who, surveys show, want to learn and improve. But every time he had to submit a report and asked for feedback, his boss couldn't say anything negative. "He would visibly dance around the aspects of my reports that needed improvement," he says. "I never really knew exactly where I stood."

Bosses who want to avoid any discomfort, "use generalities so people really don't know what they're talking about," says Laura Collins, an HR consultant. Instead, they tend toward one size-fits-all comments: "pay a little more attention to detail" and "improve the way you communicate" and "develop better organization skills."

Such avoidance is a recipe for an employee blindsiding. During the year she worked for one such boss, Maxine Erlwein got glowing 90-day and six-month reviews, and held daily meetings with her boss to whom she'd tell her plans. Then, in the annual review, her former boss "tried to claim my

performance was not meeting any of the minimum requirements of the position," she says. The stress leveled her appetite, memory and sleep. "Nonconfrontational people will nurse a grudge," she says.

No one appreciates the deceptive peace and quiet. Lawrence Levine, program analyst, has witnessed a colleague spending much of his day on eBay, among other online time-killers. There's no doubt the supervisor saw it, too. It mystified the staff.

"We all pondered in the absence of any action why the heck this person drawing a decent salary was allowed to do this stuff," he says. "The anger was that all the rest of us were evaluated on what we produced."

But John Traylor, a chief engineer who once experienced a similar frustration over a lazy colleague, sees a different side now that he's a conflict-avoiding manager himself. He hates to give an employee news that would "crush his spirit."

He even once quietly arranged to have an employee transferred at the request of others. "He could leave with the dignity of having been asked by higher levels to move to a more important project—and I didn't have to confront the real issue," he says.

He concedes that his handling didn't help the employee improve. He also says that the management training he received from the company didn't teach him how to deal with such conflict. "It would have been helpful," he says.[1]

**Should an employee confront her or his manager when conflict is being avoided? Explain your rationale. For an interpretation of this case and additional comments, visit our Online Learning Center at**

**www.mhhe.com/kinickiob4e**

FOR DISCUSSION

# A Modern View of Conflict

**conflict**

**One party perceives its interests are being opposed or set back by another party.**

**1 learning objective**

Define the term *conflict,* distinguish between functional and dysfunctional conflict, and identify three desired outcomes of conflict.

A comprehensive review of the conflict literature yielded this consensus definition: "**conflict** is a process in which one party perceives that its interests are being opposed or negatively affected by another party."[4] The word *perceives* reminds us that sources of conflict and issues can be real or imagined. The resulting conflict is the same. Conflict can escalate (strengthen) or deescalate (weaken) over time. "The conflict process unfolds in a context, and whenever conflict, escalated or not, occurs the disputants or third parties can attempt to manage it in some manner."[5] Consequently, current and future managers need to understand the dynamics of conflict and know how to handle it effectively (both as disputants and as third parties).

## A Conflict Continuum

Ideas about managing conflict underwent an interesting evolution during the 20th century. Initially, scientific management experts such as Frederick W Taylor believed all conflict ultimately threatened management's authority and thus had to be avoided or quickly resolved.[6] Later, human relationists recognized the inevitability of conflict and advised managers to learn to live with it. Emphasis remained on resolving conflict whenever possible, however. Beginning in the 1970s, OB specialists realized conflict had both positive and negative outcomes, depending on its nature and intensity. This perspective introduced the revolutionary idea that organizations could suffer from *too little* conflict.

Work groups, departments, or organizations experiencing too little conflict tend to be plagued by apathy, lack of creativity, indecision, and missed deadlines. Excessive conflict, on the other hand, can erode organizational performance because of political infighting, dissatisfaction, lack of teamwork, and turnover. Workplace aggression and violence can be manifestations of excessive conflict.[7] Appropriate types and levels of conflict energize people in constructive directions.[8]

# Functional versus Dysfunctional Conflict

The distinction between **functional conflict** and **dysfunctional conflict** pivots on whether the organization's interests are served. According to one conflict expert,

> **functional conflict**
> Serves organization's interests.
>
> **dysfunctional conflict**
> Threatens organization's interests.

> Some [types of conflict] support the goals of the organization and improve performance; these are functional, constructive forms of conflict. They benefit or support the main purposes of the organization. Additionally, there are those types of conflict that hinder organizational performance; these are dysfunctional or destructive forms. They are undesirable and the manager should seek their eradication.[9]

Functional conflict is commonly referred to in management circles as constructive or cooperative conflict.[10]

Often, a simmering conflict can be defused in a functional manner or driven to dysfunctional proportions, depending on how it is handled. For example, consider the two very different outcomes to conflicts that surfaced at Airbus and at Snokist Growers. For Airbus, critical problems arose in installing the complex wiring for its A380 aircraft. With 30,000 cables in the new luxury liner to power standard tasks plus video consoles, satellite phones, and more, the wiring was harder to engineer and install than planners had expected. As the company was forced to announce delays, managers started blaming one another—conflict that further slowed progress. Airbus executives, concluding that the solution was firm leadership to get everyone focused on mutual goals, appointed Rüdiger Fuchs to take charge of assembly operations. Fuchs gathered information from all his managers, ordered engineers to move to the factory floor, and began bringing together production managers and engineers for daily meetings to identify and solve problems. These changes brought in transparency that made it harder for the parties to focus on blame and easier to focus on solutions, so the project began moving forward again.[11]

In contrast, at Snokist, a Washington State fruit-packing and canning cooperative owned by 350 fruit growers, conflict between management and cannery employees has persisted. Problems began several years ago, when CEO Valerie Woerner tried to save the nearly bankrupt company by reducing inventories, automating tasks, laying off workers, and slashing benefits for the remaining employees. Frightened and angry, the employees responded by voting for union representation and then demanding better wages and benefits. When Snokist hired a Texas labor attorney, the union walked away from negotiations, saying his "arrogant" attitude created a hostile environment, and the union voted to strike. The eight-month strike, which started during harvest season, was ugly and expensive. Eventually, the workers accepted a contract that gave them only a small part of what they had demanded. This resolution might seem like a victory for Snokist, but the contract was for a three-year period, meaning workers and management will soon be at the bargaining table again. Union representative Sherry Scott says, "We think we deserve a better deal from the company, and we look forward to talking to them about it."[12]

**Test Your Knowledge**
Styles of Handling Conflict

Consider the conflict at Snokist between management and cannery employees. What could have been done to come to a better resolution for both parties?

**Layoff survivors typically complain about being overworked, thus paving the way for stress and conflict. What can managers do to help employees cope with the stress associated with surviving a large layoff?**

# Antecedents of Conflict

Certain situations produce more conflict than others. By knowing the antecedents of conflict, managers are better able to anticipate conflict and take steps to resolve it if it becomes dysfunctional. Among the situations that tend to produce either functional or dysfunctional conflict are

- Incompatible personalities or value systems.
- Overlapping or unclear job boundaries.
- Competition for limited resources.
- Interdepartment/intergroup competition.
- Inadequate communication.
- Interdependent tasks (e.g., one person cannot complete his or her assignment until others have completed their work).
- Organizational complexity (conflict tends to increase as the number of hierarchical layers and specialized tasks increase).
- Unreasonable or unclear policies, standards, or rules.
- Unreasonable deadlines or extreme time pressure.
- Collective decision making (the greater the number of people participating in a decision, the greater the potential for conflict).
- Decision making by consensus (dissenters may feel coerced).
- Unmet expectations (employees who have unrealistic expectations about job assignments, pay, or promotions are more prone to conflict).
- Unresolved or suppressed conflicts.[13]

Proactive managers carefully read these early warnings and take appropriate action (see Skills & Best Practices on page 279). For example, group conflict sometimes can be reduced by making decisions on the basis of majority approval rather than striving for a consensus.

# Why People Avoid Conflict

Are you uncomfortable in conflict situations? Do you go out of your way to avoid conflict? If so, you're not alone. Many of us avoid conflict for a variety of both good and bad reasons. Tim Ursiny, in his entertaining and instructive book, *The Coward's Guide to Conflict,* contends that we avoid conflict because we fear various combinations of the following things: "harm"; "rejection"; "loss of relationship"; "anger"; "being seen as selfish"; "saying the wrong thing"; "failing"; "hurting someone else"; "getting what you want"; and "intimacy."[14] This list is self-explanatory, except for the fear of "getting what you want." By this, Ursiny is referring to those who, for personal reasons, feel undeserving and/or fear the consequences of success (so they tend to sabotage themselves). Of course, avoiding conflict doesn't make it go away; the same situation is likely to continue and even to escalate.[15] What, then, is the alternative? For our present purposes, it is sufficient to become consciously aware of our fears and practice overcoming them. Reading, understanding, and acting upon the material in this chapter are steps in a positive direction.

# Desired Outcomes of Conflict

Within organizations, conflict management is more than simply a quest for agreement. If progress is to be made and dysfunctional conflict minimized, a broader agenda is in order. Tjosvold's cooperative conflict model calls for three desired outcomes:

1. *Agreement.* But at what cost? Equitable and fair agreements are best. An agreement that leaves one party feeling exploited or defeated will tend to breed resentment and subsequent conflict.

2. *Stronger relationships.* Good agreements enable conflicting parties to build bridges of goodwill and trust for future use. Moreover, conflicting parties who trust each other are more likely to keep their end of the bargain.

3. *Learning.* Functional conflict can promote greater self-awareness and creative problem solving. Like the practice of management itself, successful conflict handling is learned primarily by doing. Knowledge of the concepts and techniques in this chapter is a necessary first step, but there is no substitute for hands-on practice. In a contentious world, there are plenty of opportunities to practice conflict management.[16]

# Major Forms of Conflict

Certain antecedents of conflict deserve a closer look. This section explores the nature and organizational implications of three common forms of conflict: personality conflict, intergroup conflict, and cross-cultural conflict. Our discussion of each type of conflict includes some practical tips.

## Personality Conflicts

As discussed in Chapter 5, your *personality* is the package of stable traits and characteristics creating your unique identity. According to experts on the subject:

Each of us has a unique way of interacting with others. Whether we are seen as charming, irritating, fascinating, nondescript, approachable, or intimidating depends in part on our personality, or what others might describe as our style.[17]

Given the many possible combinations of personality traits, it is clear why personality conflicts are inevitable. We define a **personality conflict** as interpersonal opposition based on personal dislike and/or disagreement. This is an important topic, as evidenced by a recent survey of

learning objective 2

Define *personality conflicts,* and explain how they should be managed.

**personality conflict**

Interpersonal opposition driven by personal dislike or disagreement.

Pictured here is Joseph Tucci of EMC, a leading data storage company. His personality has been described as low key and unruffled, while prone to make decisions and take action quickly. Direct and easy to talk to, "He is not the imperial CEO," says his company's chief financial officer. These qualities help people trust and believe in him, and he has succeeded in leading more than one company out of a steep decline.

173 managers in the U.S. When the managers were asked what makes them most uncomfortable, an overwhelming 73% said, "Building relationships with people I dislike." "Asking for a raise" (25%) and "speaking to large audiences" (24%) were the distant second and third responses.[18]

**Workplace Incivility: The Seeds of Personality Conflict**    Somewhat akin to physical pain, chronic personality conflicts often begin with seemingly insignificant irritations. For instance, consider the following mentors with difficult personalities:

> When Adrian Gonzalez started his new job at a manufacturer, he was assigned to share a cubicle with a senior peer assigned to mentor him. All his mentor really wanted was an ally in his stab-in-the-back criticisms of their colleagues. . . .
>
> "If the guy were in a more influential position," says Mr. Gonzalez, "he could have made my life a living hell."
>
> You don't have to tell that to Joe Silverman, whose mentor in a former job in personnel research was his boss. The man, he says, lived in his own world, evidenced by his droning on despite the glazed eyes and lack of any follow-up questions.[19]

The apparently difficult personalities of these mentors were all the more frustrating in light of the junior employee's expectation that a mentoring relationship will be positive.

Sadly, grim little scenarios such as these are all too common today, given the steady erosion of civility in the workplace.[20] Researchers say increased informality, pressure for results, and employee diversity have fostered an "anything goes" atmosphere in today's workplaces. They view incivility as a self-perpetuating vicious cycle that creates workplace stress and can even end in violence[21] (see Hands-On Exercise on page 281). A new survey of over 500 employees indicates the nature and extent of workplace incivility in the U.S.:

- 42% heard a *sexually inappropriate comment* (up 8% from the year before).
- 35% heard a *racial slur.*
- 33% heard an *ethnic slur.*
- 27% heard *age-related ridicule.*
- 23% heard *ridicule about sexual orientation.*
- 10% heard *ridicule about a person's disability.*[22]

Clearly, the need for diversity training and penalties for misconduct remains high.

Vicious cycles of incivility need to be avoided (or broken early) with an organizational culture that places a high value on respect for coworkers. This requires managers and leaders to act as caring and courteous role models. A positive spirit of cooperation, as opposed to one based on negativism and aggression, also helps. Some organizations have resorted to workplace etiquette training.[23] More specifically, constructive feedback and skillful positive reinforcement can keep a single irritating behavior from precipitating a full-blown personality conflict (or worse).

**Dealing with Personality Conflicts**    Personality conflicts are a potential minefield for managers. Let us frame the situation. Personality traits, by definition, are stable and resistant to change. Moreover, according to the American Psychiatric

## Workplace Incivility: Are *You* Part of the Problem?

*How often have you engaged in these workplace behaviors during the past year?*

|  | Never | Often |
|---|---|---|
| **1.** Paid little attention to a statement made by someone or showed little interest in their opinion. | 1—2—3—4—5 | |
| **2.** Made demeaning, rude or derogatory remarks about someone. | 1—2—3—4—5 | |
| **3.** Made unwanted attempts to draw someone into a discussion of personal matters. | 1—2—3—4—5 | |
| **4.** Made fun of someone at work. | 1—2—3—4—5 | |
| **5.** Made an ethnic, religious, or racial remark or joke at work. | 1—2—3—4—5 | |
| **6.** Cursed at someone at work. | 1—2—3—4—5 | |
| **7.** Publicly embarrassed someone at work. | 1—2—3—4—5 | |
| **8.** Played a mean prank on someone at work. | 1—2—3—4—5 | |

*What-goes-around-comes-around scale*

8–16 Good organizational citizen

17–31 Careful, your mean streak is showing

32–40 A real social porcupine

**SOURCE: Eight survey items excerpted from G Blau and L Andersson, "Testing a Measure of Instigated Workplace Incivility,"** *Journal of Occupational and Organizational Psychology,* **December 2005, Table 1, pp 595–614.**

Association's *Diagnostic and Statistical Manual of Mental Disorders,* there are 410 psychological disorders that can and do show up in the workplace.[24] This brings up legal issues. Employees in the United States suffering from psychological disorders such as depression and mood-altering diseases such as alcoholism are protected from discrimination by the Americans with Disabilities Act.[25] (Other nations have similar laws.) Also, sexual harassment and other forms of discrimination can grow out of apparent personality conflicts.[26] Finally, personality conflicts can spawn workplace aggression and violence.[27]

Traditionally, managers dealt with personality conflicts by either ignoring them or transferring one party.[28] In view of the legal implications, just discussed, both of these options may be open invitations to discrimination lawsuits. Skills & Best Practices on page 282 presents practical tips for both nonmanagers and managers who are involved in or affected by personality conflicts. Our later discussions of handling dysfunctional conflict and alternative dispute resolution techniques also apply.

# Intergroup Conflict

Conflict among work groups, teams, and departments is a common threat to organizational competitiveness. For example, when Delta and Northwest Airlines recently began to negotiate a merger of the two companies, problems arose as each airline's pilots demanded that their seniority rights be protected.[29] Pilots for Northwest are, on

learning objective 3

Discuss the role of in-group thinking in intergroup conflict, and explain what can be done to avoid cross-cultural conflict.

## How to Deal with Personality Conflicts

| Tips for Employees Having a Personality Conflict | Tips for Third-Party Observers of a Personality Conflict | Tips for Managers Whose Employees Are Having a Personality Conflict |
|---|---|---|
| • All employees need to be familiar with and *follow* company policies for diversity, antidiscrimination, and sexual harassment. | | |
| • Communicate directly with the other person to resolve the perceived conflict (emphasize problem solving and common objectives, not personalities). | • Do not take sides in someone else's personality conflict. | • Investigate and document conflict. |
| • Avoid dragging coworkers into the conflict. | • Suggest the parties work things out themselves in a constructive and positive way. | • If appropriate, take corrective action (e.g., feedback or behavior modification). |
| • If dysfunctional conflict persists, seek help from direct supervisors or human resource specialists. | • If dysfunctional conflict persists, refer the problem to the parties' direct supervisors. | • If necessary, attempt informal dispute resolution. |
| | | • Refer difficult conflicts to human resource specialists or hired counselors for formal resolution attempts and other interventions. |

average, older, which would give them an advantage in terms of pay and assignments; Delta pilots are younger, perhaps making them more economical to keep if the merger results in layoffs. Each group wants to protect its own interests, and the groups see their interests as being in conflict. Managers who understand the mechanics of intergroup conflict are better equipped to face this sort of challenge.

**In-Group Thinking: The Seeds of Intergroup Conflict** As we discussed in Chapter 9, *cohesiveness*—a "we feeling" binding group members together—can be a good or bad thing. A certain amount of cohesiveness can turn a group of individuals into a smooth-running team. Too much cohesiveness, however, can breed groupthink because a desire to get along pushes aside critical thinking. The study of in-groups by small group researchers has revealed a whole package of changes associated with increased group cohesiveness. Specifically,

- Members of in-groups view themselves as a collection of unique individuals, while they stereotype members of other groups as being "all alike."
- In-group members see themselves positively and as morally correct, while they view members of other groups negatively and as immoral.
- In-groups view outsiders as a threat.
- In-group members exaggerate the differences between their group and other groups. This typically involves a distorted perception of reality.[30]

Avid sports fans who simply can't imagine how someone would support the opposing team exemplify one form of in-group thinking. Also, this pattern of behavior is a form of ethnocentrism, discussed as a cross-cultural barrier in Chapter 3. Reflect for a moment on evidence of in-group behavior in your life. Does your circle of friends make fun of others because of their race, gender, age, nationality, weight, sexual preference, or major in college?[31]

In-group thinking is one more fact of organizational life that virtually guarantees conflict. Managers cannot eliminate in-group thinking, but they certainly should not ignore it when handling intergroup conflicts.

**Research Lessons for Handling Intergroup Conflict**   Sociologists have long recommended the contact hypothesis for reducing intergroup conflict. According to the *contact hypothesis,* the more the members of different groups interact, the less intergroup conflict they will experience. Those interested in improving race, international, and union-management relations typically encourage cross-group interaction. The hope is that *any* type of interaction, short of actual conflict, will reduce stereotyping and combat in-group thinking. But research has shown this approach to be naive and limited. For example, one study of 83 health center employees (83% female) at a Midwest U.S. university probed the specific nature of intergroup relations and concluded:

> The number of *negative* relationships was significantly related to higher perceptions of intergroup conflict. Thus, it seems that negative relationships have a salience that overwhelms any possible positive effects from friendship links across groups.[32]

Intergroup friendships are still desirable, as documented in many studies,[33] but they are readily overpowered by negative intergroup interactions. Thus, *priority number 1 for managers faced with intergroup conflict is to identify and root out specific negative linkages between (or among) groups.* A single personality conflict, for instance, may contaminate the entire intergroup experience. The same goes for an employee who voices negative opinions or spreads negative rumors about another group. Our updated contact model in Figure 11–1 is based on this and other recent research insights, such as the need to foster positive attitudes toward other groups.[34] Also, notice how conflict within the group and negative gossip from third parties are threats that need to be neutralized if intergroup conflict is to be minimized.

## Minimizing Intergroup Conflict: An Updated Contact Model   FIGURE 11–1

**Level of perceived intergroup conflict tends to increase when:**

- Conflict within the group is high.
- There are negative interactions between groups (or between members of those groups).
- Influential third-party gossip about other group is negative.

**Recommended actions:**

- Work to eliminate *specific negative* interactions between groups (and members).
- Conduct team building to reduce *intra*group conflict and prepare employees for cross-functional teamwork.
- Encourage personal friendships and good working relationships across groups and departments.
- Foster positive attitudes toward members of other groups (empathy, compassion, sympathy).
- Avoid or neutralize negative gossip across groups or departments.

SOURCE: Based on research evidence in G Labianca, D J Brass, and B Gray, "Social Networks and Perceptions of Intergroup Conflict: The Role of Negative Relationships and Third Parties," *Academy of Management Journal,* February 1998, pp 55–67; C D Batson et al., "Empathy and Attitudes: Can Feeling for a Member of a Stigmatized Group Improve Feelings toward the Group?" *Journal of Personality and Social Psychology,* January 1997, pp 105–18; and S C Wright et al., "The Extended Contact Effect: Knowledge of Cross-Group Friendships and Prejudice," *Journal of Personality and Social Psychology,* July 1997, pp 73–90.

# Cross-Cultural Conflict

Doing business with people from different cultures is commonplace in our global economy where cross-border mergers, joint ventures, outsourcing, and alliances are the order of the day.[35] Because of differing assumptions about how to think and act, the potential for cross-cultural conflict is both immediate and huge. Success or failure, when conducting business across cultures, often hinges on avoiding and minimizing actual or perceived conflict. For example, consider this cultural mismatch:

> Mexicans place great importance on saving face, so they tend to expect any conflicts that occur during negotiations to be downplayed or kept private. The prevailing attitude in the [United States], however, is that conflict should be dealt with directly and publicly to prevent hard feelings from developing on a personal level.[36]

Some cultural conflicts have resulted from the outsourcing of many jobs overseas to areas where labor is much cheaper than in the United States. This Ninestar location in India employs 850 people in three shifts, operating 24/7. What is your opinion about foreign outsourcing or "offshoring" of jobs?

This is not a matter of who is right and who is wrong; rather it is a matter of accommodating cultural differences for a successful business transaction. Awareness of the cross-cultural differences we discussed in Chapter 3 is an important first step. Beyond that, cross-cultural conflict can be moderated by using international consultants and building cross-cultural relationships.

**Using International Consultants**   In response to broad demand, there is a growing army of management consultants specializing in cross-cultural relations. Competency and fees vary widely, of course. But a carefully selected cross-cultural consultant can be helpful, as this illustration shows:

> Last year, when electronics-maker Canon planned to set up a subsidiary in Dubai through its Netherlands division, it asked consultant Sahid Mirza of Glocom, based in Dubai, to find out how the two cultures would work together.
>    Mirza sent out the test questionnaires and got a sizable response. "The findings were somewhat surprising," he recalls. "We found that, at the bedrock level, there were relatively few differences. Many of the Arab businessmen came from former British colonies and viewed business in much the same way as the Dutch."

But at the level of behavior, there was a real conflict. "The Dutch are blunt and honest in expression, and such expression is very offensive to Arab sensibilities." Mirza offers the example of a Dutch executive who says something like, "We can't meet the deadline." Such a negative expression—true or not—would be gravely offensive to an Arab. As a result of Mirza's research, Canon did start the subsidiary in Dubai, but it trained both the Dutch and the Arab executives first.[37]

Consultants also can help untangle possible personality, value, and intergroup conflicts from conflicts rooted in differing national cultures. Note: Although we have discussed basic types of conflict separately, they typically are encountered in complex, messy bundles.

## How to Build Cross-Cultural Relationships

**SKILLS & BEST PRACTICES**

| Behavior | Rank |
|---|---|
| Be a good listener | 1 |
| Be sensitive to needs of others | 2 ⎱ Tie |
| Be cooperative, rather than overly competitive | 2 ⎰ |
| Advocate inclusive (participative) leadership | 3 |
| Compromise rather than dominate | 4 |
| Build rapport through conversations | 5 |
| Be compassionate and understanding | 6 |
| Avoid conflict by emphasizing harmony | 7 |
| Nurture others (develop and mentor) | 8 |

**SOURCE:** Adapted from R L Tung, "American Expatriates Abroad: From Neophytes to Cosmopolitans," *Journal of World Business,* Summer 1998, Table 6, p 136.

### Building Relationships across Cultures

Rosalie L Tung's study of 409 expatriates from U.S. and Canadian multinational firms is very instructive.[38] Her survey sought to pinpoint success factors for the expatriates (14% female) who were working in 51 different countries worldwide. Nine specific ways to facilitate interaction with host-country nationals, as ranked from most useful to least useful by the respondents, are listed in Skills & Best Practices. Good listening skills topped the list, followed by sensitivity to others and cooperativeness rather than competitiveness. Interestingly, U.S. managers often are culturally characterized as just the opposite: poor listeners, blunt to the point of insensitivity, and excessively competitive. Some managers need to add self-management to the list of ways to minimize cross-cultural conflict.

# Managing Conflict

As we have seen, conflict has many faces and is a constant challenge for managers who are responsible for reaching organizational goals.[39] Our attention now turns to the active management of both functional and dysfunctional conflict. We discuss how to stimulate functional conflict, how to handle dysfunctional conflict, and how third parties can deal effectively with conflict.

**learning objective 4**

Explain how managers can program functional conflict, and identify the five conflict-handling styles.

## Programming Functional Conflict

Sometimes committees and decision-making groups become so bogged down in details and procedures that nothing substantive is accomplished. Carefully monitored functional conflict can help get the creative juices flowing once again. Managers basically have two options. They can fan the fires of naturally occurring conflict—although this approach can be unreliable and slow. Alternatively, managers can resort to programmed conflict. Experts in the field define **programmed conflict** as "conflict that raises different opinions *regardless of the personal feelings of the managers.*"[40] The trick is to

**programmed conflict**

**Encourages different opinions without protecting management's personal feelings.**

get contributors to either defend or criticize ideas based on relevant facts rather than on the basis of personal preference or political interests. This requires disciplined role-playing and effective leadership. Two programmed conflict techniques with proven track records are devil's advocacy and the dialectic method. Let us explore these two ways of stimulating functional conflict.

**Devil's Advocacy**     This technique gets its name from a traditional practice within the Roman Catholic Church. When someone's name came before the College of Cardinals for elevation to sainthood, it was absolutely essential to ensure that he or she had a spotless record. Consequently, one individual was assigned the role of *devil's advocate* to uncover and air all possible objections to the person's canonization. In accordance with this practice, **devil's advocacy** in today's organizations involves assigning someone the role of critic.[41] Recall from Chapter 9 that Irving Janis recommended the devil's advocate role for preventing groupthink.

**devil's advocacy**

**Assigning someone the role of critic.**

In the left half of Figure 11–2, note how devil's advocacy alters the usual decision-making process in steps 2 and 3. This approach to programmed conflict is intended to generate critical thinking and reality testing.[42] It is a good idea to rotate the job of devil's advocate so no one person or group develops a strictly negative reputation. Moreover, periodic devil's advocacy role-playing is good training for developing analytical and communication skills and emotional intelligence.

**The Dialectic Method**     Like devil's advocacy, the dialectic method is a time-honored practice. This particular approach to programmed conflict traces back to the dialectic school of philosophy in ancient Greece. Plato and his followers attempted to synthesize truths by exploring opposite positions (called *thesis* and *antithesis*). Court systems in the United States and elsewhere rely on directly opposing points of view for determining guilt or innocence. Accordingly, today's **dialectic method** calls for managers to foster a structured debate of opposing viewpoints prior to making a decision.[43] Steps 3 and 4 in the right half of Figure 11–2 set the dialectic approach apart from the normal decision-making process. Here is how Anheuser-Busch's corporate policy committee uses the dialectic method:

**dialectic method**

**Fostering a debate of opposing viewpoints to better understand an issue.**

> When the policy committee . . . considers a major move—getting into or out of a business, or making a big capital expenditure—it sometimes assigns teams to make the case for each side of the question. There may be two teams or even three. Each is knowledgeable about the subject; each has access to the same information. Occasionally someone in favor of the project is chosen to lead the dissent, and an opponent to argue for it. Pat Stokes, who heads the company's beer empire, describes the result: "We end up with decisions and alternatives we hadn't thought of previously," sometimes representing a synthesis of the opposing views. "You become a lot more anticipatory, better able to see what might happen, because you have thought through the process."[44]

A major drawback of the dialectic method is that "winning the debate" may overshadow the issue at hand. Also, the dialectic method requires more skill training than does devil's advocacy. Regarding the comparative effectiveness of these two approaches to stimulating functional conflict, however, a laboratory study ended in a tie. Compared with groups that strived to reach a consensus, decision-making groups using either devil's advocacy or the dialectic method yielded equally higher quality

**FIGURE 11–2**
Techniques
for Stimulating
Functional
Conflict:
Devil's
Advocacy and
the Dialectic
Method

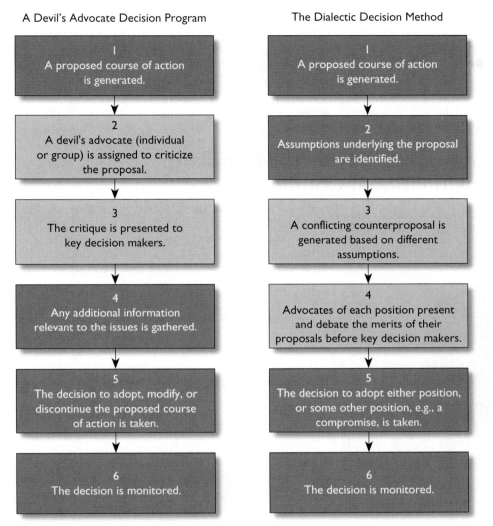

A Devil's Advocate Decision Program

The Dialectic Decision Method

1. A proposed course of action is generated.

1. A proposed course of action is generated.

2. A devil's advocate (individual or group) is assigned to criticize the proposal.

2. Assumptions underlying the proposal are identified.

3. The critique is presented to key decision makers.

3. A conflicting counterproposal is generated based on different assumptions.

4. Any additional information relevant to the issues is gathered.

4. Advocates of each position present and debate the merits of their proposals before key decision makers.

5. The decision to adopt, modify, or discontinue the proposed course of action is taken.

5. The decision to adopt either position, or some other position, e.g., a compromise, is taken.

6. The decision is monitored.

6. The decision is monitored.

SOURCE: R A Cosier and C R Schwenk, "Agreement and Thinking Alike: Ingredients for Poor Decisions," *Academy of Management Executive: The Thinking Manager's Source,* February 1990, pp 72–73. Copyright 1990 by Academy of Management. Reproduced with permission of Academy of Management via Copyright Clearance Center.

decisions.[45] But, in a more recent laboratory study, groups using devil's advocacy produced more potential solutions and made better recommendations for a case problem than did groups using the dialectic method.[46]

In light of this mixed evidence, managers have some latitude in using either devil's advocacy or the dialectic method for pumping creative life back into stalled deliberations. Personal preference and the role players' experience may well be the deciding factors in choosing one approach over the other. The important thing is to actively stimulate functional conflict when necessary, such as when the risk of blind conformity or groupthink is high. In the political arena, an important risk of conformity is that a new program may lack the wide appeal needed to win adequate public support. To encourage broader thinking from the outset, when the Massachusetts legislature set up a board to oversee the implementation of its new health insurance law, it purposely included members in the group who would be sure to have conflicts. The board brought together people from business groups, labor unions, academic institutions, and the state government. The group members clashed, as expected, but as they aired their views, they educated one another and arrived at solutions that probably would not have occurred to a more homogeneous board. The conflict was functional because the group members were willing to listen and believed in the group's mission.[47]

This meshes well with the results of a pair of laboratory studies that found a positive relationship between the degree of minority dissent and team innovation, *but only when participative decision making was used*.[48]

# Alternative Styles for Handling Dysfunctional Conflict

**Nina Olson is the IRS's National Taxpayer Advocate, a job that sometimes places her in conflict with her bosses when she has to tell them about mistakes and violations within the agency. It's particularly difficult when she must inform her immediate supervisor that he's wrong. "It is really just a nutty position," she says. "You get to say to the boss, 'This is good, but ...'" Ms Olson and her boss meet once a month to discuss and resolve issues.**

People tend to handle negative conflict in patterned ways referred to as *styles*. Several conflict styles have been categorized over the years. According to conflict specialist Afzalur Rahim's model, five different conflict-handling styles can be plotted on a 2 × 2 grid. High to low concern for *self* is found on the horizontal axis of the grid while low to high concern for *others* forms the vertical axis (see Figure 11–3). Various combinations of these variables produce the five different conflict-handling styles: integrating, obliging, dominating, avoiding, and compromising.[49] There is no single best style; each has strengths and limitations and is subject to situational constraints.[50]

**Integrating (Problem Solving)** In this style, interested parties confront the issue and cooperatively identify the problem, generate and weigh alternative solutions, and select a solution. Integrating is appropriate for complex issues plagued by misunderstanding. However, it is inappropriate for resolving conflicts rooted in opposing value systems. Its primary strength is its longer lasting impact because it deals with the underlying problem rather than merely with symptoms. The primary weakness of this style is that it is very time-consuming.

**FIGURE 11–3**
**Five Conflict-Handling Styles**

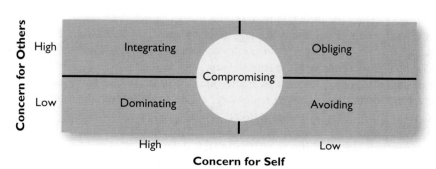

SOURCE: Reprinted by permission of Sage Publications Ltd from M A Rahim, "A Strategy for Managing Conflict in Complex Organizations," *Human Relations*, January 1985, p 84. Copyright © 1985 The Tavistock Institute.

**Obliging (Smoothing)**   "An obliging person neglects his or her own concern to satisfy the concern of the other party."[51] This style, often called smoothing, involves playing down differences while emphasizing commonalities. Obliging may be an appropriate conflict-handling strategy when it is possible to eventually get something in return. But it is inappropriate for complex or worsening problems. Its primary strength is that it encourages cooperation. Its main weakness is that it's a temporary fix that fails to confront the underlying problem.

**Dominating (Forcing)**   High concern for self and low concern for others encourages "I win, you lose" tactics. The other party's needs are largely ignored. This style is often called forcing because it relies on formal authority to force compliance. Dominating is appropriate when an unpopular solution must be implemented, the issue is minor, or a deadline is near. It is inappropriate in an open and participative climate. Speed is its primary strength. The primary weakness of this domineering style is that it often breeds resentment.[52]

**Avoiding**   This tactic may involve either passive withdrawal from the problem or active suppression of the issue. Avoidance is appropriate for trivial issues or when the costs of confrontation outweigh the benefits of resolving the conflict. It is inappropriate for difficult and worsening problems. The main strength of this style is that it buys time in unfolding or ambiguous situations. The primary weakness is that the tactic provides a temporary fix that sidesteps the underlying problem.

**Compromising**   This is a give-and-take approach involving moderate concern for both self and others. Compromise is appropriate when parties have opposite goals or possess equal power. But compromise is inappropriate when overuse would lead to inconclusive action (e.g., failure to meet production deadlines). The primary strength of this tactic is that everyone gets something, but it's a temporary fix that can stifle creative problem solving.

# Third-Party Interventions: Alternative Dispute Resolution

Disputes between employees, between employees and their employer, and between companies too often end up in lengthy and costly court battles.[53] A more constructive, less expensive approach called alternative dispute resolution has enjoyed enthusiastic growth in recent years.[54] In fact, the widely imitated "People's Court"–type television shows operating outside the formal judicial system are part of this trend toward what one writer calls "do-it-yourself justice."[55] **Alternative dispute resolution (ADR),** according to a pair of Canadian labor lawyers, "uses faster, more user-friendly methods of dispute resolution, instead of traditional, adversarial approaches (such as unilateral decision making or litigation)."[56] The following ADR techniques represent a progression of steps third parties can take to resolve organizational conflicts.[57] They are ranked from easiest and least expensive to most difficult and costly. A growing number of organizations have formal ADR policies involving an established sequence of various combinations of these techniques:

- *Facilitation.* A third party, usually a manager, informally urges disputing parties to deal directly with each other in a positive and constructive manner.

**Self-Assessment Exercise**

What Is Your Preferred Conflict-Handling Style?

**Group Exercise**

Assessing the Effectiveness of Conflict-Handling Styles

**learning objective 5**

Identify and describe at least four alternative dispute resolution (ADR) techniques.

**alternative dispute resolution (ADR)**

Avoiding costly lawsuits by resolving conflicts informally or through mediation or arbitration.

- *Conciliation.* A neutral third party informally acts as a communication conduit between disputing parties. This is appropriate when conflicting parties refuse to meet face to face. The immediate goal is to establish direct communication, with the broader aim of finding common ground and a constructive solution.

- *Peer review.* A panel of trustworthy coworkers, selected for their ability to remain objective, hears both sides of a dispute in an informal and confidential meeting. Any decision by the review panel may or may not be binding, depending on the company's ADR policy. Membership on the peer review panel often is rotated among employees.[58]

- *Ombudsman.* Someone who works for the organization, and is widely respected and trusted by his or her coworkers, hears grievances on a confidential basis and attempts to arrange a solution. This approach, more common in Europe than North America, permits someone to get help from above without relying on the formal hierarchy chain.

- *Mediation.* "The mediator—a trained, third-party neutral—actively guides the disputing parties in exploring innovative solutions to the conflict. Although some companies have in-house mediators who have received ADR training, most also use external mediators who have no ties to the company."[59] Unlike an arbitrator, a mediator does *not* render a decision. It is up to the disputants to reach a mutually acceptable decision.

- *Arbitration.* Disputing parties agree ahead of time to accept the decision of a neutral arbitrator in a formal courtlike setting, often complete with evidence and witnesses. Statements are confidential. Decisions are based on legal merits. Trained arbitrators, typically from outside agencies such as the American Arbitration Association, are versed in relevant laws and case precedents. Historically, employee participation in arbitration was voluntary. A 2001 U.S. Supreme Court decision changed things. As part of the employment contract with nonunion workers, employers in the United States now have the legal right to insist upon *mandatory* arbitration in lieu of a court battle. A vigorous debate now rages over the fairness and quality of mandatory arbitration.[60]

# Negotiating

**negotiation**

Give-and-take process between conflicting interdependent parties.

Formally defined, **negotiation** is a give-and-take decision-making process involving interdependent parties with different preferences.[61] Common examples include labor-management negotiations over wages, hours, and working conditions and negotiations between supply chain specialists and vendors involving price, delivery schedules, and credit terms. Self-managed work teams with overlapping task boundaries also need to rely on negotiated agreements. Negotiating skills are more important than ever today.[62]

6 learning objective

Draw a distinction between distributive and integrative negotiation, and explain the concept of added-value negotiation.

## Two Basic Types of Negotiation

Negotiation experts distinguish between two types of negotiation—*distributive* and *integrative.* Understanding the difference requires a change in traditional "fixed-pie" thinking:

A *distributive* negotiation usually involves a single issue—a "fixed-pie"—in which one person gains at the expense of the other. For example, haggling over the price of a rug in a bazaar is a distributive negotiation. In most conflicts, however, more than one issue is at stake, and each party values the issues differently. The outcomes available are no longer a fixed-pie divided among all parties. An agreement can be found that is better for both parties than what they would have reached through distributive negotiation. This is an *integrative* negotiation.

However, parties in a negotiation often don't find these beneficial trade-offs because each *assumes* its interests *directly* conflict with those of the other party. "What is good for the other side must be bad for us" is a common and unfortunate perspective that most people have. This is the mind-set we call the *mythical* "fixed-pie."[63]

Distributive negotiation involves traditional win–lose thinking. Integrative negotiation calls for a progressive win–win strategy.[64] For example, as president of Environmental Defense, Fred Krupp helps the nonprofit organization achieve more of its objectives by seeking win–win negotiations with businesses. Environmental Defense opened a Bentonville, Arkansas, office near Wal-Mart's headquarters to help that company achieve goals for energy efficiency and packaging reduction, and when other environmental groups wanted to combat acid rain with strict limits on sulfur dioxide emissions, Environmental Defense partnered with utilities to push for a cap-and-trade system that offers business greater flexibility while still reducing emissions. Regarding the latter effort, William Reilly, the Environmental Protection Agency's leader at the time, says Krupp's willingness to take a business-friendly stance "helped us in Congress and in the eyes of the public" to get the new regulations enacted.[65] Finding areas of common ground can be difficult; successful negotiators are able to weigh multiple issues affecting a problem and gather information about which issues are most important to the other parties and why.[66]

# Added-Value Negotiation

One practical application of the integrative approach is **added-value negotiation (AVN).** During AVN, the negotiating parties cooperatively develop multiple deal packages while building a productive long-term relationship. AVN consists of these five steps:

1. *Clarify interests.* After each party identifies its tangible and intangible needs, the two parties meet to discuss their respective needs and find *common ground* for negotiation.

2. *Identify options.* A *marketplace of value* is created when the negotiating parties discuss desired elements of value (such as property, money, behavior, rights, and risk reduction).

---

## Negotiating Your Salary

Experts offer this advice for getting the best compensation you can.

- **Know the market rate.** Research what companies are paying for other employees with similar jobs in the same area.

- **Consider the economy.** When the economy is slowing or in recession, don't expect big raises. For example, if you're a recent graduate, salaries won't be bigger than the previous year's. In tough times, show that you understand the business's challenges.

- **Know your own value.** Can you justify making more than the market rate? Be ready to offer specific examples of your experience and accomplishments; tell how you benefited your past and present employers.

- **Be honest.** Don't exaggerate your pay or accomplishments.

- **Don't go first.** Try to wait for the other person to name a number. You might say you want to be paid the going rate for someone with your qualifications. If you have to give an answer, give a range, not a specific dollar figure.

- **Consider benefits, too.** Some of the most valuable parts of your compensation package may be insurance and retirement savings. Retirement may seem like eons away, but an employer match of 5% to your 401(k) plan is like an extra 5% of pay—without an immediate tax bite.

- **Look at the long term.** If you can't get a big pay package, consider whether you can ask for something else that will help your long-term career—say, a chance to work on an important assignment.

SOURCES: Based on B Brophy, "Bargaining for Bigger Bucks: A Step-by-Step Guide to Negotiating Your Salary," *Business 2.0*, May 2004, p 107; S Curran, "Compensation Advice for New Grads," *BusinessWeek*, April 30, 2007, www.businessweek.com; and F Di Meglio, "Job Searchers Face a New Reality," *BusinessWeek*, April 3, 2008, www.businessweek.com.

SKILLS & BEST PRACTICES

**added-value negotiation (AVN)**

Give-and-take process between conflicting interdependent parties.

3. *Design alternative deal packages.* While aiming for *multiple deals,* each party mixes and matches elements of value from both parties in workable combinations.

4. *Select a deal.* Each party analyzes deal packages proposed by the other party. Jointly, the parties discuss and select from feasible deal packages, with a spirit of *creative agreement.*

5. *Perfect the deal.* Together the parties discuss unresolved issues, develop a written agreement, and *build relationships* for future negotiations.[67]

"*Never, EVER purr during the negotiating process, Derwood!*"

COPYRIGHT Scott Arthur Masear. Reprinted with permission.

## Applying What You Have Learned: How to Negotiate Your Pay and Benefits

*Fact:* Women and other minorities too often come up short when it comes to negotiating fair compensation, in addition to being *under*-represented in top-management positions. *Harvard Business Review* recently offered this interpretation:

Research has shown that both conscious and subconscious biases contribute to this problem. But we've discovered another, subtler source of inequality: Women often don't get what they want and deserve because they don't ask for it. In three separate studies, we found that men are more likely than women to negotiate for what they want. . . .

Women are less likely than men to negotiate for themselves for several reasons. First, they often are socialized from an early age not to promote their own interests and to focus instead on the needs of others. . . . Women tend to assume that they will be recognized and rewarded for working hard and doing a good job. Unlike men, they haven't been taught that they can ask for more.

Second, many companies' cultures penalize women when they do ask—further discouraging them from doing so.[68]

Consequently, women (and any other employees) who feel they are being shortchanged in pay and/or promotions need to polish their integrative negotiation skills (see Skills & Best Practices on page 291). Employers, meanwhile, need to cultivate a diversity ethic, grant rewards equitably, and foster a culture of dignity and fair play.

# key terms

# chapter summary

- *Define the term* conflict, *distinguish between functional and dysfunctional conflict, and identify three desired outcomes of conflict.* Conflict is a process in which one party perceives that its interests are being opposed or negatively affected by another party. It is inevitable and not necessarily destructive. Too little conflict, as evidenced by apathy or lack of creativity, can be as great a problem as too much conflict. Functional conflict enhances organizational interests while dysfunctional conflict is counterproductive. Three desired conflict outcomes are agreement, stronger relationships, and learning.

- *Define* personality conflicts, *and explain how they should be managed.* Personality conflicts involve interpersonal opposition based on personal dislike and/or disagreement (or as an outgrowth of workplace incivility). Care needs to be taken with personality conflicts in the workplace because of the legal implications of diversity, discrimination, and sexual harassment. Managers should investigate and document personality conflicts, take corrective actions such as feedback or behavior modification if appropriate, or attempt informal dispute resolution. Difficult or persistent personality conflicts need to be referred to human resource specialists or counselors.

- *Discuss the role of in-group thinking in intergroup conflict, and explain what can be done to avoid cross-cultural conflict.* Members of in-groups tend to see themselves as unique individuals who are more moral than outsiders, whom they view as a threat and stereotypically as all alike. In-group thinking is associated with ethnocentric behavior.

International consultants can prepare people from different cultures to work effectively together. Cross-cultural conflict can be minimized by having expatriates build strong cross-cultural relationships with their hosts (primarily by being good listeners, being sensitive to others, and being more cooperative than competitive).

- *Explain how managers can program functional conflict, and identify the five conflict-handling styles.* Functional conflict can be stimulated by permitting antecedents of conflict to persist or programming conflict during decision making with devil's advocates or the dialectic method. The five conflict-handling styles are integrating (problem solving), obliging (smoothing), dominating (forcing), avoiding, and compromising. There is no single best style.

- *Identify and describe at least four alternative dispute resolution (ADR) techniques.* Alternative dispute resolution (ADR) involves avoiding costly court battles with more informal and user-friendly techniques such as facilitation, conciliation, peer review, ombudsman, mediation, and arbitration.

- *Draw a distinction between distributive and integrative negotiation, and explain the concept of added-value negotiation.* Distributive negotiation involves fixed-pie and win–lose thinking. Integrative negotiation is a win–win approach to better results for both parties. The five steps in added-value negotiation are as follows: Step 1, clarify interests; Step 2, identify options; Step 3, design alternative deal packages; Step 4, select a deal; and Step 5, perfect the deal. Elements of value, multiple deals, and creative agreement are central to this approach.

# discussion questions

1. Based on reading this chapter, how might John Hardcastle and Lawrence Levine (see the chapter-opening case) deal with their conflict-avoiding bosses? Explain.
2. What examples of functional and dysfunctional conflict have you observed in organizations lately? What were the outcomes? What caused the dysfunctional conflict?
3. Which of the five conflict-handling styles is your strongest? Your weakest? How can you improve your ability to handle conflict?
4. Which of the six ADR techniques appeals the most to you? Why?
5. How could added-value negotiation make your life a bit easier? Explain in terms of a specific problem, conflict, or deadlock.

# ethical dilemma

## Is Flagler Productions Unfairly Exploiting Wal-Mart?

For nearly 30 years, Wal-Mart Stores Inc. employed a video production company [Flager Productions] here to capture footage of its top executives, sometimes in unguarded moments. Two years ago, the retailing giant stopped using the tiny company. . . .

In recent months, Flagler has opened its trove of some 15,000 Wal-Mart tapes to the outside world, with an eye toward selling clips. The material is proving irresistible to everyone from business historians and documentary film-makers to plaintiffs lawyers and union organizers.

Among the revealing moments: A former executive vice president and board member challenges store managers in 2004 to continue his work opposing unionization. Male managers in drag lead thousands of coworkers in the company cheer. In another meeting, managers mock foolish or dangerous use of products sold in its stores. . . .

The best part, maintains plaintiffs lawyer Gene P. Graham Jr., is that "Wal-Mart has no control over this stuff."

Wal-Mart isn't pleased. "It's difficult to understand how the company could now sell to third parties the material we paid it to produce on our behalf," says a Wal-Mart spokeswoman. "Needless to say, we did not pay Flagler Productions to tape internal meetings with this aftermarket in mind."

The production company's founder and former owner, Mike Flagler, says he was hired on a handshake in the 1970s to help produce the events Wal-Mart holds each year for managers and shareholders, including entertainment portions of its annual meeting and important sales meetings. He filmed them as well.[69]

Mr. Flagler tried to sell the videos to Wal-Mart for several million dollars. Wal-Mart refused and countered with an offer of $500,000. Flagler's new owners declined because they think they can make more money selling the clips to others.

### Are Flagler Productions' actions unethical?

1. Yes. The company was paid to produce the videos and it is just plain wrong for Flagler to try and sell these videos to others who want to sue Wal-Mart.

2. No. Flagler never signed a contract specifying that the videos were owned by Wal-Mart. It's a market opportunity and Flagler should exploit it.

3. Yes. Flagler made a deal on a handshake and it is unethical to assume that it is okay to sell damaging videos to others because there is no signed contract to this effect. What happened to doing business based on your word?

4. No. Wal-Mart deserves what it gets because they discontinued using Flagler. Wal-Mart represented 90% of Flagler's revenue and Flagler must do what is needed to survive.

5. Invent other options. Discuss.

For an interpretation of this situation, visit our Web site, at
**www.mhhe.com/kinickiob4e**

# part Four

# Managing Organizational Processes

# chapter twelve

# Communicating
# in the Digital Age

**LEARNING OBJECTIVES**

**After reading the material in this chapter, you should be able to:**

1. Describe the perceptual process model of communication.

2. Describe the process, personal, physical, and semantic barriers to effective communication.

3. Contrast the communication styles of assertiveness, aggressiveness, and nonassertiveness.

4. Discuss the primary sources of nonverbal communication.

5. Review the five dominant listening styles and 10 keys to effective listening.

6. Explain the information technology of Internet/intranet/extranet, e-mail, instant messaging, handheld devices, blogs, videoconferencing/telepresence, and group support systems, and explain the related use of teleworking.

Yogesh Gupta, the CEO of Fatwire, is highlighted in the opening vignette. How does he successfully communicate, and what is the outcome for his business?

Executives know success in business depends on identifying and fixing problems before they become crises. It is the most basic rule in management: No matter how smart your strategies seem on paper, if you don't know how they're being executed and whether there are urgent problems, you won't be successful.

The higher executives climb, the less likely they are to know what is and isn't working at their companies. Many are surrounded by yes people who filter information; others dismiss or ignore bearers of bad news.

"I've heard so many executives tell employees to be candid and then jump down their throats if they bring up a problem or ask a critical question," says Yogesh Gupta, president and CEO of Fatwire, a software company that helps businesses manage their Web sites.

Mr. Gupta was determined not to do that when he was recruited to Fatwire from CA in August. Since then, he has spent hours talking with his 200 employees and seeking the advice of his nine senior managers—all but one of whom are veterans of the company. He has frequent private meetings with each member of the management team so they will feel freer to be candid with him. In that way, he can ask the important questions: What am I doing wrong? What

would you do differently if you were running the company? What's the biggest thing getting in the way of you doing your job well?

Already, he learned from these talks that Fatwire should beef up its staff in marketing and in product development. Others have counseled him to improve Fatwire's customer-support processes. Every time he has gotten good advice privately, he has found a way to publicly praise the manager so others will come forward with suggestions. . . .

Executives at big companies who have many layers of management between themselves and front-line employees face the biggest challenge finding out how their strategies are actually working. Those who want accurate information must commit to spending time in the field—often and on their own—where they are away from handlers and can coax employees to be forthcoming about problems.

Kathleen Murphy, CEO of ING's U.S. Wealth Management unit, which sells a variety of products, from annuities to financial-planning services, oversees 3,000 employees. She holds town-hall meetings with large groups of employees but admits the sessions "are mostly for me to push my message out because people are less candid at big meetings." So, she also meets regularly with smaller groups of managers at all levels of her division.

Once, when an operations group complained about a convoluted work process, she agreed the change they proposed was more efficient.

But she says she doesn't always act on what she hears, believing that executives have to filter out the inevitable complaints from the crucial information and ideas that create a productive and congenial workplace.

An upbeat executive, Ms. Murphy has teamwork in her DNA. She grew up negotiating with her five siblings for elbow room at the dinner table and played lots of sports. She says she has a "low tolerance" for people who are complainers. "There's a big difference between candor that stems from caring about doing things better and negative energy, which can be toxic," she says.

After reorganizing her division recently, Ms. Murphy sat through several meetings at which managers made suggestions and expressed their concerns. She encouraged everyone to voice their objections, but made her case that the changes would help them expand the business and better serve their customers.

They went through "a few rough sessions," she admits. But in the end, they found common ground. Her listening made all the difference. Now moving to a new building, she'll be next door to her customer-service staff.[1]

**What does this case teach you about effective communication? For an interpretation of this case and additional comments, visit our Online Learning Center at**

**www.mhhe.com/kinickiob4e**

FOR DISCUSSION

**A FEW YEARS AGO,** Dell saw its reputation dive, and poor communication perpetuated the problem. The company had been widely respected for making customized PCs available at affordable prices, but efforts to keep costs low began to erode product and service quality. Industry blogs and their readers complained about Dell's laptops and frustrating calls to unhelpful customer service technicians. Eventually, Dell's leaders realized that its employees should be part of the conversation. They began offering to help bloggers who posted complaints, and they launched the company's own Direct2Dell blog to deal with issues as they arise, as well as IdeaStorm .com, a Web site that invites ideas from customers. Dell also began improving customer service conversations by training technicians to listen more empathetically and then to solve problems more effectively. Negative blog posts about Dell have dropped sharply, and customer satisfaction measures are on the rise. Chief marketing officer Mark Jarvis says, "Listening to our customers . . . is actually the most perfect form of marketing you could have."[2]

Effective communication also is critical for career success, employee motivation, and job satisfaction. For example, a recent national survey of 636 employees revealed that interpersonal communication was ranked as the number-one skill needed for career advancement. Another polling of 336 organizations revealed that 66% of the respondents did not know or understand their organization's mission and business strategy, which subsequently led them to feel disengaged at work. The apparent lack of communication in these organizations is a problem because employee disengagement is associated with lower productivity and product quality, and higher labor costs and turnover.[3]

Moreover, organizational communication has been dramatically affected by the introduction and explosive use of computers and information technology. Who would have guessed that companies would use blogs to communicate with customers and to obtain input during internal strategic planning meetings? Managers need more than good interpersonal skills to effectively communicate in today's workplace. They also need to understand the pros and cons of different types of communication media and information technology.

This chapter will help you to better understand how managers can both improve their communication skills and design more effective communication programs. We discuss (1) basic dimensions of the communication processes, focusing on a perceptual process model and barriers to effective communication; (2) interpersonal communication; and (3) communicating in the computerized information age.

# Basic Dimensions of the Communication Process

**communication**

Interference exchange of information and understanding.

**Communication** is defined as "the exchange of information between a sender and a receiver, and the inference (perception) of meaning between the individuals involved."[4] Managers who understand this process can analyze their own communication patterns as well as design communication programs that fit organizational needs. This section reviews a perceptual process model of communication and discusses the barriers to effective communication.

# A Perceptual Process Model of Communication

learning objective    1

Describe the perceptual process model of communication.

As we all know, communicating is not that simple or clear-cut. Communication is fraught with miscommunication. In recognition of this, researchers have begun to examine communication as a form of social information processing (recall the discussion in Chapter 4) in which receivers interpret messages by cognitively processing information. This view led to development of a perceptual model of communication that depicts communication as a process in which receivers create meaning in their own minds. Let us consider the parts of this process and then integrate them with an example.

**Sender, Message, and Receiver**    The sender is the person wanting to communicate information—the message. The receiver is the person, group, or organization for whom the message is intended.

**Encoding**    Communication begins when a sender encodes an idea or thought. Encoding entails translating thoughts into a code or language that can be understood by others. This forms the foundation of the message. For example, if a professor wants to communicate to you about an assignment, he or she must first think about what information he or she wants to communicate. Once the professor resolves this issue in his or her mind (encoding), he or she can select a medium with which to communicate.

**Selecting a Medium**    Managers can communicate through a variety of media. Potential media include face-to-face conversations, telephone calls, e-mail, voice mail, videoconferencing, written memos or letters, photographs or drawings, meetings, bulletin boards, computer output, and charts or graphs. Choosing the appropriate

Although managers can communicate through a variety of media, face-to-face communication is useful for delivering sensitive or important issues that require feedback, intensive interaction, or nonverbal cues. **Do you think that the people in this meeting are having fun?**

media depends on many factors, including the nature of the message, its intended purpose, the type of audience, proximity to the audience, time horizon for disseminating the message, and personal preferences.[5] Janice Fields, chief operating officer of McDonald's USA, spends 85% of her time traveling for face-to-face meetings with franchise owners.[6] No doubt, Fields's personal preferences as a manager shape this preference for communicating in person, but the medium also is suitable for the complex task of motivating franchisees and identifying problems and opportunities.

All media have advantages and disadvantages. Face-to-face conversations, for example, are useful for communicating about sensitive or important issues that require feedback and intensive interaction.[7] In contrast, telephones are convenient, fast, and private, but lack nonverbal information. Although writing memos or letters is time-consuming, it is a good medium when it is difficult to meet with the other person, when formality and a written record are important, and when face-to-face interaction is not necessary to enhance understanding. Electronic communication, which is discussed later in this chapter, can be used to communicate with a large number of dispersed people and is potentially a very fast medium. Electronic communications also tend to save money compared with paper-based alternatives, but experts disagree over whether paper or electronic messages are more secure.[8]

### Decoding and Creating Meaning
Decoding occurs when receivers receive a message. It is the process of interpreting and making sense of a message. Returning to our example of a professor communicating about an assignment, decoding would occur among students when they receive the message from the professor.

In contrast to the conduit model's assumption that meaning is directly transferred from sender to receiver, the perceptual model is based on the belief that a receiver creates the meaning of a message in his or her mind. This means that the same message can be interpreted differently by different people. Consider the following example that occurred to a reporter from *The Wall Street Journal* when he was on assignment in China.

> I was riding the elevator a few weeks ago with a Chinese colleague here in the *Journal's* Asian headquarters. I smiled and said, "Hi." She responded, "You've gained weight." I might have been appalled, but at least three other Chinese co-workers also have told me I'm fat. I probably should cut back on the pork dumplings. In China, such an intimate observation from a colleague isn't necessarily an insult. It's probably just friendliness.[9]

This example highlights that decoding and creating the meaning of a message are influenced by cultural norms and values.

### Feedback
Have you ever been on your cell phone and thought that you lost your connection with the person you were talking to? If yes, something like the following probably occurred. "Hello, Joyce are you there?" "Joyce, can you hear me?" The other person may say back, "Yes, I can hear you, but your voice is fading in and out." This is an example of feedback—the receiver expresses a reaction to the sender's message.

Feedback from managers can significantly shape the nature of communication at work (see Skills & Best Practices on page 301).

**noise**

Interference with the transmission and understanding of a message.

### Noise
Noise represents anything that interferes with the transmission and understanding of a message. It affects all linkages of the communication process. Noise includes factors such as a speech impairment, poor telephone connections, illegible handwriting, inaccurate statistics in a memo or report, poor hearing and eyesight, environmental noises,

people talking or whistling, and physical distance between sender and receiver. Modern electronic devices can introduce noise literally, as when a BlackBerry or Treo buzzes near an audio system, or figuratively, as when someone listening to a speaker is also trying to check a text message.[10] Nonverbal communication, discussed later in this chapter, also is a source of noise, as are cross-cultural differences between senders and receivers (recall our discussion in Chapter 3).

Noise and the other elements of the communication process all play a role in the example in Figure 12–1. Notice that the communication process is sequential.

# Barriers to Effective Communication

For communication to be effective, senders must accurately communicate their intended message, and receivers must perceive and interpret the message accurately. Anything that gets in the way of the accurate transmission and reception of a message is a barrier to effective communication. You should understand these barriers so that you can be aware of their existence and try to reduce their impact.

Some barriers are actually part of the communication process itself (see Table 12–1). The communication process will fail if any step in the process is blocked. From a practical point of view, however, three types of barriers are likely to influence communication's effectiveness: (1) personal barriers, (2) physical barriers, and (3) semantic barriers.

**Personal Barriers**  Have you ever communicated with someone and felt totally confused? This may have led you to wonder: is it them or is it me? Personal

## Managing Gossip and Rumors

In almost any organization, an informal network called the grapevine spreads gossip and rumors. When those stories reach a manager's ears, what should he or she do?

- Gossip about members of the organization, true or not, damages morale and divides the team. To signal that this behavior is inappropriate and restore group cohesiveness, the manager should call together the whole group (including the person gossiped about), state that rumors are unacceptable, and apologize on behalf of the team. This brings the situation into the open, where rumors do not thrive.

- When a manager hears an employee gossiping or spreading rumors, the manager should point out how that behavior hurts the team and state clearly that it is unacceptable.

- Managers should clarify that they *do* need to hear about situations that may involve serious misconduct, such as harassment, discrimination, or potential violence at work.

SOURCE: Based on P Falcone, "Tattletales Spell Trouble," *HR Magazine,* November 2007, pp 91–94.

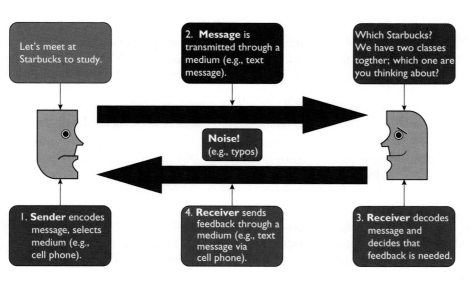

# FIGURE 12–1
## Communication Process in Action

learning objective 2

Describe the process, personal, physical, and semantic barriers to effective communication.

**TABLE 12–1**
Communication
Barriers
within the
Communication
Process

- **Sender barrier—no message gets sent.** Have you ever had an idea but were afraid to voice it because you feared criticism? Then obviously no message got sent.

  But the barrier need not be for psychological reasons. Suppose as a new manager you simply didn't realize (because you weren't told) that supervising your subordinates' expense accounts was part of your responsibility. In that case, it may be understandable why you never call them to task about fudging their expense reports—why, in other words, no message got sent.

- **Encoding barrier—the message is not expressed correctly.** No doubt you've sometimes had difficulty trying to think of the correct word to express how you feel about something. If English is not your first language, perhaps, then you may have difficulty expressing to a supervisor, coworker, or subordinate what it is you mean to say.

- **Medium barrier—the communication channel is blocked.** You never get through to someone because his or her phone always has a busy signal. The computer network is down and the e-mail message you sent doesn't go through. These are instances of the communication medium being blocked.

- **Decoding barrier—the recipient doesn't understand the message.** Your boss tells you to "lighten up" or "buckle down," but because English is not your first language, you don't understand what the messages mean. Or perhaps you're afraid to show your ignorance when someone is throwing computer terms at you and says that your computer connection has "a bandwidth problem."

- **Receiver barrier—no message gets received.** Because you were talking to a coworker, you weren't listening when your supervisor announced today's work assignments, and so you have to ask him or her to repeat the announcement.

- **Feedback barrier—the recipient doesn't respond enough.** No doubt you've had the experience of giving someone street directions, but since they only nod their heads and don't repeat the directions back to you, you don't really know whether you were understood. The same thing can happen in many workplace circumstances.

SOURCE: A Kinicki and B Williams, *Management: A Practical Introduction,* 3rd ed. (Burr Ridge, IL: McGraw-Hill, 2008), p 493.

barriers represent any individual attributes that hinder communication. Let's examine nine common personal barriers that foster miscommunication.

1. *Variable skills in communicating effectively.* Some people are simply better communicators than others. They have the speaking and listening skills, the ability to use gestures for dramatic effect, the vocabulary to alter the message to fit the audience, the writing skills to convey concepts in simple and concise terms, and the social skills to make others feel comfortable.[11] In contrast, others lack these skills. Don't worry, communication skills can be enhanced with training.[12]

2. *Variations in how information is processed and interpreted.* Did you grow up in the country, in the suburbs, or in a city? Did you attend private or public school? What were your parents' attitudes about your doing chores and playing sports? Are you from a loving home or one marred with fighting, yelling, and lack of structure?

   Answers to these questions are relevant because they make up the different frames of references and experiences people use to interpret the world around them. As you may recall from Chapter 4, people selectively attend to various stimuli based on their unique frames of reference. This means that these differences affect our interpretations of what we see and hear.

3. *Variations in interpersonal trust.* Chapter 9 discussed the manner in which trust affects interpersonal relationships. Communication is more likely to be distorted when people do not trust each other. Rather than focusing on the message, a lack of trust is likely to cause people to be defensive and question the accuracy of what is being communicated. For example, as a young employee, George Franks tried to foster communication with his boss by regularly asking how he could help; the boss, however, interpreted the frequent questions as evidence that Franks thought the boss couldn't handle his job.[13]

4. *Stereotypes and prejudices.* We noted in Chapter 4 that stereotypes are oversimplified beliefs about specific groups of people. They potentially distort communication because their use causes people to misperceive and recall information. It is important for all of us to be aware of our potential stereotypes and to recognize that they may subconsciously affect the interpretation of a message. At the same time, people often worry that well-intentioned words will be interpreted as "politically incorrect" slurs against members of one group or another. Valda Boyd Ford, CEO of the Center for Human Diversity, says learning about our own stereotypes can help us prepare for sticky situations. She also advises an open-minded attitude that treats these situations as an opportunity for learning, rather than defensiveness.[14]

5. *Big egos.* Our egos, whether due to pride, self-esteem, superior ability, or arrogance, are a communication barrier. Egos can cause political battles, turf wars, and pursuit of power, credit, and resources. Egos influence how we treat others as well as our receptiveness to being influenced by others. Have you ever had someone put you down in public? Then you know how ego feelings can influence communication.

6. *Poor listening skills.* How many times have you been in class when one student asks the same question that was asked minutes earlier? How about going to a party and meeting someone who only talks about him- or herself and never asks questions about you? This experience certainly doesn't make one feel important or memorable. It's hard to communicate effectively when one of the parties is not listening. We discuss listening skills in a later section of this chapter.

7. *Natural tendency to evaluate others' messages.* What do you say to someone after watching the latest movie in a theater? What did you think of the movie? He or she might say, "It was great, best movie I've seen all year." You then may say "I agree," or alternatively, "I disagree, that movie stunk." The point is that we all have a natural tendency, according to renowned psychologist Carl Rogers, to evaluate messages from our own point of view or frame of reference, particularly when we have strong feelings about the issue.[15]

8. *Inability to listen with understanding.* Listening with understanding occurs when a receiver can "see the expressed idea and attitude from the other person's point of view, to sense how it feels to him, to achieve his frame of reference in regard to the thing he is talking about."[16] Try to listen with understanding; it will make you less defensive and can improve your accuracy in perceiving messages.

9. *Nonverbal communication.* Communication accuracy is enhanced when one's facial expression and gestures are consistent with the intent of a message. Interestingly, people may not even be aware of this issue. More is said about this important aspect of communication later in this chapter.

**Physical Barriers: Sound, Time, Space, and More**   Have you ever been talking to someone on a cell phone while standing in a busy area with traffic noise and people talking next to you? You know what physical barriers are. Other such barriers include time-zone differences, telephone-line static, distance from others, and crashed computers. Office design is another physical barrier, which is why more organizations are hiring experts to design facilities that promote open interactions, yet provide space for private meetings.[17]

Some managers tell employees they have an open-door policy to invite communication but, in fact, erect physical barriers by literally closing their door. Of course, managers need uninterrupted periods of time. David Mammano, CEO of Next Step Publishing, acknowledges both needs. He and Next Step's other employees each have a foot-shaped loofah they can hang on their door or outside their cubicle for an hour each day. While the foot is displayed, they are not to be disturbed; the rest of the time, the door really is open for communication.[18]

**Semantic Barriers: When Words Matter**   When your boss tells you, "We need to complete this project right away," what does it mean? Does "we" mean just you? You and your coworkers? Or you, your coworkers, and the boss? Does "right away" mean today, tomorrow, or next week? These are examples of semantic barriers. **Semantics** is the study of words.

**semantics**

**The study of words.**

Semantic barriers are more likely in today's multicultural workforce. Their frequency also is fueled by the growing trend to outsource customer service operations to foreign countries, particularly India. Unfortunately, some Americans are incensed over having to communicate with customer-service employees working in such call centers. Consider the message that Mitul Pandley, a specialist working in a call center located in India, received from a customer living in Mt. Pleasant, Pennsylvania. "I wish not to have anyone from India or any foreign country or anyone with an Indian accent or foreign accent continue handling my case."[19] Exchanges like this prompted Wipro BPO, Mitul's employer, to institute training programs aimed at reducing semantic barriers.

**jargon**

**Language or terminology that is specific to a particular profession, group, or company.**

Jargon is another key semantic barrier. **Jargon** represents language or terminology that is specific to a particular profession, group, or company. The use of jargon has been increasing as our society becomes more technologically oriented. (For example, "The CIO wants the RFP to go out ASAP" means "The Chief Information Officer wants the Request for Proposal to go out as soon as possible.") It is important to remember that words that are ordinary to you may be mysterious to outsiders. If we want to be understood more clearly, it is important to choose our language more carefully.[20]

**Test Your Knowledge**

Barriers to Effective Communication

# Interpersonal Communication

The quality of interpersonal communication within an organization is very important. People with good communication skills helped groups to make more innovative decisions and were promoted more frequently than individuals with less developed abilities.[21] Although there is no universally accepted definition of **communication competence,** it is a performance-based index of an individual's abilities to effectively use communication behaviors in a given context.[22] Business etiquette, for example, is one component of communication competence. At this time we would like you to complete the business etiquette test in the Hands-On Exercise. How did you score?

**communication competence**

**Ability to effectively use communication behaviors in a given context.**

# What Is Your Business Etiquette?

**INSTRUCTIONS:** Business etiquette is one component of communication competence. Test your business etiquette by answering the following questions. After circling your response for each item, calculate your score by reviewing the correct answers listed in note 23 in the Endnotes section of the book.[23] Next, use the norms at the end of the test to interpret your results.

1. The following is an example of a proper introduction: "Ms Boss, I'd like you to meet our client, Mr Smith."
   True   False

2. If someone forgets to introduce you, you shouldn't introduce yourself, you should just let the conversation continue.
   True   False

3. If you forget someone's name, you should keep talking and hope no one will notice. This way you don't embarrass yourself or the person you are talking to.
   True   False

4. When shaking hands, a man should wait for a woman to extend her hand.
   True   False

5. Who goes through a revolving door first?
   *a.* Host  *b.* Visitor

6. It is all right to hold private conversations, either in person or on a cell phone in office bathrooms, elevators, and other public spaces.
   True   False

7. When two U.S. businesspeople are talking to one another, the space between them should be approximately
   *a.* 1.5 feet *b.* 3 feet *c.* 7 feet

8. Business casual attire requires socks for men and hose for women.
   True   False

9. To signal that you do not want a glass of wine, you should turn your wine glass upside down.
   True   False

10. If a call is disconnected, it's the caller's responsibility to redial.
    True   False

11. When using a speakerphone, you should tell the caller if there is anyone else in the room.
    True   False

12. You should change your voicemail message if you are going to be out of the office.
    True   False

## ARBITRARY NORMS

Low business etiquette (0–4 correct): Consider buying an etiquette book or hiring a coach to help you polish your professional image.

 Moderate business etiquette (5–8 correct): Look for a role model or mentor, and look for ways you can improve your business etiquette.

 High business etiquette (9–12 correct): Good for you. You should continue to practice good etiquette and look for ways to maintain your professional image.

**SOURCE: This test was adapted from material contained in M Brody, "Test Your Etiquette," *Training & Development*, February 2002, pp 64–66. Copyright © February 2002 from *Training & Development* by M Brody. Reprinted with permission of American Society for Training & Development.**

Howard Schultz, CEO of Starbucks, has some definite ideas about interpersonal communication, which both starts and fills his day. He likes to keep it personal. "In the early morning I focus on Europe. I'll call Greece or Spain or whatever, either at home or on the drive into work, to talk about challenges . . . or to congratulate them. These personal conversations are very important. . . . I'm not a big e-mailer, though; it's a crutch that hinders person-to-person communication."

**Self-Assessment Exercise**

What Is Your Communication Under Stress?

Communication competence is determined by three components: communication abilities and traits, situational factors, and the individuals involved in the interaction (see Figure 12–2). Cross-cultural awareness, for instance, is an important communication ability/trait. Individuals involved in an interaction also affect communication competence. People are likely to withhold information and react emotionally or defensively when interacting with someone they dislike or do not trust. You can improve your communication competence through five communication styles/abilities/traits under your control: assertiveness, aggressiveness, nonassertiveness, nonverbal communication, and active listening. We conclude this section by discussing gender differences in communication.

**FIGURE 12–2**
Communication Competence Affects Upward Mobility

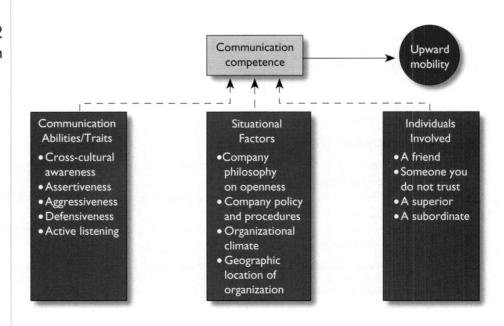

# Assertiveness, Aggressiveness, and Nonassertiveness

learning objective 3
Contrast the communication styles of assertiveness, aggressiveness, and nonassertiveness.

The saying "You can attract more flies with honey than with vinegar" captures the difference between using an assertive communication style and an aggressive style. Research studies indicate that assertiveness is more effective than aggressiveness in both work-related and consumer contexts.[24] An **assertive style** is expressive and self-enhancing and is based on the "ethical notion that it is not right or good to violate our own or others' basic human rights, such as the right to self-expression or the right to be treated with dignity and respect."[25] In contrast, an **aggressive style** is expressive and self-enhancing and strives to take unfair advantage of others. A **nonassertive style** is characterized by timid and self-denying behavior. Nonassertiveness is ineffective because it gives the other person an unfair advantage.

Managers may improve their communication competence by trying to be more assertive and less aggressive or nonassertive. This can be achieved by using the appropriate nonverbal and verbal behaviors listed in Table 12–2. For instance, managers should attempt to use the nonverbal behaviors of good eye contact, a strong, steady, and audible voice,

**assertive style**

Expressive and self-enhancing, but does not take advantage of others.

**aggressive style**

Expressive and self-enhancing, but takes unfair advantage of others.

**nonassertive style**

Timid and self-denying behavior.

Communication Styles   **TABLE 12–2**

| Communication Style | Description | Nonverbal Behavior Pattern | Verbal Behavior Pattern |
|---|---|---|---|
| Assertive | Pushing hard without attacking; permits others to influence outcome; expressive and self-enhancing without intruding on others | Good eye contact<br>Comfortable but firm posture<br>Strong, steady, and audible voice<br>Facial expressions matched to message<br>Appropriately serious tone<br>Selective interruptions to ensure understanding | Direct and unambiguous language<br>No attributions or evaluations of others' behavior<br>Use of "I" statements and cooperative "we" statements |
| Aggressive | Taking advantage of others; expressive and self-enhancing at others' expense | Glaring eye contact<br>Moving or leaning too close<br>Threatening gestures (pointed finger; clenched fist)<br>Loud voice<br>Frequent interruptions | Swear words and abusive language<br>Attributions and evaluations of others' behavior<br>Sexist or racist terms<br>Explicit threats or put-downs |
| Nonassertive | Encouraging others to take advantage of us; inhibited; self-denying | Little eye contact<br>Downward glances<br>Slumped posture<br>Constantly shifting weight<br>Wringing hands<br>Weak or whiny voice | Qualifiers ("maybe"; "kind of")<br>Fillers ("uh," "you know," "well")<br>Negaters ("It's not really that important"; "I'm not sure") |

SOURCE: Adapted in part from J A Waters, "Managerial Assertiveness," *Business Horizons,* September/October 1982, pp 24–29.

and selective interruptions. They should avoid nonverbal behaviors such as glaring or little eye contact, threatening gestures, slumped posture, and a weak or whiny voice. Appropriate verbal behaviors include direct and unambiguous language and the use of "I" messages instead of "you" statements. For example, when you say, "Mike, I was disappointed with your report because it contained typographical errors," rather than "Mike, your report was poorly done," you reduce defensiveness. "I" statements describe your feelings about someone's performance or behavior instead of laying blame on the person.

# Sources of Nonverbal Communication

**Nonverbal communication** is "Any message, sent or received independent of the written or spoken word . . . [It] includes such factors as use of time and space, distance between persons when conversing, use of color, dress, walking behavior, standing, positioning, seating arrangement, office locations and furnishings."[26]

Experts estimate that 65% to 90% of every conversation is partially interpreted through nonverbal communication.[27] It thus is important to ensure that your nonverbal signals are consistent with your intended verbal messages. Because of the prevalence of nonverbal communication and its significant effect on organizational behavior (including, but not limited to, perceptions of others, hiring decisions, work attitudes, turnover, and the acceptance of one's ideas in a presentation), it is important that managers become consciously aware of the sources of nonverbal communication.

**nonverbal communication**

Messages sent outside of the written or spoken word.

**Body Movements and Gestures**   Body movements, such as leaning forward or backward, and gestures, such as pointing, provide additional nonverbal information that can either enhance or detract from the communication process. Open body positions, such as leaning backward, communicate *immediacy,* a term used to represent openness, warmth, closeness, and availability for communication. *Defensiveness* is communicated by gestures such as folding arms, crossing hands, and crossing one's legs. Although it is both easy and fun to interpret body movements and gestures, it is important to remember that body-language analysis is subjective, easily misinterpreted, and highly dependent on the context and cross-cultural differences.[28] Thus, managers need to be careful when trying to interpret body movements. Inaccurate interpretations can create additional "noise" in the communication process.

**Touch**   Touching is another powerful nonverbal cue. People tend to touch those they like. A meta-analysis of gender differences in touching indicated that women do more touching during conversations than men.[29] Touching conveys an impression of warmth and caring and can be used to create a personal bond between people. Be careful about touching people from diverse cultures, however, as norms for touching vary significantly around the world.[30]

**Facial Expressions**   Facial expressions convey a wealth of information. Smiling, for instance, typically represents warmth, happiness, or friendship, whereas frowning conveys dissatisfaction or anger. Do you think these interpretations apply to different cross-cultural groups? A summary of relevant research revealed that the association between facial expressions and emotions varies across cultures.[31] A smile, for example, does not convey the same emotion in different countries. Therefore, managers need to be careful in interpreting facial expressions among diverse groups of employees.

**Eye Contact**   Eye contact is a strong nonverbal cue that varies across cultures. Westerners are taught at an early age to look at their parents when spoken to. In contrast, Asians are taught to avoid eye contact with a parent or superior in order to show obedience and subservience.[32] Once again, managers should be sensitive to different orientations toward maintaining eye contact with diverse employees.

**Practical Tips**   It is important to have good nonverbal communication skills in light of the fact that they are related to the development of positive interpersonal relationships. The Skills & Best Practices offers insights into improving your nonverbal communication skills. Practice these tips by turning the sound off while watching television and then trying to interpret emotions and interactions. Honest feedback from your friends about your nonverbal communication style also may help.

# Active Listening

Some communication experts contend that listening is the keystone communication skill for employees involved in sales, customer service, or management. In support of this conclusion, listening effectiveness was positively associated with customer satisfaction and negatively associated with employee intentions to quit. Poor communication between employees and management also was cited as a primary cause of employee discontent and turnover.[33] Listening skills are particularly important for all of us because we spend a great deal of time listening to others.

Listening involves much more than hearing a message. Hearing is merely the physical component of listening. **Listening** is the process of *actively* decoding and interpreting verbal messages. Listening requires cognitive attention and information processing; hearing does not. With these distinctions in mind, we examine listening styles and offer some practical advice for becoming a more effective listener.

**Listening Styles**   Communication experts believe that people listen with a preferred listening style. While people may lean toward one dominant listening style, we tend to use a combination of two or three. There are five dominant listening styles: appreciative, empathetic, comprehensive, discerning, and evaluative.[34] Let us consider each style.

An *appreciative* listener listens in a relaxed manner, preferring to listen for pleasure, entertainment, or inspiration. He or she tends to tune out speakers who provide no amusement or humor in their communications. *Empathetic* listeners interpret messages by focusing on the emotions and body language being displayed by the speaker as well as the presentation media. They also tend to listen without judging. A *comprehensive* listener makes sense of a message by first organizing specific thoughts and actions and then integrates this information by focusing on relationships among ideas. These listeners prefer logical

**Group Exercise**

Nonverbal Communication: A Twist on Charades

**Manager's Hot Seat Application**

Listening Skills: Yeah, Whatever

**listening**

**Actively decoding and interpreting verbal messages.**

learning objective 5

Review the five dominant listening styles and 10 keys to effective listening.

presentations without interruptions. *Discerning* listeners attempt to understand the main message and determine important points. They like to take notes and prefer logical presentations. Finally, *evaluative* listeners listen analytically and continually formulate arguments and challenges to what is being said. They tend to accept or reject messages based on personal beliefs, ask a lot of questions, and can become interruptive.

You can improve your listening skills by first becoming aware of the effectiveness of the different listening styles you use in various situations. This awareness can then help you to modify your style to fit a specific situation. For example, if you are listening to a presidential debate, you may want to focus on using a comprehensive and discerning style. In contrast, an evaluative style may be more appropriate if you are listening to a sales presentation.[35]

**Self-Assessment Exercise**

Active Listening Skills Inventory

**Becoming a More Effective Listener**    Effective listening is a learned skill that requires effort and motivation. That's right, it takes energy and desire to really listen to others. Unfortunately, it may seem like there are no rewards for listening, but there are negative consequences when we don't. Think of a time, for example, when someone did not pay attention to you by looking at his or her watch or doing some other activity such as typing on a keyboard. How did you feel? You may have felt put down, unimportant, or offended. In turn, such feelings can erode the quality of interpersonal relationships as well as fuel job dissatisfaction, lower productivity, and poor customer service. Listening is an important skill that can be improved by avoiding the 10 habits of bad listeners while cultivating the 10 good listening habits (see Table 12–3).

In addition, a communication expert suggests that we can all improve our listening skills by adhering to the following three fundamental recommendations:[36]

1. Attending closely to what's being said, not to what you want to say next.

2. Allowing others to finish speaking before taking our turn.

3. Repeating back what you've heard to give the speaker the opportunity to clarify the message.

# Women and Men Communicate Differently

Women and men have communicated differently since the dawn of time. Gender-based differences in communication are partly caused by linguistic styles commonly used by women and men. Deborah Tannen, a communication expert, defines **linguistic style** as follows:

**linguistic style**

**A person's typical speaking pattern.**

Linguistic style refers to a person's characteristic speaking pattern. It includes such features as directness or indirectness, pacing and pausing, word choice, and the use of such elements as jokes, figures of speech, stories, questions, and apologies. In other words, linguistic style is a set of culturally learned signals by which we not only communicate what we mean but also interpret others' meaning and evaluate one another as people.[37]

Linguistic style not only helps explain communication differences between women and men, but it also influences our perceptions of others' confidence, competence, and abilities. Increased awareness of linguistic styles can thus improve communication accuracy and your communication competence. This section strives to increase your understanding of interpersonal communication between women and men by discussing alternative explanations for differences in linguistic styles, various communication differences

The Keys to Effective Listening    TABLE 12–3

| Keys to Effective Listening | The Bad Listener | The Good Listener |
| --- | --- | --- |
| 1. Capitalize on thought speed | Tends to daydream | Stays with the speaker, mentally summarizes the speaker, weighs evidence, and listens between the lines |
| 2. Listen for ideas | Listens for facts | Listens for central or overall ideas |
| 3. Find an area of interest | Tunes out dry speakers or subjects | Listens for any useful information |
| 4. Judge content, not delivery | Tunes out dry or monotone speakers | Assesses content by listening to entire message before making judgments |
| 5. Hold your fire | Gets too emotional or worked up by something said by the speaker and enters into an argument | Withholds judgment until comprehension is complete |
| 6. Work at listening | Does not expend energy on listening | Gives the speaker full attention |
| 7. Resist distractions | Is easily distracted | Fights distractions and concentrates on the speaker |
| 8. Hear what is said | Shuts out or denies unfavorable information | Listens to both favorable and unfavorable information |
| 9. Challenge yourself | Resists listening to presentations of difficult subject matter | Treats complex presentations as exercise for the mind |
| 10. Use handouts, overheads, or other visual aids | Does not take notes or pay attention to visual aids | Takes notes as required and uses visual aids to enhance understanding of the presentation |

SOURCES: Derived from N Skinner, "Communication Skills," *Selling Power*, July/August 1999, pp 32–34; and G Manning, K Curtis, and S McMillen, *Building the Human Side of Work Community* (Cincinnati, OH: Thomson Executive Press, 1996), pp 127–54.

between women and men, and recommendations for improving communication between the sexes.

**Why Linguistic Styles Vary between Women and Men**    Although researchers do not completely agree on the cause of communication differences between women and men, there are two competing explanations that involve the well-worn debate between *nature* and *nurture*. Some researchers believe that interpersonal differences between women and men are due to inherited biological differences between the sexes. More specifically, this perspective, which also is called the "Darwinian perspective" or "evolutionary psychology," attributes gender differences in communication to drives, needs, and conflicts associated with reproductive strategies used by women and men. For example, proponents would say that males

Research reveals that men and women possess different communication styles. For example, men are more boastful about their accomplishments whereas women are more modest. How might differences in male and female communication patterns affect how men and women are perceived during group problem-solving meetings?

communicate more aggressively, interrupt others more than women, and hide their emotions because they have an inherent desire to possess features attractive to females in order to compete with other males for purposes of mate selection. Although males are certainly not competing for mate selection during a business meeting, evolutionary psychologists propose that men cannot turn off the biologically based determinants of their behavior.[38]

In contrast, social role theory is based on the idea that females and males learn ways of speaking as children growing up. Research shows that girls learn conversational skills and habits that focus on rapport and relationships, whereas boys learn skills and habits that focus on status and hierarchies. Accordingly, women come to view communication as a network of connections in which conversations are negotiations for closeness. This orientation leads women to seek and give confirmation and support more so than men. Men, on the other hand, see conversations as negotiations in which people try to achieve and maintain the upper hand. It thus is important for males to protect themselves from others' attempts to put them down or push them around. This perspective increases a male's need to maintain independence and avoid failure.[39]

**Gender Differences in Communication**    Research demonstrates that women and men communicate differently in a number of ways.[40] Women, for example, are more likely to share credit for success, to ask questions for clarification, to tactfully give feedback by mitigating criticism with praise, and to indirectly tell others what to do. In contrast, men are more likely to boast about themselves, to bluntly give feedback, and to withhold compliments, and are less likely to ask questions and to admit fault or weaknesses.

There are two important issues to keep in mind about these trends. First, the trends identified cannot be generalized to include all women and men. Some men are less likely to boast about their achievements while some women are less likely to share the credit. The point is that there are always exceptions to the rule. Second, your linguistic style influences perceptions about your confidence, competence, and authority. These judgments may, in turn, affect your future job assignments and subsequent promotability.

**Improving Communications between the Sexes**    Deborah Tannen recommends that everyone needs to become aware of how linguistic styles work and how they influence our perceptions and judgments. She believes that knowledge of linguistic styles helps to ensure that people with valuable insights or ideas get heard. Consider how gender-based linguistic differences affect who gets heard at a meeting:

> Those who are comfortable speaking up in groups, who need little or no silence before raising their hands, or who speak out easily without waiting to be recognized are far more likely to get heard at meetings. Those who refrain from talking until it's clear that the previous speaker is finished, who wait to be recognized, and who are inclined to link their comments to those of others will do fine at a meeting where everyone else is following the same rules but will have a hard time getting heard in a meeting with people whose styles are more like the first pattern. Given the socialization typical of boys and girls, men are more likely to have learned the first style and women the second, making meetings more congenial for men than for women.[41]

Knowledge of these linguistic differences can assist managers in devising methods to ensure that everyone's ideas are heard and given fair credit both in and out of meetings. Furthermore, it is useful to consider the organizational strengths and limitations of your linguistic style. You may want to consider modifying a linguistic characteristic that is a detriment to perceptions of your confidence, competence, and authority. In conclusion, communication between the sexes can be improved by remembering that women and men have different ways of saying the same thing.

# Communication in the Computerized Information Age

As discussed in Chapter 1, the use of computers and information technology is dramatically affecting many aspects of organizational behavior. For example, when Adecco, a staffing company, received a request to supply 300 factory workers immediately, senior vice president Steve Baruch used instant messaging to collaborate with managers in three states to find the workers in a matter of hours—a task that would have taken a few days using other communication technology.[42] And Tyco International, which makes and services fire and safety products, uses handheld devices called PDAs to get information to its service technicians. The technicians are responsible for servicing more than 200 kinds of equipment, so instead of trying to memorize every procedure, they look up schematics, procedures, and animation clips on their PDAs—far more practical than toting and thumbing through bulky manuals.[43]

A recent study of 2,032 youth by the Kaiser Family Foundation suggests that young people are also multitasking and spending a great deal of time using electronics. A

subsample who kept detailed diaries indicated that they spent about an hour a day using a computer and almost three-quarters of an hour reading. More than half of that time, they were multitasking—for example, listening to music or checking instant messages. Kids also spent nearly four hours a day watching television, and they were multitasking 45% of that time.[44] These teens may think they are well prepared for today's fast-paced workplace. Indeed, some managers assume that multitasking is the way to get more done. However, research shows that people can't actually think about two tasks at the same time, and employees may be more productive if they can organize their time so they aren't constantly switching between tasks.[45]

In addition to multitasking, researchers have uncovered another modern trend in communication—multicommunicating. **Multicommunicating** represents "the use of technology to participate in several interactions at the same time."[46] Examples would be answering e-mail messages during a lecture, texting someone during a dinner conversation with a friend, and text messaging while participating in a group conference call. As you probably know, multicommunicating has both positive and negative consequences. While it enables us to get more things done in a shorter amount of time, it also can create miscommunication and can foster stress and hurt feelings for those involved. Our advice, multicommunicate with caution, and be aware that there are times and places when it is inappropriate.[47]

Multicommunicating is an emerging trend in modern day communication. How effective a tool is the ability to multicommunicate?

**Multicommunicating**

Using technology to participate in two or more social interactions at the same time.

**"The webcam and electric prod? Oh, it's just something we're trying out."**

*Copyright © Ted Goff. Reprinted with permission.*

**Internet**

A global network of computer networks.

**intranet**

An organization's private Internet.

**extranet**

Connects internal employees with selected customers, suppliers, and strategic partners.

The computerized information age is radically changing communication patterns in both our personal and work lives. For example, recent statistics reveal that 72% of the population in North America uses the Internet. Cross-culturally, this percentage is higher than the percentage of the population using the Internet in Africa (5%), Asia (14%), Europe (47%), the Middle East (17%), Latin America/Caribbean (22%), and Oceania/Australia (56%).[48] This section explores key components of information technology that influence communication patterns and management within a computerized workplace: Internet/intranet/extranet, electronic mail and instant messaging, handheld devices, blogs, videoconferencing, group support systems, and teleworking.

# Internet/Intranet/Extranet

The Internet, or more simply, the Net, is more than a computer network. It is a network of computer networks. The **Internet** is a global network of independently operating but interconnected computers. The Internet connects everything from supercomputers, to large mainframes contained in businesses, government, and universities, to the personal computers in our homes and offices. An **intranet** is nothing more than an organization's private Internet. Intranets also have *firewalls* that block outside Internet users from accessing internal information. This is done to protect the privacy and confidentiality of company documents. In contrast to the internal focus of an intranet, an **extranet** is an extended intranet in that it connects internal employees with selected customers, suppliers, and other strategic partners. Enterprise Rent-A-Car, which specializes in renting cars to people whose autos are in the shop for repair, has an extranet that connects its offices with insurance companies and body shops. Use of this technology has increased customer satisfaction because it enables people to receive their repaired cars two days faster than average.[49]

The primary benefit of the Internet, intranets, and extranets is that they can enhance the ability of employees to find, create, manage, and distribute information. The effectiveness of these systems, however, depends on how organizations set up and manage their intranet/extranet and how employees use the acquired information (see Skills & Best Practices on page 315). For example, communication effectiveness actually can decrease if a corporate intranet becomes a dumping ground of unorganized information. In this case, employees will find themselves flailing in a sea of information. To date, however, no rigorous research studies have been conducted that directly demonstrate productivity increases from using the Internet, intranets, or extranets. But there are case studies that reveal other organizational benefits. For example, American Electric Power, an electric utility in Ohio with 20,000 employees, experienced significant cost savings by placing all of its human resource policies, procedures, and forms on its intranet.[50] United Parcel Service (UPS) also estimated that productivity increased 35% after the implementation of high-speed wireless Internet access via

Wi-Fi.[51] Employee training is another online application that has saved companies millions of dollars.[52]

In contrast to these positive case studies, a recent study by Harris Interactive revealed that 51% admitted using the Internet at work from one to five hours a week for personal matters. Another survey of 474 human resource professionals indicated that 43% found that employees were viewing pornography while at work.[53] All told, International Data Corp. estimated personal use of the Internet during work hours contributes to a 30% to 40% decrease in productivity.[54] Organizations are taking these statistics to heart and are attempting to root out cyberslackers by tracking employee behavior with electronic monitoring.[55]

There is one last aspect of the Internet worth noting— cybercrime. It strikes individuals and organizations alike. For example, Figure 12–3 shows the amount of cyber-crime committed for three categories of illegal behavior. All told, cyber-fraud cost businesses about $1.5 billion in 2005.[56] Interestingly, almost 50% of this criminal activity originates inside an organization. It may occur as the result of employee carelessness, for example, leaving a laptop unsecured or sending confidential, unencrypted information over the Internet. Alternatively, employees can steal trade secrets or sell customer information. Organizations can combat this problem by educating employees about security, classifying data as open or sensitive and confidential, using encryption for sensitive and confidential information, monitoring employee activities, and holding employees accountable for failure to follow rules regarding information security.[57]

# Electronic Mail and Instant Messaging

Electronic mail, or e-mail, uses the Internet/intranet to send computer-generated text and documents between people. The use of e-mail throughout the world has exploded due to four key benefits: (1) reduced costs of distributing information, (2) increased teamwork, (3) reduced paper costs, and (4) increased flexibility. On the other hand, there are four drawbacks: It can result in (1) wasted time and effort, as in dealing with spam and unsolicited junk mail, (2) information overload, (3) increased costs to organize, store, and monitor usage, and (4) neglect of other media (see Table 12–4).[58] Users also need to appreciate that e-mail, for practical purposes, is not confidential.[59]

## What Your Intranet Should Offer

**SKILLS & BEST PRACTICES**

The best intranets help employees efficiently find the information they need. Employee surveys and Web tracking software can pinpoint what employees want and what they actually use. In general, the following features improve an intranet:

- A simple design that makes it easy for employees to find important content. The home page can be customized to the needs of particular departments or pay levels, or to an individual's interests.

- Easy-to-find links to commonly used forms, news about the company and its industry, and information about employee benefits and training.

- Practical facts, such as holiday schedules and the week's menu in the company cafeteria.

- Frequent updates, so information is current and material is circulated, rather than every department's story being featured at once in an overwhelming mass.

- Opportunities to contribute, such as wikis, where employees can add their ideas on a shared site. Employees should be required to sign contributions, not contribute anonymously, to discourage nastiness and silliness.

- Photos and video clips of actual employees are more motivating than stock photos of models in phony situations.

- An effective search engine that uses the language of employees (for example, company and industry jargon used in each department).

**SOURCES:** Based on J Taylor Arnold, "Improving Intranet Usefulness," *HR Magazine,* April 2008, pp 103–6; and V Vara, "The Winning Formula," *The Wall Street Journal,* May 14, 2007, http://online.wsj.com.

**FIGURE 12–3**
The Costs of
Cybercrime

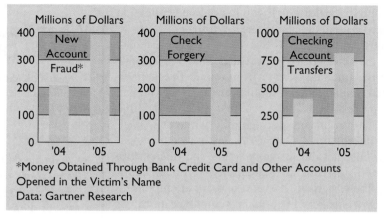

*Money Obtained Through Bank Credit Card and Other Accounts
Opened in the Victim's Name
Data: Gartner Research

SOURCE: S E Ante and B Grow, "Meet the Hackers," *BusinessWeek,* May 29, 2006, p. 60.

**TABLE 12–4    E-Mail: Benefits, Drawbacks, and Suggestions for Managing It**

**Benefits**

- *Reduced costs of distributing information.* E-mail allows information to be sent electronically, thereby reducing the costs of sending information to employees and customers.
- *Increased teamwork.* Users can send messages to colleagues anywhere in the world and receive immediate feedback.
- *Reduced paper costs.* An expert estimates these savings at $9,000 per employee.
- *Increased flexibility.* Employees with laptops, cell phones, and handheld devices can access e-mail from anywhere.

**Drawbacks**

- *Wasted time and effort.* E-mail can distract people from completing their work responsibilities. People spend too much time searching.
- *Information overload.* The average corporate employee receives 171 messages a day, and 10 to 40% are unimportant.
- *Increased costs to organize, store, and monitor.* Systems are needed to protect privacy. The Federal Rules of Civil Procedures require organizations to keep tabs on e-mail and produce them in case of litigation.
- *Neglect of other media.* People unsuccessfully attempt to solve complex problems with e-mail. E-mail reduces the amount of face-to-face communication.

**Managing E-Mail**

- *Do not assume e-mail is confidential.* Employers are increasingly monitoring all e-mail. Assume your messages can be read by anyone.
- *Be professional and courteous.* Recommendations include: delete trailing messages, don't send chain letters and jokes, don't type in all caps—it's equivalent to shouting, don't respond immediately to a nasty e-mail, refrain from using colored text and background, don't expose your contact list to strangers, and be patient about receiving replies.
- *Avoid sloppiness.* Use a spell checker or reread the message before sending.
- *Don't use e-mail for volatile or complex issues.* Use a medium that is appropriate for the situation at hand.
- *Keep messages brief and clear.* Use accurate subject headings and let the reader know what you want right up front.
- *Save people time.* Type "no reply necessary" in the subject line or at the top of your message if appropriate.
- *Be careful with attachments.* Large attachments can crash someone's systems and use up valuable time downloading. Send only what is necessary, and get permission to send multiple attachments.

SOURCES: C Graham, "In-Box Overload," *The Arizona Republic,* March 16, 2007, p A14; M Totty, "Rethinking the Inbox," *The Wall Street Journal,* March 26, 2007, p R8; A Smith, "Federal Rules Define Duty to Preserve Work E-Mails," *HR Magazine,* January 2007, pp 27, 36; M Totty, "Letter of the Law," *The Wall Street Journal,* March 26, 2007, p R10; and "The Top 10 E-Mail Courtesy Suggestions," *Coachville Coach Training,* March 22, 2000, http://topten.org.content/tt.BN122.htm.

A more immediate alternative to e-mail is instant messaging, which until recently was largely used for personal communications at home. IM usage has become more popular at work because users can see which of their contacts are currently online and can have chats in real time simultaneously with several people. A recent survey found that about one-third of U.S. employees use instant messaging at work, although this use is not always authorized.[60] Individuals who are skilled at multitasking and modern technology may use carefully placed IMs to coach others during meetings.

## Handheld Devices

Handheld devices, which also are referred to as PDAs (personal digital assistants), offer users the portability to do work from any location. They are used by millions of people and were designed to allow users to multitask from any location. For example, PDAs can be used to make and track appointments, do word processing, crunch numbers on a spreadsheet, receive and send e-mail, display training documents and videos, and complete a variety of other tasks.[61] Of course, users also enjoy nonwork-related applications—downloading and playing music, videos, and games. The question from an OB perspective is whether or not these devices actually lead to higher productivity.

Although many people seem addicted to their handheld devices, some academics are skeptical about their real value. Consider the following comments made by several professors to a reporter from *BusinessWeek*.

> The idea that gadgets always make us more efficient, "is a scam, and illusion," says David Greenfield, director of the Hartford-based Center for Internet Studies. That's because at their heart, gadgets enable multitasking. And a growing body of evidence suggests that multitasking can easily turn into multislacking. It also increases errors, short-circuits attention spans, induces air-traffic-controller-like stress, and elongates the time it takes to accomplish the most basic tasks by up to 50% or more, according to University of Michigan psychology professor David Meyer. . . .
>
> Gadgets also trigger cognitive overload, says Harvard Medical School psychiatry instructor Dr Edward M. Hallowell. . . . All that toggling back and forth "dilutes performance and increases irritability," says Hallowell, causing steady managers to become disorganized and underachievers.[62]

Given these considerations, we wonder why sales of handheld devices continue to explode. Dr Meyer offers one potential explanation. He notes that the use of PDAs activates our dopamine-reward system, which induces a pleasurable state for approximately 6% of the population. Dr Meyer says that this effect is clinically addictive.[63] Alternatively, people may view these devices as one way to cope with increasing pressures to accomplish more in the face of ever increasing informational demands. In the end, time and additional research will determine the actual value of handheld devices.

## Blogs

A **blog** is an online journal in which people write whatever they want about any topic. Blogging is one of the latest Internet trends. Experts estimate that there are around 100 million blogs in existence worldwide.[64] The benefits of blogs include the opportunity for people to discuss issues in a casual format. These discussions serve much like a chat group and thus provide managers with insights from a wide segment of the employee and customer base as well as the general public. Executives like Jonathan Schwartz, president and COO of Sun Microsystems, and Paul Otellini, the CEO of Intel, are both using blogs at work to discuss issues of importance.[65] Blogs also give people the opportunity to air their opinions, grievances, and creative ideas. Blogs can also be used to obtain feedback. For example, Christopher Barger, a blogger from IBM, reads other people's blogs to

> **blog**
> **Online journal in which people comment on any topic.**

see what people are saying about IBM's products. Other companies with blogs include Microsoft, Hewlett-Packard, Sun Microsystems, General Motors, and Boeing.[66]

Blogs also have pitfalls. One entails the lack of legal and organizational guidelines regarding what can be posted online. For example, flight attendant Ellen Simonetti and Google employee Mark Jen were both fired for information they included on their blogs. Simonetti posted suggestive pictures of herself in uniform, and Jen commented about his employer's finances.[67] Another involves the potential for employees to say unflattering things about their employer and to leak confidential information. Finally, one can waste a lot of time reading silly and unsubstantiated postings. For example, a recent study showed that 25% of employees read blogs at work, losing approximately 9% of their workweek.[68]

We cannot make any overall conclusion regarding blogs because there has not been any research into their effectiveness as a communication, marketing, or managerial tool. Once again, time will tell.

# Videoconferencing/Telepresence

Videoconferencing, also known as teleconferencing, uses video and audio links along with computers to enable people in different locations to see, hear, and talk with one another. This allows people from many locations to conduct a meeting without having to travel.

**telepresence**

**Communicating with the most advanced videoconferencing systems.**

**Telepresence** is an advanced form of videoconferencing. It represents a method of communicating that is based on using the most sophisticated videoconferencing systems. Here is how these two systems were described in *The Wall Street Journal*.

HP Halo Telepresence Solutions, as seen in this photo, utilize hardware and software technologies to create immersive collaboration rooms that make users feel like they are in the same location, even if they are on different continents. What do you see as the advantages of this type of videoconferencing?

Traditional videoconferencing setups are essentially a monitor, camera and microphone, placed in a conventional conference room. Telepresence systems, by contrast, require specially designed rooms with multiple cameras, sound-damping equipment and high-definition video screens. They simulate the sensation of two groups of people at identical tables facing each other through windows.

Participants appear life-sized and move smoothly—not like small, herky-jerky figures on a TV screen. The sound quality is high; there is little lag or audio distortion. The systems are also designed to allow groups of workers to share documents, such as engineering drawings or marketing plans, or perform product demonstrations. Also, people in more than two locations can participate in the same meeting.[69]

Telepresence systems can cost anywhere between $200,000 and $500,000.

There are three key benefits of videoconferencing and telepresence. These systems can reduce an organization's travel expenses. Additionally, such systems help organizations to be more innovative because they allow people working across the world to participate in the innovation process on an as-needed basis. Finally, both systems allow employees to speed up the decision-making process (recall our discussion in Chapter 10).

# Group Support Systems

**Group support systems (GSSs)** entail using state-of-the-art computer software and hardware to help people work better together. They enable people to share information without the constraints of time and space. This is accomplished by utilizing computer networks to link people across a room or across the globe. Collaborative applications include messaging and e-mail systems, calendar management, videoconferencing, computer teleconferencing, electronic whiteboards, and the type of computer-aided decision-making systems discussed in Chapter 10.

**group support systems (GSSs)**

Computer software and hardware that help people work better together.

GSS applications have demonstrated increased productivity and cost savings. A recent meta-analysis of 48 experiments also revealed that groups using GSSs during brainstorming experienced greater participation and influence quality, a greater quantity of ideas generated, and less domination by individual members than did groups meeting face-to-face.[70]

Organizations that use full-fledged GSSs have the ability to create virtual teams or to operate as a virtual organization. Virtual organizations are discussed in Chapter 15. You may recall from Chapter 9 that a virtual team represents a physically dispersed task group that conducts its business by using the types of information technology currently being discussed. Specifically, virtual teams tend to use Internet/intranet systems, GSSs, and videoconferencing systems. These real-time systems enable people to communicate with anyone at any time.[71]

It is important to keep in mind that modern-day information technology only enables people to interact virtually; it doesn't guarantee effective communications. For example, in some organizations, shared calendars have become a tool for power plays as employees try to schedule others for meetings while their colleagues scramble for ways to claim being busy in spite of a calendar showing a block of unscheduled time.[72] Interestingly, there are a whole host of unique communication problems associated with using the information technology needed to operate virtually.[73]

# Teleworking

**Teleworking,** also referred to as telecommuting, is a work practice in which an employee does part of his or her job in a remote location, typically at home, using a variety of information technologies. That said, any employee with a laptop, Internet access, and a phone can work from almost anywhere. Experts estimate that, by 2010, about 100 million people will telework from home at least one day a month in the United States.[74] Telework is more common for jobs involving computer work, writing, and phone work that require concentration and limited interruptions.

**teleworking**

Doing work that is generally performed in the office away from the office using different information technologies.

A recent meta-analysis of 46 studies involving 12,883 employees uncovered the following benefits of teleworking: (1) increased autonomy, job satisfaction, and performance and (2) reduced work–family conflict, intentions to quit, and role stress. Further, results also indicated that the quality of relationships between teleworkers and their managers remained positive. This suggests that teleworkers' careers are not necessarily derailed because they do not have the same amount of face time as other workers.[75]

Although telecommuting represents an attempt to accommodate employee needs and desires, it requires adjustments and is not for everybody. Many people thoroughly enjoy the social camaraderie that exists within an office setting. These individuals probably would not like to telecommute. Others lack the self-discipline needed to work at home. To overcome these concerns, organizations such as Hewlett-Packard are using personality tests, which were discussed in Chapter 5, to identify people most suited to working off site.[76]

# key terms

# chapter summary

- *Describe the perceptual process model of communication.* Communication is a process of consecutively linked elements. This model of communication depicts receivers as information processors who create the meaning of messages in their own mind. Because receivers' interpretations of messages often differ from those intended by senders, miscommunication is a common occurrence.

- *Describe the process, personal, physical, and semantic barriers to effective communication.* Every element of the perceptual model of communication is a potential process barrier. There are eight personal barriers that commonly influence communication: (a) the ability to effectively communicate, (b) the way people process and interpret information, (c) the level of interpersonal trust between people, (d) the existence of stereotypes and prejudices, (e) the egos of the people communicating, (f) the ability to listen, (g) the natural tendency to evaluate or judge a sender's message, and (h) the inability to listen with understanding. Physical barriers pertain to distance, physical objects, time, and work and office noise. Semantic barriers show up as encoding and decoding errors because these phases of communication involve transmitting and receiving words and symbols. Cultural diversity is a key contributor to semantic barriers.

- *Contrast the communication styles of assertiveness, aggressiveness, and nonassertiveness.* An assertive style is expressive and self-enhancing but does not violate others' basic human rights. In contrast, an aggressive style is expressive and self-enhancing but takes unfair advantage of others. A nonassertive style is characterized by timid and self-denying behavior. An assertive communication style is more effective than either an aggressive or nonassertive style.

- *Discuss the primary sources of nonverbal communication.* There are several identifiable sources of nonverbal communication effectiveness. Body movements and gestures, touch, facial expressions, and eye contact are important nonverbal cues. The interpretation of these nonverbal cues significantly varies across cultures.

- *Review the five dominant listening styles and 10 keys to effective listening.* The five dominant listening styles are appreciative, empathetic, comprehensive, discerning, and evaluative. Good listeners use the following 10 listening habits: (1) capitalize on thought speed by staying with the speaker and listening between the lines, (2) listen for ideas rather than facts, (3) identify areas of interest between the speaker and listener, (4) judge content and not delivery, (5) do not judge until the speaker has completed his or her message, (6) put energy and effort into listening, (7) resist distractions, (8) listen to both favorable and unfavorable information, (9) read or listen to complex material to exercise the mind, and (10) take notes when necessary and use visual aids to enhance understanding.

- *Explain the information technology of Internet/intranet/extranet, e-mail, instant messaging, handheld devices, blogs, videoconferencing/telepresence, and group support systems, and explain the related use of teleworking.* The Internet is a global network of computer networks. An intranet is an organization's private Internet. It contains a firewall that blocks outside Internet users from accessing private internal information. An extranet connects an organization's internal employees with selected customers, suppliers, and strategic partners. The primary benefit of these "nets" is that they can enhance the ability of employees to find, create, manage, and distribute information. E-mail uses the Internet/intranet/extranet to send computer-generated text and documents between people. Handheld devices, also known as PDAs (personal digital assistants), offer users the portability to do work from any location. They serve as minicomputers and communication devices. A blog is an online journal in which people write whatever they want about any topic. Blogging is the latest Internet trend. Videoconferencing uses video and audio links along with computers to enable people located at different locations to see, hear, and talk with one another. GSSs use state-of-the-art computer software and hardware to help people work better together. Information is shared across time and space by linking people with computer networks. Teleworking involves doing work that is generally performed in the office away from the office using different information technologies.

# discussion questions

1. Returning to the chapter-opening case, what concepts discussed in this chapter were used by Yogesh Gupta and Kathleen Murphy?
2. What are some sources of noise that interfere with communication during a class lecture, an encounter with a professor in his or her office, or a movie?
3. Which of the keys to effective listening are most difficult to follow when listening to a class lecture? Explain.
4. Which barrier to effective communication is most difficult to reduce? Explain
5. What are the pros and cons of using PDAs? Discuss.

# ethical dilemma

## Should People Making False Statements in Blogs Be Prosecuted?[77]

It bills itself as the world's "most prestigious college discussion board," giving a glimpse into law school admissions policies, postgraduate social networking, and the hiring practices of major law firms.

But the AutoAdmit site, widely used by law students for information on schools and firms, is also known as a venue for racist and sexist remarks and career-damaging rumors. Now it's at the heart of a defamation lawsuit that legal experts say could test the anonymity of the Internet.

After facing lewd comments and threats by posters, two women at Yale Law School filed a suit on June 8 in U.S. District Court in New Haven, Connecticut, that includes subpoenas for 28 anonymous users of the site, which has generated more than 7 million posts since 2004. According to court documents, a user on the site named "STAN-FORDtrol" began a thread in 2005 seeking to warn Yale students about one of the women in the suit, entitled "Stupid Bitch to Enter Yale Law." Another threatened to rape and sodomize her, the documents said.

The plaintiff, a respected Stanford University graduate identified only as "Doe I" in the lawsuit, learned of the Internet attack in the summer of 2005 before moving to Yale in Connecticut. The posts gradually became more menacing. Some posts made false claims about her academic record and urged users to warn law firms or accused her of bribing Yale officials to gain admission and of forming a lesbian relationship with a Yale administrator, the court papers said.

The plaintiff said she believes the harassing remarks, which lasted nearly two years, cost her an important summer internship. After interviewing with 16 firms, she received only four callbacks and ultimately had no offers—a result considered unusual given her qualifications.

Another woman, identified as Doe II, endured similar attacks. The two, who say they suffered substantial "psychological and economic injury," also sued a former manager of the site because he refused to remove disparaging messages. The manager had cited free speech protections.

## What Is Your Opinion about the Issue of False, Negative Blogs?

1. The Constitution of the U.S. allows free speech, and people should be allowed to say whatever they want. Further, it is normal for people to have different perceptions about others. As such, it does not seem fair to prosecute someone who has a unique, negative perception about someone else.

2. The reputations of these two women were damaged by malicious, negative statements that were untrue. Although the individuals posting these statements should be punished, the AutoAdmit site should not. The site cannot police the accuracy of posted blogs.

3. Both the individuals making the malicious, negative statements and the blog site, AutoAdmit, should be punished. AutoAdmit should be held accountable because the women asked management of the site to remove the false posts.

4. Invent other options.

For an interpretation of this situation, visit our Web site, at **www.mhhe.com/kinickiob4e**

If you're looking for additional study materials, be sure to check out the Online Learning Center at

**www.mhhe.com/kinickiob4e**

for more information and interactivities that correspond to this chapter.

# Influence, Power, and Politics: An Organizational Survival Kit

**After reading the material in this chapter, you should be able to:**

1. Name five "soft" and four "hard" influence tactics, and summarize Cialdini's principles of influence and persuasion.

2. Identify and briefly describe French and Raven's five bases of power.

3. Define the term *empowerment*, and explain how to make it succeed.

4. Define *organizational politics*, explain what triggers it, and specify the three levels of political action in organizations.

5. Distinguish between favorable and unfavorable impression management tactics.

6. Explain how to manage organizational politics.

Shai Agassi is working on an electric only car and believes can make this dream a reality. Would you buy into Project Better Place?

Just over a year ago, on Dec. 31, 2006, Shai Agassi settled into a leather couch in the office of Ehud Olmert to meet with the Israeli Prime Minister. Agassi, then a top executive at German software giant SAP, had come to pitch the idea of his native Israel reducing its dependence on oil by replacing gas-powered cars with electric ones. Olmert liked the concept but laid down a steep challenge: He wanted Agassi to raise hundreds of millions in venture capital and get an auto industry CEO on board before he would pledge his support. "You go find the money and find a major automaker who will commit to this, and I'll give you the policy backing you need," Olmert said.

Within a year, Agassi had pulled off everything Olmert had asked. He raised $200 million in venture capital and, with help from Israeli President Shimon Peres, persuaded Carlos Ghosn, the chief executive of Renault and Nissan, to make a new kind of electric car for the Israeli market. On Jan. 21, Agassi, Olmert, Peres, and Ghosn unveiled the novel project, under which Agassi's Silicon Valley company, Better Place, will sell electric cars and build a network of locations where drivers can charge and replace batteries. Olmert has done his part, too. Israel just boosted the sales tax on gasoline-powered cars to as much as 60% and pledged to buy up old gas cars to get them off the road.

Agassi contends that Israel is just the start. He hopes to expand his business into several other countries over the next few years, with China, France, and Britain among the potential markets. Ultimately, he believes that his company and others like it could shake two pillars of the global economy, the $1.5 trillion-a-year auto industry and the $1.5 trillion-a-year market for gasoline. "If what I'm saying is right, this would be the largest economic dislocation in the history of capitalism," says Agassi. . . .

Agassi's other unusual idea is for Better Place to operate as something akin to a mobile-phone carrier. He plans to sell electric cars to consumers at a relatively low price and then charge them monthly operating fees. The total cost of owning an electric car, including the up-front price and ongoing operating expenses, is expected to be less than that of a conventional car. At first, consumers will buy cars directly from Better Place, though later they could buy them from auto dealers with a Better Place service plan. Agassi hopes to begin testing the system by the end of this year and have tens of thousands of electric cars on Israel's roads by 2011.

The approach has won Agassi support from some unlikely corners. Idan Ofer, chairman of Israel Corp., a leading refiner of oil in Israel, is one of his biggest backers even though Agassi's technology could cut into demand for gasoline. "If I didn't do it, somebody else will," says Ofer. "What's the point of fighting something that's inevitable?" . . .

While Olmert held the power, it was Peres who quickly emerged as the godfather for Agassi's project. He helped broker meetings with automakers at the World Economic Forum's annual meeting in Davos. During a snowstorm last Jan. 26, he volunteered his hotel suite for meetings with car company executives. First, a vice-chairman at one Japanese automaker listened to the presentation and was cool to the idea. But then Ghosn came in, and he had precisely the opposite reaction. He invited Agassi to talk things over with operational executives at Renault.

What got Ghosn excited was Israel's willingness to slash import taxes for green vehicles and alter domestic sales taxes in ways that would make the economics of the plan work. "This is a unique situation," says Ghosn. "It's the first mass marketplace for electric cars under conditions that make sense for all the parties." As a result of getting involved, the Nissan-Renault Alliance has made electric autos a top priority. Initially, the companies expect to produce electric cars for Israel and other countries by modifying existing models, but eventually they plan to introduce new models designed from the ground up to run on batteries developed by Nissan.

Immediately after the Davos meetings, Peres urged Agassi to take on Project Better Place as his own business. Agassi was in line for the CEO job at SAP, but Peres challenged him to change course: "In your young life, there's nothing better you could do." A few days later Hasso Plattner, SAP's chairman, called Agassi to say CEO Henning Kagermann had signed on for two more years. Since that would push back Agassi's opportunity to move into the CEO spot, he saw it as a sign that he was free to leave and pursue other career paths. He quit on the spot, though two months went by before his departure was final. . . .

In December, Agassi saw his dream come one step closer to reality. With his backers in place and the company's launch scheduled, he took a test drive in a Renault that his employees had converted to run on electricity. The modified Renault Mégane is capable of going from zero to 60 in eight seconds and has a top speed of 130. Agassi and his beaming father, Reuven, tooled around a Tel Aviv suburb for half an hour.

Better Place now has talks under way with about a dozen other countries. Agassi hopes to pilot the project in a few countries this year and begin mass deployments in 2011. He's optimistic that he'll be able to defy the odds, but he's also realistic enough to know there are many difficult days ahead. "There will be a very loud splat when I hit the ground," he says, "or there's going to be a revolution."[1]

**Why was Agassi successful in raising money for his venture? Explain.** For an interpretation of this case and additional comments, visit our Online Learning Center at

www.mhhe.com/ kinickiob4e

FOR DISCUSSION

illustrates how important it is for you to develop the interpersonal skills needed to influence others. Shai Aggasi was able to use these skills to influence Ehud Olmert, Shimon Peres, and Carlos Ghosn while overcoming a lack of power and political agendas. Who knows, Agassi's influence skills may revolutionize the world.

In a perfect world, individual and collective interests would be closely aligned and everyone would move forward as one. Instead, we typically find a rather messy situation in which self-interests often override the collective mission. Personal hidden agendas are pursued, political coalitions are formed, false impressions are made, and people end up working at cross purposes. Managers need to be able to guide diverse individuals, who are often powerfully motivated to put their own self-interests first, to pursue common objectives. At stake in this tug-of-war between individual and collective interests is no less than the ultimate survival of the organization.

The purpose of this chapter is to give you a survival kit for the rough-and-tumble side of organizational life. We do so by exploring the interrelated topics of organizational influence and persuasion, social power, employee empowerment, organizational politics, and impression management.

# Influencing and Persuading Others

How do you get others to carry out your wishes? Do you simply tell them what to do? Or do you prefer a less direct approach, such as promising to return the favor? Whatever approach you use, the crux of the issue is *social influence*. A large measure of interpersonal interaction involves attempts to influence others, including parents, bosses, coworkers, spouses, teachers, friends, and children.

Let's start sharpening your influence skills with a familiarity of the following research insights.

## Nine Generic Influence Tactics

1 learning objective

Name five "soft" and four "hard" influence tactics, and summarize Cialdini's principles of influence and persuasion.

A particularly fruitful stream of research, initiated by David Kipnis and his colleagues in 1980, reveals how people influence each other in organizations. The Kipnis methodology involved asking employees how they managed to get their bosses, coworkers, or subordinates to do what they wanted them to do.[2] Statistical refinements and replications by other researchers over a 13-year period eventually yielded nine influence tactics. The nine tactics, ranked in diminishing order of use in the workplace are as follows:

1. *Rational persuasion.* Trying to convince someone with reason, logic, or facts.
2. *Inspirational appeals.* Trying to build enthusiasm by appealing to others' emotions, ideals, or values.
3. *Consultation.* Getting others to participate in planning, making decisions, and changes.
4. *Ingratiation.* Getting someone in a good mood prior to making a request; being friendly, helpful, and using praise, flattery, or humor.[3]
5. *Personal appeals.* Referring to friendship and loyalty when making a request.
6. *Exchange.* Making express or implied promises and trading favors.
7. *Coalition tactics.* Getting others to support your effort to persuade someone.
8. *Pressure.* Demanding compliance or using intimidation or threats.

9. *Legitimating tactics.* Basing a request on one's authority or right, organizational rules or policies, or express or implied support from superiors.[4]

These approaches can be considered *generic* influence tactics because they characterize social influence in all directions. Researchers have found this ranking to be fairly consistent regardless of whether the direction of influence is downward, upward, or lateral.[5]

Some call the first five influence tactics—rational persuasion, inspirational appeals, consultation, ingratiation, and personal appeals—"soft" tactics because they are friendlier and not as coercive as the last four tactics. Exchange, coalition, pressure, and legitimating tactics accordingly are called "hard" tactics because they involve more overt pressure.

## Three Influence Outcomes

According to researchers, an influence attempt has three possible outcomes:

1. *Commitment:* Substantial agreement followed by initiative and persistence in pursuit of common goals.

2. *Compliance:* Reluctant or insincere agreement requiring subsequent prodding to satisfy minimum requirements.

3. *Resistance:* Stalling, unproductive arguing, or outright rejection.[6]

Commitment is the best outcome in the workplace because the target person's intrinsic motivation will energize good performance.[7] A G Lafley, the highly respected CEO of 100,000-employee Procter & Gamble, made commitment the cornerstone of his growth plan after taking charge in 2000:

> I always talk about this hierarchy of commitment. On the high end it's disciples—people who really believe in what you're doing and in you. And on the low end it's saboteurs. And there's everything in between. So I had to make sure that we got rid of the saboteurs, built a strong cadre of disciples, and moved all fence sitters to the positive side.[8]

**As CEO of Procter & Gamble, A G Lafley uses persuasive power to win commitment to company goals.**

The fence sitters required Lafley's best powers of influence and persuasion during a hectic schedule of face-to-face meetings with P&G employees worldwide. Too often in today's hurried workplaces managers must settle for compliance or face resistance because they do not invest themselves in the situation, as Lafley did.

## Practical Research Insights

Laboratory and field studies have taught us useful lessons about the relative effectiveness of influence tactics along with other instructive insights:

- Commitment is more likely when people rely on consultation, strong rational persuasion, and inspirational appeals and *do not* rely on pressure and coalition tactics (see Skills & Best Practices).[9] Interestingly, in one study, managers were

## How a Winning Coach Obtains Commitment

How does coach Pat Summitt, who has led the University of Tennessee women's basketball team to eight national championship titles, keep the Lady Volunteers committed to winning? Notice her influence tactics in this description:

Selecting players, she looks for competitiveness and a deep desire for improvement. . . . But it's her channeling of that drive that has defined careers, both hers and her players'. "When you're in the room with her," says Shelley Collier, captain of the 1986–1987 national championship team, "You just stand up. She doesn't even have to talk."

Yet when Summitt does talk, her players listen. In a tournament game . . . against the University of North Carolina, the Lady Vols were down by 12 in the second half, with eight minutes to play. Summitt called for a time-out. Other coaches might have barked commands, pulled out a notebook, drawn lines. But Summitt calmly inquired: "What type of defense do we want to run?" The team answered, "Can we make a stop?" (Could they hold them scoreless on their next possession?) Forward Candace Parker upped the ante. "Can we make five consecutive stops?" They could, the team said. And they went on a 20–2 run to win the game.

There was a time when Summitt, 55, might have acted differently. She has learned to be more communicative, she says, and less confrontational. . . . "You have to be very secure to stop and think about what the players need from you."

**SOURCE:** Excerpted from K Garber, "Showing How the Game Is Played," *U.S. News & World Report,* November 19, 2007, p 60. Also see J Balloch, "Fans Celebrate 8th National Title with Lady Vols," *Knoxville News Sentinel govolsxtra,* April 10, 2008, www .govolsxtra.com.

not very effective at *downward* influence. They relied most heavily on inspiration (an effective tactic), ingratiation (a moderately effective tactic), and pressure (an ineffective tactic).[10]

- Commitment is more likely when the influence attempt involves something *important* and *enjoyable* and is based on a *friendly* relationship.[11]
- Credible (believable and trustworthy) people tend to be the most persuasive.[12]
- In a survey of 101 employees from two different organizations, employees were more likely to resist change when managers used a legitimating tactic and more apt to accept change when managers relied on a consultative strategy.[13]

## How to Do a Better Job of Influencing and Persuading Others

Practical, research-based advice has been offered by Robert B Cialdini, a respected expert at Arizona State University. Based on many years of research by himself and others, Cialdini (pronounced Chal-*dee*-knee) derived the following six principles of influence and persuasion:[14]

1. *Liking.* People tend to like those who like them. Learning about another person's likes and dislikes through informal conversations builds friendship bonds. So do sincere and timely praise, empathy, and recognition.

2. *Reciprocity.* The belief that both good and bad deeds should be repaid in kind is virtually universal. Managers who act unethically and treat employees with contempt can expect the same in return. Worse, those employees, in turn, are likely to treat each other and their customers unethically and with contempt. Managers need to be positive and constructive role models and fair-minded to benefit from the principle of reciprocity.

3. *Social proof.* People tend to follow the lead of those most like themselves. Role models and peer pressure are powerful cultural forces in social settings. Managers are advised to build support for workplace changes by first gaining the enthusiastic support of informal leaders who will influence their peers.

4. *Consistency.* People tend to do what they are personally committed to do. A manager who can elicit a verbal commitment from an employee has taken an important step toward influence and persuasion.

5. *Authority.* People tend to defer to and respect credible experts. According to Cialdini, too many managers and professionals take their expertise for granted, as in the case of a hospital where he consulted:

> The physical therapy staffers were frustrated because so many of their stroke patients abandoned their exercise routines as soon as they left the hospital. No matter how often the staff emphasized the importance of regular home exercise—it is, in fact, crucial to the process of regaining independent function—the message just didn't sink in.
> Interviews with some of the patients helped us pinpoint the problem. They were familiar with the background and training of their physicians, but the patients knew little about the credentials of the physical therapists who were urging them to exercise. It was a simple matter to remedy that lack of information: We merely asked the therapy director to display all the awards, diplomas, and certifications of her staff on the walls of the therapy rooms. The result was startling: Exercise compliance jumped 34% and has never dropped since.[15]

6. *Scarcity.* People want items, information, and opportunities that have limited availability. Special opportunities and privileged information are influence builders for managers.

Importantly, Cialdini recommends using these six principles in combination, rather than separately, for maximum impact. Because of major ethical implications, one's goals need to be worthy and actions need to be sincere and genuine when using these six principles.

By demonstrating the rich texture of social influence, the foregoing research evidence and practical advice whet our appetite for learning more about how today's managers can and do reconcile individual and organizational interests. Let us focus on social power.

# Social Power and Empowerment

The term *power* evokes mixed and often passionate reactions. To skeptics, Lord Acton's time-honored declaration that "power corrupts and absolute power corrupts absolutely" is truer than ever.[16] However, OB specialists remind us that, like it or not, power is a fact of life in modern organizations. According to one management writer:

> Power must be used because managers must influence those they depend on. Power also is crucial in the development of managers' self-confidence and willingness to support subordinates. From this perspective, power should be accepted as a natural part of any organization. Managers should recognize and develop their own power to coordinate and support the work of subordinates; it is powerlessness, not power, that undermines organizational effectiveness.[17]

Thus, power is a necessary and generally positive force in organizations.[18] As the term is used here, **social power** is defined as "the ability to marshal the human, informational, and material resources to get something done."[19]

**social power**

Ability to get things done with human, informational, and material resources.

Importantly, the exercise of social power in organizations is not necessarily a downward proposition. Employees can and do exercise power upward and laterally. Their power also can affect people in other organizations—an increasingly important consideration as today's organizations collaborate on a variety of projects. For example, as Steve Jobs has led Apple to innovate in personal computers, operating systems, desktop publishing, music players, and cell phones, he has reshaped the competitive landscape in several industries. His history of game-changing moves has given Jobs more power in negotiating contracts with other firms and has earned him widespread respect as a master of technology marketing, whom others want to emulate:

> No other high-tech impresario could walk into the annual sales meeting of one of his fiercest rivals and get a standing ovation. That's what happened back in 2002, when [Intel's CEO] Andy Grove invited Jobs to talk about innovating. It would be two more years before Apple agreed to start using Intel chips in its computers. But the Intel salespeople couldn't help themselves. Star power: He has that too.[20]

**2** **learning objective**

Identify and briefly describe French and Raven's five bases of power.

**reward power**

Obtaining compliance with promised or actual rewards.

**coercive power**

Obtaining compliance through threatened or actual punishment.

# Five Bases of Power

A popular classification scheme for social power traces back to the landmark work of John French and Bertram Raven. They proposed that power arises from five different bases: reward power, coercive power, legitimate power, expert power, and referent power.[21] Each involves a different approach to influencing others. Each has advantages and drawbacks.

**Reward Power**  Managers have **reward power** if they can obtain compliance by promising or granting rewards. Pay-for-performance plans and positive reinforcement programs attempt to exploit reward power.

The text gives an example of this Volkswagon executive and his use of coercive power. Do you think his strategy is effective?

**Coercive Power**  Threats of punishment and actual punishment give an individual **coercive power.** For instance, consider this favorite technique of Wolfgang Bernhard, a Volkswagen executive and "ruthless cost-cutter": "He routinely locks staffers in meeting rooms, then refuses to open the doors until they've stripped $1,500 in costs from a future model."[22] Bathroom break, anyone?

**Legitimate Power**  This base of power is anchored to one's formal position or authority.[23] Thus, managers who obtain compliance primarily because of their formal authority to make decisions have **legitimate power.** Legitimate power may be expressed either positively or negatively. Positive legitimate power focuses constructively on job performance. Negative legitimate power tends to be threatening and demeaning to those being influenced. Its main purpose is to build the power holder's ego.

**legitimate power**

Obtaining compliance through formal authority.

**expert power**

Obtaining compliance through one's knowledge or information.

**Expert Power**  Valued knowledge or information gives an individual **expert power** over those who need such knowledge or information. The power of supervisors is enhanced because they know about work assignments and schedules before their employees do. Skillful use of expert power played a key role in the effectiveness of team leaders in a study of three physician medical diagnosis teams.[24] When growth slowed at Starbucks, the company brought back its former CEO, Howard Schultz, because he was seen as someone with enough expert power to bring about significant change. A reporter described Schultz as "highly respected for turning Starbucks into one of the hottest growth stocks in the 1990s and creating a retail powerhouse."[25]

Because of this track record, the board of directors and investors expect that the company's employees will believe Schultz has good ideas for success and therefore will follow his lead. Knowledge *is* power in today's high-tech workplaces. Just ask any IT (information technology) manager who is struggling to maintain control over the company's computer network even as tech-savvy workers download the latest Internet applications and software updates.[26]

**referent power**

**Obtaining compliance through charisma or personal attraction.**

**Referent Power**    Also called charisma, **referent power** comes into play when one's personality becomes the reason for compliance. Role models have referent power over those who identify closely with them.[27]

To further your understanding of these five bases of power, take a moment to complete the questionnaire in the Hands-On Exercise. What is your power profile? Where do you need improvement?

**Test Your Knowledge**

Sources of Power

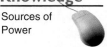

## From Teammate to Manager: Taking Charge

If you've been promoted to lead your group, you suddenly have more legitimate power. But to be an effective leader, you need to exercise that power carefully in a way that doesn't alienate but motivates your former coworkers:

- *Don't show off.* It might be tempting to strengthen your leadership role with an aggressive, dominating style, overseeing every detail. But that approach stirs resentment.

- *Do accept responsibility.* Trying to stay buddies with group members will undermine your ability to get the job done and will erode respect for you and your ability to handle the position. Collaborate when it's the best way to accomplish goals, not to save a friendship.

- *Do your homework.* Work with your new supervisor to define goals for yourself and your team. Strengthen your network of mentors to improve your management skills. Meet with your staff to go over your vision and expectations. Setting a direction for the team enhances your credibility (expert power).

- *Pay attention to team members' concerns.* Show them how meeting the group's goals will put them on track toward meeting their own needs.

SOURCE: Based on E Garone, "Managing Your Former Peers Takes Extra Effort," *The Wall Street Journal,* March 10, 2008, http://online.wsj.com.

## Practical Lessons from Research

Researchers have identified the following relationships between power bases and work outcomes such as job performance, job satisfaction, and turnover:

- Expert and referent power had a generally positive effect.
- Reward and legitimate power had a slightly positive effect.
- Coercive power had a slightly negative effect.[28]

A follow-up study involving 251 employed business school seniors looked at the relationship between influence styles and bases of power. This was a bottom-up study. In other words, employee perceptions of managerial influence and power were examined. Rational persuasion was found to be a highly acceptable managerial influence tactic. Why? Because employees perceived it to be associated with the three bases of power they viewed positively: legitimate, expert, and referent.[29]

In summary, expert and referent power appear to get the best *combination* of results and favorable reactions from lower-level employees.[30] For some practical advice on putting these lessons into practice as a new manager, see Skills & Best Practices. A good example is Lorraine Bolsinger, a vice president in charge of General Electric's Ecomagination program, which focuses on GE's environmentally friendly products and promotes GE activities with a positive impact on climate change. This position gave Bolsinger a tenuous degree of legitimate power, because she has no direct authority over the heads of the GE business units whose decisions she needs to influence. Bolsinger increased her expert power by tracking sales of Ecomagination products, demonstrating that the Ecomagination brand is contributing to GE's bottom-line success. Her track record at results-oriented GE has made her a respected leader in that company.[31]

**empowerment**

Sharing varying degrees of power with lower-level employees to tap their full potential.

## Employee Empowerment

An exciting trend in today's organizations centers on giving employees a greater say in the workplace. This trend wears various labels, including "participative management" and "open-book management."[32] Regardless of the label one prefers, it is all about empowerment. Management consultant and writer W Alan Rudolph offers this definition of **empowerment:** "recognizing and releasing into the organization the power that people already have in their wealth of useful knowledge, experience, and internal motivation."[33]

A recent study used 45 in-depth interviews to determine the meaning of empowerment from an employee point of view. Interestingly, employees interpreted empowerment in terms of how much personal responsibility and control over their work they experienced. Results also showed that employees varied in terms of how much empowerment they desired. Some employees liked to have responsibility and freedom, and others did not.[34] This conclusion is similar to what we learned about the job characteristics model of job design in Chapter 6.

The concept of empowerment requires some adjustment in traditional thinking. First and foremost, power is *not* a zero-sum situation where one person's gain is another's loss. Social power is unlimited. This requires win–win thinking. Frances Hesselbein, the woman credited with modernizing the Girl Scouts of the USA, put it this way: "The more power you give away, the more you have."[35] Authoritarian managers who view employee empowerment as a threat to their personal power are missing the point because of their win–lose thinking.[36]

The second adjustment to traditional thinking involves seeing empowerment as *a matter of degree* not as an either–or proposition.[37] Figure 13–1 illustrates how power can be shifted to the hands of nonmanagers step by step. The overriding goal is to increase productivity and competitiveness in leaner organizations. Each step in this evolution increases the power of organizational contributors who traditionally were told what, when, and how to do things. For example, at the level of consultation (influence sharing), Norman Regional Health System implements hundreds of employee suggestions each year, sending explanations to employees whose ideas are not accepted, so that everyone can see management's response. At the delegation level (power distribution), coffee and tea trader Equal Exchange lives out its "fair trade" mission by organizing as a democracy; each employee has one vote on decisions including what to sell and where to operate.[38]

**Group Exercise**
The Effects of Abusing Power

# Participative Management

Confusion exists about the exact meaning of participative management (PM). Management experts have clarified this situation by defining **participative management** as the process whereby employees play a direct role

> **participative management**
> Involving employees in various forms of decision making.

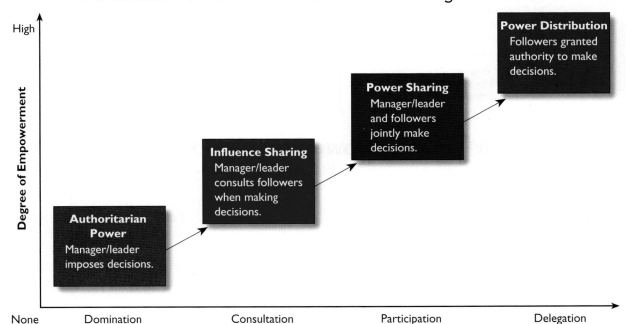

## The Evolution of Power: From Domination to Delegation    FIGURE 13–1

Degree of Empowerment (vertical axis, High)

**Power Distribution**
Followers granted authority to make decisions.

**Power Sharing**
Manager/leader and followers jointly make decisions.

**Influence Sharing**
Manager/leader consults followers when making decisions.

**Authoritarian Power**
Manager/leader imposes decisions.

None          Domination          Consultation          Participation          Delegation

## Participative Management at Linden Lab

Linden Lab is best known for creating an online virtual world Second Life. The 250-employee company's management style is just as innovative. Employees have a voice in management decisions and contribute to evaluating one another's performance.

At a traditional company, managers decide which tasks their employees will work on; at Linden Lab, employees decide how they will allocate their hours. How does the company ensure that the decisions are beneficial? Through "transparency," which means everyone sees what the projects are and has input into prioritizing them. Employees receive points when they invest in projects they think will be most beneficial to the company and in employees they believe are deserving. When a project is complete, the points are divided up among employees according to each person's contribution to the project. At the end of each quarter, employees receive a bonus based on dividing a share of quarterly profits among employees according to the number of points they earned.

Employees participate in performance feedback through a program called the Love Machine. When they notice someone doing exceptional work or appreciate a favor, they log in to the Love Machine, select the person's name from a menu, and type a short message of appreciation. Everyone in the company can see the messages, and at the end of each quarter, employees get a dollar for every favorable message. Again, transparency is how Linden Lab prevents employees from misusing their power.

**SOURCE: Based on M Wagner, "One-on-One with Second Life Creator Philip Rosedale,"** *Information Week,* **March 18, 2008, www.informationweek.com.**

in (1) setting goals, (2) making decisions, (3) solving problems, and (4) making changes in the organization. Participative management includes, but goes beyond, simply asking employees for their ideas or opinions.

Advocates of PM claim employee participation increases employee satisfaction, commitment, and performance (see Skills & Best Practices). Consistent with both Maslow's need theory and the job characteristics model of job design (see Chapter 6), participative management is predicted to increase motivation because it helps employees fulfill three basic needs: (1) autonomy, (2) meaningfulness of work, and (3) interpersonal contact. Satisfaction of these needs enhances feelings of acceptance and commitment, security, challenge, and satisfaction. In turn, these positive feelings supposedly lead to increased innovation and performance.[39]

Participative management does not work in all situations. The design of work, the level of trust between management and employees, and the employees' competence and readiness to participate represent three factors that influence the effectiveness of PM. With respect to the design of work, individual participation is counterproductive when employees are highly interdependent on each other, as on an assembly line. The problem with individual participation in this case is that interdependent employees generally do not have a broad understanding of the entire production process. Participative management also is less likely to succeed when employees do not trust management. Finally, PM is more effective when employees are competent, prepared, and interested in participating. 3M Corporation, a culture of innovation coupled with a talented workforce, provides fertile ground for the company's 3P (Pollution Prevention Pays) program. Thousands of employee ideas for being more environmentally friendly by reducing wasted energy and materials saved 3M more than $1 billion in the program's first year alone.[40]

# Making Empowerment Work

Empowerment has its fair share of critics and suffers from unrealistic expectations.[41] Research results to date are mixed, with a recent trend favoring empowerment.[42] We believe empowerment has good promise if managers go about it properly. Managers committed to the idea of employee empowerment need to follow the path of continuous improvement, learning from their successes and failures. Eight years of research with 10 "empowered" companies led consultant W Alan Randolph to formulate an empowerment plan that combines (1) information sharing to build trust, (2) creation of a structure in which employees have autonomy to make decisions aimed at a clear vision, and (3) development of effective teams.[43] This model requires clear goals and lots of relevant training, and the process may take several years to unfold.

# Organizational Politics and Impression Management

Most students of OB find the study of organizational politics intriguing. Perhaps this topic owes its appeal to the antics of television's corporate villains on *The Office, Ugly Betty,* and many other shows. As we will see, however, organizational politics includes, but is not limited to, dirty dealing. Organizational politics is an ever-present and sometimes annoying feature of modern work life. One expert recently observed, "Many 'new economy' companies use the acronym 'WOMBAT'—or waste of money, brains, and time—to describe office politics."[44] On the other hand, organizational politics is often a positive force in modern work organizations. Skillful and well-timed politics can help you get your point across, neutralize resistance to a key project, relieve stress, or get a choice job assignment.[45]

**learning objective 4**

Define *organizational politics,* explain what triggers it, and specify the three levels of political action in organizations.

We explore this important and interesting area by (1) defining the term *organizational politics,* (2) identifying three levels of political action, (3) discussing eight specific political tactics, (4) considering a related area called *impression management,* and (5) discussing how to curb organizational politics.

## Definition and Domain of Organizational Politics

"**Organizational politics** involves intentional acts of influence to enhance or protect the self-interest of individuals or groups."[46] An emphasis on *self-interest* distinguishes this form of social influence. Managers are endlessly challenged to achieve a workable balance between employees' self-interests and organizational interests, as discussed at the beginning of this chapter. When a proper balance exists, the pursuit of self-interest may serve the organization's interests. Political behavior becomes a negative force when self-interests erode or defeat organizational interests. For example, researchers have documented the political tactic of filtering and distorting information flowing up to the boss. This self-serving practice put the reporting employees in the best possible light.[47]

Donald Trump is known for being both political and influential. Fans of *The Apprentice* have seen Trump and the contestants on the show prove this to be true. How has he used his power and influence to his advantage?

**organizational politics**

Intentional enhancement of self-interest.

**Political Behavior Triggered by Uncertainty** Political maneuvering is triggered primarily by *uncertainty.* Five common sources of uncertainty within organizations are

1. Unclear objectives.
2. Vague performance measures.
3. Ill-defined decision processes.
4. Strong individual or group competition.[48]
5. Any type of change.

Closely akin to the second factor—vague performance measures—is the problem of *unclear performance–reward linkages* (recall our discussion of expectancy motivation theory in Chapter 7). This is a significant problem, according to the results of a recent survey of 10,000 employees. Regarding the statement "Employees who do a better job get paid more," 48% of the responding managers agreed, whereas only 31% of the nonmanagers agreed.[49] Employees tend to resort to political games when they are unsure about what it takes to get ahead. Relative to the fifth factor—any type of change—organization development specialist Anthony Raia noted, "Whatever we attempt to change, the political subsystem becomes active. Vested interests are almost always at stake and the distribution of power is challenged."[50]

We would expect a field sales representative, striving to achieve an assigned quota, to be less political than a management trainee working on a variety of projects. While some management trainees stake their career success on hard work, competence, and a bit of luck, many do not. These people attempt to gain a competitive edge through some combination of the political tactics discussed below. Meanwhile, the salesperson's performance is measured in actual sales, not in terms of being friends with the boss or taking credit for others' work. Thus, the management trainee would tend to be more political than the field salesperson because of greater uncertainty about management's expectations. Similarly, a manager placed in charge of a well-planned project is motivated to proceed with its implementation, while a manager charged with a project expected to fail is more likely to be preoccupied with political questions such as why he or she was selected for the assignment, whether management might be persuaded to change course, and how to salvage his or her reputation if the project is a disaster.[51]

Because employees generally experience greater uncertainty during the earlier stages of their careers, are junior employees more political than more senior ones? The answer is yes, according to a survey of 243 employed adults in upstate New York. In fact, one senior employee nearing retirement told the researcher: "I used to play political games when I was younger. Now I just do my job."[52]

**Three Levels of Political Action**    Although much political maneuvering occurs at the individual level, it also can involve group or collective action. Figure 13–2 illustrates three different levels of political action: the individual level, the coalition level, and the network level.[53] Each level has its distinguishing characteristics. At the individual level, personal self-interests are pursued by the individual. The political aspects of coalitions and networks are not so obvious, however.

**coalition**

Temporary groupings of people who actively pursue a single issue.

People with a common interest can become a political coalition by fitting the following definition. In an organizational context, a **coalition** is an informal group bound together by the *active* pursuit of a *single* issue. Coalitions may or may not coincide with formal group

## FIGURE 13–2
Levels of Political Action in Organizations

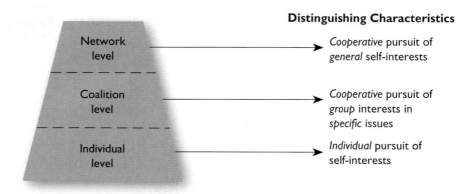

**Distinguishing Characteristics**

Network level → *Cooperative* pursuit of *general* self-interests

Coalition level → *Cooperative* pursuit of *group* interests in *specific* issues

Individual level → *Individual* pursuit of self-interests

membership. When the target issue is resolved (a sexually harassing supervisor is fired, for example), the coalition disbands. Experts note that political coalitions have "fuzzy boundaries," meaning they are fluid in membership, flexible in structure, and temporary in duration.[54]

Coalitions are a potent political force in organizations. In recent years, coalitions on the corporate boards of Home Depot, Computer Associates, and Hewlett-Packard ousted the heads of those companies.

A third level of political action involves networks.[55] Unlike coalitions, which pivot on specific issues, networks are loose associations of individuals seeking social support for their general self-interests. Politically, networks are people oriented, while coalitions are issue oriented. Networks have broader and longer term agendas than do coalitions. For instance, Avon's Hispanic and Latino employees have built a network to enhance the members' career opportunities.

**Frequently Used Political Tactics**    Anyone who has worked in an organization has firsthand knowledge of blatant politicking. Blaming someone else for your mistake is an obvious political ploy. So is trafficking in favors, as reported in *The Wall Street Journal*:

> In his study of customer-service agents, Frank Flynn, an associate professor at Stanford's Graduate School of Business who studies favor exchange, found that soon after the completion of a favor, its recipient thought it was more valuable than the person who granted it. Over time, however, they reversed roles: "The person who received it didn't think it was that big a deal, but the person who granted the favor thought it was a bigger deal."
>
> Understanding the shelf life of a favor granted, some colleagues require immediate favor redemption. Richard Vandagriff occasionally worked with a contractor who was one of those favor accountants. "He doesn't keep a book, but might as well," he says. Once, the man even counterfeited a favor—resetting furnace controls that didn't need resetting.
>
> "Now I need a favor from you," he told Mr. Vandagriff.
>
> "It was a setup to get me to get one of my people to help him."
>
> It worked.[56]

But other political tactics are more subtle. Researchers have identified a range of political behavior.

Although researchers have proposed many different categories of political tactics, two studies put these ideas to the test by asking samples of 87 U.S. and 250 British managers to identify the types of political behaviors they had experienced. Top-, middle-, and low-level managers were included in the samples. The following set of tactics was perceived as happening more frequently.[57]

1. Building a network of useful contacts.
2. Using "key players" to support initiatives.
3. Making friends with power brokers.
4. Bending the rules to fit the situation.
5. Self-promotion.
6. Creating a favorable image. (Also known as *impression management*.)[58]
7. Praising others (ingratiation).
8. Attacking or blaming others.
9. Using information as a political tool.

The researchers distinguished between reactive and proactive political tactics. Some of the tactics, such as scapegoating, were *reactive* because the intent was to *defend* one's self-interest. Other tactics, such as building a network of useful contacts, were *proactive* because they sought to *promote* the individual's self-interest.[59]

5 learning objective

Distinguish between favorable and unfavorable impression management tactics.

# Impression Management

**Impression management** is defined as "the process by which people attempt to control or manipulate the reactions of others to images of themselves or their ideas."[60] This encompasses how one talks, behaves, and looks. Most impression management attempts are directed at making a *good* impression on relevant others. But, as we will see, some employees strive to make a *bad* impression. For purposes of conceptual clarity, we will focus on *upward* impression management (trying to impress one's immediate supervisor) because it is most relevant for managers. Still, it is good to remember that *anyone* can be the intended target of impression management. Parents, teachers, peers, employees, and customers are all fair game when it comes to managing the impressions of others.

**impression management**

**Getting others to see us in a certain manner.**

"So, with just a few extra lines and a splash of color, our dismal sales become a lovely mountain scene."

*Mark Anderson, Andertoons.com. Reprinted with permission.*

Impression management would appear to be a low priority for Jim Buckmaster, CEO of craigslist.org. Buckmaster wears casual dress to work, shares an office with company founder Craig Newmark, and takes public transportation to his rented house. His wife picks him up at the ferry landing.

**Good Impressions** If you "dress for success," project an upbeat attitude at all times, and avoid offending others, you are engaging in favorable impression management—particularly so if your motive is to improve your chances of getting what you want in life.[61] There are questionable ways to create a good impression, as well. For instance, Stewart Friedman, director of the University of Pennsylvania's Leadership Program, offered this gem:

> Last year, I was doing some work with a large bank. The people there told me a story that astounded me: After 7 PM, people would open the door to their office, drape a spare jacket on the back of their chair, lay a set of glasses down on some reading material on their desk—and then go home for the night. The point of this elaborate gesture was to create the illusion that they were just out grabbing dinner and would be returning to burn the midnight oil.[62]

Impression management often strays into unethical territory.

A statistical factor analysis of the influence attempts reported by a sample of 84 bank employees (including 74 women) identified three categories of favorable upward impression management tactics.[63] Favorable upward impression management tactics can be *job-focused* (manipulating information about one's job performance), *supervisor-focused* (praising and doing favors for one's supervisor), and *self-focused* (presenting oneself as a polite and nice person). A moderate amount of upward impression management is a necessity for the average employee today. For example, a review of 69 studies suggests ingratiation can slightly improve your performance appraisal results and make your boss like you significantly more.[64] Too little impression management, and busy managers are liable to overlook some of your valuable contributions when they make job assignment, pay, and promotion decisions. Too much, and you run the risk of being branded a "schmoozer," a "phony," and other unflattering things by your coworkers.[65] Noticeable flattery and ingratiation can backfire by embarrassing the target person and damaging one's credibility.[66] Also, the risk of unintended insult is very high when impression management tactics cross gender, racial, ethnic, and cultural lines.[67] International management experts warn:

> The impression management tactic is only as effective as its correlation to accepted norms about behavioral presentation. In other words, slapping a Japanese subordinate on the back with a rousing "Good work, Hiro!" will not create the desired impression in Hiro's mind that the expatriate intended. In fact, the behavior will likely create the opposite impression.[68]

**Bad Impressions**   At first glance, the idea of consciously trying to make a bad impression in the workplace seems absurd.[69] But an interesting new line of impression management research has uncovered both motives and tactics for making oneself look *bad*. In a survey of the work experiences of business students at a large northwestern U.S. university, more than half "reported witnessing a case of someone intentionally looking bad at work."[70] Why? Four motives came out of the study:

> (1) *Avoidance:* Employee seeks to avoid additional work, stress, burnout, or an unwanted transfer or promotion. (2) *Obtain concrete rewards:* Employee seeks to obtain a pay raise or a desired transfer, promotion, or demotion. (3) *Exit:* Employee seeks to get laid off, fired, or suspended, and perhaps also to collect unemployment or workers' compensation. (4) *Power:* Employee seeks to control, manipulate, or intimidate others, get revenge, or make someone else look bad.[71]

Within the context of these motives, *unfavorable* upward impression management makes sense.

Five unfavorable upward impression management tactics identified by the researchers are as follows:

- *Decreasing performance*—restricting productivity, making more mistakes than usual, lowering quality, neglecting tasks.
- *Not working to potential*—pretending ignorance, having unused capabilities.
- *Withdrawing*—being tardy, taking excessive breaks, faking illness.
- *Displaying a bad attitude*—complaining, getting upset and angry, acting strangely, not getting along with coworkers.
- *Broadcasting limitations*—letting coworkers know about one's physical problems and mistakes (both verbally and nonverbally).[72]

Recommended ways to manage employees who try to make a bad impression can be found throughout this book. They include more challenging work, greater autonomy, better feedback, supportive leadership, clear and reasonable goals, and a less stressful work setting.

# Keeping Organizational Politics in Check

learning objective 6

Explain how to manage organizational politics.

A recent meta-analysis of 59 studies involving 25,059 people revealed that perceptions of organizational politics were negatively associated with job satisfaction and organizational commitment, and positively related to job stress and intentions to quit.[73] Do these results suggest that managers should attempt to stop people from being political? Good luck. Organizational politics cannot be eliminated. A manager would be naive to expect such an outcome. But political maneuvering can and should be managed to keep it constructive and within reasonable bounds. Harvard's Abraham

## SKILLS & BEST PRACTICES

# How to Keep Organizational Politics within Reasonable Bounds

- Screen out overly political individuals at hiring time.
- Create an open-book management system.
- Make sure every employee knows how the business works and has a personal line of sight to key results with corresponding measureable objectives for individual accountability.
- Have nonfinancial people interpret periodic financial and accounting statements for all employees.
- Establish formal conflict resolution and grievance processes.
- As an ethics filter, do only what you would feel comfortable doing on national television.
- Publicly recognize and reward people who get real results without political games.

**SOURCE: Adapted in part from discussion in L B MacGregor Serven, *The End of Office Politics as Usual* (New York: American Management Association, 2002), pp 184–99.**

Zaleznik put the issue this way: "People can focus their attention on only so many things. The more it lands on politics, the less energy—emotional and intellectual—is available to attend to the problems that fall under the heading of real work."[74]

An individual's degree of politicalness is a matter of personal values, ethics, and temperament. People who are either strictly nonpolitical or highly political generally pay a price for their behavior. The former may experience slow promotions and feel left out, while the latter may run the risk of being called self-serving and lose their credibility. People at both ends of the political spectrum may be considered poor team players. A moderate amount of prudent political behavior generally is considered a survival tool in complex organizations. Experts remind us that

> political behavior has earned a bad name only because of its association with politicians. On its own, the use of power and other resources to obtain your objectives is not inherently unethical. It all depends on what the preferred objectives are.[75]

With this perspective in mind, the practical steps in Skills & Best Practices are recommended. Notice the importance of reducing uncertainty through clear performance–reward linkages. Measurable objectives are management's first line of defense against negative expressions of organizational politics. General Electric studiously cultivates a no-nonsense culture where political maneuvering and impression management are discouraged. Kevin Sharer, the CEO of bio-tech giant Amgen, who was a GE executive, explains:

> It has . . . set a standard in candor—that is, dealing with reality and rigor in communicating around the company. Everybody has a real chance to know exactly where they are. There is no puffery. That is buttressed by rigorous, fact-based, honest assessment of the business situation. There isn't an ounce of denial in the place.[76]

# key terms

# chapter summary

- *Name five "soft" and four "hard" influence tactics, and summarize Cialdini's principles of influence and persuasion.* Five soft influence tactics are rational persuasion, inspirational appeals, consultation, ingratiation, and personal appeals. They are more friendly and less coercive than the four hard influence tactics: exchange, coalition tactics, pressure, and legitimating tactics. According to research, soft tactics are better for generating commitment and are perceived as more fair than hard tactics. Cialdini's six principles of influence and persuasion are *liking* (favoring friends), *reciprocity* (belief that one good or bad turn deserves to be repaid in kind), *social proof* (following those similar to oneself), *consistency* (following through on personal commitments), *authority* (deferring to credible and respected experts), and *scarcity* (seeking things of limited availability).

- *Identify and briefly describe French and Raven's five bases of power.* French and Raven's five bases of power are reward power (rewarding compliance), coercive power (punishing noncompliance), legitimate power (relying on formal authority), expert power (providing needed information), and referent power (relying on personal attraction).

- *Define the term* empowerment, *and explain how to make it succeed.* Empowerment involves sharing varying degrees of power and decision-making authority with lower-level employees to better serve the customer. According to Randolph's model, empowerment requires active sharing of key information, structure that encourages autonomy, transfer of control from managers to teams, and persistence. Trust and training also are very important.

- *Define organizational politics,* explain what triggers it, *and specify the three levels of political action in organizations.* Organizational politics is defined as intentional acts of influence to enhance or protect the self-interests of individuals or groups. Uncertainty triggers most politicking in organizations. Political action occurs at individual, coalition, and network levels. Coalitions are informal, temporary, and single-issue alliances.

- *Distinguish between favorable and unfavorable impression management tactics.* Favorable upward impression management can be job-focused (manipulating information about one's job performance), supervisor-focused (praising or doing favors for the boss), or self-focused (being polite and nice). Unfavorable upward impression management tactics include decreasing performance, not working to potential, withdrawing, displaying a bad attitude, and broadcasting one's limitations.

- *Explain how to manage organizational politics.* Although organizational politics cannot be eliminated, managers can keep it within reasonable bounds. Measurable objectives for personal accountability are key. Participative management also helps, especially in the form of open-book management. Formal conflict resolution and grievance programs are helpful. Overly political people should not be hired, and employees who get results without playing political games should be publicly recognized and rewarded. The "how-would-it-look-on-TV" ethics test can limit political maneuvering.

# discussion questions

1. What influence and political tactics were used by Shai Agassi in the chapter-opening case? Explain.
2. Before reading this chapter, did the term *power* have a negative connotation for you? Do you view it differently now? Explain.
3. In your opinion, how much empowerment is too much in today's workplaces?
4. Why do you think organizational politics is triggered primarily by uncertainty?
5. How much impression management do you see in your classroom or workplace today? Citing specific examples, are those tactics effective?

# ethical dilemma

## Should Workers Be Suspended for Lying about Smoking?

Whirlpool charges smokers $500 a year more than non-smokers for insurance coverage. This surcharge created feelings of inequity and motivated employees to lie about their smoking habits on their insurance application forms. Recently, 39 workers were suspended because they were seen smoking outside a factory in Evansville, Indiana. Consider what led to these suspensions.

> The workers' union challenged the smoker fees in 2006, citing a state law, and an arbiter ruled the company had to pay back the surcharges collected during a 28-month period through June 2006. The amount was expected to be $1,000 per employee. . . .
>
> Last month, Whirlpool's suit to overturn the ruling was dismissed in a sealed settlement, setting the stage for rebates.
>
> The suspended workers drew attention to their smoking when they asked for the rebates, prompting the company to check to see whether they had paid the fees. Apparently they hadn't.
>
> Whirlpool suspended the employees because it has a policy stating that "falsifying company documents is a serious offense" punishable by suspension or termination.[77]

While you consider what should be done in this case, keep in mind that a study by Mercer, a consulting firm, indicated that only 5 percent of companies with 500 or more employees charge smokers more than nonsmokers for insurance.

### What Is Your Position about the Suspended Employees?

1. The employees lied and thus violated corporate policy. They should be terminated. If the company doesn't hold the line on this policy, what does it say about holding employees accountable for other corporate policies?

2. The company should give rebates only to those who paid the surcharges. Further, the smokers who lied on the insurance applications should be asked to complete a new form, but should not be suspended or terminated. They simply showed bad judgment and deserve a break.

3. The company should not be asking about health-related habits on an insurance enrollment form. As such, employees should not be suspended or terminated for lying. The lying employees should not receive a rebate.

4. The organization needs to be supportive and offer some type of wellness program to help employees quit smoking. This program should be part of the benefit package. The lying employees should be reinstated, but not given any rebates.

For an interpretation of this situation, visit our Web site, at
**www.mhhe.com/kinickiob4e**

---

If you're looking for additional study materials, be sure to check out the Online Learning Center at

**www.mhhe.com/kinickiob4e**

for more information and interactivities that correspond to this chapter.

# chapter Fourteen

# Leadership

**LEARNING OBJECTIVES**

**After reading the material in this chapter, you should be able to:**

1. Review trait theory research, and discuss the takeaways from both the trait and behavioral styles theories of leadership.

2. Explain, according to Fiedler's contingency model, how leadership style interacts with situational control.

3. Discuss House's revised path–goal theory and Hersey and Blanchard's situational leadership theory.

4. Describe the difference between transactional and transformational leadership and discuss how transformational leadership transforms followers and work groups.

5. Explain the leader–member exchange (LMX) model of leadership and the concept of shared leadership.

6. Review the principles of servant-leadership and discuss Level 5 leadership.

7. Describe the follower's role in the leadership process.

Indra Nooyi, CEO of PepsiCo.

Indra Nooyi is an entirely different kind of CEO, a product of her native India as well as of PepsiCo's family-values approach to grooming CEOs. She is not hung up on pay. She's not shy about asking for help when she needs it. She's 52 years old and does not plan for this job to be her last. Her friend Henry Kissinger predicts that it's only a matter of time before she is plucked for a big Washington post, possibly a cabinet job, and Nooyi acknowledges that at some point, she'd like that. She's cosmopolitan, rigorously educated, and a strategic thinker—her background is Boston Consulting Group—much more interested in the burgeoning markets in Russia and China than in the noisy U.S. cola wars.

Since becoming CEO, she has reorganized PepsiCo to make it less fixated on the U.S. and broadened the power structure by doubling her executive team to 29. . . . She has created a motto—"Performance With Purpose"—that puts a positive spin on how she wants PepsiCo to do business both at home and abroad.

It essentially boils down to balancing the profit motive with making healthier snacks, striving for a net-zero impact on the environment, and taking care of your workforce. "If all you want is to screw this company down tight and get double-digit earnings growth and nothing else, then I'm the wrong person," she says. "Companies today are bigger than many economies. We are little republics. We are engines of efficiency. If companies don't do [responsible] things, who is going to? Why not start making change now?" . . .

Indra Krishnamurthy Nooyi has one of those incredible, impeccable track records. She grew up in Chennai (formerly Madras), on the southeast coast of

India, the daughter of an accountant and a stay-at-home mother who "encouraged us but held us back, told us we could rule the country as long as we kept the home fires burning," she says. Her grandfather, a retired judge, scrutinized report cards, presided over homework, and in his later years prepared her in advance for all the theorems in her geometry book to be sure she'd be able to excel if he were to die before the school year ended. Every night at dinner her mother would present a world problem to Nooyi and her sister and have them compete to solve it as if they were a President or Prime Minister. Though her family is Hindu, Nooyi attended a Catholic school, was an avid debater, played cricket, badgered her parents (and the nuns) until she was allowed to play the guitar, and then formed an all-girl rock band—the first ever at the Holy Angels Convent. . . .

One of Nooyi's most stunning talents is the art of suasion. She can rouse an audience and rally them around something as mind-numbing as a new companywide software installation. Her new motto, "Performance With Purpose," is both a means of "herding the organization" and of presenting PepsiCo globally. Because these days, she knows, you can't take even an emerging market for granted. . . .

Nooyi sells her ideas with a famous intensity. Her colleagues say she "brings her whole self" to the office. She insists that everybody's birthday is celebrated with a cake . . . and everyone is forever 35. Her karaoke machine is the ubiquitous party game at every PepsiCo gathering. She talks about being a mother. In December one executive recalls how Nooyi described to her whole team what it felt like to be a soccer mom whose week it was to bring the treats. You get a very specific list. You can't have nuts. You can't have wheat. The situation confounds the CEO mom, she confesses, urging them to "make it easy for me so I don't have to think. We can do this. We already have the products."

Just as she was held to very high standards in her youth, she expects everyone

around her to measure up. She has red, green, and purple pens and uses them liberally to mark up everything that crosses her desk. "My scribbles are legendary—*legendary*," she says with a twinkle. Like "I have never seen such gross incompetence." Or " 'This is unacceptable,' and I underline 'unacceptable' three times," she says. She's joking, but she gets her point across. One of her so-called love letters once scared some secretaries so badly that she had to go assure them that their bosses were not about to lose their jobs.

"She challenges you," says Tim Minges, president of the Asia Pacific region. When his team couldn't find an inexpensive alternative to palm oil for its products in Thailand last year, she kept pushing and pushing, saying, "I hear you, I hear you, so what's the right solution?" until they came up with one: rice bran oil. "But don't try to delegate up, because she will bounce it right back in your face," he says. . . .

With her team, there's nothing remote about Nooyi. She is part schoolmarm, part mother hen. She once told Hugh Johnston, who worked for her in corporate strategy, that he was dressed like a bum. At the time he was helping roll out the company's IT program, and he replied, "Indra, these are IT people; this is what we do. We don't go out of the building." When he moved to headquarters, she told him where to shop, and he has acquired a whole new wardrobe. She knows she is demanding, and she worries about it. She throws dinners for members of her team and their spouses, including Q&A sessions in which she insists on getting questions from the spouses and won't sit down until she does.

She appreciates the support from families, she says, because her career has been tough on her own family.[1]

**Would you like to work for Indra Nooyi? Explain why. For an interpretation of this case and additional comments, visit our Online Learning Center at**

**www.mhhe.com/ kinickiob4e.**

FOR DISCUSSION

SOMEONE ONCE OBSERVED THAT a leader is a person who finds out which way the parade is going, jumps in front, and yells "Follow me!" The plain fact is that this approach to leadership has little chance of working in today's rapidly changing world. As illustrated in the chapter opening case, leadership involves more than simply taking charge. Indra Nooyi is focused on more than PepsiCo's profits. She wants the firm to benefit consumers' health, reduce its impact on the environment, and provide satisfying work for employees. In short, successful leaders are those individuals who can step into a situation and make a noticeable difference. But how much of a difference can leaders make in modern organizations?

OB researchers have discovered that leaders can make a difference.[2] One study, for instance, revealed that leadership was positively associated with net profits from 167 companies over a time span of 20 years.[3] Research also showed that a coach's leadership skills affected the success of his or her team. Specifically, teams in both Major League Baseball and college basketball won more games when players perceived the coach to be an effective leader.[4] Rest assured, leadership make a difference!

After formally defining the term *leadership,* this chapter focuses on the following areas: (1) trait and behavioral approaches to leadership, (2) alternative situational theories of leadership, (3) the full-range model of leadership, and (4) additional perspectives on leadership. Because there are many different leadership theories within each of these areas, it is impossible to discuss them all. This chapter reviews those theories with the most research support.

# What Does Leadership Involve?

Disagreement about the definition of leadership stems from the fact that it involves a complex interaction among the leader, the followers, and the situation. For example, some researchers define leadership in terms of personality and physical traits, while others believe leadership is represented by a set of prescribed behaviors. In contrast, other researchers believe that leadership is a temporary role that can be filled by anyone. There is a common thread, however, among the different definitions of leadership. The common thread is social influence.

**leadership**

Influencing employees to voluntarily pursue organizational goals.

As the term is used in this chapter, **leadership** is defined as "a social influence process in which the leader seeks the voluntary participation of subordinates in an effort to reach organizational goals."[5] This definition implies that leadership involves more than wielding power and exercising authority and is exhibited at different levels. At the individual level, for example, leadership involves mentoring, coaching, inspiring, and motivating. Leaders build teams, create cohesion, and resolve conflict at the group level. Finally, leaders build culture and create change at the organizational level.[6]

There are two components of leadership missing from the above definition: the moral and follower perspectives. Leadership is not a moral concept. History is filled with examples of effective leaders who were killers, corrupt, and morally bankrupt. Barbara Kellerman, a leadership expert, commented on this notion by concluding "Leaders are like the rest of us: trustworthy and deceitful, cowardly and brave, greedy and generous. To assume that all good leaders are good people is to be willfully blind to the reality of the human condition, and it more severely limits our scope for becoming more effective at leadership."[7] The point is that good leaders develop a keen sense of their strengths and weaknesses and build on their positive attributes.

Moreover, research on leadership has only recently begun to recognize that the expectations, attitudes, and behavior of followers also affect how well the presumed leader can lead. "Followership" is discussed in the last section of this chapter.

# Trait and Behavioral Theories of Leadership

This section examines the two earliest approaches used to explain leadership. Trait theories focused on identifying the personal traits that differentiated leaders from followers. Behavioral theorists examined leadership from a different perspective. They tried to uncover the different kinds of leader behaviors that resulted in higher work group performance. Both approaches to leadership can teach current and future managers valuable lessons about leading.

**learning objective 1**

Review trait theory research, and discuss the takeaways from both the trait and behavioral styles theories of leadership.

## Trait Theory

Trait theory is the successor to what was called the "great man" theory of leadership. This approach was based on the assumption that leaders such as Abraham Lincoln, Martin Luther King, or Jack Welch were born with some inborn ability to lead. In contrast, trait theorists believed that leadership traits were not innate, but could be developed through experience and learning. A **leader trait** is a physical or personality characteristic that can be used to differentiate leaders from followers.

Before World War II, hundreds of studies were conducted to pinpoint the traits of successful leaders. Dozens of leadership traits were identified. During the postwar period, however, enthusiasm was replaced by widespread criticism. Researchers simply were unable to uncover a consistent set of traits that accurately predicted which individuals became leaders in organizations.

**leader trait**

**Personal characteristic that differentiates leaders from followers.**

**Contemporary Trait Research**   Two OB researchers concluded in 1983 that past trait data may have been incorrectly analyzed. By applying modern statistical techniques to an old database, they demonstrated that the majority of a leader's behavior could be attributed to stable underlying traits.[8] Unfortunately, their methodology did not single out specific traits.

More recently, results from three separate meta-analyses shed light on important leadership traits. The first was conducted in 1986 by Robert Lord and his associates. Based on a reanalysis of past studies, Lord concluded that people have leadership *prototypes* that affect our perceptions of who is and who is not an effective leader. Your **leadership prototype** is a mental representation of the traits and behaviors that you believe are possessed by leaders. We thus tend to perceive that someone is a leader when he or she exhibits traits or behaviors that are consistent with our prototypes.[9] Lord's research demonstrated that people are perceived as being leaders when they exhibit the traits associated with intelligence, masculinity, and dominance. However, a recent study of almost 6,000 middle managers in 33 countries found that prototypes varied somewhat, depending on the organization's structure.[10] Another study of 6,052 middle-level managers from 22 European countries revealed that leadership prototypes are culturally based. In other words, leadership prototypes are influenced by national cultural values.[11] Researchers have not yet identified a set of global leadership prototypes.

**leadership prototype**

**Mental representation of the traits and behaviors possessed by leaders.**

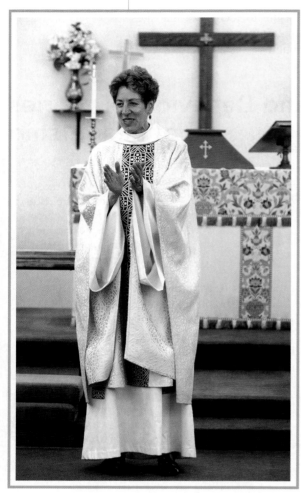

**Bishop Katharine Jefferts Schori was recently appointed the first woman bishop in the American Episcopal Church. Among the personal traits that contribute to her leadership ability are her appetite for challenge and risk-taking—she holds a pilot's license, is a skilled mountaineer, and entered the Episcopal priesthood at 40 after a successful career in oceanography. She is also fluent in Spanish. Another trait, her sex, may prove controversial for some, but Jefferts Shori views it as a means "to build a holy community."**

The next two meta-analyses were completed by Timothy Judge and his colleagues. The first examined the relationship among the Big Five personality traits (see Table 5–1 for a review of these traits) and leadership emergence and effectiveness in 94 studies. Results revealed that extraversion was most consistently and positively related to both leadership emergence and effectiveness. Conscientiousness and openness to experience also were positively correlated with leadership effectiveness.[12] Judge's second meta-analysis involved 151 samples and demonstrated that intelligence was modestly related to leadership effectiveness. Judge concluded that personality is more important than intelligence when selecting leaders.[13]

This conclusion is supported by research that examined emotional and political intelligence. Recall that *emotional intelligence,* which was discussed in Chapter 5, is the ability to manage oneself and one's relationships in mature and constructive ways. Given that leadership is an influence process, it should come as no surprise that emotional intelligence is associated with leadership effectiveness.[14] Political intelligence is a recently proposed leadership trait and represents an offshoot of emotional intelligence. Politically intelligent leaders use power and intimidation to push followers in the pursuit of an inspiring vision and challenging goals. Although these leaders can be insensitive, hard to work with, and demanding, they tend to be effective when faced with stagnant and change-resistant situations.[15] Consider the following description of Apple's CEO, Steve Jobs:

> Jobs is among the most controversial figures in business. He oozes smug superiority, lacing his public comments with ridicule of Apple's rivals. . . . No CEO is more willful, or more brazen, at making his own rules, in ways both good and bad. And no CEO is more personally identified with— and controlling of—the day-to-day affairs of his business. . . . He has listed himself as "co-inventor" on 103 separate Apple patents, everything from the user interface for the iPod to the support system for the glass staircase used in Apple's dazzling retail stores. . . .
>
> Jobs' personal abuses are also legend: He parks his Mercedes in handicapped spaces, periodically reduces subordinates to tears, and fires employees in angry tantrums. Yet many of his top deputies at Apple have worked with him for years, and even some of those who have departed say that although it's often brutal and Jobs hogs the credit, they've never done better work. . . .
>
> Stanford management science professor Robert Sutton . . . says . . . , "The degree to which people in Silicon Valley are afraid of Jobs is unbelievable. . . . He made

people feel terrible; he made people cry. But he was almost always right, and even when he was wrong, it was so creative it was still amazing."[16]

Politically intelligent leaders seem to walk a fine line between using intimidation to achieve organizational goals and humiliation and bullying to make themselves feel good. Future research is needed to examine the long-term effectiveness of leaders with political intelligence.

Another open question with regard to trait theory is whether more of a trait is necessarily better. In a series of studies of MBA students, those with a moderate level of assertiveness were seen as the most effective leaders, as measured in terms of positive relationships and goal achievement. Individuals who scored very high or very low in assertiveness rated as less effective leaders.[17] Thus, it might be important to consider not only *which* traits are associated with leadership but also *what degree* of those traits contributes to leadership effectiveness.

**Farcus**

by David Waisglass
Gordon Coulthart

© 1992 Farcus Cartoons    WAISGLASS/COULTHART    www.farcus.com

**"Because I'm the boss, that's why!"**

**Gender and Leadership**    The increase of women in the workforce has generated much interest in understanding the similarities and differences in female and male leaders. Three separate meta-analyses and a series of studies conducted by consultants across the country uncovered the following differences: (1) Men and women were seen as displaying more task and social leadership, respectively;[18] (2) women used a more democratic or participative style than men, and men used a more autocratic and directive style than women;[19] (3) men and women were equally assertive;[20] and (4) women executives, when rated by their peers, managers, and direct reports, scored higher than their male counterparts on a variety of effectiveness criteria.[21]

**What Are the Takeaways from Trait Theory?**    We can no longer afford to ignore the implications of leadership traits. Traits play a central role in how we perceive leaders, and they ultimately impact leadership effectiveness.[22] What can be learned from the previous research on traits? Integrating across past studies leads to the extended list of positive traits shown in Table 14–1. This list provides guidance regarding the leadership traits you should attempt to cultivate if you want to assume a leadership role. Personality tests, which were discussed in Chapter 5, and other trait assessments can be used to evaluate your strengths and weaknesses vis-à-vis these traits. Results can then be used to prepare a personal development plan.[23]

There are two organizational applications of trait theory. First, organizations may want to include personality and trait assessments into their selection and promotion processes. It is important to remember that this should only be done with valid measures of leadership traits.[24] Second, management development programs can be used to enhance employees' leadership traits. Hasbro, Inc., for example, sent a targeted group of managers to a program that included a combination of 360-degree feedback, trait assessments, executive coaching, classroom training, and problem-solving assignments on real-life projects. Hasbro is very excited and pleased with the results of their leadership development program.[25]

**Group Exercise**

What Is Your Motivation to Lead?

**Self-Assessment Exercise**

Do You Have What It Takes to Be a Leader?

**TABLE 14–1** | Key Positive Leadership Traits

| Positive Traits | |
| --- | --- |
| Intelligence | Sociability |
| Self-confidence | Emotional intelligence |
| Determination | Extraversion |
| Honesty/integrity | Conscientiousness |

# Behavioral Styles Theory

This phase of leadership research began during World War II as part of an effort to develop better military leaders. It was an outgrowth of two events: the seeming inability of trait theory to explain leadership effectiveness and the human relations movement, an outgrowth of the Hawthorne Studies. The thrust of early behavioral leadership theory was to focus on leader behavior, instead of on personality traits. It was believed that leader behavior directly affected work group effectiveness. This led researchers to identify patterns of behavior (called leadership styles) that enabled leaders to effectively influence others.

**The Ohio State Studies**    Researchers at Ohio State University began by generating a list of behaviors exhibited by leaders. Ultimately, the Ohio State researchers concluded there were only two independent dimensions of leader behavior: consideration and initiating structure. **Consideration** involves leader behavior associated with creating mutual respect or trust and focuses on a concern for group members' needs and desires. **Initiating structure** is leader behavior that organizes and defines what group members should be doing to maximize output. These two dimensions of leader behavior were oriented at right angles to yield four behavioral styles of leadership: low structure–high consideration, high structure–high consideration, low structure–low consideration, and high structure–low consideration.

**consideration**

Creating mutual respect and trust with followers.

**initiating structure**

Organizing and defining what group members should be doing.

It initially was hypothesized that a high-structure–high-consideration style would be the one best style of leadership. Through the years, the effectiveness of the high–high style has been tested many times. Overall, results have been mixed and there has been very little research about these leader behaviors until just recently. Findings from a 2004 meta-analysis of 130 studies and more than 20,000 individuals demonstrated that consideration and initiating structure had a moderately strong, significant relationship with leadership outcomes. Results revealed that followers performed more effectively for structuring leaders even though they preferred considerate leaders.[26] All told, results do not support the idea that there is one best style of leadership, but they do confirm the importance of considerate and structuring leader behaviors. Follower satisfaction, motivation, and performance are significantly associated with these two leader behaviors. Future research is needed to incorporate them into more contemporary leadership theories.

**University of Michigan Studies**    As in the Ohio State studies, this research sought to identify behavioral differences between effective and ineffective leaders.

Researchers identified two different styles of leadership: one was employee centered, the other was job centered. These behavioral styles parallel the consideration and initiating-structure styles identified by the Ohio State group.

### What Are the Takeaways from Behavioral Styles Theory?

By emphasizing leader *behavior,* something that is learned, the behavioral style approach makes it clear that leaders are made, not born. Given what we know about behavior shaping and model-based training, leader *behaviors* can be systematically improved and developed.[27]

Behavioral styles research also revealed that there is no one best style of leadership. The effectiveness of a particular leadership style depends on the situation at hand. For instance, employees prefer structure over consideration when faced with role ambiguity.[28] Finally, research also reveals that it is important to consider the difference between how frequently and how effectively managers exhibit various leader behaviors. For example, a manager might ineffectively display a lot of considerate leader behaviors. Such a style is likely to frustrate employees and possibly result in lowered job satisfaction and performance. Because the frequency of exhibiting leadership behaviors is secondary in importance to effectiveness, managers are encouraged to concentrate on improving the effective execution of their leader behaviors.[29] Finally, Peter Drucker, an internationally renowned management expert and consultant, recommended a set of nine behaviors (see Skills & Best Practices) managers can focus on to improve their leadership effectiveness. The first two practices provide the knowledge leaders need. The next four help leaders convert knowledge into effective action, and the following two ensure that the whole organization feels responsible and accountable. Drucker refers to the last recommendation as a managerial rule.

---

**SKILLS & BEST PRACTICES**

## Peter Drucker's Tips for Improving Leadership Effectiveness

1. Determine what needs to be done.

2. Determine the right thing to do for the welfare of the entire enterprise or organization.

3. Develop action plans that specify desired results, probable restraints, future revisions, check-in points, and implications for how one should spend his or her time.

4. Take responsibility for decisions.

5. Take responsibility for communicating action plans and give people the information they need to get the job done.

6. Focus on opportunities rather than problems. Do not sweep problems under the rug, and treat change as an opportunity rather than a threat.

7. Run productive meetings. Different types of meetings require different forms of preparation and different results. Prepare accordingly.

8. Think and say "we" rather than "I." Consider the needs and opportunities of the organization before thinking of your own opportunities and needs.

9. Listen first, speak last.

---

# Situational Theories

Situational leadership theories grew out of an attempt to explain the inconsistent findings about traits and styles. **Situational theories** propose that the effectiveness of a particular style of leader behavior depends on the situation. As situations change, different styles become appropriate. This directly challenges the idea of one best style of leadership. Let us closely examine three alternative situational theories of leadership that reject the notion of one best leadership style.

**situational theories**

**Propose that leader styles should match the situation at hand.**

# Fiedler's Contingency Model

Fred Fiedler, an OB scholar, developed a situational model of leadership. It is the oldest and one of the most widely known models of leadership. Fiedler's model is based on the following assumption:

> The performance of a leader depends on two interrelated factors: (1) the degree to which the situation gives the leader control and influence—that is, the likelihood that [the leader] can successfully accomplish the job; and (2) the leader's basic motivation—that is, whether [the leader's] self-esteem depends primarily on accomplishing the task or on having close supportive relations with others.[30]

With respect to a leader's basic motivation, Fiedler believes that leaders are either task motivated or relationship motivated. These basic motivations are similar to initiating structure/concern for production and consideration/concern for people.

Fiedler's theory also is based on the premise that leaders have one dominant leadership style that is resistant to change. He suggests that leaders must learn to manipulate or influence the leadership situation in order to create a "match" between their leadership style and the amount of control within the situation at hand. After discussing the components of situational control and the leadership matching process, we review relevant research and managerial implications.[31]

**Situational Control** Situational control refers to the amount of control and influence the leader has in her or his immediate work environment. Situational control ranges from high to low. High control implies that the leader's decisions will produce predictable results because the leader has the ability to influence work outcomes. Low control implies that the leader's decisions may not influence work outcomes because the leader has very little influence. There are three dimensions of situational control: leader–member relations, task structure, and position power. These dimensions vary independently, forming eight combinations of situational control (see Figure 14–1).

The three dimensions of situational control are defined as follows:

- *Leader–member relations* reflect the extent to which the leader has the support, loyalty, and trust of the work group.

- *Task structure* is concerned with the amount of structure contained within tasks performed by the work group.

- *Position power* refers to the degree to which the leader has formal power to reward, punish, or otherwise obtain compliance from employees.

**Linking Leadership Motivation and Situational Control** Fiedler's complete contingency model is presented in Figure 14–1. The last row under the Situational Control column shows that there are eight different leadership situations. Each situation represents a unique combination of leader–member relations, task structure, and position power. Situations I, II, and III represent high control situations. Figure 14–1 shows that task-motivated leaders are hypothesized to be most effective in situations of high control. Under conditions of moderate control (situations IV, V, VI, and VII), relationship-motivated leaders are expected to be more effective. Finally, the results orientation of task-motivated leaders is predicted to be more effective under the condition of very low control (situation VIII).

**Research and Managerial Implications** Research has provided mixed support for Fiedler's model, suggesting that the model needs theoretical refinement.[32]

Representation of Fiedler's Contingency Model    **FIGURE 14–1**

| Situational Control | High Control Situations | | | Moderate Control Situations | | | | Low Control Situations |
|---|---|---|---|---|---|---|---|---|
| Leader–member relations | Good | Good | Good | Good | Poor | Poor | Poor | Poor |
| Task structure | High | High | Low | Low | High | High | Low | Low |
| Position power | Strong | Weak | Strong | Weak | Strong | Weak | Strong | Weak |
| Situation | I | II | III | IV | V | VI | VII | VIII |

| **Optimal Leadership Style** | **Task-Motivated Leadership** | **Relationship-Motivated Leadership** | **Task-Motivated Leadership** |
|---|---|---|---|

SOURCE: Adapted from F E Fiedler, "Situational Control and a Dynamic Theory of Leadership," in *Managerial Control and Organizational Democracy,* eds B King, S Streufert, and F E Fiedler (New York: John Wiley & Sons, 1978), p 114.

That said, the major contribution of Fiedler's model is that it prompted others to examine the contingency nature of leadership. This research, in turn, reinforced the notion that there is no one best style of leadership. Leaders are advised to alter their task and relationship orientation to fit the demands of the situation at hand. Likewise, organizations preparing employees for leadership roles should keep in mind that leadership is about more than just inspiring others or just pushing hard until the job is done. In fact, many leadership development programs target an organization's high achievers, but some of these individuals push so hard to meet difficult goals that they have not learned to foster teamwork or listen well to other people's ideas. Coaching and rewards can encourage individuals to become adept at using a combination of task- and relationship-motivated behaviors.[33]

# Path–Goal Theory

Path–goal theory was originally proposed by Robert House in the 1970s.[34] He developed a model that describes how leadership effectiveness is influenced by the interaction between four leadership styles (directive, supportive, participative, and achievement-oriented) and a variety of contingency factors. **Contingency factors** are situational variables that cause one style of leadership to be more effective than another. Path–goal theory has two groups of contingency variables. They are employee characteristics and environmental factors. Five important employee characteristics are locus of control, task ability, need for achievement, experience, and need for clarity. Two relevant environmental factors are task structure (independent versus interdependent tasks) and work group dynamics. In order to gain a better understanding of how

**Test Your Knowledge**
Fiedler's Contingency Model of Leadership

learning objective **3**

Discuss House's revised path–goal theory and Hersey and Blanchard's situational leadership theory.

**contingency factors**

**Variables that influence the appropriateness of a leadership style.**

these contingency factors influence leadership effectiveness, we illustratively consider locus of control (see Chapter 5), task ability and experience, and task structure.

Employees with an internal locus of control are more likely to prefer participative or achievement-oriented leadership because they believe they have control over the work environment. Such individuals are unlikely to be satisfied with directive leader behaviors that exert additional control over their activities. In contrast, employees with an external locus tend to view the environment as uncontrollable, thereby preferring the structure provided by supportive or directive leadership. An employee with high task ability and experience is less apt to need additional direction and thus would respond negatively to directive leadership. This person is more likely to be motivated and satisfied by participative and achievement-oriented leadership. Oppositely, an inexperienced employee would find achievement-oriented leadership overwhelming as he or she confronts challenges associated with learning a new job. Supportive and directive leadership would be helpful in this situation. Finally, directive and supportive leadership should help employees experiencing role ambiguity. However, directive leadership is likely to frustrate employees working on routine and simple tasks. Supportive leadership is most useful in this context. In the following situation, which contingency factors do you think the company president failed to apply?

> The president of a small manufacturing company in Cleveland told his top marketing manager that he wasn't going to be reachable during a recent weeklong safari in Africa. But midway through the week, the manager received a voice-mail message from his boss inquiring whether he had completed a particular assignment—and telling him which task to tackle next.
>
> "I felt he didn't trust that I knew how to do my job," the marketing manager says. "When he got back from vacation . . . he confessed he'd programmed the voice-mail message to me before he left."
>
> Fed up with being micromanaged, the manager quit shortly afterward.[35]

There have been about 50 studies testing various predictions derived from House's original model. Results have been mixed, with some studies supporting the theory and others not.[36] House thus proposed a new version of path–goal theory in 1996 based on these results and the accumulation of new knowledge about OB.

**A Reformulated Theory**   The revised theory is presented in Figure 14–2.[37] There are three key changes in the new theory. First, House now believes that leadership is more complex and involves a greater variety of leader behavior. He thus identifies eight categories of leadership styles or behavior (see Table 14–2). The need for an expanded list of leader behaviors is supported by current research and descriptions of business leaders.[38] Consider how Benoit Vincent, chief technical officer of TaylorMade-adidas Golf, improved his leadership by broadening his repertoire of leadership behaviors.

> A pedigreed engineer with decades of experience, Vincent's education, background, and technical abilities were more than enough to garner the respect he needed to effectively manage the 100-plus engineers and other staffers who report to him. . . .
>
> [But] in executive meetings, Vincent tended to whiz through finely detailed technical information, leaving his fellow execs, all of whom lack an engineering background, more baffled than informed. Turnover in his department was commonplace. . . . If employees completed a task, he says, "My idea of a reward was to let them keep their job."
>
> To witness Vincent in action at TMaG today, you might be inclined to wonder whether his evil twin was surreptitiously replaced by his better half. . . . Now he listens to people, many of whom come to him first with their issues, difficulties, and concerns, he says, because they feel safe and listened to.[39]

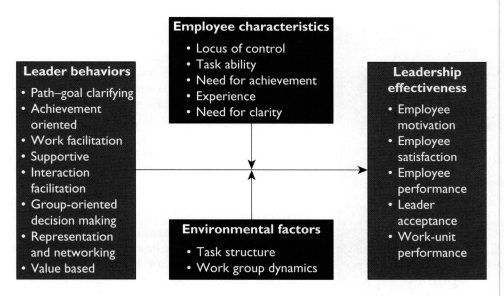

FIGURE 14–2
A General Representation of House's Revised Path–Goal Theory

Categories of Leader Behavior within the Revised Path–Goal Theory

TABLE 14–2

| Category of Leader Behavior | Description of Leader Behaviors |
|---|---|
| Path–goal clarifying behaviors | Clarifying employees' performance goals; providing guidance on how employees can complete tasks; clarifying performance standards and expectations; use of positive and negative rewards contingent on performance |
| Achievement-oriented behaviors | Setting challenging goals; emphasizing excellence; demonstrating confidence in employees' abilities |
| Work facilitation behaviors | Planning, scheduling, organizing, and coordinating work; providing mentoring, coaching, counseling, and feedback to assist employees in developing their skills; eliminating roadblocks; providing resources; empowering employees to take actions and make decisions |
| Supportive behaviors | Showing concern for the well-being and needs of employees; being friendly and approachable; treating employees as equals |
| Interaction facilitation behaviors | Resolving disputes; facilitating communication; encouraging the sharing of minority opinions; emphasizing collaboration and teamwork; encouraging close relationships among employees |
| Group-oriented decision-making behaviors | Posing problems rather than solutions to the work group; encouraging group members to participate in decision making; providing necessary information to the group for analysis; involving knowledgeable employees in decision making |
| Representation and networking behaviors | Presenting the work group in a positive light to others; maintaining positive relationships with influential others; participating in organizationwide social functions and ceremonies; doing unconditional favors for others |
| Value-based behaviors | Establishing a vision, displaying passion for it, and supporting its accomplishment; demonstrating self-confidence; communicating high performance expectations and confidence in others' abilities to meet their goals; giving frequent positive feedback |

SOURCE: Descriptions were adapted from R J House, "Path–Goal Theory of Leadership: Lessons, Legacy, and a Reformulated Theory," *Leadership Quarterly*, 1996, pp 323–52.

**The leadership style of Jamie Dimon, CEO of J P Morgan Chase, wins admiration from some but can include aggression and rudeness.**

As a result of coaching, Vincent learned to augment his use of path–goal clarifying behaviors and achievement-oriented behaviors with work facilitation behaviors (based on what he learned, he now coaches others), supportive behaviors, and interaction facilitation behaviors.

The second key change involves the role of intrinsic motivation (discussed in Chapter 6) and empowerment (discussed in Chapter 13) in influencing leadership effectiveness. House places much more emphasis on the need for leaders to foster intrinsic motivation through empowerment. Shared leadership represents the final change in the revised theory. That is, path–goal theory is based on the premise that an employee does not have to be a supervisor or manager to engage in leader behavior. Rather, House believes that leadership is shared among all employees within an organization. More is said about shared leadership in the final section of this chapter.

**Research and Managerial Implications**
There are not enough direct tests of House's revised path–goal theory using appropriate research methods and statistical procedures to draw overall conclusions. Future research is clearly needed to assess the accuracy of this model. That said, there still are two important managerial implications. First, effective leaders possess and use more than one style of leadership. Managers are encouraged to familiarize themselves with the different categories of leader behavior outlined in path–goal theory and to try new behaviors when the situation calls for them. Second, a small set of employee characteristics (i.e., ability, experience, and need for independence) and environmental factors (task characteristics of autonomy, variety, and significance) are relevant contingency factors.[40] Managers are advised to modify their leadership style to fit these various employee and task characteristics.

# Hersey and Blanchard's Situational Leadership Theory

Situational leadership theory (SLT) was developed by management writers Paul Hersey and Kenneth Blanchard.[41] According to the theory, effective leader behavior depends on the readiness level of a leader's followers. **Readiness** is defined as the extent to which a follower possesses the ability and willingness to complete a task. Willingness is a combination of confidence, commitment, and motivation.

**readiness**

Follower's ability and willingness to complete a task.

The SLT model is summarized in Figure 14–3. The appropriate leadership style is found by cross-referencing follower readiness, which varies from low to high, with one of four leadership styles. The four leadership styles represent combinations of

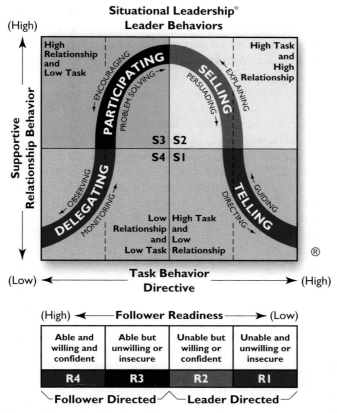

**FIGURE 14–3**
Situational
Leadership
Model

SOURCE: Paul Hersey, *The Management of Organizational Behavior: Utilizing Human Resources,* Center for Leadership Studies, Escondido, CA, 1984. Reprinted with permission. Situational Leadership® is a registered trademark of the Center for Leadership Studies, Inc. Copyright © 2002, Center for Leadership Studies, Inc. All Rights Reserved.

task and relationship-oriented leader behaviors ($S_1$ to $S_4$). Leaders are encouraged to use a "telling style" for followers with low readiness. This style combines high task-oriented leader behaviors, such as providing instructions, with low relationship-oriented behaviors, such as close supervision (see Figure 14–3). As follower readiness increases, leaders are advised to gradually move from a telling, to a selling, to a participating, and, ultimately, to a delegating style.[42]

Although SLT is widely used as a training tool, it is not strongly supported by scientific research. Finally, researchers have concluded that the self-assessment instrument used to measure leadership style and follower readiness is inaccurate and should be used with caution.[43] In summary, managers should exercise discretion when using prescriptions from SLT.

# The Full-Range Model of Leadership: From Laissez-Faire to Transformational Leadership

One of the most recent approaches to leadership is referred to as a full-range model of leadership.[44] The authors of this theory, Bernard Bass and Bruce Avolio, proposed that leadership behavior varied along a continuum from laissez-faire leadership (i.e., a general failure to take responsibility for leading) to transactional leadership to transformational leadership. Of course, laissez-faire leadership is a terrible way for any manager to behave and should be avoided.[45] In contrast, transactional and transformational leadership are both positively related to a variety of employee attitudes and behaviors and represent different aspects of being a good leader. Let us consider these two important dimensions of leadership.

**Transactional leadership** focuses on clarifying employees' role and task requirements and providing followers with positive and negative rewards contingent on performance. Further, transactional leadership encompasses the fundamental managerial activities of setting goals, monitoring progress toward goal achievement, and rewarding and punishing people for their level of goal accomplishment.[46] You can see from this description that transactional leadership is based on using extrinsic motivation (recall our discussion in Chapter 6) to increase employee productivity. Consider how Bijan Khosrowshahi, chief executive of Fuji Fire and Marine Insurance, used transactional leadership to pick up the pace of growth at what had been a slow-moving company.

**transactional leadership**

Focuses on clarifying employees' roles and providing rewards contingent on performance.

Bijan Khosrowshahi, CEO of Fuji Fire and Marine Insurance, uses both transactional and transformational leadership to influence his followers. His leadership is credited with increase financial performance for the firm. Would you like to work for Mr. Khosrowshahi? Why?

He changed reporting lines so more managers talked directly to him. Then he forbade participants from reading prepared reports word-for-word in meetings, as had been customary. . . .

To assess talent, he grilled about 40 senior managers on the details of their jobs, discussing issues from reinsurance schemes to the chances of getting business from Toyota Motor Corp. . . .

Mr. Khosrowshahi is prodding managers to identify solutions as well as problems, and urging employees to take more initiative. Early on, he solicited volunteers to develop new-product ideas. . . .

[Yasunobu] Aoki's team was asked to create a new auto-insurance policy. . . . When Mr. Aoki presented the plan to a Fuji committee including Mr. Khosrowshahi, he was taken aback by their tough questions.

"That's when I realized this wasn't a game," says Mr. Aoki.[47]

In contrast, **transformational leaders** "engender trust, seek to develop leadership in others, exhibit self-sacrifice and serve as moral agents, focusing themselves and followers on objectives that transcend the more immediate needs of the work group."[48] Transformational leaders can produce significant organizational change and results because this form of leadership fosters higher levels of intrinsic motivation, trust, commitment, and loyalty from followers than does transactional leadership. That said, however, it is important to note that transactional leadership is an essential prerequisite to effective leadership,

**transformational leadership**

Transforms employees to pursue organizational goals over self-interests.

and that the best leaders learn to display both transactional and transformational leadership to various degrees. In support of this proposition, research reveals that transformational leadership leads to superior performance when it "augments" or adds to transactional leadership.[49] Let us return to the example of Fuji's Bijan Khosrowshahi to see how he augmented transactional leadership with transformational leadership so that employees would be inspired to work in new ways.

> Mr. Khosrowshahi also worked on boosting morale, scheduling lunches with employees and launching a training program with Tokyo's Hitotsubashi University. To commemorate Fuji's improved earnings last year, he gave each of its employees 10,000 yen, or around $95, accompanied by thank-you notes in envelopes decorated with his caricature.
>
> Hiroko Ikeno, an office worker who was a member of Mr. Aoki's team, says Mr. Khosrowshahi is so popular that some colleagues have taped his photo to their PCs.[50]

Khosrowshahi's leadership has helped Fuji's net premiums written (equivalent to revenues) rise for the first time in several years. We now turn our attention to examining the process by which transformational leadership influences followers.

## How Does Transformational Leadership Transform Followers?

Transformational leaders transform followers by creating changes in their goals, values, needs, beliefs, and aspirations. They accomplish this transformation by appealing to followers' self-concepts—namely their values and personal identity. Figure 14–4 presents a model of how leaders accomplish this transformation process.

A Transformational Model of Leadership    **FIGURE 14–4**

SOURCE: Based in part on D A Waldman and F J Yammarino, "CEO Charismatic Leadership: Levels-of-Management and Levels-of-Analysis Effects," *Academy of Management Review,* April 1999, pp 266–85; B Shamir, R J House, and M B Arthur, "The Motivational Effects of Charismatic Leadership: A Self-Concept Based Theory," *Organization Science,* November 1993, pp 577–94; and A E Colbert, A L Kristof-Brown, B H Bradley, and M R Barrick, "CEO Transformational Leadership: The Role of Goal Importance Congruence in Top Management Teams," *Academy of Management Journal,* February 2008, pp 81–96.

Figure 14–4 shows that transformational leader behavior is first influenced by various individual and organizational characteristics. For example, research reveals that transformational leaders tend to have personalities that are more extraverted, agreeable, and proactive than nontransformational leaders, and female leaders use transformational leadership more than male leaders.[51] Organizational culture also influences the extent to which leaders are transformational. Cultures that are adaptive and flexible rather than rigid and bureaucratic are more likely to create environments that foster the opportunity for transformational leadership to be exhibited.

Transformational leaders engage in four key sets of leader behavior (see Figure 14–4).[52] The first set, referred to as *inspirational motivation,* involves establishing an attractive vision of the future, the use of emotional arguments, and exhibition of optimism and enthusiasm. A vision is "a realistic, credible, attractive future for your organization."[53] According to Burt Nanus, a leadership expert, the "right" vision unleashes human potential because it serves as a beacon of hope and common purpose. It does this by attracting commitment, energizing workers, creating meaning in employees' lives, establishing a standard of excellence, promoting high ideals, and bridging the gap between an organization's present problems and its future goals and aspirations. Leo Kiely, chief executive of Molson Coors Brewing, applies inspirational motivation by enthusiastically defining a vision ("a big, hairy, audacious goal") and empowering people ("Turn the team loose and let them play").[54] Virgin Atlantic's president, Richard Branson, has shared a vision of creating a "green" airline that uses biofuels; he announced a test flight by tasting a sample of jet fuel made of coconuts and babassu nuts.[55]

*Idealized influence,* the second set of leader behaviors, includes behaviors such as sacrificing for the good of the group, being a role model, and displaying high ethical standards. For example, the behaviors described in Skills & Best Practices are intended to provide this type of influence. Through their actions, transformational leaders model the desired values, traits, beliefs, and behaviors needed to realize the vision. The third set, *individualized consideration,* entails behaviors associated with providing support, encouragement, empowerment, and coaching to employees. *Intellectual stimulation,* the fourth set of leadership behaviors, involves behaviors that encourage employees to question the status quo and to seek innovative and creative solutions to organizational problems. These behaviors are consistent with the finding by management expert Roger Martin that successful leaders tend to see problems and opportunities in all their complexity, rather than as either-or choices. In their search for a fresh

## Leadership through Business Decencies

Steve Harrison, chairman of Lee Hecht Harrison, says leaders can improve a company's culture by using *business decencies*—gestures "offered without expectation of reward" that show respect for and interest in others. The most effective decencies are actionable (that is, behavior, not just a warm feeling), tangible (something that can be observed or that changes the environment in an observable way), pragmatic (making business sense), affordable (immediately and in terms of setting a precedent), replicable (so others can imitate it), and sustainable (generating goodwill for the long haul).

Harrison offers a few examples:

- Rearrange seating at meetings to dissolve barriers and make it easier to connect with attendees.

- Write one thank-you note on paper or via e-mail each day.

- Give praise in public, criticism in private.

- Take time to talk to receptionists, administrative assistants, and maintenance people.

- Acknowledge the family, friends, and outside interests of people who work for you.

- Convey bad news in person.

- Make yourself easily accessible by having regular open office hours.

**SOURCE: Based on S Harrison, "Deliberate Acts of Decency,"** *HR Magazine,* **July 2007, pp 97–99 (list quoted from p 99).**

perspective, these leaders are more likely to bring together people with different viewpoints, rather than break a problem into components so that, for example, the finance staff looks only at the financial implications while the sales managers look only for ways to push their product to new customers.[56]

# Research and Managerial Implications

Components of the transformational model of leadership have been the most widely researched leadership topic over the last decade. Overall, the relationships outlined in Figure 14–4 generally were supported by previous research. For example, transformational leader behaviors were positively associated with the extent to which employees identified with both their leaders and immediate work groups.[57] Followers of transformational leaders also were found to set goals that were consistent with those of the leader, to be happier and more engaged in their work, to have higher levels of intrinsic motivation, to have higher levels of group cohesion, and to be more committed to change initiatives.[58] With respect to the direct relationship between transformational leadership and work outcomes, a meta-analysis of 49 studies indicated that transformational leadership was positively associated with measures of leadership effectiveness and employees' job satisfaction.[59] However, recent research suggests that it is important to use all the forms of transformational behavior. Restaurant managers who used transformational leadership obtained more employee ideas for improvement *if* they communicated they were open to new ideas.[60] You can probably imagine that if your boss conveyed a passion only for his or her own vision, you might actually be less eager to share your ideas; the same thing seems to have happened in the restaurants studied. At the organizational level, a second meta-analysis demonstrated that transformational leadership was positively correlated with organizational measures of effectiveness.[61]

These results underscore four important managerial implications. First, the best leaders are not just transformational; they are both transactional and transformational. Leaders should attempt to use these two types of leadership while avoiding a "laissez-faire" or "wait-and-see" style.

Second, transformational leadership not only affects individual-level outcomes like job satisfaction, organizational commitment, and performance, but it also influences group dynamics and group-level outcomes. Managers can thus use the four types of transformational leadership shown in Figure 14–4 as a vehicle to improve group dynamics and work-unit outcomes. This is important in today's organizations because most employees do not work in isolation. Rather, people tend to rely on the input and collaboration of others, and many organizations are structured around teams. The key point to remember is that transformational leadership transforms individuals as well as teams and work groups. We encourage you to use this to your advantage.

Third, employees at any level in an organization can be trained to be more transactional and transformational.[62] This reinforces the organizational value of developing and rolling out a combination of transactional and transformational leadership training for all employees. Also, whether or not organizations offer formal leadership training programs, individuals can develop their own leadership skills (see Skills & Best Practices on page 362).

Fourth, transformational leaders can be ethical or unethical. Whereas ethical transformational leaders enable employees to enhance their self-concepts, unethical ones

## Experimenting with Leadership

Management professor Stewart Friedman has developed a program called Total Leadership, in which participants develop their strengths "in all of life's domains—work, home, community, and self." The goal is to try short-term changes aimed at improvements in one area spilling over into others as individuals become "more focused, passionate, and committed to what they're doing."

To begin, you identify your core values and how well your actions are aligned with those values, as well as the needs of key people in each of your life's domains. You should then be able to identify areas where you want to improve. Friedman recommends experimenting with small changes designed to fulfill goals in each domain. A successful experiment generally involves nine components:

1. *Tracking and reflecting.* Record activities, thoughts, and feelings to assess progress.

2. *Planning and organizing.* Take actions to manage time and plan for the future.

3. *Rejuvenating and restoring.* Quit unhealthy activities and add ones that renew your commitment and health.

4. *Appreciating and caring.* Have fun, enjoy relationships, and serve others.

5. *Focusing and concentrating.* Pay attention to those who matter most.

6. *Revealing and engaging.* Share your vision, mentor others, listen carefully.

7. *Time shifting and "re-placing."* Adjust work times and places to reach your goals.

8. *Delegating and developing.* Reallocate and eliminate tasks to free time and develop others.

9. *Exploring and venturing.* Move toward activities, jobs, and a career that better fits your values.

SOURCE: Based on S D Friedman, "Be a Better Leader, Have a Richer Life," *Harvard Business Review,* April 2008, pp 112–18.

select or produce obedient, dependent, and compliant followers. Top management can create and maintain ethical transformational leadership by

1. Creating and enforcing a clearly stated code of ethics.

2. Recruiting, selecting, and promoting people who display ethical behavior.

3. Developing performance expectations around the treatment of employees—these expectations can then be assessed in the performance appraisal process.

4. Training employees to value diversity.

5. Identifying, rewarding, and publicly praising employees who exemplify high moral conduct.[63]

# Additional Perspectives on Leadership

This section examines four additional perspectives to leadership: leader–member exchange theory, shared leadership, servant-leadership, and Level 5 leadership. We spend more time discussing leader–member exchange theory because it has been more thoroughly investigated.

## The Leader–Member Exchange Model of Leadership

The leader–member exchange (LMX) model of leadership revolves around the development of dyadic relationships between managers and their direct reports. This model is quite different from those previously discussed in that it focuses on the quality of relationships between managers and subordinates as opposed to the behaviors or traits of either leaders or followers. It also is different in that it does not assume that leader behavior is characterized by a stable or average leadership style as does behavioral styles theory and Fiedler's contingency theory. In other words, these models assume a leader treats all employees in about the same way. In contrast, the LMX model is based on the assumption that leaders develop unique one-to-one relationships with each of the people reporting to them. Behavioral scientists call this sort of relationship a *vertical dyad.* The forming of vertical dyads is said to be a naturally occurring process, resulting from the leader's attempt to delegate and assign work roles. As a result of this process, two distinct types of leader–member exchange relationships are expected to evolve.[64]

One type of leader–member exchange is called the **in-group exchange.** In this relationship, leaders and followers develop a partnership characterized by reciprocal influence, mutual trust, respect and liking, and a sense of common fates. In the second type of exchange, referred to as an **out-group exchange,** leaders are characterized as overseers who fail to create a sense of mutual trust, respect, or common fate.[65]

**Research Findings**    If the leader–member exchange model is correct, there should be a significant relationship between the type of leader–member exchange and job-related outcomes. Research supports this prediction. For example, a positive leader–member exchange was positively associated with less resistance to change[66] and greater job satisfaction, job performance, goal commitment, trust between managers and employees, work climate, and satisfaction with leadership.[67] The type of leader–member exchange also was found to predict not only turnover among nurses and computer analysts but also career outcomes, such as promotability, salary level, and receipt of bonuses over a seven-year period.[68]

Studies also have identified a variety of variables that influence the quality of an LMX. For example, LMX was related to personality similarity and demographic similarity.[69] Further, the quality of an LMX was positively related with the extent to which leaders and followers like each other, the leaders' positive expectations of their subordinates, the frequency of communications between managers and their direct reports, the extent to which a leader's traits match the follower's leadership prototypes, and organizational culture.[70]

**Managerial Implications**    There are three important implications associated with the LMX model of leadership. First, leaders are encouraged to establish high-performance expectations for all of their direct reports because setting high-performance standards fosters high-quality LMXs. Second, because personality and demographic similarity between leaders and followers is associated with higher LMXs, managers need to be careful that they don't create a homogeneous work environment in the spirit of having positive relationships with their direct reports. Our discussion of diversity in Chapter 4 clearly documented that there are many positive benefits of having a diverse workforce. The third implication pertains to those of us who find ourselves in a poor LMX. Before providing advice about what to do in this situation, we would like you to assess the quality of your current leader–member exchange. The Hands-On Exercise on page 364 contains a measure of leader–member exchange that segments an LMX into four subdimensions: mutual affection, loyalty, contribution to work activities, and professional respect.

What is the overall quality of your LMX? Do you agree with this assessment? Which subdimensions are high and low? If your overall LMX and associated subdimensions are all high, you should be in a very good situation with respect to the relationship between you and your manager. Having a low LMX overall score or a low dimensional score, however, reveals that part of the relationship with your manager may need improvement. A management consultant offers the following tips for improving the quality of leader–member exchanges.[71]

1. Stay focused on your department's goals and remain positive about your ability to accomplish your goals. An unsupportive boss is just another obstacle to be overcome.

**learning objective**

Explain the leader–member exchange (LMX) model of leadership and the concept of shared leadership.

**Group Exercise**

What Kind of Leader Do You Prefer?

**in-group exchange**

A partnership characterized by mutual trust, respect, and liking.

**out-group exchange**

A partnership characterized by a lack of mutual trust, respect, and liking.

# Assessing Your Leader–Member Exchange

**INSTRUCTIONS:** For each of the items shown below, use the following scale to circle the answer that best represents how you feel about the relationship between you and your current manager/supervisor. If you are not currently working, complete the survey by thinking about a previous manager. Remember, there are no right or wrong answers. After circling a response for each of the 12 items, use the scoring key to compute scores for the subdimensions within your leader–member exchange.

1 = Strongly disagree
2 = Disagree
3 = Neither agree nor disagree
4 = Agree
5 = Strongly agree

1. I like my supervisor very much as a person.    1 2 3 4 5

2. My supervisor is the kind of person one would like to have as a friend.    1 2 3 4 5

3. My supervisor is a lot of fun to work with.    1 2 3 4 5

4. My supervisor defends my work actions to a superior, even without complete knowledge of the issue in question.    1 2 3 4 5

5. My supervisor would come to my defense if I were "attacked" by others.    1 2 3 4 5

6. My supervisor would defend me to others in the organization if I made an honest mistake.    1 2 3 4 5

7. I do work for my supervisor that goes beyond what is specified in my job description.    1 2 3 4 5

8. I am willing to apply extra efforts, beyond those normally required, to meet my supervisor's work goals.    1 2 3 4 5

9. I do not mind working my hardest for my supervisor.    1 2 3 4 5

10. I am impressed with my supervisor's knowledge of his/her job.    1 2 3 4 5

11. I respect my supervisor's knowledge of and competence on the job.    1 2 3 4 5

12. I admire my supervisor's professional skills.    1 2 3 4 5

## SCORING KEY

Mutual affection (add items 1–3) _____
Loyalty (add items 4–6) _____
Contribution to work activities (add items 7–9) _____
Professional respect (add items 10–12) _____
Overall score (add all 12 items) _____

## ARBITRARY NORMS

Low mutual affection = 3–9
High mutual affection = 10–15
Low loyalty = 3–9
High loyalty = 10–15
Low contribution to work activities = 3–9
High contribution to work activities = 10–15
Low professional respect = 3–9
High professional respect = 10–15
Low overall leader–member exchange = 12–38
High overall leader–member exchange = 39–60

2. Do not fall prey to feeling powerless, and empower yourself to get things done.

3. Exercise the power you have by focusing on circumstances you can control and avoid dwelling on circumstances you cannot control.

4. Work on improving your relationship with your manager. Begin by examining the level of trust between the two of you and then try to improve it by frequently and effectively communicating. You can also increase trust by following through on your commitments and achieving your goals.

5. Use an authentic, respectful, and assertive approach to resolve differences with your manager. It also is useful to use a problem-solving approach when disagreements arise.

**Self-Assessment Exercise**

Assessing Your Leader–Member Exchange

# Shared Leadership

A pair of OB scholars noted that "there is some speculation, and some preliminary evidence, to suggest that concentration of leadership in a single chain of command may be less optimal than shared leadership responsibility among two or more individuals in certain task environments."[72] This perspective is quite different from the previous theories and models discussed in this chapter, which assume that leadership is a vertical, downward-flowing process. In contrast, the notion of shared leadership is based on the idea that people need to share information and collaborate to get things done at work. This, in turn, underscores the need for employees to adopt a horizontal process of influence or leadership. **Shared leadership** entails a simultaneous, ongoing, mutual influence process in which individuals share responsibility for leading regardless of formal roles and titles.

> **shared leadership**
> Simultaneous, ongoing, mutual influence process in which people share responsibility for leading.

Shared leadership is most likely to be needed when people work in teams, when people are involved in complex projects, and when people are doing knowledge work—work that requires voluntary contributions of intellectual capital by skilled professionals.[73] Interestingly, a group of management professors points out that these are the conditions in which leaders direct teams (often called guilds) in online role-playing games.[74] Interviews with and observations of people who excel as leaders in these games showed that they build expertise at assessing complex situations, making speedy decisions, taking risks, and moving in and out of leadership roles as the situation's needs match their capabilities and willingness to step forward or accept the group's nomination. The researchers found that this type of shared leadership was especially effective when leaders could offer nonmonetary incentives and information was available to the entire team—conditions that could readily exist in the modern workplace.

Researchers are just now beginning to explore the process of shared leadership, and results are promising. For example, shared leadership in teams was positively associated with group cohesion, group citizenship, and group effectiveness.[75] Table 14–3 contains a list of key questions and answers that managers should consider when determining how they can develop shared leadership.

**learning objective 6**

Review the principles of servant-leadership and discuss Level 5 leadership.

# Servant-Leadership

Servant-leadership is more a philosophy of managing than a testable theory. The term *servant-leadership* was coined by Robert Greenleaf in 1970. Greenleaf believes that great leaders act as servants, putting the needs of others, including employees, customers, and community, as their first priority. **Servant-leadership** focuses on increased service to

> **servant-leadership**
> Focuses on increased service to others rather than to oneself.

## TABLE 14–3    Key Questions and Answers to Consider When Developing Shared Leadership

| Key Questions | Answers |
|---|---|
| What task characteristics call for shared leadership? | Tasks that are highly *interdependent.* |
| | Tasks that require a great deal of *creativity.* |
| | Tasks that are highly *complex.* |
| What is the role of the leader in developing shared leadership? | *Designing the team,* including clarifying purpose, securing resources, articulating vision, selecting members, and defining team processes. |
| | *Managing the boundaries* of the team. |
| How can organizational systems facilitate the development of shared leadership? | *Training and development systems* can be used to prepare both designated leaders and team members to engage in shared leadership. |
| | *Reward systems* can be used to promote and reward shared leadership. |
| | *Cultural systems* can be used to articulate and to demonstrate the value of shared leadership. |
| What vertical and shared leadership behaviors are important to team outcomes? | *Directive leadership* can provide task-focused directions. |
| | *Transactional leadership* can provide both personal and material rewards based on key performance metrics. |
| | *Transformational leadership* can stimulate commitment to a team vision, emotional engagement, and fulfillment of higher-order needs. |
| | *Empowering leadership* can reinforce the importance of self-motivation. |
| What are the ongoing responsibilities of the vertical leader? | The vertical leader needs to be able to step in and *fill voids* in the team. |
| | The vertical leader needs to continue to *emphasize the importance of the shared leadership approach,* given the task characteristics facing the team. |

SOURCE: C L Pearce, "The Future of Leadership: Combining Vertical and Shared Leadership to Transform Knowledge Work," *Academy of Management Executive: The Thinking Manager's Source,* February 2004, p 48. Copyright 2004 by Academy of Management. Reproduced with permission of Academy of Management via Copyright Clearance Center.

others rather than to oneself.[76] Because the focus of servant-leadership is serving others over self-interest, servant-leaders are less likely to engage in self-serving behaviors that hurt others. Embedding servant-leadership into an organization's culture requires actions as well as words. For example, a servant-leader might decide to forgo a hefty bonus if the bonus's impact on employees—assuming they don't receive comparable incentives—will be demoralizing.

According to Jim Stuart, cofounder of the leadership circle in Tampa, Florida, "Leadership derives naturally from a commitment to service. You know that you're practicing servant-leadership if your followers become wiser, healthier, more autonomous—and more likely to become servant-leaders themselves."[77] Servant-leadership is not a quick-fix approach to leadership. Rather, it is a long-term, transformational approach to life and work.

Servant-leaders have the characteristics listed in Table 14–4. An example of someone with these characteristics is Patricia Woertz, chief executive of Archer

Daniels Midland. A plant manager with a former employer said Woertz was "the first person from the executive ranks who ever actually listened to what the folks at the refinery were saying." Besides listening, Woertz has been praised for her ability to conceptualize the company's future and her commitment to employee development.

> Pointing out that the rest of the world, including ADM's competition, is constantly changing and improving, [Woertz] says she's working to build an attitude of continuous learning in the ADM culture.
>
> The bio-fuels giant does business in 60 countries, and Woertz promotes diversity among its leaders. In addition to hiring local leaders in each country, she likes to "[mix] the salad," placing a U.S. leader in Hamburg, a German leader in China, a Chinese leader in Australia, and so forth.
>
> As Woertz plans for the future, she communicates her enthusiasm for the challenges that lie ahead. . . . Such opportunities are "what people come to work for," she says.[78]

An organization can hardly go wrong by trying to adopt these and the other characteristics in Table 14–4.

### Characteristics of the Servant-Leader    TABLE 14–4

| Servant–Leadership Characteristics | Description |
|---|---|
| 1. Listening | Servant-leaders focus on listening to identify and clarify the needs and desires of a group. |
| 2. Empathy | Servant-leaders try to empathize with others' feelings and emotions. An individual's good intentions are assumed even when he or she performs poorly. |
| 3. Healing | Servant-leaders strive to make themselves and others whole in the face of failure or suffering. |
| 4. Awareness | Servant-leaders are very self-aware of their strengths and limitations. |
| 5. Persuasion | Servant-leaders rely more on persuasion than positional authority when making decisions and trying to influence others. |
| 6. Conceptualization | Servant-leaders take the time and effort to develop broader based conceptual thinking. Servant-leaders seek an appropriate balance between a short-term, day-to-day focus and a long-term, conceptual orientation. |
| 7. Foresight | Servant-leaders have the ability to foresee future outcomes associated with a current course of action or situation. |
| 8. Stewardship | Servant-leaders assume that they are stewards of the people and resources they manage. |
| 9. Commitment to the growth of people | Servant-leaders are committed to people beyond their immediate work role. They commit to fostering an environment that encourages personal, professional, and spiritual growth. |
| 10. Building community | Servant-leaders strive to create a sense of community both within and outside the work organization. |

SOURCE: These characteristics and descriptions were derived from L C Spears, "Introduction: Servant-Leadership and the Greenleaf Legacy," in *Reflections on Leadership: How Robert K Greenleaf's Theory of Servant-Leadership Influenced Today's Top Management Thinkers*, ed L C Spears (New York: John Wiley & Sons, 1995), pp 1–14.

Patricia Woertz of Archer Daniels Midland has been praised for being a servant leader. Which characteristics of servant-leaders shown in Table 14–4 did she exhibit?

# Level 5 Leadership

This model of leadership was not derived from any particular theory or model of leadership. Rather, it was developed from a longitudinal research study attempting to answer the following question: Can a good company become a great company and, if so, how? The study was conducted by a research team headed by Jim Collins, a former university professor who started his own research-based consulting company. He summarized his work in the best seller *Good to Great.*[79]

To answer the research question, Collins identified a set of companies that shifted from good performance to great performance. Great performance was defined as "cumulative stock returns at or below the general stock market for 15 years, punctuated by a transition point, then cumulative returns at least three times the market over the next 15 years."[80] Beginning with a sample of 1,435 companies on the Fortune 500 from 1965 to 1995, he identified 11 good-to-great companies: Abbot, Circuit City, Fannie Mae, Gillette, Kimberly-Clark, Kroger, Nucor, Philip Morris, Pitney Bowes, Walgreens, and Wells Fargo. His next step was to compare these 11 companies with a targeted set of direct comparison companies. This comparison enabled him to uncover the drivers of good-to-great transformations. One of the key drivers was called Level 5 leadership (see Figure 14–5). In other words, every company that experienced good-to-great performance was led by an individual possessing the characteristics associated with Level 5 leadership. Let us consider this leadership hierarchy.

Figure 14–5 reveals that a Level 5 leader possesses the characteristics of humility and a fearless will to succeed. American president Abraham Lincoln is an example of such an individual. Although he was soft-spoken and shy, he possessed great will to accomplish his goal of uniting his country during the Civil War in the 1860s. This determination resulted in the loss of 250,000 Confederates, 360,000 Union soldiers, and ultimately to a united country.[81] Being humble and determined, however, was not enough for Lincoln to succeed at his quest. Rather, a Level 5 leader must also possess the capabilities associated with the other levels in the hierarchy. Although an individual does not move up the hierarchy in a stair-step fashion, a Level 5 leader must possess the capabilities contained in Levels 1 to 4 before he or she can use the Level 5 characteristics to transform an organization.

It is important to note the overlap between the capabilities represented in this model and the previous leadership theories discussed in this chapter. For example, Level 1 is consistent with research on trait theory. Trait research tells us that leaders are intelligent, self-confident, determined, honest, sociable, emotionally intelligent, extraverted, and conscientious. Levels 3 and 4 also seem to contain behaviors associated with transactional and transformational leadership, respectively. The novel and unexpected component of this theory revolves around the conclusion that good-to-great leaders are not only transactional and transformational, but most importantly, they are humble and fiercely determined.

There are three points to keep in mind about Level 5 leadership. First, Collins notes that there are additional drivers for taking a company from good to great other than being a Level 5 leader.[82] Level 5 leadership enables the implementation of these additional drivers. Second, to date there has not been any additional research testing

The Level 5 Hierarchy    **FIGURE 14–5**

Level 5    **Level 5 Executive**

Builds enduring greatness through a paradoxical blend of personal humility and professional will.

Level 4    **Effective leader**

Catalyzes commitment to and vigorous pursuit of a clear and compelling vision, stimulating higher performance standards.

Level 3    **Competent manager**

Organizes people and resources toward the effective and efficient pursuit of predetermined objectives.

Level 2    **Contributing team member**

Contributes individual capabilities to the achievement of group objectives and works effectively with others in a group setting.

Level I    **Highly capable individual**

Makes productive contributions through talent, knowledge, skills, and good work habits.

SOURCE: Figure from *Good to Great: Why Some Companies Make the Leap and Others Don't* by J Collins. Copyright © 2001 by J Collins. Reprinted with permission from Jim Collins.

Collins's conclusions. Future research is clearly needed to confirm the Level 5 hierarchy. Finally, Collins believes that some people will never become Level 5 leaders because their narcissistic and boastful tendencies do not allow them to subdue their own ego and needs for the greater good of others. In contrast, Amy Woods Brinkley, global risk executive for Bank of America, says, "It's very important to operate with a confident humility," that is, recognizing "what you know and what you don't know," so that the leader knows when to draw on other people's expertise.[83]

# The Role of Followers in the Leadership Process

learning objective 7

Describe the follower's role in the leadership process.

All of the previous theories discussed in this chapter have been leader-centric. That is, they focused on understanding leadership effectiveness from the leader's point of view. We conclude this chapter by discussing the role of followers in the leadership process. Although very little research has been devoted to this topic, it is an important issue to consider because the success of both leaders and followers is contingent on the dynamic relationship among the people involved.[84] For example, people who are feeling strong emotions in general tend to have stronger feelings about how charismatic their leader is.[85] Thus, a charismatic individual's impact as a leader will depend in part on the followers' emotional states. Similarly, leaders' behaviors will have a different impact on employees who are content simply to come to work and carry out their tasks than on those who are highly dedicated to, even consumed by, the organization's mission.[86]

Leaders and followers alike are responsible for the quality of their mutual relationship. If something is wrong with the relationship, one or the other needs to intervene. Poor relationships between leaders and followers are frequently caused by unmet expectations—recall our discussion of job satisfaction in Chapter 6. Let us thus consider the nature of leaders' and employees' expectations.

Leaders want followers to be productive, reliable, honest, cooperative, proactive, and flexible.[87] Leaders do not benefit from followers who hide the truth, withhold information, fail to generate ideas, are unwilling to collaborate, provide inaccurate feedback, or are unwilling to take the lead on projects and initiatives.[88] In contrast, research shows that followers seek, admire, and respect leaders who foster three emotional responses in others: Followers want organizational leaders to create feelings of *significance* (what one does at work is important and meaningful), *community* (a sense of unity encourages people to treat others with respect and dignity and to work together in pursuit of organizational goals), and *excitement* (people are engaged and feel energy at work).[89] What then can followers do to enhance the achievement of these mutual expectations?

A pair of OB experts developed a four step process for followers to use in managing the leader–follower relationship.[90] First, it is critical for followers to understand their boss. Followers should attempt to gain an appreciation for their manager's leadership style, interpersonal style, goals, expectations, pressures, and strengths and weaknesses. Second, followers need to understand their own style, needs, goals, expectations, and strengths and weaknesses.[91] The next step entails conducting a gap analysis between the understanding a follower has about his or her boss and the understanding the follower has about him- or herself. With this information in mind, followers are ready to proceed to the final step of developing and maintaining a relationship that fits both parties' needs and styles.

This final step requires followers to build on mutual strengths and to adjust or accommodate the leader's divergent style, goals, expectations, and weaknesses.[92] For example, a follower might adjust his or her style of communication in response to the boss's preferred method for receiving information. Other adjustments might be made in terms of decision making. If the boss prefers a participative approach, then followers should attempt to involve their manager in all decisions regardless of the follower's decision-making style—recall our discussion of decision-making styles in Chapter 10. Good use of time and resources is another issue for followers to consider. Most managers are pushed for time, energy, and resources and are more likely to appreciate followers who save rather than cost them time and energy. Followers should not use up their manager's time discussing trivial matters.

There are two final issues to consider. First, a follower may not be able to accommodate a leader's style, expectations, or weaknesses and may have to seek a transfer or quit his or her job to reconcile the discrepancy. We recognize that there are personal and ethical trade-offs that one may not be willing to make when managing the leader–follower relationship. Second, we can all enhance our boss's leadership effectiveness and our employer's success by becoming better followers. Remember, it is in an individual's best interest to be a good follower because leaders need and want competent employees.

# key terms

# chapter summary

- *Review trait theory, and discuss the takeaways from both the trait and behavioral styles theories of leadership.* Historical leadership research does not support the notion that effective leaders possess traits unique from followers. More recent research shows that effective leaders possess the following traits: intelligence, self-confidence, determination, honesty/integrity, sociability, emotional intelligence, extraversion, and conscientiousness. Research also demonstrates that men and women exhibit different styles of leadership. The takeaways from trait theory are that (a) we can no longer ignore the implications of traits; traits influence leadership effectiveness; (b) organizations may want to include personality and trait assessments into their selection and promotion processes; and (c) management development programs can be used to enhance employees' leadership traits. The takeaways from behavioral styles theory are as follows: (a) leaders are made, not born; (b) there is no one best style of leadership; (c) the effectiveness of a particular style depends on the situation at hand; and (d) managers are encouraged to concentrate on improving the effective execution of their leadership behaviors.

- *Explain, according to Fiedler's contingency model, how leadership style interacts with situational control.* Fiedler believes leader effectiveness depends on an appropriate match between leadership style and situational control. Leaders are either task motivated or relationship motivated. Situation control is composed of leader–member relations, task structure, and position power. Task-motivated leaders are effective under situations of both high and low control. Relationship-motivated leaders are more effective when they have moderate situational control.

- *Discuss House's revised path–goal theory and Hersey and Blanchard's situational leadership theory.* There are three key

changes in the revised path–goal theory. Leaders now are viewed as exhibiting eight categories of leader behavior (see Table 14–2) instead of four. In turn, the effectiveness of these styles depends on various employee characteristics and environmental factors. Second, leaders are expected to spend more effort fostering intrinsic motivation through empowerment. Third, leadership is not limited to people in managerial roles. Rather, leadership is shared among all employees within an organization. According to situational leadership theory (SLT), effective leader behavior depends on the readiness level of a leader's followers. As follower readiness increases, leaders are advised to gradually move from a telling to a selling to a participating and, finally, to a delegating style. Research does not support SLT.

- *Describe the difference between transactional and transformational leadership and discuss how transformational leadership transforms followers and work groups.* There is an important difference between transactional and transformational leadership. Transactional leaders focus on clarifying employees' role and task requirements and provide followers with positive and negative rewards contingent on performance. Transformational leaders motivate employees to pursue organizational goals over their own self-interests. Both forms of leadership are important for organizational success. Individual characteristics and organizational culture are key precursors of transformational leadership, which is comprised of four sets of leader behavior. These leader behaviors, in turn, positively affect followers' and work groups' goals, values, beliefs, aspirations, and motivation. These positive effects are then associated with a host of preferred outcomes.

- *Explain the leader–member exchange (LMX) model of leadership and the concept of shared leadership.* The LMX model revolves around the development of dyadic relationships between managers and their direct reports. These leader–member exchanges qualify as either in-group or out-group relationships. Research supports this model of leadership. Shared leadership involves a simultaneous, ongoing, mutual influence process in which individuals share responsibility for leading regardless of formal roles and titles. This type of leadership is most likely to be needed when people work in teams, when people are involved in complex projects, and when people are doing knowledge work.

- *Review the principles of servant-leadership and discuss Level 5 leadership.* Servant-leadership is more a philosophy than a testable theory. It is based on the premise that great leaders act as servants, putting the needs of others, including employees, customers, and community, as their first priority. Level 5 leadership represents a hierarchy of leadership capabilities that are needed to lead companies in transforming from good to great.

- *Describe the follower's role in the leadership process.* Followers can use a four-step process for managing the leader–follower relationship. Followers need to understand their boss and themselves. They then conduct a gap analysis between the understanding they have about their boss and themselves. The final step requires followers to build on mutual strengths and to adjust or accommodate the leader's divergent style, goals, expectations, and weaknesses.

# discussion questions

1. Citing examples, which different leadership traits and styles were displayed by Indra Nooyi?
2. Is everyone cut out to be a leader? Explain.
3. Does it make more sense to change a person's leadership style or the situation? How would Fred Fiedler and Robert House answer this question?
4. Have you ever worked for a transformational leader? Describe how she or he transformed followers.
5. In your view, which leadership theory has the greatest practical application? Why?

# ethical dilemma

## Should You Support Your Friend?

You are a manager at a call center and are faced with the difficult task of having to lay off a friend who works for the company. This employee has performed wonderfully in the past and you would hate to see him go. Nonetheless, your company lost a contract with a major client and his position is obsolete. You are aware that this employee has been building a house and is 10 days from closing. He has sold his other home and now is living with his in-laws. The employee has come to you and is asking for a favor. He wants you to extend his employment for 10 more days so that he can qualify for the loan for his new home. Unfortunately, you do not have the authority to do so, and you told him you cannot grant this favor. He then told you that the mortgage company will be calling sometime soon to get a verbal confirmation of his employment. This confirmation is an essential prerequisite in order for your friend to obtain the loan for his new home. Because you can't extend his employment, he now is asking for another favor. He wants you to tell the mortgage company that he is still employed.

## Solving the Dilemma

As a manager at this call center, what would you do?

**1.** Tell the mortgage company he is still working for the company. Your friend needs a break and you are confident that he'll find a job in the near future.

**2.** Refuse to lie. It is unethical to falsify information regarding employment.

**3.** Simply avoid the mortgage company's phone call.

**4.** Invent other options. Discuss.

For an interpretation of this situation, visit our Web site, at
**www.mhhe.com/kinickiob4e**

If you're looking for additional study materials, be sure to check out the Online Learning Center at

**www.mhhe.com/kinickiob4e**

for more information and interactivities that correspond to this chapter.

# part Five

# Managing Evolving Organizations

# Designing Effective Organizations

**After reading the material in this chapter, you should be able to:**

1. Describe the four characteristics common to all organizations.

2. Explain the difference between closed and open systems.

3. Define seven basic ways organizations are structured.

4. Discuss Burns and Stalker's findings regarding mechanistic and organic organizations.

5. Identify when each of the seven organization structures is the right fit.

6. Describe the four generic organizational effectiveness criteria.

**Sergey Brin (on left) and Larry Page cofounded Google and believe there is an optimal size for all organizations. Do you agree?**

Over the years Google co-founders Sergey Brin and Larry Page have become understandably judicious about their time. After all, multibillionaires are constantly in demand. Yet the engineering-grad-students-turned-media-moguls made time for FORTUNE when informed that Google had been chosen, for the second year running, as America's best company to work for. . . .

On the subject of culture, one of the key components to building a great long-term company, Page and Brin by turns again display the art of spin and candor. Page recently visited some new Google offices in the Seattle area and says he's amazed at how much these newer, smaller offices resemble Google in its early days.

"You walk into an office with 200 people and it's amazing the extent it feels like Google did when it was a startup," he says. "I think that's really healthy for a culture." Page believes human organizations have an optimal size he calls

"natural units." He waxes for a bit on their virtues. "I think as we get bigger, that's the way we're going to try to maintain our culture—to make sure we have the right sized groups."

Brin isn't so sure. The founders famously say they bicker privately, and Brin offers a glimpse by contradicting Page. "I don't think keeping the culture is a goal." Brin says. "I don't think we should be looking back to our golden years in the garage. The goal is to improve as we grow, and we certainly have more resources to bring to bear on the cultural issues and whatnot as we gain scale."

In other words, for Page it's about maintaining the culture; for Brin it's about improving it. Interestingly, Schmidt (Google's CEO), who'll often interrupt the founders when he thinks it's necessary, sits by silently.

Ask if they think Microsoft erred by allowing itself to get too big, and Page returns to his natural-units kick.

"Microsoft, as I understand it, grew mostly in one location, which certainly is not the case for us." Page says. "We have different groups of people that are doing different kinds of things, like, for example, YouTube, which has remained largely a division. They're in San Bruno [about 20 minutes up the freeway from Google's Mountain View, Calif., headquarters], and they have their own culture, which is different and cool. If you look at companies that are really big and successful at doing many different things, like GE, they certainly have a complex organizational structure. But they're able to keep it together."

This notion of YouTube's being a separate entity is certain to raise eyebrows among certain factions within Google. Yes, YouTube is physically apart, and its founders, Chad Hurley and Steve Chen, appear to be still very much engaged. YouTube, in fact, hasn't been Google-ized. But Google insiders make it clear that Google guides the show at YouTube,

including the fact that most department heads at YouTube report to a superior at Google. And while General Electric is famous for its decentralized approach, it has a unified culture nurtured from headquarters. More to the point, there aren't many companies that have pulled off the balancing act GE (GE, Fortune 500) has.

The founders clearly are thinking ahead as Google becomes more acquisitive. I wonder, for example, how Google will do at integrating the people of DoubleClick, none of whom will have been vetted by the famously rigorous—and often annoying—Google hiring process.

"We don't really know that the way we hire at Google is optimal, and we're trying to improve it all the time," says Page. "We obviously hire a lot of smart people. We also hire people who have different kinds of skills, and we hire people who work on computers, and do construction, and many, many other things."

With companies Google has acquired, their hiring culture may be different, "but they've had something that really worked for them in their space," Page adds. "For a company like DoubleClick, they understand what they're doing. The company has been around for a long time, is pretty mature, and they're obviously serving the customers well. So, we're not religious about the way we do it. In fact, we're trying to learn from how other people operate as well."[1]

**Do you agree with Larry Page's conclusion that all human organizations have an optimal size? Explain your rationale. For an interpretation of this case and additional comments, visit our Online Learning Center at**

**www.mhhe.com/kinickiob4e**

FOR DISCUSSION

**VIRTUALLY EVERY ASPECT OF LIFE** is affected at least indirectly by some type of organization. We look to organizations to feed, clothe, house, educate, and employ us. Organizations attend to our needs for entertainment, police and fire protection, insurance, recreation, national security, transportation, news and information, legal assistance, and health care. Modern organizations have one thing in common: They are the primary context for *organizational behavior*. In a manner of speaking, organizations are the chessboard upon which the game of organizational behavior is played. Therefore, present and future managers need a working knowledge of modern organizations to improve their chances of making the right moves when managing people at work.

The chapter-opening case illustrates that there is not one type of organizational design that works best in all situations. The best design depends on the extent to which it matches the demands of the situation at hand. This type of contingency design is discussed later in this chapter. The Google case also reinforces a conclusion we made in Chapter 2. That is, organizational structure is related to an organization's culture. This underscores how important it is for managers to consider the interplay between organizational culture and organizational design. This chapter will help you to manage this dynamic and important relationship.

We begin by defining the term *organization,* discussing important dimensions of organization charts, and contrasting views of organizations as closed or open systems. Our attention then turns to the various ways organizations are designed, from traditional divisions of work to more recent, popular ideas about lowering barriers between departments and companies. Next, we discuss the contingency approach to designing organizations. We conclude by describing criteria for assessing an organization's effectiveness.

# Organizations: Definition and Dimensions

**1 learning objective**

Describe the four characteristics common to all organizations.

As a necessary springboard for this chapter, we need to formally define the term *organization* and clarify the meaning of organization charts.

## What Is an Organization?

According to Chester I Barnard's classic definition, an **organization** is "a system of consciously coordinated activities or forces of two or more persons."[2] Embodied in the *conscious coordination* aspect of this definition are four common denominators of all organizations: coordination of effort, a common goal, division of labor, and a hierarchy of authority.[3] Organization theorists refer to these factors as the organization's *structure.*

> **organization**
>
> System of consciously coordinated activities of two or more people.

Coordination of effort is achieved through formulation and enforcement of policies, rules, and regulations. Division of labor occurs when the common goal is pursued by individuals performing different but related tasks. The hierarchy of authority, also called the chain of command, is a control mechanism dedicated to making sure the right people do the right things at the right time. Historically, managers have maintained the integrity of the hierarchy of authority by adhering to the unity of command principle. The **unity of command principle** specifies that each employee should report to only one manager. Otherwise, the argument goes, inefficiency would prevail because of conflicting orders

> **unity of command principle**
>
> Each employee should report to a single manager.

and lack of personal accountability. (Indeed, these are problems in today's more fluid and flexible organizations based on innovations such as cross-functional and self-managed teams.) Managers in the hierarchy of authority also administer rewards and punishments. When operating in concert, the four definitional factors—coordination of effort, a common goal, division of labor, and a hierarchy of authority—enable an *organization* to come to life and function.

## Organization Charts

An **organization chart** is a graphic representation of formal authority and division of labor relationships. To the casual observer, the term *organization chart* means the family tree–like pattern of boxes and lines posted on workplace walls. Within each box one usually finds the names and titles of current position holders. To organization theorists, however, organization charts reveal much more. The partial organization chart in Figure 15–1 reveals four basic dimensions of

**Test Your Knowledge**
Allocating Authority

> **organization chart**
> **Boxes-and-lines illustration showing chain of formal authority and division of labor.**

**Sample Organization Chart for a Hospital** | **FIGURE 15–1**
(executive and director levels only)

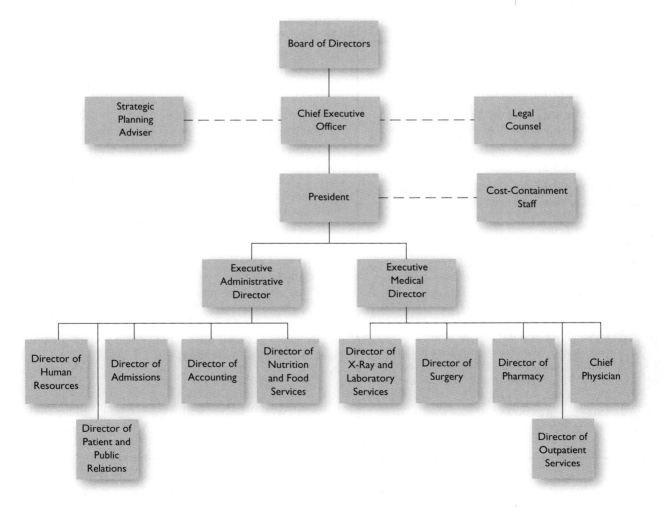

organizational structure: (1) hierarchy of authority (who reports to whom), (2) division of labor, (3) spans of control, and (4) line and staff positions.

**Hierarchy of Authority**   As Figure 15–1 illustrates, there is an unmistakable hierarchy of authority.[4] Working from bottom to top, the 10 directors report to the two executive directors who report to the president who reports to the chief executive officer. Ultimately, the chief executive officer answers to the hospital's board of directors. The chart in Figure 15–1 shows strict unity of command up and down the line. A formal hierarchy of authority also delineates the official communication network.

**span of control**

**The number of people reporting directly to a given manager.**

**Division of Labor**   In addition to showing the chain of command, the sample organization chart indicates extensive division of labor. Immediately below the hospital's president, one executive director is responsible for general administration while another is responsible for medical affairs. Each of these two specialties is further subdivided as indicated by the next layer of positions. At each successively lower level in the organization, jobs become more specialized.

**Spans of Control**   The **span of control** refers to the number of people reporting directly to a given manager.[5] Spans of control can range from narrow to wide. For example, the president in Figure 15–1 has a narrow span of control of two. (Staff assistants usually are not included in a manager's span of control.) The executive administrative director in Figure 15–1 has a wider span of control of five. Spans of control exceeding 30 can be found in assembly-line operations where machine-paced and repetitive work substitutes for close supervision. Historically, spans of five to six were considered best. Despite years of debate, organization theorists have not arrived at a consensus regarding the ideal span of control.

Generally, the narrower the span of control, the closer the supervision and the higher the administrative costs as a result of a higher manager-to-worker ratio. Recent emphasis on leanness and administrative efficiency dictates spans of control as wide as possible but guarding against inadequate supervision and lack of coordination. Wider spans also complement the trend toward greater worker autonomy and empowerment (see Skills & Best Practices).

**Line and Staff Positions**   The organization chart in Figure 15–1 also distinguishes between line and staff positions. Line managers such as the president, the two executive directors, and the various directors occupy

## Managing a Wide Span

In some situations, a manager can successfully lead a group of 30 or even more employees. The following conditions and practices help.

- Jobs are similar to one another, so training and goal-setting are simpler.

- Employees have the knowledge, talent, and motivation to work independently.

- Employees are empowered to make decisions.

- Pay is linked to results, so employees have an incentive to excel.

- Communication technology keeps managers in touch with their employees and helps everyone share knowledge.

At Gemesa, PepsiCo's cookie business in Mexico, supervisors are responsible for the work of 56 employees each. That span of control succeeds because employees are so familiar with company goals and processes that they can handle greater responsibility. Also, incentive pay is linked to productivity, quality, service, and teamwork. The efficiency of this organizational structure has enhanced Gemesa's business results.

SOURCE: Based on G Anders, "Overseeing More Employees—with Fewer Managers," *The Wall Street Journal*, March 24, 2008, p B6.

formal decision-making positions within the chain of command. Line positions generally are connected by solid lines on organization charts. Dotted lines indicate staff relationships. **Staff personnel** do background research and provide technical advice and recommendations to their **line managers,** who have the authority to make decisions. For example, the cost-containment specialists in the sample organization chart merely advise the president on relevant matters. Apart from supervising the work of their own staff assistants, they have no line authority over other organizational members. Modern trends such as cross-functional teams and reengineering are blurring the distinction between line and staff.

> **staff personnel**
>
> Provide research, advice, and recommendations to line managers.
>
> **line managers**
>
> Have authority to make organizational decisions

According to a study of 207 police officers in Israel, line personnel exhibited greater job commitment than did their staff counterparts.[6] This result was anticipated because the line managers' decision-making authority empowered them and gave them comparatively more control over their work situations.

# An Open-System Perspective of Organizations

**learning objective** 2

Explain the difference between closed and open systems.

To understand how organizations have evolved, we need to know the difference between closed and open systems.[7] A **closed system** is said to be a self-sufficient entity. It is "closed" to the surrounding environment. In contrast, an **open system** depends on constant interaction with the environment for survival. The distinction between closed and open systems is a matter of degree. Because every worldly system is partly closed and partly open, the key question is: How great a role does the environment play in the functioning of the system? For instance, a battery-powered clock is a relatively closed system. Once the battery is inserted, the clock performs its time-keeping function hour after hour until the battery goes dead. The human body, on the other hand, is a highly open system because it requires a constant supply of life-sustaining oxygen from the environment. Nutrients also are imported from the environment. Open systems are capable of self-correction, adaptation, and growth, thanks to characteristics such as homeostasis and feedback control.

> **closed system**
>
> A relatively self-sufficient entity.
>
> **open system**
>
> Organism that must constantly interact with its environment to survive

Historically, management theorists downplayed the environment as they used closed-system thinking to characterize organizations as either well-oiled machines or highly disciplined military units.[8] They believed rigorous planning and control would eliminate environmental uncertainty. But that proved unrealistic. Drawing upon the field of general systems theory that emerged during the 1950s, organization theorists suggested a more dynamic model for organizations.[9] The resulting open-system model likened organizations to the human body.[10] Accordingly, the model in Figure 15–2 reveals the organization to be a living organism that transforms inputs into various outputs. The outer boundary of the organization is permeable. People, information, capital, and goods and services move back and forth across this boundary. Moreover, each of the five organizational subsystems—goals and values, technical, psychosocial, structural, and managerial—is dependent on the others. Feedback about such things as sales and customer satisfaction or dissatisfaction enables the organization to self-adjust and survive despite uncertainty and change. In effect, the organization is alive.

## FIGURE 15–2 | The Organization as an Open System

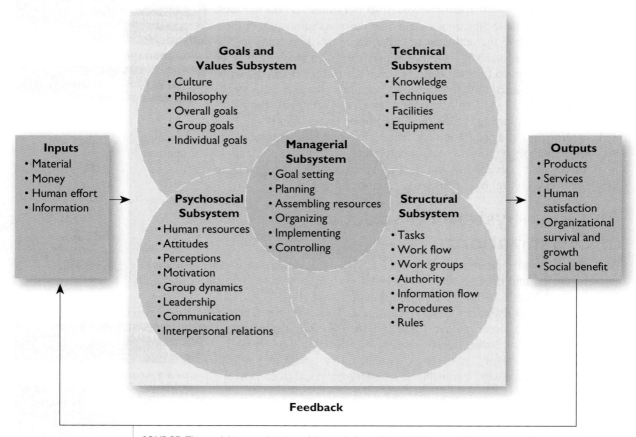

**SOURCE:** This model is a combination of Figures 5–2 and 5–3 in F E Kast and J E Rosenzweig, *Organization and Management: A Systems and Contingency Approach,* 4th ed (New York: McGraw-Hill, 1986), pp 112, 114. Copyright © 1986 by the McGraw-Hill Companies. Reprinted with permission

# Organization Design in a Changing World

**3** learning objective

Define seven basic ways organizations are structured.

Until a few decades ago, most management theorists thought about organizations' structures mainly in terms of how each organization arranged its hierarchy from top to bottom.[11] More recently, many organizations have emphasized horizontal relationships to carry out entire processes or to operate with teams. In addition, some companies' managers have seen alternatives to working within the boundaries that have traditionally defined organizations. In this section, we look at the types of structures that have resulted from each of these three points of view.

## Traditional Designs

Organizations defined by the traditional approach may have functional, divisional, and/or matrix structures. A functional structure groups people according to the business functions they perform, for example, manufacturing, marketing, and finance. A manager is responsible for the performance of each of these functions, and employees tend to identify strongly with their particular function, such as sales or engineering.

The organization chart in Figure 15–1 illustrates a functional structure. Responsibility at this hospital is first divided into administrative and medical functions, and within each category, directors are responsible for each of the functions. This arrangement puts together people who are experts in the same or similar activities. Thus, as a small company grows and hires more production workers, salespeople, and accounting staff, it typically groups them together with a supervisor who understands their function.

In a divisional structure, the organization groups together activities related to outputs, such as type of product or type (or location) of customer. For example, General Electric has six businesses (major product divisions): GE Commercial Finance, GE Healthcare, GE Industrial, GE Infrastructure, GE Money, and NBC Universal. These major business areas are subdivided into either product or geographic divisions. GE Healthcare is divided into product divisions such as Clinical Systems and Diagnostic Imaging; and GE Money is divided into three geographic divisions, Americas, Asia Pacific, and Europe, Middle East and Africa.[12] The people in a division can become experts at making a particular type of product or serving the particular needs of their customer group or geographic area. Typically, each division has a functional structure.

"YOU KNOW, EVER SINCE I STARTED WORKING HERE, I'VE HAD THIS CRAVING FOR CHEESE."

*Reprinted by permission of Dave Carpenter from Harvard Business Review, April 2004.*

Some organizations have concluded that using a functional or divisional structure divides people too much. Either employees don't collaborate across functions well enough to meet customer needs or they don't share expertise across divisions well enough to operate efficiently. One way to address this problem while still focusing on hierarchy is to create a matrix structure. A matrix structure combines functional and divisional chains of command to form a grid with two command structures, one shown vertically according to function, and the other shown horizontally, by product line, brand, customer group, or geographic region. In the example shown in Figure 15–3, Ford might set up vice presidents for each functional group and project managers for each make of car. Employees would report to two managers: one in charge of the function they perform and the other in charge of the project they are working on.[13]

# Focus on Collaboration: Horizontal Design

The traditional approach of dividing up work according to functions, products, and customers is dissatisfying to managers who want to focus on bringing people together, without internal boundaries keeping them apart. If you want people to share knowledge and continually improve the way things are done, you need to create an environment in which collaboration feels easy and natural. Many organizations with this viewpoint have emphasized horizontal relationships among people who are working on shared tasks more than vertical relationships in a traditional organizational design.

This horizontal approach to organizational design tends to focus on work processes. A process consists of every task and responsibility needed to meet a customer need, such as developing a new product or filling a customer order. Completing a process requires input from people in different functions, typically organized into a cross-functional team (described in Chapter 9). Thus, teamwork is a feature of organizations

**FIGURE 15–3**    Sample Matrix Structure That Ford Might Use

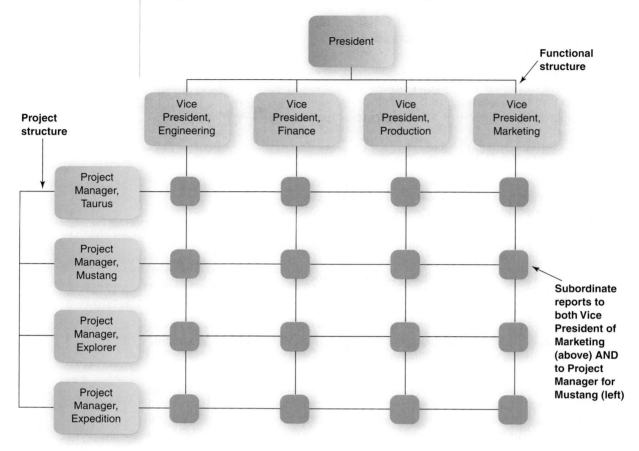

designed horizontally. Two experts in organization design have identified five principles for designing a horizontal organization:

1.  Organize around complete workflow processes rather than tasks.
2.  Flatten hierarchy and use teams to manage everything.
3.  Appoint process team leaders to manage internal team processes.
4.  Let supplier and customer contact drive performance.
5.  Provide required expertise from outside the team as required.[14]

# Opening Boundaries between Organizations

While the horizontal organization aims to break down barriers within organizations, some structures are based on the idea that not even barriers *between* organizations are always ideal. Sometimes organizations can perform better by creating structures in which they can pool their resources to work toward a shared goal. The result of applying this thinking may be a hollow, modular, or virtual organization.

A hollow organization results from strategic application of the trend toward outsourcing. The organization's managers identify core competencies—functions the organization can do better and more profitably than other organizations. An athletic shoe company, for example, might decide that it can excel at developing new designs, owing to its design talent and knowledge of the market. Then it might find outsourcing partners to handle other activities such as manufacturing, order taking, shipping, and managing employee benefits. The more processes that are outsourced, the more the resulting organization is "hollow"—and focused on what it does best. Furniture company Herman Miller goes outside the organization for design expertise. CEO Brian Walker explains the advantages:

> This external network ensures that we are always taking a fresh look at problems faced by our customers without subjecting it to our own filters. If you have only an internal design staff, even an enormously talented one, you are inherently limited by their existing world view and experiences. Our ability to tap into a broader outside network lets us . . . get a fresh perspective on existing or emerging problems.[15]

Herman Miller also uses other organizations for manufacturing; Walker says the company is "more . . . an integrator than a manufacturer," which makes it less resistant to new product ideas because it doesn't have to change manufacturing processes itself.

A modular organization, like a hollow organization, uses outsourcing. But instead of outsourcing processes, it outsources parts of a product, such as components of a jet or subroutines of a software program. The modular organization is responsible for ensuring that the parts meet quality requirements, that the parts arrive in a timely fashion, and that the organization is capable of efficiently combining the parts into the final whole. A well-known example is Boeing, in its production of the 787 Dreamliner.

> When [Boeing] decided to engineer a new aircraft, the company also decided to engineer a new engineering process. That process includes dozens of partners around the globe that build and pre-assemble big pieces of the plane.
>
> Boeing's job is to manage this far-flung supply chain and to make sure the parts fit together flawlessly on the factory floor in Everett, Wash.[16]

Finally, an organization may identify partners to create a virtual organization, "a company outside a company created specifically to respond to an exceptional market opportunity that is often temporary."[17] Just as "virtual memory" in a computer causes it to seem as if it has more memory, so a virtual organization does more than what its founding organization could do with the resources within the organization's boundaries. The organization identifies partners with the needed talents and negotiates an agreement in which the participants typically work in separate facilities. The facilities are linked by technology as they work toward a common goal, such as developing a new product or entering a new market. For instance, this level of collaboration can help in developing cell phones for the U.S. market. AT&T and Verizon dominate the market for wireless service to such a degree that phone producers must work with them to create compatible products and to develop a pipeline for selling them. Nokia, which had trouble gaining market share in the United States, recently shifted its strategy "to develop phones in partnership with U.S. carriers, in part by assigning 300 product developers each to AT&T and Verizon."[18] Salespeople and R&D personnel also are assigned

Nokia is the leading supplier of mobile phones around the world. Part of the company's success is related to its approach to product development. Nokia develops phones in partnership with **AT&T** and other phone carriers. What characteristics must this and other virtual organizations have in order to survive?

## How to Manage Geographically Dispersed Employees

The three keys are **sharing knowledge, building trust, and maintaining connectedness.** Other steps include:

**Hire carefully:** People working in remote locations, especially at home, need to be self-starters who are well-organized, self-motivated, and effective communicators.

**Communicate regularly:** Daily e-mails and weekly phone conversations, at a minimum, help nip problems in the bud, address complaints, and build strong working relationships.

**Practice "management by wandering around":** Get out of the home office and regularly visit remote employees on their turf to get a first-hand view of what is happening. These visits also afford opportunities for coaching, feedback, and positive reinforcement.

**Conduct regular audits:** Formal audits ensure compliance with company policies, legal requirements, and ethical standards.

**Use technology as a tool, not a weapon:** Rely on cost-effective new technologies to enhance productivity. Be sensitive to privacy rights and employee morale when engaging in electronic performance monitoring (e.g., videotaping, monitoring e-mail and Internet use, and counting keystrokes).

**Achieve a workable balance between online and live training.** Live face-to-face training is expensive, but can build trust and teamwork.

**SOURCE:** Adapted from J W Janove, "Management by Remote Control," *HR Magazine*, April 2004, pp 119–24.

to work with particular wireless carriers. In general, a virtual organization demands flexibility, and managers must be able to lead and motivate people in separate locations (see Skills & Best Practices).

# The Contingency Approach to Designing Organizations

According to the **contingency approach to organization design,** organizations tend to be more effective when they are structured to fit the demands of the situation.[19] The purpose of this section is to introduce you to the contingency approach to organization design by reviewing a landmark study, drawing a distinction between centralized and decentralized decision making, and discussing when each of the organization designs is best suited to the context.

## Mechanistic versus Organic Organizations

A landmark contingency design study was reported by a pair of British behavioral scientists, Tom Burns and G M Stalker. In the course of their research, they drew a very instructive distinction between what they called mechanistic and organic organizations. **Mechanistic organizations** are rigid bureaucracies with strict rules, narrowly defined tasks, and top-down communication. A mechanistic organization generally would have one of the traditional organization designs described earlier in this chapter. Ironically, it is at the cutting edge of technology that this seemingly out-of-date approach has found a home. In the highly competitive business of Web hosting—running clients' Web sites in high-security facilities humming with Internet servers—speed and reliability are everything. Enter military-style managers who require strict discipline, faithful adherence to thick rule books, and flawless execution. But, as *BusinessWeek* observed, "The regimented atmosphere and military themes . . . may be tough to stomach for skilled workers used to a more free-spirited atmosphere."[20]

Oppositely, **organic organizations** are flexible networks of multitalented individuals who perform a variety of tasks.[21] An example is Eileen Fisher, Inc., which designs and manufactures women's clothing. The company's leadership includes Susan Schor, who—in the words of founder Eileen Fisher—"came in and created her own place": heading all aspects of "people and culture," including employee development, social consciousness, human resources, and internal communications. Schor's accomplishments include crafting an organizational structure in which all employees work in

**contingency approach to organization design**

Creating an effective organization–environment fit.

**4  learning objective**

Discuss Burns and Stalker's findings regarding mechanistic and organic organizations.

# HANDS-ON EXERCISE

## Mechanistic or Organic?

**INSTRUCTIONS:** Think of your present (or a past) place of employment and rate it on the following eight factors. Calculate a total score and compare it to the scale.

### Characteristics

| | | | | | | | | | |
|---|---|---|---|---|---|---|---|---|---|
| **1.** Task definition and knowledge required ............................ | Narrow, technical | 1 | 2 | 3 | 4 | 5 | 6 | 7 | Broad; general |
| **2.** Linkage between individual's contribution and organization's purpose ............................ | Vague or indirect | 1 | 2 | 3 | 4 | 5 | 6 | 7 | Clear or direct |
| **3.** Task flexibility ........................... | Rigid; routine | 1 | 2 | 3 | 4 | 5 | 6 | 7 | Flexible; varied |
| **4.** Specification of techniques, obligations, and rights ............... | Specific | 1 | 2 | 3 | 4 | 5 | 6 | 7 | General |
| **5.** Degree of hierarchical control ............................ | High | 1 | 2 | 3 | 4 | 5 | 6 | 7 | Low (self-control emphasized) |
| **6.** Primary communication pattern ............................ | Top-down | 1 | 2 | 3 | 4 | 5 | 6 | 7 | Lateral (between peers) |
| **7.** Primary decision-making style ............................ | Authoritarian | 1 | 2 | 3 | 4 | 5 | 6 | 7 | Democratic; participative |
| **8.** Emphasis on obedience and loyalty ............................ | High | 1 | 2 | 3 | 4 | 5 | 6 | 7 | Low |

Total score = _____

### Scale

 8–24 = Relatively mechanistic
25–39 = Mixed
40–56 = Relatively organic

**SOURCE:** Adapted from discussion in T Burns and G M Stalker, *The Management of Innovation* (London: Tavistock, 1961), pp 119–25.

teams run by facilitators and "no one reports to anyone. Instead, we 'connect into' someone else."[22] These qualities of an organic organization are easiest to maintain with the lowered boundaries of horizontal and virtual organizations. Internet technology has made such arrangements more practical by enabling individuals to develop networks of people with whom they can readily share information as needed—a kind of "ecosystem" of people and knowledge.[23] The organization's job then becomes a matter of helping people create and use an optimal network for learning and collaborating.

**A Matter of Degree** Importantly, as illustrated in the Hands-On Exercise, each of the mechanistic-organic characteristics is a matter of degree. Organizations tend to be *relatively* mechanistic or *relatively* organic. Pure types are rare because divisions, departments, or units in the same organization may be more or less mechanistic or organic. From an employee's standpoint, which organization structure would you prefer?

**Test Your Knowledge**
Mechanistic vs. Organic Organizations

**mechanistic organizations**

Rigid, command-and-control bureaucracies.

**organic organizations**

Fluid and flexible network of multitalented people.

**centralized decision making**

Top managers make all key decisions.

**decentralized decision making**

Lower-level managers are empowered to make important decisions.

**Different Approaches to Decision Making**    Decision making tends to be centralized in mechanistic organizations and decentralized in organic organizations. **Centralized decision making** occurs when key decisions are made by top management. **Decentralized decision making** occurs when important decisions are made by middle- and lower-level managers. Generally, centralized organizations are more tightly controlled while decentralized organizations are more adaptive to changing situations.[24] Semco, a Brazilian manufacturer, turned to a more decentralized structure when it needed to spark dramatic change. Ricardo Semler became CEO when Semco was headed for bankruptcy; he eliminated most senior-management jobs and pushed decision making down to lower levels of self-managed teams. The outcomes have been promising.

> The move initially caused inefficiencies and higher costs but eventually allowed low-level innovation to flourish. . . . Inventory backlogs have eased, product lines have expanded, and sales have jumped. . . . After the company's reorganization, revenues climbed from $4 million to $212 million.[25]

Experts on the subject warn against extremes of centralization or decentralization. The challenge is to achieve a workable balance between the two extremes. A management consultant put it this way:

> The modern organization in transition will recognize the pull of two polarities: a need for greater centralization to create low-cost shared resources; and, a need to improve market responsiveness with greater decentralization. Today's winning organizations are the ones that can handle the paradox and tensions of both pulls. These are the firms that analyze the optimum organizational solution in each particular circumstance, without prejudice for one type of organization over another. The result is, almost invariably, a messy mixture of decentralized units sharing cost-effective centralized resources.[26]

Centralization and decentralization are not an either-or proposition; they are an *and-also* balancing act.

**Practical Research Insights**    When they classified a sample of actual companies as either mechanistic or organic, Burns and Stalker discovered one type was not superior to the other. Each type had its appropriate place, depending on the environment. When the environment was relatively *stable and certain,* the successful organizations tended to be *mechanistic. Organic* organizations tended to be the successful ones when the environment was *unstable and uncertain.*[27]

In a more recent study of 103 department managers from eight manufacturing firms and two aerospace organizations, managerial skill was found to have a greater impact on a global measure of department effectiveness in organic departments than in mechanistic departments. This led the researchers to recommend the following contingencies for management staffing and training:

> If we have two units, one organic and one mechanistic, and two potential applicants differing in overall managerial ability, we might want to assign the more competent to the organic unit since in that situation there are few structural aids available to the manager in performing required responsibilities. It is also possible that managerial training is especially needed by managers being groomed to take over units that are more organic in structure.[28]

Another interesting finding comes from a study of 42 voluntary church organizations. As the organizations became more mechanistic (more bureaucratic) the intrinsic motivation of their members decreased. Mechanistic organizations apparently undermined the volunteers' sense of freedom and self-determination. Additionally, the researchers believe their findings help explain why bureaucracy tends to feed on itself: "A mechanistic organizational structure may breed the need for a more extremely mechanistic system because of the reduction in intrinsically motivated behavior."[29] Thus, bureaucracy begets greater bureaucracy.

Most recently, field research in two factories, one mechanistic and the other organic, found expected communication patterns. Command-and-control (downward) communication characterized the mechanistic factory. Consultative or participative (two-way) communication prevailed in the organic factory.[30]

### Both Mechanistic and Organic Structures Have Their Places
Although achievement-oriented students of OB typically express a distaste for mechanistic organizations, not all organizations or subunits can or should be organic. For example, McDonald's could not achieve its admired quality and service standards without extremely mechanistic restaurant operations. Imagine the food and service you would get if McDonald's employees used their own favorite ways of doing things and worked at their own pace! On the other hand, mechanistic structure alienates some employees because it erodes their sense of self-control.

# Getting the Right Fit
All of the organization structures described in this chapter are used today because each structure has advantages and disadvantages that make it appropriate in some cases. For example, the clear roles and strict hierarchy of an extremely mechanistic organization are beneficial when careful routines and a set of checks and balances are important, as at a nuclear power facility. In a fast-changing environment with a great deal of uncertainty, an organization would benefit from a more organic structure that lowers boundaries between functions and organizations. Let us consider each of the seven basic organization designs.

A functional structure can save money by grouping together people who need similar materials and equipment. Quality standards can be maintained because supervisors understand what department members do and because people in the same function develop pride in their specialty. Workers can devote more of their time to what they do best. These benefits are easiest to realize in a stable environment, where the organization doesn't depend on employees to coordinate their efforts to solve varied problems. Today fewer organizations see their environment as stable, so more are moving away from strictly functional structures.

Divisional structures increase employees' focus on customers and products. Managers have the flexibility to make decisions that affect several functions in order to serve customer needs. This enables the organization to move faster if a new customer need arises or if a competitor introduces an important product. However, duplicating functions in each division can add to costs, so this structure may be too expensive for some organizations. Also, divisions sometimes focus on their own customer groups or products to the exclusion of the company's overall mission. Ford Motor Company has struggled to unify its geographic and brand divisions to save money by sharing design, engineering, and manufacturing. Managers of geographic divisions have introduced new car models on different time lines and insisted that their customers want different features.[31] In contrast, geographic divisions have helped McDonald's grow by freeing managers to introduce menu items and décor that locals appreciate.[32]

**Self-Assessment Exercise**

Identify Your Preferred Organization Structure

learning objective **5**

Identify when each of the seven organization structures is the right fit.

A matrix structure tries to combine the advantages of functional and divisional structures. This advantage is also the structure's main drawback: it violates the unity of command principle, described previously in the chapter. Employees have to balance the demands of a functional manager and a product or project manager. When they struggle with this balance, decision making can slow to a crawl, and political behavior can overpower progress. The success of a matrix organization therefore requires superior managers who communicate extensively, foster commitment and collaboration, manage conflict, and negotiate effectively to establish goals and priorities consistent with the organization's strategy. One organization that has made matrix structures work for decades is Procter & Gamble. To manage 138,000 employees in more than 80 countries, the company has a matrix structure in which global business units are responsible for a brand's development and production, while market development organizations focus on the customer needs for particular regions and the way the brands can meet those needs. Employees have to meet objectives both for the brand and for the market, with different managers responsible for each.[33]

Horizontal designs generally improve coordination and communication in organizations.[34] Cross-functional teams can arrive at creative solutions to problems that arise in a fast-changing environment. Teams can develop new products faster and more efficiently than can functions working independently in a traditional structure. Horizontal designs also encourage knowledge sharing. However, because lines of authority are less clear, managers must be able to share responsibility for the organization's overall performance, build commitment to a shared vision, and influence others even when they lack direct authority.[35] This type of structure is a good fit when specialization is less important than the ability to respond to varied or changing customer needs. It requires employees who can rise to the challenges of empowerment. A horizontal design is a good fit for Research in Motion (RIM) because it builds on employees' deep product and customer knowledge. All employees use the company's BlackBerry pocket computers, so they know what works and what doesn't. RIM's chief executive maintains that because employees know the details of what makes the BlackBerry work, they are

**This $2,500 Tata Motors compact car is the result of an organization that adopted a modular structure. How did this structure enable the company to cut costs and inefficiencies?**

well positioned to continue improving it: "We didn't just buy an operating system from one company and a radio technology from another, and then have them assembled somewhere in Asia. We actually built the whole thing. . . . I don't mind investing in it because I know there's a return."[36] RIM applies that knowledge by creating teams to brainstorm new ideas in every aspect of the company's operations.

Finally, organizations that open their boundaries to become hollow, modular, or virtual can generate superior returns by focusing on what they do best.[37] Like functional organizations, they tap people in particular specialties, who may be more expert than the generalists of a divisional or horizontal organization. The downside of these structures is that organizations give up expertise and control in the functions or operations that are outsourced. Still, like divisional and horizontal organizations, they can focus on customers or products, leaving their partners to focus on their own specialty area. In India, when Tata Motors wanted to develop a $2,500 compact car, it decided its own engineers needed assistance, so Tata adopted a modular structure. Each of its suppliers tackled designing particular components to be as inexpensive as possible while still meeting quality standards, and Tata focused on coordinating their work.[38] An example of a successful hollow organization is one global manufacturer that shifted its focus to developing products and contracted with outsourcing firms to make the products in the manufacturer's own facilities, handling the process from ordering materials to shipping the finished product. The arrangement maintained quality while cutting labor costs by 40% by avoiding inefficiency and duplication of work.[39]

The success of organizations that work across boundaries depends on managers' ability to get results from people over whom they do not have direct formal authority by virtue of their position in the organization. For example, Boeing has been embarrassed by its setbacks in manufacturing the Dreamliner from components provided by a network of suppliers, which did not always meet their commitments to Boeing.[40] Also, individuals in these organizations may not have the same degree of commitment as employees of a traditional organization, so motivation and leadership may be more difficult. Therefore, these designs are the best fit when organizations have suitable partners they trust; efficiency is very important; the organization can identify functions, processes, or product components to outsource profitably; and in the case of a virtual organization, when the need to be met is temporary. In a study of managers in 20 organizations that extensively collaborate with other companies, these efforts most often succeeded in companies that select and train for teamwork skills, invest in processes that promote collaboration, set up tools and systems for sharing information, and treat collaboration as one of the company's ongoing programs requiring leadership.[41]

# Striving for Organizational Effectiveness

Assessing organizational effectiveness is an important topic for an array of people, including managers, stockholders, government agencies, and OB specialists. The purpose of this section is to introduce a widely applicable and useful model of organizational effectiveness.

learning objective 6

Describe the four generic organizational effectiveness criteria.

## Generic Effectiveness Criteria

A good way to better understand this complex subject is to consider four generic approaches to assessing an organization's effectiveness (see Figure 15–4). These effectiveness criteria apply equally well to large or small and profit or not-for-profit organizations. Moreover, as denoted by the overlapping circles in Figure 15–4, the four effectiveness criteria can be used in various combinations. The key thing to remember is "no single approach to the evaluation of effectiveness is appropriate in all circumstances or for all organization types."[42] What do Coca-Cola and France Télécom, for example, have in common, other than being large profit-seeking corporations? Because a multidimensional approach is required, we need to look more closely at each of the four generic effectiveness criteria before we can answer this question.

**Goal Accomplishment** Goal accomplishment is the most widely used effectiveness criterion for organizations. Key organizational results or outputs are compared with previously stated goals or objectives. Deviations, either plus or minus, require

**One criterion for organizational effectiveness is the respect of your peers. Under CEO Jeff Immelt, General Electric has been among *Fortune*'s most admired companies in the United States for several years in a row.**

**FIGURE 15–4**    Four Dimensions of Organizational Effectiveness

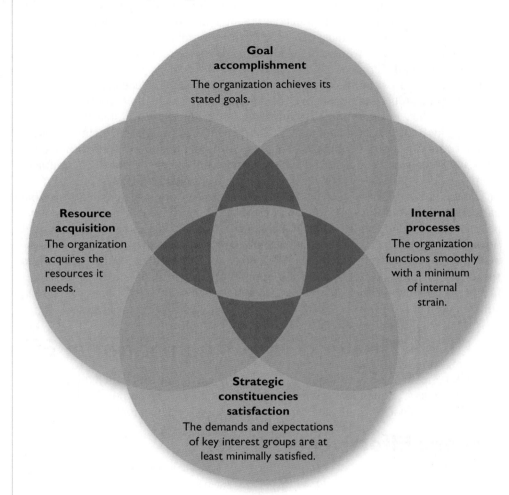

**Goal accomplishment**
The organization achieves its stated goals.

**Resource acquisition**
The organization acquires the resources it needs.

**Internal processes**
The organization functions smoothly with a minimum of internal strain.

**Strategic constituencies satisfaction**
The demands and expectations of key interest groups are at least minimally satisfied.

SOURCES: Adapted from discussion in K Cameron, "Critical Questions in Assessing Organizational Effectiveness," *Organizational Dynamics,* Autumn 1980, pp 66–80; and K S Cameron, "Effectiveness as Paradox: Consensus and Conflict in Conceptions of Organizational Effectiveness," *Management Science,* May 1986, pp 539–53.

corrective action. This is simply an organizational variation of the personal goal-setting process discussed in Chapter 7.[43] Effectiveness, relative to the criterion of goal accomplishment, is gauged by how well the organization meets or exceeds its goals.[44]

Productivity improvement, involving the relationship between inputs and outputs, is a common organization-level goal.[45] Goals also may be set for organizational efforts such as minority recruiting, pollution prevention, and quality improvement. Given today's competitive pressures and e-commerce revolution, *innovation* and *speed* are very important organizational goals worthy of measurement and monitoring.[46] At Xerox, innovation is a key goal under the leadership of chief technology officer Sophie Vandebroek. In contrast to some companies, such as Google, that give employees wide latitude to create, Xerox asks researchers to target their efforts on "six *S*s": innovations that make systems simpler, speedier, smaller, smarter, and more

secure, and that are socially responsible (for example, using less energy to operate). To ensure that innovation contributes to other business goals, Vandebroek defines three roles for innovation at Xerox: "an explorer role, where we push the limits of the technology . . . the partnership role, [where Xerox people] work with the business-group engineers to make sure these cool technologies actually end up in a product or service . . . [and] the incubator, [in which] we try to understand fully the business value of these ideas."[47] In this way, the structure of Xerox's Innovation Group keeps innovation efforts directed toward practical goals.

**Resource Acquisition**   The second criterion, resource acquisition, relates to inputs rather than outputs. An organization is deemed effective in this regard if it acquires necessary factors of production such as raw materials, labor, capital, and managerial and technical expertise. An organizational design that made resource acquisition more difficult caused major problems for Boeing in the production of its 787 Dreamliner. To achieve the goal of operating faster and more efficiently, the company had outsourced the production—and even the design—of components to manufacturers around the world. However, as the planned launch date for the new jet came and went, Boeing was forced to acknowledge that suppliers were running into quality and scheduling problems, and in some cases, Boeing's management wasn't even fully aware of the extent of the difficulties.[48]

**Internal Processes**   Some refer to the third effectiveness criterion—internal processes—as the "healthy systems" approach. An organization is said to be a healthy system if information flows smoothly and if employee loyalty, commitment, job satisfaction, and trust prevail. Goals may be set for any of these internal processes. Healthy systems, from a behavioral standpoint, tend to have a minimum of dysfunctional conflict and destructive political maneuvering. M Scott Peck, the physician who wrote the highly regarded book, *The Road Less Traveled,* characterizes healthy organizations in ethical terms:

> A healthy organization, Peck says, is one that has a genuine sense of community: It's a place where people are emotionally present with one another, and aren't afraid to talk about fears and disappointments—because that's what allows us to care for one another. It's a place where there is authentic communication, a willingness to be vulnerable, a commitment to speaking frankly and respectfully—and a commitment not to walk away when the going gets tough.[49]

Betty Eaton Keyes would likely say that these qualities exist at her workplace, Richardson, Texas–based AMX, which develops remote controls and electronic touch panels. Keyes tried retiring but found that she missed the people too much and returned as a part-time receptionist. Bobby Ramoz echoes her sentiments: "Coming to work every day is like going to a friend's house." AMX's chief executive, Rashid Skaf, explains that these attitudes are actively pursued by management as a way to help the company thrive: "When people are happy, they are more productive, and they achieve more than even they thought was possible."[50]

**strategic constituency**

Any group of people with a stake in the organization's operation or success.

**Strategic Constituencies Satisfaction**   Organizations both depend on people and affect the lives of people. Consequently, many consider the satisfaction of key interested parties to be an important criterion of organizational effectiveness.

A **strategic constituency** is any group of individuals who have some stake in the organization—for example, resource providers, users of the organization's products or services, producers of the organization's output, groups whose cooperation is essential for the organization's survival, or those whose lives are significantly affected by the organization.[51]

Strategic constituencies (or *stakeholders*) generally have competing or conflicting interests.[52] This forces executives to do some strategic juggling to achieve workable balances. For example, in recent years, it has been difficult for many organizations to satisfy the needs and preferences of employees, in part because of investors' pressure to operate more efficiently to withstand global competition at the same time many employees are demanding more flexibility so that they can fulfill competing roles.[53] Besides employees and investors, another key constituency is, of course, customers. To learn how Citigroup designed its organization to help satisfy an important segment of this constituency, see Skills & Best Practices.

## SKILLS & BEST PRACTICES

## How Citigroup Organized to Serve Big Customers

Citigroup, like many companies today, has some big customers with global operations. Serving these major customers is complicated. Traditional structures, often with sales and service representatives specializing in particular countries or product lines, fall short of helping these customers meet their needs. Citigroup has addressed that problem with global account management, a structure in which a manager is assigned to ensure that a single customer's worldwide needs are satisfied by whichever experts in the organization can provide the necessary products and services.

Citigroup began moving toward global account management in the 1960s when it began assigning people to serve as client specialists, developing marketing plans for large customers. In the 1970s, Citigroup devoted an entire division to global clients. Today, Citigroup serves more than 1,400 major clients through its Global Relationship Banking division.

In that division, account managers work directly with the chief financial officer or equivalent executive of the clients they serve. The managers' performance is measured by asking clients to score how well Citigroup has helped them meet business goals such as innovation and product quality. The company also measures how well each business relationship is performing in terms of Citigroup's own goals for profits and risk management.

**SOURCE: Based on C Senn and A Thoma, "Worldly Wise,"** *The Wall Street Journal,* **March 3, 2007, http:// online.wsj.com.**

## Mixing Effectiveness Criteria: Practical Guidelines

Experts on the subject recommend a multidimensional approach to assessing the effectiveness of modern organizations. This means no single criterion is appropriate for all stages of the organization's life cycle. Nor will a single criterion satisfy competing stakeholders. Well-managed organizations mix and match effectiveness criteria to fit the unique requirements of the situation.[54] For example, Irdeto Holdings, which provides content protection for pay TV and video recordings, decided on a structural change after determining that sales were growing fastest in Asia, which already accounted for almost 40% of the company's revenues. To meet business goals for serving this important geographic market, Irdeto's executives decided to convert the company's Beijing office into a second headquarters (the first headquarters is located near Amsterdam). This change serves an important constituency—Asian customers—but raised concerns with Amsterdam employees. Responding to that second constituency, Irdeto's CEO, Graham Kill, announced plans to build a new Amsterdam office building and explained that employees can enjoy an exciting career path if they are willing to rotate between the two headquarters cities. Management also has had to address internal processes, especially in developing Chinese managers to take initiative in decision making and to think about issues affecting the entire corporation, not just Asian markets.[55]

Managers need to identify and seek input from strategic constituencies. This information, when merged with the organization's stated mission and philosophy, enables management to derive an appropriate *combination* of effectiveness criteria. The following guidelines are helpful in this regard:

- *The goal accomplishment approach* is appropriate when "goals are clear, consensual, time-bounded, measurable."[56]

- *The resource acquisition approach* is appropriate when inputs have a traceable effect on results or output. For example, the amount of money the American Red Cross receives through donations dictates the level of services provided.

- *The internal processes approach* is appropriate when organizational performance is strongly influenced by specific processes (e.g., cross-functional teamwork).

- *The strategic constituencies approach* is appropriate when powerful stakeholders can significantly benefit or harm the organization.[57]

# key terms

# chapter summary

- *Describe the four characteristics common to all organizations.* They are coordination of effort (achieved through policies and rules), a common goal (a collective purpose), division of labor (people performing different but related tasks), and a hierarchy of authority (the chain of command).

- *Explain the difference between closed and open systems.* Closed systems, such as a battery-powered clock, are relatively self-sufficient. Open systems, such as the human body, are highly dependent on the environment for survival.

- *Define seven basic ways organizations are structured.* Traditional designs include (1) functional structures, in which work is divided according to function; (2) divisional structures, in which work is divided according to product or customer type or location; and (3) matrix structures, with dual reporting structures based on product and function. Organizations also may be designed (4) horizontally, with cross-functional teams responsible for entire processes. Organization design also may reduce barriers between organizations, becoming (5) hollow organizations, which outsource functions; (6) modular organizations, which outsource the production of a product's components; or (7) virtual organizations, which temporarily combine the efforts of members of different companies in order to complete a project.

- *Discuss Burns and Stalker's findings regarding mechanistic and organic organizations.* British researchers Burns and Stalker found that mechanistic (bureaucratic, centralized) organizations tended to be effective in stable situations. In unstable situations, organic (flexible, decentralized) organizations were more effective. These findings underscored the need for a contingency approach to organization design.

- *Identify when each of the seven organization structures is the right fit.* Mechanistic organizations and functional structures may be necessary when tight control is important and the environment is stable. Organic organizations allow for innovation in a rapidly changing environment. Divisional structures are a good fit when the organization needs deep knowledge of varied customer groups and the ability to respond to customer demands quickly. A matrix organization can deliver the advantages of functional and divisional structures if the company has superior managers who communicate extensively, foster commitment and collaboration, and negotiate effectively to establish goals and priorities consistent with the organization's strategy. A horizontal design is a good fit when specialization is less important than the ability to respond to varied or changing customer needs. Hollow, modular, and virtual designs are best when organizations have suitable partners they trust; efficiency is very important; the organization can identify functions, processes, or product components to outsource; and in the case of a virtual organization, when the need to be met is temporary.

- *Describe the four generic organizational effectiveness criteria.* They are goal accomplishment (satisfying stated objectives), resource acquisition (gathering the necessary productive inputs), internal processes (building and maintaining healthy organizational systems), and strategic constituencies satisfaction (achieving at least minimal satisfaction for all key stakeholders).

# discussion questions

1. Based on the chapter-opening case, what type of organizational structure does Google use? Explain.
2. What would an organization chart of your current (or last) place of employment look like? Does the chart you have drawn reveal the hierarchy (chain of command), division of labor, span of control, and line–staff distinctions? Does it reveal anything else? Explain.
3. Why is it appropriate to view modern organizations as open systems?
4. In a nutshell, what does contingency organization design entail?
5. If organic organizations are popular with most employees, why can't all organizations be structured in an organic fashion?

# ethical dilemma

## Has Electronic Monitoring Gone Too Far?

Results from an American Management Association national survey: The Electronic Monitoring & Surveillance Survey revealed that 25% of employers have fired employees who misused email (e.g., offensive language or excessive personal use), while roughly 33% discharged people for using the Internet inappropriately (e.g., surfing for pornography).[58] "Computer monitoring takes many forms, with 45% of employers tracking content, keystrokes, and time spent at the keyboard. Another 43% store and review computer files. In addition, 12% monitor the blogosphere to see what is being written about the company, and another 10% monitor social networking sites."[59] Consider how electronic monitoring impacted Kary Nagel.

Kary Nagel, 24, was regarded as a good employee until she criticized the owners of a credit-repair agency on her personal email. She was immediately fired after the owners read her email. "I never signed anything saying it was OK to monitor my email or Internet activity," Nagel said. "So I assumed it wasn't, which was a horrible assumption."[60]

Companies believe that electronic monitoring will reduce the estimated 30 to 40% decrease in productivity associated with Internet surfing during work hours. Interestingly, companies such as WakeMed Health & Hospitals and Butterball do not even inform employees that they are being monitored at work. Some people believe that the failure to tell employees about monitoring activities is just plain wrong.[61]

### How Much Electronic Surveillance in the Workplace Is Too Much?

1. Electronic surveillance signals a distrust in employees, erodes morale, and ultimately hampers productivity. Explain your rationale.

2. Employers sign the paychecks and own the equipment, so they have the right to make sure they are getting their money's worth and their equipment is being used properly. Explain.

3. This sort of "snoopervision" creates a cat-and-mouse game in which "beating the system" becomes more important than productivity. Explain.

4. Electronic surveillance is unnecessary if properly trained and equipped employees are held accountable for meeting challenging but fair performance goals. Explain your rationale.

5. No amount of electronic performance monitoring can make up for poor hiring decisions, inadequate training, a weak performance-reward system, and inept supervision. Explain.

6. Invent other interpretations or options. Discuss.

For an interpretation of this situation, visit our Web site, **www.mhhe.com/kinickiob4e.**

---

If you're looking for additional study materials, be sure to check out the Online Learning Center at

**www.mhhe.com/kinickiob4e**

for more information and interactivities that correspond to this chapter.

# chapter Sixteen

# Managing Change and Organizational Learning

**LEARNING OBJECTIVES**

**After reading the material in this chapter, you should be able to:**

1. Discuss the external and internal forces that create the need for organizational change.

2. Describe Lewin's change model and the systems model of change.

3. Explain Kotter's eight steps for leading organizational change.

4. Review the 11 reasons employees resist change.

5. Identify alternative strategies for overcoming resistance to change.

6. Discuss the process organizations use to build their learning capabilities.

Ten thousand layoffs here, twelve hundred there: There's a lot of anxiety in the workplace, and a lot of empty offices, too. As the recession takes hold, there is likely to be more of both. So here come the interior designers trying to persuade executives to do something—anything—with the space where employees used to be. "It's kind of an exciting time because we consider ourselves change managers," says Jo Heinz, the president of office design firm Staffelbach Design Associates in Dallas. "Downsizing is often essential, and of course no one looks forward to it. But if it's handled well, it can help the company become more efficient and effective."

**Empty cubicles like this are common in today's poor economy. How would it benefit an organization to change the layout of the office to eliminate empty cubicles?**

It's pretty obvious why leaving employees surrounded by suddenly vacated offices isn't a great idea: It's depressing. "I feel unstable. Who knows when more layoffs will come?" says a woman who sits in a row of eight cubes, only four of which are occupied after job cuts at the automotive company where she works. As all manner of consultants do, designers see opportunity amid all this uncertainty, and not just for themselves, of course. "It's a business imperative to transform the physical space quickly to send a clear message to the remaining employees, to say we value you and we're a viable, healthy company," says James Ludwig, vice-president of design for office furniture maker Steelcase.

Many executives, though, are loath to spend money after cutting jobs. If they do move people closer together, it's often so the company can try to lease some of the unused space. "Rearranging folks might improve morale, but it's a cost decision," says a facilities planner at a homebuilder that has gone through a series of layoffs. "We're not making people work on orange crates. It will continue to be a comfortable layout," he adds. . . .

Clients call in Heinz and her team before any layoffs are announced, sometimes as early as four months in advance. They walk around the office late at night and during weekends to get a feel for the space without arousing suspicions. They meet with executives to help them think about how to reorganize the workplace to reflect new business realities: which departments are going to be working more closely together, which ones might shrink further. Designers often suggest turning empty offices into quiet rooms, where massage chairs, sofas, and plasma TVs on mute are common, or caucus rooms, where comfortable seating, good coffee, and Internet access are supposed to encourage brainstorming. And if that doesn't go over well, they might propose creating informal meeting spaces—no espresso machines required.

When the layoffs are imminent, Heinz's staff moves into a hotel near the client and sets up a command center. They coordinate the work of movers, liquidators, contractors, and furniture installers. After the announcement, the designers come into the office to oversee the move and deal with employees about to be uprooted. "We see people feeling disappointed and downtrodden. We bring in energy, a positive attitude. We tell them we're here to help," Heinz says. The most common complaint, she says, is about how much more work employees will be expected to do. "We always say: 'We're going to have your workspace so fine-tuned that it should be easier to be more productive.' "

MANAGING THE MANAGERS
As often happens after a major change, many employees at one energy company were moved from private offices to a smaller, open area to save space (and encourage collaboration—the new workplace buzzword). No walls, not such a problem. But no white boards? So Heinz found white boards that could fit in the workstations and encouraged the managers to let people write on the glass walls of the conference rooms with water-based markers. "After that, they were really happy," she says. "They got control over their environment."

At a company in Dallas, it was the executives who became cube dwellers. Heinz had to talk up the change as a way to allow more effective communication with their staffs. "And we had to show them where the closest conference rooms were and how to book them," she says. Indeed, several designers say they spend a lot of time talking to managers about the rules for the new, open workspace.[1]

Are you surprised that organizations hire outside firms to help redesign the physical layout after layoffs? Discuss your rationale. For an interpretation of this case, and additional comments, visit our Online Learning Center at

www.mhhe.com/kinickiob4e

**INCREASED GLOBAL COMPETITION,** startling breakthroughs in information technology, changes in consumer preferences, and calls for greater corporate ethics are forcing companies to change the way they do business. Employees want satisfactory work environments, customers are demanding greater value, and investors want more integrity in financial disclosures. The rate of organizational and societal change is clearly accelerating.

As exemplified in the opening case, organizations must change in order to satisfy customers and shareholders. Furthermore, any type of change, whether it be product driven, personal, or organizational, is likely to encounter resistance even when it represents an appropriate course of action. Even when employees don't actively resist a change, the goal of the change might not be realized if employees feel so negative about it that absenteeism and turnover rise.[2] Peter Senge, a well-known expert on the topic of organizational change, made the following comment about organizational change during an interview with *Fast Company* magazine:

> When I look at efforts to create change in big companies over the past 10 years, I have to say that there's enough evidence of success to say that change is possible—and enough evidence of failure to say that it isn't likely.[3]

If Senge is correct, then it is all the more important for current and future managers to learn how they can successfully implement organizational change.

This final chapter was written to help managers navigate the journey of change. Specifically, we discuss the forces that create the need for organization change, models of planned change, resistance to change, and creating a learning organization.

# Forces of Change

**1** learning objective

Discuss the external and internal forces that create the need for organizational change.

Major organizational changes can involve the organization's strategy, leadership, culture, work processes, and organizational structure. In a recent survey by the Society for Human Resource Management, 8 out of 10 HR professionals said their company had planned or carried out a major organizational change in the preceding two years.[4] How do organizations know when they should change? What cues should an organization look for? Although there are no clear-cut answers to these questions, the "cues" that signal the need for change are found by monitoring the forces for change.

Organizations encounter many different forces for change. These forces come from external sources outside the organization and from internal sources. This section examines the forces that create the need for change. Awareness of the forces of change can help managers determine when they should consider implementing an organizational change.

## External Forces

**external forces for change**

Originate outside the organization.

**External forces for change** originate outside the organization. Because these forces have global effects, they may cause an organization to question the essence of what business it is in and the process by which products and services are produced. There are four key external forces for change: demographic characteristics, technological advancements, market changes, and social and political pressures. Each is now discussed.

**Demographic Characteristics** Chapter 4 provided a detailed discussion of the demographic changes occurring in the U.S. workforce. We concluded that organizations need to effectively manage diversity if they are to receive maximum contribution and commitment from employees. An aging U.S. workforce has become an important force for change at Toyota. For years, the company has had an edge in efficiency; its workers were paid less than those at U.S. based automakers, so its labor cost for producing each car was less. But as the U.S. employees have been with the company nearly two decades, their wages have climbed, even as Toyota's U.S. competitors have laid off many of their older workers and negotiated contracts that pay newer workers lower rates. Now Toyota has to work harder than ever to improve efficiency, cut the cost of health care benefits, and find other ways to keep its competitive edge.[5]

**Technological Advancements**  Both manufacturing and service organizations are increasingly using technology as a means to improve productivity, competitiveness, and customer service while also cutting costs. For example, information technology is enabling more and more forms of self-service, from Internet stores and banks for customers to online help for employees who want to learn about their benefits packages. Visitors to Adour Alain Ducasse restaurant in New York City can choose their wines by looking up information on a touch screen in the bar. The restaurant's management sees the technology not as a

substitute for an educated sommelier but as a way for customers to enjoy learning about and trying new wines.[6] In other applications, including use of robots in factories, technology is intended to improve efficiency without adding employees. There is no question that the development and use of technological advancements is probably one of the biggest forces for change.

**Customer and Market Changes**  Increasing customer sophistication is requiring organizations to deliver higher value in their products and services. Customers are simply demanding more now than they did in the past. Moreover, customers are more likely to shop elsewhere if they do not get what they want because of lower customer switching costs. A big challenge for toy companies is that today's children are increasingly interested in electronics rather than toys. This force for change, which leads the companies to shift product lines to include more online activities, demands not only that the companies revamp what they sell, but also that they revise the mix of talent they need in their workforces to develop new product ideas and bring them to market.[7]

  With respect to market changes, companies are experiencing increased pressure to obtain more productivity because global competition is fierce. Swings in the economic cycle also spur a need to change in response to surging or falling demand for products, requiring companies to produce more or survive on less.

Under its new CEO Robert Siegel, the venerable clothier Lacoste is responding to market forces. Shifting tastes among U.S. shoppers inspired the company to restore its brand's luxury image with better fabrics, higher prices, more exclusive distribution, and newly designed multiseason fashions like stylish boots and shearling jackets that appeal to a new generation of shoppers. "When you think back to Lacoste 10 years ago," says Siegel, "we never had the young customer that we have now."

Exelon is the largest nuclear power operator in the United States. Under CEO John Rowe, its response to internal forces must include increased capacity and a better safety record.

**Social and Political Pressures**    These forces are created by social and political events. For example, widespread concern about the impact of climate change and rising energy costs have been important forces for change in almost every industry around the world. Companies have gone "green," looking for ways to use less energy themselves and to sell products that consume less energy. Employees of Microsoft are eagerly claiming spots on the company's free shuttle buses, leaving their cars at home, and employees at 3M have submitted thousands of ideas to the company's 3P (Pollution Prevention Pays) program, saving the company more than $1 billion in the first year alone.[8]

In general, social and political pressure is exerted through legislative bodies that represent the American populace. Political events also can create substantial change. For example, the war in Iraq created tremendous opportunities for defense contractors and organizations like Halliburton that are involved in rebuilding the country. Although it is difficult for organizations to predict changes in political forces, many organizations hire lobbyists and consultants to help them detect and respond to social and political changes. In the case of climate change, experts predict that some degree of regulation is likely. Harvard business professor Forest Reinhardt advises that companies take bold action, rather than waiting for government constraints:

> Business leaders must be courageous in betting on the long-term future that will benefit their companies the most. . . . By betting on the future they want, corporations will make that future all the more likely. Prudent businesspeople may balk at the idea that they should stick their necks out and, in some cases, act unilaterally on climate change. But their necks are already exposed.[9]

## Internal Forces

**Internal forces for change** come from inside the organization. These forces can be subtle, such as low job satisfaction, or can manifest in outward signs, such as low productivity or high turnover and conflict. Investors, too, pressure companies to improve their sales and profits. As a result, boards of directors expect fast results from today's chief executives, who, in turn, pressure their managers to shake up the way things are done.[10] At McDonald's, for example, CEO Jim Skinner acknowledged that the company's profits had been falling. "We proved that we were getting bigger but not better. And we have to be better." Skinner launched his new strategy, Plan to Win, which aims for changes that improve service, food quality, store ambience, and marketing.[11] In general, internal forces for change come from both human resource problems and managerial behavior/decisions. At Amazon, internal forces for change include a culture that values a constant search for ways to improve the customer's shopping experience, even if an innovation takes years to deliver bottom-line improvements.[12] Finally, small changes in an organization, such as a decision to empower employees, can lead to a series of changes that were not initially planned but amount to a dramatic overall change in what the organization does and how it operates.[13]

# Models of Planned Change

American managers are criticized for emphasizing short-term, quick-fix solutions to organizational problems. When applied to organizational change, this approach is doomed from the start. Quick-fix solutions do not really solve underlying causes of problems and they have little staying power. Researchers and managers alike thus have tried to identify effective ways to manage the change process. This section reviews three models of planned change—Lewin's change model, a systems model of change, and Kotter's eight steps for leading organizational change—and organizational development.

## Lewin's Change Model

Most theories of organizational change originated from the landmark work of social psychologist Kurt Lewin. Lewin developed a three-stage model of planned change which explained how to initiate, manage, and stabilize the change process.[14] The three stages are unfreezing, changing, and refreezing.

**learning objective** 2

Describe Lewin's change model and the systems model of change.

**Unfreezing**  The focus of this stage is to create the motivation to change. In so doing, individuals are encouraged to replace old behaviors and attitudes with those desired by management. Managers can begin the unfreezing process by disconfirming the usefulness or appropriateness of employees' present behaviors or attitudes. In other words, employees need to become dissatisfied with the old way of doing things. Managers frequently create the motivation for change by presenting data regarding levels of effectiveness, efficiency, or customer satisfaction. Declines in the stock price and same-store sales of Starbucks, along with the reappointment of Howard Schultz as CEO of the company he once built into an internationally known brand, signaled a need for change in how Starbucks operated. Schultz communicated that in a memo complaining that the company was losing its vision and growing dull in terms of product innovation. He has attempted to create a sense of urgency and motivate a commitment to change through his intense leadership style and frequent trips to meet directly with employees and urge them "not to be 'bystanders' who tolerate mediocrity."[15]

Benchmarking is another technique that can be used to unfreeze an organization. **Benchmarking** "describes the overall process by which a company compares its performance with that of other companies, then learns how the strongest-performing companies achieve their results."[16] For example, one company for which we consulted discovered through benchmarking that their costs to develop software were twice as high as the best companies in the industry, and the time it took to get a new product to market was four times longer than the benchmarked organizations. These data were ultimately used to unfreeze employees' attitudes and motivate people to change the organization's internal processes in order to remain competitive. Managers also need to devise ways to reduce the barriers to change during this stage.

**benchmarking**

**Process by which a company compares its performance with that of high-performing organizations.**

**Changing**  Organizational change, whether large or small, is undertaken to improve some process, procedure, product, service, or outcome of interest to management. Because change involves learning and doing things differently, this stage entails providing employees with new information, new behavioral models, new processes or procedures, new equipment, new technology, or new ways of getting the job done. How does management know what to change?

## Refreezing Change at Lloyd's

Lloyd's, the London-based insurance marketer known for providing unusual and sometimes risky coverage for valuables including satellites, skyscrapers, and Keith Richards's hands, also generates a not so environmentally friendly by-product: about four tons of paper every day. Richard Ward, CEO of Lloyd's, is trying to make a major move away from paper documents to electronic accounting, contracts, and claims handling.

Recognizing that getting a 300-year-old company to change work habits is difficult, Ward has the company adopt one process at a time, rewarding those who move forward and prodding those who don't. In a recent August, Ward reported that 30% of Lloyd's claims are being processed electronically, with a goal of 100% paperless claims processing by the end of the year.

Writing to the insurers who jointly own Lloyd's as its members, Ward "threatened to publish lists of people falling behind his targets [for going paperless] and to potentially limit the amount of coverage sold by those who keep relying on paper slips," according to *The Wall Street Journal.* Ward is also considering praise for those who lead in the change: "You might say here are the 10 best, now where are the rest of you?" Ward is considering ways to celebrate paper-free work methods. One idea is to crush one of the unmarked vans that transport documents for storing or shredding. The crushed van could be mounted at headquarters as a monument to the company's transformation.

**SOURCE: Based on I McDonald, "Making Paperless Trails at Lloyd's,"** *The Wall Street Journal,* **August 13, 2007, pp B1, B6.**

There is no simple answer to this question. Organizational change can be aimed at improvement or growth, or it can focus on solving a problem such as poor customer service or low productivity. Change also can be targeted at different levels in an organization. For example, sending managers to leadership training programs can be a solution to improving individuals' job satisfaction and productivity. In contrast, installing new information technology may be the change required to increase work group productivity and overall corporate profits. The point to keep in mind is that change should be targeted at some type of desired end-result. The systems model of change, which is the next model to be discussed, provides managers with a framework to diagnose the target of change.

**Refreezing**    Change is stabilized during refreezing by helping employees integrate the changed behavior or attitude into their normal way of doing things. This is accomplished by first giving employees the chance to exhibit the new behaviors or attitudes. Once these have been exhibited, positive reinforcement is used to reinforce the desired change (see Skills & Best Practices). Additional coaching and modeling also are used at this point to reinforce the stability of the change. Extrinsic rewards, particularly monetary incentives (recall our discussion in Chapter 8), are frequently used to reinforce behavioral change.

## A Systems Model of Change

A systems approach takes a "big picture" perspective of organizational change. It is based on the notion that any change, no matter how large or small, has a cascading effect throughout an organization.[17] For example, promoting an individual to a new work group affects the group dynamics in both the old and new groups. Similarly, creating project or work teams may necessitate the need to revamp compensation practices. These examples illustrate that change creates additional change. Today's solutions are tomorrow's problems.

A systems model of change offers managers a framework or model to use for diagnosing *what* to change and for determining *how* to evaluate the success of a change effort. To further your understanding about this model, we first describe its components and then discuss a brief application. The four main components of a systems model of change are inputs, strategic plans, target elements of change, and outputs (see Figure 16–1).

**mission statement**

Summarizes "why" an organization exists.

**Inputs**    All organizational changes should be consistent with an organization's mission, vision, and resulting strategic plan. A **mission statement** represents the "reason" an organization exists, and an organization's

A Systems Model of Change | **FIGURE 16–1**

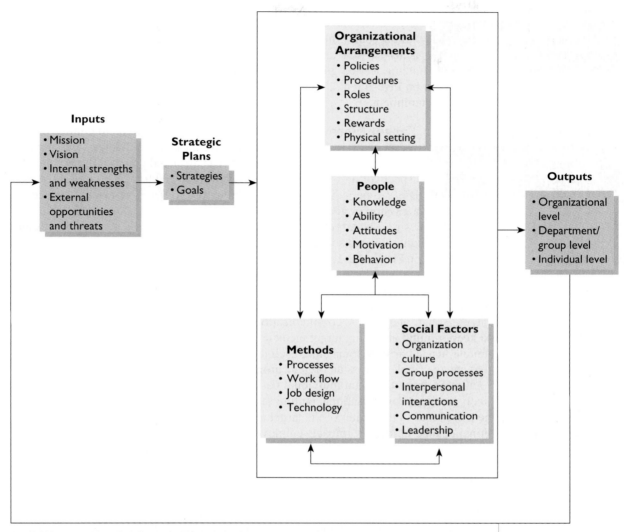

**Target Elements of Change**

**Organizational Arrangements**
• Policies
• Procedures
• Roles
• Structure
• Rewards
• Physical setting

**Inputs**
• Mission
• Vision
• Internal strengths and weaknesses
• External opportunities and threats

**Strategic Plans**
• Strategies
• Goals

**People**
• Knowledge
• Ability
• Attitudes
• Motivation
• Behavior

**Outputs**
• Organizational level
• Department/ group level
• Individual level

**Methods**
• Processes
• Work flow
• Job design
• Technology

**Social Factors**
• Organization culture
• Group processes
• Interpersonal interactions
• Communication
• Leadership

SOURCES: Adapted from D R Fuqua and D J Kurpius, "Conceptual Models in Organizational Consultation," *Journal of Counseling & Development,* July/August 1993, pp 602–18; and D A Nadler and M L Tushman, "Organizational Frame Bending: Principles for Managing Reorientation," *Academy of Management Executive,* August 1989, pp 194–203.

*vision* is a long-term goal that describes "what" an organization wants to become. Consider how the difference between mission and vision affects organizational change. Your university probably has a mission to educate people. This mission does not necessarily imply anything about change. It simply defines the university's overall purpose. In contrast, the university may have a vision to be recognized as the "best" university in the country. This vision requires the organization to benchmark itself against other world-class universities and to create plans for achieving the vision. For example, the vision of the W. P. Carey School of Business at Arizona State University is to be among the top 25 business schools in the world. An assessment of an organization's internal strengths and weaknesses against its environmental opportunities and threats (SWOT) is another key input within the systems model. This SWOT analysis is a key component of the strategic planning process.

**Strategic Plans**   A **strategic plan** outlines an organization's long-term direction and the actions necessary to achieve planned results. Among other things, strategic plans are based on results from a SWOT analysis. This analysis aids in developing an organizational strategy to attain desired goals such as profits, customer satisfaction, quality, adequate return on investment, and acceptable levels of turnover and employee satisfaction and commitment.

> **strategic plan**
>
> A long-term plan outlining actions needed to achieve desired results.

**Target Elements of Change**   **Target elements of change** are the components of an organization that may be changed. They essentially represent change levers that managers can push and pull to influence various aspects of an organization. The choice of which lever to pull, however, is based on a diagnosis of a problem, or problems, or the actions needed to accomplish a vision or goal: A problem exists when managers are not obtaining the results they desire. The target elements of change are used to diagnose problems and to identify change-related solutions.

> **target elements of change**
>
> Components of an organization that may be changed.

As shown in Figure 16–1, there are four targeted elements of change: organizational arrangements, social factors, methods, and people.[18] Each target element of change contains a subset of more detailed organizational features. For instance, the "social factors" component includes consideration of an organization's culture, group processes, interpersonal interactions, communication, and leadership. There are two final issues to keep in mind about the target elements of change shown in Figure 16–1. First, the double-headed arrows connecting each target element of change convey the message that change ripples across an organization. For example, changing a reward system to reinforce team rather than individual performance (an organizational arrangement) is likely to impact organizational culture (a social factor). Second, the "people" component is placed in the center of the target elements of change box because all organizational change ultimately impacts employees. Organizational change is more likely to succeed when managers proactively consider the impact of change on its employees.

**Outputs**   Outputs represent the desired end-results of a change. Once again, these end-results should be consistent with an organization's strategic plan. Figure 16–1 indicates that change may be directed at the organizational level, department/group level, or individual level. Change efforts are more complicated and difficult to manage when they are targeted at the organizational level. This occurs because organizational-level changes are more likely to affect multiple target elements of change shown in the model.

**Applying the Systems Model of Change**   There are two different ways to apply the systems model of change. The first is as an aid during the strategic planning process. Once a group of managers has determined its vision and strategic goals, the target elements of change can be considered when developing action plans to support the accomplishment of goals. For example, following the merger of Adolph Coors Company and Molson, the management team of Molson Coors Brewing established goals of cutting costs by $180 million, making Coors Light a global brand, and developing new high-end brands of beer. Target elements of change have included strengthening shared values of the predecessor companies (social factors), keeping production and distribution employees focused on their existing functions (motivation, a people factor), creating a general-management development program (another people factor), and establishing a subsidiary to specialize in new products (organizational arrangements).[19]

For another application of the systems model to strategy development, see Skills & Best Practices.

The second application involves using the model as a diagnostic framework to determine the causes of an organizational problem and to propose solutions. We highlight this application by considering a consulting project in which we used the model. We were contacted by the CEO of a software company and asked to figure out why the presidents of three divisions were not collaborating with each other—the problem. It turned out that two of the presidents submitted a proposal for the same $4 million project from a potential customer. Our client did not get the work because the customer was appalled at having received two proposals from the same company; hence the CEO's call to us. We decided to interview employees by using a structured set of questions that pertained to each of the target elements of change. For instance, we asked employees to comment on the extent to which the reward system, organizational culture, work flow, and physical setting contributed to collaboration across divisions. The interviews taught us that the lack of collaboration among the division presidents was due to the reward system (an organizational arrangement), a competitive culture and poor communications (social factors), and poor work flow (a methods factor). Our recommendation was to change the reward systems, restructure the organization, and redesign the work flow.

# Kotter's Eight Steps for Leading Organizational Change

John Kotter, an expert in leadership and change management, believes that organizational change typically fails because senior management makes a host of implementation errors. Kotter proposed an eight-step process for leading change (see Table 16–1) based on these errors.[20] Unlike the systems model of change, this model is not diagnostic in orientation. Its application will not help managers to diagnose *what* needs to be changed. Rather, this model is more like Lewin's model of change in that it prescribes *how* managers should sequence or lead the change process.

Kotter's eight steps shown in Table 16–1 subsume Lewin's model of change. The first four steps represent Lewin's "unfreezing" stage. Steps 5, 6, and 7 represent "changing," and step 8 corresponds to "refreezing." The value of Kotter's steps is that they provide specific recommendations about behaviors that managers need to exhibit to successfully lead organizational change. It is

SKILLS & BEST PRACTICES

## Navigating a Turnaround at Circuit City

The Circuit City chain of electronics stores has been struggling with recent losses. The company's chief executive, Philip J Schoonover, instituted some difficult changes, including layoffs, new store formats, greater emphasis on services, and more efficient back-office systems. While Circuit City's future is still uncertain, Schoonover has gained experience in leading people forward despite difficulties. He offers the following five ideas for turning a company around:

1. *Listen to employees.* The best strategies come from the bottom up, not the top down.

2. *Refresh management.* Different stages of a turnaround require different skill sets.

3. *Embrace your heritage.* Play to and upgrade your company's historic strengths.

4. *Protect the future.* A CEO must make decisions that protect the company after a turnaround.

5. *Stay the course.* There will be bumps along the way; stay focused on the big picture.

**SOURCE: Based on a list quoted from G McWilliams, "Can Circuit City Survive Boss's Cure?"** *The Wall Street Journal,* **February 11, 2008, pp B1, B3.**

**Do you think Circuit City's CEO has the right ideas to turn the company around? Explain.**

**TABLE 16–1**  Steps to Leading Organizational Change

| Step | Description |
|------|-------------|
| 1. Establish a sense of urgency | Unfreeze the organization by creating a compelling reason for why change is needed. |
| 2. Create the guiding coalition | Create a cross-functional, cross-level group of people with enough power to lead the change. |
| 3. Develop a vision and strategy | Create a vision and strategic plan to guide the change process. |
| 4. Communicate the change vision | Create and implement a communication strategy that consistently communicates the new vision and strategic plan. |
| 5. Empower broad-based action | Eliminate barriers to change, and use target elements of change to transform the organization. Encourage risk taking and creative problem solving. |
| 6. Generate short-term wins | Plan for and create short-term "wins" or improvements. Recognize and reward people who contribute to the wins. |
| 7. Consolidate gains and produce more change | The guiding coalition uses credibility from short-term wins to create more change. Additional people are brought into the change process as change cascades throughout the organization. Attempts are made to reinvigorate the change process. |
| 8. Anchor new approaches in the culture | Reinforce the changes by highlighting connections between new behaviors and processes and organizational success. Develop methods to ensure leadership development and succession. |

SOURCE: The steps were developed by J P Kotter, *Leading Change* (Boston: Harvard Business School Press, 1996).

important to remember that Kotter's research reveals that it is ineffective to skip steps and that successful organizational change is 70% to 90% leadership and only 10% to 30% management. Senior managers are thus advised to focus on leading rather than managing change.[21] For example, PepsiCo's chief executive, Indra Nooyi, is highly visible in her leadership role, articulating her vision to make PepsiCo "known around the world as a good company" that offers more healthful snacks, limits its environmental impact, and "offers employees 'a career, not just a job.'"[22]

# Creating Change through Organization Development

Organization development (OD) is different from the previously discussed models of change. OD does not entail a structured sequence as proposed by Lewin and Kotter, but it does possess the same diagnostic focus associated with the systems model of change. That said, OD is much broader in orientation than any of the previously discussed models. Specifically, a pair of experts in this field of study and practice defined **organization development** as follows:

> OD consists of planned efforts to help persons work and live together more effectively, over time, in their organizations. These goals are achieved by applying behavioral science principles, methods, and theories adapted from the fields of psychology, sociology, education, and management.[23]

**organization development**

**A set of techniques or tools that are used to implement organizational change.**

As you can see from this definition, OD constitutes a set of techniques or interventions that are used to implement "planned" organizational change aimed at increasing "an organization's ability to improve itself as a humane and effective system."[24] OD techniques or interventions apply to each of the change models discussed in this section. For example, OD is used during Lewin's "changing" stage. It also is used to identify and implement targeted elements of change within the systems model of change. Finally, OD might be used during Kotter's steps 1, 3, 5, 6, and 7. In this section, we briefly review the four identifying characteristics of OD and its research and practical implications.[25]

**OD Involves Profound Change**    Change agents using OD generally desire deep and long-lasting improvement. OD consultant Warner Burke, for example, who strives for fundamental *cultural* change, wrote: "By fundamental change, as opposed to fixing a problem or improving a procedure, I mean that some significant aspect of an organization's culture will never be the same."[26]

**OD Is Value Loaded**    Owing to the fact that OD is rooted partially in humanistic psychology, many OD consultants carry certain values or biases into the client organization. They prefer cooperation over conflict, self-control over institutional control, and democratic and participative management over autocratic management. In addition to OD being driven by a consultant's values, OD practitioners now believe that there is a broader "value perspective" that should underlie any organizational change. Specifically, OD should always be customer focused and it should help an organization achieve its vision and strategic goals. This approach implies that organizational interventions should be aimed at helping to satisfy customers' needs and thereby provide enhanced value of an organization's products and services.

**OD Is a Diagnosis/Prescription Cycle**    OD theorists and practitioners have long adhered to a medical model of organization. Like medical doctors, internal and external OD consultants approach the "sick" organization, "diagnose" its ills, "prescribe" and implement an intervention, and "monitor" progress. Table 16–2 presents a list of several different OD interventions that can be used to change individual, group, or organizational behavior as whole.

**OD Is Process Oriented**    Ideally, OD consultants focus on the form and not the content of behavioral and administrative dealings. For example, product design engineers and market researchers might be coached on how to communicate more effectively with one another without the consultant knowing the technical details of their conversations. In addition to communication, OD specialists focus on other processes, including problem solving, decision making, conflict handling, trust, power sharing, and career development.

**OD Research and Practical Implications**    Before discussing OD research, it is important to note that many of the topics contained in this book are used during OD interventions. Team building, for example, is commonly used as an OD technique.

**TABLE 16–2** | Some OD Interventions for Implementing Change

- **Survey feedback:** A questionnaire is distributed to employees to ascertain their perceptions and attitudes. The results are then shared with them. The questionnaire may ask about such matters as group cohesion, job satisfaction, and managerial leadership. Once the survey is done, meaningful results can be communicated with employees so that they can then engage in problem solving and constructive changes.

- **Process consultation:** An OD consultant observes the communication process—interpersonal-relations, decision-making, and conflict-handling patterns—occurring in work groups and provides feedback to the members involved. In consulting with employees (particularly managers) about these processes, the change agent hopes to give them the skills to identify and improve group dynamics on their own.

- **Team building:** Work groups are made to become more effective by helping members learn to function as a team. For example, members of a group might be interviewed independently by the OD change agent to establish how they feel about the group, then a meeting may be held away from their usual workplace to discuss the issues. To enhance team cohesiveness, the OD consultant may have members work together on a project such as rock climbing, with the consultant helping with communication and conflict resolution. The objective is for members to see how they can individually contribute to the group's goals and efforts.

- **Intergroup development:** Intergroup development resembles team building in many of its efforts. However, intergroup development attempts to achieve better cohesiveness among several work groups, not just one. During the process, the change agent tries to elicit misperceptions and stereotypes that the groups have for each other so that they can be discussed, leading to better coordination among them.

- **Technostructural activities:** Technostructural activities are interventions concerned with improving the work technology or organizational design with people on the job. An intervention involving a work-technology change might be the introduction of e-mail to improve employee communication. An intervention involving an organizational-design change might be making a company less centralized in its decision making.

SOURCE: A Kinicki and B Williams, *Management: A Practical Introduction,* 3rd ed. (Burr Ridge: IL: McGraw-Hill/Irwin, 2008), p 330.

It is used to improve the functioning of work groups. The point is that OD research has practical implications for a variety of OB applications previously discussed. OD-related interventions produced the following insights:

- A meta-analysis of 18 studies indicated that employee satisfaction with change was higher when top management was highly committed to the change effort.[27]

- A meta-analysis of 52 studies provided support for the systems model of organizational change. Specifically, varying one target element of change created changes in other target elements. Also, there was a positive relationship between individual behavior change and organizational-level change.[28]

- A meta-analysis of 126 studies demonstrated that multifaceted interventions using more than one OD technique were more effective in changing job attitudes and work attitudes than interventions that relied on only one human-process or technostructural approach.[29]

- A survey of 1,700 firms from China, Japan, the United States, and Europe revealed that (1) U.S. and European firms used OD interventions more frequently than firms from China and Japan and (2) some OD interventions are culture free and some are not.[30]

Four practical implications are derived from this research. First, planned organizational change works. However, management and change agents are advised to rely on multifaceted interventions. As indicated elsewhere in this book, goal setting, feedback, recognition and rewards, training, participation, and challenging job design have good track records relative to improving performance and satisfaction. Second, change programs are more successful when they are geared toward meeting both short-term and long-term results. Managers should not engage in organizational change for the sake of change. Change efforts should produce positive results. Third, organizational change is more likely to succeed when top management is truly committed to the change process and the desired goals of the change program. This is particularly true when organizations pursue large-scale transformation. Finally, the effectiveness of OD interventions is affected by cross-cultural considerations. Managers and OD consultants should not blindly apply an OD intervention that worked in one country to a similar situation in another country.[31]

# Understanding and Managing Resistance to Change

We are all creatures of habit. It generally is difficult for people to try new ways of doing things. It is precisely because of this basic human characteristic that most employees do not have enthusiasm for change in the workplace. Rare is the manager who does not have several stories about carefully cultivated changes that died on the vine because of resistance to change. It is important for managers to learn to manage resistance because failed change efforts are costly. Costs include decreased employee loyalty, lowered probability of achieving corporate goals, waste of money and resources, and difficulty in fixing the failed change effort. This section examines employee resistance to change and practical ways of dealing with the problem.

## Why People Resist Change in the Workplace

No matter how technically or administratively perfect a proposed change may be, people make or break it. Individual and group behavior following an organizational change can range from enthusiastic support to outright hostility. A survey of human resource executives found that "the top two obstacles encountered during major organizational change are communication breakdown and employee resistance."[32] **Resistance to change** is an emotional/behavioral response to real or imagined threats to an established work routine. Resistance can be as subtle as passive resignation and as overt as deliberate sabotage. Let us now consider the reasons employees resist change in the first place. Eleven of the leading reasons are listed here:[33]

**learning objective 4**
Review the 11 reasons employees resist change.

**resistance to change**
Emotional/behavioral response to real or imagined work changes.

1. *An individual's predisposition toward change.* This predisposition is highly personal and deeply ingrained. It is an outgrowth of how one learns to handle change and ambiguity as a child. While some people are distrustful and suspicious of change, others see change as a situation requiring flexibility, patience, and understanding.[34]

© 2004 Ted Goff

*Copyright © Ted Goff. Reprinted with permission.*

2. *Surprise and fear of the unknown.* When innovative or radically different changes are introduced without warning, affected employees become fearful of the implications. Grapevine rumors fill the void created by a lack of official announcements. This is exactly what happened when General Motors announced its negotiated plan to reduce its workforce through a carefully designed attrition program. The reduction in workforce was needed to help GM lower its operating costs.

> Almost as soon as yesterday's buyout offer from General Motors Corp was announced, news—and rumors—began sweeping through the company's truck assembly plant in Pontiac, Mich. "It spread like wildfire," said 52-year-old Larry Walker, a 33-year veteran of the plant, which employs 2,500 hourly workers and makes the GMC Sierra Truck and Chevrolet Silverado. "I talked about it with my buddies all day long. We're all trying to figure out what we should do."[35]

3. *Climate of mistrust.* Trust, as discussed in Chapter 9, involves reciprocal faith in others' intentions and behavior. Mutual mistrust can doom to failure an otherwise well-conceived change. Mistrust encourages secrecy, which begets deeper mistrust. Managers who trust their employees make the change process an open, honest, and participative affair. Employees who, in turn, trust management are more willing to expend extra effort and take chances with something different.

4. *Fear of failure.* Intimidating changes on the job can cause employees to doubt their capabilities. Self-doubt erodes self-confidence and cripples personal growth and development.

5. *Loss of status and/or job security.* Administrative and technological changes that threaten to alter power bases or eliminate jobs generally trigger strong resistance. For example, most corporate restructuring involves the elimination of managerial jobs. One should not be surprised when middle managers resist restructuring and participative management programs that reduce their authority and status.

6. *Peer pressure.* Someone who is not directly affected by a change may actively resist it to protect the interest of his or her friends and coworkers.

7. *Disruption of cultural traditions and/or group relationships.* Whenever individuals are transferred, promoted, or reassigned, cultural and group dynamics are thrown into disequilibrium.

8. *Personality conflicts.* Just as a friend can get away with telling us something we would resent hearing from an adversary, the personalities of change agents can breed resistance.

9. *Lack of tact and/or poor timing.* Undue resistance can occur because changes are introduced in an insensitive manner or at an awkward time.

10. *Nonreinforcing reward systems.* Individuals resist when they do not foresee positive rewards for changing. For example, an employee is unlikely to support a change effort that is perceived as requiring him or her to work longer with more pressure.

**11.** *Past success.* Success can breed complacency. It also can foster a stubbornness to change because people come to believe that what worked in the past will work in the future. Decades ago the Green Revolution alleviated hunger in Asia and Latin America by equipping farmers with more productive strains of wheat and rice. But in the words of Usha Tuteja, who heads the Agricultural Economics Research Center at Delhi University, "People got complacent." Governments, believing that the problem of feeding a growing population had been solved, stopped funding agricultural research. Unfortunately, today new challenges have again made food supply a major problem, and the solutions will require years of investment in further research.[36]

# Alternative Strategies for Overcoming Resistance to Change

**learning objective 5**

Identify alternative strategies for overcoming resistance to change.

Before recommending specific approaches to overcome resistance, there are five key conclusions that should be kept in mind. First, an organization must be ready for change. Just as a table must be set before you can eat, so must an organization be ready for change before it can be effective.[37] Establishing a climate of trust, in which leaders are respected for their integrity, not only is part of ethical leadership but also can lay a foundation in which change will be accepted. Leaders also may consider how employees are likely to react to a change: Is resistance inevitable or even likely? If so, what concerns are employees likely to have, and are these concerns legitimate? Employees don't always resist, and when they do, it is sometimes in response to leaders' behavior.[38]

Second, people are more likely to resist change when they do not agree on the causes of current problems and the need for change. This is a "cognitive" hurdle that must be overcome by increasing employees' commitment to change.[39] **Commitment to change** is defined as a mind-set "that binds an individual to a course of action deemed necessary for the successful implementation of a change initiative."[40] A study of 343 employees in 30 organizations found that the employees had greater change commitment when they had transformational leaders (described in Chapter 14), while change management practices—such as those described in this chapter—contributed more to commitment when the leader was not described as transformational.[41] Another study, which looked at 553 employees in 25 organizations, found that commitment to change was lower when employees were experiencing pervasive, overlapping changes, rather than just one change.[42] One manager who appreciates this hurdle is Pfizer's Toni Hoover, who leads the company's largest research facility, located in Connecticut. Hoover says the scientists there have "change fatigue" because of cost cutting following two mergers, so she places priority on fostering communication and a positive work environment.[43] To further illustrate the idea of commitment to change, complete the Hand-On Exercise on page 414, a shortened version of an instrument measuring this commitment. Were you committed to the change? Did this level of commitment affect your behavioral support for what management was trying to accomplish?

**commitment to change**

A mind-set of doing whatever it takes to effectively implement change.

Third, organizational change is less successful when top management fails to keep employees informed about the process of change. Fourth, do not assume that people are consciously resisting change. Managers are encouraged to use the systems model of change to identify the obstacles that are affecting the implementation process. Fifth, employees' perceptions or interpretations of a change significantly affect resistance. Employees are less likely to resist when they perceive that the benefits of

# Does Your Commitment to a Change Initiative Predict Your Behavioral Support for the Change?

**INSTRUCTIONS:** First, think of a time in which a previous or current employer was undergoing a change initiative that required you to learn something new or to discontinue an attitude, behavior, or organizational practice. Next, evaluate your commitment to this change effort by indicating the extent to which you agree with the following survey items. Use the rating scale shown below. Finally, assess your behavioral support for the change.

1 = Strongly disagree
2 = Disagree
3 = Neither agree nor disagree
4 = Agree
5 = Strongly agree

1. I believe in the value of this change.  1—2—3—4—5
2. This change serves an important purpose.  1—2—3—4—5
3. This change is a good strategy for the organization.  1—2—3—4—5
4. I have no choice but to go along with this change.  1—2—3—4—5
5. It would be risky to speak out against this change.  1—2—3—4—5
6. It would be too costly for me to resist this change.  1—2—3—4—5
7. I feel a sense of duty to work toward this change.  1—2—3—4—5
8. It would be irresponsible of me to resist this change.  1—2—3—4—5
9. I feel obligated to support this change.  1—2—3—4—5

Total score = _____

## ARBITRARY NORMS

9–18 = Low commitment
19–35 = Moderate commitment
36–45 = High commitment

## BEHAVIORAL SUPPORT FOR THE CHANGE

Overall, I modified my attitudes and behavior in line with what management was trying to accomplish  1—2—3—4—5

**SOURCE:** Survey items were obtained from L Herscovitch and J P Meyer, "Commitment to Organizational Change: Extension of a Three-Component Model," *Journal of Applied Psychology*, June 2002, p 477.

a change overshadow the personal costs. At a minimum then, managers are advised to (1) provide as much information as possible to employees about the change, (2) inform employees about the reasons/rationale for the change, (3) conduct meetings to address employees' questions regarding the change, and (4) provide employees the opportunity to discuss how the proposed change might affect them.[44] These recommendations underscore the importance of communicating with employees throughout the process of change. Recall also from Chapter 12 that communication is a two-way process.

Change leaders should not merely argue for the change but also listen to the resisters' point of view to be sure not to miss new perspectives that might suggest ways to improve the planned change.[45]

In addition to communication, employee participation in the change process is another generic approach for reducing resistance. That said, however, organizational change experts have criticized the tendency to treat participation as a cure-all for resistance to change. They prefer a contingency approach because resistance can take many forms and, furthermore, because situational factors vary (see Table 16–3).[46] As shown in Table 16–3, Participation + Involvement does have its place, but it takes time that is not always available. Also as indicated in Table 16–3, each of the other five methods has its situational niche, advantages, and drawbacks. In short, there is no universal strategy for overcoming resistance to change. Managers need a complete repertoire of change strategies.

**Group Exercise**

Overcoming Resistance to Change

### Six Strategies for Overcoming Resistance to Change    TABLE 16–3

| Approach | Commonly Used in Situations | Advantages | Drawbacks |
|---|---|---|---|
| Education + Communication | Where there is a lack of information or inaccurate information and analysis. | Once persuaded, people will often help with the implementation of the change. | Can be very time consuming if lots of people are involved. |
| Participation + Involvement | Where the initiators do not have all the information they need to design the change and where others have considerable power to resist. | People who participate will be committed to implementing change, and any relevant information they have will be integrated into the change plan. | Can be very time consuming if participators design an inappropriate change. |
| Facilitation + Support | Where people are resisting because of adjustment problems. | No other approach works as well with adjustment problems. | Can be time consuming, expensive, and still fail. |
| Negotiation + Agreement | Where someone or some group will clearly lose out in a change and where that group has considerable power to resist. | Sometimes it is a relatively easy way to avoid major resistance. | Can be too expensive in many cases if it alerts others to negotiate for compliance. |
| Manipulation + Co-optation | Where other tactics will not work or are too expensive. | It can be a relatively quick and inexpensive solution to resistance problems. | Can lead to future problems if people feel manipulated. |
| Explicit + Implicit coercion | Where speed is essential and where the change initiators possess considerable power. | It is speedy and can overcome any kind of resistance. | Can be risky if it leaves people angry at the initiators. |

# Creating a Learning Organization

Organizations are finding that yesterday's competitive advantage is becoming the minimum entrance requirement for staying in business. This puts tremendous pressure on organizations to learn how best to improve and stay ahead of competitors. In fact, both researchers and practicing managers agree that an organization's capability to learn is a key strategic weapon. It thus is important for organizations to enhance and nurture their capability to learn.

So what is organizational learning and how do organizations become learning organizations? To help clarify what this process entails, this section begins by defining organizational learning and a learning organization. We then present a model of organizational learning and conclude by reviewing new roles and skills required of leaders to create a learning organization.

## Defining Organizational Learning and a Learning Organization

Organizational learning (OL) and a learning organization (LO) are not the same thing. Susan Fisher and Margaret White, experts on organizational change and learning, define organizational learning as follows:

> Organizational learning is a reflective process, played out by members at all levels of the organization, that involves the collection of information from both the external and internal environments. This information is filtered through a collective sensemaking process, which results in shared interpretations that can be used to instigate actions resulting in enduring changes to the organization's behavior and theories in use.[47]

This definition highlights that organizational learning represents a process by which information is gathered and then interpreted through a cognitive, social process. The accumulated information from this interpretative process represents an organization's knowledge base. This knowledge in turn is stored in organizational "memory," which consists of files, records, procedures, policies, and organizational culture. In contrast, learning organizations use organizational knowledge to foster innovation and organizational effectiveness.

Peter Senge, a professor at the Massachusetts Institute of Technology, popularized the term *learning organization* in his best-selling book entitled *The Fifth Discipline*. He described a learning organization as "a group of people working together to collectively enhance their capacities to create results that they truly care about."[48] A practical interpretation of these ideas results in the following definition. A **learning organization** is one that proactively creates, acquires, and transfers knowledge and that changes its behavior on the basis of new knowledge and insights.

**learning organization**

Proactively creates, acquires, and transfers knowledge throughout the organization.

By breaking this definition into its three component parts, we can clearly see the characteristics of a learning organization. First, new ideas are a prerequisite for learning. Learning organizations actively try to infuse their organizations with new ideas and information. They do this by constantly scanning their external environments, hiring new talent and expertise when needed, and devoting significant resources to train and develop their employees. Second, new knowledge must be transferred throughout the organization. Learning organizations strive to reduce structural, process, and interpersonal barriers to the sharing of information, ideas, and knowledge among organizational members. Finally, behavior must change as a result of new knowledge. Learning organizations are results oriented. They foster an environment in which employees are encouraged to use new behaviors and operational processes to achieve corporate goals.

# Building an Organization's Learning Capability

Figure 16.2 presents a model of how organizations build and enhance their learning capability. **Learning capabilities** represent the set of core competencies, which are defined as the special knowledge, skills, and technological know-how that differentiate an organization from its competitors, and processes that enable an organization to adapt to its environment. The general idea underlying Figure 16.2 is that learning capabilities are the fuel for organizational success. Just like gasoline enables a car's engine to perform, learning capabilities equip an organization to foresee and respond to internal and external changes. This capability, in turn, increases the chances of satisfying customers and boosting sales and profitability. Let us now consider the two major contributors to an organization's learning capability: facilitating factors and learning mode.

**learning capabilities**

**The set of core competencies and internal processes that enable an organization to adapt to its environment.**

**Facilitating Factors**   *Facilitating factors* represent "the internal structure and processes that affect how easy or hard it is for learning to occur and the amount of effective learning that takes place."[49] These conditions are most likely in an organization with "a supportive learning environment, concrete learning processes and practices, and leadership behavior that provides reinforcement."[50] Table 16–4 details qualities that help a department or organization meet each of those requirements. Many organizations fulfill one or another of the requirements; an organization gains an advantage by outdoing others in areas where it sees a way to excel.

**Learning Mode**   **Learning modes** represent the various ways in which organizations attempt to create and maximize their learning. Figure 16.2 shows that learning modes are directly influenced by an organization's culture and experience or history.[51] The history of EMC Corporation has included a transformation of its industry—information storage—that

**learning modes**

**The various ways in which organizations attempt to create and maximize their learning.**

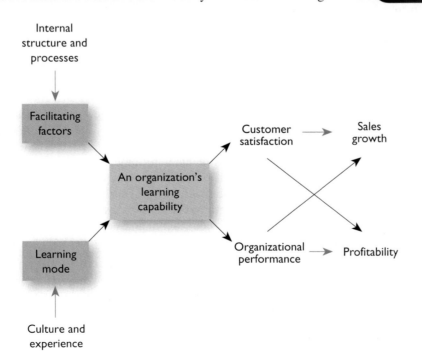

**FIGURE 16–2**
Building an Organization's Learning Capability

**TABLE 16–4** Criteria for a Learning Organization

| **Supportive learning environment** |
| --- |
| Psychological safety: People are not afraid to speak up, share information, discuss problems, and try ideas. |
| Appreciation of differences: Different ideas and opinions are valued. |
| Openness to new ideas: New ideas and approaches are welcome. |
| Time for reflection: People are not too busy to maintain quality, improve processes, and review their work. |
| **Concrete learning processes and practices** |
| Experimentation: The unit frequently tries new ideas and has processes for evaluating them. |
| Information collection: The unit systematically gathers information on customers, competitors, and trends. |
| Analysis: The unit effectively discusses issues, including underlying assumptions and conflicting viewpoints. |
| Education and training: New and experienced employees receive training, and time is made available for training. |
| Information transfer: Employees meet with customers, suppliers, and experts inside and outside the organization, and activities are formally reviewed. |
| **Leadership that reinforces learning** |
| Managers recognize the limits of their knowledge and invite input from others. |
| Managers ask questions and listen effectively. |
| Managers encourage expression of multiple viewpoints. |
| Managers provide time and resources for identifying problems, analyzing performance, and reflecting on new ideas. |

SOURCE: Based on D A Garvin, A C Edmondson, and F Gino, "Is Yours a Learning Organization?" *Harvard Business Review*, March 2008, pp 109–16.

shifted EMC from a focus on data storage hardware to software. Along with that change came a need for EMC's employees to learn entirely new skills, so management made development of learning capabilities part of its strategy. With a culture that places greater value on learning, EMC devoted a sum equal to 5% of payroll to learning and development programs. These activities include an immersion program to teach new employees about EMC's culture and vision, lessons on the information storage industry, a sales training program that emphasizes role-playing and on-the-job learning, a global job rotation program, and mentoring relationships, as well as tuition reimbursement for employees who want to pursue educational goals at an outside school.[52]

OB researcher Danny Miller reviewed the literature on organizational learning and identified six dominant modes of learning:[53]

I. *Analytic learning.* Learning occurs through systematic gathering of internal and external information. Information tends to be quantitative and analyzed via formal systems. The emphasis is on using deductive logic to numerically analyze objective data.

2. *Synthetic learning.* Synthetic learning is more intuitive and generic than the analytic mode. It emphasizes the synthesis of large amounts of complex information by using systems thinking. That is, employees try to identify interrelationships between issues, problems, and opportunities.

3. *Experimental learning.* This mode is a rational methodological approach that is based on conducting small experiments and monitoring the results.

4. *Interactive learning.* This mode involves learning-by-doing. Rather than using systematic methodological procedures, learning occurs primarily through the exchange of information. Learning is more intuitive and inductive.

5. *Structural learning.* This mode is a methodological approach that is based on the use of organizational routines. Organizational routines represent standardized processes and procedures that specify how to carry out tasks and roles. People learn from routines because they direct attention, institutionalize standards, and create consistent vocabularies.

6. *Institutional learning.* This mode represents an inductive process by which organizations share and model values, beliefs, and practices either from their external environments or from senior executives. Employees learn by observing environmental examples or senior executives. Socialization and mentoring play a significant role in institutional learning.

## Leadership Is the Foundation of a Learning Organization

Leadership is the key to fostering organizational learning and the creation of a learning organization. The most effective leaders are those who use both transactional and transformational leadership (recall our discussion in Chapter 14) to facilitate organizational learning.[54] To make this happen, however, leaders must adopt new roles and associated activities. Specifically, leaders perform three key functions in building a learning organization: (1) building a commitment to learning, (2) working to generate ideas with impact, and (3) working to generalize ideas with impact.[55]

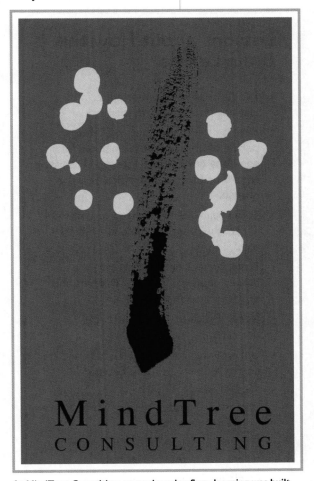

At MindTree Consulting, an engineering firm, learning was built in from the company's founding. Its corporate logo was designed by a child with cerebral palsy, which signifies, according to Chief Operating Officer Subroto Bagchi, that "We believe there is much we can learn from everyone." To "break the engineering mindset," the company invites people from widely diverse backgrounds such as dance, space exploration, and writing to present lectures for its 3,500 employees.

### Building a Commitment to Learning

Leaders need to instill an intellectual and emotional commitment to learning. Thomas Tierney, former CEO of Bain & Company, proposes that leaders foster this commitment by building a culture that promotes the concept of "teacher-learners." His concept is based on the idea that organizational learning and innovation are enhanced when employees behave like both teachers and learners.[56] Of course, leaders also need to invest the financial resources needed to create a learning infrastructure.

**Working to Generate Ideas with Impact**     Ideas with impact are those that add value to one or more of an organization's three key stakeholders: employees, customers, and shareholders. Experts suggest the following ways to generate ideas with impact:

- Implement continuous improvement programs.
- Increase employee competence through training, or buy talent from outside the organization.
- Experiment with new ideas, processes, and structural arrangements.
- Go outside the organization to identify world-class ideas and processes.
- Instill systems thinking throughout the organization.

**Working to Generalize Ideas with Impact**     Leaders must make a concerted effort to reduce interpersonal, group, and organizational barriers to learning. This can be done by creating a learning infrastructure.[57] This is a large-scale effort that includes the following activities:

- Measuring and rewarding learning.
- Increasing open and honest dialogue among organizational members.
- Reducing conflict.
- Increasing horizontal and vertical communication.
- Promoting teamwork.
- Rewarding risk taking and innovation.
- Reducing the fear of failure.
- Increasing the sharing of successes, failures, and best practices across organizational members.
- Reducing stressors and frustration.
- Reducing internal competition.
- Increasing cooperation and collaboration.
- Creating a psychologically safe and comforting environment.[58]

The reasons these ideas work, as well as some additional suggestions for reducing barriers to learning, come from neuroscience, the study of brain functioning (see Skills & Best Practices).

SKILLS & BEST PRACTICES

## Lessons about How the Brain Learns

- People need sufficient sleep to integrate learning into long-term memory.
- Because the brain "shuts off" after a period of time [about 20 minutes for someone paying close attention], learning should be broken down into bite-size nuggets.
- Social pain—being rejected or berated—affects the brain the same as physical pain.
- Social fairness and respect give the brain a chemical boost. Unfairness and disrespect do the opposite.
- Stress can cause people to think unclearly.
- Uncertainty arouses fear circuits and can decrease ability to make decisions.
- Employees need some ownership over situations to better accept changes. Even a little choice helps.
- Engaging people in more active learning techniques improves retention.
- Employees' ability to think clearly can be hindered when employers fail to meet expectations or create uncertainty in the workplace.

SOURCE: A Fox, "The Brain at Work," *HR Magazine*, March 2008, pp 37–42.

# Unlearning the Organization

In addition to implementing the ideas discussed earlier, organizations must concurrently unlearn organizational practices and paradigms that made them successful. Quite simply, traditional organizations and the associated organizational behaviors they created have outlived their usefulness. Management must seriously question and challenge the ways of thinking that worked in the past if they want to create a learning organization.[59] For example, the old management paradigm of planning, organizing, and control might be replaced with one of vision, values, and empowerment. The time has come for management and employees to think as owners, not as "us" and "them" adversaries.

# key terms

benchmarking   403
commitment to change   413
external forces for change   400
internal forces for change   402

learning capabilities   417
learning modes   417
learning organization   416
mission statement   404

organization development   409
resistance to change   411
strategic plan   406
target elements of change   406

# chapter summary

- *Discuss the external and internal forces that create the need for organizational change.* Organizations encounter both external and internal forces for change. There are four key external forces for change: demographic characteristics, technological advancements, customer and market changes, and social and political pressures. Internal forces for change come from both human resource problems and managerial behavior/decisions.

- *Describe Lewin's change model and the systems model of change.* Lewin developed a three-stage model of planned change that explained how to initiate, manage, and stabilize the change process. The three stages were *unfreezing*, which entails creating the motivation to change, *changing*, and stabilizing change through *refreezing*. A systems model of change takes a big picture perspective of change. It focuses on the interaction among the key components of change. The three main components of change are inputs, target elements of change, and outputs. The target elements of change represent the components of an organization that may be changed. They include organizing arrangements, social factors, methods, goals, and people.

- *Discuss Kotter's eight steps for leading organizational change.* John Kotter believes that organizational change fails for one or more of eight common errors. He proposed eight steps that organizations should follow to overcome these errors. The eight steps are as follows: (*a*) establish a sense of urgency, (*b*) create the guiding coalition, (*c*) develop a vision and strategy, (*d*) communicate the change vision, (*e*) empower broad-based action, (*f*) generate short-term wins, (*g*) consolidate gains and produce more change, and (*h*) anchor new approaches in the culture.

- *Discuss the 11 reasons employees resist change.* Resistance to change is an emotional/behavioral response to real or imagined threats to an established work routine. Eleven reasons employees resist change are (*a*) an individual's predisposition toward change, (*b*) surprise and fear of the unknown, (*c*) climate of mistrust, (*d*) fear of failure, (*e*) loss of status and/or job security, (*f*) peer pressure, (*g*) disruption of cultural traditions and/or group relationships, (*h*) personality conflicts, (*i*) lack of tact and/or poor timing, (*j*) nonreinforcing reward systems, and (*k*) past success.

- *Identify alternative strategies for overcoming resistance to change.* Organizations must be ready for change. Assuming an organization is ready for change, the alternative strategies for overcoming resistance to change are education + communication, participation + involvement, facilitation + support, negotiation + agreement, manipulation + cooperation, and explicit + implicit coercion. Each has its situational appropriateness and advantages and drawbacks.

- *Discuss the process organizations use to build their learning capabilities.* Learning capabilities represent the set of core competencies and processes that enable an organization to adapt to its environment. Learning capabilities are directly affected by organizational facilitating factors and learning modes. Facilitating factors constitute the internal structure and processes that either encourage or impede learning within an organization. Learning modes represent the various ways by which organizations attempt to create and maximize their learning. Researchers believe that there is some type of optimal matching between the facilitating factors and learning modes that affects learning capability.

# discussion questions

1. Returning to the chapter-opening case, how can an effective office redesign reduce the employees' resistance to change following company layoffs? Explain.
2. How would you respond to a manager who made the following statement? "Unfreezing is not important; employees will follow my directives."
3. Have you ever gone through a major organizational change at work? If yes, what type of organizational development intervention was used? Was it effective? Explain.
4. Which source of resistance to change do you think is the most common? Which is the most difficult for management to deal with?
5. How would you assess the extent to which an organization is truly a learning organization? Discuss different alternative methods.

# ethical dilemma

## Is There an Ethical Way to Implement Downsizing without Hurting Your Best Employees?[60]

Intel has restructured and eliminated about 10,500 jobs during the past 20 months. The company decided to make these cuts owing to declining revenue and market share. Intel used a quantitative approach in making the cuts. That is, the company studied workforce demographics and determined what areas were most in need of cuts and then reassigned people based on where they might best contribute to the company's future plans. The managerial ranks were reduced the most. Corporate executives are pleased with the process because the company is now more profitable and competitive.

In contrast, some employees believe that the company "botched the restructuring in ways that have harmed morale, employee development and long-term leadership quality." Interviews with employees uncovered complaints that "Intel disregarded employees' passions in reorganizing, squandered the talents of HR specialists and unwisely shifted leadership training efforts from lower-level managers to upper-level executives." Disgruntled employees believe that Intel did not consider employees interests during the restructuring. An internal memo obtained by *Workforce Management* indicated that senior management knew they would be losing quality employees. The memo states: "We know we are losing good people in this move. But we have too many managers, and this manager reduction is necessary to improve our decision making and communication and to resize the company. In addition, since we need to become a leaner company and are limiting job openings, redeploying their skills, as individual contributors or as managers, is not a reasonable option."

## Solving the Dilemma: How Would You Have Handled the Layoffs at Intel?

1. Intel's approach sounds logical to me. Revenues are up, and the company just unveiled a new processing chip that *Time* called the best invention of the year. You can't make everyone happy when you let go more than 10,000 people.

2. Downsizing solely by the numbers is bad. Management should have accommodated employees' passions and interests when restructuring even if it resulted in less cuts than desired. In the long run, this will lead to higher employee satisfaction and performance.

3. It sounds like the criticisms are being leveled by people who don't like their new assignments. They should quit complaining and be happy that they are still employed.

4. I am not sure that there is an optimum approach. It is impossible to balance the short-term goal of reducing costs while maintaining a positive work environment in which people are doing the type of work they are passionate about.

5. Invent other interpretations or options. Discuss.

For an interpretation of this situation, visit our Web site, **www.mhhe.com/kinickiob4e.**

If you're looking for additional study materials, be sure to check out the Online Learning Center at

**www.mhhe.com/kinickiob4e**

for more information and interactivities that correspond to this chapter.

# Chapter I

[1] Excerpted from Margery Weinstein, "Accounting for Success," *Training,* February 2008, pp 66, 68, 70, 72.

[2] As quoted in D Reed, "Kelly Must Build on Success," *USA Today,* August 16, 2004, p 4B. Also see "The Best Advice I Ever Got: Herb Kelleher, Founder and Chairman of Southwest Airlines," *Fortune,* March 21, 2005, pp 116, 118; and D Kirkpatrick, "Star Power: Kevin Johnson, Microsoft," *Fortune,* February 6, 2006, p 58.

[3] Data from "Southwest Airlines Co. (LUV): Company Profile," *Yahoo Finance,* http://finance.yahoo.com, accessed February 22, 2008.

[4] J Pfeffer and J F Veiga, "Putting People First for Organizational Success," *Academy of Management Executive,* May 1999, p 37.

[5] Adapted from ibid. Also see J K Harter, F L Schmidt, and T L Hayes, "Business-Unit-Level Relationship Between Employee Satisfaction, Employee Engagement, and Business Outcomes: A Meta-Analysis," *Journal of Applied Psychology,* April 2002, pp 268–79; J Pfeffer, "Producing Sustainable Competitive Advantage Through the Effective Management of People," *Academy of Management Executive,* November 2005, pp 95–106; J Pfeffer and R I Sutton, "Evidence-Based Management," *Harvard Business Review,* January 2006, pp 62–74; J Pfeffer and R I Sutton, *Hard Facts, Dangerous Half-Truths & Total Nonsense* (Boston: Harvard Business School Press, 2006); and J McGregor, "Forget Going with Your Gut," *BusinessWeek,* March 20, 2006, p 112.

[6] C B Gibson, C L Porath, G S Benson, and E E Lawler III, "What Results When Firms Implement Practices: The Differential Relationship between Specific Practices, Firm Financial Performance, Customer Service, and Quality," *Journal of Applied Psychology* 92(6) (2007): 1467–80.

[7] See J Pfeffer, "The Myth of the Disposable Worker," *Business 2.0,* October 2005, p 78; W F Cascio, "Strategies for Responsible Restructuring," *Academy of Management Executive,* November 2005, pp 39–50; and M Conlin, "The Shortsighted Solution," *BusinessWeek,* April 10, 2006, p 110.

[8] T Minton-Eversole, "Less Engagement, Less Profit, Research Finds," *HR Magazine,* December 2007, p 20.

[9] For inspiring discussion and examples, see A Pomeroy, "CEO of GE Values People, HR," *HR Magazine,* July 2007, p 12; S Shellenbarger, "Rules of Engagement," *The Wall Street Journal,* October 1, 2007, p R3; and A Lashinsky, "Can Google Three-Peat?" *Fortune,* January 31, 2008, http://money.cnn.com.

[10] "100 Best Companies to Work For, 2008," *Fortune,* February 4, 2008, http://money.cnn.com.

[11] See I S Fulmer, B Gerhart, and K S Scott, "Are the 100 Best Better? An Empirical Investigation of the Relationship Between Being a 'Great Place to Work' and Firm Performance," *Personnel Psychology,* Winter 2003, pp 965–93.

[12] "Wanted: Employees Who Get Things Done," *HR Magazine,* January 2008, p 10.

[13] H Mintzberg, "The Manager's Job: Folklore and Fact," *Harvard Business Review,* July–August 1975, p 61. Also see M M Clark, "NLRB General Counsel's Office Issues Liberal Criteria for Defining 'Supervisor,'" *HR Magazine,* February 2004, p 30.

[14] See, for example, H Mintzberg, "Managerial Work: Analysis from Observation," *Management Science,* October 1971, pp B97–B110; and F Luthans, "Successful vs. Effective Real Managers," *Academy of Management Executive,* May 1988, pp 127–32. For an instructive critique of the structured observation method, see M J Martinko and W L Gardner, "Beyond Structured Observation: Methodological Issues and New Directions," *Academy of Management Review,* October 1985, pp 676–95. Also see N Fondas, "A Behavioral Job Description for Managers," *Organizational Dynamics,* Summer 1992, pp 47–58.

[15] See L B Kurke and H E Aldrich, "Mintzberg Was Right! A Replication and Extension of *The Nature of Managerial Work,*" *Management Science,* August 1983, pp 975–84.

[16] For example, see J Gosling and H Mintzberg, "The Five Minds of a Manager," *Harvard Business Review,* November 2003, pp 54–63; G Yukl and R Lepsinger, "Why Integrating the Leading and Managing Roles Is Essential for Organizational Effectiveness," *Organizational Dynamics,* no. 4, 2005, pp 361–75; A I Kraut, P R Pedigo, D D McKenna, and M D Dunnette, "The Role of the Manager: What's Really Important in Different Management Jobs," *Academy of Management Executive,* November 2005, pp 122–29; G Hamel, "The Why, What, and How of Management Innovation," *Harvard Business Review,* February 2006, pp 72–84; K R Brousseau, M J Driver, G Hourihan, and R Larsson, "The Seasoned Executive's Decision-Making Style," *Harvard Business Review,* February 2006, pp 111–21; "Secrets of Greatness: How I Work," *Fortune,* March 20, 2006, pp 66–85; and J Jenkins, "Getting Up to Full Speed," *HR Magazine,* April 2006, pp 117–20.

[17] Validation studies can be found in E Van Velsor and J B Leslie, *Feedback to Managers, Volume II: A Review and Comparison of Sixteen Multi-Rater Feedback Instruments* (Greensboro, NC: Center for Creative Leadership, 1991); F Shipper, "A Study of the Psychometric Properties of the Managerial Skill Scales of the Survey of Management Practices," *Educational and Psychological Measurement,* June 1995, pp 468–79; and C L Wilson, *How and Why Effective Managers Balance Their Skills: Technical, Teambuilding, Drive* (Columbia, MD: Rockatech Multimedia Publishing, 2003).

[18] For example, see J Sandberg, "Understanding Competence at Work," *Harvard Business Review,* March 2001, pp 24–28; D Bartram, "The Great Eight Competencies: A Criterion-Centric Approach to Validation," *Journal of Applied Psychology,* November 2005, pp 1185–203; "Do Your Leaders Have 'Executive Intelligence'?" *Industry Week,* June 6, 2007, www.industryweek.com (interview of Justin Menkes); M Weinstein, "Prescriptions for Success," *Training,* May 2007, pp 30–37; and A Jordan-Nowe, "'Soft Skills' Again Treasured," *The Arizona Republic,* July 29, 2007, p EC1.

[19] See F Shipper, "Mastery and Frequency of Managerial Behaviors Relative to Sub-Unit Effectiveness," *Human Relations,* April 1991, pp 371–88.

[20] Ibid; and Wilson, *How and Why Effective Managers Balance Their Skills.*

[21] Data from F Shipper, "A Study of Managerial Skills of Women and Men and Their Impact on Employees' Attitudes and Career Success in a Nontraditional Organization," paper presented at the Academy of Management Meeting, August 1994, Dallas, Texas. The same outcome for on-the-job studies is reported in A H Eagly and B T Johnson, "Gender and Leadership Style: A Meta-Analysis," *Psychological Bulletin,* September 1990, pp 233–56.

[22] For instance, see J B Rosener, "Ways Women Lead," *Harvard Business Review,* November–December 1990, pp 119–25; C Lee, "The Feminization of Management," *Training,* November 1994, pp 25–31; and A Fels, "Do Women Lack Ambition?" *Harvard Business Review,* April 2004, pp 50–60.

[23] See T W Malone, *The Future of Work: How the New Order of Business Will Shape Your Organization, Your Management Style, and Your Life* (Boston: Harvard Business School Press, 2004); and P Aburdene, *Megatrends 2010: The Rise of Conscious Capitalism* (Charlottesville, VA: Hampton Roads Publishing Co., 2005).

[24] Essential sources on reengineering are M Hammer and J Champy, *Reengineering the Corporation: A Manifesto for Business Revolution* (New York: HarperCollins, 1993); and J Champy, *Reengineering Management: The Mandate for New Leadership* (New York: HarperCollins, 1995). Also see "Anything Worth Doing Is Worth Doing from Scratch," *Inc.,* May 18, 1999 (20th Anniversary Issue), pp 51–52.

[25] See J Weber, "'Mosh Pits' of Creativity," *BusinessWeek,* November 7, 2005, pp 98–100; R D Hof, "Collaboration: Teamwork, Supercharged," *BusinessWeek,* November 21, 2005, pp 90–94; M Goldsmith, "Building a Better Team," *BusinessWeek,* September 11, 2007, www.businessweek.com; and N Mourkogiannis, "How to Build a Winning Team," *BusinessWeek,* December 20, 2007.

[26] See C L Pearce and C C Manz, "The New Silver Bullets of Leadership: The Importance of Self- and Shared Leadership in Knowledge Work," *Organizational Dynamics,* no. 2, 2005, pp 130–40; A Houlihan, "Empower Your Employees to Make Smart Decisions," *Supervision,* July 2007, pp 3–5; and N R Lockwood, "Leveraging Employee Engagement for Competitive Advantage: HR's Strategic Role," *HR Magazine,* March 2007, General Reference Center Gold, http://find.galegroup.com.

[27] See K Carnes, D Cottrell, and M C Layton, *Management Insights: Discovering the Truths to Management Success* (Dallas: CornerStone Leadership Institute, 2004).

[28] For details, see J B Miner, "The Rated Importance, Scientific Validity, and Practical Usefulness of Organizational Behavior Theories: A Quantitative Review," *Academy of Management Learning and Education,* September 2003, pp 250–68.

[29] B S Lawrence, "Historical Perspective: Using the Past to Study the Present," *Academy of Management Review,* April 1984, p 307. Also see H Rubin, "Past Track to the Future," *Fast Company,* May 2001, pp 166–73.

[30] Evidence indicating that the original conclusions of the famous Hawthorne studies were unjustified may be found in R G Greenwood, A A Bolton, and R A Greenwood, "Hawthorne a Half Century Later: Relay Assembly Participants Remember," *Journal of Management,* Fall–Winter 1983, pp 217–31; and R H Franke and J D Kaul, "The Hawthorne Experiments: First Statistical Interpretation," *American Sociological Review,* October 1978, pp 623–43. For a positive interpretation of the Hawthorne studies, see J A Sonnenfeld, "Shedding Light on the Hawthorne Studies," *Journal of Occupational Behaviour,* April 1985, pp 111–30.

[31] See M Parker Follett, *Freedom and Coordination* (London: Management Publications Trust, 1949).

[32] See D McGregor, *The Human Side of Enterprise* (New York: McGraw-Hill, 1960). Also see D Jacobs, "Book Review Essay: Douglas McGregor—The Human Side of Enterprise in Peril," *Academy of Management Review,* April 2004, pp 293–96.

[33] J Hall, "Americans Know How to Be Productive If Managers Will Let Them," *Organizational Dynamics,* Winter 1994, p 38.

[34] For an interesting historical perspective on the behavioral sciences, see J Adler, "Freud in Our Midst," *Newsweek,* March 27, 2006, pp 42–49.

[35] See, for example, R Zemke, "TQM: Fatally Flawed or Simply Unfocused?" *Training,* October 1992, p 8; and D Dickson, R C Ford, and B Laval, "The Top Ten Excuses for Bad Service (and How to Avoid Needing Them)," *Organizational Dynamics,* no. 2, 2005, pp 168–84.

[36] R Morton, "Visibility Makes Service More than Bearable," *Logistics Today,* November 2007, pp 1, 9, 10.

[37] Robert Half Management Resources, "The Quest for Talent: Recruiting Remains Executives' Top Concern, Survey Shows," news release, February 1, 2008, www.roberthalfmr.com.

[38] Instructive background articles on TQM are R R Gehani, "Quality Value-Chain: A Meta-Synthesis of Frontiers of Quality Movement," *Academy of Management Executive,* May 1993, pp 29–42; P Mears, "How to Stop Talking About, and Begin Progress Toward, Total Quality Management," *Business Horizons,* May–June 1993, pp 11–14; the Total Quality Special Issue of *Academy of Management Review,* July 1994; and R J Vokurka, Rhonda R Lummus, and D Krumwiede, "Improving Manufacturing Flexibility: The Enduring Value of JIT and TQM," *SAM Advanced Management Journal,* Winter 2007, pp 14–21.

[39] M Sashkin and K J Kiser, *Putting Total Quality Management to Work* (San Francisco: Berrett-Koehler, 1993), p 39.

[40] R J Schonberger, "Total Quality Management Cuts a Broad Swath—Through Manufacturing and Beyond," *Organizational Dynamics,* Spring 1992, p 18. Other quality-related articles include H Liao and A Chuang, "A Multilevel Investigation of Factors Influencing Employee Service Performance and Customer Outcomes," *Academy of Management Journal,* February 2004, pp 41–58; L Heuring, "Six Sigma in Sight," *HR Magazine,* March 2004, pp 76–80; N Brodsky, "You're Fired!" *Inc.,* May 2004, pp 51–52; and D McDonald, "Roll Out the Blue Carpet," *Business 2.0,* May 2004, pp 53–54.

[41] Deming's landmark work is W E Deming, *Out of the Crisis* (Cambridge, MA: MIT, 1986). Also see J Henry, "Company's Quality Crusade Was Launched by an American: Deming Inspired Toyota and Then Everyone Else Played Catch-Up," *Automotive News,* October 29, 2007, General Reference Center Gold, http://find.galegroup.com.

[42] See M Trumbull, "What Is Total Quality Management?" *The Christian Science Monitor,* May 3, 1993, p 12; and J Hillkirk, "World-Famous Quality Expert Dead at 93," *USA Today,* December 21, 1993, pp 1B–2B.

[43] Based on discussion in M Walton, *Deming Management at Work* (New York: Putnam/Perigee, 1990).

[44] Ibid., p 20.

[45] Adapted from D E Bowen and E E Lawler III, "Total Quality-Oriented Human Resources Management," *Organizational Dynamics,* Spring 1992, pp 29–41. Also see L Selden and I C MacMillan, "Manage Customer-Centric Innovation—Systematically," *Harvard Business Review,* April 2006, pp 108–16.

[46] J Tayman, "The Enormous Engine That Could," *Business 2.0,* April 2005, p 122. Also see Y Kageyama, "Toyota Spreads Quality Globally," *The Arizona Republic,* April 16, 2006, p D5.

[47] As quoted in P LaBarre, "The Industrialized Revolution," *Fast Company,* November 2003, pp 116, 118.

[48] See J M Ivancevich, T N Duening, and W Lidwell, "Bridging the Manager-Organizational Scientist Collaboration Gap," *Organizational Dynamics,* no. 2, 2005, pp 103–17; E W Ford, W J Duncan, A G Bedeian, P M Ginter, M D Rousculp, and A M Adams, "Mitigating Risks, Visible Hands, Inevitable Disasters, and Soft Variables: Management Research That Matters to Managers," *Academy of Management Executive,* November 2005, pp 24–38; and J M Bartunek, S L Rynes, and R D Ireland, "What Makes Management Research Interesting, and Why Does It Matter?" *Academy of Management Journal,* February 2006, pp 9–15.

[49] B E Becker, M A Huselid, and D Ulrich, *The HR Scorecard: Linking People, Strategy, and Performance* (Boston: Harvard Business School Press, 2001), p 4. Also see J McGregor, "The World's Most Innovative Companies," *BusinessWeek,* April 24, 2006, pp 63–74.

[50] See L Bassi and D McMurrer, "How's Your Return on People?" *Harvard Business Review,* March 2004, p 18; B Hall, "Here Comes Human Capital Management," *Training,* March 2004, pp 16–17; "Employers Say Measuring Is Vital But Still Don't Do It," *HR Magazine,* April 2004, p 18; R J Grossman, "Developing Talent," *HR Magazine,* January 2006, pp 40–46; J Schlosser, "Infosys U.," *Fortune,* March 20, 2006, pp 41–42; M Bolch, "Bearing Fruit," *HR Magazine,* March 2006, pp 56–60; and E Woyke, "The Boss is Watching—So Watch Your iPod," *BusinessWeek,* April 24, 2006, p 16.

[51] A Pomeroy, "C-Suite Worries over Succession Planning," *HR Magazine,* December 2007, p 22.

[52] V Fuhrmans, "The 50 Women to Watch," *The Wall Street Journal,* November 19, 2007, pp R3–R4, R8–R12.

[53] See L Bassi and D McMurrer, "Developing Measurement Systems for Managing in the Knowledge Era," *Organizational Dynamics,* no. 2, 2005, pp 185–196.

[54] Inspired by P S Adler and S Kwon, "Social Capital: Prospects for a New Concept," *Academy of Management Review,* January 2002, pp 17–40. Also see "Social Capitalists: The Top 20 Groups That Are Changing the World," *Fast Company,* January 2004, pp 45–57; and R Takeuchi, D P Lepak, H Wang, and K Takeuchi, "An Empirical Examination of the Mechanisms Mediating between High-Performance Work Systems and the Performance of Japanese Organizations," *Journal of Applied Psychology* 92(4) (2007): 1069–83.

[55] L Prusak and D Cohen, "How to Invest in Social Capital," *Harvard Business Review,* June 2001, p 93.

[56] Data from "What Makes a Job OK," *USA Today,* May 15, 2002, p 1B.

[57] J L Schenker, "Ex-SAP CEO Launches African Venture Fund," *BusinessWeek,* February 15, 2008, www.businessweek.com; "Agents of Change: Social Entrepreneurs," *The Economist,* February 2, 2008, General Reference Center Gold, http://find.galegroup.com; and J Rauch, "'This Is Not Charity,'" *Atlantic Monthly,* October 2007, pp 65–76.

[58] M E P Seligman and M Csikszentmihalyi, "Positive Psychology: An Introduction," *American Psychologist,* January 2000, p 5. Also see the other 15 articles in the January 2000 issue of *American Psychologist;* M Elias, "There's a Recipe for Resilience," *USA Today,* June 29, 2005, pp 1D–2D; B L Fredrickson and M F Losada, "Positive Affect and the Complex Dynamics of Human Flourishing," *American Psychologist,*

October 2005, pp 678–86; and S Jayson, "Unhappiness Has Risen in the Past Decade," *USA Today,* January 9, 2006, p 7D.

[59] See F Luthans, K W Luthans, and B C Luthans, "Positive Psychological Capital: Beyond Human and Social Capital," *Business Horizons,* January–February 2004, pp 45–50.

[60] F Luthans, "The Need for and Meaning of Positive Organizational Behavior," *Journal of Organizational Behavior,* September 2002, p 698. Also see T A Wright, "Positive Organizational Behavior: An Idea Whose Time Has Truly Come," *Journal of Organizational Behavior,* June 2003, pp 437–42; S Fineman, "On Being Positive: Concerns and Counterpoints," *Academy of Management Review,* April 2006, pp 270–91; and L M Roberts, "Shifting the Lens on Organizational Life: The Added Value of Positive Scholarship," *Academy of Management Review,* April 2006, pp 292–305.

[61] See A Marsh, "The Art of Work," *Fast Company,* August 2005, pp 76–79; and S J Peterson and B K Spiker, "Establishing the Positive Contributory Value of Older Workers: A Positive Psychology Perspective," *Organizational Dynamics,* no. 2, 2005, pp 153–67.

[62] Supportive findings can be found in A Giardini and M Frese, "Linking Service Employees' Emotional Competence to Customer Satisfaction: A Multilevel Approach," *Journal of Organizational Behavior,* February 2008, pp 155–70; L Muse, S Harris, W Giles, and H Field, "Work-Life Benefits and Positive Organizational Behavior: Is There a Connection?" *Journal of Organizational Behavior,* February 2008, pp 171–92; and F Luthans, S Norman, B Avolio, and J Avey, "The Mediating Role of Psychological Capital in the Supportive Organizational Climate—Employee Performance Relationship," *Journal of Organizational Behavior,* February 2008, pp 219–38.

[63] "The 100 Best Companies to Work For: and the Winners Are," *Fortune,* January 23, 2006, p 90.

[64] "100 Best Companies to Work For, 2008."

[65] See S Baker, "Wiser About the Web," *BusinessWeek,* March 27, 2006, pp 54–58; S Levy and B Stone, "The New Wisdom of the Web," *Newsweek,* April 3, 2006, pp 46–53; and A Lashinsky, "The Boom Is Back," *Fortune,* May 1, 2006, pp 70–87.

[66] E Krell, "HR Challenges in Virtual Worlds," *HR Magazine,* November 2007, pp 85–87.

[67] K Tyler, "The Tethered Generation," *HR Magazine,* May 2007, pp 41–46; and J Levco, "Hoofing It to the Office Passe," *Chicago Tribune,* January 6, 2008.

[68] T J Mullaney and A Weintraub, "The Digital Hospital," *BusinessWeek,* March 28, 2005, p 77.

[69] See M A Tucker, "E-Learning Evolves," *HR Magazine,* October 2005, pp 74–78; S Boehle, "Putting the 'Learning' Back in E-Learning," *Training,* January 2006, pp 30–34; B West, "Online, It's All About Design," *Training,* March 2006, p 76; and J Gordon, "Seven Revelations About E-Learning," *Training,* April 2006, pp 28–31.

[70] J Merritt, "You Mean Cheating Is Wrong?" *BusinessWeek,* December 9, 2002, p 8. Also see R M Henig, "Looking for the Lie," *The New York Times Magazine,* February 5, 2006, pp 46–53, 76, 80, 83.

[71] See Kathy Gurchiek, "Ethics, Schmethics, U.S. Teens Say," *HR Magazine,* February 2008, p 26.

## Ethics Learning Module

[1] Excerpted from J Puzzangbera, "Yahoo Taken to Task over China," *Los Angeles Times,* November 7, 2007; www.latimes.com/business/la-fi-yahoo7nov07,0,5198009.story?coll=la-home-center.

[2] For a related discussion, see D J Moberg, "Ethics Blind Spots in Organizations: How Systematic Errors in Person Perception Undermine Moral Agency," *Organization Studies,* 2006, pp 413–28; and C J Fombrun, "Corporate Governance," *Corporate Reputation Review,* Winter 2006, pp 267–71.

[3] Data from N Varchaver, "Long Island Confidential," *Fortune,* November 27, 2006, pp 172–86. Also see M Orey, "Enron's Last Mystery," *BusinessWeek,* June 12, 2006, pp 28, 30; R W Clement, "Just How Unethical Is American Business?" *Business Horizons,* July–August 2006, pp 313–27; and H Maurer, "Hyundai's Black Eye," *BusinessWeek,* February 19, 2007, pp 30–31.

[4] See A Pomeroy, "Slashing SOX Costs Faster," *HR Magazine,* January 2007, pp 14, 16; and D Henry, "Not Everyone Hates SarbOx," *BusinessWeek,* January 29, 2007, p 37.

[5] Results can be found in "HR Poll Results," http://hr2.blr.com/index.cfm/Nav/11.0.0.0/Action/Poll_Question/qid/170, accessed April 8, 2005; also see K Gurchiek, "Ethics, Schmethics, U.S. Teens Say," *HR Magazine,* February 2008, p 26.

[6] See "Doctors Don't Turn in Colleagues," *The Arizona Republic,* December 12, 2007, p A16.

[7] P Babcock, "Spotting Lies," *HR Magazine,* October 2003, p 47. Also see J Gill, "Smart Questions for Your Hiring Manager," *Inc.,* February 2007, p 47.

[8] See www.josephsoninstitute.org/pdf/workplace-flier_0604.pdf, accessed April 8, 2005.

[9] See R Alsop, "How Boss's Deeds Buff a Firm's Reputation," *The Wall Street Journal,* January 31, 2007, pp B1–B2; A Fox, "Corporate Social Responsibility Pays Off," *HR Magazine,* August 2007, pp 43–47; and J Collier and R Esteban, "Corporate Social Responsibility and Employee Commitment," *Business Ethics: A European Review,* January 2007, pp 19–33.

[10] Results can be found in "Tarnished Employment Brands Affect Recruiting," *HR Magazine,* November 2004, pp 16, 20.

[11] T M Jones, "Corporate Social Responsibility Revisited, Redefined," *California Management Review,* Spring 1980, pp 59–60. Also see P Engardio, "Beyond the Green Corporation," *BusinessWeek,* January 29, 2007, pp 50–64.

[12] See the related discussion in A Fox, "Be an Insider on Social Responsibility," *HR Magazine,* February 2008, pp 75, 77.

[13] A B Carroll, "Managing Ethically with Global Stakeholders: A Present and Future Challenge," *Academy of Management Executive,* May 2004, p 118.

[14] Ibid., pp 117–18.

[15] See, for example, S J Reynolds and T L Ceranic, "The Effects of Moral Judgment and Moral Identity on Moral Behavior: An Empirical Examination of the Moral Individual," *Journal of Applied Psychology* 92(6) (November 2007), pp 1610–24. Also see R L Hotz, "Scientists Draw Link between Morality and Brain's Wiring," *The Wall Street Journal,* May 11, 2007, p B1.

[16] See C Gilligan, "In a Different Voice: Women's Conceptions of Self and Morality," *Harvard Educational Review,* November 1977, pp 481–517.

[17] S Jaffee and J Hyde, "Gender Differences in Moral Orientation: A Meta-Analysis," *Psychological Bulletin,* September 2000, pp 703–26.

[18] The following discussion is based on A J Daboub, A M A Rasheed, R L Priem, and D A Gray, "Top Management Team Characteristics and Corporate Illegal Activity," *Academy of Management Review,* January 1995, pp 138–70.

[19] S Nance-Nash, "Ethics Reigns," *Insight* (Illinois CPA Society), September–October 2007, www.icpas.org.

[20] See M E Schweitzer, L Ordóñez, and B Douma, "Goal Setting as a Motivator of Unethical Behavior," *Academy of Management Journal,* June 2004, pp 422–32.

[21] S Jayson, "Teens Face up to Ethics Choices—If You Can Believe Them," *USA Today,* December 6, 2006, p 6D.

[22] Results can be found in T Jackson, "Cultural Values and Management Ethics: A 10-Nation Study," *Human Relations,* October 2001, pp 1267–1302.

[23] The following discussion is based on A J Daboub, A M A Rasheed, R L Priem, and D A Gray, "Top Management Team Characteristics and Corporate Illegal Activity," *Academy of Management Review,* January 1995, pp 138–70.

[24] This discussion is based on Constance E Bagley, "The Ethical Leader's Decision Tree," *Harvard Business Review,* February 2003, pp 18–19.

[25] See E E Schultz and T Francis, "Financial Surgery: How Cuts in Retiree Benefits Fatten Companies' Bottom Lines," *The Wall Street Journal,* March 1, 2004, p A1.

[26] See Ch. 6 in K Hodgson, *A Rock and a Hard Place: How to Make Ethical Business Decisions When the Choices Are Tough* (New York: AMACOM, 1992), pp 66–77.

[27] S Welch, "The Uh-Oh Feeling," *O,* November 2007, pp 117–20.

**28** Adapted from W E Stead, D L Worrell, and J Garner Stead, "An Integrative Model for Understanding and Managing Ethical Behavior in Business Organizations," *Journal of Business Ethics,* March 1990, pp 233–42, and D C Kayes, D Stirling, and T M Nielsen, "Building Organizational Integrity," *Business Horizons,* January–February 2007, pp 61–70.

**29** Integrity testing is discussed by D Armstrong, "Malingerer Test Roils Personal-Injury Law," *The Wall Street Journal,* March 5, 2008, pp A1, A13.; and C M Berry, P R Sackett, and S Wiemann, "A Review of Recent Development in Integrity Test Research," *Personnel Psychology,* Summer 2007, pp 271–301.

**30** Guidelines for ethics training are discussed by D Zielinski, "The Right Direction: Can Ethics Training Save Your Company?" *Training,* June 2005, pp 26–32.

**31** Whistle-blowing is discussed by B Levisohn, "Getting More Workers to Whistle," *BusinessWeek,* January 28, 2008, p 18; and A Pasztor, "FAA Seeks to Fine Southwest $10.2 Million," *The Wall Street Journal,* March 7, 2008, p A4.

**32** As quoted in D Jones, "Military a Model for Execs," *USA Today,* June 9, 2004, p 4B.

**33** A good discussion of values and courage is provided by K K Reardon, "Courage," *Harvard Business Review,* January 2007, pp 58–64.

## Chapter 2

**1** Excerpted from B Morris, "What Makes Apple Golden," *Fortune,* March 17, 2008, pp 68, 70.

**2** E H Schein, "Culture: The Missing Concept in Organization Studies," *Administrative Science Quarterly,* June 1996, p 236.

**3** This figure and related discussion are based on C Ostroff, A Kinicki, and M Tamkins, "Organizational Culture and Climate," in *Handbook of Psychology,* vol. 12, eds W C Borman, D R Ilgen, and R J Klimoski (New York: Wiley & Sons, 2003), pp 565–93.

**4** This discussion is based on E H Schein, *Organizational Culture and Leadership,* 2nd ed (San Francisco: Jossey-Bass, 1992), pp 16–48.

**5** Excerpted from J McGregor, "The 2008 Winners," *BusinessWeek,* March 3, 2008, p 49.

**6** S H Schwartz, "Universals in the Content and Structure of Values: Theoretical Advances and Empirical Tests in 20 Countries," in *Advances in Experimental Social Psychology,* ed M P Zanna (New York: Academic Press, 1992), p 4.

**7** See P Engardio, "Beyond the Green Corporation," *BusinessWeek,* January 29, 2007, pp 50–64. Also see M Jarman, "Profitable & Sustainable," *The Arizona Republic,* February 7, 2008, pp D1–D2.

**8** R Sidel, "Amid Turmoil, a Shake-Up at Citi," *The Wall Street Journal,* November 5, 2007, pp A1, A16.

**9** R M Price, "Infusing Innovation into Corporate Culture," *Organizational Dynamics,* 2007, pp 320–28.

**10** See the related discussion in J Welch and S Welch, "Employee Polls: A Vote in Favor," *BusinessWeek,* January 28, 2008, p 90.

**11** A description of Google's innovative culture is discussed by J Larson, "Maintaining Culture of Innovation," *The Arizona Republic,* April 13, 2006, pp D1, D3.

**12** Adapted from L Smircich, "Concepts of Culture and Organizational Analysis," *Administrative Science Quarterly,* September 1983, pp 339–58.

**13** Statistics and data contained in the Southwest Airlines example can be found in the Southwest Airlines Fact Sheet, updated December 11, 2007, www.southwest.com.

**14** K D Godsey, "Slow Climb to New Heights," *Success,* October 1996, p 21.

**15** Southwest's mission statement can be found in "Customer Service Commitment," www.southwest.com, accessed February 26, 2008.

**16** See the related discussion in S Ten Have, W Ten Have, A F Stevens, M Vander Elst, and F Pol-Coyne, *Key Management Models: The Management Tools and Practices That Will Improve Your Business* (San Francisco: Jossey-Bass, 2003).

**17** A thorough description of the CVF is provided in K S Cameron, R E Quinn, J Degraff, and A V Thakor, *Creating Values Leadership* (Northampton, MA: Edward Elgar, 2006).

**18** T F Shea, "Badger Mining Stages an Encore," *HR Magazine,* July 2007, pp 44–45.

**19** Excerpted from J McGregor, "How Failure Breeds Success," *BusinessWeek,* July 10, 2006, pp 45–46.

**20** These examples were taken from D Welch, D Kiley, and M Ihlwan, "My Way or the Highway at Hyundai," *BusinessWeek,* March 17, 2008, pp 48–51; and E Frauenheim, "Culture Crash," *Workforce Management,* January 14, 2008, pp 12–17.

**21** See C Daniels, "Meet Mr. Nuke," *Fortune,* May 15, 2006, pp 140–46.

**22** The Ritz-Carlton's culture is discussed in J Gordon, "Redefining Elegance," *Training,* March 2007, pp 14–18.

**23** E A Goodman, R F Zammuto, and B D Gifford, "The Competing Values Framework: Understanding the Impact of Organizational Culture on the Quality of Work Life," *Organization Development Journal,* Fall 2001, pp 58–68; P A Balthazard, R A Cooke, and R E Potter, "Dysfunctional Culture, Dysfunctional Organization," *Journal of Managerial Psychology,* 2006, pp 709–32; and B Erdogan, R C Liden, and M L Kraimer, "Justice and Leader-member Exchange: The Moderating Role of Organizational Culture," *Academy of Management Journal,* April 2006, pp 395–406.

**24** Supportive results can be found in W Arthur Jr, S T Bell, A J Villado, and D Doverspike, "The Use of Person-Organization Fit in Employment Decision Making: An Assessment of Its Criterion-Related Validity," *Journal of Applied Psychology,* July 2006, pp 786–801.

**25** Culture and performance were examined by M Skerlavaj, M I Stemberger, R Skrinjar, and V Dimovski, "Organizational Learning Culture: The Missing Link between Business Process Change and Organizational Learning," *International Journal of Production Economics,* April 2007, pp 346–67; and A Xenikou and M Simosi, "Organizational Culture and Transformational Leadership as Predictors of Business Unit Performance," *Journal of Managerial Performance,* 2006, pp 566–79.

**26** See C W Hart, "Beating the Market with Customer Satisfaction," *Harvard Business Review,* March 2007, pp 30–31.

**27** J Combs, Y Liu, A Hall, and D Ketchen, "How Much Do High-Performance Work Practices Matter? A Meta-Analysis of Their Effects on Organizational Performance," *Personnel Psychology,* Autumn 2006, pp 501–28.

**28** J P Kotter and J L Heskett, *Corporate Culture and Performance* (New York: Free Press, 1992). For a contrasting example, see A Lucchetti and M Langley, "Perform-or-Die Culture Leaves Thin Talent Pool for Top Wall Street Jobs," *The Wall Street Journal,* November 5, 2007, pp A1, A16.

**29** The success rate of mergers is discussed in M J Epstein, "The Drivers of Success in Post-Merger Integration," *Organizational Dynamics,* May 2004, pp 174–89. Also see R Popely and J Mateja, "Long, Silent Car Ride for Pair," *Chicago Tribune,* April 8, 2007, sec 5, pp 1, 12; and "Dealing with Cultural Misfits," *HR Magazine,* March 2007, pp 14, 16.

**30** V Sathe and E J Davidson, "Toward a New Conceptualization of Culture Change," in *Handbook of Organizational Culture and Climate,* ed N M Ashkanasay, C P M Wilderom, and M F Peterson (Thousand Oaks, CA: Sage, 2000), pp 279–96; and J Welch and S Welch, "Miscreants Among Us," *BusinessWeek,* February 18, 2008, p 84.

**31** The mechanisms were based on material contained in E H Schein, "The Role of the Founder in Creating Organizational Culture," *Organizational Dynamics,* Summer 1983, pp 13–28.

**32** See N Byrnes, "The Art of Motivation," *BusinessWeek,* May 1, 2006, pp 57–62.

**33** D Clark, "Why Silicon Valley Is Rethinking the Cubicle Office," *The Wall Street Journal,* October 15, 2007, http://online.wsj.com.

**34** D Moss, "Triage: Methodically Developing Its Employees," *HR Magazine,* July 2007, p 45.

**35** Ibid.

**36** C Jarnagin and J W Slocum Jr, "Creating Corporate Cultures through Mythopoetic Leadership," *Organizational Dynamics,* 2007, pp 288–302.

**37** C Hymowitz, "New CEOs May Spur Resistance if They Try to Alter Firm's Culture," *The Wall Street Journal,* August 13, 2007, p B1.

**38** A good example is provided by B Hindo, "Making the Elephant Dance," *BusinessWeek,* May 1, 2006, pp 88–90.

**39** Hymowitz, "New CEOs May Spur Resistance."

[40] These examples are explored in B Roberts, "Social Networking at the Office," *HR Magazine,* March 2008, pp 81–83.

[41] J Van Maanen, "Breaking In: Socialization to Work," in *Handbook of Work, Organization, and Society,* ed R Dubin (Chicago: Rand-McNally, 1976), p 67.

[42] This example was described in J Stearns, "Sedona Company Wants Happy Employees," *Arizona Republic,* April 10, 2005, p D2.

[43] Onboarding programs are discussed by D Moscato, "Using Technology to Get Employees on Board," *HR Magazine,* March 2005, pp 107–09.

[44] K Shermach, "Training de Luxe," *Training,* October 2007, pp 32, 34.

[45] T N Bauer, T Bodner, B Erdogan, D M Truxillo, and J S Tucker, "Newcomer Adjustment during Organizational Socialization: A Meta-Analytic Review of Antecedents, Outcomes, and Methods," *Journal of Applied Psychology,* May 2007, pp 707–21.

[46] Excerpted from S Reed, "The Stealth Oil Giant," *BusinessWeek,* January 14, 2008, p 45.

[47] See J Durett, "Training 101," *Training,* March 2006, pp 70–71.

[48] See D Cable and C Parsons, "Socialization Tactics and Person-Organization Fit," *Personnel Psychology,* Spring 2001, pp 1–23.

[49] R Levering and M Moskowitz, "The 100 Best Companies to Work For: And the Winners Are . . ." *Fortune,* January 23, 2006, p 94.

[50] See A M Saks and B E Ashforth, "Proactive Socialization and Behavioral Self-Management," *Journal of Vocational Behavior,* June 1996, pp 301–23.

[51] For a thorough review of research on the socialization of diverse employees with disabilities see A Colella, "Organizational Socialization of Newcomers with Disabilities: A Framework for Future Research," in *Research in Personnel and Human Resources Management,* ed G R Ferris (Greenwich, CT: JAI Press, 1996), pp 351–417.

[52] This definition is based on the network perspective of mentoring proposed by M Higgins and K Kram, "Reconceptualizing Mentoring at Work: A Development Network Perspective," *Academy of Management Review,* April 2001, pp 264–88.

[53] Supportive results can be found in Monica L Forret and Thomas W Dougherty, "Networking Behaviors and Career Outcomes: Differences for Men and Women?" *Journal of Organizational Behavior,* May 2004, pp 419–37.

[54] Career functions are discussed in detail in K Kram, *Mentoring of Work: Developmental Relationships in Organizational Life* (Glenview, IL: Scott, Foresman, 1985).

[55] T J DeLong, J J Gabarro, and R J Lees, "Why Mentoring Matters in a Hypercompetitive World," *Harvard Business Review,* January 2008, pp 115–21.

[56] This discussion is based on Higgins and Kram, "Reconceptualizing Mentoring at Work."

[57] See T D Allen, L T Eby, and E Lentz, "The Relationship between Formal Mentoring Program Characteristics and Perceived Program Effectiveness," *Personnel Psychology,* Spring 2006, pp 125–53.

[58] Results can be found in "Leadership Needs Development," *Training,* February 2006, p 7.

[59] DeLong et al., "Why Mentoring Matters."

[60] A Pomeroy, "Internal Mentors and Coaches Are Popular," *HR Magazine,* September 2007, p 12.

[61] This example was based on material in J Hagerty and D Paletta, "Lender's CEO Regrets Email Tone," *The Wall Street Journal,* March 10, 2008, http://online.wsj.com/article/SB120509573190722773.html; and G Simpson and E Perez, "FBI Investigates Countrywide," *The Wall Street Journal,* March 8, 2008, http://online.wsj.com/article/SB1204946266424521739.html.

## Chapter 3

[1] Excerpted from S Hamm, "International Isn't Just IBM's First Name," *BusinessWeek,* January 28, 2008, pp 37–39.

[2] See B Einhorn, "Outsourcing the Patients," *BusinessWeek,* March 24, 2008, p 36; K Epstein and J Crown, "Globalization Bites Boeing," *BusinessWeek,* March 24, 2008, p 32; M Herbst, "Guess Who's Getting the Most Work Visas," *BusinessWeek,* March 17, 2008, pp 62, 64; and J Welch and S Welch, "Fear Not the Foreign Investor," *BusinessWeek,* January 21, 2008, p 80.

[3] D J Lynch, "Developing Nations Poised to Challenge USA as King of the Hill," *USA Today,* February 8, 2007, p 2B.

[4] H Dolezalek, "It's a Small World," *Training,* January 2008, pp 22–26.

[5] Descriptions of Mr. Kent are provided in "The Coca-Cola Company Board of Directors Nominates Muhtar Kent as Director," *Business Wire,* February 21, 2008, http://news.moneycentral.msn.com; and B McKay, "Coke Makes It Official, Taps Kent as CEO," *The Wall Street Journal Online,* December 7, 2007, p A3.

[6] M A Carpenter, W G Sanders, and H B Gregersen, "Bundling Human Capital with Organizational Context: The Impact of International Assignment Experience on Multinational Firm Performance and CEO Pay," *Academy of Management Journal,* June 2001, pp 493–511.

[7] See L Nardon and R M Steers, "The New Global Manager: Learning Cultures on the Fly," *Organizational Dynamics,* January–March 2008, pp 47–59.

[8] M Javidan and R J House, "Cultural Acumen for the Global Manager: Lessons from Project GLOBE," *Organizational Dynamics,* Spring 2001, p 292. For an example, G A Fowler, "China Tightens Web-Video Rules," *The Wall Street Journal,* January 4, 2008, p A2.

[9] F Trompenaars and C Hampden-Turner, *Riding the Waves of Culture: Understanding Cultural Diversity in Global Business,* 2nd ed (New York: McGraw-Hill, 1998), pp 6–7. Also see C Wan, C Chiu, S Peng, and K Tam, "Measuring Cultures through Intersubjective Cultural Norms," *Journal of Cross-Cultural Psychology,* March 2007, pp 213–26.

[10] See M Mendenhall, "A Painless Approach to Integrating 'International' into OB, HRM, and Management Courses," *Organizational Behavior Teaching Review,* no. 3 (1988–89), pp 23–27. For an example, see P Dvorak and L Abboud, "SAP's Plan to Globalize Hits Cultural Barriers," *The Wall Street Journal,* May 11, 2007, http://online.wsj.com.

[11] See C L Sharma, "Ethnicity, National Integration, and Education in the Union of Soviet Socialist Republics," *The Journal of East and West Studies,* October 1989, pp 75–93.

[12] E Flitter, "How to Tell When Yes Really Means No," *The Wall Street Journal,* October 31, 2007, http://online.wsj.com.

[13] M Pudelko and M E Mendenhall, "What Western Executives Need to Know about Current Japanese Management Practices," *Organizational Dynamics,* 2007, p 284.

[14] See G A Sumner, *Folkways* (New York: Ginn, 1906).

[15] D A Heenan and H V Perlmutter, *Multinational Organization Development* (Reading, MA: Addison-Wesley, 1979), p 17.

[16] Data from R Kopp, "International Human Resource Policies and Practices in Japanese, European, and United States Multinationals," *Human Resource Management,* Winter 1994, pp 581–99.

[17] See R M Kanter, "Transforming Giants," *Harvard Business Review,* January 2008, pp 43–52; and R Strack, J Baier, A Fahlander, "Managing Demographic Risk," *Harvard Business Review,* February 2008, pp 119–28; and S Hamm, "Yound and Impatient in India," *BusinessWeek,* January 28, 2008, pp 45–48.

[18] Data from B Hagerty, "Trainers Help Expatriate Employees Build Bridges to Different Cultures," *The Wall Street Journal,* June 14, 1993, pp B1, B3.

[19] C M Farkas and P De Backer, "There Are Only Five Ways to Lead," *Fortune,* January 15, 1996, p 111.

[20] For related research, see G S Van Der Vegt, E Van De Vliert, and X Huang, "Location-Level Links Between Diversity and Innovative Climate Depend on National Power Distance," *Academy of Management Journal,* December 2005, pp 1171–182.

[21] For complete details, see G Hofstede, *Culture's Consequences: International Differences in Work-Related Values,* abridged ed (Newbury Park, CA: Sage Publications, 1984); G Hofstede, "The Interaction between National and Organizational Value Systems," *Journal of Management Studies,* July 1985, pp 347–57; and G Hofstede, "Management Scientists Are Human," *Management Science,* January 1994, pp 4–13; and B L Kirkman, K B Lowe, and C B Gibson, "A Quarter Century of *Culture's Consequences:* A Review of Empirical Research Incorporating Hofstede's Cultural Values Framework," *Journal of International Business Studies,* May 2006, pp 285–320.

[22] A similar conclusion is presented in the following replication of Hofstede's work: A Merritt, "Culture in the Cockpit: Do Hofstede's

Dimensions Replicate?" *Journal of Cross-Cultural Psychology,* May 2000, pp 283–301.

[23] See Global Deception Research Team, "A World of Lies," *Journal of Cross-Cultural Psychology,* January 2006, pp 60–74.

[24] J S Osland and A Bird, "Beyond Sophisticated Stereotyping: Cultural Sensemaking in Context," *Academy of Management Executive,* February 2000, p 67.

[25] "Fujio Mitarai: Canon," *BusinessWeek,* January 14, 2002, p 55.

[26] P C Earley and E Mosakowski, "Cultural Intelligence," *Harvard Business Review,* October 2004, p 140; and I Alon and J M Higgins, "Global Leadership Success Through Emotional and Cultural Intelligences," *Business Horizons,* November–December 2005, pp 501–512.

[27] See R J House, P J Hanges, M Javidan, P W Dorfman, and V Gupta, eds, *Culture, Leadership, and Organizations: The GLOBE Study of 62 Societies* (Thousand Oaks, CA: Sage, 2004).

[28] R House, M Javidan, P Hanges, and P Dorfman, "Understanding Cultures and Implicit Leadership Theories across the Globe: An Introduction to Project GLOBE," *Journal of World Business,* Spring 2002, p 4.

[29] See M Javidan and A Dastmalchian, "Culture and Leadership in Iran: The Land of Individual Achievers, Strong Family Ties, and Powerful Elite," *Academy of Management Executive,* November 2003, pp 127–42; and M Javidan, G K Stahl, F Brodbeck, and C P M Wilderom, "Cross-Border Transfer of Knowledge: Cultural Lessons from Project GLOBE," *Academy of Management Executive,* May 2005, pp 59–76.

[30] Adapted from the list in House, Javidan, Hanges, and Dorfman, "Understanding Cultures and Implicit Leadership Theories across the Globe," pp 5–6.

[31] M Irvine, "Young Workers Saving to Retire," *The Arizona Republic,* December 28, 2003, p D5.

[32] L E Atwater, J F Brett, and A C Charles, "The Delivery of Workplace Discipline: Lessons Learned," *Organizational Dynamics,* 2007, pp 392–403.

[33] M Edwards, "As Good as It Gets," *AARP: The Magazine,* November–December 2004, p 48.

[34] Data from Trompenaars and Hampden-Turner, *Riding the Waves of Culture: Understanding Cultural Diversity in Global Business,* Ch 5. For relevant research evidence, see E G T Green and J Deschamps, "Variation of Individualism and Collectivism within and between 20 Countries," *Journal of Cross-Cultural Psychology,* May 2005, pp 321–39; and J L Xie, J Roy, and Z Chen, "Cultural and Individual Differences in Self-Rating Behavior: An Extension and Refinement of the Cultural Relativity Hypothesis," *Journal of Organizational Behavior,* May 2006, pp 341–64.

[35] See J A Vandello and D Cohen, "Patterns of Individualism and Collectivism across the United States," *Journal of Personality and Social Psychology,* August 1999, pp 279–92.

[36] As quoted in E E Schultz, "Scudder Brings Lessons to Navajo, Gets Some of Its Own," *The Wall Street Journal,* April 29, 1999, p C12.

[37] Trompenaars and Hampden-Turner, *Riding the Waves of Culture: Understanding Cultural Diversity in Global Business,* p 56.

[38] See W L Adair, L Weingart, and J Brett, "The Timing and Function of Offers in U.S. and Japanese Negotiations," *Journal of Applied Psychology,* July 2007, pp 1056–68.

[39] I Adler, "Between the Lines," *Business Mexico,* October 2000, p 24.

[40] R Drew, "Working with Foreigners," *Management Review,* September 1999, p 6.

[41] See C Saunders, C Van Slyke, and D R Vogel, "My Time or Yours? Managing Time Visions in Global Virtual Teams," *Academy of Management Executive,* February 2004, pp 19–31.

[42] D J Lynch, "Building Explosion in China Pumps Up Exports from USA," *USA Today,* April 20, 2006, p 2B.

[43] R W Moore, "Time, Culture, and Comparative Management: A Review and Future Direction," in *Advances in International Comparative Management,* vol. 5, ed S B Prasad (Greenwich, CT: JAI Press, 1990), pp 7–8.

[44] See A C Bluedorn, C F Kaufman, and P M Lane, "How Many Things Do You Like to Do at Once? An Introduction to Monochronic and Polychronic Time," *Academy of Management Executive,* November 1992, pp 17–26.

[45] See N Hellmich, "Most People Multitask, so Most People Don't Sit Down to Eat," *USA Today,* September 30, 2004, p 8D; and D H Freedman, "Why Interruption, Distraction, and Multitasking Are Not Such Awful Things After All," *Inc.,* February 2007, pp 67–68.

[46] See M Archer, "Too Busy to Read This Book? Then You Really Need To," *USA Today,* April 17, 2006, p 10B.

[47] O Port, "You May Have To Reset This Watch—In a Million Years," *BusinessWeek,* August 30, 1993, p 65.

[48] See M Javidan, P W Dorfman, M S de Luque, and R J House, "In the Eye of the Beholder: Cross Cultural Lessons in Leadership from Project GLOBE," *Academy of Management Perspectives,* February 2006, pp 67–90; G B Graen, "In the Eye of the Beholder: Cross-Cultural Lesson in Leadership from Project GLOBE: A Response Viewed from the Third Culture Bonding (TCB) Model of Cross-Cultural Leadership," *Academy of Management Perspectives,* November 2006, pp 95–101; and R J House, M Javidan, P W Dorfman, and M Sully de Luque, "A Failure of Scholarship: Response to George Graen's Critique of GLOBE," *Academy of Management Perspectives,* November 2006, pp 102–14.

[49] J Guyon, "David Whitwam," *Fortune,* July 26, 2004, p 174.

[50] See "China's Talent Gap," *Training,* April 2007, p 7; and J McGregor and S Hamm, "Managing the Workforce," *BusinessWeek,* January 28, 2008, p 34.

[51] A Fisher, "Five Ways to Ignite Your Career," *Fortune,* February 6, 2006, p 50.

[52] J S Black and H B Gregersen, "The Right Way to Manage Expats," *Harvard Business Review,* March–April 1999, p 53.

[53] Results are presented in A Maingault, L Albright, and V Neal, "Policy Tips, Repatriation, Safe Harbor Rules," *HR Magazine,* March 2008, pp 34–35.

[54] These insights come from R L Tung, "Female Expatriates: The Model Global Manager?" *Organizational Dynamics,* no. 3, 2004, pp 243–53; and A Varma, S M Toh, and P Budhwar, "A New Perspective on the Female Expatriate Experience: The Role of Host Country National Categorization," *Journal of World Business,* June 2006, pp 112–20.

[55] An excellent reference book on this topic is J S Black, H B Gregersen, and M E Mendenhall, *Global Assignments: Successfully Expatriating and Repatriating International Managers* (San Francisco: Jossey-Bass, 1992). Also see M Orey, "People Movers," *BusinessWeek,* January 28, 2008, p 44; and M Wang and R Takeuchi, "The Role of Goal Orientation during Expatriation: A Cross-Sectional and Longitudinal Investigation," *Journal of Applied Psychology,* September 2007, pp 1437–45.

[56] See P C Earley, "Intercultural Training for Managers: A Comparison of Documentary and Interpersonal Methods," *Academy of Management Journal,* December 1987, pp 685–98; and J S Black and M Mendenhall, "Cross-Cultural Training Effectiveness: A Review and a Theoretical Framework for Future Research," *Academy of Management Review,* January 1990, pp 113–36.

[57] M Bolch, "Going Global," *Training,* January 2008, pp 28–29.

[58] T Lowry and F Balfour, "It's All About the Face-to-Face," *BusinessWeek,* January 28, 2008, pp 50–51.

[59] L Yuan, "Personal Lives, Office Lives," *The Wall Street Journal,* February 19, 2008, http://online.wsj.com.

[60] P Dvorak, "Plain English Gets Harder in Global Era," *The Wall Street Journal,* November 5, 2007, pp B1, B3.

[61] K L Miller, "How a Team of Buckeyes Helped Honda Save a Bundle," *BusinessWeek,* September 13, 1993, p 68.

[62] Bolch, "Going Global." Also see L Grensing-Pophal, "Expat Lifestyles Take a Hit," *HR Magazine,* March 2008, pp 51–54.

[63] B Newman, "For Ira Caplan, Re-Entry Has Been Strange," *The Wall Street Journal,* December 12, 1995, p A12.

[64] See H B Gregersen, "Commitments to a Parent Company and a Local Work Unit During Repatriation," *Personnel Psychology,* Spring 1992, pp 29–54; and H B Gregersen and J S Black, "Multiple Commitments upon Repatriation: The Japanese Experience," *Journal of Management,* no. 2, 1996, pp 209–29.

[65] Ibid., pp 226–27.

[66] This case was based on L P Cohen, "Chiquita Under the Gun," *The Wall Street Journal,* August 2, 2007, pp A1, A9.

# Chapter 4

[1] Excerpted from A M Chaker, "High Schools Add Classes Scripted by Corporations," *The Wall Street Journal,* March 16, 2008, pp A1, A3.

[2] A Kingsbury, "More Proof that Mentors Matter," *U.S. News & World Report,* November 19, 2007, p 59.

[3] Research on object perception is thoroughly discussed by L J Rips, S Blok, and G Newman, "Tracing the Identity of Objects," *Psychological Review,* January 2006, pp 1–30.

[4] L Landro, "Hospitals Combat Dangerous Bedsores," *The Wall Street Journal,* September 5, 2007, pp D1–D2.

[5] The negativity bias was examined by N Kyle Smith, J T Larsen, T L Chartrand, and J T Cacioppo, "Being Bad Isn't Always Good: Affective Context Moderates the Attention Bias Toward Negative Information," *Journal of Personality and Social Psychology,* February 2006, pp 210–20.

[6] S Miller, "Survey: Employees Undervalue Benefits," *HR Magazine,* August 2007, p 30.

[7] E Rosch, C B Mervis, W D Gray, D M Johnson, and P Boyes-Braem, "Basic Objects in Natural Categories," *Cognitive Psychology,* July 1976, p 383.

[8] For other examples of encoding information using a schema, see T Parker-Pope, "Latest Weight-Loss Advice: Slow Down and Pay Attention," *The Wall Street Journal,* January 16, 2007, p D1; T Parker-Pope, "The Accidental Binge Drinker: How Much We Really Pour," *The Wall Street Journal,* May 1, 2007, p D1; A Cynkar, "Seeing Red Impairs Test Performance," *Monitor on Psychology,* May 2007, p 11; and S Dingfelder, "Good for Sales, Bad for Boys," *Monitor on Psychology,* September 2007, p 11.

[9] C M Judd and B Park, "Definition and Assessment of Accuracy in Social Stereotypes," *Psychological Review,* January 1993, p 110.

[10] See, for example, "Promoting Positive Prejudice May Beat Damping Negative," *The Wall Street Journal,* January 7, 2008, p B8; and R R Hastings, "The Forgotten Minority," *HR Magazine,* July 2007, pp 63–67.

[11] Results can be found in "Accounting and Race: A Long Way to Go," *Training,* April 2006, p 15.

[12] Results are reported in C Daniels, "Young, Gifted, Black—and Out of Here," *Fortune,* May 3, 2004, p 48. Supportive results can be found in P W Hom, L Roberson, and A D Ellis, "Challenging Conventional Wisdom About Who Quits: Revelations from Corporate America," *Journal of Applied Psychology,* January 2008, pp 1–34.

[13] M R Mehl, S Vazire, N Ramírez-Esparza, R B Slatcher, and J W Pennebaker, "Are Women Really More Talkative than Men?" *Science,* July 6, 2007, p 82.

[14] This discussion is based on material presented in G V Bodenhausen, C N Macrae, and J W Sherman, "On the Dialectics of Discrimination," in *Dual-Process Theories in Social Psychology,* eds S Chaiken and Y Trope (New York: Guilford Press, 1999), pp 271–90. Also see C Munsey, "Training Helps Police Officers Overcome Racial Bias," *Monitor on Psychology,* September 2007, p 13.

[15] For a thorough discussion about the structure and organization of memory, see L R Squire, B Knowlton, and G Musen, "The Structure and Organization of Memory," in *Annual Review of Psychology,* eds L W Porter and M R Rosenzweig (Palo Alto, CA: Annual Reviews Inc., 1993), vol. 44, pp 453–95.

[16] Various training approaches are discussed by P Babcock, "Detecting Hidden Bias," *HR Magazine,* February 2006, pp 51–55.

[17] Results can be found in C M Marlowe, S L Schneider, and C E Nelson, "Gender and Attractiveness Biases in Hiring Decisions: Are More Experienced Managers Less Biased?" *Journal of Applied Psychology,* February 1996, pp 11–21.

[18] Details of this study can be found in C K Stevens, "Antecedents of Interview Interactions, Interviewers' Ratings, and Applicants' Reactions," *Personnel Psychology,* Spring 1998, pp 55–85.

[19] See R C Mayer and J H Davis, "The Effect of the Performance Appraisal System on Trust for Management: A Field Quasi-Experiment," *Journal of Applied Psychology,* February 1999, pp 123–36. Also see I Dennis, "Halo Effects in Grading Student Projects," *Journal of Applied Psychology,* July 2007, pp 1169–76.

[20] Results can be found in W H Bommer, J L Johnson, G A Rich, P M Podsakoff, and S B Mackenzie, "On the Interchangeability of Objective and Subjective Measures of Employee Performance: A Meta-Analysis," *Personnel Psychology,* Autumn 1995, pp 587–605.

[21] The effectiveness of rater training was supported by D V Day and L M Sulsky, "Effects of Frame-of-Reference Training and Information Configuration on Memory Organization and Rating Accuracy," *Journal of Applied Psychology,* February 1995, pp 158–67.

[22] Results can be found in J S Phillips and R G Lord, "Schematic Information Processing and Perceptions of Leadership in Problem-Solving Groups," *Journal of Applied Psychology,* August 1982, pp 486–92. Also see G F Seib, "Issues Recede in 08 Contest As Voters Focus on Character," *The Wall Street Journal,* February 5, 2008, pp A1, A14; and R P Vecchio and D M Brazil, "Leadership and Sex-Similarity: A Comparison in a Military Setting," *Personnel Psychology,* Summer 2007, pp 303–35.

[23] See S Begley, "All in Your Head? Yes, and Scientists Are Figuring Out Why," *The Wall Street Journal,* March 17, 2006, p B1; and "How Racism Affects the Mind—and Body," *The Wall Street Journal,* July 16, 2007, p B5.

[24] See E C Baig, "Survey Offers a 'Sneak Peek' into Net Surfers' Brains," *USA Today,* March 27, 2006, p 4B; and L Winerman, "Screening Surveyed," *Monitor on Psychology,* January 2006, pp 28–29. Also see B White, "Watching What You See on the Web," *The Wall Street Journal,* December 6, 2007, pp B1, B2.

[25] Excerpted from E C Baig, "Survey Offers a 'Sneak Peek' into Net Surfers' Brains," *USA Today,* March 27, 2006, p 4B.

[26] Kelley's model is discussed in detail in H H Kelley, "The Processes of Causal Attribution," *American Psychologist,* February 1973, pp 107–28.

[27] For examples, see J Susskind, K Maurer, V Thakkar, D L Hamilton, and J W Sherman, "Perceiving Individuals and Groups: Expectancies, Dispositional Inferences, and Causal Attributions," *Journal of Personality and Social Psychology,* February 1999, pp 181–91. Also see K White, D R Lehman, K J Hemphill, and D R Mandel, "Causal Attributions, Perceived Control, and Psychological Adjustment: A Study of Chronic Fatigue Syndrome," *Journal of Applied Social Psychology,* 2006, pp 75–99.

[28] Results from these studies can be found in D A Hofmann and A Stetzer, "The Role of Safety Climate and Communication in Accident Interpretation: Implications for Learning from Negative Events," *Academy of Management Journal,* December 1998, pp 644–57; and I Choi, R E Nisbett, and A Norenzayan, "Causal Attribution across Cultures: Variation and Universality," *Psychological Bulletin,* January 1999, pp 47–63.

[29] These cases are discussed in J A Segal, "Woman in the Moon," *HR Magazine,* August 2007, pp 107–14.

[30] Details may be found in S E Moss and M J Martinko, "The Effects of Performance Attributions and Outcome Dependence on Leader Feedback Behavior Following Poor Subordinate Performance," *Journal of Organizational Behavior,* May 1998, pp 259–74; and E C Pence, W C Pendelton, G H Dobbins, and J A Sgro, "Effects of Causal Explanations and Sex Variables on Recommendations for Corrective Actions Following Employee Failure," *Organizational Behavior and Human Performance,* April 1982, pp 227–40.

[31] See D Konst, R Vonk, and R V D Vlist, "Inferences about Causes and Consequences of Behavior of Leaders and Subordinates," *Journal of Organizational Behavior,* March 1999, pp 261–71.

[32] See J Silvester, F Patterson, E Ferguson, "Comparing Two Attributional Models of Job Performance in Retail Sales: A Field Study," *Journal of Occupational and Organizational Psychology,* March 2003, pp 115–32.

[33] The following discussion is based on L Gardenswartz and A Rowe, *Diverse Teams at Work* (New York: McGraw-Hill, 1994), pp 31–57. Also see R Hastings, "SHRM Diversity Report a Call to Action," *HR Magazine,* April 2008, p 34.

[34] H Collingwood, "Who Handles a Diverse Work Force Best?" *Working Women,* February 1996, p 25.

[35] S Meisinger, "Diversity: More than Just Representation," *HR Magazine,* January 2008, p 8; and L Ryan, "Diversity: Beyond a

Numbers Game," *BusinessWeek,* January 14, 2008, www.businessweek
.com.

[36] See "Best Practices & Outstanding Initiatives," *Training,* February 2008, pp 114–20; and "Training Top 125 2008," *Training,* February 2008, pp 76–11.

[37] For information on equal employment opportunity legislation, see K M Pyburn Jr, R E Ployhart, and D A Kravitz, "The Diversity-Validity Dilemma: Overview and Legal Context," *Personnel Psychology,* Spring 2008, pp 143–51; R E Polyhart and B C Holtz, "The Diversity-Validity Dilemma: Strategies for Reducing Racioethnic and Sex Subgroup Differences and Adverse Impact in Selection," *Personnel Psychology,* Spring 2008, pp 153–72; and M Heller, "Special Report: Background Checking—Digging Deeper," *Workforce Management,* March 3, 2008, pp 35–39.

[38] Results can be found in D A Harrison, D A Kravitz, D M Mayer, L M Leslie, and D Lev-Arey, "Understanding Attitudes Toward Affirmative Action Programs in Employment: Summary and Meta-Analysis of 35 Years of Research," *Journal of Applied Psychology,* September, 2006, pp 1013–36.

[39] For a thorough review of relevant research, see M E Heilman, "Affirmative Action: Some Unintended Consequences for Working Women," in *Research in Organizational Behavior,* vol 16, ed B M Staw and L L Cummings (Greenwich, CT: JAI Press, 1994), pp 125–69.

[40] M E Heilman, W S Battle, C E Keller, and R A Lee, "Type of Affirmative Action Policy: A Determinant of Reactions to Sex-Based Preferential Selection?" *Journal of Applied Psychology,* April 1998, pp 190–205.

[41] K Miner-Rubino and L M Cortina, "Beyond Targets: Consequences of Vicarious Exposure to Misogyny at Work," *Journal of Applied Psychology,* September 2007, pp 1254–69. Also see C Farrell, "Is the Workplace Getting Raunchier?" *BusinessWeek,* March 17, 2008, p 19.

[42] A M Morrison, *The New Leaders: Guidelines on Leadership Diversity in America* (San Francisco: Jossey-Bass, 1992), p 78.

[43] Bureau of Labor Statistics, "Labor Force Statistics from the Current Population Survey," http://data.bls.gov, accessed March 14, 2008.

[44] See the related discussion by S M Colarelli, J L Spranger, and M A R Hechanova, "Women, Power, and Sex Composition in Small Groups: An Evolutionary Perspective," *Journal of Organizational Behavior,* March 2006, pp 163–84; and L Scott, "Expert: Women in Business Face Maze," *The Arizona Republic,* April 13, 2008, pp D1, D2.

[45] Bureau of Labor Statistics, *Women in the Labor Force: A Databook,* www.bls.gov/cps/wlf-databook2007.htm, last modified October 24, 2007.

[46] Results can be found in K S Lyness and D E Thompson, "Above the Glass Ceiling: A Comparison of Matched Samples of Female and Male Executives," *Journal of Applied Psychology,* June 1997, pp 359–75.

[47] This study was conducted by K S Lyness and M K Judiesch, "Are Women More Likely to Be Hired or Promoted into Management Positions?" *Journal of Vocational Behavior,* February 1999, pp 158–73.

[48] Jenny Mero, "Fortune 500 Women CEOs," *Fortune,* April 30, 2007, http://money.cnn.com; Del Jones, "Female CEOs Make More Gains in 2007," *USA Today,* January 3, 2008, http://usatoday.com; and Catalyst, "2007 Census: Board Directors," www.catalyst.org. Also see A J Hillman, C Shropshire, and A A Cannella Jr, "Organizational Predictors of Women on Corporate Boards," *Academy of Management Journal,* August 2007, pp 941–52; and D Brady, "A Little Shame Goes a Long Way," *BusinessWeek,* April 16, 2007, pp 34–35.

[49] Here are the ranks for each career strategy: Strategy 1 = 12; Strategy 2 = 6; Strategy 3 = 5; Strategy 4 = 11; Strategy 5 = 9; Strategy 6 = 3; Strategy 7 = 10; Strategy 8 = 1; Strategy 9 = 7; Strategy 10 = 8; Strategy 11 = 4; Strategy 12 = 2; and Strategy 13 = 13.

[50] Details of this study can be found in B R Ragins, B Townsend, and M Mattis, "Gender Gap in the Executive Suite: CEOs and Female Executives Report on Breaking the Glass Ceiling," *Academy of Management Executive,* February 1998, pp 28–42. Also see K R Browne, "Evolved Sex Differences and Occupational Segregation," *Journal of Organizational Behavior,* March 2006, pp 143–62.

[51] S Steckner, "Damned or Doomed?" *Arizona Republic,* November 12, 2007, pp B1, B7.

[52] Census Bureau, "Minority Population Tops 100 Million," news release, May 17, 2007, www.census.gov; and Census Bureau, *Statistical Abstract*

*of the United States 2008,* Table 11, p. 15, "Resident Population by Race, Hispanic Origin Status, and Age—Projections: 2010 and 2015," www.census.gov.

[53] Bureau of Labor Statistics, "Characteristics of the Employed," *Labor Force Statistics from the Current Population Survey,* www.bls.gov, accessed March 14, 2008.

[54] Equal Employment Opportunity Commission, "Race-Based Charges, FY 1997–FY 2007," www.eeoc.gov, last updated February 26, 2008.

[55] Bureau of Labor Statistics, "Weekly and Hourly Earnings Data from the Current Population Survey," http://data.bls.gov, accessed March 14, 2008. But see Hastings, "The Forgotten Minority."

[56] For a review of this research, see L Roberson and C J Block, "Racioethnicity and Job Performance: A Review and Critique of Theoretical Perspectives on the Causes of Group Differences," in *Research in Organizational Behavior,* vol 23, eds B M Staw and R I Sutton (New York: JAI Press, 2001), pp 247–326. Also see M Schoeff Jr, "Clamping Down on Race Bias," *Workforce Management,* January 14, 2008, pp 1, 3; and K Maher, "Lockheed Settles Racial-Discrimination Suit," *The Wall Street Journal,* January 3, 2008, p A4.

[57] Census Bureau, *Statistical Abstract of the United States,* 2008, Table 27, "Educational Attainment by Race and Hispanic Origin," www.census.gov.

[58] See E Vance, "College Graduates Lack Key Skills, Report Says," *Chronicle of Higher Education,* February 2, 2007, p A30.

[59] National Center for Education Statistics (NCES), U.S. Department of Education, *Mini-Digest of Education Statistics 2007,* March 2008, NCES 2008-023, http://nces.ed.gov/pubs2008/2008023.pdf; and NCES, "National Assessment of Adult Literacy: Key Findings," http://nces.ed.gov/naal/, accessed March 14, 2008.

[60] "Facts on Literacy," *National Literacy Facts,* August 27, 1998, www.svs.net/wpci/Litfacts.htm.

[61] Literacy statistics can be found in A Aston and R Vella, "Reading, Writing, and Rankings: America and the World," *BusinessWeek,* March 24, 2008, p 15; and J Mehring and L Daunis-Allen, "Education: The Next Generation of U.S. Workers Is Falling Behind," *BusinessWeek,* February 25, 2008, p 17.

[62] New Commission on the Skills of the American Workforce, *Tough Choices or Tough Times* (San Francisco: Jossey-Bass, 2007), pp xvi–xvii.

[63] See the related discussion in ibid.; C Boles, "Last Call? Gates Pushes Globalism in Remarks," *The Wall Street Journal,* March 13, 2008, p B3; and R Strack, J Baier, and A Fahlander, "Managing Demographic Risk," *Harvard Business Review,* February 2008, pp 119–28.

[64] Census Bureau, *Statistical Abstract of the United States 2008,* Table 10, "Resident Population Projections by Sex and Age: 2010 to 2050," www.census.gov. Also see Census Bureau, "U.S. Interim Projections by Age, Sex, Race, and Hispanic Origin," www.census.gov/ipc/www/usinterimproj/, last modified May 31, 2007.

[65] For examples, see M Schoeff Jr, "Diversity's Strategic Role," *Workforce Management,* January 14, 2008, p 5; S Vranica, "Ads Made for Women, by Women," *The Wall Street Journal,* November 21, 2007, p B3; E White, "Deloitte Tries a Different Sales Pitch for Women," *The Wall Street Journal,* October 8, 2007, pp B1, B6; and S Skidmore, "Nike Designs Shoe for Indians," *Arizona Republic,* September 26, 2007, p A20.

[66] For examples, see Eagly and Carli, "Women and the Labyrinth of Leadership"; E White, "The New Recruits: Older Workers," *The Wall Street Journal,* January 14, 2008, p B3; K Hedlund, "Say Goodbye to 9 to 5," *Phoenix Woman,* Fall 2007, p 20; and M P McQueen, "Workplace Disabilities Are on the Rise," *The Wall Street Journal,* May 1, 2007, pp D1, D5.

[67] See R Levering and M Moskowitz, "The 100 Best Companies to Work For," *Fortune,* January 24, 2005, p 76.

[68] Y Wingett, "Hospital Translators Filling Void," *Arizona Republic,* June 3, 2007, pp B1, B4. Also see "Hispanics in Business: New Initiatives Propel a New Generation of Leaders," *Fortune,* May 28, 2007, p 130; and Ruiz, "BLS: Hispanics, Nurses Poised for Big Gains in U.S. Workforce," *Workforce Management,* January 14, 2008, pp 5–6.

[69] See the related discussion in N Byrnes, "Get' Em While They're Young," *BusinessWeek,* May 22, 2006, pp 86–87; and K Tyler, "Generation Gaps," *HR Magazine,* January 2008, pp 69–72.

[70] Managerial issues and solutions for an aging workforce are discussed by J W Hedge, W C Borman, and S E Lammelein, *The Aging Workforce: Realities, Myths, and Implications for Organizations,* 2006, Washington, DC: American Psychological Association; D R Avery, P F McKay, and D C Wilson, "Engaging the Aging Workforce: The Relationship between Perceived Age Similarity, Satisfaction with Coworkers, and Employee Engagement," *Journal of Applied Psychology,* November 2007, pp 1542–56; For more about managing young workers, see R R Hastings, "Millennials Expect a Lot from Leaders," *HR Magazine,* January 2008, p 30; and H Mackay, "New Generation Doesn't Play by Old Rules," *Arizona Republic,* January 6, 2008, p D2. Also see D Dauten, "When It Comes to Hiring, 50 Is the New 25," *Boston Globe,* February 17, 2008, www.boston.com.

[71] See D Cadrain, "Employers Prepare to Keep, Not Lose, Baby Boomers." *2008 HR Trendbook,* pp 23–24; and K Tyler, "Leveraging Long Tenure." *HR Magazine,* May 2007, pp 55–60.

[72] These barriers were taken from discussions in Loden, *Implementing Diversity;* E E Spragins, "Benchmark: The Diverse Work Force," *Inc.,* January 1993, p 33; and Morrison, *The New Leaders: Guidelines on Leadership Diversity in America.* For examples of these barriers, see C T Kulik, M B Pepper, L Roberson, and S K Parker, "The Rich Get Richer: Predicting Participation in Voluntary Diversity Training," *Journal of Organizational Behavior,* August 2007, pp 753–69; and B R Ragins, R Singh, and J M Cornwell, "Making the Invisible Visible: Fear and Disclosure of Sexual Orientation at Work," *Journal of Applied Psychology,* July 2007, pp 1103–18.

[73] See the related discussion in A Fisher, "The Sky's the Limit," *Fortune,* May 1, 2006, pp 124B–124H.

[74] A C Homan, "Bridging Faultlines by Valuing Diversity: Diversity Beliefs, Information Elaboration, and Performance in Diverse Work Groups," *Journal of Applied Psychology,* September 2007, pp 1189–99.

[75] This discussion is based on R R Thomas Jr, *Redefining Diversity* (New York: AMACOM, 1996).

[76] D J Gaiter, "Eating Crow: How Shoney's, Belted by a Lawsuit, Found the Path to Diversity," *The Wall Street Journal,* April 16, 1996, pp A1, A11.

[77] P Dass and B Parker, "Strategies for Managing Human Resource Diversity: From Resistance to Learning," *Academy of Management Executive,* May 1999, p 69.

[78] Gaiter, "Eating Crow."

[79] E White, "Fostering Diversity to Aid Business," *The Wall Street Journal,* May 20, 2006, p B3.

[80] M Gunther, "Queer Inc.," *Fortune,* December 11, 2006, p 102.

[81] Ibid.

[82] For a good example, see D Brady, "The Holy Cross Fraternity," *BusinessWeek,* March 12, 2007, pp 70–76.

[83] Excerpted from A McConnon, "Mad Ave: If I Only Had a Brain Scan," *BusinessWeek,* January 22, 2007, p 19.

# Chapter 5

[1] Excerpted from S Steckner, "Ms. Personality," *Arizona Woman,* February/March 2008, pp 37, 41–42.

[2] D Seligman, "The Trouble with Buyouts," *Fortune,* November 30, 1992, p 125. Also see A N Salvaggio, B Schneider, L H. Nishii, D M Mayer, A Ramesh, and J S Lyon, "Manager Personality, Manager Service Quality Orientation, and Service Climate: Test of a Model," *Journal of Applied Psychology,* November 2007, pp 1741–50.

[3] Data from "If We Could Do It Over Again," *USA Today,* February 19, 2001, p 4D.

[4] See J Sandberg, "Global-Market Woes Are More Personality Than Nationality," *The Wall Street Journal,* January 29, 2008, p B1; and M Weinstein, "Leadership: Leadership," *Training,* February 2008, pp 41–46.

[5] V Gecas, "The Self-Concept," in *Annual Review of Sociology,* eds R H Turner and J F Short, Jr. (Palo Alto, CA: Annual Reviews Inc., 1982), vol. 8, p 3. Also see R Johnson, C Rosen, and P Levy, "Getting to the Core Self-Evaluation: A Review and Recommendations," *Journal of Organizational Behavior,* April 2008, pp 391–413.

[6] L Festinger, *A Theory of Cognitive Dissonance* (Stanford, CA: Stanford University Press, 1957), p 3.

[7] A Canadian versus Japanese comparison of self-concept can be found in J D Campbell, P D Trapnell, S J Heine, I M Katz, L F Lavallee, and D R Lehman, "Self-Concept Clarity: Measurement, Personality Correlates, and Cultural Boundaries," *Journal of Personality and Social Psychology,* January 1996, pp 141–56.

[8] See D C Barnlund, "Public and Private Self in Communicating with Japan," *Business Horizons,* March/April 1989, pp 32–40; and the section on "Doing Business with Japan" in P R Harris and R T Moran, *Managing Cultural Differences,* 4th ed (Houston: Gulf Publishing, 1996), pp 267–76.

[9] As quoted in A Deutschman, "What I Know Now," *Fast Company,* September 2005, p 96.

[10] Based in part on a definition found in Gecas, "The Self-Concept." Also see N Branden, *Self-Esteem at Work: How Confident People Make Powerful Companies* (San Francisco: Jossey-Bass, 1998).

[11] H W Marsh, "Positive and Negative Global Self-Esteem: A Substantively Meaningful Distinction or Artifacts?" *Journal of Personality and Social Psychology,* April 1996, p 819.

[12] Ibid.

[13] See P Borghesi, "I Was Out of a Job—And an Identity," *Newsweek,* January 30, 2006, p 13.

[14] E Diener and M Diener, "Cross-Cultural Correlates of Life Satisfaction and Self-Esteem," *Journal of Personality and Social Psychology,* April 1995, p 662. For cross-cultural evidence of a similar psychological process for self-esteem, see T M Singelis, M H Bond, W F Sharkey, and C S Y Lai, "Unpackaging Culture's Influence on Self-Esteem and Embarrassability," *Journal of Cross-Cultural Psychology,* May 1999, pp 315–41.

[15] See C Kobayashi and J D Brown, "Self-Esteem and Self-Enhancement in Japan and America," *Journal of Cross-Cultural Psychology,* September 2003, pp 567–80.

[16] Based on data in F L Smoll, R E Smith, N P Barnett, and J J Everett, "Enhancement of Children's Self-Esteem through Social Support Training for Youth Sports Coaches," *Journal of Applied Psychology,* August 1993, pp 602–10.

[17] W J McGuire and C V McGuire, "Enhancing Self-Esteem by Directed-Thinking Tasks: Cognitive and Affective Positivity Asymmetries," *Journal of Personality and Social Psychology,* June 1996, p 1124.

[18] S Begley, "Real Self-Esteem Builds on Achievement, Not Praise for Slackers," *The Wall Street Journal,* April 18, 2003, p B1. Also see W B Swann Jr., C Chang-Schneider, and K L McClarty, "Do People's Self-Views Matter? Self-Concept and Self-Esteem in Everyday Life," *American Psychologist,* February–March 2007, pp 84–94; and T A Judge and C Hurst, "Capitalizing on One's Advantages: Role of Core Self-Evaluations," *Journal of Applied Psychology,* September 2007, pp 1212–27.

[19] M E Gist, "Self-Efficacy: Implications for Organizational Behavior and Human Resource Management," *Academy of Management Review,* July 1987, p 472. Also see A Bandura, "Self-Efficacy: Toward a Unifying Theory of Behavioral Change," *Psychological Review,* March 1977, pp 191–215; and M E Gist and T R Mitchell, "Self-Efficacy: A Theoretical Analysis of Its Determinants and Malleability," *Academy of Management Review,* April 1992, pp 183–211.

[20] C Brennan, "Tiger Loses Favorite Driver," *USA Today,* May 4, 2006, p 3C.

[21] Based on D H Lindsley, D A Brass, and J B Thomas, "Efficacy-Performance Spirals: A Multilevel Perspective," *Academy of Management Review,* July 1995, pp 645–78.

[22] See, for example, V Gecas, "The Social Psychology of Self-Efficacy," in *Annual Review of Sociology,* eds W R Scott and J Blake (Palo Alto, CA: Annual Reviews, Inc., 1989), vol. 15, pp 291–316; and K van Dam, S Oreg, and B Schyns, "Daily Work Contexts and Resistance to Organizational Change: The Role of Leader-Member Exchange, Development Climate, and Change Process Characteristics," *Applied Psychology,* April 2008, pp 313–34.

[23] For more on learned helplessness, see Gecas, "The Social Psychology of Self-Efficacy"; M J Martinko and W L Gardner, "Learned Helplessness: An Alternative Explanation for Performance Deficits," *Academy of Management Review,* April 1982, pp 195–204; and C R Campbell and M J Martinko, "An Integrative Attributional Perspective of Empowerment and Learned Helplessness: A Multimethod Field Study," *Journal of Management,* no. 2, 1998, pp 173–200.

[24] For an update on Bandura, see D Smith, "The Theory Heard 'Round the World," *Monitor on Psychology,* October 2002, pp 30–32.

[25] Research on this connection is reported in R B Rubin, M M Martin, S S Bruning, and D E Powers, "Test of a Self-Efficacy Model of Interpersonal Communication Competence," *Communication Quarterly,* Spring 1993, pp 210–20.

[26] Excerpted from T Petzinger Jr, "Bob Schmonsees Has a Tool for Better Sales, and It Ignores Excuses," *The Wall Street Journal,* March 26, 1999, p B1.

[27] Data from A D Stajkovic and F Luthans, "Self-Efficacy and Work-Related Performance: A Meta-Analysis," *Psychological Bulletin,* September 1998, pp 240–61.

[28] Based in part on discussion in Gecas, "The Social Psychology of Self-Efficacy."

[29] See S K Parker, "Enhancing Role Breadth Self-Efficacy: The Roles of Job Enrichment and Other Organizational Interventions," *Journal of Applied Psychology,* December 1998, pp 835–52.

[30] The positive relationship between self-efficacy and readiness for retraining is documented in L A Hill and J Elias, "Retraining Midcareer Managers: Career History and Self-Efficacy Beliefs," *Human Resource Management,* Summer 1990, pp 197–217.

[31] See A D Stajkovic and Fred Luthans, "Social Cognitive Theory and Self-Efficacy: Going beyond Traditional Motivational and Behavioral Approaches," *Organizational Dynamics,* Spring 1998, pp 62–74.

[32] See P C Earley and T R Lituchy, "Delineating Goal and Efficacy Effects: A Test of Three Models," *Journal of Applied Psychology,* February 1991, pp 81–98.

[33] See P Tierney and S M Farmer, "Creative Self-Efficacy: Its Potential Antecedents and Relationship to Creative Performance," *Academy of Management Journal,* December 2002, pp 1137–48.

[34] See W S Silver, T R Mitchell, and M E Gist, "Response to Successful and Unsuccessful Performance: The Moderating Effect of Self-Efficacy on the Relationship between Performance and Attributions," *Organizational Behavior and Human Decision Processes,* June 1995, pp 286–99.

[35] For a comprehensive update, see S W Gangestad and M Snyder, "Self-Monitoring: Appraisal and Reappraisal," *Psychological Bulletin,* July 2000, pp 530–55.

[36] M Snyder and S Gangestad, "On the Nature of Self-Monitoring: Matters of Assessment, Matters of Validity," *Journal of Personality and Social Psychology,* July 1986, p 125.

[37] Data from M Kilduff and D V Day, "Do Chameleons Get Ahead? The Effects of Self-Monitoring on Managerial Careers," *Academy of Management Journal,* August 1994, pp 1047–60.

[38] Data from D B Turban and T W Dougherty, "Role of Protege Personality in Receipt of Mentoring and Career Success," *Academy of Management Journal,* June 1994, pp 688–702.

[39] See F Luthans, "Successful vs. Effective Managers," *Academy of Management Executive,* May 1988, pp 127–32.

[40] G Toegel, N Anand, and M Kilduff, "Emotion Helpers: The Role of High Positive Affectivity and High Self-Monitoring Managers," *Personnel Psychology,* Summer 2007, pp 337–65.

[41] See R Arvey, Z Zhand, B Avolio, and R Krueger, "Developmental and Genetic Determinants of Leadership Role Occupancy Among Women," *Journal of Applied Psychology,* May 2007, pp 693–706.

[42] The landmark report is J M Digman, "Personality Structure: Emergence of the Five-Factor Model," *Annual Review of Psychology,* vol. 41, 1990, pp 417–40. Also see M K Mount, M R Barrick, S M Scullen, and J Rounds, "Higher-Order Dimensions of the Big Five Personality Traits and the Big Six Vocational Interest Types," *Personnel Psychology,* Summer 2005, pp 447–78; and P Warr, D Bartram, and A Brown, "Big Five Validity: Aggregation Method Matters," *Journal of Occupational and Organizational Psychology,* September 2005, pp 377–86.

[43] For more on personality measurement and assessment, see P Sackett and F Lievens, "Personnel Selection," *Annual Review of Psychology,* 2008, pp 419–50. and J R Matthews and L H Matthews, "Personality Assessment Training: View from a Licensing Board," *Journal of Personality Assessment,* February 2006, pp 46–50.

[44] Data from S V Paunonen et al., "The Structure of Personality in Six Cultures," *Journal of Cross-Cultural Psychology,* May 1996, pp 339–53.

[45] J Allik and R R McCrae, "Escapable Conclusions: Toomela (2003) and the Universality of Trait Structure," *Journal of Personality and Social Psychology,* August 2004, p 261. For more supporting evidence, see D P Schmitt, J Allik, R R McCrae, and V Benet-Martinez, "The Geographic Distribution of Big Five Personality Traits," *Journal of Cross-Cultural Psychology,* March 2007, pp 173–212.

[46] See M R Barrick and M K Mount, "The Big Five Personality Dimensions and Job Performance: A Meta-Analysis," *Personnel Psychology,* Spring 1991, pp 1–26. Also see R P Tett, D N Jackson, and M Rothstein, "Personality Measures as Predictors of Job Performance: A Meta-Analytic Review," *Personnel Psychology,* Winter 1991, pp 703–42; and S E Seibert and M L Kraimer, "The Five-Factor Model of Personality and Career Success," *Journal of Vocational Behavior,* February 2001, pp 1–21.

[47] Barrick and Mount, "The Big Five Personality Dimensions and Job Performance: A Meta-Analysis," p 18. Also see D Kamdar and L Van Dyne, "The Joint Effects of Personality and Workplace Social Exchange Relationships in Predicting Task Performance and Citizenship Performance," *Journal of Applied Psychology,* September 2007, pp 1286–98; and C J Resick, B B Baltes, and C W Shantz, "Person–Organization Fit and Work-Related Attitudes and Decisions: Examining Interactive Effects with Job Fit and Conscientiousness," *Journal of Applied Psychology,* September 2007, pp 1446–55.

[48] B Marcus, K Lee, and M C Ashton, "Personality Dimensions Explaining Relationships between Integrity Tests and Counterproductive Behavior: Big Five, or One in Addition?" *Personnel Psychology,* Spring 2007, pp 1–34.

[49] For details, see S Clarke and I T Robertson, "A Meta-Analytic Review of the Big Five Personality Factors and Accident Involvement in Occupational and Non-Occupational Settings," *Journal of Occupational and Organizational Psychology,* September 2005, pp 355–76.

[50] Barrick and Mount, "The Big Five Personality Dimensions and Job Performance: A Meta-Analysis," p 21.

[51] For details, see L A Witt and G R Ferris, "Social Skill as Moderator of the Conscientiousness-Performance Relationship: Convergent Results across Four Studies," *Journal of Applied Psychology,* October 2003, pp 809–20.

[52] Lead researcher William Fleeson, as quoted in M Dittmann, "Acting Extraverted Spurs Positive Feelings, Study Finds," *Monitor on Psychology,* April 2003, p 17.

[53] F P Morgeson, M A Campion, R L Dipboye, J R Hollenbeck, K Murphy, and N Schmitt, "Reconsidering the Use of Personality Tests in Personnel Selection Contexts," *Personnel Psychology,* Autumn 2007, pp 683–729. Also see D Armstrong, "Malingerer Test Roils Personal-Injury Law," *The Wall Street Journal,* March 5, 2008, pp A1, A3; and M Conlin, "Telecommuting: Out of Sight, Yes. Out of Mind, No," *BusinessWeek,* February 18, 2008, p 60.

[54] J M Crant, "Proactive Behavior in Organizations," *Journal of Management,* no. 3, 2000, p 439.

[55] Ibid., pp 439–41. Also see J A Thompson, "Proactive Personality and Job Performance: A Social Capital Perspective," *Journal of Applied Psychology,* September 2005, pp 1011–017; and B Erdogan and T N Bauer, "Enhancing Career Benefits of Employee Proactive Personality: The Role of Fit with Jobs and Organizations," *Personnel Psychology,* Winter 2005, pp 859–91.

[56] D Hannah, "How I Did It: Joaquin Galan, CEO, Galypso International," *Inc.,* The 2007 Inc. 5000, www.inc.com/inc5000/, accessed March 26, 2008; and T Snyder, "How I Did It: Rachel Coleman, CEO, Two Little Hands Productions," *Inc.,* The 2007 Inc. 5000, www.inc.com/inc5000/, accessed March 26, 2008.

[57] See S B Gustafson and M D Mumford, "Personal Style and Person-Environment Fit: A Pattern Approach," *Journal of Vocational Behavior,* April 1995, pp 163–88; T M Glomb and E T Walsh, "Can Opposites Attract? Personality Heterogeneity in Supervisor-Subordinate Dyads as a Predictor of Subordinate Outcomes," *Journal of Applied Psychology,* July 2005, pp 749–57; "Personality Assessment Soars at Southwest," *Training,* January 2008, p 14; J Sandberg, "The Office Pessimists May Not Be Lovable, but Are Often Right," *The Wall Street Journal,* November 27, 2007, p B1; and F Zakaria, "The Power of Personality," *Newsweek,* December 24, 2007, p 41.

[58] For an instructive update, see J B Rotter, "Internal versus External Control of Reinforcement: A Case History of a Variable," *American Psychologist,* April 1990, pp 489–93. A critical review of locus of control and a call for a meta-analysis can be found in R W Renn and R J Vandenberg, "Differences in Employee Attitudes and Behaviors Based on Rotter's (1966) Internal-External Locus of Control: Are They All Valid?" *Human Relations,* November 1991, pp 1161–77.

[59] For an overall review of research on locus of control, see P E Spector, "Behavior in Organizations as a Function of Employee's Locus of Control," *Psychological Bulletin,* May 1982, pp 482–97; the relationship between locus of control and performance and satisfaction is examined in D R Norris and R E Niebuhr, "Attributional Influences on the Job Performance–Job Satisfaction Relationship," *Academy of Management Journal,* June 1984, pp 424–31; salary differences between internals and externals were examined by P C Nystrom, "Managers' Salaries and Their Beliefs about Reinforcement Control," *Journal of Social Psychology,* August 1983, pp 291–92.

[60] Robert Solomon, as quoted in D Vera and A Rodriguez-Lopez, "Strategic Virtues: Humility as a Source of Competitive Advantage," *Organizational Dynamics,* no. 4, 2004, pp 394–95.

[61] Ibid., p 395.

[62] As quoted in "Believe in Something Bigger than Yourself," *Business 2.0,* December 2005, p 126.

[63] These results are discussed in L Winerman, "A Healthy Mind, a Longer Life," *Monitor on Psychology,* November 2006, pp 42–44.

[64] D A Harrison, D A Newman, and P L Roth, "How Important Are Job Attitudes? Meta-Analytic Comparisons of Integrative Behavioral Outcomes and Time Sequences," *Academy of Management Journal,* April 2006, pp 305–25.

[65] M Fishbein and I Ajzen, *Belief, Attitude, Intention and Behavior: An Introduction to Theory and Research* (Reading, MA: Addison-Wesley, 1975), p 6.

[66] The components or structure of attitudes is thoroughly discussed in A P Brief, *Attitudes in and around Organizations* (Thousand Oaks, CA: Sage, 1998), pp 49–84.

[67] S Meisinger, "Management Holds Key to Employee Engagement," *HR Magazine,* February 2008, p 8; Towers Perrin, "Towers Perrin Study Finds Significant 'Engagement Gap' among Global Workforce," news release, October 22, 2007, www.towersperrin.com; Towers Perrin, "2007 Global Workforce Study: Key Facts and Figures," 2007, www.towersperrin.com; and Towers Perrin, "2007–2008 Towers Perrin Global Workforce Study," Publications, www.towersperrin.com.

[68] Research cited in J Sandberg, "Another Meeting? Good. Another Chance to Hear Myself Talk," *The Wall Street Journal,* March 11, 2008, http://online.wsj.com. The following examples also are from this article.

[69] For details about this theory, see L Festinger, *A Theory of Cognitive Dissonance* (Stanford, CA: Stanford University Press, 1957). Also see J V Petrocelli, Z L Tormala, and D D Rucker, "Unpacking Attitude Certainty: Attitude Clarity and Attitude Correctness," *Journal of Personality and Social Psychology,* January 2007, pp 30–41.

[70] B M Staw and J Ross, "Stability in the Midst of Change: A Dispositional Approach to Job Attitudes," *Journal of Applied Psychology,* August 1985, pp 469–80.

[71] P S Visser and J A Krosnick, "Development of Attitude Strength over the Life Cycle: Surge and Decline," *Journal of Personality and Social Psychology,* December 1998, pp 389–410.

[72] I Ajzen, "The Theory of Planned Behavior," *Organizational Behavior and Human Decision Processes,* vol 50 (1991), p 188.

[73] R P Steel and N K Ovalle II, "A Review and Meta-Analysis of Research on the Relationship between Behavioral Intentions and Employee Turnover," *Journal of Applied Psychology,* November 1984, pp 673–86.

[74] M R Barrick and R D Zimmerman, "Reducing Voluntary Turnover through Selection," *Journal of Applied Psychology,* January 2005, pp 159–66.

[75] See I Ajzen and M Fishbein, *Understanding Attitudes and Predicting Social Behavior* (Englewood Cliffs, NJ: Prentice Hall, 1980); A Anderson, and D Lavallee, "Applying the Theories of Reasoned Action and Planned Behavior to Athlete Training Adherence Behavior," *Applied Psychology,* April 2008, pp 304–12; T Cronan and S Al-Rafee,

"Factors that Influence the Intention to Pirate Software and Media," *Journal of Business Ethics,* April 2008, pp 527–45; M Reid and A Wood, "An Investigation into Blood Donation Intentions among Non-Donors," *International Journal of Nonprofit and Voluntary Sector Marketing,* February 2008, pp 31–43; and J Ramsey, B Punnett, and D Greenidge, "A Social Psychological Account of Absenteeism in Barbados," *Human Resource Management Journal,* April 2008, pp 97–117.

[76] E A J Hooft, M P Born, T W Taris, and H V D Flier, "The Cross-Cultural Generalizability of the Theory of Planned Behavior," *Journal of Cross-Cultural Psychology,* March 2006, pp 127–35.

[77] For supportive research, see T L Webb and P Sheeran, "Does Changing Behavioral Intentions Engender Behavior Change: A Meta-Analysis of the Experimental Evidence," *Psychological Bulletin,* March 2006, pp 249–68.

[78] M L Kraimer, S J Wayne, R C Liden, and R T Sparrowe, "The Role of Job Security in Understanding the Relationship between Employees' Perceptions of Temporary Workers and Employees' Performance," *Journal of Applied Psychology,* March 2005, pp 389–98.

[79] For interesting reading on intelligence, see J R Flynn, "Searching for Justice: The Discovery of IQ Gains over Time," *American Psychologist,* January 1999, pp 5–20; and E Benson, "Intelligent Intelligence Testing," *Monitor on Psychology,* February 2003, pp 48–54.

[80] For an excellent update on intelligence, including definitional distinctions and a historical perspective of the IQ controversy, see R A Weinberg, "Intelligence and IQ," *American Psychologist,* February 1989, pp 98–104.

[81] Ibid.

[82] S L Wilk, L Burris Desmarais, and P R Sackett, "Gravitation to Jobs Commensurate with Ability: Longitudinal and Cross-Sectional Tests," *Journal of Applied Psychology,* February 1995, p 79.

[83] B Azar, "People Are Becoming Smarter—Why?" *APA Monitor,* June 1996, p 20.

[84] See D Lubinski, "Introduction to the Special Section on Cognitive Abilities: 100 Years after Spearman's (1904) 'General Intelligence,' Objectively Determined and Measured," *Journal of Personality and Social Psychology,* January 2004, pp 96–111.

[85] See F L Schmidt and J E Hunter, "Employment Testing: Old Theories and New Research Findings," *American Psychologist,* October 1981, p 1128; and N R Kuncel, S A Hezlett, and D S Ones, "Academic Performance, Career Potential, Creativity, and Job Performance: Can One Construct Predict Them All?" *Journal of Personality and Social Psychology,* January 2004, pp 148–61. A brief overview of the foregoing study can be found in M Greer, "General Cognition Also Makes the Difference on the Job, Study Finds," *Monitor on Psychology,* April 2004, p 12.

[86] H Gardner, *Frames of Mind: The Theory of Multiple Intelligences,* 10th ed (New York: Basic Books, 1993). Also see H Gardner, *Intelligence Reframed: Multiple Intelligences for the 21st Century* (New York: Basic Books, 2000).

[87] For a good overview of Gardner's life and work, see M K Smith, "Howard Gardner and Multiple Intelligences," *Encyclopedia of Informal Education,* 2002, www.infed.org/thinkers/gardner.htm. Also see B Fryer, "The Ethical Mind: A Conversation with Psychologist Howard Gardner," *Harvard Business Review,* March 2007, pp 51–56.

[88] R J Sternberg, "WICS: A Model of Leadership in Organizations," *Academy of Management Learning and Education,* December 2003, p 388.

[89] See K Albrecht, "Social Intelligence: Beyond IQ," *Training,* December 2004, pp 26–31; and A A Loort, "Multiple Intelligences: A Comparative Study between the Preferences of Males and Females," *Social Behavior and Personality,* no 1, 2005, pp 77–88.

[90] G Colvin, "Spitzer's Bully Pulpit," *Fortune,* March 31, 2008, p 18.

[91] D Lieberman, "Fear of Failing Drives Diller," *USA Today,* February 10, 1999, p 3B.

[92] L Abboud, "16: Patricia Russo, Chief Executive, Alcatel-Lucent," *The Wall Street Journal,* 50 Women to Watch 2007, November 19, 2007, p R4.

[93] R S Lazarus, *Emotion and Adaptation* (New York: Oxford University Press, 1991), p 6.

[94] Based on discussion in R D Arvey, G L Renz, and T W Watson, "Emotionality and Job Performance: Implications for Personnel

Selection," in *Research in Personnel and Human Resources Management,* vol. 16, ed G R Ferris (Stamford, CT: JAI Press, 1998), pp 103–47.

[95] For more on crying at work, see M Diamond, S Shellenbarger, "Read This and Weep: Crying at Work Gains Acceptance," *The Wall Street Journal,* April 26, 2007, p D1.

[96] See M Fugate, A Kinicki, and G Prussia, "Employee Coping with Organizational Change: An Examination of Alternative Theoretical Perspectives and Models," *Personnel Psychology,* Spring 2008, pp 1–36.

[97] J McGregor, "#1 Taryn Rose," *Fast Company,* May 2005, p 69.

[98] D Goleman, *Emotional Intelligence* (New York: Bantam Books, 1995), p 34. For more, see B Wall, "Being Smart Only Takes You So Far," *Training and Development,* January 2007, pp 64–68.

[99] See the box titled "Get Happy Carefully" on p 49 of D Goleman, R Boyatzis, and A McKee, "Primal Leadership: The Hidden Driver of Great Performance," *Harvard Business Review,* Special Issue: Breakthrough Leadership, December 2001, pp 43–51.

[100] See J Mayer, R Roberts, and S Barsade, "Human Abilities: Emotional Intelligence," *Annual Review of Psychology,* 2008, pp 507–36; D Eilerman, "The Significance of Emotional Engagement in Conflict Management," Mediate.com, January 2008, http://www.mediate .com/articles/eilermanD10.cfm; G A Van Kleef and S Côté, "Expressing Anger in Conflict: When It Helps and When It Hurts," *Journal of Applied Psychology,* November 2007, pp 1557–69; and J Rode, C H Mooney, M L Arthaud-Day, J P Near, T T Baldwin, R S Rubin, and W H Bommer, "Emotional Intelligence and Individual Performance: Evidence of Direct and Moderated Effects," *Journal of Organizational Behavior,* May 2007, pp 399–421.

[101] Data from S D Pugh, "Service with a Smile: Emotional Contagion in the Service Encounter," *Academy of Management Journal,* October 2001, pp 1018–27.

[102] Drawn from P Totterdell, S Kellett, K Teuchmann, and R B Briner, "Evidence of Mood Linkage in Work Groups," *Journal of Personality and Social Psychology,* June 1998, pp 1504–15. Also see R Ilies, D T Wagner, and F P Morgeson, "Explaining Affective Linkages in Teams: Individual Differences in Susceptibility to Contagion and Individualism– Collectivism," *Journal of Applied Psychology,* July 2007, pp 1140–48.

[103] "Impact of Emotions in the Work Environment," Knowledge@ Wharton, April 23, 2007, reprinted in *News Journal,* Wilmington, DE, www.delawareonline.com.

[104] N M Ashkanasy and C S Daus, "Emotion in the Workplace: The New Challenge for Managers," *Academy of Management Executive,* February 2002, p 79.

[105] S G Barsade and D E Gibson, "Why Does Affect Matter in Organizations?" *Academy of Management Perspectives,* February 2007, pp 36–59; and "Impact of Emotions in the Work Environment."

[106] Data from A M Kring and A H Gordon, "Sex Differences in Emotions: Expression, Experience, and Physiology," *Journal of Personality and Social Psychology,* March 1998, pp 686–703.

[107] Excerpted from P Bathurst, "Workplace Policies on Body Art Differ," *The Arizona Republic,* October 22, 2006, p EC1.

# Chapter 6

[1] Excerpted from J Sandberg, "Cubicle Culture: For Many Employees, a Dream Job Is One That Isn't a Nightmare," *The Wall Street Journal,* April 15, 2008, p B1.

[2] T R Mitchell, "Motivation: New Direction for Theory, Research, and Practice," *Academy of Management Review,* January 1982, p 81.

[3] This discussion is based on T R Mitchell and D Daniels, "Motivation," in *Handbook of Psychology,* vol 12, eds W C Borman, D R Ilgen, and R J Klimoski (Hoboken, NJ: John Wiley & Sons, Inc., 2003), pp 225–54. Also see D Kamdar and L Van Dyne, "The Joint Effects of Personality and Workplace Social Exchange Relationships in Predicting Task Performance and Citizenship Performance," *Journal of Applied Psychology,* September 2007, pp 1286–98.

[4] A Pomeroy, "Accountants with 'HEART,'" *HR Magazine,* July 2007, p 48.

[5] See J Mehring, "What's Lifting Productivity," *BusinessWeek,* May 24, 2004, p 32. For further support, see A Johnson, "It's True: A Nicer

Office Can Boost Morale," *Arizona Republic,* September 3, 2007, pp D1, D3.

[6] T Haerem and D Rau, "The Influence of Degree of Expertise and Objective Task Complexity on Perceived Task Complexity and Performance," *Journal of Applied Psychology,* September 2007, pp 1320–31.

[7] For a complete description of Maslow's theory, see A H Maslow, "A Theory of Human Motivation," *Psychological Review,* July 1943, pp 370–96.

[8] M Hofman, "The Idea That Saved My Company," *Inc.,* October 2007, www.inc.com. Another application of Maslow's theory is provided by C Conley, *How Great Companies Get Their Mojo from Maslow* (San Francisco, CA: Jossey-Bass, 2007).

[9] The use of surveys is discussed by J Welch and S Welch, "Employee Polls: A Vote in Favor," *BusinessWeek,* January 28, 2008, p 90.

[10] H A Murray, *Explorations in Personality* (New York: John Wiley & Sons, 1938), p 164.

[11] See K G Shaver, "The Entrepreneurial Personality Myth," *Business and Economic Review,* April/June 1995, pp 20–23.

[12] See the following series of research reports: D K McNeese-Smith, "The Relationship between Managerial Motivation, Leadership, Nurse Outcomes and Patient Satisfaction," *Journal of Organizational Behavior,* March 1999, pp 243–59; A M Harrell and M J Stahl, "A Behavioral Decision Theory Approach for Measuring McClelland's Trichotomy of Needs," *Journal of Applied Psychology,* April 1981, pp 242–47; and M J Stahl, "Achievement, Power and Managerial Motivation: Selecting Managerial Talent with the Job Choice Exercise," *Personnel Psychology,* Winter 1983, pp 775–89.

[13] Evidence for the validity of motivation training can be found in H Heckhausen and S Krug, "Motive Modification," in *Motivation and Society,* ed A J Stewart (San Francisco: Jossey-Bass, 1982).

[14] Results can be found in D B Turban and T L Keon, "Organizational Attractiveness: An Interactionist Perspective," *Journal of Applied Psychology,* April 1993, pp 184–93.

[15] See T W H Ng, K L Sorensen, and D C Feldman, "Dimensions, Antecedents, and Consequences of Workaholism: A Conceptual Integration and Extension," *Journal of Organizational Behavior,* January 2007, pp 111–36.

[16] J L Bowditch and A F Buono, *A Primer on Organizational Behavior* (New York: John Wiley & Sons, 1985), p 210.

[17] This framework was proposed by M A Campion and P W Thayer, "Development and Field Evaluation of an Interdisciplinary Measure of Job Design," *Journal of Applied Psychology,* February 1985, pp 29–43.

[18] See the related discussion in S Wagner-Tsukamoto, "An Institutional Economic Reconstruction of Scientific Management: On the Lost Theoretical Logic of Taylorism," *Academy of Management Review,* January 2007, pp 105–17.

[19] This type of program was developed and tested by M A Campion and C L McClelland, "Follow-Up and Extension of the Interdisciplinary Costs and Benefits of Enlarged Jobs," *Journal of Applied Psychology,* June 1993, pp 339–51.

[20] Excerpted from R J Grossman, "Putting HR in Rotation," *HR Magazine,* March 2003, p 53.

[21] See F Herzberg, B Mausner, and B B Snyderman, *The Motivation to Work* (New York: John Wiley & Sons, 1959).

[22] J Mero, "You Do What?" *Fortune,* April 3, 2006, p 33.

[23] F Herzberg, "One More Time: How Do You Motivate Employees?" *Harvard Business Review,* January/February 1968, p 56.

[24] For a thorough review of research on Herzberg's theory, see C C Pinder, *Work Motivation: Theory, Issues, and Applications* (Glenview, IL: Scott, Foresman, 1984). For supportive results, see N R Lockwood, "Leveraging Employee Engagement for Competitive Advantage," *2007 SHRM Quarterly,* 2007, pp 1–11.

[25] J R Hackman, G R Oldham, R Janson, and K Purdy, "A New Strategy for Job Enrichment," *California Management Review,* Summer 1975, p 58.

[26] Definitions of the job characteristics were adapted from J R Hackman and G R Oldham, "Motivation through the Design of Work: Test of a Theory," *Organizational Behavior and Human Performance,* August 1976, pp 250–79.

[27] A review of this research can be found in M L Ambrose and C T Kulik, "Old Friends, New Faces: Motivation Research in the 1990s," *Journal of Management,* 1999, pp 231–92.

[28] R S Gajendran and D A Harrison, "The Good, the Bad, and the Unknown about Telecommuting: Meta-Analysis of Psychological Mediators and Individual Consequences," *Journal of Applied Psychology,* November 2007, pp 1524–41.

[29] Supportive results can be found in R F Piccolo and J A Colquitt, "Transformational Leadership and Job Behaviors: The Mediating Role of Core Job Characteristics," *Academy of Management Journal,* April 2006, pp 327–40; and and A Grant, "Does Intrinsic Motivation Fuel the Prosocial Fire? Motivational Synergy in Predicting Persistence, Performance, and Productivity," *Journal of Applied Psychology,* January 2008, pp 48–58.

[30] The turnover meta-analysis was conducted by R W Griffeth, P W Hom, and S Gaertner, "A Meta-Analysis of Antecedents and Correlates of Employee Turnover: Update, Moderator Tests, and Research Implications for the Next Millennium," *Journal of Management,* 2000, pp 463–88. Absenteeism results are discussed in Y Fried and G R Ferris, "The Validity of the Job Characteristics Model: A Review and Meta-Analysis," *Personnel Psychology,* Summer 1987, pp 287–322. For additional support from a third meta-analysis, see S E Humphrey, J D Nahrgang, and F P Morgeson, "Integrating Motivational, Social, and Contextual Work Design Features: A Meta-Analytic Summary and Theoretical Extension of the Work Design Literature," *Journal of Applied Psychology,* September 2007, pp 1332–56.

[31] Results can be found in M R Kelley, "New Process Technology, Job Design, and Work Organization: A Contingency Model," *American Sociological Review,* April 1990, pp 191–208.

[32] Productivity studies are reviewed in R E Kopelman, *Managing Productivity in Organizations* (New York: McGraw-Hill, 1986).

[33] A thorough discussion of reengineering and associated outcomes can be found in J Champy, *Reengineering Management: The Mandate for New Leadership* (New York: HarperBusiness, 1995).

[34] See S Sonnentag and F R H Zijlstra, "Job Characteristics and Off-Job Activities as Predictors of Need for Recovery, Well-Being, and Fatigue," *Journal of Applied Psychology,* March 2006, pp 330–50; and D Moyer, "Best with Rest," *Harvard Business Review,* March 2006, p 152.

[35] C Vander Doelen, "Virtual Assembly Weeds Out 'Bad' Jobs," *Windsor (ON) Star,* December 15, 2007, www.canada.com.

[36] This description was taken from J R Edwards, J A Scully, and M D Brtek, "The Nature and Outcome of Work: A Replication and Extension of Interdisciplinary Work-Design Research," *Journal of Applied Psychology,* December 2000, pp 860–68.

[37] M Maynard, "At Toyota, a Global Giant Reaches for Agility," *New York Times,* February 22, 2008, www.nytimes.com. See N Woodward, "Easing Back Pain," *HR Magazine,* April 2008, pp 57–60.

[38] National Institute of Neurological Disorders and Stroke, "NINDS Repetitive Motion Disorders Information Page," www.ninds.nih.gov, last updated February 14, 2007.

[39] Bureau of Labor Statistics, "Nonfatal Occupational Injuries and Illnesses Requiring Days Away from Work, 2006," news release, November 8, 2007, www.bls.gov.

[40] C A Sprigg, C B Stride, T D Wall, D J Holman, and P R Smith, "Work Characteristics, Musculoskeletal Disorders, and the Mediating Role of Psychological Strain: A Study of Call Center Employees," *Journal of Applied Psychology,* November 2007, pp 1456–66.

[41] Definitions of engagement and results from the survey can be found in "Dilbert Is Right, Says Gallup Study," *Gallup Management Journal,* http://gmj.gallup.com/content/defajult.asp?ci=22381, accessed April 13, 2006.

[42] See A Gopal, "Worker Disengagement Continues to Cost Singapore," *Gallup Management Journal,* http://gmj.gallup.com/content/defajult .asp?ci=22720, accessed May 11, 2006.

[43] The definition and discussion of intrinsic motivation were drawn from R M Ryan and E L Deci, "Intrinsic and Extrinsic Motivations: Classic Definitions and New Directions," *Contemporary Educational Psychology,* January 2000, pp 54–67. Also see A Fox, "The Brain's Limitations," *HR Magazine,* March 2008, p 40.

[44] The definition and discussion of extrinsic motivation were drawn from Ryan and Deci, "Intrinsic and Extrinsic Motivations."

[45] See K W Thomas, E Jansen, and W G Tymon, Jr, "Navigating in the Realm of Theory: An Empowering View of Construct Development," in *Research in Organizational Change and Development,* vol. 10, eds W A Pasmore and R W Woodman (Greenwich, CT: JAI Press, 1997), pp 1–30.

[46] See E L Deci and R M Ryan, "The 'What' and 'Why' of Goal Pursuits: Human Needs and Self-Determination of Behavior," *Psychological Inquiry,* December 2000, pp 227–68.

[47] K Thomas, *Intrinsic Motivation at Work: Building Energy and Commitment* (San Francisco: Berrett-Koehler Publishers, 2000), p 44.

[48] J Sandberg, "A Modern Conundrum: When Work's Invisible, so Are Its Satisfactions," *The Wall Street Journal,* February 19, 2008, http://online.wsj.com.

[49] Thomas, *Intrinsic Motivation at Work,* p 44.

[50] See "The 100 Best Companies to Work For," p 100.

[51] Thomas, *Intrinsic Motivation at Work,* p 44.

[52] Thomas, *Intrinsic Motivation at Work,* p 44.

[53] Sandberg, "A Modern Conundrum."

[54] Preliminary supportive results can be found in B Kuvaas, "Work Performance, Affective Commitment, and Work Motivation: The Roles of Pay Administration and Pay Level," *Journal of Organizational Behavior,* May 2006, pp 365–85.

[55] M M Grynbaum, "Starbucks Takes a Three-Hour Coffee Break," *New York Times,* February 27, 2008, www.nytimes.com.

[56] Other methods for increasing competence are discussed by J Welch and S Welch, "When a Star Slacks Off," *BusinessWeek,* March 17, 2008, p 88; and by J Welch and S Welch, "When Growth Is the Only Solution," *BusinessWeek,* March 31, 2008, p 110.

[57] C Taylor, "On-the-Spot Incentives," *HR Magazine,* May 2004, p 82.

[58] Supportive results can be found in A Giardini and M Frese, "Linking Service Employees' Emotional Competence to Customer Satisfaction: A Multilevel Approach," *Journal of Organizational Behavior,* February 2008, pp 155–70.

[59] For norms on this survey, see D J Weiss, R V Dawis, G W England, and L H Lofquist, *Manual for the Minnesota Satisfaction Questionnaire* (Minneapolis: Industrial Relations Center, University of Minnesota, 1967).

[60] Results are reported in M Boyle, "Happiness Index: Nothing Is Rotten in Denmark," *Fortune,* February 19, 2001, p 242.

[61] For a review of these models, see A P Brief, *Attitudes In and Around Organizations* (Thousand Oaks, CA: Sage Publications, 1998).

[62] S Miller, "HR, Employees Vary on Job Satisfaction," *HR Magazine,* August 2007, p 32.

[63] For a review of need satisfaction models, see E F Stone, "A Critical Analysis of Social Information Processing Models of Job Perceptions and Job Attitudes," in *Job Satisfaction: How People Feel about Their Jobs and How It Affects Their Performance,* eds C J Cranny, P Cain Smith, and E F Stone (New York: Lexington Books, 1992), pp 21–52.

[64] See J P Wanous, T D Poland, S L Premack, and K S Davis, "The Effects of Met Expectations on Newcomer Attitudes and Behaviors: A Review and Meta-Analysis," *Journal of Applied Psychology,* June 1992, pp 288–97.

[65] M Weinstein, "Retention Redux," *Training,* October 2007, p 8.

[66] A complete description of this model is provided by E A Locke, "Job Satisfaction," in *Social Psychology and Organizational Behavior,* eds M Gruneberg and T Wall (New York: John Wiley & Sons, 1984).

[67] For a test of the value fulfillment value, see W A Hochwarter, P L Perrewé, G R Ferris, and R A Brymer, "Job Satisfaction and Performance: The Moderating Effects of Value Attainment and Affective Disposition," *Journal of Vocational Behavior,* April 1999, pp 296–313.

[68] Results can be found in J Cohen-Charash and P E Spector, "The Role of Justice in Organizations: A Meta-Analysis," *Organizational Behavior and Human Decision Processes,* November 2001, pp 278–321.

[69] A thorough discussion of this model is provided by C L Hulin, and T A Judge, "Job Attitudes," in *Handbook of Psychology,* vol 12, eds W C Borman, D R Ilgen, and R J Klimoski (Hoboken, NJ: John Wiley & Sons, Inc., 2003), pp 255–76.

[70] Supportive results can be found in R Ilies and T A Judge, "On the Heritability of Job Satisfaction: The Mediating Role of Personality," *Journal of Applied Psychology,* August 2003, pp 750–59; and B M Staw and J Ross, "Stability in the Midst of Change: A Dispositional Approach

to Job Attitudes," *Journal of Applied Psychology,* August 1985, pp 69–80.

71 See R D Arvey, T J Bouchard, Jr, N L Segal, and L M Abraham, "Job Satisfaction: Environmental and Genetic Components," *Journal of Applied Psychology,* April 1989, pp 187–92. Also see S E Hammpson, L R Goldberg, T M Vogt, and J P Dubanoski, "Mechanisms by Which Childhood Personality Traits Influence Adult Health Status: Educational Attainment and Healthy Behaviors," *Health Psychology,* January 2007, pp 121–25.

72 See C Dormann and D Zapf, "Job Satisfaction: A Meta-Analysis of Stabilities," *Journal of Organizational Behavior,* August 2001, pp 483–504.

73 Results can be found in A J Kinicki, F M McKee-Ryan, C A Schriesheim, and K P Carson, "Assessing the Construct Validity of the Job Descriptive Index (JDI): A Review and Analysis," *Journal of Applied Psychology,* February 2002, pp 14–32.

74 See S P Brown, "A Meta-Analysis and Review of Organizational Research on Job Involvement," *Psychological Bulletin,* September 1996, pp 235–55.

75 Results can be found in A Cooper-Hakim and C Viswesvaran, "The Construct of Work Commitment: Testing an Integrative Framework," *Psychological Bulletin,* March 2005, pp 241–59. Also see O Solinger, W Olffen, and R Roe, "Beyond the Three-Component Model of Organizational Commitment," *Journal of Applied Psychology,* January 2008, pp 70–83.

76 D W Organ, "The Motivational Basis of Organizational Citizenship Behavior," in *Research in Organizational Behavior,* eds B M Staw and L L Cummings (Greenwich, CT: JAI Press, 1990), p 46.

77 B J Hoffman, C A Blair, J P Meriac, and D J Woehr, "Expanding the Criterion Domain? A Quantitative Review of the OCB Literature," *Journal of Applied Psychology,* March 2007, pp 555–66.

78 Supportive results can be found in B J Tepper, M K Duffy, J Hoobler, and M D Ensley, "Moderators of the Relationship between Coworkers' Organizational Citizenship Behavior and Fellow Employees' Attitudes," *Journal of Applied Psychology,* June 2004, pp 455–65.

79 See S C Payne and S S Webber, "Effects of Service Provider Attitudes and Employment Status on Citizenship Behaviors and Customers' Attitudes and Loyalty Behavior," *Journal of Applied Psychology,* March 2006, pp 365–78; and A A Luchak and I R Gellatly, "A Comparison of Linear and Nonlinear Relations between Organizational Commitment and Work Outcomes," *Journal of Applied Psychology,* May 2007, pp 786–93.

80 Results can be found in D J Koys, "The Effects of Employee Satisfaction, Organizational Citizenship Behavior, and Turnover on Organizational Effectiveness: A Unit-Level, Longitudinal Study," *Personnel Psychology,* Spring 2001, pp 101–14.

81 D M Bergeron, "The Potential Paradox of Organizational Citizenship Behavior: Good Citizens at What Cost?" *Academy of Management Review,* October 2007, pp 1078–95.

82 Results are reported in "Sick Day or Just Sick and Tired?" *Training,* December 2005, p 8.

83 See R D Hackett, "Work Attitudes and Employee Absenteeism: A Synthesis of the Literature," *Journal of Occupational Psychology,* 1989, pp 235–48.

84 Results can be found in P W Hom and A J Kinicki, "Toward a Greater Understanding of How Dissatisfaction Drives Employee Turnover," *Academy of Management Journal,* October 2001, pp 975–87.

85 A Fisher, "Playing for Keeps," *Fortune,* January 22, 2007, p 85; and "CFO: All Pain, No Gain," *Fortune,* February 5, 2007, p 18.

86 Y Lermusiaux, "Calculating the High Cost of Employee Turnover," www.ilogos.com/en/expertviews/articles/strategic/200331007_YL.html, accessed April 15, 2005, p 1.

87 See Lermusiaux, "Calculating the High Cost of Employee Turnover." An automated program for calculating the cost of turnover can be found at "Calculate Your Turnover Costs," www.keepemployees.com/turnovercalc.htm, accessed April 3, 2008.

88 Results can be found in R W Griffeth, P W Hom, and S Gaertner, "A Meta-Analysis of Antecedents and Correlates of Employee Turnover: Update, Moderator Tests, and Research Implications for the Next Millennium," *Journal of Management,* 2000, pp 463–88. Also see P Hom, L Roberson, and A Ellis, "Challenging Conventional Wisdom About Who Quits: Revelations from Corporate America," *Journal of Applied Psychology,* January 2008, pp 1–34.

89 Results can be found in M A Blegen, "Nurses' Job Satisfaction: A Meta-Analysis of Related Variables," *Nursing Research,* January/February 1993, pp 36–41.

90 The various models are discussed in T A Judge, C J Thoresen, J E Bono, and G K Patton, "The Job Satisfaction–Job Performance Relationship: A Qualitative and Quantitative Review," *Psychological Bulletin,* May 2001, pp 376–407.

91 Results can be found in ibid.

92 One example is provided by D J Schleicher, J D Watt, and G J Greguras, "Reexamining the Job Satisfaction–Performance Relationship: The Complexity of Attitudes," *Journal of Applied Psychology,* February 2004, pp 165–77.

93 These issues are discussed by C Ostroff, "The Relationship between Satisfaction, Attitudes, and Performance: An Organizational Level Analysis," *Journal of Applied Psychology,* December 1992, pp 963–74.

94 Results can be found in J K Harter, F L Schmidt, and T L Hayes, "Business-Unit-Level Relationship between Employee Satisfaction, Employee Engagement, and Business Outcomes: A Meta-Analysis," *Journal of Applied Psychology,* April 2002, pp 268–79.

95 D S Ones, "Introduction to the Special Issue on Counterproductive Behaviors at Work," *International Journal of Selection and Assessment* 10/1–2 (2002), pp 1–4 (quoting p 1).

96 H R Weber, "Ex-Coke Secretary Sentenced to Eight Years," *Yahoo News,* May 23, 2007, http://news.yahoo.com; H R Weber, "Former Coca-Cola Secretary Guilty," *Yahoo News,* February 2, 2007, http://news.yahoo.com; and H R Weber, "Prosecutor Says Greed Drove Coke Theft," *Yahoo News,* January 22, 2007, http://news.yahoo.com.

97 B Leonard, "Study: Bully Bosses Prevalent in U.S.," *HR Magazine,* May 2007, pp 22, 28.

98 M S Mitchell and M L Ambrose, "Abusive Supervision and Workplace Deviance and the Moderating Effects of Negative Reciprocity Beliefs," *Journal of Applied Psychology,* July 2007, pp 1159–68.

99 J B Olson-Buchanan and W R Boswell, "An Integrative Model of Experiencing and Responding to Mistreatment at Work," *Academy of Management Review,* January 2008, pp 76–96.

100 C Hymowitz, "Bosses Have to Learn How to Confront Troubled Employees," *The Wall Street Journal,* April 23, 2007, p B1.

101 Ibid.

102 B W Roberts, P D Harms, A Caspi, and T E Moffitt, "Predicting the Counterproductive Employee in a Child-to-Adult Prospective Study," *Journal of Applied Psychology,* September 2007, pp 1427–36. Also see M N Bing, S M Stewart, H K Davison, P D Green, M D McIntyre, and L R James, "An Integrative Typology of Personality Assessment for Aggression: Implications for Predicting Counterproductive Workplace Behavior," *Journal of Applied Psychology,* May 2007, pp 722–44.

103 S Dilchert, D S Ones, R D Davis, and C D Rostow, "Cognitive Ability Predicts Objectively Measured Counterproductive Work Behaviors," *Journal of Applied Psychology,* May 2007, pp 616–27.

104 J R Detert, L K Treviño, E R Burris, and M Andiappan, "Managerial Modes of Influence and Counterproductivity in Organizations: A Longitudinal Business-Unit-Level Investigation," *Journal of Applied Psychology,* July 2007, pp 993–1005.

105 J Janove, "Jerks at Work," *HR Magazine,* May 2007, pp 111–17.

106 K W Smola and C D Sutton, "Generational Differences: Revisiting Generational Work Values for the New Millennium," *Journal of Organizational Behavior,* June 2002, p 379.

107 A Pomeroy, "Work/Life Balance Not a Gender Issue," *HR Magazine,* April 2007, p 16; S Shellenbarger, "Men on the Daddy Track Find a Place of Their Own at Home," *The Wall Street Journal,* November 8, 2007, p D1; and T DeAngelis, "Making Time for Family Time," *Monitor on Psychology,* January 2008, pp 38–39. Also see J Herzlich, "Work/Life Balance Tops List," *Arizona Republic,* January 6, 2008, p EC1.

108 P L Perrewé and W A Hochwarter, "Can We Really Have It All? The Attainment of Work and Family Values," *Current Directions in Psychological Science,* February 2001, p 31.

109 M Valcour, "Work-Based Resources as Moderators of the Relationship between Work Hours and Satisfaction with Work–Family Balance," *Journal of Applied Psychology,* November 2007, pp 1512–23.

Also see R Ilies, K M Schwind, D T Wagner, M D Johnson, D S DeRue, and D R Ilgen, "When Can Employees Have a Family Life? The Effects of Daily Workload and Affect on Work–Family Conflict and Social Behaviors at Home," *Journal of Applied Psychology,* September 2007, pp 1368–79.
[110] C Hymowitz, "View from the Top," *The Wall Street Journal,* November 19, 2007, pp R6–R7.
[111] See, for example, "100 Best Companies to Work For 2008," *Fortune,* February 4, 2008, http://money.cnn.com, especially, "100 Best Companies to Work For 2008: Best Benefits," February 4, 2008, http://money.cnn.com.
[112] K Gurchiek, "U.S. Lags in Policies That Are Worker-Friendly," *HR Magazine,* April 2007, pp 29, 32. Also see A Athavaley, "Vacation Deflation: Breaks Get Shorter," *The Wall Street Journal,* August 15, 2007, pp D1, D3.
[113] An integrated approach is discussed by J H Greenhaus and G N Powell, "When Work and Family Are Allies: A Theory of Work-Family Enrichment," *Academy of Management Review,* January 2006, pp 72–92.
[114] "View from the Top," *The Wall Street Journal,* November 19, 2007, p R6.
[115] Excerpted from S Carey, "Cranky Skies: Fliers Behave Badly Again As 9/11 Era Fades," *The Wall Street Journal,* September 12, 2007, p A16.

## Chapter 7

[1] Excerpted from G Colvin, "Rewarding Failure," *Fortune,* April 28, 2008, p 22.
[2] See L Festinger, *A Theory of Cognitive Dissonance* (Stanford, CA: Stanford University Press, 1957).
[3] See, for example, H Zhao, S J Wayne, B C Glibkowski, and J Bravo, "The Impact of Psychological Contract Breach on Work-Related Outcomes: A Meta-Analysis," *Personnel Psychology,* Autumn 2007, pp 647–80; L M Cortina, "Unseen Injustice: Incivility as Modern Discrimination in Organizations," *Academy of Management Review,* January 2008, pp 55–75; "Counterattack of the Week," *BusinessWeek,* June 11, 2007, p 29; and J McGregor, "Sweet Revenge," *BusinessWeek,* January 22, 2007, pp 65–66.
[4] Inputs and outputs are discussed by J S Adams, "Toward an Understanding of Inequity," *Journal of Abnormal and Social Psychology,* November 1963, pp 422–36.
[5] The generalizability of the equity norm was examined by L K Scheer, N A Kumar, and J-B E M Steenkamp, "Reactions to Perceived Inequity in U.S. and Dutch Interorganizational Relationships," *Academy of Management Journal,* June 2003, pp 303–16. An alternative perspective is offered by M Bolino and W Turnley, "Old Faces, New Places: Equity Theory in Cross-Cultural Contexts," *Journal of Organizational Behavior,* January 2008, pp 29–50.
[6] L M Sixel, "They Want to Climb Fire Ladder, but Can't," *Houston Chronicle,* January 4, 2008, downloaded from General Reference Center Gold, http://find.galegroup.com.
[7] M N Bing and S M Burroughs, "The Predictive and Interactive Effects of Equity Sensitivity in Teamwork-Oriented Organizations," *Journal of Organizational Behavior,* May 2001, p 271.
[8] Types of equity sensitivity are discussed by ibid., pp 271–90; and K S Sauley and A G Bedeian, "Equity Sensitivity: Construction of a Measure and Examination of Its Psychometric Properties," *Journal of Management,* 2000, pp 885–910.
[9] Y Cohen-Charash and J S Mueller, "Does Perceived Unfairness Exacerbate or Mitigate Interpersonal Counterproductive Work Behaviors Related to Envy?" *Journal of Applied Psychology,* May 2007, pp 666–80. Also see B Beard, "Don't Get Mad Get Even," *The Arizona Republic,* April 20, 2008, pp D1, D5.
[10] J Sandberg, "If That Guy Got a Promotion, Mine Can't Be Far Behind," *The Wall Street Journal,* September 18, 2007, p B1.
[11] For a thorough review of organizational justice theory and research, see R Cropanzano, D E Rupp, C J Mohler, and M Schminke, "Three Roads to Organizational Justice," in *Research in Personnel and Human Resources Management,* vol. 20, ed G R Ferris (New York: JAI Press, 2001), pp 269–329.
[12] J S Lublin, "More CEOs Are Saying No (Voluntarily) to Bonuses," *The Wall Street Journal,* April 7, 2008, http://online.wsj.com. For another example, see J Mackey, "I No Longer Want to Work for Money," *Fast Company,* February 2007, p 112.
[13] J A Colquitt, D E Conlon, M J Wesson, C O L H Porter, and K Y Ng, "Justice at the Millennium: A Meta-Analytic Review of 25 Years of Organizational Justice Research," *Journal of Applied Psychology,* June 2001, p 426.
[14] E Tahmincioglu, "Electronic Workplace Vulnerable to Revenge," *Arizona Republic,* August 6, 2001, p D1.
[15] Results can be found in C Spitzmüller, D M Glenn, C D Barr, S G Rogelberg, and P Daniel, "'If You Treat Me Right, I Reciprocate': Examining the Role of Exchange in Organizational Survey Response," *Journal of Organizational Behavior,* February 2006, pp 19–35; and J Greenberg, "Losing Sleep Over Organizational Injustice: Attenuating Insomniac Reactions to Underpayment Inequity with Supervisory Training in Interactional Justice," *Journal of Applied Psychology,* January 2006, pp 58–69.
[16] Supportive results can be found in R A Posthuma, C P Maertz Jr, and J B Dworkin, "Procedural Justice's Relationship with Turnover: Explaining Past Inconsistent Findings," *Journal of Organizational Behavior,* May 2007, pp 381–98; J Choi and C C Chen, "The Relationships of Distributive Justice and Compensation System Fairness to Employee Attitudes in International Joint Ventures," *Journal of Organizational Behavior,* August 2007, pp 687–703; H Moon, D Kamdar, D Mayer, and R Takeuchi, "Me or We? The Role of Personality and Justice as Other-Centered Antecedents to Innovative Citizenship Behaviors Within Organizations," *Journal of Applied Psychology,* January 2008, pp 84–94; and S Tangirala and R Ramanujam, "Employee Silence on Critical Work Issues: The Cross Level Effects of Procedural Justice Climate," *Personnel Psychology,* Spring 2008, pp 37–68.
[17] See B W Heineman Jr., "Avoiding Integrity Land Mines," *Harvard Business Review,* April 2007, pp 100–8.
[18] See S Whiting and P Podsakoff, and J Pierce, "Effects of Task Performance, Helping, Voice, and Organizational Loyalty on Performance Appraisal Ratings," *Journal of Applied Psychology,* January 2008, pp 125–39.
[19] The role of equity in organizational change is thoroughly discussed by A T Cobb, R Folger, and K Wooten, "The Role Justice Plays in Organizational Change," *Public Administration Quarterly,* Summer 1995, pp 135–51.
[20] Group level effects of justice were examined by S E Naumann and N Bennett, "A Case for Procedural Justice Climate: Development and Test of a Multilevel Model," *Academy of Management Journal,* October 2000, pp 881–89.
[21] See W R Boswell and J B Olson-Buchanan, "Experiencing Mistreatment at Work: The Role of Grievance Filing, Nature of Mistreatment, and Employee Withdrawal," *Academy of Management Journal,* February 2004, pp 129–39. For recent studies that support the impact of justice on a variety of individual and organizational outcomes, see S Thau, K Aquino, and R Wittek, "An Extension of Uncertainty Management Theory to the Self: The Relationship between Justice, Social Comparison Orientation, and Antisocial Work Behaviors," *Journal of Applied Psychology,* January 2007, pp 250–58; and A Barsky and S A Kaplan, "If You Feel Bad, It's Unfair: A Quantitative Synthesis of Affect and Organizational Justice Perceptions," *Journal of Applied Psychology,* January 2007, pp 286–95.
[22] J Brockner, A Y Fishman, J Reb, B Goldman, S Spiegel, and C Garden, "Procedural Fairness, Outcome Favorability, and Judgments of an Authority's Responsibility," *Journal of Applied Psychology,* November 2007, pp 1657–71.
[23] The relationship between justice perceptions and leadership was examined by B Erdogan and R C Liden, "Collectivism As a Moderator of Responses to Organizational Justice: Implications for Leader-Member Exchange and Ingratiation," *Journal of Organizational Behavior,* February 2006, pp 1–17; and J Sandberg, "Too-Nice Boss?" *The Arizona Republic,* March 2, 2008, p EC1.
[24] B A Scott, J A Colquitt, and C P Zapata-Phelan, "Justice as a Dependent Variable: Subordinate Charisma as a Predictor of Interpersonal and Informational Justice Perceptions," *Journal of Applied Psychology,* November 2007, pp 1597–1609.

[25] M G Ehrhart, "Leadership and Procedural Justic Climate as Antecedents of Unit-Level Organizational Citizenship Behavior," *Personnel Psychology,* Spring 2004, pp 61–94; and J Yang, K W Mossholder, and T K Peng, "Procedural Justice Climate and Group Power Distance: An Examination of Cross-Level Interaction Effects," *Journal of Applied Psychology,* May 2007, pp 681–92.

[26] For a complete discussion of Vroom's theory, see V H Vroom, *Work and Motivation* (New York: John Wiley & Sons, 1964).

[27] See J Chowdhury, 'The Motivational Impact of Sales Quotas on Effort," *Journal of Marketing Research,* February 1993, pp 28–41; and C C Pinder, *Work Motivation* (Glenview, IL: Scott, Foresman, 1984), ch 7.

[28] J R Detert and E R Burris, "Leadership Behavior and Employee Voice: Is the Door Really Open?" *Academy of Management Journal,* August 2007, pp 869–84. Another example of instrumentality is found in R Smith, "Utilities Amp Up Push to Slash Energy Use," *The Wall Street Journal,* January 9, 2008, pp A1, A12.

[29] Excerpted from "Federal Express's Fred Smith," *Inc.,* October 1986, p 38.

[30] Results can be found in W van Eerde and H Thierry, "Vroom's Expectancy Models and Work-Related Criteria: A Meta-Analysis," *Journal of Applied Psychology,* October 1996, pp 575–86.

[31] See J P Wanous, T L Keon, and J C Latack, "Expectancy Theory and Occupational/Organizational Choices: A Review and Test," *Organizational Behavior and Human Performance,* August 1983, pp 66–86.

[32] See the discussion in T R Mitchell and D Daniels, "Motivation," in *Handbook of Psychology,* vol. 12, eds W C Borman, D R Ilgen, and R J Klimoski (Hoboken, NJ: John Wiley & Sons, Inc., 2003), pp 225–54.

[33] This issue is discussed by S J Dubner, "The Freaky Side of Business," *Training,* February 2006, pp 8–9.

[34] See D R Spitzer, "Power Rewards: Rewards That Really Motivate," *Management Review,* May 1996, pp 45–50; and A Kohn, *Punished by Rewards: The Trouble with Gold Stars, Incentive Plans, A's, Praise, and Other Bribes* (Boston: Houghton Mifflin, 1993).

[35] Result can be found in G D Jenkins, Jr, A Mitra, N Gupta, and J D Shaw, "Are Financial Incentives Related to Performance? A Meta-Analytic Review of Empirical Research," *Journal of Applied Psychology,* October 1998, pp 777–87.

[36] See S Bates, "Top Pay for Best Performance," *HR Magazine,* January 2003, pp 31–38.

[37] "100 Best Companies to Work For 2008," *Fortune,* February 4, 2008, http://money.cnn.com; and G Colvin, "AmEx Gets CEO Pay Right," *Fortune,* January 21, 2008, pp. 22, 24.

[38] "Baptist Health Care's Standards of Performance," *Healthcare Financial Management,* January 2007, pp 105–6. Also see C Wallis, "How to Make Great Teachers," *Time,* February 25, 2008, pp 28–34.

[39] R Charan, "Conquering a Culture of Indecision," *Harvard Business Review,* April 2001, pp 75–82.

[40] E A Locke, K N Shaw, L M Saari, and G P Latham, "Goal Setting and Task Performance: 1969–1980," *Psychological Bulletin,* July 1981, p 126.

[41] Results from both studies can be found in R Rodgers and J E Hunter, "Impact of Management by Objectives on Organizational Productivity," *Journal of Applied Psychology,* April 1991, pp 322–36; and R Rodgers, J E Hunter, and D L Rogers, "Influence of Top Management Commitment on Management Program Success," *Journal of Applied Psychology,* February 1993, pp 151–55.

[42] The following discussion is based on E A Locke and G P Latham, "Building a Practically Useful Theory of Goal Setting and Task Motivation," *American Psychologist,* September 2002, pp 705–17.

[43] See A Barrett, "Cracking the Whip at Wyeth," *BusinessWeek,* February 6, 2006, pp 70–71; and H Dolezalek, "Winning Ways: Wyeth Pharmaceuticals," *Training,* February 6, 2008, www.trainingmag.com.

[44] S Miller, "Many Don't Disclose Executive Pay Goals," *HR Magazine,* March 2008, p 33.

[45] R Millward, "Harrington Hungry for More," *Arizona Republic,* July 24, 2007, p C6. Also see S Banjo, "Shared Goals," *The Wall Street Journal,* April 14, 2008, p R3.

[46] M Frese, S I Krauss, N Keith, S Escher, R Grabarkiewicz, S T Luneng, C Heers, J Unger, and C Friedrich, "Business Owners' Action Planning and Its Relationship to Business Success in Three African Countries," *Journal of Applied Psychology,* November 2007, pp 1481–98.

[47] Results can be found in P M Wright, "Operationalization of Goal Difficulty as a Moderator of the Goal Difficulty–Performance Relationship," *Journal of Applied Psychology,* June 1990, pp 227–34.

[48] See Locke, Shaw, Saari, and Latham, "Goal Setting and Task Performance: 1969–1980"; and A J Mento, R P Steel, and R J Karren, "A Meta-Analytic Study of the Effects of Goal Setting on Task Performance: 1966–1984," *Organizational Behavior and Human Decision Processes,* February 1987, pp 52–83.

[49] Results can be found in R E Wood, A J Mento, and E A Locke, "Task Complexity as a Moderator of Goal Effects: A Meta-Analysis," *Journal of Applied Psychology,* August 1987, pp 416–25.

[50] See Locke and Latham, "Building a Practically Useful Theory of Goal Setting and Task Motivation."

[51] See R P DeShon and R A Alexander, "Goal Setting Effects on Implicit and Explicit Learning of Complex Tasks," *Organizational Behavior and Human Decision Processes,* January 1996, pp 18–36.

[52] Supportive results can be found in K L Langeland, C M Johnson, and T C Mawhinney, "Improving Staff Performance in a Community Mental Health Setting: Job Analysis, Training, Goal Setting, Feedback, and Years of Data," *Journal of Organizational Behavior Management,* 1998, pp 21–43.

[53] See Locke and Latham, "Building a Practically Useful Theory of Goal Setting and Task Motivation."

[54] See ibid.

[55] See J J Donovan and D J Radosevich, "The Moderating Role of Goal Commitment on the Goal Difficulty–Performance Relationship: A Meta-Analytic Review and Critical Reanalysis," *Journal of Applied Psychology,* April 1998, pp 308–15. Also see A Sykes, "The Secrets to Success in Wellness Programs: Leadership, Incentives, Healthy Workplace," *Industry Week,* January 1, 2008, http://www.industryweek.com/ReadArticle.aspx?ArticleID=15506.

[56] See the related discussion in T P Flannery, D A Hofrichter, and P E Platten, *People, Performance, & Pay* (New York: The Free Press, 1996). Also see D C Kayes, "The Destructive Pursuit of Idealized Goals," *Organizational Dynamics,* November 2005, pp 391–401.

[57] See F M Moussa, "Determinants, Process, and Consequences of Personal Goals and Performance," *Journal of Management,* 2000, pp 1259–85; and P M Wright, J M George, S R Farnsworth, and G C McMahan, "Productivity and Extra-Role Behavior: The Effects of Goals and Incentives on Spontaneous Helping," *Journal of Applied Psychology,* June 1993, pp 374–81.

[58] Results are presented in "Coming Up Short? Join the Club," *Training,* April 2006, p 14.

[59] See J A Colquitt and M J Simmering, "Conscientiousness, Goal Orientation, and Motivation to Learn during the Learning Process: A Longitudinal Study," *Journal of Applied Psychology,* August 1998, pp 654–65.

[60] C L Porath and T S Bateman, "Self-Regulation: From Goal Orientation to Job Performance," *Journal of Applied Psychology,* January 2006, pp 185–86.

[61] Ibid., pp 185–92; Y Gong and J Fan, "Longitudinal Examination of the Role of Goal Orientation in Cross-Cultural Adjustment," *Journal of Applied Psychology,* January 2006, pp 176–84.

[62] See DeShon and Gillespie, "A Motivated Action Theory Account of Goal Orientation."

[63] M Weinstein, "Business Driven," *Training,* March 2007, pp 40, 42.

[64] T R Mitchell, "Motivation: New Directions for Theory, Research, and Practice," *Academy of Management Review,* January 1982, p 81.

[65] G Colvin, "What Makes GE Great?" *Fortune,* March 6, 2006, p 96.

[66] "HMO Clerks Who Pare Doctor Visits Rewarded," *Arizona Republic,* May 18, 2002, p A10.

[67] This issue is discussed in E White, "The Best vs. the Rest," *The Wall Street Journal,* January 30, 2006, pp B1, B3.

[68] A M Schmidt and R P DeShon, "What to Do? The Effects of Discrepancies, Incentives, and Time on Dynamic Goal Prioritization," *Journal of Applied Psychology,* July 2007, pp 928–41.

[69] Excerpted from C Bellamy, "Teacher Resigns as School Backs Plagiarizing Kids," *Arizona Republic,* February 10, 2002, p A21.

# Chapter 8

[1] Excerpted from J Reingold, "You Got Served," *Fortune,* October 1, 2007, pp 55–58.

[2] B Tulgan, "The Under-Management Epidemic," *HR Magazine,* October 2004, p 119.

[3] See H Aguinis and C Pierce, "Enhancing the Relevance of Organizational Behavior by Embracing Performance Management Research," *Journal of Organizational Behavior,* January 2008, pp 139–45; and P Falcone, "Big-Picture Performance Appraisal," *HR Magazine,* August 2007, pp 97–100.

[4] This distinction is drawn from G P Latham, J Almost, S Mann, and C Moore, "New Developments in Performance Management," *Organizational Dynamics,* no. 1, 2005, pp 77–87.

[5] See K Tyler, "Performance Art," *HR Magazine,* August 2005, pp 57–63; J Welch and S Welch, "The Global Warming Wager," *BusinessWeek,* February 26, 2007, p 130; J Sandberg, "Performance Reviews Need Some Work, Don't Meet Potential," *The Wall Street Journal,* November 20, 2007, p B1; and S Westcott, "Putting an End to End-of-Year Reviews," *Inc,* December 2007, www.inc.com.

[6] See A Clancy, "Managers Can Make Dreaded Employee Reviews More Helpful," *Long Island Business News,* September 14, 2007, downloaded from General Reference Center Gold, http://find.galegroup.com; and J Welch and S Welch, "Ideas the WelchWay: The Global Warming Wager," *BusinessWeek,* February 26, 2007, p 130.

[7] As quoted in C Fishman, "Fred Smith," *Fast Company,* June 2001, pp 64, 66.

[8] K Tyler, "One Bad Apple," *HR Magazine,* December 2004, p 85.

[9] C D Lee, "Feedback, Not Appraisal," *HR Magazine,* November 2006, p 111. Also see J Gill, "How to Help an Underachiever," *Inc,* March 2007, p 44.

[10] Both the definition of feedback and the functions of feedback are based on discussion in D R Ilgen, C D Fisher, and M S Taylor, "Consequences of Individual Feedback on Behavior in Organizations," *Journal of Applied Psychology,* August 1979, pp 349–71; and R E Kopelman, *Managing Productivity in Organizations: A Practical People-Oriented Perspective* (New York: McGraw-Hill, 1986), p 175.

[11] See P C Earley, G B Northcraft, C Lee, and T R Lituchy, "Impact of Process and Outcome Feedback on the Relation of Goal Setting to Task Performance," *Academy of Management Journal,* March 1990, pp 87–105.

[12] Based on C C Rosen, P E Levy, and R J Hall, "Placing Perceptions of Politics in the Context of the Feedback Environment, Employee Attitudes, and Job Performance," *Journal of Applied Psychology,* January 2006, pp 211–20.

[13] For relevant research, see J S Goodman, "The Interactive Effects of Task and External Feedback on Practice Performance and Learning," *Organizational Behavior and Human Decision Processes,* December 1998, pp 223–52.

[14] See J M Jackman and M H Strober, "Fear of Feedback," *Harvard Business Review,* April 2003, pp 101–7; and J Sandberg, "When Part of Your Job Is Caring for a Boss Who Is Too Needy," *The Wall Street Journal,* May 15, 2007, p B1.

[15] See B D Bannister, "Performance Outcome Feedback and Attributional Feedback: Interactive Effects on Recipient Responses," *Journal of Applied Psychology,* May 1986, pp 203–10.

[16] For complete details, see P M Podsakoff and J-L Farh, "Effects of Feedback Sign and Credibility on Goal Setting and Task Performance," *Organizational Behavior and Human Decision Processes,* August 1989, pp 45–67.

[17] See "How to Take the Venom Out of Vitriol," *Training,* June 2000, p 28.

[18] W S Silver, T R Mitchell, and M E Gist, "Responses to Successful and Unsuccessful Performance: The Moderating Effect of Self-Efficacy on the Relationship between Performance and Attributions," *Organizational Behavior and Human Decision Processes,* June 1995, p 297.

[19] L E Atwater, J F Brett, and A C Charles, "The Delivery of Workplace Discipline: Lessons Learned," *Organizational Dynamics,* 2007, pp 392–403.

[20] See T J DeLong and V Vijayaraghavan, "Let's Hear It for B Players," *Harvard Business Review,* June 2003, pp 96–102.

[21] See S Boehle, "True Vision," *Training,* February 2008, pp 32–39.

[22] See J Smither, M London, and R Reilly, "Does Performance Improve Following Multisource Feedback? A Theoretical Model, Meta-analysis, and Review of Empirical Findings," *Personnel Psychology,* Spring 2005, pp 33–66.

[23] M Weinstein, "Study: HR Execs Don't Trust Employee Evaluations," *Training,* April 2006, p 11.

[24] See M R Edwards, A J Ewen, and W A Verdini, "Fair Performance Management and Pay Practices for Diverse Work Forces: The Promise of Multisource Assessment," *ACA Journal,* Spring 1995, pp 50–63.

[25] See G D Huet-Cox, T M Nielsen, and E Sundstrom, "Get the Most from 360-Degree Feedback: Put It on the Internet," *HR Magazine,* May 1999, pp 92–103.

[26] This list is based in part on discussion in H J Bernardin, "Subordinate Appraisal: A Valuable Source of Information about Managers," *Human Resource Management,* Fall 1986, pp 421–39.

[27] "50 Best Small and Medium Companies to Work for in America," *HR Magazine,* July 2007, pp 43–61.

[28] Data from D Antonioni, "The Effects of Feedback Accountability on Upward Appraisal Ratings," *Personnel Psychology,* Summer 1994, pp 349–56.

[29] See L Atwater, P Roush, and A Fischthal, "The Influence of Upward Feedback on Self- and Follower Ratings of Leadership," *Personnel Psychology,* Spring 1995, pp 35–59.

[30] Data from JW Smither, M London, NL Vasilopoulos, RR Reilly, RE Millsap, and N Salvemini, "An examination of the Effects of an Upward Feedback Program over Time, Personnel Psychology, Spring 1995, pp. 1–34.

[31] See "Training Top 125 2008," *Training,* February 2008, p 81.

[32] Results can be found in J Smither, M London, and R Reilly, "Does Performance Improve Following Multisource Feedback: A Theoretical Model, Meta-Analysis, and Review of Empirical Findings," *Personnel Psychology,* Spring 2005, p 33.

[33] D Jones, "It's Lonely—and Thin-Skinned—at the Top," *USA Today,* January 16, 2007, p 1B.

[34] See D E Coates, "Don't Tie 360 Feedback to Pay," *Training,* September 1998, pp 68–78.

[35] "Friendly Feedback," *Training,* May 2007, p 11. Also see J Sammer, "Calibrating Consistency," *HR Magazine,* January 2008, pp. 73–75.

[36] Adapted from C Bell and R Zemke, "On-Target Feedback," *Training,* June 1992, pp 36–44. A model feedback program is discussed by M Weinstein, "Leadership Leader," *Training,* February 2008, pp 41–46.

[37] See J Kerr and J W Slocum, Jr., "Managing Corporate Culture through Reward Systems," *Academy of Management Executive,* November 2005, pp 130–38.

[38] See J Welch and S Welch, "When Growth Is the Only Solution," *BusinessWeek,* March 31, 2008, p 110; and J Welch and S Welch, "When a Star Slacks Off," *BusinessWeek,* March 17, 2008, p 88.

[39] For example, see B Nelson, *1001 Ways to Reward Employees,* 2nd ed (NY: Workman Publishing, 2005); M J Conyon, "Executive Compensation and Incentives," *Academy of Management Perspectives,* February 2006, pp 25–44; and S Curran, "Compensation Advice for New Grads," *BusinessWeek Online,* April 30, 2007, www.businessweek.com.

[40] W J Wiatrowski, "Family-Related Benefits in the Workplace," *Monthly Labor Review,* March 1990, p 28.

[41] For complete discussions, see A P Brief and R J Aldag, "The Intrinsic-Extrinsic Dichotomy: Toward Conceptual Clarity," *Academy of Management Review,* July 1977, pp 496–500; and E L Deci, R Koestner, and R M Ryan, "A Meta-Analytic Review of Experiments Examining the Effects of Extrinsic Rewards on Intrinsic Motivation," *Psychological Bulletin,* November 1999, pp 627–68.

[42] "50 Best Small and Medium Companies to Work for in America."

[43] A Zimmerman, "49: Carol Tomé," *The Wall Street Journal,* November 19, 2007, p R12.

[44] M Von Glinow, "Reward Strategies for Attracting, Evaluating, and Retaining Professionals," *Human Resource Management,* Summer 1985, p 193.

[45] A Markels and J S Lublin, "Longevity-Reward Programs Get Short Shrift," *The Wall Street Journal,* April 27, 1995, p B1.

[46] Six reward system objectives are discussed in E E Lawler III, "The New Pay: A Strategic Approach," *Compensation & Benefits Review,* July/August 1995, pp 14–22.

[47] See D Cadrain, "Put Success in Sight," *HR Magazine,* May 2003, pp 84–92; J Kiska, "Customer Satisfaction Pays Off," *HR Magazine,* February 2004, 87–93; and C Taylor, "On-the-Spot Incentives," *HR Magazine,* May 2004, pp 80–84.

[48] For both sides of the "Does money motivate?" debate, see N Gupta and J D Shaw, "Let the Evidence Speak: Financial Incentives *Are* Effective!!" *Compensation & Benefits Review,* March/April 1998, pp 26, 28–32; A Kohn, "Challenging Behaviorist Dogma: Myths about Money and Motivation," *Compensation & Benefits Review;* March/April 1998, pp 27, 33–37; and B Ettorre, "Is Salary a Motivator?" *Management Review,* January 1999, p 8.

[49] Data from D Kiley, "Crafty Basket Makers Cut Downtime, Waste," *USA Today,* May 10, 2001, p 3B.

[50] See M V Copeland, "The Shrink Shrinker," *Business 2.0,* April 2006, p 86.

[51] C B Cadsby, F Song, and F Tapon, "Sorting and Incentive Effects of Pay for Performance: An Experimental Investigation," *Academy of Management Journal,* April 2007, pp 387–405.

[52] Data from M Bloom and G T Milkovich, "Relationships among Risk, Incentive Pay, and Organizational Performance," *Academy of Management Journal,* June 1998, pp 283–97.

[53] For details, see G D Jenkins, Jr, N Gupta, A Mitra, and J D Shaw, "Are Financial Incentives Related to Performance? A Meta-Analytic Review of Empirical Research," *Journal of Applied Psychology,* October 1998, pp 777–87.

[54] See M J Mandel, "Those Fat Bonuses Don't Seem to Boost Performance," *BusinessWeek,* January 8, 1990, p 26; L A Bebchuk and J M Fried, "Pay without Performance: Overview of the Issues," *Academy of Management Perspectives,* February 2006, pp 5–24; and A Pomeroy, "Pay for Performance Is Working, Says a New Study," *HR Magazine,* January 2007, pp 14, 16.

[55] G Koretz, "Bad Marks for Pay-by-Results," *BusinessWeek,* September 4, 1995, p 28. Also see L King, "School Systems Argue the Merits of Teacher 'Bonuses' Tied to Test Scores," *USA Today,* March 21, 2006, p 8D.

[56] Excerpted from "How Effective Is Incentive Pay?" *HR Magazine,* January 2008, p 12.

[57] List adapted from D R Spitzer, "Power Rewards: Rewards That Really Motivate," *Management Review,* May 1996, pp 45–50. Also see R Eisenberger and J Cameron, "Detrimental Effects of Reward: Reality or Myth?" *American Psychologist,* November 1996, pp 1153–66; S Miller, "Satisfaction with Pay, Benefits Falling," *HR Magazine,* January 2007, pp 38–39; and C Palmeri, "Workers Say: 'We Want an Upgrade'," *BusinessWeek,* April 16, 2007, p 11.

[58] See M Weinstein, "Performance Anxiety: When Performance Management Doesn't Work," *Training,* January 2006, p 9; and M D Johnson, J R Hollenbeck, S E Humphrey, D R Ilgen, D Jundt, and C J Meyer, "Cutthroat Cooperation: Asymmetrical Adaptation to Changes in Team Reward Structures," *Academy of Management Journal,* February 2006, pp 103–19.

[59] D Robb, "A Total View of Employee Rewards," *HR Magazine,* August 2007, pp 93–95.

[60] K M Kroll, "Let's Get Flexible," *HR Magazine,* April 2007, pp 97–100.

[61] See B E Litzky, K A Eddleston, and D L Kidder, "The Good, the Bad, and the Misguided: How Managers Inadvertently Encourage Deviant Behaviors," *Academy of Management Perspectives,* February 2006, pp 91–103.

[62] For a recent unconventional perspective, see R J DeGrandpre, "A Science of Meaning? Can Behaviorism Bring Meaning to Psychological Science?" *American Psychologist,* July 2000, pp 721–38.

[63] See E L Thorndike, *Educational Psychology: The Psychology of Learning,* vol. II (New York: Columbia University Teachers College, 1913).

[64] Discussion of an early behaviorist who influenced Skinner's work can be found in P J Kreshel, "John B Watson at J Walter Thompson: The Legitimation of 'Science' in Advertising," *Journal of Advertising,* no. 2, 1990, pp 49–59. Recent discussions involving behaviorism include M R Ruiz, "B F Skinner's Radical Behaviorism: Historical Misconstructions

and Grounds for Feminist Reconstructions," *Psychology of Women Quarterly,* June 1995, pp 161–79.

[65] For more recent discussion, see J W Donahoe, "The Unconventional Wisdom of B F Skinner: The Analysis-Interpretation Distinction," *Journal of the Experimental Analysis of Behavior,* September 1993, pp 453–56.

[66] See B F Skinner, *The Behavior of Organisms* (New York: Appleton-Century-Crofts, 1938).

[67] For modern approaches to respondent behavior, see B Azar, "Classical Conditioning Could Link Disorders and Brain Dysfunction, Researchers Suggest," *APA Monitor,* March 1999, p 17.

[68] For interesting discussions of Skinner and one of his students, see M B Gilbert and T F Gilbert, "What Skinner Gave Us," *Training,* September 1991, pp 42–48.

[69] See F Luthans and R Kreitner, *Organizational Behavior Modification and Beyond: An Operant and Social Learning Approach* (Glenview, IL: Scott, Foresman, 1985), pp 49–56.

[70] See K Blanchard and S Johnson, *The One Minute Manager* (New York: Berkley Books, 1981); and K Blanchard and R Lorber, *Putting the One Minute Manager to Work* (New York: Berkley Books, 1984).

[71] A Zimmerman, "Staying on Target," *The Wall Street Journal,* May 7, 2007, pp B1, B13. Also see J Reingold, "Target's Inner Circle," *Fortune,* March 31, 2008, pp 74–86.

[72] Ibid.

[73] Research on punishment is reported in B P Niehoff, R J Paul, and J F S Bunch, "The Social Effects of Punishment Events: The Influence of Violator Past Performance Record and Severity of the Punishment on Observers' Justice Perceptions and Attitudes," *Journal of Organizational Behavior,* November 1998, pp 589–602.

[74] See C B Ferster and B F Skinner, *Schedules of Reinforcement* (New York: Appleton-Century-Crofts, 1957).

[75] See L M Saari and G P Latham, "Employee Reactions to Continuous and Variable Ratio Reinforcement Schedules Involving a Monetary Incentive," *Journal of Applied Psychology,* August 1982, pp 506–8.

[76] P Brinkley-Rogers and R Collier, "Along the Colorado, the Money's Flowing," *Arizona Republic,* March 4, 1990, p A12.

[77] R Levering and M Moskowitz, "Fortune 100 Best Companies to Work For: 2007," *Fortune,* January 22, 2007, p 96.

[78] The topic of managerial credibility is covered in J M Kouzes and B Z Posner, *Credibility* (San Francisco: Jossey-Bass, 1993).

[79] An on-the-job example of behavior shaping can be found in J Case, "Are Your Meetings Like This?" *Inc.,* March 2003, p 79.

[80] Data from K L Alexander, "Continental Airlines Soars to New Heights," *USA Today,* January 23, 1996, p 4B.

[81] Continental Airlines, "Continental Airlines to Pay Record $158 Million Profit Sharing to Its Employees," news release, February 11, 2008, www.continental.com.

[82] L Gerdes, "You Have 20 Minutes to Surf. Go." *BusinessWeek,* December 26, 2005, p 16.

## Chapter 9

[1] Excerpted from E White, "How a Company Made Everyone a Team Player," *The Wall Street Journal,* August 13, 2007, pp B1, B7.

[2] E Van Velsor and J Brittain Leslie, "Why Executives Derail: Perspectives across Time and Cultures," *Academy of Management Executive,* November 1995, p 62.

[3] Ibid. p 63. Also see D S DrRue, J R Hollenbeck, M D Johnson, D R Ilgen, and D K Jundt, "How Different Team Downsizing Approaches Influence Team-Level Adaptation and Performance," *Academy of Management Journal,* February 2008, pp 182–96.

[4] See R Mirchandani, "Postmodernism and Sociology: From the Episte-mological to the Empirical," *Sociological Theory,* March 2005, pp 86–115.

[5] This definition is based in part on one found in D Horton Smith, "A Parsimonious Definition of 'Group': Toward Conceptual Clarity and Scientific Utility," *Sociological Inquiry,* Spring 1967, pp 141–67.

[6] E H Schein, *Organizational Psychology,* 3rd ed (Englewood Cliffs, NJ: Prentice Hall, 1980), p 145. For more, see L R Weingart, "How Did They Do That? The Ways and Means of Studying Group Process," in *Research*

*in Organizational Behavior,* vol. 19, eds L L Cummings and B M Staw (Greenwich, CT: JAI Press, 1997), pp 189–239.

[7] See R Cross, N Nohria, and A Parker, "Six Myths about Informal Networks—and How to Overcome Them," *MIT Sloan Management Review,* Spring 2002, pp 67–75; and C Shirky, "Watching the Patterns Emerge," *Harvard Business Review,* February 2004, pp 34–35.

[8] Data from "Co-workers Support Each Other," *USA Today,* May 28, 2003, p 1B.

[9] Excerpted from S Armour, "Company 'Alumni' Groups Keep Word Out after Workers Go," *USA Today,* August 30, 2005, p 4B.

[10] See J Janove, "FOB: Friend of Boss," *HR Magazine,* June 2005, pp 153–56.

[11] See Schein, *Organizational Psychology,* pp 149–53.

[12] "50 Best Small and Medium Companies to Work for in America," *HR Magazine,* July 2007, pp 43–61; and InsureMe, "About Us," www .insureme.com, accessed April 16, 2008.

[13] For an instructive overview of five different theories of group development, see J P Wanous, A E Reichers, and S D Malik, "Organizational Socialization and Group Development: Toward an Integrative Perspective," *Academy of Management Review,* October 1984, pp 670–83.

[14] See B W Tuckman, "Developmental Sequence in Small Groups," *Psychological Bulletin,* June 1965, pp 384–99; and B W Tuckman and M A C Jensen, "Stages of Small-Group Development Revisited," *Group & Organization Studies,* December 1977, pp 419–27.

[15] See T Postmes, R Spears, A T Lee, and R J Novak, "Individuality and Social Influence in Groups: Inductive and Deductive Routes to Group Identity," *Journal of Personality and Social Psychology,* November 2005, pp 747–63.

[16] J McGregor, "Forget Going with Your Gut," *BusinessWeek,* March 20, 2006, p 112.

[17] A useful resource book is T Ursiny, *The Coward's Guide to Conflict: Empowering Solutions for Those Who Would Rather Run than Fight* (Naperville, IL: Sourcebooks, 2003).

[18] For related research, see M Van Vugt and C M Hart, "Social Identity as Social Glue: The Origins of Group Loyalty," *Journal of Personality and Social Psychology,* April 2004, pp 585–98.

[19] See C M Mason and M A Griffin, "Group Task Satisfaction: The Group's Shared Attitude to Its Task and Work Environment," *Group and Organization Management,* December 2005, pp 625–52.

[20] G Graen, "Role-Making Processes within Complex Organizations," in *Handbook of Industrial and Organizational Psychology,* ed M D Dunnette (Chicago: Rand McNally, 1976), p 1201.

[21] See D J McAllister, D Kamdar, E W Morrison, and D B Turban, "Disentangling Role Perceptions: How Perceived Role Breadth, Discretion, Instrumentality, and Efficacy Relate to Helping and Taking Charge," *Journal of Applied Psychology,* September 2007, pp 1200–11.

[22] See K D Benne and P Sheats, "Functional Roles of Group Members," *Journal of Social Issues,* Spring 1948, pp 41–49.

[23] E C Dierdorff and F P Morgeson, "Consensus in Work Role Requirements: The Influence of Discrete Occupational Context on Role Expectations," *Journal of Applied Psychology,* September 2007, pp 1228–41.

[24] See H J Klein and P W Mulvey, "Two Investigations of the Relationships among Group Goals, Goal Commitment, Cohesion, and Performance," *Organizational Behavior and Human Decision Processes,* January 1995, pp 44–53; and D Knight, C C Durham, and E A Locke, "The Relationship of Team Goals, Incentives, and Efficacy to Strategic Risk, Tactical Implementation, and Performance," *Academy of Management Journal,* April 2001, pp 326–38.

[25] A Zander, "The Value of Belonging to a Group in Japan," *Small Group Behavior,* February 1983, pp 7–8.

[26] R R Blake and J Srygley Mouton, "Don't Let Group Norms Stifle Creativity," *Personnel,* August 1985, p 28.

[27] See D Kahneman, "Reference Points, Anchors, Norms, and Mixed Feelings," *Organizational Behavior and Human Decision Processes,* March 1992, pp 296–312.

[28] A Lashinsky, "Can Google Three-Peat," *Fortune,* January 31, 2008, http://money.cnn.com; K McKeough, "1: The Best of the Best—Google,"

*Crain's Chicago Business,* March 3, 2008, downloaded from General Reference Center Gold, http://find.galegroup.com; and G Colvin, "Xerox's Inventor-in-Chief," *Fortune,* June 27, 2007, http://money.cnn .com.

[29] See J Pfeffer, "Bring Back Shame," *Business 2.0,* September 2003, p 80.

[30] D Michaels, "Airbus, Amid Turmoil, Revives Troubled Plane," *The Wall Street Journal,* October 15, 2007, pp A1, A19.

[31] L Meckler, "How 10 People Reshaped Massachusetts Health Care," *The Wall Street Journal,* May 30, 2007, pp A1, A13.

[32] D C Feldman, "The Development and Enforcement of Group Norms," *Academy of Management Review,* January 1984, pp 50–52.

[33] Ibid.

[34] "Top 10 Leadership Tips from Jeff Immelt," *Fast Company,* April 2004, p 96.

[35] See P Bathurst, "Gen X is Taking Over With Rules of Its Own," *The Arizona Republic,* April 27, 2008, p EC1; and M Vella, "White-Collar Workers Shoulder Together—Like It Or Not," *BusinessWeek Indata,* April 28, 2008, p 58.

[36] "How Three Bosses Got to the Top," *Arizona Republic,* August 5, 2007, p D5.

[37] J R Katzenbach and D K Smith, *The Wisdom of Teams: Creating the High-Performance Organization* (New York: HarperBusiness, 1999), p 45.

[38] Condensed and adapted from ibid., p 214. Also see R Rico, M Sánchez-Manzanares, F Gil, and C Gibson, "Team Implicit Coordination Processes: A Team Knowledge-Based Approach," *Academy of Management Review,* January 2008, pp 163–84.

[39] "Company Is a Team, Not a Family," *HR Magazine,* April 2007, p 18.

[40] See M P Hillmann, P Dongier, R P Murgallis, M Khosh, E K Allen, and R Evernham, "When Failure Isn't an Option," *Harvard Business Review,* July/August 2005, pp 41–50.

[41] J R Katzenbach and D K Smith, "The Discipline of Teams," *Harvard Business Review,* March/April 1993, p 112.

[42] "A Team's-Eye View of Teams," *Training,* November 1995, p 16; and L Gratton and T J Erickson, "Eight Ways to Build Collaborative Teams," *Harvard Business Review,* November 2007, pp 101–9.

[43] P Burrows, "Cisco's Comeback," *BusinessWeek,* November 24, 2003, p 124.

[44] See P Falcone, "On the Brink of Failure," *HR Magazine,* February 2008, pp 82–84; and "Sound of Teambuilding," *Training,* February 2008, p 16.

[45] Excerpted from S Max, "Seagate's Morale-athon," *BusinessWeek,* April 3, 2006, p 110–12.

[46] B Kiviat, "It's What's on the Outside That Counts," *Time,* September 3, 2007, Global Business, p 6. Also see J Schaubroeck, S S K Lam, and S E Cha, "Embracing Transformational Leadership: Team Values and the Impact of Leader Behavior on Team Performance," *Journal of Applied Psychology,* July 2007, pp 1020–30.

[47] D Ancona and H Bresman, "Thinking Outside the Team," *HR Magazine,* September 2007, pp 133–36. Also see D Ancona and H Bresman, *X-Teams: How to Build Teams That Lead, Innovate, and Succeed* (Boston: Harvard Business School Press, 2007).

[48] C Johnson, "Merck to Pay $650 Million in Medicaid Settlement," *Washington Post,* February 8, 2008, www.washingtonpost.com.

[49] J Bachman, "Why's the MD-80 Still Flying?" *BusinessWeek,* April 10, 2008, www.businessweek.com.

[50] Harris Interactive, "Microsoft Jumps to No. 1 in National Corporate Reputation Survey," news release, February 1, 2007, www .harrisinteractive.com.

[51] L Prusak and D Cohen, "How to Invest in Social Capital," *Harvard Business Review,* June 2001, p 90.

[52] D De Cremer and T R Tyler, "The Effects of Trust in Authority and Procedural Fairness on Cooperation," *Journal of Applied Psychology,* May 2007, pp 639–49.

[53] See D M Rousseau, S B Sitkin, R S Burt, and C Camerer, "Not So Different After All: A Cross-Discipline View of Trust," *Academy of Management Review,* July 1998, pp 393–404.

[54] J D Lewis and A Weigert, "Trust as a Social Reality," *Social Forces,* June 1985, p 971. Trust is examined as an *indirect* factor in K T Dirks, "The Effects of Interpersonal Trust on Work Group Performance," *Journal of Applied Psychology,* June 1999, pp 445–55. Also see

J A Colquitt, B A Scott, and J A LePine, "Trust, Trustworthiness, and Trust Propensity: A Meta-Analytic Test of Their Unique Relationships with Risk Taking and Job Performance," *Journal of Applied Psychology,* July 2007, pp 909–27.

[55] Adapted from C Johnson-George and W C Swap, "Measurement of Specific Interpersonal Trust: Construction and Validation of a Scale to Assess Trust in a Specific Other," *Journal of Personality and Social Psychology,* December 1982, pp 1306–17; and D J McAllister, "Affect- and Cognition-Based Trust as Foundations for Interpersonal Cooperation in Organizations," *Academy of Management Journal,* February 1995, pp 24–59.

[56] See R Zemke, "Little Lies," *Training,* February 2004, p 8.

[57] J Katz, "Red Shirts to the Rescue," *Industry Week,* March 2008, downloaded from General Reference Center Gold, http://find.galegroup.com.

[58] Adapted from F Bartolomé, "Nobody Trusts the Boss Completely— Now What?" *Harvard Business Review,* March/April 1989, pp 135–42.

[59] Data from C Joinson, "Teams at Work," *HR Magazine,* May 1999, pp 30–36.

[60] McKeough, "1: The Best of the Best—Google."

[61] Adapted from Table 1 in V U Druskat and J V Wheeler, "Managing from the Boundary: The Effective Leadership of Self-Managing Work Teams," *Academy of Management Journal,* August 2003, pp 435–57.

[62] See A E Randal and K S Jaussi, "Functional Background Identity, Diversity, and Individual Performance in Cross-Functional Teams," *Academy of Management Journal,* December 2003, pp 763–74.

[63] Excerpted from "Fast Talk," *Fast Company,* February 2004, p 50. For cross-functional teams in action, see C Edwards, "Inside Intel," *BusinessWeek,* January 9, 2006, pp 46–54; "How to Break Out of Commodity Hell," *BusinessWeek,* March 27, 2006, p 76; and B Finn, "Outside-In R&D," *Business 2.0,* April 2006, p 85.

[64] S Gregory, "Cool Runnings," *Time,* October 15, 2007, Global Business, pp 9–10.

[65] See "1996 Industry Report: What Self-Managing Teams Manage," *Training,* October 1996, p 69.

[66] See L L Thompson, *Making the Team: A Guide for Managers* (Upper Saddle River, NJ: Prentice Hall, 2000).

[67] See P S Goodman, R Devadas, and T L Griffith Hughson, "Groups and Productivity: Analyzing the Effectiveness of Self-Managing Teams," in *Productivity in Organizations,* eds J P Campbell, R J Campbell and Associates (San Francisco: Jossey-Bass, 1988), pp 295–327. and S Kauffeld, "Self-Directed Work Groups and Team Competence," *Journal of Occupational and Organizational Psychology,* March 2006, pp 1–21.

[68] Drawn from H van Mierlo, C G Rutte, M A Kompier, and H A C M Doorewaard, "Self-Managing Teamwork and Psychological Well-Being: Review of a Multilevel Research Domain," *Group and Organization Management,* April 2005, pp 211–35.

[69] J E Mathieu, M T Maynard, S R Taylor, L L Gilson, and T M Ruddy, "An Examination of the Effects of Organizational District and Team Contexts on Team Processes and Performance: A Meso-Mediational Model," *Journal of Organizational Behavior,* October 2007, pp 891–910. Also see Z-X Zhang, P S Hempel, Y-L Han, and D Tjosvold, "Transactive Memory System Links Work Team Characteristics and Performance," *Journal of Applied Psychology,* November 2007, pp 1722–30.

[70] C W Langfred, "The Downside of Self-Management: A Longitudinal Study of the Effects of Conflict on Trust, Autonomy, and Task Interdependence in Self-Managing Teams," *Academy of Management Journal,* August 2007, pp 885–900.

[71] S T Bell, "Deep-Level Composition Variables as Predictors of Team Performance: A Meta-Analysis," *Journal of Applied Psychology,* May 2007, pp 595–615. Also see S E Humphrey, J R Hollenbeck, C J Meyer, and D R Ilgen, "Trait Configurations in Self-Managed Teams: A Conceptual Examination of the Use of Seeding for Maximizing and Minimizing Trait Variance in Teams," *Journal of Applied Psychology,* May 2007, pp 885–92.

[72] R Ilies, D T Wagner, and F P Morgeson, "Explaining Affective Linkages in Teams: Individual Differences in Susceptibility to Contagion and Individualism–Collectivism," *Journal of Applied Psychology,* July 2007, pp 1140–48.

[73] Excerpted from M Conlin, "The Easiest Commute of All," *BusinessWeek,* December 12, 2005, pp 78–79. Also see J T Arnold, "Making the Leap," *HR Magazine,* May 2006, pp 80–86.

[74] See A M Townsend, S M DeMarie, and A R Hendrickson, "Virtual Teams: Technology and the Workplace of the Future," *Academy of Management Executive,* August 1998, pp 17–29.

[75] See C Saunders, C Van Slyke, and D R Vogel, "My Time or Yours? Managing Time Visions in Global Virtual Teams," *Academy of Management Executive,* February 2004, pp 19–31.

[76] Excerpted from K Naughton, "Styling with Digital Clay," *Newsweek,* April 28, 2003, pp 46–47. For a large-scale example, see S E Ante, "Collaboration: IBM," *BusinessWeek,* November 24, 2003, p 84.

[77] Based on P Bordia, N DiFonzo, and A Chang, "Rumor as Group Problem Solving: Development Patterns in Informal Computer-Mediated Groups," *Small Group Research,* February 1999, pp 8–28.

[78] See K A Graetz, E S Boyle, C E Kimble, P Thompson, and J L Garloch, "Information Sharing in Face-to-Face, Teleconferencing, and Electronic Chat Groups," *Small Group Research,* December 1998, pp 714–43.

[79] Based on F Niederman and R J Volkema, "The Effects of Facilitator Characteristics on Meeting Preparation, Set Up, and Implementation," *Small Group Research,* June 1999, pp 330–60.

[80] Based on J J Sosik, B J Avolio, and S S Kahai, "Inspiring Group Creativity: Comparing Anonymous and Identified Electronic Brainstorming," *Small Group Research,* February 1998, pp 3–31.

[81] See B L Kirkman, B Rosen, C B Gibson, P E Tesluk, and S O McPherson, "Five Challenges to Virtual Team Success: Lessons from Sabre, Inc.," *Academy of Management Executive,* August 2002, pp 67–79; and Y Shin, "Conflict Resolution in Virtual Teams," *Organizational Dynamics,* November 2005, pp 331–45.

[82] See E Kelley, "Keys to Effective Virtual Global Teams," *Academy of Management Executive,* May 2001, pp 132–33; in "Virtual Teams that Work," *HR Magazine,* July 2003, p 121; and R F Maruca, "How Do You Manage an Off-Site Team?" *BusinessWeek,* September 30, 2007, www.businessweek.com.

[83] For a comprehensive update on groupthink, see the entire February/March 1998 issue of *Organizational Behavior and Human Decision Processes* (12 articles).

[84] I L Janis, *Groupthink,* 2nd ed (Boston: Houghton Mifflin, 1982), p 9. Alternative models are discussed in K Granstrom and D Stiwne, "A Bipolar Model of Groupthink: An Expansion of Janis's Concept," *Small Group Research,* February 1998, pp 32–56.

[85] Ibid. For an alternative model, see R J Aldag and S Riggs Fuller, "Beyond Fiasco: A Reappraisal of the Groupthink Phenomenon and a New Model of Group Decision Processes," *Psychological Bulletin,* May 1993, pp 533–52.

[86] Adapted from Janis, *Groupthink,* pp 174–75. Also see J M Wellen and M Neale, "Deviance, Self-Typicality, and Group Cohesion: The Corrosive Effects of the Bad Apples on the Barrel," *Small Group Research,* April 2006, pp 165–86.

[87] A Stuart, "Group Therapy," *CFO,* November 2007, pp 31–33.

[88] D D Henningsen, M L M Henningsen, J Eden, and M G Cruz, "Examining the Symptoms of Groupthink and Retrospective Sensemaking," *Small Group Research,* February 2006, pp 36–64.

[89] Stuart, "Group Therapy."

[90] Based on discussion in B Latane, K Williams, and S Harkins, "Many Hands Make Light the Work: The Causes and Consequences of Social Loafing," *Journal of Personality and Social Psychology,* June 1979, pp 822–32; and D A Kravitz and B Martin, "Ringelmann Rediscovered: The Original Article," *Journal of Personality and Social Psychology,* May 1986, pp 936–41.

[91] See S J Karau and K D Williams, "Social Loafing: Meta-Analytic Review and Theoretical Integration," *Journal of Personality and Social Psychology,* October 1993, pp 681–706.

[92] See S J Zaccaro, "Social Loafing: The Role of Task Attractiveness," *Personality and Social Psychology Bulletin,* March 1984, pp 99–106.

[93] For complete details, see K Williams, S Harkins, and B Latane, "Identifiability as a Deterrent to Social Loafing: Two Cheering Experiments," *Journal of Personality and Social Psychology,* February 1981, pp 303–11.

[94] See J M Jackson and S G Harkins, "Equity in Effort: An Explanation of the Social Loafing Effect," *Journal of Personality and Social Psychology*, November 1985, pp 1199–1206.

[95] Both studies are reported in S G Harkins and K Szymanski, "Social Loafing and Group Evaluation," *Journal of Personality and Social Psychology*, June 1989, pp 934–41.

[96] Data from J A Wagner III, "Studies of Individualism-Collectivism: Effects on Cooperation in Groups," *Academy of Management Journal*, February 1995, pp 152–72. Also see P W Mulvey, L Bowes-Sperry, and H J Klein, "The Effects of Perceived Loafing and Defensive Impression Management on Group Effectiveness," *Small Group Research*, June 1998, pp 394–415.

[97] See S G Scott and W O Einstein, "Strategic Performance Appraisal in Team-Based Organizations: One Size Does Not Fit All," *Academy of Management Executive*, May 2001, pp 107–16.

[98] Excerpted from J O'Donnell, "Should Business Execs Meet at Strip Clubs?" *USA Today*, March 23, 2006, pp 1A–2A.

## Chapter 10

[1] Excerpted from J Adamy, "McDonald's Takes On a Weakened Starbucks," *The Wall Street Journal*, January 7, 2008, pp A1, A10.

[2] T A Stewart, "Did You Ever Have to Make Up Your Mind?" *Harvard Business Review*, January 2006, p 12.

[3] Results are presented in P A Salz, "High Performance: Intelligent Use of Information Is a Powerful Corporate Tool," April 27, 2006, p A10. Also see T H Davenport, "Competing on Analytics," *Harvard Business Review*, January 2006, pp 99–108; and J Pfeffer and R I Sutton, "Evidence-Based Management," *Harvard Business Review*, January 2006, pp 63–74.

[4] A thorough discussion of the rational model can be found in M H Bazerman, *Judgment in Managerial Decision Making* (Hoboken, NJ: John Wiley & Sons, 2006).

[5] J L Yang, "Mattel's CEO Recalls a Rough Summer," *Fortune*, January 22, 2008, http://cnn.money.com (interview with Bob Eckert).

[6] Results can be found in J P Bymes, D C Miller, and W D Schafer, "Gender Differences in Risk Taking: A Meta-Analysis," *Psychological Bulletin*, May 1999, pp 367–83.

[7] Yang, "Mattel's CEO Recalls a Rough Summer."

[8] H A Simon, "Rational Decision Making in Business Organizations," *American Economic Review*, September 1979, p 510. S T Certo, B L Connelly, and L Tihanyi, "Managers and Their Not-So Rational Decisions, *Business Horizons*, 2008, pp 113–19.

[9] R Brown, *Rational Choice and Judgment* (Hoboken, NJ: John Wiley & Sons, 2005), p 9.

[10] For a complete discussion of bounded rationality, see H A Simon, *Administrative Behavior*, 2nd ed (New York: Free Press, 1957). Also see M H Bazerman and D Chugh, "Decisions without Blinders," *Harvard Business Review*, January 2006, pp 88–97.

[11] "Poor Decisions Hurt Company Performance," *HR Magazine*, February 2007, p 16.

[12] See M D Cohen, J G March, and J P Olsen, "A Garbage Can Model of Organizational Choice," *Administrative Science Quarterly*, March 1981, pp 1–25.

[13] Ibid, p 2.

[14] This discussion is based on material in J G March and R Weisinger-Baylon, *Ambiguity and Command* (Marshfield, MA: Pitman Publishing, 1986), pp 11–35.

[15] See A Carter, "Lighting a Fire under Campbell," *BusinessWeek*, December 4, 2006, pp 96, 99.

[16] For more on garbage can processes, see J L Bower and C G Gilbert, "How Managers' Everyday Decisions Create or Destroy Your Company's Strategy," *Harvard Business Review*, February 2007, pp 72–79.

[17] D J Snowden and M E Boone, "A Leader's Framework for Decision Making," *Harvard Business Review*, November 2007, pp 69–76.

[18] Ibid, p 76.

[19] See A Tversky and D Kahneman, "Judgment under Uncertainty: Heuristics and Biases," *Science*, September 1974, pp 1124–31.

[20] Study reported in E Hoffman, "Fooled by Nice Duds and a Fancy Degree," *BusinessWeek*, February 11, 2008, p 72.

[21] These biases are discussed in S F Dingfelder, "Taking Stock of Your Stock," *Monitor on Psychology*, January 2007, pp 18–19; and Bazerman, *Judgment in Managerial Decision Making*.

[22] R A Lowe and A A Ziedonis, "Overoptimism and the Performance of Entrepreneurial Firms," *Management Science*, February 2006, pp 173–86. Also see S Perman, "Intrapreneurs and Adaptive Persistence," *BusinessWeek*, April 2, 2008, www.businessweek.com.

[23] G Flaccus, "Risky Decisions Are Faulted in Death of California Firefighters," *Arizona Republic*, May 23, 2007, p A13.

[24] This scenario was taken from Bazerman, *Judgment in Managerial Decision Making*, p 41.

[25] See J Ross and B M Staw, "Organizational Escalation and Exit: Lessons from the Shoreham Nuclear Power Plant," *Academy of Management Journal*, August 1993, pp 701–32. For a sports-related example, see E Ramstad, "Why Korea Makes the World's Best Women Golfers," *The Wall Street Journal*, April 25, 2007, pp A1, A11.

[26] Ibid. Also see J W Mullins, "Good Money after Bad?" *Harvard Business Review*, March 2007, pp 37–48.

[27] M-G Seo and L F Barrett, "Being Emotional during Decision Making—Good or Bad? An Empirical Investigation," *Academy of Management Journal*, August 2007, pp 923–40; Also see D Malhotra, G Ku, and J K Murnighan, "When Winning Is Everything," *Harvard Business Review*, May 2008, pp 78–86.

[28] D W De Long and P Seemann, "Confronting Conceptual Confusion and Conflict in Knowledge Management," *Organizational Dynamics*, Summer 2000, p 33.

[29] See T H Davenport, L Prusak, and B Strong, "Organization: Putting Ideas to Work," *The Wall Street Journal*, March 10, 2008, p R11.

[30] R Lubit, "Tacit Knowledge and Knowledge Management: The Keys to Sustainable Competitive Advantage," *Organizational Dynamics*, 2001, p 166.

[31] The role of intuition in decision making is discussed by C C Miller and R D Ireland, "Intuition in Strategic Decision Making: Friend or Foe in the Fast-Paced 21st Century," *Academy of Management Executive*, February 2005, pp 19–30.

[32] K K Spors, "Getting Workers to Share Know-How with Their Peers," *The Wall Street Journal*, April 3, 2008, http://online.wsj.com.

[33] T O'Driscoll, "Join the Webvolution," *Training*, February 2008, p 24.

[34] R Cross, A Parker, L Prusak, and S P Borgatti, "Knowing What We Know: Supporting Knowledge Creation and Sharing in Social Networks," *Organizational Dynamics*, Fall 2001, p 109.

[35] Ibid.

[36] This definition was derived from A J Rowe and R O Mason, *Managing with Style: A Guide to Understanding, Assessing and Improving Decision Making* (San Francisco: Jossey-Bass, 1987).

[37] The discussion of styles was based on material contained in ibid.

[38] Excerpted from B Gimbel, "Keeping Planes Apart," *Fortune*, June 27, 2005, p 112.

[39] B Bremner and D Roberts, "A Billion Tough Sells," *BusinessWeek*, March 20, 2006, p 44.

[40] Y I Kane and P Dvorak, "Howard Stringer, Japanese CEO," *The Wall Street Journal*, March 3–4, 2007, pp A1, A6.

[41] Norms were obtained from Rowe and Mason, *Managing with Style*.

[42] See ibid.; and M J Dollinger and W Danis, "Preferred Decision-Making Styles: A Cross-Cultural Comparison," *Psychological Reports*, 1998, pp 755–61.

[43] L Kopeikina, "The Elements of a Clear Decision," *MIT Sloan Management Review*, Winter 2006, p 19.

[44] E Sadler-Smith and E Shefy, "The Intuitive Executive: Understanding and Applying 'Gut Feel' in Decision-Making," *Academy of Management Executive*, November 2004, p 77.

[45] C C Miller and R D Ireland, "Intuition in Strategic Decision Making: Friend or Foe in the Fast-Paced 21st Century," *Academy of Management Executive*, February 2005, p 20.

[46] Ibid, pp 19–30.

[47] See E Dane and M G Pratt, "Exploring Intuition and Its Role in Managerial Decision Making," *Academy of Management Review,* January 2007, pp 33–54.

[48] N M Tichy and W G Bennis, "Making Judgment Calls: The Ultimate Act of Leadership," *Harvard Business Review,* October 2007, p 99.

[49] See D Begley, "You Might Help a Teen Avoid Dumb Behavior by Nurturing Intuition," *The Wall Street Journal,* November 3, 2006, p B1.

[50] Courage and intuition are discussed in K K Reardon, "Courage as a Skill," *Harvard Business Review,* January 2007, pp 58–64.

[51] This definition was based on R J Sternberg, "What Is the Common Thread of Creativity?" *American Psychologist,* April 2001, pp 360–62.

[52] J Y Kim, "A Lifelong Battle against Disease," *U.S. News & World Report,* November 19, 2007, pp 62, 64.

[53] Quoted on pp 48–49 of D Coutu, "Creativity Step by Step," *Harvard Business Review,* April 2008, pp 47–51 (interview with Twyla Tharp).

[54] S Holmes, "Just Plain Genius," *BusinessWeek,* April 17, 2006, p 20.

[55] Results can be found in E Tahmincioglu, "Gifts that Gall," *Workforce Management,* April 2004, p 45.

[56] Details of this study can be found in M Basadur, "Managing Creativity: A Japanese Model," *Academy of Management Executive,* May 1992, pp 29–42.

[57] See R Berner, "How P&G Pampers New Thinking," *BusinessWeek,* April 14, 2008, pp 73–74; A K-Y Leung, W W Maddux, A D Galinsky, and C-Y Chiu, "Multicultural Experience Enhances Creativity," *American Psychologist,* April 2008, pp 169–81; and J Welch and S Welch, "Finding Innovation Where It Lives," *BusinessWeek,* April 21, 2008, p 84.

[58] B Hindo, "At 3M, a Struggle between Efficiency and Creativity," *BusinessWeek,* June 2007, pp 8–14.

[59] Results can be found in C K W De Dreu and M A West, "Minority Dissent and Team Innovation: The Importance of Participation in Decision Making," *Journal of Applied Psychology,* December 2001, pp 1191–201.

[60] S J Shin and J Zhou, "When Is Educational Specialization Heterogeneity Related to Creativity in Research and Development Teams? Transformational Leadership as a Moderator," *Journal of Applied Psychology,* November 2007, pp 1709–21.

[61] These recommendations were derived from R Y Hirokawa, "Group Communication and Decision-Making Performance: A Continued Test of the Functional Perspective," *Human Communication Research,* October 1988, pp 487–515.

[62] See the related discussion in B B Baltes, M W Dickson, M P Sherman, C C Bauer, and J S LaGanke, "Computer-Mediated Communication and Group Decision Making: A Meta-Analysis," *Organizational Behavior and Human Decision Processes,* January 2002, pp 156–79.

[63] These guidelines were derived from G P Huber, *Managerial Decision Making* (Glenview, IL: Scott, Foresman, 1980), p 149.

[64] G W Hill, "Group versus Individual Performance: Are $N + 1$ Heads Better than One?" *Psychological Bulletin,* May 1982, p 535.

[65] See T Connolly and L Ordóñez, "Judgment and Decision Making," in *Handbook of Psychology,* vol. 12, eds W C Borman, D R Ilgen, and R J Klimoski (Hoboken, NJ: John Wiley & Sons, 2003), pp 493–518. Also see S Dingfelder, "Groups May Find More Elegant Solutions than Individuals," *Monitor on Psychology,* May 2006, p 15.

[66] G M Parker, *Team Players and Teamwork: The New Competitive Business Strategy* (San Francisco: Jossey-Bass, 1990).

[67] The effect of group dynamics on brainstorming is discussed by P B Paulus and H-C Yang, "Idea Generation in Groups: A Basis for Creativity in Organizations," *Organizational Behavior and Human Decision Processes,* May 2000, pp 76–87.

[68] These recommendations were obtained from Parker, *Team Players and Teamwork.*

[69] See A F Osborn, *Applied Imagination: Principles and Procedures of Creative Thinking,* 3rd ed (New York: Scribners, 1979).

[70] See W H Cooper, R Brent Gallupe, S Pollard, and J Cadsby, "Some Liberating Effects of Anonymous Electronic Brainstorming," *Small Group Research,* April 1998, pp 147–78.

[71] These recommendations and descriptions were derived from B Nussbaum, "The Power of Design," *BusinessWeek,* May 17, 2004, pp 88–94.

[72] The NGT procedure is discussed by L Thompson, "Improving the Creativity of Organizational Work Groups," *Academy of Management Executive,* February 2003, pp 96–109.

[73] See ibid.

[74] See N C Dalkey, D L Rourke, R Lewis, and D Snyder, *Studies in the Quality of Life: Delphi and Decision Making* (Lexington, MA: Lexington Books: D C Heath and Co., 1972).

[75] A thorough description of computer-aided decision-making systems is provided by M C Er and A C Ng, "The Anonymity and Proximity Factors in Group Decision Support Systems," *Decision Support Systems,* May 1995, pp 75–83.

[76] M Weinstein, "So Happy Together," *Training,* May 2006, p 38.

[77] Supportive results can be found in S S Lam and J Schaubroeck, "Improving Group Decisions by Better Polling Information: A Comparative Advantage of Group Decision Support Systems," *Journal of Applied Psychology,* August 2000, pp 565–73; and I Benbasat and J Lim, "Information Technology Support for Debiasing Group Judgments: An Empirical Evaluation," *Organizational Behavior and Human Decision Processes,* September 2000, pp 167–83.

[78] Results can be found in Baltes, Dickson, Sherman, Bauer, and LaGanke, "Computer-Mediated Communication and Group Decision Making."

[79] Excerpted from J Kelley, "Westwood Students Get OK for Eagle Feathers," *The Mesa Republic,* May 25, 2006, p 15.

## Chapter 11

[1] Excerpted from J Sandberg, "Avoiding Conflicts, The T00-Nice Boss Makes Matters Worse," *The Wall Street Journal,* February 26, 2008, p B1.

[2] P E Spector, "Introduction: Conflict in Organizations," *Journal of Organizational Behavior,* January 2008, p 3.

[3] See C K W De Dreu, "The Virtue and Vice of Workplace Conflict: Food For (Pessimistic) Thought," *Journal of Organizational Behavior,* January 2008, pp 5–18; and D Tjosvold, "The Conflict-Positive Organization: It Depends Upon Us," *Journal of Organizational Behavior,* January 2008, pp 19–28.

[4] J A Wall, Jr, and R Robert Callister, "Conflict and Its Management," *Journal of Management,* no. 3, 1995, p 517.

[5] Ibid., p 544.

[6] See O Jones, "Scientific Management, Culture and Control: A First-Hand Account of Taylorism in Practice," *Human Relations,* May 2000, pp 631–53.

[7] See J Thilmany, "In Case of Emergency," *HR Magazine,* November 2007, pp 79–83; P Falcone, "Tattletales Spell Trouble," *HR Magazine,* November 2007, pp 91–94; and "Employer's Legal Guide to Issues of the Modern Workplace," *Fulton County Daily Report,* January 24, 2008, downloaded from General Reference Center Gold, http://find.galegroup.com.

[8] See S Alper, D Tjosvold, and K S Law, "Interdependence and Controversy in Group Decision Making: Antecedents to Effective Self-Managing Teams," *Organizational Behavior and Human Decision Processes,* April 1998, pp 33–52.

[9] S P Robbins, "'Conflict Management' and 'Conflict Resolution' Are Not Synonymous Terms," *California Management Review,* Winter 1978, p 70.

[10] Cooperative conflict is discussed in Tjosvold, *Learning to Manage Conflict.* Also see A C Amason, "Distinguishing the Effects of Functional and Dysfunctional Conflict on Strategic Decision Making: Resolving a Paradox for Top Management Teams," *Academy of Management Journal,* February 1996, pp 123–48.

[11] D Michaels, "Airbus, Amid Turmoil, Revives Troubled Plane," *The Wall Street Journal,* October 15, 2007, pp A1, A19.

[12] A Salkever, "Anatomy of a Business Decision: The Union Wanted Wage and Benefit Increases; Management Saw That as the Path to Bankruptcy; Was a Strike Inevitable?" *Inc,* May 2007, pp 55–58.

[13] Adapted in part from discussion in A C Filley, *Interpersonal Conflict Resolution* (Glenview, IL: Scott, Foresman, 1975), pp 9–12; and B Fortado, "The Accumulation of Grievance Conflict," *Journal of Management Inquiry,* December 1992, pp 288–303. Also see D Tjosvold and M Poon, "Dealing with Scarce Resources: Open-Minded Interaction for Resolving Budget Conflicts," *Group & Organization Management,* September 1998, pp 237–55.

[14] Excerpted from T Ursiny, *The Coward's Guide to Conflict: Empowering Solutions for Those Who Would Rather Run than Fight* (Naperville, IL: Sourcebooks, 2003), p 27.

[15] Sandberg, "Avoiding Conflicts, the Too-Nice Boss Makes Matters Worse."

[16] Adapted from discussion in Tjosvold, *Learning to Manage Conflict,* pp 12–13.

[17] L Gardenswartz and A Rowe, *Diverse Teams at Work: Capitalizing on the Power of Diversity* (New York: McGraw-Hill, 1994), p 32.

[18] Data from "Do I Have It?" *BusinessWeek,* July 7, 2003, p 14.

[19] J Sandberg, "With Bad Mentors, It's Better to Break Up than to Make Up," *The Wall Street Journal,* March 18, 2008, p B1.

[20] S Lim, L M Cortina, and V J Magley, "Personal and Workgroup Incivility: Impact on Work and Health Outcomes," *Journal of Applied Psychology,* January 2008, pp 95–107; and L M Cortina, "Unseen Injustice: Incivility As Modern Discrimination in Organizations," *Academy of Management Review,* January 2008, pp 55–75.

[21] S Lim and L M Cortina, "Interpersonal Mistreatment in the Workplace: The Interface and Impact of General Incivility and Sexual Harassment," *Journal of Applied Psychology,* May 2005, pp 483–96; and K Torres, "Ill Effects of Workplace Bullying," *Occupational Hazards,* April 2008, downloaded from General Reference Center Gold, http://find.galegroup.com.

[22] Novations Group, "Sharp Rise Seen in Sexual Remarks in Workplace," news release, February 25, 2008, www.novations.com.

[23] See D L Coutu, "In Praise of Boundaries: A Conversation with Miss Manners," *Harvard Business Review,* December 2003, pp 41–45; L Buchanan, "The Bully Rulebook: How to Deal with Jerks," *Inc,* February 2007, pp 43–44; H Green, "How to Get Rid of the, uh, Jerks," *BusinessWeek,* March 19, 2007, p 14; and C M Dalton, "The Bully Down the Hall," *Business Horizons,* March–April 2007, pp 89–91.

[24] Data from D Stamps, "Yes, Your Boss Is Crazy," *Training,* July 1998, pp 35–39. Also see and J Scelfo, "Men and Depression: Facing Darkness," *Newsweek,* February 26, 2007, pp 42–49.

[25] See D Riddle and R Bales, "Disability Claims for Alcohol-Related Misconduct," *St John's Law Review,* Spring 2008, pp 699–734.

[26] See N W Janove, "Sexual Harassment and the Three Big Surprises," *HR Magazine,* November 2001, pp 123–30.

[27] Se J B. Olson-Buchanan and W R Boswell, "An Integrative Model of Experiencing and Responding to Mistreatment at Work," *Academy of Management Review,* January 2008, pp 76–96; and C Hymowitz, "Bosses Have to Learn How to Confront Troubled Employees," *The Wall Street Journal,* April 23, 2007, p B1.

[28] For practical advice, see N Nicholson, "How to Motivate Your Problem People," *Harvard Business Review,* Special Issue: Motivating People, January 2003, pp 56–65.

[29] A Marks, "Delta–Northwest Merger: Pilots' Demands Hold Any Deal Up," *Christian Science Monitor,* March 4, 2008, downloaded from General Reference Center Gold, http://find.galegroup.com.

[30] Based on discussion in G Labianca, D J Brass, and B Gray, "Social Networks and Perceptions of Intergroup Conflict: The Role of Negative Relationships and Third Parties," *Academy of Management Journal,* February 1998, pp 55–67.

[31] See J Barbian, "Racism Shrugged," *Training,* February 2003, p 68; R J Eidelson and J I Eidelson, "Dangerous Ideas: Five Beliefs That Propel Groups toward Conflict," *American Psychologist,* March 2003, pp 182–92; and T M Glomb and H Liao, "Interpersonal Aggression in Work Groups: Social Influence, Reciprocal, and Individual Effects," *Academy of Management Journal,* August 2003, pp 486–96.

[32] Labianca, Brass, and Gray, "Social Networks and Perceptions of Intergroup Conflict," p 63 (emphasis added).

[33] For example, see S C Wright, A Aron, T McLaughlin-Volpe, and S A Ropp, "The Extended Contact Effect: Knowledge of Cross-Group Friendships and Prejudice," *Journal of Personality and Social Psychology,* July 1997, pp 73–90.

[34] See C D Batson, M P Polycarpou, E Harmon-Jones, H J Imhoff, E C Mitchener, L L Bednar, T R Klein, and L Highberger, "Empathy and Attitudes: Can Feeling for a Member of a Stigmatized Group Improve Feelings toward the Group?" *Journal of Personality and Social Psychology,* January 1997, pp 105–18.

[35] For more, see R L Tung, V Worm, and T Fang, "Sino-Western Business Negotiations Revisted—30 Years After China's Open Door Policy," *Organizational Dynamics,* January–March 2008, pp 60–74; and D Welch, D Kiley, and M Ihlwan, "My Way the Highway at Hyundai," *BusinessWeek,* March 6, 2008, http://www.businessweek.com/print/magazine/content/08_11/.

[36] "Negotiating South of the Border," *Harvard Management Communication Letter,* August 1999, p 12.

[37] Reprinted from A Rosenbaum, "Testing Cultural Waters," *Management Review,* July/August 1999, p 43. Copyright 1999 American Management Association. Reproduced with permission of American Management Association via Copyright Clearance Center.

[38] See R L Tung, "American Expatriates Abroad: From Neophytes to Cosmopolitans," *Journal of World Business,* Summer 1998, pp 125–44.

[39] See H M Guttman, "Conflict Management as a Core Leadership Competency," *Training,* November 2005, pp 34–39.

[40] R A Cosier and C R Schwenk, "Agreement and Thinking Alike: Ingredients for Poor Decisions," *Academy of Management Executive,* February 1990, p 71.

[41] For example, see "Facilitators as Devil's Advocates," *Training,* September 1993, p 10.

[42] Good background reading on devil's advocacy can be found in C R Schwenk, "Devil's Advocacy in Managerial Decision Making," *Journal of Management Studies,* April 1984, pp 153–68. Also see the critique of devil's advocacy in T Kelley and J Littman, *The Ten Faces of Innovation* (NY: Currency Doubleday, 2005), pp 2–3.

[43] See G Katzenstein, "The Debate on Structured Debate: Toward a Unified Theory," *Organizational Behavior and Human Decision Processes,* June 1996, pp 316–32.

[44] W Kiechel III, "How to Escape the Echo Chamber," *Fortune,* June 18, 1990, p 130.

[45] See D M Schweiger, W R Sandberg, and P L Rechner, "Experiential Effects of Dialectical Inquiry, Devil's Advocacy, and Consensus Approaches to Strategic Decision Making," *Academy of Management Journal,* December 1989, pp 745–72.

[46] See J S Valacich and C Schwenk, "Devil's Advocacy and Dialectical Inquiry Effects on Face-to-Face and Computer-Mediated Group Decision Making," *Organizational Behavior and Human Decision Processes,* August 1995, pp 158–73.

[47] L Meckler, "How 10 People Reshaped Massachusetts Health Care," *The Wall Street Journal,* May 30, 2007, pp A1, A13.

[48] Based on C K W De Dreu and M A West, "Minority Dissent and Team Innovation: The Importance of Participation in Decision Making," *Journal of Applied Psychology,* December 2001, pp 1191–201.

[49] A statistical validation for this model can be found in M A Rahim and N R Magner, "Confirmatory Factor Analysis of the Styles of Handling Interpersonal Conflict: First-Order Factor Model and Its Invariance across Groups," *Journal of Applied Psychology,* February 1995, pp 122–32.

[50] See, for example, K J Behfar, R S Peterson, E A Mannix, and W M K Trochim, "The Critical Role of Conflict Resolution in Teams: A Close Look at the Links Between Conflict Type, Conflict Management Strategies, and Team Outcomes," *Journal of Applied Psychology,* January 2008, pp 170–88; and G A Van Kleef and S Côté, "Expressing Anger in Conflict: When It Helps and When It Hurts," *Journal of Applied Psychology,* November 2007, pp 1557–69.

[51] M A Rahim, "A Strategy for Managing Conflict in Complex Organizations," *Human Relations,* January 1985, p 84.

[52] See R Rubin, "Study: Bullies and Their Victims Tend to Be More Violent," *USA Today,* April 15, 2003, p 9D; and D Salin, "Ways of Explaining Workplace Bullying: A Review of Enabling, Motivating and Precipitating Structures and Processes in the Work Environment," *Human Relations,* October 2003, pp 1213–32.

[53] See, for example, M Orey, "Fear of Firing," *BusinessWeek,* April 23, 2007, p 54.

[54] See C Bendersky, "Organizational Dispute Resolution Systems: A Complementarities Model," *Academy of Management Review,* October 2003, pp 643–56.

[55] See M Bordwin, "Do-It-Yourself Justice," *Management Review,* January 1999, pp 56–58.

[56] B Morrow and L M Bernardi, "Resolving Workplace Disputes," *Canadian Manager,* Spring 1999, p 17. For related research, see J M Brett, M Olekalns, R Friedman, N Goates, C Anderson, and C Cherry Lisco, "Sticks and Stones: Language, Face, and Online Dispute Resolution," *Academy of Management Journal,* February 2007, pp 85–99.

[57] Adapted from discussion in K O Wilburn, "Employment Disputes: Solving Them Out of Court," *Management Review,* March 1998, pp 17–21; and Morrow and Bernardi, "Resolving Workplace Disputes," pp 17–19, 27.

[58] For more, see M M Clark, "A Jury of Their Peers," *HR Magazine,* January 2004, pp 54–59.

[59] Wilburn, "Employment Disputes: Solving Them Out of Court," p 19.

[60] For background on this contentious issue, see S Armour, "Arbitration's Rise Raises Fairness Issue," *USA Today,* June 12, 2001, pp 1B–2B; T J Heinsz, "The Revised Uniform Arbitration Act: An Overview," *Dispute Resolution Journal,* May–July 2001, pp 28–39; and J B Thelen, "Manager Who Refused to Sign Agreement Must Arbitrate," *HR Magazine,* January 2007, p 111.

[61] Based on a definition in M A Neale and M H Bazerman, "Negotiating Rationally: The Power and Impact of the Negotiator's Frame," *Academy of Management Executive,* August 1992, pp 42–51.

[62] See, for example, P Prada and S Carey, "Delta Chief's Fancy Footwork," *The Wall Street Journal,* April 22, 2008, pp B1, B2; E Pooley, "Get a Killer Raise in 2007," *Canadian Business,* January 14, 2007, pp 61–62; and J R Curhan and A Pentland, "Thin Slices of Negotiation: Predicting Outcomes from Conversational Dynamics within the First Five Minutes," *Journal of Applied Psychology,* May 2007, pp 802–11.

[63] M H Bazerman and M A Neale, *Negotiating Rationally* (New York: Free Press, 1992), p 16. Also see and P H Kim, R L Pinkley, and A R Fragale, "Power Dynamics in Negotiation," *Academy of Management Review,* October 2005, pp 799–822.

[64] Good win–win negotiation strategies can be found in R R Reck and B G Long, *The Win–Win Negotiator: How to Negotiate Favorable Agreements That Last* (New York: Pocket Books, 1987); R Fisher and W Ury, *Getting to YES: Negotiating Agreement without Giving In* (Boston: Houghton Mifflin, 1981); R Fisher and D Ertel, *Getting Ready to Negotiate: The Getting to YES Workbook* (New York: Penguin Books, 1995); C Woodyard, "Working Hand-in-Hand," *USA Today,* February 6, 2007, pp 1B–2B; E A Grant, "Playing Hard to Get," *Inc,* March 2007, pp 104–9; and N Brodsky, "The Paranoia Moment: Are They Stalling? Is This Deal about to Fall Apart?" *Inc,* April 2007, pp 67–68.

[65] B Schulte, "Teaming Up with the Enemy," *U.S. News & World Report,* November 19, 2007, pp 54, 56.

[66] D Malhotra and M H Bazerman, "Investigative Negotiation," *Harvard Business Review,* September 2007, pp 72–78.

[67] Adapted from K Albrecht and S Albrecht, "Added Value Negotiating," *Training,* April 1993, pp 26–29.

[68] L Babcock, S Laschever, M Gelfand, and D Small, "Nice Girls Don't Ask," *Harvard Business Review,* October 2003, p 14. Also see H R Bowles, L Babcock, and L Lai, "Social Incentives for Gender Differences in the Propensity to Initiate Negotiations: Sometimes It Does Hurt to Ask," *Organizational Behavior and Human Decision Processes,* May 2007, pp 84–103; and E Agnvall, "Women and Negotiation," *HR Magazine,* December 2007, pp 69–73.

[69] Excerpted from G McWilliams, "Candid Camera: Trove of Videos Vexes Wal-Mart," *The Wall Street Journal,* April 9, 2008, http://online .wsj.com/article_print/SB120770260120100.

## Chapter 12

[1] Excerpted from C Hymowitz, "Sometimes, Moving Up Make It Harder to See What Goes On Below," *The Wall Street Journal,* October 15, 2007, p B1.

[2] J Jarvis, "Dell Learns to Listen," *BusinessWeek,* October 17, 2007, www.businessweek.com. Also see J Jarvis, "Love the Customers Who Hate You," *BusinessWeek,* March 3, 2008, p 58.

[3] Results can be found in K Gurchiek, "Survey: 'Key' Skills Advance HR Career," *HR Magazine,* April 2008, p 38; and "Why Am I Here," *Training,* April 2006, p 13.

[4] J L Bowditch and A F Buono, *A Primer on Organizational Behavior,* 4th ed (New York: John Wiley & Sons, 1997), p 120.

[5] For a detailed discussion about selecting an appropriate medium, see B Barry and I Smithey-Fulmer, "The Medium and the Message: The Adaptive Use of Communication Media in Dyadic Influence," *Academy of Management Review,* April 2004, pp 272–92.

[6] J Adamy, "38: Janice Fields, Executive Vice President and Chief Operating Officer, McDonald's USA," *The Wall Street Journal,* November 19, 2007, p R10.

[7] The appropriateness of using different media to terminate employees is discussed by J Welch and S Welch, "The Right Way to Say Goodbye," *BusinessWeek,* March 26, 2007, p 144; and D Levine, A Maingault, and D Lacy, "Cobra, Evasive Poor Performers, Illegal Workers," *HR Magazine,* March 2007, pp 41–42.

[8] E Laise, "Pushing Paperless: The Pros and Cons," *The Wall Street Journal,* May 2, 2007, pp D1, D10. Also see B Grow, K Epstein, and C-C Tschang, "The New E-Spionage Threat," *BusinessWeek,* April 21, 2008, pp 33–41.

[9] G A Fowler, "In China's Offices, Foreign Colleagues Might Get an Earful," *The Wall Street Journal,* February 13, 2007, p B1.

[10] See D Searcey and J E Vascellaro, "Trying to Minimize a Lot of the Buzz about BlackBerrys," *The Wall Street Journal,* May 11, 2007, pp A1, A7. Also see J Sandberg, "From Crib to Cubicle, A Familiar Voice—Our Own—Reassures," *The Wall Street Journal,* March 25, 2008, p B1.

[11] Ideas for improving personal communication skills are discussed in R Tucker, "Four Key Skills to Master Now," *Fortune,* October 30, 2006, p 123; J Welch and S Welch, "Keeping Morale Up in a Downturn," *BusinessWeek,* May 5, 2008, p 80; and J Lublin, "Talking Too Much on a Job Interview May Kill Your Chance," *The Wall Street Journal,* October 30, 2007, http://online.wsj.com.

[12] See "Interpersonal Effectiveness Training: Beyond the Water Cooler," *Training,* April 2006, p 10.

[13] For this and other examples, see J Sandberg, "Not Communicating with Your Boss? Count Your Blessings," *The Wall Street Journal,* May 22, 2007, p B1.

[14] V Boyd Ford, "The Paralysis of Political Correctness," *HR Magazine,* November 2007, pp 69–71. Also see R J Grossman, "Keep Pace with Older Workers," *HR Magazine,* May 2008, pp 39–46.

[15] For a thorough discussion of these barriers, see C R Rogers and F J Roethlisberger, "Barriers and Gateways to Communication," *Harvard Business Review,* July/August 1952, pp 46–52.

[16] Ibid, p 47.

[17] Physical barriers are discussed by S Shellenbarger, "Time-Zoned: Working around the Round-the-Clock Workday," *The Wall Street Journal,* February 15, 2007, p D1; and E Woyke, "Wanted: A Clutter Cutter," *BusinessWeek,* April 9, 2007, p 12.

[18] L Buchanan, "Do Not Disturb," *Inc,* November 2007, p 144.

[19] J Sandberg, "It Says Press Any Key; Where's the Any Key?" *The Wall Street Journal,* February 20, 2007, p B1.

[20] The use of jargon and acronyms is discussed by C Hymowitz, "Mind Your Language: To Do Business Today, Consider Delayering," *The Wall Street Journal,* March 27, 2006, p B1.

[21] Results can be found in J D Johnson, W A Donohue, C K Atkin, and S Johnson, "Communication, Involvement, and Perceived Innovativeness," *Group & Organization Management,* March 2001, pp 24–52; and B Davenport Sypher and T E Zorn, Jr, "Communication-Related Abilities and Upward Mobility: A Longitudinal Investigation," *Human Communication Research,* Spring 1986, pp 420–31. Also see

K Gurchiek, "Survey: 'Key' Skills Advance HR Career," *HR Magazine,* April 2008, p 38.

22 The measurement of communication competence is discussed by J M Schirmer, L Mauksch, F Lang, M K Marvel, K Zoppi, R E Epstein, D Brock, and M Pryzbylski, "Assessing Communication Competence: A Review of Current Tools," *Family Medicine,* March 2005, pp 184–192.

23 1. *False.* Clients always take precedence, and people with the greatest authority or importance should be introduced first.

2. *False.* You should introduce yourself. Say something like "My name is _____. I don't believe we've met."

3. *False.* It's OK to admit you can't remember. Say something like "My mind just went blank, your name is?" Or offer your name and wait for the other person to respond with his or hers.

4. *False.* Business etiquette has become gender neutral.

5. *a. Host.* This enables him or her to lead their guest to the meeting place.

6. *False.* Not only is it rude to invade public areas with your conversation, but you never know who might hear details of your business transaction or personal life.

7. *b. 3 feet.* Closer than this is an invasion of personal space. Farther away forces people to raise their voices. Because communication varies from country to country, you should also inform yourself about cultural differences.

8. *True.* An exception to this would be if your company holds an event at the beach or the pool.

9. *False.* Just wave your hand over it when asked, or say "No thank you."

10. *True.* The person who initiated the call should redial if the connection is broken.

11. *True.* If you must use a speakerphone, you should inform all parties who's present.

12. *True.* You should record a greeting such as "I'm out of the office today, March 12. If you need help, please dial _____ at extension . . ."

24 See F Timmins and C McCabe, "How Assertive Are Nurses in the Workplace? A Preliminary Pilot Study," *Journal of Nursing Management,* January 2005, pp 61–67.

25 J A Waters, "Managerial Assertiveness," *Business Horizons,* September/October 1982, p 25.

26 Ibid., p 27. Also see C Binkley, "Want to Be CEO? You Have to Dress the Part," *The Wall Street Journal,* January 10, 2008, pp D1, D12.

27 This statistic was provided by A Fisher, "How Can I Survive a Phone Interview?" *Fortune,* April 19, 2004, p 54.

28 Problems with body language analysis are discussed by A Pihulyk, "Communicate with Clarity: The Key to Understanding and Influencing Others," *Canadian Manager,* Summer 2003, pp 12–13.

29 Related research is summarized by J A Hall, "Male and Female Nonverbal Behavior," in *Multichannel Integrations of Nonverbal Behavior,* eds A W Siegman and S Feldstein (Hillsdale, NJ: Lawrence Erlbaum, 1985), pp 195–226.

30 See R E Axtell, *Gestures: The Do's and Taboos of Body Language around the World* (New York: John Wiley & Sons, 1991); and E Flitter, "Touchy Subject: Doing Business Where Hugs Replace Handshakes," *The Wall Street Journal,* December 19, 2007, http://online.wsj.com.

31 See J A Russell, "Facial Expressions of Emotion: What Lies Beyond Minimal Universality?" *Psychological Bulletin,* November 1995, pp 379–91. Also see B Azar, "A Case for Angry Men and Happy Women," *Monitor on Psychology,* April 2007, pp 18–19.

32 Norms for cross-cultural eye contact are discussed by C Engholm, *When Business East Meets Business West: The Guide to Practice and Protocol in the Pacific Rim* (New York: John Wiley & Sons, 1991).

33 See D Knight, "Perks Keeping Workers out of Revolving Door," *The Wall Street Journal,* April 30, 2005, p D3; and G Rooper, "Managing Employee Relations," *HR Magazine,* May 2005, pp 101–104.

34 The discussion of listening styles is based on "5 Listening Styles," http://www.crossroadsinstitute.org/listyle.html, June 19, 2004.

35 See the related discussion in J Condrill, "What Is Your Listening Style?" *AuthorsDen,* July 7, 2004, http://www.authorsden.com/visit/viewarticle.asp?id=18707.

36 These recommendations were excerpted from J Jay, "On Communicating Well," *HR Magazine,* January 2005, pp 87–88.

37 D Tannen, "The Power of Talk: Who Gets Heard and Why," *Harvard Business Review,* September/October 1995, p 139.

38 For a thorough review of the evolutionary explanation of sex differences in communication, see A H Eagly and W Wood, "The Origins of Sex Differences in Human Behavior," *American Psychologist,* June 1999, pp 408–23.

39 See D Tannen, "The Power of Talk: Who Gets Heard and Why," in *Negotiation: Readings, Exercises, and Cases,* 3rd ed, eds R J Lewicki and D M Saunders (Boston, MA: Irwin/McGraw-Hill, 1999), pp 160–73; and D Tannen, *You Just Don't Understand: Women and Men in Conversation* (New York: Ballantine Books, 1990). Also see J Ewers, "Ladies, Cool It if You Want Cash," *U.S. News & World Report,* September 24, 2007, p 57.

40 See M Dainton and E D Zelley, *Applying Communication Theory for Professional Life: A Practical Introduction* (Thousand Oaks, CA: Sage, 2005).

41 Tannen, "The Power of Talk: Who Gets Heard and Why," pp 147–48.

42 C Mamberto, "Instant Messaging Invades the Office," *The Wall Street Journal,* July 24, 2007, pp B1–B2.

43 M Weinstein, "Mobility Movement," *Training,* September 2007, pp 14–16.

44 Henry J Kaiser Family Foundation, "Key Findings: Media Multitasking among American Youth; Prevalence Predictors and Pairings," Pub No 7593, December 12, 2006, www.kff.org; A Cynkar, "Socially Wired," *Monitor on Psychology,* November 2007, pp 47–49; and K Joy, "Generation Distraction," *Columbus (OH) Dispatch,* January 15, 2008, downloaded from General Reference Center Gold, http://find.galegroup.com.

45 C Gibbons and A Johnson, "The Tasks at Hand," *Arizona Republic,* September 19, 2007, pp D1–D2.

46 N L Reinsch, Jr, J W Turner, and C H Tinsley, "Multicommunicating: A Practice Whose Time Has Come?" *Academy of Management Review,* April 2008, p 391.

47 See Ibid., pp. 391–403, for a complete discussion of multi-communicating.

48 Miniwatts Marketing Group, "Internet Usage Statistics: The Internet Big Picture," *Internet World Stats,* March 31, 2008, www.internetworldstats.com.

49 See J McGregor, "The 2008 Winners," *BusinessWeek,* March 3, 2008, pp 47–50.

50 See J T Arnold, "Improving Intranet Usefulness," *HR Magazine,* April 2008, pp 103–6; and D M Owens, "Managing Corporate Policies Online," *HR Magazine,* May 2008, pp 69–72.

51 This statistic was reported in H Green, S Rosenbush, R O Crockett, and S Holmes, "Wi-Fi Means Business," *BusinessWeek,* April 28, 2003, pp 86–92.

52 Online training is discussed by L Bealko, "Running Effective Online Trainings," January 12, 2006, *Techsoup,* http://www.techsoup.org/howto/articles/training/page4245.cfm.

53 See M E Medland, "Time Squeeze," *HR Magazine,* November 2004, pp 66–70; and "X-Rated," *Training,* p 10.

54 See D Buss, "Spies Like Us," *Training,* December 2001, pp 44–48.

55 See, for example, A Fox, "Caught in the Web," *HR Magazine,* December 2007, pp 35–39; and J McGregor, "A Way to Tell if They're Slaving Away or Surfing," *BusinessWeek,* January 14, 2008, p 56.

56 See B Grow, "The Mind Games Cybercrooks Play," *BusinessWeek,* April 17, 2006, pp 54, 58.

57 Information security is discussed by W S Mossberg, "How to Avoid Cons That Can Lead to Identity Theft," *The Wall Street Journal,* May 1, 2008, p D1; and S H Wildstrom, "Public Wi-Fi: Be Very Paranoid," *BusinessWeek,* March 24, 2008, pp 85–86.

58 Pros and cons of e-mail are discussed in K Byron, "Carrying Too Heavy a Load? The Communication and Miscommunication of Emotion by Email," *Academy of Management Review,* April 2008, pp 309–27; C Graham, "In-Box Overload," *Arizona Republic,* April 16, 2007, p A14; J Saranow, "Deleting the Habit: How Email Junkies Do in Withdrawal," *The Wall Street Journal,* February 14, 2007, pp A1, A18; and A Smith, "Federal Rules Define Duty to Preserve Work E-Mails," *HR Magazine,* January 2007, pp 27, 36.

59 See, for example, S Eldridge, "Sexist E-Mail Backfires," *HR Magazine,* August 2007, pp 103–4; and J S Lublin, "How to Network without Sabotaging Your Own Job Hunt," *The Wall Street Journal,* December 4, 2007, p B1.

60 Mamberto, "Instant Messaging Invades the Office."

61 See descriptions in "Labor Notes: The Boss Is Watching—so Watch Your iPod," *BusinessWeek,* April 24, 2006, p 16; "Podcast Popularity Grows," *Training,* April 2006, p 14; and Weinstein, "Mobility Movement."

62 Excerpted from M Conlin, "Take a Vacation from Your BlackBerry," *BusinessWeek,* December 20, 2004, p 56.

63 See Conlin, "Take a Vacation from Your BlackBerry." Also see A Athavaley, "The New BlackBerry Addicts," *The Wall Street Journal,* January 23, 2007, pp D1–D2; "Can't Disconnect? You Are Not Alone," *HR Magazine,* February 2007, p 14; C Hymowitz, "A Vacationing Boss Should Take a Break; Let Staffers Step Up," *The Wall Street Journal,* August 20, 2007, p B1; and E Simon, "Phantom Vibes," *Arizona Republic,* October 11, 2007, p D3.

64 This statistic was reported in "ITU Corporate Strategy Newslog—Estimated 100 Million Blogs Worldwide in Early 2006," http:www.itu.int/osg/spu/newslog/estimated+100Million+Blogs+Worldwide+In+Early+. . ., January 11, 2007.

65 Cell phone blogging is discussed by "The Son Rises at Qualcomm," *Fortune,* April 18, 2005, p 45.

66 See Alterio, "IBM Taps into Blogosphere."

67 This example is discussed in "Firms Taking Action against Worker Blogs," *MSNBC News,* posted March 7, 2005, www.msnbc.msn.com/id/7116338, accessed March 7, 2005.

68 See J Gordon, "Straight Talk: Wasting Time on the Company Dime," *Training,* May 2006, p 6.

69 Excerpted from J Scheck and B White, "'Telepresence' Is Taking Hold," *The Wall Street Journal,* May 6, 2008, p B6.

70 Results can be found in S A Rains, "Leveling the Organizational Playing Field—Virtually: A Meta-Analysis of Experimental Research Assessing the Impact of Group Support System Use on Member Influence Behaviors," *Communication Research,* April 2005, pp 193–234.

71 See J Forster, "Virtual Call Centers Cyberagents on Rise," *The Arizona Republic,* March 4, 2006, p D3.

72 J Sandberg, "Shared Calendars Mean Never Getting to Fib, 'I'm Booked,'" *The Wall Street Journal,* June 19, 2007, p B1.

73 Challenges associated with virtual operations are discussed by S O'Mahony and S R Barley, "Do Digital Telecommunications Affect Work and Organization? The State of Our Knowledge," in *Research in Organizational Behavior,* vol. 21, eds R I Sutton and B M Staw (Stamford, CT: JAI Press, 1999), pp 125–61.

74 WorldatWork, "Telework Trending Upward, Survey Says," news release, February 8, 2007, www.worldatwork.org.

75 See R S Gajendran and D A Harrison, "The Good, the Bad, and the Unknown About Telecommuting: Meta-Analysis of Psychological Mediators and Individual Consequences," *Journal of Applied Psychology,* November 2007, pp 1524–41.

76 M Conlin, "Telecommuting: Out of Sight, Yes. Out of Mind, No," *BusinessWeek,* February 18, 2008, p 60.

77 Excerpted from "Bulletin Board Suit Tests Online Anonymity," *PC Magazine Online,* January 27, 2008. http://find.galegroup.com.ezproxy.crystallakelibrary.org/itx/start.do?prodId=GRGM>.

## Chapter 13

1 Excerpted from S Hamm, "The Electric Car Acid Test," *BusinessWeek,* February 4, 2008, pp 43–46.

2 See D Kipnis, S M Schmidt, and J Wilkinson, "Intraorganizational Influence Tactics: Explorations in Getting One's Way," *Journal of Applied Psychology,* August 1980, pp 440–52. Also see P Lyons, "A Leadership Development Model to Improve Organizational Competitiveness," *Advances in Competitiveness Research,* 2007, pp 103–15.

3 For more on humor, see C D Cooper, "Just Joking Around? Employee Humor Expression as an Ingratiatory Behavior," *Academy of Management Review,* October 2005, pp 765–76; and T Musbach, "Everyone Wants a Funny Boss," *Yahoo HotJobs: Career Articles,* 2007, http://hotjobs.yahoo.com, accessed October 16, 2007.

4 Based on Table 1 in G Yukl, C M Falbe, and J Y Youn, "Patterns of Influence Behavior for Managers," *Group & Organization Management,* March 1993, pp 5–28. An additional influence tactic is presented in B P Davis and E S Knowles, "A Disrupt-then-Reframe Technique of Social Influence," *Journal of Personality and Social Psychology,* February 1999, pp 192–99.

5 For related reading, see K D Elsbach, "How to Pitch a Brilliant Idea," *Harvard Business Review,* September 2003, pp 117–23.

6 Based on discussion in G Yukl, H Kim, and C M Falbe, "Antecedents of Influence Outcomes," *Journal of Applied Psychology,* June 1996, pp 309–17.

7 See R E Boyatzis, M L Smith, and N Blaize, "Developing Sustainable Leaders through Coaching and Compassion," *Academy of Management Learning and Education,* March 2006, pp 8–24.

8 C Tkaczyk, "Follow These Leaders," *Fortune,* December 12, 2005, p 125.

9 Supportive results can be found in S Hysong, "The Role of Technical Skill in Perceptions of Managerial Performance," *The Journal of Management Development,* 2008, pp 275–90; and R W Kolodinsky, D C F Treadway, and G R Ferris, "Political Skill and Influence Effectiveness: Testing Portions of An Expanded Ferris and Judge (1991) Model," *Human Relations,* December 2007, pp 1747–78. Also see T R Clark, "Engaging the Disengaged," *HR Magazine,* April 2008, pp 109–12.

10 Data from G Yukl and J B Tracey, "Consequences of Influence Tactics Used with Subordinates, Peers, and the Boss," *Journal of Applied Psychology,* August 1992, pp 525–35. Also see C M Falbe and G Yukl, "Consequences for Managers of Using Single Influence Tactics and Combinations of Tactics," *Academy of Management Journal,* August 1992, pp 638–52.

11 Data from Yukl, Kim, and Falbe, "Antecedents of Influence Outcomes."

12 Based on C Pornpitakpan, "The Persuasiveness of Source Credibility: A Critical Review of Five Decades' Evidence," *Journal of Applied Social Psychology,* February 2004, pp 243–81.

13 S A Furst and D M Cable, "Employee Resistance to Organizational Change: Managerial Influence Tactics and Leader-Member Exchange," *Journal of Applied Psychology,* March 2008, pp 453–62.

14 Adapted from R B Cialdini, "Harnessing the Science of Persuasion," *Harvard Business Review,* October 2001, pp 72–79.

15 Ibid, p 77.

16 See A D Wright, "Survey: Nonprofits Fall Short on Ethics," *HR Magazine,* May 2008, p 24; and R. Riney, "Heal Leadership Disorders," *HR Magazine,* May 2008, pp 62–66.

17 D Tjosvold, "The Dynamics of Positive Power," *Training and Development Journal,* June 1984, p 72. Also see T A Stewart, "Get with the New Power Game," *Fortune,* January 13, 1997, pp 58–62.

18 See J Welch and S Welch, "Tough Guys Finish First," *BusinessWeek,* April 24, 2006, p 112; and W B Werther, "From Manager to Executive," *Organizational Dynamics,* no. 2, 2006, pp 196–204.

19 M W McCall Jr, *Power, Influence, and Authority: The Hazards of Carrying a Sword,* Technical Report No. 10 (Greensboro, NC: Center for Creative Leadership, 1978), p 5. For an excellent overview of power, see E P Hollander and L R Offermann, "Power and Leadership in Organizations," *American Psychologist,* February 1990, pp 179–89.

20 B Schlender, "Power 25: 1, Steve Jobs, Chairman and CEO, Apple," *Fortune,* December 10, 2007, pp 116–17.

21 See J R P French and B Raven, "The Bases of Social Power," in *Studies in Social Power,* ed D Cartwright (Ann Arbor: University of Michigan Press, 1959), pp 150–67.

22 G Edmondson, "Power Play at VW," *BusinessWeek,* December 4, 2006, p 45.

23 See S M Farmer and H Aguinis, "Accounting for Subordinate Perceptions of Supervisor Power: An Identity-Dependence Model," *Journal of Applied Psychology,* November 2005, pp 1069–83.

[24] Data from J R Larson, Jr, C Christensen, A S Abbott, and T M Franz, "Diagnosing Groups: Charting the Flow of Information in Medical Decision-Making Teams," *Journal of Personality and Social Psychology,* August 1996, pp 315–30.

[25] J Adamy, "Schultz Takes Over to Try to Perk Up Starbucks," *The Wall Street Journal,* January 8, 2008, pp B1–B2.

[26] "Who Needs the IT Guy Any More?" *ExtremeTech.com,* March 7, 2008, downloaded from General Reference Center Gold, http://find.galegroup.com. Also see N Sivanathan, M M Pillutla, and J K Murnighan, "Power Gained, Power Lost," *Organizational Behavior and Human Decision Processes,* March 2008, pp 135–46.

[27] See D Jones, "Meeting a CEO's Spouse Can Affect Job, in a Good Way, or Bad," *USA Today,* August 29, 2005, pp 1B–2B.

[28] See B Gupta and N K Sharma, "Compliance with Bases of Power and Subordinates' Perception of Superiors: Moderating Effect of Quality of Interaction," *Singapore Management Review,* 2008, pp 1–24; P M Podsakoff and C A Schriesheim, "Field Studies of French and Raven's Bases of Power: Critique, Reanalysis, and Suggestions for Future Research," *Psychological Bulletin,* May 1985, p 388; and C A Schriesheim, T R Hinkin, and P M Podsakoff, "Can Ipsative and Single-Item Measures Produce Erroneous Results in Field Studies of French and Raven's (1950) Five Bases of Power? An Empirical Investigation," *Journal of Applied Psychology,* February 1991, pp 106–14.

[29] See T R Hinkin and C A Schriesheim, "Relationships between Subordinate Perceptions and Supervisor Influence Tactics and Attributed Bases of Supervisory Power," *Human Relations,* March 1990, pp 221–37.

[30] See J A Clair, R DuFresne, N Jackson, and J Ladge, "Being the Bearer of Bad News: Challenges Facing Downsizing Agents in Organizations," *Organizational Dynamics,* no. 2, 2006, pp 131–44; and A Carter, "Curiously Strong Teamwork," *BusinessWeek,* February 26, 2007, pp 90, 92.

[31] K Kranhold, "29: Lorraine Bolsinger, Vice President, General Electric," *The Wall Street Journal,* November 19, 2007, p R9.

[32] See C L Pearce and C C Manz, "The New Silver Bullets of Leadership: The Importance of Self- and Shared Leadership in Knowledge Work," *Organizational Dynamics,* no. 2, 2005, pp 130–40.

[33] W A Randolph and M Sashkin, "Can Organizational Empowerment Work in Multinational Settings?" *Academy of Management Executive,* February 2002, p 104. Also see N R Lockwood, "Leveraging Employee Engagement for Competitive Advantage: HR's Strategic Role," *HR Magazine,* 2007 SHRM Research Quarterly, March 2007, pp 1–12. Also see R C Liden and S Arad, "A Power Perspective of Empowerment and Work Groups: Implications for Human Resources Management Research," in *Research in Personnel and Human Resources Management,* vol. 14, ed G R Ferris (Greenwich, CT: JAI Press, 1996), pp 205–51.

[34] K. Greasley, A Bryman, A Dainty, and A Price, et al., "Understanding Empowerment from An Employee Perspective; What Does It Mean and Do They Want it?" *Team Performance Management,* 2008, pp 39–55. "A Power Perspective of Empowerment and Work Groups"; and G M Spreitzer, "Social Structural Characteristics of Psychological Empowerment," *Academy of Management Journal,* April 1996, pp 483–504.

[35] L Shaper Walters, "A Leader Redefines Management," *Christian Science Monitor,* September 22, 1992, p 14.

[36] See S Zuboff, "Ranking Ourselves to Death," *Fast Company,* November 2004, p 125.

[37] See P C Hemlin, "A Delegate Situation," *Supply Management,* March 13, 2008, p 36; and B. Kenney, "Whatever Happened to Quality," *Industry Week,* April 2008, pp 42–47.

[38] "Creating a 'Magnetic Culture," *Modern Healthcare,* December 3, 2007, downloaded from General Reference Center Gold, http://find.galegroup.com; and R Rayasam, "Equal Exchange Serves Up a Cup of Cooperation," *U.S. News & World Report,* April 24, 2008, http://find.galegroup.com.

[39] For an extended discussion of this model, see M Sashkin, "Participative Management Is an Ethical Imperative," *Organizational Dynamics,* Spring 1984, pp 4–22.

[40] B Kenney, "Continuous Improvement Gets a Green Makeover," *Industry Week,* December 2007, pp 28–32.

[41] See J A Belasco and R C Stayer, "Why Empowerment Doesn't Empower: The Bankruptcy of Current Paradigms," *Business Horizons,* March April 1994, pp 29–41; and W A Randolph, "Re-thinking Empowerment: Why Is It So Hard to Achieve?" *Organizational Dynamics,* Fall 2000, pp 94–107.

[42] B D Cawley, L M Keeping, and P E Levy, "Participation in the Performance Appraisal Process and Employee Reactions: A Meta-Analytic Review of Field Investigations," *Journal of Applied Psychology,* August 1998, pp 615–33; J A Wagner III, C R Leana, E A Locke, and D M Schweiger, "Cognitive and Motivational Frameworks in U.S. Research on Participation: A Meta-Analysis of Primary Effects," *Journal of Organizational Behavior,* 1997, pp 49–65; C D Zatzick and R D Iverson, "High-Involvement Management and Workforce Reduction: Competitive Advantage or Disadvantage?" *Academy of Management Journal,* October 2006, pp 999–1015; and A Srivastava, K M Bartol, and E A Locke, "Empowering Leadership in Management Teams: Effects on Knowledge Sharing, Efficacy, and Performance," *Academy of Management Journal,* December 2006, pp 1239–51.

[43] W A Randolph, "Navigating the Journey to Empowerment," *Organizational Dynamics,* Spring 1995, p 31.

[44] L B MacGregor Serven, *The End of Office Politics as Usual* (New York: American Management Association, 2002), p 5. Also see K J McGregor, "Sweet Revenge: The Power of Retribution, Spite, and Loathing in the World of Business," *BusinessWeek,* January 22, 2007, pp 64–70.

[45] See J Sandberg, "From the Front Lines: Bosses Muster Staffs for Border Skirmishes," *The Wall Street Journal,* February 18, 2004, p B1; K Hannon, "Change the Way You Play: Small Things You Can Do to Get Ahead," *USA Today,* March 15, 2004, p 6B; G R Ferris, S L Davidson, and P L Perrewe, *Political Skill at Work* (Palo Also, CA: Davies-Black, 2005); and G Ferris, S Davidson, and P Perrewe, "Developing Political Skill at Work," *Training,* November 2005, pp 40–45.

[46] R W Allen, D L Madison, L W Porter, P A Renwick, and B T Mayes, "Organizational Politics: Tactics and Characteristics of Its Actors," *California Management Review,* Fall 1979, p 77. A comprehensive overview can be found in K M Kacmar and R A Baron, "Organizational Politics: The State of the Field, Links to Related Processes, and an Agenda for Future Research," in *Research in Personnel and Human Resources Management,* vol. 17, ed G R Ferris (Stamford, CT: JAI Press, 1999), pp 1–39.

[47] See P M Fandt and G R Ferris, "The Management of Information and Impressions: When Employees Behave Opportunistically," *Organizational Behavior and Human Decision Processes,* February 1990, pp 140–58.

[48] First four based on discussion in D R Beeman and T W Sharkey, "The Use and Abuse of Corporate Politics," *Business Horizons,* March–April 1987, pp 26–30.

[49] Quote and data from "The Big Picture: Reasons for Raises," *BusinessWeek,* May 29, 2006, p 11.

[50] A Raia, "Power, Politics, and the Human Resource Professional," *Human Resource Planning,* no. 4, 1985, p 203.

[51] See J S Lublin, "Assigned to a Flop? You Could Wind Up Looking Like a Winner," *The Wall Street Journal,* May 1, 2007, p B1.

[52] A J DuBrin, "Career Maturity, Organizational Rank, and Political Behavioral Tendencies: A Correlational Analysis of Organizational Politics and Career Experience," *Psychological Reports,* October 1988, p 535.

[53] This three-level distinction comes from A T Cobb, "Political Diagnosis: Applications in Organizational Development," *Academy of Management Review,* July 1986, pp 482–96.

[54] An excellent historical and theoretical perspective of coalitions can be found in W B Stevenson, J L Pearce, and L W Porter, "The Concept of 'Coalition' in Organization Theory and Research," *Academy of Management Review,* April 1985, pp 256–68.

[55] See D Kirkpatrick, "Web 2.0 Gets Over Its Goofing-Off Phase," *Fortune,* March 31, 2008, pp 32–34; S H Ibarra and M Hunter, "How Leaders Create and Use Networks," *Harvard Business Review,* January 2007, pp 40–47; and N Anand and J A Conger, "Capabilities of the Consummate Networker," *Organizational Dynamics,* no 1, 2007, pp 13–27.

[56] J Sandberg, "People Can't Resist Doing a Big Favor—or Asking for One," *The Wall Street Journal,* December 18, 2007, http://online.wsj.com.

[57] See D A Buchanan, "You Stab My Back, I'll Stab Yours: Management Experience and Perceptions of Organization Political Behavior," *British Journal of Management,* March 2008, pp 49–64; and Allen, Madison, Porter, Renwick, and Mayes, "Organizational Politics," p 77.

[58] See W L Gardner III, "Lessons in Organizational Dramaturgy: The Art of Impression Management," *Organizational Dynamics,* Summer 1992, pp 33–46.

[59] See G Brown, T B Lawrence, and S L Robinson, "Territoriality in Organizations," *Academy of Management Review,* July 2005, pp 577–94.

[60] A Rao, S M Schmidt, and L H Murray, "Upward Impression Management: Goals, Influence Strategies, and Consequences," *Human Relations,* February 1995, p 147. Also see M C Andrews and K M Kacmar, "Impression Management by Association: Construction and Validation of a Scale," *Journal of Vocational Behavior,* February 2001, pp 142–61.

[61] See N T Nguyen, A Seers, and N S Hartman, "Putting a Good Face on Impression Management: Team Citizenship and Team Satisfaction," *Journal of Behavioral and Applied Management,* January 2008, pp 148–68; K M Kacmar, K J Harris, and B G Nagy, "Further Validation of the Bolino and Turnley Impression Management Scale," *Journal of Behavioral and Applied Management,* September 2007, pp 16–32; and C H V Iddekinge, L A McFarland, and P H Raymark, "Antecedents of Impression Management Use and Effectiveness in a Structured Interview," *Journal of Management,* October 2007, pp 752–73.

[62] S Friedman, "What Do You Really Care About? What Are You Most Interested In?" *Fast Company,* March 1999, p 90. Also see B M DePaulo and D A Kashy, "Everyday Lies in Close and Casual Relationships," *Journal of Personality and Social Psychology,* January 1998, pp 63–79.

[63] See S J Wayne and G R Ferris, "Influence Tactics, Affect, and Exchange Quality in Supervisor-Subordinate Interactions: A Laboratory Experiment and Field Study," *Journal of Applied Psychology,* October 1990, pp 487–99. For another version, see Table 1 (p 246) in S J Wayne and R C Liden, "Effects of Impression Management on Performance Ratings: A Longitudinal Study," *Academy of Management Journal,* February 1995, pp 232–60.

[64] See R A Gordon, "Impact of Ingratiation on Judgments and Evolutions: A Meta-Analytic Investigation," *Journal of Personality and Social Psychology,* July 1996, pp 54–70.

[65] See Y-Y Chen and W Fang, "The Moderating Effect of Impression Management on the Organizational Politics-Performance Relationship," *Journal of Business Ethics,* May 2008, pp 263–77. Also see R Vonk, "The Slime Effect: Suspicion and Dislike of Likeable Behavior toward Superiors," *Journal of Personality and Social Psychology,* April 1998, pp 849–64.

[66] See, for example, D C Treadway, G R Ferris, A B Duke, G L Adams, and J B Thatcher, "The Moderating Role of Subordinate Political Skill on Supervisors' Impressions of Subordinate Ingratiation and Ratings of Subordinate Interpersonal Facilitation," *Journal of Applied Psychology,* May 2007, pp 848–55.

[67] See P Rosenfeld, R A Giacalone, and C A Riordan, "Impression Management Theory and Diversity: Lessons for Organizational Behavior," *American Behavioral Scientist,* March 1994, pp 601–4; and R A Giacalone and J W Beard, "Impression Management, Diversity, and International Management," *American Behavioral Scientist,* March 1994, pp 621–36.

[68] M E Mendenhall and C Wiley, "Strangers in a Strange Land: The Relationship between Expatriate Adjustment and Impression Management," *American Behavioral Scientist,* March 1994, pp 605–20.

[69] For a humorous discussion of making a bad impression, see P Hellman, "Looking BAD," *Management Review,* January 2000, p 64.

[70] T E Becker and S L Martin, "Trying to Look Bad at Work: Methods and Motives for Managing Poor Impressions in Organizations," *Academy of Management Journal,* February 1995, p 191.

[71] Ibid., p 181. Also see S L Grover, "The Truth, the Whole Truth, and Nothing But the Truth: The Causes and Management of Workplace Lying," *Academy of Management Executive,* May 2005, pp 148–57.

[72] Adapted from ibid., pp 180–81.

[73] B K Miller, M A Rutherford, and R W Kolodinsky, "Perceptions of Organizational Politics: A Meta-Analysis of Outcomes," *Journal of Business and Psychology,* March 2008, pp 209–23.

[74] A Zaleznik, "Real Work," *Harvard Business Review* January/February 1989, p 60.

[75] C M Koen Jr, and S M Crow, "Human Relations and Political Skills," *HR Focus,* December 1995, p 11.

[76] As quoted in B Morris, "The GE Mystique," *Fortune,* March 6, 2006, p 98.

[77] B Rose, "Smokers' Health Fee Hazy Issue for Firms," *Chicago Tribune,* April 28, 2008, pp 1–2.

# Chapter 14

[1] Excerpted from B Morris, "The Pepsi Challenge: Can This Snack and Soda Giant Go Healthy?" *Fortune,* March 3, 2008, pp 55–66.

[2] See, for example, B J Avolio, R J Reichard, S T Hannah, F O Walumbwa, and A Chan, "A Meta-Analytic Review of Leadership Impact Research: Experimental and Quasi-Experimental Studies," *Leadership Quarterly* (in press).

[3] See S Lieberson and J F O'Connor, "Leadership and Organizational Performance: A Study of Large Corporations," *American Sociological Review,* April 1972, pp 117–30. Also see M Maremont, "Scholars Link Success of Firms to Lives of CEOs," *The Wall Street Journal,* September 5, 2007, pp A1, A15.

[4] Results can be found in K T Dirks, "Trust in Leadership and Team Performance: Evidence from NCAA Basketball," *Journal of Applied Psychology,* December 2000, pp 1004–12; and D Jacobs and L Singell, "Leadership and Organizational Performance: Isolating Links between Managers and Collective Success," *Social Science Research,* June 1993, pp 165–89.

[5] C A Schriesheim, J M Tolliver, and O C Behling, "Leadership Theory: Some Implications for Managers," *MSU Business Topics,* Summer 1978, p 35.

[6] The different levels of leadership are thoroughly discussed by F J Yammarino, F Dansereau, and C J Kennedy, "A Multiple-Level Multidimensional Approach to Leadership: Viewing Leadership through an Elephant's Eye," *Organizational Dynamics,* 2001, pp 149–62.

[7] B Kellerman, "Leadership Warts and All," *Harvard Business Review,* January 2004, p 45. Also see M G Harvey, M R Buckley, J T Heames, R Zinko, R L Brouer, and G R Ferris, "A Bully as an Archetypal Destructive Leader," *Journal of Leadership and Organizational Studies,* November 2007, pp 117–29.

[8] See D A Kenny and S J Zaccaro, "An Estimate of Variance Due to Traits in Leadership," *Journal of Applied Psychology,* November 1983, pp 678–85.

[9] See J S Phillips and R G Lord, "Schematic Information Processing and Perceptions of Leadership in Problem-Solving Groups," *Journal of Applied Psychology,* August 1982, pp 486–92. Also see B A Ritter and R G Lord, "The Impact of Previous Leaders on the Evaluation of New Leaders: An Alternative to Prototype Matching," *Journal of Applied Psychology,* November 2007, pp 1683–95; C Binkley, "Want to Be CEO? You Have to Dress the Part," *The Wall Street Journal,* January 10, 2008, pp D1, D12; C Binkley, "Women in Power: Finding Balance in the Wardrobe," *The Wall Street Journal,* January 24, 2008, pp D1, D7; and C Hymowitz, "Top Executives Value Advice from a Spouse: Some Won't Ask for It," *The Wall Street Journal,* February 11, 2008, p B1.

[10] M W Dickson, C J Resick, and P J Hanges, "Systemic Variation in Organizationally-Shared Cognitive Prototypes of Effective Leadership Based on Organizational Form," *Leadership Quarterly,* October 2006, pp 487–505.

[11] Results from this study can be found in F C Brodbeck et al., "Cultural Variation of Leadership Prototypes across 22 European Countries," *Journal of Occupational and Organizational Psychology,* March 2000, pp 1–29.

[12] Results can be found in T A Judge, J E Bono, R Ilies, and M W Gerhardt, "Personality and Leadership: A Qualitative and Quantitative Review," *Journal of Applied Psychology,* August 2002, pp 765–80.

[13] See T A Judge, A E Colbert, and R Ilies, "Intelligence and Leadership: A Quantitative Review and Test of Theoretical Propositions," *Journal of Applied Psychology,* June 2004, pp 542–52.

[14] Supportive results can be found in S Xavier, "Are You at the Top of Your Game? Checklist for Effective Leaders," *Journal of Business Strategy,* 2005, pp 35–42. Also see B Fryer, "Timeless Leadership," *Harvard Business Review,* March 2008, pp 45–49 (interview with David McCullough).

[15] Political intelligence is discussed by R M Kramer, "The Great Intimidators," *Harvard Business Review,* February 2006, pp 88–96.

[16] P Elkind, "The Trouble with Steve," *Fortune,* March 17, 2008, downloaded from General Reference Center Gold, http://find.galegroup.com.

[17] D R Ames and F J Flynn, "What Breaks a Leader? The Curvilinear Relationship between Assertiveness and Leadership," *Journal of Personality and Social Psychology,* February 2007, pp 307–24.

[18] Gender and the emergence of leaders was examined by A H Eagly and S J Karau, "Gender and the Emergence of Leaders: A Meta-Analysis," *Journal of Personality and Social Psychology,* May 1991, pp 685–710; and R K Shelly and P T Munroe, "Do Women Engage in Less Task Behavior than Men?" *Sociological Perspectives,* Spring 1999, pp 49–67.

[19] See A H Eagly, S J Karau, and B T Johnson, "Gender and Leadership Style among School Principals: A Meta-Analysis," *Educational Administration Quarterly,* February 1992, pp 76–102.

[20] Supportive findings are contained in J M Twenge, "Changes in Women's Assertiveness in Response to Status and Roles: A Cross-Temporal Meta-Analysis, 1931–1993," *Journal of Personality and Social Psychology,* July 2001, pp 133–45.

[21] For a summary of this research, see R Sharpe, "As Leaders, Women Rule," *BusinessWeek,* November 20, 2000, pp 74–84.

[22] See M Van Vugt, R Hogan, and R B Kaiser, "Leadership, Followership, and Evolution: Some Lessons from the Past," *American Psychologist,* April 2008, pp 182–96. For some examples, see J Welch and S Welch, "Chief Executive Officer-in-Chief," *BusinessWeek,* February 4, 2008, p 88.

[23] The process of preparing a development plan is discussed by L Morgan, G Spreitzer, J Dutton, R Quinn, E Heaphy, and B Barker, "How to Play to Your Strengths," *Harvard Business Review,* January 2005, pp 75–80. Also see M Kets de Vries, "Executive 'Complexes,'" *Organizational Dynamics,* 2007, pp 377–91; C Hymowitz, "Too Many Companies Lack Succession Plans, Wasting Time, Talent," *The Wall Street Journal,* November 26, 2007, p B1; M J Frase, "Smart Selections," *HR Magazine,* December 2007, pp 63–67; and M Weinstein, "Leadership Leader," *Training,* February 2008, pp 41–46.

[24] See, for example, P Hemp, "Where Will We Find Tomorrow's Leaders? A Conversation with Linda A Hill," *Harvard Business Review,* January 2008, pp 124–29; "Gail Holton: Running Show in Small Business," *Arizona Republic,* August 5, 2007, p D5; and "Becky Kuhn: Best Boss Works with the Best People," *Arizona Republic,* August 5, 2007, p D5.

[25] Details on Hasbro's program can be found in A Pomeroy, "Head of the Class," *HR Magazine,* January 2005, pp 54–58. Leadership development is also discussed in D A Ready and J A Conger, "Make Your Company a Talent Factory," *Harvard Business Review,* June 2007, pp 68–77; J L Bower, "Solve the Succession Crisis by Growing Inside–Outside Leaders," *Harvard Business Review,* November 2007, pp 91–96; C Hymowitz, "They Ponder Layoffs, but Executives Still Face Gaps in Talent," *The Wall Street Journal,* January 28, 2008, p B1; S Boehle, "True Vision," *Training,* February 2008, pp 32–39; "Training Top 125," *Training,* February 2008, pp 76–111; N M Davis, "Build Leaders from Within," *HR Magazine,* February 2008, p 10; P Cappelli, "Talent Management for the Twenty-First Century," *Harvard Business Review,* March 2008, pp 74–81; E E Lawler III, "The HR Department: Give It More Respect," *The Wall Street Journal,* March 10, 2008, p R8; "Succession Planning Not Limited to the C-Suite," *HR Magazine,* April 2008, p 16; and H Dolezalek, "We Train to Please," *Training,* April 2008, pp 34–35. Also see R D Arvey, Z Zhang, B J Avolio, and R F Krueger, "Developmental and Genetic Determinants of Leadership Role Occupancy among Women," *Journal of Applied Psychology,* May 2007,

pp 693–706. Also see P Dvorak and J Badal, "This Is Your Brain on the Job," *The Wall Street Journal,* September 20, 2007, http://online.wsj.com.

[26] Results can be found in T A Judge, R F Piccolo, and R Ilies, "The Forgotten Ones? The Validity of Consideration and Initiating Structure in Leadership Research," *Journal of Applied Psychology,* February 2004, pp 36–51. For a description of supportive research, see G Anders, "Tough CEOs Often Most Successful, a Study Finds," *The Wall Street Journal,* November 19, 2007, http://online.wsj.com.

[27] For more on the leader behaviors needed in particular management situations, see P Dvorak, "A Different Animal Seeks the No. 1 Post; Often, It's Not No. 2," *The Wall Street Journal,* October 22, 2007, p B1.

[28] See B M Bass, *Bass & Stogdill's Handbook of Leadership: Theory, Research, and Managerial Applications,* 3rd ed (New York: The Free Press, 1990), chs 20–25.

[29] The relationships between the frequency and mastery of leader behavior and various outcomes were investigated by F Shipper and C S White, "Mastery, Frequency, and Interaction of Managerial Behaviors Relative to Subunit Effectiveness," *Human Relations,* January 1999, pp 49–66.

[30] F E Fiedler, "Job Engineering for Effective Leadership: A New Approach," *Management Review,* September 1977, p 29.

[31] For more on this theory, see F E Fiedler, "A Contingency Model of Leadership Effectiveness," in *Advances in Experimental Social Psychology,* vol. 1, ed L Berkowitz (New York: Academic Press, 1964); and F E Fiedler, *A Theory of Leadership Effectiveness* (New York: McGraw-Hill, 1967).

[32] See L H Peters, D D Hartke, and J T Pohlmann, "Fiedler's Contingency Theory of Leadership: An Application of the Meta-Analyses Procedures of Schmidt and Hunter," *Psychological Bulletin,* March 1985, pp 274–85; and C A Schriesheim, B J Tepper, and L A Tetrault, "Least Preferred Co-Worker Score, Situational Control, and Leadership Effectiveness: A Meta-Analysis of Contingency Model Performance Predictions," *Journal of Applied Psychology,* August 1994, pp 561–73.

[33] D B Peterson, "High Potential, High Risk," *HR Magazine,* March 2008, pp 85–87.

[34] For more detail on this theory, see R J House, "A Path–Goal Theory of Leader Effectiveness," *Administrative Science Quarterly,* September 1971, pp 321–38.

[35] C Hymowitz, "A Vacationing Boss Should Take a Break; Let Staffers Step Up," *The Wall Street Journal,* August 20, 2007, p B1.

[36] This research is summarized by R J House, "Path–Goal Theory of Leadership: Lessons, Legacy, and a Reformulated Theory," *Leadership Quarterly,* Autumn 1996, pp 323–52.

[37] See ibid.

[38] See, for example, R Berner, "Chanel's American in Paris," *BusinessWeek,* January 29, 2007, pp 70–71; J Welch and S Welch, "When to Talk, When to Balk," *BusinessWeek,* April 30, 2007, p 102; and "Lisa Glow: Cross-Collaboration a Key Skill," *Arizona Republic,* August 5, 2007, p D5.

[39] Quoted from pages 22–23 of S Boehle, "Crafting a Coaching Culture," *Training,* May 2007, pp 22–24.

[40] Results can be found in P M Podsakoff, S B MacKenzie, M Ahearne, and W H Bommer, "Searching for a Needle in a Haystack: Trying to Identify the Illusive Moderators of Leadership Behaviors," *Journal of Management,* 1995, pp 422–70. Also see H Liao and M Subramony, "Employee Customer Orientation in Manufacturing Organizations: Joint Influences of Customer Proximity and the Senior Leadership Team," *Journal of Applied Psychology,* March 2008, pp 317–28.

[41] A thorough discussion of this theory is provided by P Hersey and K H Blanchard, *Management of Organizational Behavior: Utilizing Human Resources,* 5th ed (Englewood Cliffs, NJ: Prentice Hall, 1988).

[42] A comparison of the original theory and its latest version is provided by P Hersey and K H Blanchard, "Great Ideas Revisited," *Training & Development,* January 1996, pp 42–47.

[43] See D C Lueder, "Don't Be Misled by LEAD," *Journal of Applied Behavioral Science,* May 1985, pp 143–54; and C L Graeff, "The Situational Leadership Theory: A Critical View," *Academy of Management Review,* April 1983, pp 285–91.

[44] For a complete description of this theory, see B J Bass and B J Avolio, *Revised Manual for the Multi-Factor Leadership Questionnaire* (Palo Alto, CA: Mindgarden, 1997).

[45] For an example of a laissez-faire leader, see K Kelly, "Cayne to Step Down as Bear Stearns CEO," *The Wall Street Journal,* January 8, 2008, pp A1, A18.

[46] A definition and description of transactional leadership is provided by J Antonakis and R J House, "The Full-Range Leadership Theory: The Way Forward," in *Transformational and Charismatic Leadership: The Road Ahead,* ed B J Avolio and F J Yammarino (New York: JAI Press, 2002), pp 3–34. Also see M Gottfredson, S Schaubert, and H Saenz, "The New Leader's Guide to Diagnosing the Business," *Harvard Business Review,* February 2008, pp 63–73. For an example of transactional leadership behavior, see J Nocera, "A C E O Sells the Store," *New York Times,* March 1, 2008, pp B1, B8.

[47] Quoted from page B4 of P Dvorak, "Outsider CEO Translates a New Message in Japan," *The Wall Street Journal,* March 10, 2008, pp B1, B4.

[48] U R Dumdum, K B Lowe, and B J Avolio, "A Meta-Analysis of Transformational and Transactional Leadership Correlates of Effectiveness and Satisfaction: An Update and Extension," in *Transformational and Charismatic Leadership: The Road Ahead,* ed B J Avolio and F J Yammarino (New York: JAI Press, 2002), p 38.

[49] Supportive research is summarized by J Antonakis and R J House, "The Full-Range Leadership Theory: The Way Forward." For an example of the need for transactional leadership, see S Carey and P Prada, "Course Change: Why JetBlue Shuffled Top Rank," *The Wall Street Journal,* May 11, 2007, pp B1–B2.

[50] Dvorak, "Outsider CEO Translates a New Message in Japan," p B4.

[51] Supportive results can be found in R S Rubin, D C Munz, and W H Bommer, "Leading from Within: The Effects of Emotion Recognition and Personality on Transformational Leadership Behavior," *Academy of Management Journal,* October 2005, pp 845–58; and T A Judge and J E Bono, "Five-Factor Model of Personality and Transformational Leadership," *Journal of Applied Psychology,* October 2000, pp 751–65.

[52] These definitions are derived from R Kark, B Shamir, and C Chen, "The Two Faces of Transformational Leadership: Empowerment and Dependency," *Journal of Applied Psychology,* April 2003, pp 246–55.

[53] B Nanus, *Visionary Leadership* (San Francisco: Jossey-Bass, 1992), p 8.

[54] Quoted on page B5 of D Kesmodel, "How 'Chief Beer Taster' Blended Molson, Coors," *The Wall Street Journal,* October 1, 2007, pp B1, B5.

[55] S McCartney, "Virgin Puts Biofuels on Maiden Voyage," *The Wall Street Journal,* February 29, 2008, pp D1, D4.

[56] R Martin, "How Successful Leaders Think," *Harvard Business Review,* June 2007, pp 60–67.

[57] See R Kark, B Shamir, and G Chen, "The Two Faces of Transformational Leadership," *Journal of Applied Psychology,* April 2003, pp 246–55.

[58] Supportive results can be found in W H Bommer, G A Rich, and R S Rubin, "Changing Attitudes about Change: Longitudinal Effects of Transformational Leader Behavior on Employee Cynicism about Organizational Change," *Journal of Organizational Behavior,* November 2005, pp 733–53; B M Bass, B J Avolio, D I Jung, and Y Berson, "Predicting Unit Performance by Assessing Transformational and Transactional Leadership," *Journal of Applied Psychology,* April 2003, pp 207–18; J P Wang and F O Walumbwa, "Family-Friendly Programs, Organizational Commitment, and Work Withdrawal: The Moderating Role of Transformational Leadership," *Personnel Psychology,* Summer 2007, pp 397–427; J E Bono, H J Foldes, G Vinson, and J P Muros, "Workplace Emotions: The Role of Supervision and Leadership," *Journal of Applied Psychology,* September 2007, pp 1357–67; and D M Herold, D B Fedor, S Caldwell, and Y Liu, "The Effects of Transformational and Change Leadership on Employees' Commitment to a Change: A Multilevel Study," *Journal of Applied Psychology,* March 2008, pp 346–57.

[59] Results can be found in U R Dumdum, K B Lowe, and B J Avolio, "A Meta-Analysis of Transformational and Transactional Leadership Correlates of Effectiveness and Satisfaction: An Update and Extension."

[60] J R Detert and E R Burris, "Leadership Behavior and Employee Voice: Is the Door Really Open?" *Academy of Management Journal,* August 2007, pp 869–84.

[61] See K B Lowe, K G Kroeck, and N Sivasubramaniam, "Effectiveness Correlates of Transformational and Transactional Leadership: A Meta-Analytic Review of the MLQ Literature," *Leadership Quarterly,* 1996, pp 385–425. Also see H Liao and A Chuang, "Transforming Service Employees and Climate: A Multilevel, Multisource Examination of Transformational Leadership in Building Long-Term Service Relationships," *Journal of Applied Psychology,* July 2007, pp 1006–19; and J Schaubroeck, S S K Lam, and S E Cha, "Embracing Transformational Leadership: Team Values and the Impact of Leader Behavior on Team Performance," *Journal of Applied Psychology,* July 2007, pp 1020–30.

[62] See A J Towler, "Effects of Charismatic Influence Training on Attitudes, Behavior, and Performance," *Personnel Psychology,* Summer 2003, pp 363–81; and L A DeChurch and M A Marks, "Leadership in Multiteam Systems," *Journal of Applied Psychology,* March 2006, pp 311–29.

[63] These recommendations were derived from J M Howell and B J Avolio, "The Ethics of Charismatic Leadership: Submission or Liberation," *The Executive,* May 1992, pp 43–54.

[64] See F Dansereau, Jr, G Graen, and W Haga, "A Vertical Dyad Linkage Approach to Leadership within Formal Organizations," *Organizational Behavior and Human Performance,* February 1975, pp 46–78; and R M Dienesch and R C Liden, "Leader–Member Exchange Model of Leadership: A Critique and Further Development," *Academy of Management Review,* July 1986, pp 618–34.

[65] These descriptions were taken from D Duchon, S G Green, and T D Taber, "Vertical Dyad Linkage: A Longitudinal Assessment of Antecedents, Measures, and Consequences," *Journal of Applied Psychology,* February 1986, pp 56–60.

[66] S A Furst and D M Cable, "Employee Resistance to Organizational Change: Managerial Influence Tactics and Leader–Member Exchange," *Journal of Applied Psychology,* March 2008, pp 453–62.

[67] Supportive results can be found in T N Bauer, B Erodgan, R C Liden, and S J Wayne, "A Longitudinal Study of the Moderating Role of Extraversion: Leader-Member Exchange, Performance, and Turnover During New Executive Development," *Journal of Applied Psychology,* March 2006, pp 298–310; and C A Schriesheim, S L Castro, and F J Yammarino, "Investigating Contingencies: An Examination of the Impact of Span of Supervision and Upward Controllingness on Leader–Member Exchange Using Traditional and Multivariate within—and between— Entities Analysis," *Journal of Applied Psychology,* October 2000, pp 659–77.

[68] A turnover study was conducted by G B Graen, R C Liden, and W Hoel, "Role of Leadership in the Employee Withdrawal Process," *Journal of Applied Psychology,* December 1982, pp 868–72. The career progress study was conducted by M Wakabayashi and G B Graen, "The Japanese Career Progress Study: A 7-Year Follow-Up," *Journal of Applied Psychology,* November 1984, pp 603–14. Also see B Groysberg, "How Star Women Build Portable Skills," *Harvard Business Review,* February 2008, pp 74–81.

[69] See D O Adebayo and I B Udegbe, "Gender in the Boss-Subordinate Relationship: A Nigerian Study," *Journal of Organizational Behavior,* June 2004, pp 515–25.

[70] Supportive results can be found in B Erdogan, R C Liden, and M L Kraimer, "Justice and Leader-Member Exchange: The Moderating Role of Organizational Culture," *Academy of Management Journal,* April 2006, pp 395–406; K M Kacmar, L A Witt, S Zivnuska, and S M Gully, "The Interactive-Effect of Leader–Member Exchange and Communication Frequency on Performance Ratings," *Journal of Applied Psychology,* August 2003, pp 764–72; and O Epitropaki and R Martin, "From Ideal to Real: A Longitudinal Study of the Role of Implicit Leadership Theories on Leader–Member Exchanges and Employee Outcomes," *Journal of Applied Psychology,* July, 2005, pp 659–76.

[71] These recommendations were derived from G C Mage, "Leading Despite Your Boss," *HR Magazine,* September 2003, pp 139–44. Also

see W Lam, X Huang, and E Snape, "Feedback-Seeking Behavior and Leader-Member Exchange: Do Supervisor-Attributed Motives Matter?" *Academy of Management Journal,* April 2007, pp 348–63.

[72] R J House and R N Aditya, "The Social Scientific Study of Leadership: Quo Vadis?" *Journal of Management,* 1997, p 457.

[73] A thorough discussion of shared leadership is provided by C L Pearce, "The Future of Leadership: Combining Vertical and Shared Leadership to Transform Knowledge Work," *Academy of Management Executive,* February 2004, pp 47–57.

[74] B Reeves, T W Malone, and T O'Driscoll, "Leadership's Online Labs," *Harvard Business Review,* May 2008, pp 59–66.

[75] This research is summarized in B J Avolio, J J Soskik, D I Jung, and Y Berson, "Leadership Models, Methods, and Applications," in *Handbook of Psychology,* ed W C Borman, D R Ilgen, R J Klimoski (Hobohen, NJ: John Wiley & Sons, 2003), vol 12, pp 277–307.

[76] An overall summary of servant-leadership is provided by L C Spears, *Reflections on Leadership: How Robert K Greenleaf's Theory of Servant-Leadership Influenced Today's Top Management Thinkers* (New York: John Wiley & Sons, 1995).

[77] J Stuart, *Fast Company,* September 1999, p 114.

[78] A Pomeroy, "Communication Skills Essential for Leaders," *HR Magazine,* December 2007, p 10.

[79] See J Collins, *Good to Great* (New York: Harper Business, 2001).

[80] J Collins, "Level 5 Leadership: The Triumph of Humility and Fierce Resolve," *Harvard Business Review,* January 2001, p 68.

[81] For a discussion of maturity gained in response to life's losses, see L A King and J A Hicks, "Whatever Happened to 'What Might Have Been'?" *American Psychologist,* October 2007, pp 625–36.

[82] See Collins, *Good to Great.*

[83] V Bauerlein, "13: Amy Woods Brinkley, Global Risk Executive, Bank of America," *The Wall Street Journal,* November 19, 2007, p R4.

[84] The role of followers is discussed in J M Howell and B Shamir, "The Role of Followers in the Charismatic Leadership Process: Relationships and Their Consequences," *Academy of Management Review,* January 2005, pp 96–112; B Kellerman, "Followers Flex Their Muscles," *U.S. News and World Report,* November 19, 2007, p 78; and Van Vugt, Hogan, and Kaiser, "Leadership, Followership, and Evolution."

[85] J C Pastor, M Mayo, and B Shamir, "Adding Fuel to the Fire: The Impact of Followers' Arousal on Ratings of Charisma," *Journal of Applied Psychology,* November 2007, pp 1584–96. For a real-life example, see M Useem, "The Ultimate Trial by Fire," *U.S. News and World Report,* November 19, 2007, p 70.

[86] G Anders, "Management Leaders Turn Attention to Followers," *The Wall Street Journal,* December 24, 2007, p B3.

[87] This point was made in J J Gabarro and J P Kotter, "Managing Your Boss," *Harvard Business Review,* January 2005, pp 92–99.

[88] See L Bossidy, "What Your Leader Expects of You and What You Should Expect in Return," *Harvard Business Review,* April 2007, pp 58–65.

[89] See R Goffee and G Jones, "Followership: It's Personal, Too," *Harvard Business Review,* December 2001, p 148.

[90] Gabarro and Kotter, "Managing Your Boss."

[91] See B George, P Sims, A N McLean, and D Mayer, "Discovering Your Authentic Leadership," *Harvard Business Review,* February 2007, pp 129–38.

[92] The following suggestions were discussed in Gabarro and Kotter, "Managing Your Boss."

## Chapter 15

[1] Excerpted from A Lashinsky, "Can Google Three-Peat?" *Fortune,* January 31, 2008, http://money.cnn.com/2008/01/28/news/companies/google.qa.fortune/index.htm.

[2] C I Barnard, *The Functions of the Executive* (Cambridge, MA: Harvard University Press, 1938), p 73.

[3] Drawn from E H Schein, *Organizational Psychology,* 3rd ed (Englewood Cliffs, NJ: Prentice Hall, 1980), pp 12–15.

[4] For an interesting historical perspective of hierarchy, see P Miller and T O'Leary, "Hierarchies and American Ideals, 1900–1940," *Academy of Management Review,* April 1989, pp 250–65. Also see H J Leavitt, "Why Hierarchies Thrive," *Harvard Business Review,* March 2003, pp 96–102.

[5] For an excellent overview of the span of control concept, see D D Van Fleet and A G Bedeian, "A History of the Span of Management," *Academy of Management Review,* July 1977, pp 356–72.

[6] M Koslowsky, "Staff/Line Distinctions in Job and Organizational Commitment," *Journal of Occupational Psychology,* June 1990, pp 167–73.

[7] For open-systems perspectives, see A Deutschman, "Open Wide: The Traditional Business Organizational Meets Democracy," *Fast Company,* March 2007, pp 40–41; and K M Hmieleski and M D Ensley, "A Contextual Examination of New Venture Performance: Entrepreneur Leadership Behavior, Top Management Team Heterogeneity, and Environmental Dynamism," *Journal of Organizational Behavior,* October 2007, pp 865–89.

[8] For discussion of organizational metaphors, see C Oswick and P Jones, "Beyond Correspondence? Metaphor in Organization Theory," *Academy of Management Review,* April 2006, pp 483–85; and J Cornelissen, "Metaphor in Organization Theory: Progress and the Past," *Academy of Management Review,* April 2006, pp 485–88.

[9] For a management-oriented discussion of general systems theory, see K E Boulding, "General Systems Theory: The Skeleton of Science," *Management Science,* April 1956, pp 197–208.

[10] See L Buchanan, "No More Metaphors," *Harvard Business Review,* March 2005, p 19; and L Prusak, "The Madness of Individuals," *Harvard Business Review,* June 2005, p 22.

[11] The three categories of thinking about organizational design are based on N Anand and R L Daft, "What Is the Right Organization Design?" *Organizational Dynamics,* 2007, pp 329–44.

[12] General Electric Company, "Fact Sheet," Our Company: Our Businesses, GE Web site, www.ge.com, accessed May 22, 2008. Also see M Vella, "Why GE Is Getting Out of the Kitchen," *BusinessWeek,* May 16, 2008, www.businessweek.com.

[13] See A Taylor III, "Can This Car Save Ford?" *Fortune,* May 5, 170–78.

[14] Anand and Daft, "What Is the Right Organization Design?" p 332.

[15] P Lawrence, "Herman Miller's Creative Network," *BusinessWeek,* February 15, 2008, www.businessweek.com (interview with Brian Walker).

[16] M V Copeland, "Boeing's Big Dream," *Fortune,* April 24, 2008, http://money.cnn.com.

[17] Anand and Daft, "What Is the Right Organization Design?" p 338.

[18] D Kiley, "Nokia Starts Listening," *BusinessWeek,* May 5, 2008, p 30.

[19] For updates, see M Goold and A Campbell, "Do You Have a Well-Designed Organization?" *Harvard Business Review,* March 2002, pp 117–24; and J A A Silence, "A Contingency Theory of Rhetorical Congruence," *Academy of Management Review,* July 2005, pp 608–21.

[20] B Elgin, "Running the Tightest Ships on the Net," *BusinessWeek,* January 29, 2001, p 126.

[21] See D A Morand, "The Role of Behavioral Formality and Informality in the Enactment of Bureaucratic versus Organic Organizations," *Academy of Management Review,* October 1995, pp 831–72. Also see F Shipper and C C Manz, "Employee Self-Management without Formally Designated Teams: An Alternative Road to Empowerment," *Organizational Dynamics,* Winter 1992, pp 48–61; and A Deutschman, "The Fabric of Creativity," *Fast Company,* December 2004, pp 54–62.

[22] A Pomeroy, "Passion, Obsession Drive the 'Eileen Fisher Way,'" *HR Magazine,* July 2007, p 55.

[23] T O'Driscoll, "Join the Webvolution," *Training,* February 2008, p 24.

[24] See G P Huber, C C Miller, and W H Glick, "Developing More Encompassing Theories about Organizations: The Centralization-Effectiveness Relationship as an Example," *Organization Science,* no. 1, 1990, pp 11–40; and C Handy, "Balancing Corporate Power: A New Federalist Paper," *Harvard Business Review,* November/December 1992, pp 59–72. Also see A Slywotzky and D Nadler, "The Strategy Is the Structure," *Harvard Business Review,* February 2004, p 16.

[25] J Ewers, "No Ideas? You're Not Alone," *U.S. News & World Report,* June 18, 2007, pp 50–52, quoting from p 51.

[26] P Kaestle, "A New Rationale for Organizational Structure," *Planning Review,* July/August 1990, p 22.

[27] Details of this study can be found in T Burns and G M Stalker, *The Management of Innovation* (London: Tavistock, 1961). Also see W D Sine, H Mitsuhashi, and D A Kirsch, "Revisiting Burns and Stalker: Formal Structure and New Venture Performance in Emerging Economic Sectors," *Academy of Management Journal,* February 2006, pp 121–32; and N Nohria, "Survival of the Adaptive," *Harvard Business Review,* May 2006, p 23.

[28] D J Gillen and S J Carroll, "Relationship of Managerial Ability to Unit Effectiveness in More Organic versus More Mechanistic Departments," *Journal of Management Studies,* November 1985, pp 674–75.

[29] J D Sherman and H L Smith, "The Influence of Organizational Structure on Intrinsic versus Extrinsic Motivation," *Academy of Management Journal,* December 1984, p 883.

[30] See J A Courtright, G T Fairhurst, and L E Rogers, "Interaction Patterns in Organic and Mechanistic Systems," *Academy of Management Journal,* December 1989, pp 773–802.

[31] A Taylor III, "Can This Car Save Ford?" *Fortune,* April 22, 2008, http://money.cnn.com.

[32] P Gumbel, "Big Mac's Local Flavor," *Fortune,* May 2, 2008, http://money.cnn.com.

[33] Procter & Gamble, "Corporate Info: Structure," Careers page of P&G Web site, www.pg.com, accessed May 22, 2008; and Procter & Gamble, "Facts about P&G," 2007, www.pg.com.

[34] Anand and Daft, "What Is the Right Organization Design?" pp 331–33.

[35] Y L Doz and M Kosonen, "The New Deal at the Top," *Harvard Business Review,* June 2007, pp 98–104; and E White, "Art of Persuasion Becomes Key," *The Wall Street Journal,* May 19, 2008, http://onlines.wsj.com.

[36] A Hesseldahl, "BlackBerry: Innovation behind the Icon," *BusinessWeek,* April 4, 2008, www.businessweek.com.

[37] Anand and Daft, "What Is the Right Organization Design?" pp 333–40.

[38] M Kripalani, "Inside the Tata Nano Factory," *BusinessWeek,* May 9, 2008, www.businessweek.com.

[39] J Holland, "Innovative Outsourcing Model Saves Company Millions," *Industry Week,* April 25, 2007, www.industryweek.com.

[40] Copeland, "Boeing's Big Dream."

[41] A MacCormack and T Forbath, "Learning the Fine Art of Global Collaboration," *Harvard Business Review,* January 2008, pp 24, 26.

[42] K Cameron, "Critical Questions in Assessing Organizational Effectiveness," *Organizational Dynamics,* Autumn 1980, p 70.

[43] See G H Seijts, G P Latham, K Tasa, and B W Latham, "Goal Setting and Goal Orientation: An Integration of Two Different yet Related Literatures," *Academy of Management Journal,* April 2004, pp 227–39.

[44] For discussion of a very goal-oriented company, see "What Makes GE Great?" *Fortune,* March 6, 2006, pp 90–96.

[45] See, for example, R O Brinkerhoff and D E Dressler, *Productivity Measurement: A Guide for Managers and Evaluators* (Newbury Park, CA: Sage Publications, 1990).

[46] See S Baker, "Wiser about the Web," *BusinessWeek,* March 27, 2006, pp 54–58.

[47] G Colvin, "Xerox's Inventor-in-Chief," *Fortune,* June 27, 2007, http://money.cnn.com.

[48] J L Lunsford, "Boeing Scrambles to Repair Problems with New Plane," *The Wall Street Journal,* December 7, 2007, http://online.wsj.com.

[49] "Interview: M Scott Peck," *Business Ethics,* March/April 1994, p 17. Also see C B Gibson and J Birkinshaw, "The Antecedents, Consequences, and Mediating Role of Organizational Ambidexterity," *Academy of Management Journal,* April 2004, pp 209–26.

[50] R Zeidner, "Working at AMX Is 'Like Going to a Friend's House,'" *HR Magazine,* July 2007, p 56.

[51] Cameron, "Critical Questions in Assessing Organizational Effectiveness," p 67. Also see W Buxton, "Growth from Top to Bottom," *Management Review,* July/August 1999, p 11.

[52] See R K Mitchell, B R Agle, and D J Wood, "Toward a Theory of Stakeholder Identification and Salience: Defining the Principle of Who and What Really Counts," *Academy of Management Review,* October 1997, pp 853–96; T J Rowley and M Moldoveanu, "When Will Stakeholder Groups Act? An Interest- and Identity-Based Model of Stakeholder Group Mobilization," *Academy of Management Review,* April 2003, pp 204–19.

[53] See A L Kalleberg, "The Mismatched Worker: When People Don't Fit Their Jobs," *Academy of Management Perspectives,* February 2008, pp 24–40.

[54] See J Welch and S Welch, "How Healthy Is Your Company?" *BusinessWeek,* May 8, 2006, p 126.

[55] P Dvorak, "How Irdeto Split Headquarters," *The Wall Street Journal,* January 7, 2008, p B3.

[56] K S Cameron, "Effectiveness as Paradox: Consensus and Conflict in Conceptions of Organizational Effectiveness," *Management Science,* May 1986, p 542.

[57] Alternative effectiveness criteria are discussed in ibid.; A G Bedeian, "Organization Theory: Current Controversies, Issues, and Directions," in *International Review of Industrial and Organizational Psychology,* eds C L Cooper and I T Robertson (New York: John Wiley & Sons, 1987), pp 1–33.

[58] See "Electronic Monitoring & Surveillance Survey: Employers Get Serious About Fighting E-Mail & Internet Abuse," *Wireless News,* March 4, 2008, NA. General Refence Center.

[59] Ibid.

[60] F Norton, "Every E-Mail You Send, Every Time You Click. . .: . . .The Boss Might Be Watching You: Count on It," *News & Observer,* March 28, 2008, http://find.galegroup.com.ezproxy.crystallakelibrary.org/itx/p.

[61] Ibid.

# Chapter 16

[1] Excerpted from S Berfield, "After the Layoff, the Redesign," *BusinessWeek,* April 14, 2008, pp 54, 56.

[2] See, for example, M Fugate, A J Kinicki, and G E Prussia, "Employee Coping with Organizational Change: An Examination of Alternative Theoretical Perspectives and Models," *Personnel Psychology,* Spring 2008, pp 1–36.

[3] A M Webber, "Learning for a Change," *Fast Company,* May 1999, p 180.

[4] Society for Human Resource Management, "Change Management: The HR Strategic Imperative as a Business Partner," *SHRM Research Quarterly,* Fourth Quarter 2007, pp 1–9.

[5] D Welch, "What Could Dull Toyota's Edge," *BusinessWeek,* April 28, 2008, p 38.

[6] S E Ante, "The iSommelier Will Take Your Order," *BusinessWeek,* February 25, 2008, p 72.

[7] See, for example, N Casey, "As Barbie Sales Fall, Mattel Looks to Simplify Its Iconic Line," *The Wall Street Journal,* April 22, 2008, p B3. Also see C Hymowitz, "CEOs Are Spending More Quality Time with Their Customers," *The Wall Street Journal,* May 14, 2007, p B1.

[8] M E Porter and F L Reinhardt, "A Strategic Approach to Climate," *Harvard Business Review,* October 2007, pp 22–23, 26; M Conlin, "Suddenly, It's Cool to Take the Bus," *BusinessWeek,* May 5, 2008, p 24; B Kenney, "Continuous Improvement Gets a Green Makeover," *Industry Week,* December 2007, pp 28–32; M Weinstein, "It's Not Easy Being Green," *Training,* April 2008, pp 20–25; D C Esty, "What Stakeholders Demand," *Harvard Business Review,* October 2007, pp 30, 34; and A J Hoffman, "If You're Not at the Table, You're on the Menu," *Harvard Business Review,* October 2007, pp 34–35. Also see B McKay, "Message in the Drink Bottle: Recycle," *The Wall Street Journal,* August 30, 2007, pp B1, B6.

[9] Quoted from p 44 of F L Reinhardt, "Place Your Bets on the Future You Want," *Harvard Business Review,* October 2007, pp 42, 44. Also see J Carey, "Lighting a Fire under Global Warming," *BusinessWeek,* April 16, 2007, p 33.

[10] See M Gottfredson, S Schaubert, and H Saenz, "The New Leader's Guide to Diagnosing the Business," *Harvard Business Review,* February 2008, pp 63–73. For an example of these pressures, see N Byrnes and P Burrows, "Where Dell Went Wrong," *BusinessWeek,* February 19, 2007, pp 62–63.

[11] J Adamy, "How Jim Skinner Flipped McDonald's," *The Wall Street Journal,* January 5, 2007, pp B1–B2.

[12] J Kirby and T A Steward, "The Institutional Yes," *Harvard Business Review,* October 2007, pp 75–82 (interview with Jeff Bezos).

[13] For an example, see D A Plowman, L T Baker, T E Beck, M Kulkarni, S T Solansky, and D V Travis, "Radical Change Accidentally: The Emergence and Amplification of Small Change," *Academy of Management Journal,* June 2007, pp 515–43.

[14] For a thorough discussion of the model, see K Lewin, *Field Theory in Social Science* (New York: Harper & Row, 1951).

[15] J Adamy, "Schultz's Second Act Jolts Starbucks," *The Wall Street Journal,* May 19, 2008, http://online.wsj.com.

[16] C Goldwasser, "Benchmarking: People Make the Process," *Management Review,* June 1995, p 40.

[17] See T A Stewart, "Architects of Change," *Harvard Business Review,* April 2006, p 10.

[18] A thorough discussion of the target elements of change can be found in M Beer and B Spector, "Organizational Diagnosis: Its Role in Organizational Learning," *Journal of Counseling & Development,* July/August 1993, pp 642–50.

[19] D Kesmodel, "How 'Chief Beer Taster' Blended Molson, Coors," *The Wall Street Journal,* October 1, 2007, pp B1, B5.

[20] These errors are discussed by J P Kotter, "Leading Change: The Eight Steps to Transformation," in *The Leader's Change Handbook,* ed J A Conger, G M Spreitzer, and E E Lawler III (San Francisco: Jossey-Bass, 1999), pp 87–99.

[21] F Ostroff, "Change Management in Government," *Harvard Business Review,* May 2006, pp 141–47.

[22] B McKay, "2: Indra Nooyi, Chairman and Chief Executive, PepsiCo," *The Wall Street Journal,* November 19, 2007, p R3.

[23] P G Hanson and B Lubin, "Answers to Questions Frequently Asked about Organization Development," in *The Emerging Practice of Organization Development,* ed W Sikes, A Drexter, and J Grant (Alexandria, VA: NTL Institute, 1989), p 16; and Society for Human Resource Management, "Organization Development: A Strategic HR Tool," *Research Quarterly,* Third Quarter 2007, pp 1–9.

[24] Different stage-based models of OD are discussed by R A Gallagher, "What Is OD?" www.orgdct.com/what_is_od.htm, accessed May 12, 2005.

[25] The stages of OD are discussed by R Cacioppe and M Edwards, "Seeking the Holy Grail of Organizational Development: A Synthesis of Integral Theory, Spiral Dynamics, Corporate Transformation and Action Inquiry," *Leadership and Organization Development Journal,* no. 2, 2005, pp 86–105.

[26] W W Burke, *Organization Development: A Normative View* (Reading, MA: Addison-Wesley, 1987), p 9.

[27] See R Rodgers, J E Hunter, and D L Rogers, "Influence of Top Management Commitment on Management Program Success," *Journal of Applied Psychology,* February 1993, pp 151–55.

[28] Results can be found in P J Robertson, D R Roberts, and J I Porras, "Dynamics of Planned Organizational Change: Assessing Empirical Support for a Theoretical Model," *Academy of Management Journal,* June 1993, pp 619–34.

[29] Results from the meta-analysis can be found in G A Neuman, J E Edwards, and N S Raju, "Organizational Development Interventions: A Meta-Analysis of Their Effects on Satisfaction and Other Attitudes," *Personnel Psychology,* Autumn 1989, pp 461–90.

[30] Results can be found in C-M Lau and H-Y Ngo, "Organization Development and Firm Performance: A Comparison of Multinational and Local Firms," *Journal of International Business Studies,* First Quarter 2001, pp 95–114.

[31] See N Orkin, "Focus on Japan," *Training,* February 2008, p 30.

[32] S Meisinger, "Change Management and HR's Role," *HR Magazine,* March 2008, p 8.

[33] Adapted in part from J D Ford, L W Ford, and A D'Amelio, "Resistance to Change: The Rest of the Story," *Academy of Management Review,* April 2008, pp 362–77; and A S Judson, *Changing Behavior in Organizations: Minimizing Resistance to Change* (Cambridge, MA: Blackwell, 1991).

[34] An individual's predisposition to change was investigated by C R Wanberg and J T Banas, "Predictors and Outcomes of Openness to Changes in a Reorganizing Workplace," *Journal of Applied Psychology,* February 2000, pp 132–42; and D M Herold, D B Fedor, and S D Caldwell, "Beyond Change Management: A Multilevel Investigation of Contextual and Personal Influences on Employees' Commitment to Change," *Journal of Applied Psychology,* July 2007, pp 942–51.

[35] G Chon, K Maher, and C Dade, "On Plant Assembly Lines and at Kitchen Tables, Worry about the Future," *The Wall Street Journal,* March 23, 2006, p A1.

[36] L Goering, "Land of Plenty No Longer," *Chicago Tribune,* May 20, 2008, sec 1, p 8.

[37] Readiness for change is discussed by S R Madsen, "Wellness in the Workplace: Preparing Employees for Change," *Organization Development Journal,* Spring 2003, pp 46–56.

[38] S D Salamon and S L Robinson, "Trust That Binds: The Impact of Collective Felt Trust on Organizational Performance," *Journal of Applied Psychology,* May 2008, pp 593–601.

[39] See D B Fedor, S Caldwell, and D M Herold, "The Effects of Organizational Changes on Employee Commitment: A Multilevel Investigation," *Personnel Psychology,* Spring 2006, pp 1–29.

[40] L Herscovitch and J P Meyer, "Commitment to Organizational Change: Extension of a Three-Component Model," *Journal of Applied Psychology,* June 2003, p 475.

[41] D M Herold, D B Fedor, S Caldwell, and Y Liu, "The Effects of Transformational and Change Leadership on Employees' Commitment to a Change: A Multilevel Study," *Journal of Applied Psychology,* March 2008, pp 346–57.

[42] Herold, Fedor, and Caldwell, "Beyond Change Management."

[43] A Johnson, "40: Toni Hoover, Senior Vice President, Pfizer," *The Wall Street Journal,* November 19, 2007, p R10.

[44] See R Charan, "Home Depot's Blueprint for Culture Change," *Harvard Business Review,* April 2006, pp 61–70; and N H Woodward, "To Make Changes, Manage Them," *HR Magazine,* May 2007, pp 63–67.

[45] Ford, Ford, and D'Amelio, "Resistance to Change."

[46] S A Furst and D M Cable, "Employee *Resistance* to Organizational Change: Managerial Influence Tactics and Leader–Member Exchange," *Journal of Applied Psychology,* March 2008, pp 453–62.

[47] S Reynolds Fisher and M A White, "Downsizing in a Learning Organization: Are There Hidden Costs?" *Academy of Management Review,* January 2000, p 245.

[48] R M Fulmer and J B Keys, "A Conversation with Peter Senge: New Development in Organizational Learning," *Organizational Dynamics,* Autumn 1998, p 35. Also see D A Garvin, A C Edmondson, and F Gino, "Is Yours a Learning Organization?" *Harvard Business Review,* March 2008, pp 109–17.

[49] A J DiBella, E C Nevis, and J M Gould, "Organizational Learning Style as a Core Capability," in *Organizational Learning and Competitive Advantage,* eds B Moingeon and A Edmondson (Thousand Oaks, CA: Sage, 1996), pp 41–42.

[50] D A Garvin, A C Edmondson, and F Gino, "Is Yours a Learning Organization?" *Harvard Business Review,* March 2008, pp 109–16, quoting p 110.

[51] The impact of organizational culture on organizational learning was demonstrated by A Jashapara, "Cognition, Culture and Competition: An Empirical Test of the Learning Organization," *The Learning Organization,* 2003, pp 31–50.

[52] S Boehle, "Core Alignment," *Training,* March 2007, pp 30–38.

[53] This discussion and definitions are based on D Miller, "A Preliminary Typology of Organizational Learning: Synthesizing the Literature," *Journal of Management,* 1996, pp 485–505.

[54] The role of leadership in organizational learning is thoroughly discussed by D Vera and M Crossan, "Strategic Leadership and Organizational Learning," *Academy of Management Review,* April 2004, pp 222–40.

[55] This discussion is based in part on D Ulrich, T Jick, and M Von Glinow, "High-Impact Learning: Building and Diffusing Learning Capability," *Organizational Dynamics,* Autumn 1993, pp 52–66.

[56] See J W Lorsch and T J Tierney, *Aligning the Stars: Organizing Professionals to Win* (Boston, MA: Harvard Business School Press, 2002).

[57] The creation of learning infrastructure is discussed by C R James, "Designing Learning Organizations," *Organizational Dynamics,* 2003, pp 46–61.

[58] See J B Quinn, "Leveraging Intellect," *Academy of Management Executive,* November 2005, pp 78–94; and M T Hansen, M L Mors, and B Lovås, "Knowledge Sharing in Organizations: Multiple Networks, Multiple Phases," *Academy of Management Journal,* October 2005, pp 776–93.

[59] See the related discussion in D Lei, J W Slocum, and R A Pitts, "Designing Organizations for Competitive Advantage: The Power of Unlearning and Learning," *Organizational Dynamics,* Winter 1999, pp 24–38. An example is provided by A Taylor III, "Can This Car Save Ford?" *Fortune,* May 5, 2008, pp 170–78.

[60] This case was based on material contained in E Frauenheim, "Culture Crash: Lost in the Shuffle," *Workforce Management,* January 14, 2008, pp 1, 12–17.

## PART ONE

Page 1 © Royalty-Free/CORBIS

## Chapter 1

Page 3 © Michael Probst/AP Photo
Page 9 Property of AT&T. Reprinted with permission of AT&T.
Page 15 © Joe Raedle/Getty Images
Page 16 © Justin Sullivan/Getty Images
Page 26 © Scott Olson/Getty Images
Page 27 © Keith Meyers/The New York Times/Redux Pictures
Page 28 © Huang Shengang, Xinhua/AP Photo
Page 32 Photo by Jamie Gaffney

## Chapter 2

Page 35 © Spencer Platt/Getty Images
Page 39 © Daniel Acker/Bloomberg News/Landov
Page 41 Courtesy of Southwest Airlines
Page 46 © Lynsey Addario/CORBIS
Page 50 © Diedra Laird Charlotte Observer/AP Photo

## Chapter 3

Page 61 © Aijaz Rahi/AP Photo
Page 65 © Tom Maruko/epa/CORBIS
Page 68 © David Butow/Redux Pictures
Page 69 © Tengku Bahar/AFP/Getty Images
Page 79 © Jim Watson/AFP/Getty Images

## PART TWO

Page 83 © RubberBall Productions

## Chapter 4

Page 85 © Syracuse Newspapers/Gary Walts/The Image Works

Page 89 © Thierry Charlier/AP Photo
Page 92 © Ryan McVay/Getty Images
Page 99 © Shannon Staphleton/Reuters/Landov
Page 102 © Larry Busacca/WireImage/Getty Images

## Chapter 5

Page 115 Photograph by Adrian Pantea
Page 117 © Brian Park Photography
Page 119 © Damian Dovarganes/AP Photo
Page 126 Copyright 2006, USA Today. Reprinted with permission
Page 130 © Kevin P. Casey/The New York Times/Redux Pictures

## Chapter 6

Page 143 © PhotoDisc/Alamy
Page 147 © Chris Weeks/WireImage/Getty Images
Page 149 © Michael Lewis
Page 153 © Windsor Star-Dan Janisse
Page 161 Courtesy of The Methodist Hospital, Houston TX

## Chapter 7

Page 173 © Ann Summa/Time Life Pictures/Getty Images
Page 177 © Bob Daemmrich/The Image Works
Page 184 © John Zich/Bloomberg News/Landov
Page 187 © Elise Amendola /AP Photo
Page 190 © AP Photo

## Chapter 8

Page 199 © Ture Lillegraven/CORBIS Outline
Page 206 © Jim Callaway Photography
Page 209 © George Widman/AP Photo
Page 212 Courtesy of Robert Kreitner
Page 214 © PhotoLink/ Getty Images

## PART THREE

Page 221 © PhotoLink/Getty Images

## Chapter 9

Page 223 Courtesy of ICU Medical, Inc.
Page 225 © Harry Cabluck/AP Photo
Page 229 © Brent Smith/Reuters/CORBIS
Page 234 Courtesy of Seagate
Page 239 Photo by Getty Images for Nike

## Chapter 10

Page 247 © Justin Sullivan/Getty Images
Page 249 © Rommel Pecson/The Image Works
Page 253 © Ryan McVay/Getty Images
Page 258 © Donald C. Johnson/CORBIS
Page 270 © Keith Brofsky/Getty Images

## Chapter 11

Page 275 © David J. Green—lifestyle themes/Alamy
Page 277 © Ed Young/CORBIS
Page 278 © Steve Cole/Getty Images
Page 280 Copyright 2008, USA Today. Reprinted with permission
Page 284 © STR/AFP/Getty Images
Page 288 Courtesy of IRS

## PART FOUR

Page 295 © Royalty-Free/CORBIS

## Chapter 12

Page 297 Chris Vultaggio Studios, Inc.
Page 299 © PhotoDisc/Getty Images
Page 306 © Laurent Rebours/AP Photo
Page 311 © John A. Rizzo/Getty Images
Page 313 © Najlah Feanny/CORBIS
Page 318 Courtesy: Hewlett-Packard Company

## Chapter 13

Page 325 © Gil Cohen Magen/Reuters/CORBIS
Page 327 © David Kohl/AP Photo
Page 330 © vario images GmbH & Co.KG/Alamy
Page 335 © Mathew Imaging/FilmMagic/Getty Images
Page 338 © Yunghi Kim/Contact Press Images

## Chapter 14

Page 345 © Neville Elder/CORBIS
Page 348 © Ethan Miller/Getty Images
Page 356 © Henny Ray Abrams/Reuters/Landov
Page 358 Courtesy of Fuji Fire and Marine Insurance Co., Ltd.
Page 368 © Kim Kulish/CORBIS

## PART FIVE

Page 375 © Cartesia/PhotoDisc/Getty Images

## Chapter 15

Page 377 © R. Magunia/Joker/SV-Bilderdienst/The Image Works
Page 385 © Nokia 2008
Page 390 © Saurabh Das, CP/AP Photo
Page 391 © Erik Freeland/CORBIS
Page 393 Courtesy of Southwest Airlines

## Chapter 16

Page 399 © Daniel Mirer/CORBIS
Page 401 The McGraw-Hill Companies, Inc./Lars A. Niki, photographer
Page 402 © Najlah Feanny/CORBIS
Page 407 © Richard Levine/Alamy
Page 419 Mind Tree Consulting

**ability**   Stable characteristic responsible for a person's maximum physical or mental performance.

**adhocracy culture**   A culture that has an external focus and values flexibility.

**added-value negotiation (AVN)**   Co-operatively developing multiple-deal packages while building a long-term relationship.

**affective component**   The feelings or emotions one has about an object or situation.

**affirmative action**   Focuses on achieving equality of opportunity in an organization.

**aggressive style**   Expressive and self-enhancing, but takes unfair advantage of others.

**alternative dispute resolution (ADR)**   Avoiding costly lawsuits by resolving conflicts informally or through mediation or arbitration.

**analytics**   A conscientious and explicit process of making decisions on the basis of the best available evidence.

**anticipatory socialization**   Occurs before an individual joins an organization, and involves the information people learn about different careers, occupations, professions, and organizations.

**assertive style**   Expressive and self-enhancing, but does not take advantage of others.

**attention**   Being consciously aware of something or someone.

**attitude**   Learned predisposition toward a given object.

**behavioral component**   How one intends to act or behave toward someone or something.

**benchmarking**   Process by which a company compares its performance with that of high-performing organizations.

**blog**   Online journal in which people comment on any topic.

**bounded rationality**   Constraints that restrict decision making.

**brainstorming**   Process to generate a quantity of ideas.

**case study**   In-depth study of a single person, group, or organization.

**causal attributions**   Suspected or inferred causes of behavior.

**centralized decision making**   Top managers make all key decisions.

**change and acquisition**   Requires employees to master tasks and roles and to adjust to work group values and norms.

**clan culture**   A culture that has an internal focus and values flexibility rather than stability and control.

**closed system**   A relatively self-sufficient entity.

**coalition**   Temporary groupings of people who actively pursue a single issue.

**coercive power**   Obtaining compliance through threatened or actual punishment.

**cognitions**   A person's knowledge, opinions, or beliefs.

**cognitive categories**   Mental depositories for storing information.

**cognitive component**   The beliefs or ideas one has about an object or situation.

**cognitive dissonance**   Psychological discomfort experienced when attitudes and behavior are inconsistent.

**collectivist culture**   Personal goals less important than community goals and interests.

**commitment to change**   A mind-set of doing whatever it takes to effectively implement change.

**communication**   Interpersonal exchange of information and understanding.

**communication competence**   Ability to effectively use communication behaviors in a given context.

**competing values framework**   A framework for categorizing organizational culture.

**conflict**   One party perceives its interests are being opposed or set back by another party.

**consensus**   Presenting opinions and gaining agreement to support a decision.

**consideration**   Creating mutual respect and trust with followers.

**contingency approach**   Using management tools and techniques in a situationally appropriate manner; avoiding the one-best-way mentality.

**contingency approach to organization design**   Creating an effective organization–environment fit.

**contingency factors**   Variables that influence the appropriateness of a leadership style.

**core job characteristics**   Job characteristics found to various degrees in all jobs.

**counterproductive work behaviors (CWBs)**   Types of behavior that harm employees and the organization as a whole.

**creativity**   Process of developing something new or unique.

**cross-cultural training**   Structured experiences to help people adjust to a new culture/country.

**cross-functionalism**   Team made up of technical specialists from different areas.

**cultural intelligence**   The ability to interpret ambiguous cross-cultural situations accurately.

**culture shock**   Anxiety and doubt caused by an overload of new expectations and cues.

**decentralized decision making**   Lower-level managers are empowered to make important decisions.

**decision making**   Identifying and choosing solutions that lead to a desired end result.

**decisiontree**   Graphical representation of process underlying decision making.

**decision-making style**   A combination of how individuals perceive and respond to information.

**delphi technique**   Process to generate ideas from physically dispersed experts.

**developmental relationship strength**   The quality of relationships among people in a network.

**devil's advocacy**   Assigning someone the role of critic.

**dialectic method**   Fostering a debate of opposing viewpoints to better understand an issue.

**discrimination**   Occurs when employment decisions are based on factors that are not job related.

**distributive justice**   The perceived fairness of how resources and rewards are distributed.

**diversity**   The host of individual differences that make people different from and similar to each other.

**diversity of developmental relationships**   The variety of people in a network used for developmental assistance.

**dysfunctional conflict**   Threatens organization's interests.

**e-business**   Running the *entire* business via the Internet.

**emotional intelligence**   Ability to manage oneself and interact with others in mature and constructive ways.

**emotions**   Complex human reactions to personal achievements and setbacks that may be felt and displayed.

**empowerment**   Sharing varying degrees of power with lower-level employees to better serve the customer.

**enacted values**   The values and norms that are exhibited by employees.

**encounter phase**   Employees learn what the organization is really like and reconcile unmet expectations.

**equity sensitivity**   An individual's tolerance for negative and positive equity.

**equity theory**   Holds that motivation is a function of fairness in social exchanges.

**espoused values**   The stated values and norms that are preferred by an organization.

**ethics**   Study of moral issues and choices.

**ethnocentrism**   Belief that one's native country, culture, language, and behavior are superior.

**expatriate**   Anyone living or working in a foreign country.

**expectancy**   Belief that effort leads to a specific level of performance.

**expectancy theory**   Holds that people are motivated to behave in ways that produce valued outcomes.

**expert power**   Obtaining compliance through one's knowledge or information.

**explicit knowledge**   Information that can be easily put into words and shared with others.

**external factors**   Environmental characteristics that cause behavior.

**external forces for change**   Originate outside the organization.

**external locus of control**   Attributing outcomes to circumstances beyond one's control.

**extinction**   Making behavior occur less often by ignoring or not reinforcing it.

**extranet**   Connects internal employees with selected customers, suppliers, and strategic partners.

**extrinsic motivation**   Motivation caused by the desire to attain specific outcomes.

**extrinsic rewards**   Financial, material, or social rewards from the environment.

**feedback**   Objective information about performance.

**field study**   Examination of variables in real-life settings.

**formal group**   Formed by the organization.

**functional conflict**   Serves organization's interests.

**fundamental attribution bias**   Ignoring environmental factors that affect behavior.

**garbage can model**   Holds that decision making is sloppy and haphazard.

**glass ceiling**   Invisible barrier blocking women and minorities from top management positions.

**goal**   What an individual is trying to accomplish.

**goal commitment**   Amount of commitment to achieving a goal.

**goal difficulty**   The amount of effort required to meet a goal.

**goal specificity**   Quantifiability of a goal.

**group**   Two or more freely interacting people with shared norms and goals and a common identity.

**group cohesiveness**   A "we feeling" binding group members together.

**group support systems (GSSs)**   Using computer software and hardware to help people work better together.

**groupthink**   Janis's term for a cohesive in-group's unwillingness to realistically view alternatives.

**hierarchy culture**   A culture that has an internal focus and values stability and control over flexibility.

**high-context cultures**   Primary meaning derived from nonverbal situational cues.

**human capital**   The productive potential of one's knowledge and actions.

**humility**   Considering the contributions of others and good fortune when gauging one's success.

**hygiene factors**   Job characteristics associated with job dissatisfaction.

**impression management**   Getting others to see us in a certain manner.

**individualistic culture**   Primary emphasis on personal freedom and choice.

**informal group**   Formed by friends.

**in-group exchange**   A partnership characterized by mutual trust, respect, and liking.

**initiating structure**   Organizing and defining what group members should be doing.

**instrumentality**   A performance → outcome perception.

**intelligence**   Capacity for constructive thinking, reasoning, problem solving.

**interactional justice**   The perceived fairness of the decision maker's behavior in the process of decision making.

**intermittent reinforcement**   Reinforcing some but not all instances of behavior.

**internal factors**   Personal characteristics that cause behavior.

**internal forces for change**   Originate inside the organization.

**internal locus of control**   Attributing outcomes to one's own actions.

**Internet**   The global system of networked computers.

**intranet**   An organization's private Internet.

**intrinsic motivation**   Motivation caused by positive internal feelings.

**intrinsic rewards**   Self-granted, psychic rewards.

**intuition**   Capacity for attaining knowledge or understanding without rational thought or logic.

**jargon**   Language or terminology that is specific to a particular profession, group, or organization.

**job design**   Changing the content and/or process of a specific job to increase job satisfaction and performance.

**job enlargement**   Putting more variety into a job.

**job enrichment**   Building achievement, recognition, stimulating work, responsibility, and advancement into a job.

**job rotation**   Moving employees from one specialized job to another.

**job satisfaction**   An affective or emotional response to one's job.

**judgmental heuristics**   Rules of thumb or shortcuts that people use to reduce information-processing demands.

**knowledge management (KM)**   Implementing systems and practices that increase the sharing of knowledge and information throughout an organization.

**laboratory study**   Manipulation and measurement of variables in contrived situations.

**law of effect**   Behavior with favorable consequences is repeated; behavior with unfavorable consequences disappears.

**leadership**   Influencing employees to voluntarily pursue organizational goals.

**leadership prototype**   Mental representation of the traits and behaviors possessed by leaders.

**leader trait**   Personal characteristics that differentiate leaders from followers.

**learned helplessness**   Debilitating lack of faith in one's ability to control the situation.

**learning capabilities**   The set of core competencies and internal processes that enable an organization to adapt to its environment.

**learning modes**   The various ways in which organizations attempt to create and maximize their learning.

**learning organization**   Proactively creates, acquires, and transfers knowledge throughout the organization.

**legitimate power**   Obtaining compliance through formal authority.

**line managers**   Have authority to make organizational decisions.

**linguistic style**   A person's typical speaking pattern.

**listening**   Actively decoding and interpreting verbal messages.

**low-context cultures**   Primary meaning derived from written and spoken words.

**maintenance roles**   Relationship-building group behavior.

**management**   Process of working with and through others to achieve organizational objectives efficiently and ethically.

**management by objectives (MBO)**   Management system incorporating participation in decision making, goal setting, and feedback.

**managing diversity**   Creating organizational changes that enable all people to perform up to their maximum potential.

**market culture**   A culture that has a strong external focus and values stability and control.

**mechanistic organizations**   Rigid, command-and-control bureaucracies.

**mentoring**   Process of forming and maintaining developmental relationships between a mentor and a junior person.

**meta-analysis**   Pools the results of many studies through statistical procedures.

**met expectations**   The extent to which one receives what he or she expects from a job.

**mission statement**   Summarizes "why" an organization exists.

**monochronic time**   Preference for doing one thing at a time because time is limited, precisely segmented, and schedule driven.

**motivation**   Psychological processes that arouse and direct goal-directed behavior.

**motivators**   Job characteristics associated with job satisfaction.

**multicommunicating**   Using technology to participate in two or more social interactions at the same time.

**need for achievement**   Desire to accomplish something difficult.

**need for affiliation**   Desire to spend time in social relationships and activities.

**need for power**   Desire to influence, coach, teach, or encourage others to achieve.

**needs**   Physiological or psychological deficiencies that arouse behavior.

**negative inequity**   Comparison in which another person receives greater outcomes for similar inputs.

**negative reinforcement**   Making behavior occur more often by contingently withdrawing something negative.

**negotiation**   Give-and-take process between conflicting interdependent parties.

**noise**   Interference with the transmission and understanding of a message.

**nominal group technique (NGT)**   Process to generate ideas and evaluate solutions.

**nonanalytic**   Using preformulated rules to make decisions.

**nonassertive style**   Timid and self-denying behavior.

**nonrational models**   Decision models that explain how decisions are actually made.

**nonverbal communication**   Messages sent outside of the written or spoken word.

**norm**   Shared attitudes, opinions, feelings, or actions that guide social behavior.

**onboarding**   Programs aimed at helping employees integrate, assimilate, and transition to new jobs.

**open system**   Organism that must constantly interact with its environment to survive.

**operant behavior**   Skinner's term for learned, consequence-shaped behavior.

**optimizing**   Choosing the best possible solution.

**organic organizations**   Fluid and flexible network of multitalented people.

**organization**   System of consciously coordinated activities of two or more people.

**organizational behavior (OB)**   Interdisciplinary field dedicated to better understanding and managing people at work.

**organizational citizenship behaviors (OCBs)**   Employee behaviors that exceed work-role requirements.

**organizational culture**   Shared values and beliefs that underlie a company's identity.

**organizational politics**   Intentional enhancement of self-interest.

**organizational socialization**   Process by which employees learn an organization's values, norms, and required behaviors.

**organization-based self-esteem**   An organization member's self-perceived value.

**organization chart**   Boxes-and-lines illustration showing chain of formal authority and division of labor.

**organization development**   A set of techniques or tools that are used to implement organizational change.

**ostracism**   Rejection by other group members.

**out-group exchange**   A partnership characterized by a lack of mutual trust, respect, and liking.

**participative management**   Involving employees in various forms of decision making.

**pay for performance**   Monetary incentives tied to one's results or accomplishments.

**performance management**   Continuous cycle of improving job performance

with goal setting, feedback and coaching, and rewards and positive reinforcement.

**perception**   Process of interpreting one's environment.

**personality**   Stable physical and mental characteristics responsible for a person's identity.

**personality conflict**   Interpersonal opposition driven by personal dislike or disagreement.

**polychronic time**   Preference for doing more than one thing at a time because time is flexible and multidimensional.

**positive inequity**   Comparison in which another person receives lesser outcomes for similar inputs.

**positive organizational behavior (POB)**   The study and improvement of employees' positive attributes and capabilities.

**positive reinforcement**   Making behavior occur more often by contingently presenting something positive.

**proactive personality**   Action-oriented person who shows initiative and perseveres to change things.

**problem**   Gap between an actual and desired situation.

**procedural justice**   The perceived fairness of the process and procedures used to make allocation decisions.

**programmed conflict**   Encourages different opinions without protecting management's personal feelings.

**punishment**   Making behavior occur less often by contingently presenting something negative or withdrawing something positive.

**rational model**   Logical four-step approach to decision making.

**readiness**   Follower's ability and willingness to complete a task.

**referent power**   Obtaining compliance through charisma or personal attraction.

**repetitive motion disorders (RMDs)**   Muscular disorder caused by repeated motions.

**resistance to change**   Emotional/behavioral response to real or imagined work changes.

**respondent behavior**   Skinner's term for unlearned stimulus–response reflexes.

**reward power**   Obtaining compliance with promised or actual rewards.

**roles**   Expected behaviors for a given position.

**sample survey**   Questionnaire responses from a sample of people.

**satisficing**   Choosing a solution that meets a minimum standard of acceptance.

**scenario technique**    A speculative forecast tool for identifying future states, given a set of conditions.

**schema**    Mental picture of an event or object.

**self-concept**    Person's self-perception as a physical, social, spiritual being.

**self-efficacy**    Belief in one's ability to do a task.

**self-esteem**    One's overall self-evaluation.

**self-managed teams**    Groups of employees granted administrative oversight for their work.

**self-monitoring**    Observing one's own behavior and adapting it to the situation.

**self-serving bias**    Taking more personal responsibility for success than failure.

**sense of choice**    The ability to use judgment and freedom when completing tasks.

**sense of competence**    Feelings of accomplishment associated with doing high-quality work.

**sense of meaningfulness**    The task purpose is important and meaningful.

**sense of progress**    Feeling that one is accomplishing something important.

**servant-leadership**    Focuses on increased service to others rather than to oneself.

**shaping**    Reinforcing closer and closer approximations to a target behavior.

**shared leadership**    Simultaneous, ongoing, mutual influence process in which people share responsibility for leading.

**situational theories**    Propose that leader styles should match the situation at hand.

**social capital**    The productive potential of strong, trusting, and cooperative relationships.

**social loafing**    Decrease in individual effort as group size increases.

**social power**    Ability to get things done with human, informational, and material resources.

**societal culture**    Socially derived, taken-for-granted assumptions about how to think and act.

**span of control**    The number of people reporting directly to a given manager.

**staff personnel**    Provide research, advice, and recommendations to line managers.

**stereotype**    Beliefs about the characteristics of a group.

**strategic constituency**    Any group of people with a stake in the organization's operation or success.

**strategic plan**    A long-term plan outlining actions needed to achieve planned results.

**tacit knowledge**    Information gained through experience that is difficult to express and formalize.

**target elements of change**    Components of an organization that may be changed.

**task roles**    Task-oriented group behavior.

**team**    Small group with complementary skills who hold themselves mutually accountable for common purpose, goals, and approach.

**team building**    Experiential learning aimed at better internal functioning of groups.

**telepresence**    Communicating with the most advanced videoconference systems.

**teleworking**    Doing work that is generally performed in the office away from the office using different information technologies.

**theory Y**    McGregor's modern and positive assumptions about employees being responsible and creative.

**360-degree feedback**    Comparison of anonymous feedback from one's superior, subordinates, and peers with self-perceptions.

**total quality management**    An organizational culture dedicated to training, continuous improvement, and customer satisfaction.

**transactional leadership**    Focuses on interpersonal interactions between managers and employees.

**transformational leadership**    Transforms employees to pursue organizational goals over self-interests.

**trust**    Reciprocal faith in others' intentions and behavior.

**unity of command principle**    Each employee should report to a single manager.

**upward feedback**    Employees evaluate their boss.

**valence**    The value of a reward or outcome.

**value attainment**    The extent to which a job allows fulfillment of one's work values.

**values**    Enduring belief in a mode of conduct or end-state.

**virtual team**    Information technology allows group members in different locations to conduct business.

**withdrawal cognitions**    Overall thoughts and feelings about quitting a job.